A History of the Jewish Experience

A History of the

ETERNAL FAITH

BEHRMAN HOUSE, INC

Jewish Experience

ETERNAL PEOPLE

by LEO TREPP

Publishers New York, N.Y.

This is a revised edition of Leo Trepp's book originally titled
Eternal Faith, Eternal People
A Journey Into Judaism

Published by Behrman House, Inc.
1261 Broadway, New York, N.Y.

Manufactured in the United States of America

LIBRARY OF CONGRESS CATALOGING IN PUBLICATION DATA

Trepp, Leo.
    A history of the Jewish experience.

    Published in 1962 under title: Eternal faith,
eternal people; a journey into Judaism.
    Bibliography: p.
    1. Judaism—History.   2. Jews—Rites and
ceremonies.   I. Title.
BM155.2.T7   1973   296   73-3142
ISBN 0-87441-072-X

To my wife Miriam
and my daughter Susan
. . . in love

Preface

This book has been in the making for many years. Started in response to a request by Jewish friends in search of a concise general outline of Judaism, it was given its specific character at the suggestion of my Christian friends, who asked for a work which would explain Judaism in simple words, addressing itself to the intelligent layman. I hope it will serve both. It is no more than an introduction, for Judaism can be fully understood only as it is lived. It is more than a set of dogmas and of principles, more than the sum total of its laws and commandments. It started as a faith. The faith has formed the people, and the people have fashioned their faith in a process of never-ending evolution. Judaism is eternal faith and eternal people, a *living dialogue* between God and the Jew, between the Jew and God, and among the Jew, his fellow Jew, and the world. Its influence upon mankind has been profound.

Judaism proclaims God is absolutely One. In calling Jews to follow Him, it holds out the ideal of wholeness to a world torn by discord, and to individual souls split by inner conflict. Judaism proclaims the coming of the Messiah, and a future in which mankind will be united in brotherhood and peace. In this Messianic ideal it offers an eternal challenge to every human being, calling him to do his utmost in promoting human welfare under God, to push forward the frontiers of human progress, and to toil unceasingly for the improvement of society.

As champion of these ideals, Judaism is vital for mankind. *Shalom* is the goal it envisions for the children of God. Shalom means peace, a peace which is more than the absence of war, for Shalom also means perfection; in Jewish tradition it is a name of God Himself.

Judaism calls for imitation of God. Its history testifies to its convictions. It is a stream, a conversation, which goes on not only between the members of any living generation but between the generations as well. Every Jew speaks to his past, as the past speaks to him. He addresses himself to the future, and the future responds. Judaism speaks to the world, and has taken the best mankind has to offer to build it into the structure of its own system.

I have tried, therefore, to arrange the ideas of Judaism around a historical framework. This book is not a Jewish history. It is selective in its inclusion of personalities and events, but it follows the historical unfolding of Jewish life and destiny. Whatever happened to the Jews at a given moment in history helped shape their outlook, their prayers and practices, their philosophy and hopes. The creative works of any Jew at any time became part of a living heritage. History, faith, and people cannot be separated, for Judaism sees God as Master of History.

The book has been guided by this principle. The discussion of doctrines and movements, of observances and practices, is introduced at the historical point in the narrative when they reached their fullest expression and concreteness. For example, Jewish holidays, dietary laws, and the "Road of Life" are discussed after an analysis of the Shulhan Arukh, the authoritative code of Jewish law. This had the advantage of permitting quotations from the Shulhan Arukh and earlier works to be introduced. In modern times new approaches to the Shulhan Arukh have evolved, and they are discussed in their historical place. From my own experience as a college teacher I consider this approach to be educationally sound. As far as possible I have permitted the teachers and sages to speak for themselves. These selections, which offer a glimpse of Jewish writing, may lead to further study. Modern works, and those easily available in translation, have been quoted less extensively than those which may be harder to obtain.

Simplicity of presentation has been my primary concern, and has influenced the choice and presentation of subject matter and ideas. In telling my story I have generally not taken a stand in defense or advocacy of specific schools of thought or philosophy. On the other hand, I have tried to include answers to questions most frequently asked.

It is my conviction that Judaism is essentially a religion of reason, and I have emphasized this aspect. I believe that Jewish history, from the Talmud to Hermann Cohen, bears out this assertion. In a sense, this too is a simplification. There are many currents, from mysticism to plain superstition, which can be traced in the stream of evolution. They have affected the character of Judaism without, in my view, changing it fundamentally. This personal conviction should be kept in mind by the reader.

The views and opinions expressed thus are mine. Judaism has no central authority which could certify a work as an official presentation of its ideas, or give it an imprimatur. I have drawn from many sources, learned from many teachers, and I am eternally indebted to all of them. The greatest of them all have been my parents, who surrounded me with love and a home filled with Jewish devotion. My father, in addition, led me into Bible and Talmud. My mother sealed her devotion to Judaism with her life, dying a Martyr's death in a Nazi camp. I have had inspiring teachers during my rabbinic training, men whose lives testified to their convictions. Men of renown have guided my university studies. Throughout the years my wife has shared with me the trials of life, in a courage born of faith, and in love which has given me strength. In my daughter I envision the future, as she grows up to be American and Jew. Without these influences and many others, the book could not have been written.

I wish to thank Mrs. Keith (Lucy) Evans for her valuable notes to the first draft of the manuscript, representing the views of the intelligent Christian reader. Dr. James Diemer, Director of Napa College, has read the final draft of the manuscript and the proofs, and aided me greatly by his comments. Goodman Library at Napa has been helpful in securing books from many sources; Mr. J. E. James drew some of the original drafts of the maps, and Mr. Karl Kultti transcribed the cantillation of Torah for me. Mr. Bernard Stein of Germany undertook the arduous task of providing me with pictures of German-Jewish historical monuments. I am grateful to all of them, and to many others who have given me encouragement, including my colleagues and students at Napa College and Santa Rosa Junior College, where I teach.

Most of the maps are adaptations of those used in Anderson, *Understanding the Old Testament* (Englewood Cliffs, N.J.: Prentice-Hall, Inc., 1957), based on maps in *The Westminster Historical Atlas to the Bible,* Revised Edition, © 1956 by W. D. Jenkins, The Westminster Press. The Oppenheim Pictures are reprinted through the courtesy of the National Federation of Temple Sisterhoods.

I would like to thank these other individuals and organizations which provided pictures used in the book: Allgemeine Wochenzeitung der Juden in Deutschland; Blackstone Studios; Supreme Grand Lodge of B'nai B'rith, Robert Shosteck, Curator, B'nai B'rith Committee on Jewish Americana, Washington, D.C.; The Consulate General of Israel; Verlag Eschkol A.-G., Berlin; The Jewish Museum, New York, Frank J. Darmstaedter; The Jewish Theological Seminary of America; Mr. Paul Lippman, Santa Rosa, California; Mr. Alex Liu; B. Manischewitz Company, Newark, New Jersey; Photographie Giraudon, Paris; Schocken Books, Inc.; Herbert S. Sonnenfeld; Spanish and Portuguese Synagogue, Amsterdam, Netherlands; Rheinland-Pfalz Ministerium für Unterricht und Kultus, Oberregierungsrat Schröder, Mainz; Staedtische Kulturinstitute, Worms; The Union of American Hebrew Congregations; and Mr. Roger Levenson for his kind advice.

The Holy Scriptures, © 1917 by the Jewish Publication Society of America, is the translation generally used in this work. I have preferred to use this translation, rather than my own, to show the Christian reader the similarities and differences between the Jewish translation and the authorized Christian ones. I hope to guide the Jewish reader toward renewed study of the authorized Jewish version from which I have quoted. Sincere appreciation is expressed to the Jewish Publication Society of America for the use of their translation. All other translations from the Hebrew, French, Latin, and German (except when indicated otherwise) are my own.

No part of Jewish experience can be understood out of the context of the whole. I have tried to show this. It is possible to read many of the chapters independently, and the reader may omit sections of greater difficulty, such as philosophy. It is my hope, however, that most readers will approach the work as a whole.

Leo Trepp

The first edition of *Eternal Faith, Eternal People* has been so well received that most of its material has been retained. The years since its first appearance have brought developments that have called for updating, which has been undertaken. My most profound appreciation is expressed to Behrman House, who have undertaken the new edition and shown me great courtesy while giving me valuable help. Since the first edition of the book, my daughter Susan has been married to Myron Greenberg, and their son, David Philip was born in 1972. The dedication is extended to them. L.T.

Contents

Introduction: The Problem of Definition 1

1 · Biblical Beginnings 4

THE FAMILY 5   THE GOD OF MOSES 8   THE LAND: CLASH OF IDEAL AND REALITY 12

2 · The Prophets and Their Message 15

DEVELOPMENT OF PROPHECY: EARLY PROPHETS 15 *Amos: The Idea of Being Chosen · Hosea: The God of Love · Isaiah: Rites and Righteousness—The Vision of the Future · Deuteronomy: Social Justice · Jeremiah: Hope of Return—The Duties of Citizenship ·* BABYLONIAN EXILE: NEW ANSWERS 25 *The Beginning of Liturgy · Ezekiel: Individual Responsibility versus Inherited Sin · The Second Isaiah: Voice of Hope · The End of the Exile*

3 · Return, Restoration, Renaissance 33

STRANGERS AND CONVERTS: THE JEWISH CONCEPT 33 *Conversion · Conversion in Historical Perspective ·* THE COVENANT 36   *What We Mean by Torah · Written and Oral Torah ·* HELLENISM 40   *Conflict and Rebellion: The Maccabees · The Inspiration of Greek Thought ·* THE SECTS: SADDUCEES, ESSENES, PHARISEES 57

4 · The Tannaim 62

THE MEN AND THEIR IDEALS 63   THE PAINTED ONES 72   ANCIENT ROOTS OF ANTI-SEMITISM 74

5 · Tenakh: The Holy Scriptures   78

THE DIVISIONS OF THE BIBLE   80   *Torah · N'vee-im: Prophets · Ketubim: Collected Writings* · HOW THE TENAKH WAS TRANSMITTED: THE MASORAH   90   HOW THE TENAKH ORIGINATED: MODERN CRITICISM   90 BIBLE IN TRANSLATION   92

6 · The Mishnah   93

ORGANIZATION OF THE MISHNAH: THE ORDERS AND THEIR CONTENT   95   EXCERPTS FROM THE MISHNAH: SANHEDRIN   98   *Palestine after the Mishnah*

7 · The Babylonian Talmud   102

BACKGROUND OF THE BABYLONIAN TALMUD   102 *Mishnah and Gemara: The Talmud · Method and Organization ·* BABYLONIAN JEWRY AFTER COMPLETION OF THE TALMUD   106   SEFARDIC AND ASHKENASIC JEWRY   108

8 · Prayer and the Prayer Book   109

WHAT WE MEAN BY PRAYER   109   THE BERAKHAH 111   STRUCTURED WORSHIP: PERIODS OF PRAYER 112   THE STRUCTURE OF THE MAIN PRAYERS   113 *The Morning Prayer · The Nineteenth Psalm and the Pattern of Jewish Worship · Amidah: The Concerns of Petition · More of the* Pledge of Allegiance *· The Afternoon Prayer · The Evening Prayer · On Retiring ·* THE STRUCTURE OF WORSHIP   120   PUBLIC AND PRIVATE WORSHIP: WHAT IS A CONGREGATION?   122   CHANTS, SINGERS, AND POETS   122   THE SIGNS: AUDIO-VISUAL REMINDERS 125   *Tallit · Tefillin · Mezuzah ·* WORSHIP AND THE JEWISH PERSONALITY   128

9 · Dissent, Disruption, Dialogue   129

PROLOGUE: PHILO OF ALEXANDRIA   129   JUDAISM IN DISSENT   133   EARLY CHRISTIANITY: THE JEWISH VIEWPOINT   136   *The Life of Jesus · The Ministry of Paul · The Period of Dissociation · The Split is Completed · The Dialogue is Resumed*

10 · Challenge and Response   142

SPAIN   142   *Hasdai and Samuel the Prince · Gabirol · Judah Halevi · Moses Maimonides · The End of Spanish Jewry ·* CENTRAL EUROPE   152   *The Life of Ashkenasic Jewry · Synagogue Buildings ·* FRENCH-GERMAN JEWRY RISES TO EMINENCE   163   *Gershom ben Judah · Rashi ·* THE STRUGGLE FOR SURVIVAL: THE CODES   167   *The Shulhan Arukh · Authority and Functions of the Orthodox Rabbi*

11 · The Jewish Year   172

THE JEWISH CALENDAR   172   THE SABBATH   176   *Work Prohibition · Traditional Sabbath Observance ·* THE DAYS OF AWE: HIGH HOLY DAYS   185   *Of Days and Seasons and Years · The Ways of Teshubah · Days of Repentance: Preparation · Rosh Hashanah · Yom Kippur: Day of Atonement ·* THE THREE PILGRIMAGE FESTIVALS   196   *Sukkot: Feast of Tabernacles (Booths) · Lights in Winter's Night: Hanukah · The Merry Feast of Purim · Pessah (Passover): Rebirth in Freedom · Shabuot · Days of Mourning*

12 · The Road of Life   216

BIRTH   216   *Circumcision · Jewish Names · An Archaic Custom: Pidyon Haben · Education and Bar Mitzvah · Toward Marriage ·* MARRIAGE   223   *Preparation · The Betrothal: First Part of the Marriage Ceremony · Marriage Rites: Second Part of the Marriage Ceremony ·* MARRIED LIFE   227   *Women's Status in Religious Law · Divorce ·* SICKNESS AND DEATH IN TRADITIONAL OBSERVANCE   231   *Health and Sickness · As Death Approaches · Preparing the Dead · Burial · The Period of Mourning · Yahrzeit ·* DIETARY LAWS   234   *Purpose and Background · The Laws ·* THE WEARING OF THE HAT   239

13 · Forces and Counterforces   242

An Example: Venice · Luther · England · Eastern Europe · Messianism · The "Gaon" of Vilna · The Baal Shem: The Hasidim · Moses Mendelssohn · Baruch Spinoza

14 · Hasidism   250

*Ezekiel · German Hasidism: Judah Hahasid and His Followers ·
Zohar: The Book of Radiance · Rabbi Isaac Luria (1534-1572) ·
Hasidism in Russia and Poland · The Impact of Hasidism*

15 · Darkness and Light   260

THE AGONY OF RUSSIAN JEWRY 260   THE DAWN OF
THE AGE OF ENLIGHTENMENT 263

16 · On Jewish Philosophy   265

SAADIA: THE BOOK OF DOCTRINES AND BELIEFS 266
Of His Ideas · JUDAH HALEVI: THE KUSARI 269
MOSES MAIMONIDES (1135-1204) 272   *Prophet and
Philosopher · God · Just Average Good People · The Meaning
of the Commandments · After Maimonides* · MOSES MEN-
DELSSOHN (1729-1786) 281   *Background · Life · Religious
Philosophy · Nature's God, His Ways, and His Works · Bibli-
cal Revelations and Miracles · Why Judaism? · Mendelssohn's
Influence*

17 · French Revolution and Aftermath   291

NAPOLEON ORGANIZES A SANHEDRIN 292   JEWS AND
THE CONGRESS OF VIENNA 293   THE STATE OR-
GANIZES THE JEWISH COMMUNITY 294   AN EX-
AMPLE: OLDENBURG 294   REORGANIZATION AND
THE DIVISION OF MINDS 297   THE SCIENCE OF
JUDAISM 298

18 · Conflicts and Conferences   299

THREE GIANTS 300   *Samuel Holdheim (1806-1860) · Abra-
ham Geiger (1810-1874) · Zachariah Frankel (1801-1875)* · CON-
TROVERSY: REFORM AND CONSERATIVE JUDAISM 302
Geiger and Holdheim · Frankel · NEO-ORTHODOXY 306
*Samson Raphael Hirsch (1808-1888) · The Character of German
Orthodoxy · Hirsch's Philosophy* · OF DENOMINATIONS AND
IDEOLOGIES: A SURVEY 314

19 · The New Anti-Semitism   316

PRESSURES AND RESULTS   317   CONTRASTS   320

20 · Zionism   321

CULTURAL ZIONISM: AHAD HA-AM   323   *Ahad Ha-Am's Life · His Ideas* · POLITICAL ZIONISM: THEODOR HERZL 326   *Herzl and the Dreyfus Affair · Herzl Learns a Lesson · The Jewish State · Reaction and Opposition* · THE PANGS OF BIRTH   330   GROWING PAINS   332

21 · An Age of Maturity   335

HERMANN COHEN (1842-1918)   337   *Life · Cohen's Answer to Basic Questions: Judaism and Christianity · God, World, and Jew · In Quest of Perfection · The Soul · Sin and Repentance · The Neighbor* · FRANZ ROSENZWEIG (1886-1929)   347   *Of His Life · Of His Thought · The Star of Redemption* · MARTIN BUBER: LIFE OF THE DIALOGUE 355   *Life · Of His Thought* · THE END OF GERMAN JEWRY   364   Leo Baeck

22 · Enter America   367

BEGINNINGS   367   *In Colonial America · Citizens of the United States · The Problems for Judaism* · GERMAN IMMIGRATION   375   ADJUSTMENT AND REFORM   377 *Isaac Leeser (1806-1868) · Isaac Meyer Wise (1819-1900): Master Builder, Father of Reform · The Development of Reform Judaism*

23 · Migration from Eastern Europe   387

Problems of Transition · Parents and Children · Prejudice · Henrietta Szold · CONSERVATIVE JUDAISM   393   *Solomon Schechter (1850-1915)* · RECONSTRUCTIONISM   397 · *Mordecai Kaplan · The Concept of God · Jewish Religion and Practice · The Character of Reconstructionism · Reconstructionism: An Example of Judaism's Flexibility* · ORTHODOXY   402 *The Character of Orthodoxy · Orthodoxy and Israel* · SOME PROBLEMS OF AMERICAN JEWRY   406   *The Impact of Circumstances · Forces of Environment and History · Cooperation in Faith, Key to the Future* · THEOLOGICAL THOUGHT   409 · THE THRUST OF THOUGHT AND TASK   412 *(Cont.)*:

SOME PRACTICAL IMPLICATIONS   414   *In Worship* •
Sabbath • *Wearing of Hats in the Synagogue* • *Divorce* • *Agunah*
• *Dietary Laws* • *Prayer and the Prayer Book*

The Next Step: A Selected Bibliography   420

Appendix   430

Index   435

A History of the Jewish Experience

Introduction: The Problem of Definition

Is there *one* nation on earth like Thy people Israel? (From Sabbath afternoon worship)." Deep and powerful has been the impact of Judaism on its adherents. It has been a force which has molded men. We need mention but one of its commandments, observance of the Sabbath; it has had the power to transform the hunted and persecuted outcasts of history into princes—for twenty-four hours, once every week. They acquired a new soul, which gave them peace amidst storms; they had the quietness of heart to meditate on God's greatness, for He had created them a unique people on earth. Thus did a faith reach into the very marrow of its faithful, to mold them and to form them, to give them vision and courage and the unconquerable urge to be God's co-workers in the shaping of a better world. Our purpose is to trace how this came about—to show how Judaism expresses itself in beliefs and doctrines, in observances and customs, in law and in folkways.

There are close to 14 million Jews in the world today, living in every part of the globe, among members of every race. Although most Jews are Caucasians, there are also Negro Jews, Indian Jews, and some Jews who are Japanese. From the very beginning of Jewish history there has been a mixture of many families on earth united by one common bond, so it is an error to speak of a Jewish race. Are they then a religious group? They are a religious communion, but they are more than that. Many Jews do not uphold any religious doctrines, yet are proud of their Jewish-

1

ness. Are they a nation in a political sense? *Some* Jews find themselves organized as a nation. Israel is a sovereign nation on its own free soil. Jews in Russia carry identity cards which designate them as Jewish *nationals,* and are presumed to be afflicted with "negative national traits." Victims of constant pressures and severe discrimination, they are not allowed to find solace in their faith, merge into the oblivion of the majority; a limited number may now emigrate. In the western world, where the Jews consider themselves primarily a *religion,* the denominations of orthodoxy, conservatism, and reform have developed, and the synagogues form religious centers of Jewish life.

Yet there is one element that elevates Jewry in all lands beyond the character of a merely religious fellowship, and that is the sense of kinship and concern which Jews feel for each other. There is no political bond between Jews in various lands, only the spirit of belongingness. The Bible expresses the nature of the Jews when it speaks of "Bet Yisrael," the House of Israel.[1] Jews form a family linked by common experiences, a common history, and a common spiritual heritage. A family acquires its character not by the house in which it dwells, but by the spirit which unites it. The family unit includes those at home and abroad, those who join by vow of marriage, and the children born of married unions. Whoever partakes of the spirit is part of the family. As the members share in common hopes and ideals, they develop the bond of love which holds them together. Jewry is a family often torn by disagreements, but with the firm base of love as its foundation.

The will to survive has its roots in Jewish conviction that Judaism and the Jewish people are the people of the Covenant, called by God to function in a unique way within mankind as a whole. The Covenant created the bond between the Jews and God, thence between Jew and Jew; it has become so internalized that even those who may be unaware of its power have retained their allegiance to the Jewish people as its embodiment. Out of the Covenant we come to understand also the place and function of Jewish law. Law is the condensation of the spirit of the Covenant into action; it is both imposed and organic; it grew out of the encounter with God and out of the spirit of the Jewish people and its needs, hence it evolved. It has served as unifying bond among Jews and contributed to their survival without making them into a legalistic community. It has deepened the spirit of unity and of purpose—although it has also been an issue of controversy, especially in modern times—calling for an active response to the divine call, it has served as a life-giving force of self-identification and spiritual awareness. It translated the Covenant into the

---

[1] In the Pentateuch we often find the term "B'nai Yisrael," the Children of Israel, signifying an even closer family unity. The term "House of Israel" occurs most frequently among the prophets of the Exile, Jeremiah and Ezekiel. They may have wished to impress the idea most forcefully upon the dispersed.

deed, its pledge into the reality of constant performance linking the Jew to God, its hope into an action program that can lead to its fulfillment for the Jew and for mankind.

Of the nearly 14 million Jews, close to six million live in the United States of America, the largest Jewish community in history. (Canada has almost 300,000.) Proud as American citizens, they have become the leaders of world Jewry, giving support and aid, offering spiritual guidance, and at the same time building a unique form of American Jewish religious life. Israel with nearly 2¾ million is the second largest free community, for the three million in Russia are not free. In Europe their number has dwindled. There are 410,000 in England and 550,000 in France, 100,000 in Rumania, 80,000 in Hungary, 40,000 in Belgium, 35,000 in Italy, 30,000 in the Netherlands, 20,000 in Switzerland, 15,000 in Sweden, 8,000 in Austria, and smaller numbers in other countries, although their life, such as among the 6,000 Danish Jews, may be active and flourishing. Only about 9,000 are left of the millions who once lived in Poland, and 30,000 of the once flourishing Jewish community of Germany. No European country is without Jews. In Africa, we find flourishing and prosperous congregations in the South of the continent (125,000), of whom the majority lives in the Republic of South Africa (120,000), while the decreasing population of Jews along the Mediterranean coast exists in poverty. On the Asian continent, outside of Israel, larger Jewish communities are found in Turkey (40,000), Iran (80,000), and in India (15,000). In South America, Brazil (150,000), Argentina (500,000), Uruguay (50,000), Mexico (35,000) and Chile (35,000) have large and well organized congregations, and in Australia (73,000) [2] they form a happy religious group.

Although we will make a careful study of the Jewish people, Judaism can be fully understood only as it is lived. It can be defined only after it is known. Professor Kaplan has called it "an evolving religious civilization."[3] Judaism is constantly changing and growing. It is religious; without its faith in God it would never have come into being, nor would it have continued beyond a few generations. It is civilization, for it includes not only religious doctrines and practices, but forms a way of life. It has created art and philosophy, language and music, folkways and cuisine. It expresses itself for some in a homeland in Israel, for others in secular culture and social service, and for the majority—as in America—in religion. Above all, Judaism cannot be understood without Jews, its living servants, the molders of this civilization.

"Is there one nation . . . like Thy people Israel?"

---

[2] These figures are based on *American Jewish Year Book 1971*, c. 1971 by The American Jewish Committee and The Jewish Publication Society, New York and Philadelphia.

[3] Mordecai M. Kaplan, *Judaism as a Civilization* (New York: Thomas Yoseloff, 1957). The idea is basic to all of Kaplan's writings and to the Reconstructionist Movement of which he is the founder.

1

Biblical
Beginnings

The ideals professed by the modern Jew are founded on those of the Bible, and his entire history, based on it, is living presence to him. The ancient masters of the Talmud permitted themselves the freedom of carrying on a dialogue with teachers long departed; the medieval commentators did the same, asking questions and answering for the teacher out of an analysis of his thoughts. The past was present; it is present still. Modern Hebrew is the only language unchanged since antiquity, although it has evolved. Were Homer to return to Greece he could not understand the tongue he helped fashion; were Isaiah to visit the places of his ministry he could, without any difficulty, continue his message in his ancient language and be understood. The orthodox Jew who prays three times a day calls upon the God of Abraham of Isaac and of Jacob; the ancestors almost stand at his side. The non-religious Jew may not be aware of it, yet his pride in the purity of Israel's concept of the absolutely One God is a link with Abraham, who found Him; his concern with ethics is a bond uniting him with Abraham and Moses and the prophets. The Ten Commandments are as contemporary today as when they were given. Creative victory over adversity was learned by the Jews in Egyptian bondage, and the story is part of present-day Jewish living, rehearsed again and again on every Passover. History reveals God today as it did to the fathers thousands of years ago, for God is Master of history. The family spirit, evolved in Abraham's clan, is still alive, and the name Israel bestowed on Jacob graces the modern state fashioned by Jews. The conflict between truth and expediency, told by the Bible, still endangers the Jewish community; the threat of dissension still hovers over it, held in check by the warning example of past experiences. The basic ideas of love and justice, of truth and righteousness, of civic duties and religious obligations, of faith and action, of dispersion and return, of purity of soul and individual responsibility, all proclaimed by the prophets and sages, are part of the living heritage of Judaism and the fabric of modern Jewish life.

The student who deals with Homer learns of a past which only dimly affects our present life; he looks for foundations of our culture which lie deeply buried and have been overlaid many times. The student examining the ideals of patriarchs, preachers, and prophets in Jewish history also deals with the past, but, at the same time, meets the immediate present. Judaism has evolved by casting off the crudities of ancient practices and views, while the great ideas of ancient Israel have remained living ideals for our time, for Jews and for all mankind.

Our examination of the past actually speaks of modern Jewry, its hopes and aspirations, its beliefs, motivations, and ideals. The Biblical and Talmudic periods are not simply the records of a majestic past but an account of our modern ideals and how they came into being, to remain effective for all eternity. In this sense the past and the present are one, and as we speak of Abraham we speak of the Jew around the corner, whose views in some ways have matured, but whose ideals are the same.

Judaism and Jewish religion have evolved, but they have never banished the past. In its highest achievements, the past is not merely a prologue; it is life. May we understand it thus.

THE FAMILY

Hebrew history begins with Abraham's migration from "Ur of the Chaldeans," a land of highest culture, to Canaan, an undeveloped country. Why did Abraham leave? He left because he had outgrown the religious and social ideas of his environment. He may have been a contemporary of Hammurabi, who lived during the second millennium before the Christian era, and known of the great code of law bearing Hammurabi's name. He may well have been familiar with the majestic creation epos, the Gilgamesh epos of Babylonia. Stories from the Gilgamesh epos and laws from the great code eventually found a place in the Bible; some of them may have been transmitted by Abraham, but with their values altered. In this alteration is the reason for Abraham's journey—he left his home in search of an ethical God. The gods of the Gilgamesh epos create the earth because they are lonely, and destroy it in a flood because they are tired of it.

The Fertile Crescent.

One man escapes the flood because he is a friend of a god, who betrays to him the secret plans of the others and advises him to build an ark. All this is unethical, especially when compared with the Bible. Here God blesses man whom He has created out of divine goodness. Rescue in the flood is the just reward of righteous living; Noah is saved because he upholds the ideal of righteousness in the midst of a wicked world. The story of Abraham's migration is the account of human ascent to the awareness of One God who is the God of righteousness. Abraham's early migration established a great principle: to follow the truth is better than culture, and to follow God is greater than all the comforts of the world. This is the beginning and the motto of Jewish history.

When Abraham arrives in Canaan he is "Hebrew," the immigrant from "across the river." [1] The society he finds is semi-nomadic, small clans huddled about the few precious water wells in an arid land. His own clan is just like the others—with one exception. It is not blood which unites the members; it is God. The stranger who accepts Abraham's God is made welcome. This is a revolutionary concept in the ancient world, where the stranger always remained a stranger.

What is he like, this God of Abraham? He is One—this is discovered by Abraham. He is loving. Other people found it necessary to appease their gods, even to offer human sacrifices. Abraham finds in a flash of revelation that God never demands any human victims, either as gift of appeasement or in token of absolute obedience. [2] God himself stays the knife which the father has poised over his son's neck. Abraham's God is a God of mercy. He has planned to destroy the city of Sodom for its wicked-

---

[1] On the relationship of the Hebrews to the Habiru see B. W. Anderson, *Understanding the Old Testament,*2nd ed., (Englewood Cliffs, N.J.: Prentice-Hall,1966). W.F. Albright regards the following interpretation as most authoritative: "Hebrew" meaning donkey driver, or huckster or caravaneer, originating from the word for "dust," as donkeys raised a lot of dust on the road. William Foxwell Albright, *The Biblical Period from Abraha to Ezra* (New York and Evanston, Ill.: Harper & Row, Inc., 1963). (Harper Torch Book, p. 5.)

[2] Genesis 22:1-12.

The stele of Hammurabi, which stands nearly eight feet high, is inscribed with a code of laws. The relief at the top depicts Hammurabi, King of Babylon, standing before the sun god, Shamash, who extends a rod and ring, symbols of royal authority, to the worshipping king.

ness, yet, because of Abraham's pleading, He will spare the city for the sake of even ten righteous people who may dwell in it.[3] This is more than justice; this is divine grace and mercy. Such is Abraham's God.

With Abraham mankind moves forward in giant step. Mythology becomes religion; Judaism has arrived. A pinnacle of progress has been reached. God is One and He is just and He is merciful. Ethical conduct determines the fate of men and nations, yet God is gracious. He permits His children to talk with Him. And Abraham, the first Jew, does approach Him. He so loves the strangers, even evildoers, that he pleads in their behalf. So encompassing is his love that he builds his family as a fellowship of faith in God and love of man. The first Jew has fully developed the eternal ideals of Judaism, to love the Lord, the One God; to love the neighbor, the stranger, for he is part of the human family.

Alone among the families of the earth, Abraham is unafraid. He has his God, "Elohe Abraham," the God of Abraham. Abraham's children will see in Him "Pahad Yitshak," Kinsman of Isaac, and "Abir Yaakob," The Mighty One of Jacob." [4] This is their heritage. God will be with them, to guide them through the trials of history. With His help Jacob tackles the forces of adversity at home and abroad and acquires a new name, "Israel; he who striveth with God." [5] Jacob's children will always bear this name and the challenge that goes with it. They have chosen God as their guide, thus may consider themselves chosen by Him, to magnify Him and to suffer for Him and to grow as a family through suffering and endurance.

Soon enough the children of Israel are tested. After migrating to Egypt to escape a severe famine, they are singled out as a subversive group with dangerous ideas, and are enslaved. In slavery they become a people, closing ranks more firmly, transcending jealousies within the group. It is this family-nation which sees the light of freedom during the rule of Rameses II, about 1280 before the Christian era, and returns home to Canaan. The return was to be one of the most momentous events in history, for on their march through the desert they were led to Mount Sinai to receive divine commandments for all mankind. Their leader was Moses.

THE GOD OF MOSES

Egypt had been an education in many ways. Advanced Egyptian religion stressed man's responsibility and his immortality of soul. After death, the soul was called to account for all its deeds before the throne of the gods. Conduct was valued above sacrifices.[6] For a fleeting moment,

---

[3] Genesis 18:20-33.
[4] Anderson, *op. cit.*, pp. 23 ff.
[5] Genesis 32:29.
[6] See "Book of the Dead," Chapter 125, the "Negative Confession."

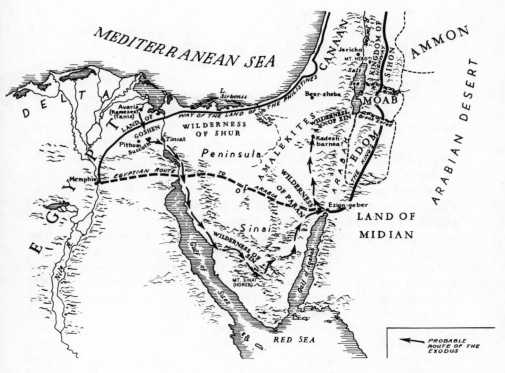

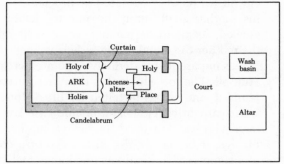

Route of the Exodus (top) and (right) Tabernacle in the Desert (Solomon's Temple followed the same basic plan).

under Pharaoh Ikhnaton, Egyptian religion even proclaimed the One God.[7] Then it fell under Canaanite fertility cults; "abominations" to Scripture. Moses rejected all pagan rites, revived the people's Hebrew traditions and purified them and used them to illumine the faith of the fathers. Thus, he transformed his band of freed slaves into a united family under God.

Moses received his call in a strange vision. Out in the desert he saw a bush ablaze in fierce flame, yet the bush was not consumed. In the midst of the fire he heard the voice of God revealing His divine Name—YHWH,

[7] See "Hymn to Aton."

9

"He Who Is What He Wishes To Be," or "He Who Causeth What Is." [8]
The bush is the symbol of Israel, surrounded by the flames of hatred,
scorched by the heat of trials, yet never consumed as God speaks through
them, and to them. He is the God of history, who calls events into being
and shapes man's destiny to His design. And history is His revelation. It
is dynamic, never static, hence His voice can be heard but His face never
seen, for the vision is static while the call is everlasting motion. Egypt,
even in its most advanced religious state, needed a visible symbol of
God. To Israel any visible image of Him is forbidden. The world will be
unable to understand it, and Israel will remain unique in the world, misunderstood and ridiculed, but champion of the God who is Master of history, shaping it to His purpose and calling man to be His helper. On this
concept of God rests the progress of mankind. At Mount Sinai they choose
to accept this God forever; they make a covenant endorsing His absolute,
categorical command, the Ten Commandments: thou shalt, thou shalt not.

The spirit of the Ten Commandments undergirds all future legislation.
Practical law has to get down to cases, but Jewish law never overlooks
the categorical imperative of the Ten Commandments. Hammurabi's law
now is overcome. No longer is there any distinction between high born
and low born, between lords and vassals. No longer is *property right* the
lawgiver's basic concern. Mosaic law is concerned with the protection of
human values. Hammurabi says, "If a son has struck his father they shall
cut off his hand." [9] Mosaic law proclaims, "He who smiteth his father or
his mother shall surely be put to death." [10] Mosaic law, superficially
viewed, seems to be harsher, yet it rests on higher principles. It makes
the mother the equal of the father; women have the same dignity as men.
It sees in parents the divinely appointed creators of life—they are like God
Himself. The son who strikes them has raised his hand against the Creator
Himself, and so has forfeited his life. "Honor thy father and thy mother"
is the categorical command behind case law. Hammurabi rules, "A nobleman who has destroyed the eye of another nobleman, they shall destroy
his eye; if he has destroyed the eye of a commoner or broken the tooth
of a commoner he shall pay one mina of silver; if he has destroyed the eye
of another nobleman's slave he shall pay one half of his value (to the
owner)." [11] The law of Moses states, "If a man smite the eye of his bondsman and destroy it, or the eye of his bondswoman and destroy it, he shall
let him go free for his eye's sake. And if he smite out his bondsman's tooth

---

[8] Exodus 3:14; Anderson, *op. cit.,* p. 34.

[9] T. J. Meek (trans.), *Code of Hammurabi,* in *Ancient Near Eastern texts relating
to the Old Testament,* ed. J. B. Pritchard (Princeton, N.J.: Princeton University Press,
1950), p. 195.

[10] Exodus 21:15.

[11] *Code of Hammurabi, op. cit.,* pp. 196, 198, 199.

Conquest of Canaan.

11

or his bondswoman's tooth he shall let him go free for his tooth's sake." [12] Man is more than property; even to his master he gives only his service. His person is free, and the master who violates it must grant full freedom in compensation. This is the law of Moses, the heritage of Israel, the imperative of the Ten Commandments. Three thousand years later, a United States Supreme Court, handing down the Dred Scot decision, did not yet understand the principle proclaimed by Judaism at the dawn of its history.

THE LAND: CLASH OF IDEAL AND REALITY

When Moses died in the desert, his disciple Joshua became the leader. The slow conquest of the land, with rivalries for the best parcels, began. The family fell apart in greed, and the national sanctuary was a weak rallying point. This weakness of the people tempted their enemies— Bedouins, who raided the farmlands, and Philistines, a great warrior group displaced from the region of Crete, and now masters of the coastal strip of Canaan. In moments of supreme danger Israel chose leaders or judges and pledged its allegiance to God. But when the battle was won and the judge had died, the pull of heathen gods, of conformity to other peoples' habits, and of selfish interests became strong again. Eventually, seeing the need for a permanent union in strength they found two roads were open to them. A revitalized religion would give them unity of purpose. They might, as the other alternative, surrender their freedom into the hands of a king.

They chose surrender. Saul was proclaimed to be their first king, to rule under God's directive. He failed because he was unstable, self-centered, and concerned primarily with the security of his own dynasty. With him, the natior collapsed. David, a man of great ability, capable of making friends and of holding them, a warrior and a hero, succeeded him. He too had weaknesses, but he had the power to see them, and the strength to repent. Deeply religious, he established the sanctuary at Jerusalem, the city he had conquered, and poetically acclaimed God as his shield and his buckler. David was the people's ideal king, for he mirrored Israel, their faults and shortcomings, but also their faith, courage, and endurance, and their unflinching trust in God. Solomon succeeded him. Politically shrewd, he developed traits of the oriental despot and built the Temple in Jerusalem, which was more a royal chapel than the center of divine inspiration. When he died, in 922, the people, groaning under the pressure of taxation and enforced service, appealed to his son Rehoboam for a redress of grievances. The king refused them, and

---

[12] Exodus 21:26-27.

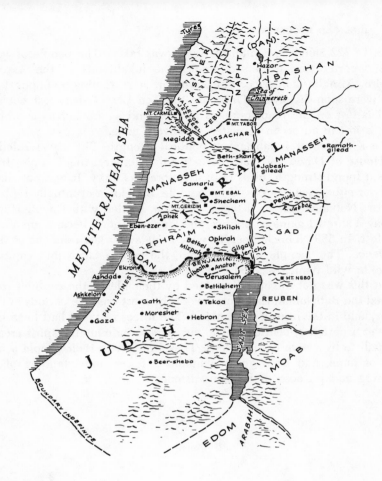

Divided Kingdom.

the result was secession. Ten of the twelve tribes fell away to form the Kingdom of Israel, only Judah and Benjamin remaining loyal to the House of David.

A house divided cannot long endure. That it endured at all is a miracle. The land of the two kingdoms, Judah and Israel, lay like a bridge between the great empires of antiquity, Egypt and the powers of the two-stream land at Tigris and Euphrates. As long as these giants balanced each other, they preferred to leave the little land alone, rather than see it in the opponent's hand. As soon as either of the two powers felt strong enough to subdue the other, the territory between them became a battle ground.

The kingdom of Israel started out in turmoil. Dynasty followed dynasty. Faith broke down, and with it the family spirit of the nation. In the East Assyria was rising to power. The eighth century saw its armies on the move. In 722 Samaria, capital of Israel, was taken. The people of Israel were deported and dispersed among the inhabitants of the Assyrian Empire. Mingling, intermarrying, without a sustaining religious faith, they were soon dissolved. These are the Ten Lost Tribes; lost not as a jewel is lost on the road, perhaps to be found again, but as a drop of wine is lost in an ocean of water, dissolved, gone.

The Kingdom of Judah lacked political strength. But it was ruled by the House of David and had the national sanctuary, the Temple. In its kings it found strength; in its faith it restored its unity. It was not spared civil war either, yet it survived for a while. Babylonia eventually replaced Assyria. Nebuchadnezzar, King of Babylon, battled with Egypt. Hoping to play a shrewd game of politics, the kings of Judah became involved—and lost. In 586 Nebuchadnezzar wiped out every last remnant of independence. The Temple was destroyed, the people taken into captivity. Some, in wild panic, escaped to Egypt.

But this was not the end. Sustained by their ideals, the captives transformed the Babylonian Exile into one of the most creative periods in their history and in the history of mankind. The forces released had been built up over a period of centuries. The men whose indomitable spirit created this will to live were the prophets. They brought to their people a message of hope, and have given mankind a fuller understanding of the meaning and purpose of human existence.

2

The Prophets
and
Their Message

The centuries of turmoil beginning in the late tenth pre-Christian century brought forth men of historical significance, the prophets. That so small a land produced so large a number of spiritual giants is a miracle. These men were challenged by the events they witnessed to ask for the purpose and meaning of life and of history. They combined deepest insights with towering courage, broadest vision with unequalled power of expression. In their hearts they felt the compelling force of divine ordination. They had to speak out. Each one became "Nabi," a speaker.[1] Called to deliver a message, they could not escape their mission even at the peril of their lives.

DEVELOPMENT OF PROPHECY: EARLY PROPHETS

There were many diviners in the ancient world, but the prophets were more than that. There were seers even among the heathens. The Bible

---

[1] Anderson, *op. cit.*, p. 184. William F. Albright considers the explanation of "Nabi" as speaker to be false. To him, Nabi means "One who is called (by God)" or "One who has a vocation (from God)." See William F. Albright, *From the Stone Age to Christianity* (New York: Doubleday Anchor Book, Doubleday & Company, Inc., 1957), p. 303.

mentions one of them—Balaam.[2] Invited by the king of Moab to pronounce a solemn curse upon Israel, he cannot do so. The king wishes to see Israel destroyed; they are his enemies. As the prophet gazes upon their encampment, it offers a picture of a peaceful society, ruled by love and justice; Balaam knows it would be unethical to voice his curse; he must bless. The inescapable relationship between ethical conduct and blessing compels him to pronounce his benediction, although he is not happy about it. The Jewish prophet, however, *is* happy—he uses the sting of his words to lead his people on the road toward blessing. This is prophecy. Balaam is a prophet among the heathens, demonstrating that the prophetic message goes out to all mankind. God's concern is for all humanity; He wishes to see all His children walk the way of righteousness, that they may be blessed. With the prophets, Judaism becomes a universalistic religion.

We have but scant reports of the very early prophets. They were diviners, who could be caught in the tremors of mystical ecstasy, but they were also leaders. This we learn from the stories of Samuel and Saul.[3] They saw the future in terms of cause and effect; if man walks with God his future is assured. Samuel makes it clear to the people who put their faith in the strong leadership of the king they have chosen: "If ye will fear the Lord and serve Him and hearken to His voice . . . and both ye and also the king that reigneth over you be followers of the Lord your God . . . but if ye will not hearken unto the voice of the Lord, then shall the hand of the Lord be against you. . . ." [4] Actually the people need no king as long as the Lord is their leader. But the people do not listen and Samuel is distressed. Has he failed them? Have they rejected his leadership of many years? Gently, with tender rebuke and a word of comfort, God sets his mind at peace: ". . . they have not rejected thee but they have rejected Me that I should not be king over them." [5] The prophet must do his duty, and having done it, need not be concerned about the outcome. He must act in utter selflessness, without any personal ambitions. Not to him do the people owe allegiance, but to God.

Like Samuel, every prophet will find that the people do not listen. He will suffer, but he will go on until the people cease rejecting God, even if they abuse God's prophet. He knows that in the end his message will prevail. It is optimism in tears, hope in sorrow, faith in despair. It has become part of the Jewish character and a Jewish message to all who labor for a better world, but it calls for courage. The history of the

---

[2] Numbers 22-24.
[3] I Samuel 9:10.
[4] I Samuel 12:24, 25.
[5] I Samuel 8:7.

prophets tells of a persistent conflict to be resolved only in the future. In the days of the Bible it was the conflict between king and prophet. In world history, it is the encounter of faith with force, of principle with expediency, of ideals and opportunism. And Jews have often been the prophets. This courage is personified and exemplified in the prophet Nathan, who accused king David of adulterous conduct to his face: "thou art the man." [6] It breaks through in the sarcasm of an Elijah, stepping boldly before a king and queen who have plotted his death and a people who have struck a religious compromise by worshipping both God and Baal: "How long halt ye between two opinions? If the Lord be God follow Him; but if Baal follow him." [7] There can be no compromise between good and evil, and the prophet has the courage to make it clear to all mankind. There will be no compromise if man will but learn to listen to the "still small voice" of human conscience and of human love,[8] so often drowned out by the mighty sounds of the thunderous forces in the world. God is not in them; His is the still small voice, and every human being has the capacity to hear it if he but lends an ear.

Of the earlier prophets we have but scant quotations; the writings of the later ones have come down to us. We speak of major prophets—Isaiah, Jeremiah, and Ezekiel—of whose speeches major portions have been passed down to us. Twelve others are called minor prophets. Their known message is equally powerful, but we have only minor portions of their total words. The basic ideas of the prophets are alike, yet each of them carries a special message, thus adding new concepts to Jewish religion. We shall hear of them. They can be harsh in rebuking their people, but it is the violence of love. They castigate their flock, not because Israel is worse than the other nations, but because Israel is *not better* than the others. To follow pragmatic ethics, to do what usage sanctions, is not enough for Israel. It may even be sinful when measured by the absolute yardstick of divine ideals. But when Israel suffers for its sins they will be the first to remind God that their people have not done worse than the others. And they will uplift Israel with a message of hope and of comfort.

Amos: The Idea of Being Chosen

The prophets come from varying backgrounds. Isaiah may have been a royal prince, Jeremiah and Ezekiel are priests, Amos is a farmer. Duty compels Amos to travel from his home town, Tecoah, in the

---

6 II Samuel 12:7.
7 I Kings 18:20 ff.
8 I Kings, 19:9-13.

Kingdom of Judah, to the Kingdom of Israel to warn and to admonish. He is not welcome and is ordered out.

He is a rugged man, and only an overpowering sense of urgency can compel him to lay down his plow. It becomes clear in his prophecies that he has sweated and prayed to wrest some blessing out of the obstinate soil of the Jerusalem countryside. He knows that he who fails to work the fields and sow the seed will gather nothing. It is an inexorable logic. Yet even the farmer who has done everything his skill and strength permit has no assurance of success. He must still pray that there be rain in right measure, that neither locust nor parching sun may kill his hopes. This is Amos' insight and he translates it into social terms for his kinsfolk in the northern kingdom, and for mankind. The sins of the people are threefold and fourfold: Religious ideals have collapsed; "they have rejected the law of the Lord (Amos 2:4)." As a result, society has lost all sense of justice: the rich oppress the poor; "they sell the righteous for silver and the needy for a pair of shoes (Amos 2:6)". They have become morally corrupt; "a man and his father go unto the same maid to profane My holy name (Amos 2:7)," and organized religion has become a mockery: "in the house of their God they drink the wine of them that have been fined (Amos 2:8)."

According to the farmer's logic can there be anything but doom? But these are principles which apply to mankind as a whole. The dramatic events of every farmer's year are universal. Amos is compelled to proclaim the God of Israel as the universal God. He preaches to the powerful nations of his day, and to all nations of all times.

Are ye not like the children of the Ethiopians unto Me, O children of Israel? says the Lord. Have I not brought forth Israel out of the land of Egypt and the Philistines from Caphtor and Aram from Kir? (Amos 9:7).

The equality includes all mankind, the dark skinned Ethiopians and the nordic Philistines. They are all one family, with equal claims to independence. Thus did Judaism raise aloft the banner of racial equality thousands of years ago, and set a standard which many nations are still reluctant to accept.

Under these conditions the concept of the "chosen people" acquires a new meaning. Israel is chosen, but only to set higher standards, to assume greater responsibility, to lead the way. "You only have I known of all the families of the earth; therefore will I visit upon you all your iniquities (Amos 3:2)." The "family of Israel" is called to prepare the way for all nations to become "families of the earth." If Israel fails it will be punished, says Amos. If it lives up to the challenge it has but done its duty. Amos thus strengthens the foundations of Judaism: social justice, moral uprightness, faith in God who is Master of mankind and whose word is addressed to all. Judaism has humbly accepted the heavy burden of its "chosenness," and hopes for the day when the rest of the world will accept it too.

Hosea: The God of Love

Amos, citizen of the austere farm community of Judah, finds the ease, the luxury, the life of comfort in Israel to be in itself a sign of decay. Hosea, citizen of the Kingdom of Israel, enjoys it. He is a tender soul, but he is deeply afflicted. The wife whom he loves has deserted him to follow other men, and returns to him only when her charms have faded. Under the compulsion of the divine command—the tenderness in his heart—he takes her back. And he raises his own emotions to acquire symbolic meaning. They stand for the love of God.

Go yet, love a woman beloved of her friend and an adulteress, even as the Lord loveth the children of Israel, though they turn unto other gods (Hos. 3:1).

Love thus becomes a key word amidst Hosea's rebukes:

When Israel was a child then I loved him (Hos. 11:1). I will heal their backsliding; I will love them freely (Hos. 14:5). I will betrothe thee unto Me forever; yea I will betrothe thee unto Me in righteousness and in justice, and in lovingkindness and in compassion. And I will betrothe thee unto Me in faithfulness; and thou shalt know the Lord (Hos. 2:21).

Truly no greater love has ever been preached, no greater compassion ever been taught. This is the Jewish concept of all-embracing love—it has never been surpassed. The world is a family, encompassing the beasts of the field and the fowls of heaven, and even the earth itself. It is a family knowing war no more. In boundless love God waits for His children to come to Him and build this world. Castigating their error and their sins, in the abundance of His compassion He will receive them. These are cornerstones of Jewish religion.

Isaiah: Rites and Righteousness—The Vision of the Future

While Amos and Hosea are preaching in the North, Isaiah raises his voice in the southern kingdom. We have his words in the Book of Isaiah; yet he did not speak all the prophecies which are contained in its pages. There were at least two authors of the book. An earlier Isaiah, the man we shall presently discuss, is perhaps author of the first 39 chapters; at least one other wrote the later chapters at a later time. We call him the second, or Deutero-Isaiah.

The first Isaiah is one of the king's close friends and advisors; some rabbis think he was a royal prince. His position is reflected in the tone of his voice. There is frankness, outspoken criticism, undisguised and cutting analysis of times and conditions. There is authority. What is the meaning of religious rites, he asks himself, and he answers boldly. They are utterly useless unless prompted by the heart and rooted in a spirit of social justice.

To what purpose is the multitude of sacrifices unto Me?—says the Lord . . . When ye come to appear before Me, who has required this at your hand to trample My courts? . . . New moon and sabbath, the holding of convocations—I cannot endure iniquity along with the solemn assembly. Yea, when ye make many prayers I will not hear; your hands are full of blood. Wash you, make you clean, put away the evil of your doings from before My eyes; Cease to do evil, Learn to do well; Seek justice, relieve the oppressed, judge the fatherless, plead for the widow. Come now and let us reason together, sayeth the Lord; Though your sins be as scarlet they shall be as white as snow . . . (Isa. 1:11-18).

These are words of command by a man who has held power; they are the promise of pardon by a man who may grant clemency. Yet they transcend the philosophy held by earthly rulers, especially those of antiquity. Obedience to practical law is not enough when it comes to God; He requires the service of the heart. Yet profession of faith remains meaningless without the deed of love. Life must testify to the sincerity of the spoken word. No religious rites, no sacraments can bring salvation. When heart and hand unite in service, no sacraments are needed. This has been the view of Judaism. The empty word, the routine "service," are mockeries, displeasing to God and corroding human character. A principle unknown to the world when it was first proclaimed by Isaiah, it has largely remained unheeded throughout the ages by the family of man. When will mankind direct its soul and sanctify its action in true service, as defined by Isaiah?

Isaiah knows that when the day of compliance comes, a new era will dawn for humanity. The prophet paints his picture of this utopia in glowing colors, but it is not merely wishful thinking. Isaiah is a statesman, and like a statesman he presents to us the reasoned blueprint of a better world. He knows government, and in this knowledge he offers to us the ideal government to which we must aspire. The prophet's picture of this "end of days" has remained Israel's guiding light through the ages, shaping Jewish hopes, beliefs, and actions. Even in the prophet's own day it left so deep an impact that Micah, his prophet-disciple, repeats it word by word as his own message, and spreads it as truly "good news" throughout the land. This is what we read in Isaiah 2:2-4, and in Micah 4:1-5:

And it shall come to pass in the end of days, that the mountain of the Lord's house shall be established as the top of the mountains, and shall be exalted above the hills; and all nations shall flow unto it. And many peoples shall go and say: 'Come ye and let us go up to the mountain of the Lord, to the house of the God of Jacob; and He will teach us of His ways, and we will walk in His paths.' For out of Zion shall go forth the law, and the word of the Lord from

Jerusalem. And He shall judge between the nations, and shall decide for many peoples; and they shall beat their swords into plowshares and their spears into pruning-hooks; nation shall not lift up sword against nation, neither shall they learn war any more (Isa. 2:2-4).

Then Isaiah continues with the appeal to the "family," the "House of Jacob":

O House of Jacob come ye and let us walk in the light of the Lord (Isa. 2:5).

And Micah adds the hope:

But they shall sit, every man under his vine and under his fig tree; and none shall make them afraid; for the mouth of the Lord of hosts has spoken (Mic. 4:4).

Thus is outlined mankind's ultimate hope, with a call to action by Isaiah and a promise of the reward by Micah. Israel is "chosen" to march ahead, but the blessings are vouchsafed to all of humanity.

The grandeur of this vision becomes clear when we compare it with other utopian ideals. Plato, in his Republic, and Sir Thomas More, who coined the name "utopia," look backward,[9] Plato to the ideal of Spartan aristocratic communism, More to the medieval corporate state he wishes to perpetuate in the face of a dynamic Renaissance society. And Christian thinking, looking forward with pessimism, can see the fulfilment of the ideal only after world shaking upheavals, when nature and society will be shaken to their foundations. The entire universe has to collapse before man acquires a new soul. This is drawn from the theology of Persian Zoroastrianism, which has also influenced Judaism.

Isaiah, however, looks forward in realistic appraisal of man's capacities, and in the spirit of equal justice for all men. How different this view is from Plato's.[10] Plato's ideas are frightening. They include a rigidly controlled caste society where philosophers rule, and the common man, denuded of his individuality, has to obey. Arrogantly the philosopher denies the average man both the right to determine his destiny and influence decisions, and the ability to grow and learn and mature. The leaders have nothing to learn from their flock. Plato, who believes that there exists an ideal, eternal pattern for everything in the world, to which all must strive, omits the most basic of ideas: the Idea of Man. To him man does not grow, while to Isaiah individuals and peoples unfold through reason, and no limit is set to their unfolding. They will all learn the truth "at the mountain of the Lord"; they will all understand it. Plato's view is static. It

---

9 Sir Thomas More, Utopia, written in Latin between 1515 and 1516.

10 A comparison of Plato and the prophets (especially the Republic and Isaiah's Utopia) can be found in Herman Cohen, Das Soziale Ideal bei Platon and den Propheten (Hermann Cohen's Jüdische Schriften, Berlin: C. A. Schwetschke & Sohn, 1924; Vol. I, pp. 306 ff.).

never moves beyond the city state in which he lives, for he does not know God as Lord of history. Isaiah's view penetrates to the moment when God, forgiving and gracious, blots out man's errors, for He has found man in earnest striving for perfection. Then "He will judge," and the verdict will be peace. Nations will live with each other in harmony, and the high-born will no longer rule over the lowly, as they eternally must in Plato's state.

Most destructive of all Plato's concepts is that of the warrior caste. To him there will always be a warrior caste, and the philosopher-ruler has to be a warrior before he can be adjudged a sage. The static society of philosophers, warriors, and artisans thus always remains an encampment. There are always barbarians, non-Greeks; they are considered inferior, and must be kept out. No fraternization shall be permitted; inequality is elevated to a permanent order, both among peoples and among individuals. They will always learn war. Isaiah predicts a time when they shall "learn war no more." To prepare for war, to train for war will then be recognized by all nations as immoral, and only then will it vanish. But the warrior caste in Plato's Republic has an additional task: to keep the third estate in check. That is why philosophers must first learn the art of war. According to Plato, there will never be a time when obedience can come spontaneously, and law will be followed freely; for in Plato's commonwealth, law is always imposed from above without the consent of the governed. Those who sit under the fig tree, to tend it as farmers do, will always be kept in fear. The prophet speaks a different language. Let man but find himself, his potential and his capacities, the compassion of his heart and the power of his mind, and he will be the builder of a better world, a society of equals.

Mankind has all too often looked backward, to recapture the past, or to far away lands, as Thomas More looked toward the New World. We are still captivated by Plato's ideal—the warrior is the man of prestige. When mankind did look forward, it found itself enveloped in fear, frightened by its inability to change; it has become fascinated by the terror of the end of days. Little has been done to follow the prophetic ideal; yet all the ideal calls for is a renewal of will. Only the Jews, defenseless and without power, have never abandoned the ideal and the vision of Isaiah. It has sustained them in trials and tribulations; it has kept alive within them an unflagging faith in human goodness and the victory of human decency; it has given purpose to their lives as they stood up for the good society, and it has given them hope. Indeed, Isaiah's vision is mankind's last and best hope; it is its only hope.

Deuteronomy: Social Justice

In the year 622 a book is found in the recesses of the Temple. Written as the farewell address of Moses, it became part of the five books of

Moses and is known as Deuteronomy. Some of its parts are old, but the spirit is that of the prophets. Once again we find the Ten Commandments, but the version is different from that of Exodus. In the early version, the Sabbath commandment reads as follows: "Remember the Sabbath day to keep it holy . . . for in six days the Lord created the heaven and the earth . . . and He rested on the seventh day . . . and hallowed it (Exod. 20:8-11)." Now, however, we are told: "Observe the Sabbath day . . . that thy manservant and thy maidservant may rest as well as thou . . . (Deut. 5:12-15)." The purpose of the Sabbath is religious; the Exodus version makes that clear. Man must recognize the Creator from Whom all blessings flow and in Whom the universe has its beginning. But the purpose of the Sabbath is also social, as Deuteronomy points out. Social justice demands that all be given respite from work. The two versions complement each other. To Judaism, religion without social justice is meaningless. Social experimentation without a religious rationale is ultimately unjustified. Why should the servant rest? Why should he be regarded as equal? Only because he is a child of God like thyself. The indivisible unity of faith and action, taught by the prophets, is thus enshrined in the Ten Commandments themselves.

In Deuteronomy, the affirmation of God's Oneness is given its most concrete and most sublime expression: "Hear O Israel, the Lord our God, the Lord is One! And thou shalt love the Lord thy God with all thy heart and all thy soul and all thy might (Deut. 6:4-9)." From earliest childhood to his dying breath, every Jew repeats these words. God is One, and God, like a lover, pleads for love. He wishes to be recognized not as majestic Creator or all-powerful Lord, but as the supreme object of our love. He has created us in love; He maintains us in love; He sustains all the living in love. All He asks of us is that we may love Him in return, and that we love all His children. "Thou shalt love thy neighbor as thyself, I am the Lord (Lev. 19:18)." By loving our neighbor we establish God as Lord of a united mankind. By loving our neighbor we love Him. The two elements—love of God and sustaining love of neighbor—are once again fused into one. Thus life becomes worship, every moment of it hallowed. Deuteronomy relates in detail how this love must permeate our daily actions. The help given the poor is simple righteousness when seen as a function of love (Deut. 24:17 ff.). The animal too has a claim to decent treatment (Deut. 25:4). Even the enemy must be treated in the spirit of love, and war be preceeded by a genuine offer of peace (Deut. 20:10), up to such time when there will be war no more. The enemies' fruit trees must be protected—even in war (Deut. 20:19). God enters all facets of human relations. That is the burden of Deuteronomy. And the book ends with a solemn covenant binding the living and all future generations to the God of love and to all neighbors in love and in service.

Jeremiah: Hope of Return—The Duties of Citizenship

Perhaps the ideal of Deuteronomy was too far removed from the generation to which it was proclaimed. Complacency set in among the people once again, and doom was soon to come. There arose a new prophet with a mighty call for spiritual rearmament—Jeremiah, a lowly priest. Bitter persecution is his reward. Yet when disaster strikes—disaster the people could have escaped by following his advice—Jeremiah becomes the most tender comforter of his stricken people.

His political advice is realistic: submit to Babylonia, give unto Caesar that which is Caesar's, that you may remain free to give unto God that which is God's. His counsel is scorned. When the enemy is at the gates, there breaks through in Jeremiah the eternal optimism of the Jew. He buys a piece of real estate, now become utterly worthless. But he pays well for it, has the deed drawn up, and instructs his disciple in public: "Thus says the Lord of hosts, the God of Israel: 'Take these deeds and put them in an earthen vessel, that they may continue many days.' For thus says the Lord of hosts, the God of Israel: 'Houses and fields and vineyards shall yet again be bought in this land.(Jer. 32).'" This is true optimism; not the optimism of the escapist and the dreamer, but an optimism born of faith, an optimism ready to accept the trials of history in the knowledge that the end is victory, for thus God has spoken.

Jeremiah's own generation was not to see it fulfilled. Family after family was led into captivity. At first they thought of it as a mere temporary exile, then, when the truth dawned on them, they lost themselves in impotent hatred and a passive hope of return.

By the rivers of Babylon there we sat down, yea we wept when we remembered Zion. Upon the willows in the midst thereof we hanged our harps. . . . O daughter of Babylon that art to be destroyed, happy shall he be that repayeth thee as thou hast served us. Happy shall he be that taketh and dasheth thy little ones against the rock (Psalm 137).

The emotion is human but it is not Jewish. It dissipates itself in hopelessness; it is not constructive, but filled with hatred instead of love. Jeremiah has to check it at its inception. He sends a message to the exiled in Babylonia:

Thus saith the Lord of hosts, the God of Israel, unto all the captivity whom I have caused to be carried away captive from Jerusalem to Babylon: "Build ye houses and dwell in them; and plant gardens and eat the fruit of them; take ye wives and beget sons and daughters; and take wives for your sons and give your daughters to husbands, that they may bear sons and daughters; and multiply ye there and be not diminished. And seek the peace of the city whither I have caused you to be carried away captives, and pray to the Lord for it; for in the peace thereof shall ye have peace (Jer. 29:4-7)."

This letter has become basic to Jewish thinking. Dispersion is willed by God; it has a purpose. It is a permanent condition of Jewish life, calling for participation in the development of the countries where Jews may live—even if they are treated unjustly there. It calls for the fullest measure of loyalty, devoted service, and constructive contributions in countries where Jews have acquired the full rights of citizenship. This is a divine law. The right of return should not be excluded, however, for those who yearn for the soil of their ancestors. The "children shall return to their own border" (Jer. 31:17) is Jeremiah's assurance.

Thus there was to be, from that day on, diaspora, a world-wide Jewish community, even during the time of the second Temple and commonwealth. The settlement in Babylonia continued to flourish, and became a center of creativity. Jeremiah himself was taken to Egypt by members of the community who sought refuge there. He died in Egypt, but the settlement grew and developed. Babylonia and Egypt were the first two diaspora centers; strong in numbers, faithful to their tradition, the Jews distinguished themselves as devoted citizens. Here lies the forecast of much of subsequent Jewish history.

BABYLONIAN EXILE: NEW ANSWERS

The Beginning of Liturgy

Babylonian Jewry had leadership. They took down their harps from the willow trees to sing again; not songs of jubilation, but still praises of God. Jeremiah had enjoined them to pray, and they met in groups for common worship. The altar was gone and with it the sacrifices. But the Book was there; they could study it and find instruction. Their leaders could explain it to them. A form of worship was started which was to become standard in all western religion. Its central feature is the reading of Holy Scripture; here God speaks. Explanation of the Word was added, in order that all might understand; it became the sermon. Prayer, hymn, and psalm expressed yearning, hope, and thanksgiving. The common pattern of religious worship is a gift of Judaism to the western world.

Scripture became the guide through life. It was the treasure house of wisdom, the mine of which limitless knowledge was dug. A great spiritual and intellectual movement was started in Babylonia; its greatest literary achievement was to be the Talmud, its most lasting contribution, Jewish love of knowledge. Study became worship; the table with the Book became an altar; the family gathered around it in holy communion. A community thus rooted in the soil of eternity could not be destroyed. It depended neither on buildings nor on priests. Wherever two or three or ten—or even one—were gathered in the name of God, His divine Presence could be found. Whoever had acquired the knowledge to teach, combining with it quality of heart and exemplary living, could be a rabbi, which means teacher. Those who joined together in common search for God became a "synagogue," a gathering. It was not a building and could not be destroyed; it has remained immune to the ravages of time and the attacks of enemies, though many synagogue buildings have been reduced to ashes. The meeting house eventually acquired the name of those who met in it: the gathering, synagogue.

The meeting places themselves followed the structural divisions of the Temple of Jerusalem. There had been three divisions in the Temple of old: the courts where the people assembled, the sanctuary where the priests performed their holy service, and the holy of holies behind the curtain, where the Ark which held the Tablets of the Ten Commandments rested. The courts were transformed into the people's gathering place; the sanctuary became the chancel where the preceptor—the cantor of today—led the people in prayer and offered their petitions to God. The holy of holies was represented by the Ark, enshrining the Holy Scriptures, which are the very essence of Israel's survival. A curtain often covers the Ark.

And so the plan of the sacred meeting place goes back to the Jews; another of their gifts to the world, to church, and to mosque. Only Judaism knew of meeting halls for the people; the other temples of antiquity were small buildings, abodes of the gods, and the common folk were excluded. Judaism has made religion democratic.

It all started in Babylonia, and is testimony to the strength of Jews and Judaism. They have been able to adjust creatively, and in adjusting they have progressed.

Ezekiel: Individual Responsibility versus Inherited Sin

Among the leaders of the people was Ezekiel, priest and prophet. He was a mystic who saw God in mighty visions, and has told us about it in great elaboration.[11] He has made it clear to all generations that God can be envisioned in all His glory wherever men seek Him.

Ezekiel is the *people's* prophet *and* the *individuals'* shepherd. Burdened by a question that weighed heavily on their minds, the children of the generation of captivity came to ask him as they had asked Jeremiah: "Are we held responsible for the sins of our fathers? They were in error, but we are still far away from home. Are we involved in their guilt?" Ezekiel, quoting Jeremiah,[12] gives an answer which establishes the basic outlook of Judaism regarding inherited sin, including original sin. His answer is categorical; there is no inherited sin

---

[11] Ezekiel 1:1 ff
[12] Jeremiah 31:29-30.

And the word of the Lord came unto me saying:

What mean ye that ye use this proverb in the land of Israel saying:

'The fathers have eaten sour grapes and the children's teeth are set on edge'?
As I live, saith the Lord God, ye shall not have occasion any more to use this
proverb in Israel. Behold all the souls are Mine; as the soul of the father so
also the soul of the son is Mine; the soul that sinneth shall die. But if a man
be just and do that which is lawful and right . . . he is just, he shall surely
live, saith the Lord God.

If he beget a son that is a robber, a shedder of blood . . . he shall not live—
he hath done all these abominations. . . .

Now, if he begets a son that sees all his father's sins , . . and considers and
doeth not such like . . . he shall not die for the iniquity of his father . . .
he shall surely live (Ezek. 18:3-17).

Judaism recognizes Yetzer-ha-Ra, the inclination to yield to sinful
temptation, but no inborn sinfulness. Victory over Yetzer-ha-Ra is won
through submission to Torah, the Rabbis maintain. No man can be
held responsible for the sins committed by his ancestors; but he is responsible for the sins committed by his fellowman, if it was within his
power to set him right. Judaism does not recognize any collective sin,
but it firmly upholds the principle of individual responsibility.

Son of man, I have set thee a watchman unto the house of Israel; therefore
when thou shalt hear the word at My mouth warn them from Me. When I say
unto the wicked: O wicked man thou shalt surely die, and thou dost not speak
to warn the wicked from his way, that wicked man shall die in his iniquity, but
his blood will I require at thy hand. Nevertheless, if thou warn the wicked of
his way to turn from it, and he turn not from his way, he shall die in his
iniquity, but thou hast delivered thy soul (Ezek. 33:7-10).

Ezekiel simply repeated an instruction the people had already received. Leviticus had pointed it out already: "Thou shalt not hate thy
brother in thy heart; thou shalt surely rebuke thy neighbor, and not bear
sin because of him (Lev. 19:17)." Conditions in the diaspora called for a
renewed emphasis on mutual responsibility, because the influences of the
environment were very strong. And the rebuke must be given in the
spirit of love, out of a deep concern for the neighbor's life, lest he die
either in spirit or in body. Man must learn to purge his own heart from
all selfishness and hatred, and take upon himself the arduous task of approaching his neighbor to help him to regain life through repentance.
Thus does man imitate God, for Whom there is no sin which cannot be
forgiven.

Say unto the children of Israel: Thus ye speak ". . . our transgressions and
our sins are upon us, we pine away in them; how can we live?" Say unto them:
"As I live, saith the Lord, I have no pleasure in the death of the wicked, but
that the wicked return from his way and live. Turn ye, turn ye from your evil
ways; for why will you die, O House of Israel (Ezek. 33:10-11)?"

Taking these pronouncements in conjunction, we find four key terms: Brother, Neighbor, Israel, Man. Out of acceptance of these terms grew the feeling of kinship which has made the Jews into one family; out of it also grew the spirit of social fervor, and the irrepressible urge to improve society and to establish social justice, that man may live. Thus has Jewry understood the message. Ezekiel, who recognizes that the feeling of guilt is akin to death, becomes the first shepherd of souls, the first pastor. As he spoke to individuals in the time of their need so does he speak across the ages to every individual soul.

The Second Isaiah: Voice of Hope

Ezekiel's answer had been incomplete. If sons do not bear guilt for the sins of their fathers, why must the good sons suffer? Why does Israel suffer so much? The second Isaiah speaks out, addressing himself to the problem. Suffering need not be regarded as the wages of sin; it may be a test of strength, a test of faith, a sign of being chosen. The suffering servant of God makes it clear to a skeptical world that nothing ean make him waver in his dedication. Were he always blessed, he would not be servant but man of privilege. It would be easy for him to love God. Were he to know that reward and punishment are always linked to man's actions as effect follows the cause, he might serve God for selfish reasons, to escape suffering or find happiness. The true servant of God must be willing to be tested, and maintain his faith in adversity. By his steadfastness he becomes a witness, and by his dedication he becomes an inspiration to the world. He illustrates that God, who commands such obedience, is truly great. His ways may be unsearchable but He commands man's allegiance. The servant of God thus suffers for all the world, which cannot help being inspired by such heroic faith. This is Isaiah's explanation for undeserved suffering.

He was despised and forsaken of men, a man of pains and acquainted with disease, . . . he was despised and we esteemed him not. Surely our diseases did he bear, and our pains he carried. . . . Yet it pleased the Lord to crush· him by disease; to see if his soul would offer itself in restitution, that he might see his seed prolong his days, and that the purpose of the Lord might prosper by his hand; Of the travail of his soul he shall see to the full, even My servant, who by his knowledge did justify the Righteous One to the many, and their iniquities did he bear (Isa. 53).

Isaiah's words, like those of Job dealing with the same problem, have been a source of inspiration to the Jew. In his encounter with the world he was told again and again that his suffering was surely evidence of sinfulness. Actually he bore the disease in behalf of his tormentors, who lived in peace, hoping they might change their ways. He bore it for the sake of his children, that they—as Jews—might carry on the task. He did not falter, though the door of escape was open if he but renounced his faith. He did all this to justify the Righteous God, knowing that some day his suffering would be justified and made worth while, having ennobled mankind to recognize God and to serve His purpose.

Such heroism in suffering is not easy. Isaiah knew he had to strengthen those who became weary and despondent at the endlessness of the trial. His words have brought new determination to the generations after him:

Why sayest thou, O Jacob, and speakest O Israel, 'My way is hidden from the Lord and my right passes over from my God'? Hast thou not known, hast thou not heard, that the everlasting God, the Creator of the ends of the earth, fainteth not, neither is weary? His discernment is past searching out. He giveth power to the faint; and to him that has no might He increaseth strength. Even youth may faint and be weary, and young men may utterly fall; but they that wait for the Lord shall renew their strength; they shall mount up with wings as eagles; they shall run and not be weary; they shall walk and not faint (Isa. 40:27-31).

Justification lies not in the reward, but in the eternal renewal of strength. Waiting should weaken; helplessness will ordinarily sap one's strength, just as failure to know God's ways should lead to doubt. The very opposite has happened in history. Nations and individuals rose in youthful strength and arrogance, cruel, ruthless, and destructive. They became weary and faint, and so they fell. But Jews have renewed their strength with every fall, with every enforced march from country to country. Walking through history they have found in their faith an everlasting source of energy. Suffering is both test and glory. Guided by this knowledge Israel has endured and will endure to the day when God will say the words: "Comfort ye, comfort ye My people (Isa. 40:1)."

The End of the Exile

Isaiah was able to witness the end of one period of trial. Events in Asia changed rapidly. Nebuchadnezzar's empire had crumbled under his successors and fallen into the hands of Cyrus, king of Persia. He permitted the exiled to go home. It was not simply an act of kindness—he wanted a friendly population in Palestine, border province of his empire toward Egypt. But to the captives the king was like a messenger of God.[13] The day of redemption had come, proving to all that steadfastness finds its reward. Jubilantly Isaiah calls out:

O thou, that tellest good tidings to Zion get thee up into the high mountain; o thou that tellest good tidings to Jerusalem lift up your voice with strength; lift it up, be not afraid; say unto the cities of Judah: "Behold your God" (Isa. 40:9).

---

13 Isaiah 44:28; 45:1.

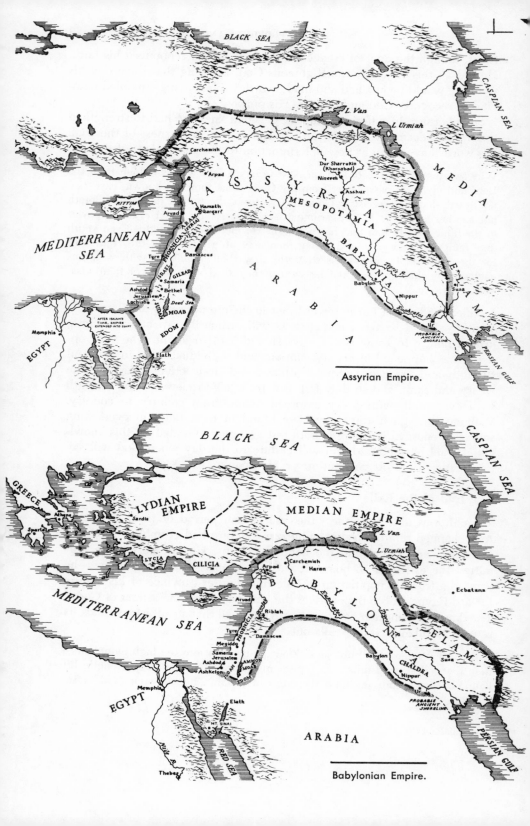

Assyrian Empire.

Babylonian Empire.

The Persian Empire.

Alexander's Empire.

They had waited and they had won. Future generations would again have to wait; but they would know that they too some day would win.

The Jewish community in Babylonia was not dissolved. Diaspora had been recognized as a permanent possibility, and many remained in their new found home. This Jewish community was destined to rise to the very summit of glory and everlasting achievement.

3

Return, Restoration, Renaissance

When the Lord brought back those that returned to Zion, we were like unto them that dreamed (Psalm 126)." The dream of the returning remnant was quickly dissolved. The land had been settled in their absence. Among the peoples who claimed it were the Samaritans, a mixed multitude. Descendants of the long destroyed kingdom of Israel had intermarried with the people of the neighborhood. They had fused Jewish ideas with heathen customs and patterns of life, and their way was not the way of Jews.[1] They could not be absorbed into the Jewish people and became hostile. Against their opposition and their intrigues, settlement and the building of a new Temple were pressed. Zerubabel, a royal prince of the House of David who had led the return, pushed the building project. He was joined by the prophets Haggai and Zachariah. In 515 the new House was solemnly consecrated.

STRANGERS AND CONVERTS: THE JEWISH CONCEPT

The Temple did not stem the tide of trouble. The settlers drew their sense of security from the land, which held the promise of survival for those who tilled it. What was more natural for the young men of the people than to marry their neighbors' daughters, whose lives and whose

---

[1] A small remnant of the Samaritans can still be found in Israel today.

ambitions were like theirs? These neighbors, however, were not Jews; they brought with them their own beliefs and drew their husbands into the folds of heathen worship. It would not be all pagan or impure, but diluted purity no longer is pure. If the family spirit broke down, the law of Moses could not long endure. This was the view of the new leader of the community. He was Ezra, a learned priest, who arrived from Babylonia c. 428, before the Christian era. He had been preceded by an equally gifted man. Nehemiah, who arrived c. 445, was a high official at the court of the Persian king; he had obtained a special leave of absence to help his brethren. The two men went to work with determination and dispatch. The walls of Jerusalem were completed, the city's population increased, and then Ezra went to the core of the problem. Marriages with heathen wives had to be dissolved; a new covenant was to be established; the people had to take a solemn pledge to obey faithfully the Law of Moses. (The dates of these two men's ministry are still controversial.)

Conversion

Ezra's act reveals an inner tension in Jewish thinking on one of the fundamental issues of religion, the admission of converts. It has contributed toward the ambivalent attitude toward conversion which is still present in Judaism. Ezra demanded complete divorce, and we can well understand his motives. He came from Babylonia, where he had learned that only through strict obedience to religion could the Jewish community expect to survive. Faith alone could hold the group together, and Ezra's one concern was the survival of the nation under God. In his strictness, he set himself in opposition to long established historical practice. From the days of Abraham, who had migrated to Canaan with "the souls . . . gotten in Haran," [2] converts had been brought into the faith with full rights and privileges as Jews. True, in moments of spiritual danger there had been a retrenchment. Abraham could not permit his son Isaac to marry any of the daughters of the land, as the Canaanite cult was an abomination. But we find Jacob proudly blessing his grandchildren, the sons of Joseph and Osnat, daughter of the priest of On in Egypt. His blessing expressed the hope that all sons in Israel might be like these two lads, Ephraim and Manasseh.[3] Moses himself had married a Midianite woman.[4] A multitude of mixed character and ancestry had joined the children of Israel on their exodus from Egypt;[5] the Canaanites and

---

[2] Genesis 12:5.
[3] Genesis 48:20.
[4] Exodus 2:15-22.
[5] Exodus 12:38.

Philistines had become absorbed in the course of Israel's life. The second Isaiah had even raised it into a principle:

Also the aliens, that join themselves to the Lord to minister unto Him; and to love the Name of the Lord to be His servants, Everyone that keepeth the sabbath from profaning it, and holdeth fast by My covenant: even them will I bring to My holy mountain; and make them joyful in My House of prayer; their burnt-offerings and their sacrifices shall be acceptable upon mine altar; for my house shall be called a house of prayer for all peoples saith the Lord God who gathereth the dispersed of Israel: Yet will I gather others to him besides those of him that are gathered (Isa. 56:6-8).

Ezra reversed this principle when he ruled that the foreign women would have to be dismissed without individual investigation regarding their worth and the sincerity of their attachment to Judaism. In doing so, he was actually agreeing with the ancient nations. Isaiah's concept was revolutionary and unique in antiquity. The barbarian could not become a Greek, the foreigner could not become a Roman citizen, simply by expressing his desire; but the stranger could become a Jew if he pledged his life by the promise "to hold fast to the covenant." Ezra's ordinance, issued at a moment of stress, did not change this universalistic outlook of Judaism. His command was obeyed without being accepted in principle. The story of Ruth has come down to us as a testimony of the unchanged outlook of the Jews.

The Book of Ruth tells a moving story. A man of Judah and his sons go to Moab to escape famine in Israel. The sons marry two daughters of the land, but their joy is brief. The two husbands and the father die, leaving only the three women—Naomi, the old widowed mother, and her two widowed daughters-in-law. Naomi decides to return home, and says farewell to the younger women. But one of them, Ruth, will not leave her, and she says:

Entreat me not to leave thee, and to return from following after thee;
for whither thou goest, I will go,
and where thou lodgest I will lodge;
thy people shall be my people, and thy God my God.
Where thou diest I will die and there I will be buried;
the Lord do so to me and more also
if aught but death part me and thee (Ruth 1:16-17).

Even in a foreign land the beauty of Judaism had wrought its miracle. By strength of conviction and nobility of love, Naomi had drawn Ruth to the inspiring fountainhead of Judaism. Converts welcomed to Judaism may bring great enrichment. Ruth marries again, finding a distinguished Jewish husband. The story proudly relates that Ruth, the Moabite, became the great-grandmother of David, the anointed of Israel.

Conversion in Historical Perspective

History shows that conversion activity continued in Judaism. The book of Esther, written during a period of severe persecution, relates with a kind of naïve pride the story of many conversions. A Jewish girl had become Queen of Persia, her uncle made prime minister, and the plot of an enemy of the Jews thwarted. With this new regime in power, "many from among the peoples of the land became Jews." [6] Although this story may never have happened, the spirit behind it, the happy acceptance of those who wished to join the faith, remains important.

Many examples could be added. In the first century before our era, Queen Helena of Adiabene and her royal family accept Judaism. During the period of the Roman empire, we find Jews travelling as missionaries all over the known world. By making converts, they make themselves unpopular among philosophers and writers, as we shall see later, and provoke an early anti-Semitic reaction. Actually, the early Christian missionaries were able to build on the foundations laid by their Jewish predecessors. With the fall of the second Temple, the rules of admission to Judaism became more stringent, and the argument for and against conversion more pointed, but the work was brought to a halt only by the edicts of the emperors and, later, by the Church prohibition of Jewish proselyting.

A person became a Jew by accepting the faith which he had studied previously, by immersion and—for men—by circumcision. A rabbinical court made the admission formal. Fundamentally, these rules have not changed.

The ideas of Ezra and the ideas of Ruth are both operative in Jewish life today; conversion as challenge and opportunity or as liability, the problem is still the same.

THE COVENANT

Ezra emphasized the genealogy of the returning flock, yet his very actions show he knew that he was not dealing with a homogeneous racial group—one cannot speak of Jews as a race. Ezra united the people by renewing the covenant. The year was 444, the place the Temple court.

All the people gathered themselves together as one man . . . and they spoke to Ezra the scribe to bring the book of the Law of Moses, which the Lord had commanded to Israel. And Ezra, the priest brought the Law before the congregation, both men and women, all that could hear with understanding . . . and he read therein. . . . And Ezra, the scribe stood upon a pulpit of

---

[6] Esther 8:17.

wood, which they had made for the purpose . . . and Ezra opened the book in the sight of all the people . . . and when he opened it, the people stood up. And Ezra blessed the Lord, the great God. And all the people answered Amen, Amen. . . . Also Jeshua and . . . the Levites caused the people to understand the Law. . . . And they read in the book in the Law of God distinctly; and they gave the sense and caused them to understand the reading (Neh. 8:1-8). Now . . . the children of Israel were assembled with fasting and with sackcloth and with earth upon them . . . and they . . . read in the book of the Law of the Lord their God a fourth part of the day; and another fourth part they confessed and prostrated themselves before the Lord their God. . . . (Then, after a review of their past history, they affirmed) . . . we make a sure covenant and subscribe to it . . . they cleaved to their brethren . . . and entered into an . . . oath to walk in God's law which was given by Moses the servant of God, and to observe and do all the commandments of the Lord our Lord, and His ordinances and His statutes (Neh. 9:1-3; 10:1, 30).

This was the moment of rebirth. The institutions established in Babylonia —Torah reading, explanation, prayer—became the universal foundation of future growth and development. The Torah with its commandments was *the* guide. This was to have far-reaching consequences. The synagogue, as the place where Torah was taught and prayer offered, now became a permanent institution, equal to the Temple. The rabbi as teacher of Torah had now become more important than the priest performing an ancient ritual. This was to lead to a centuries-long struggle for supremacy between the Temple and its priesthood and the synagogue with its rabbinic leadership and democratic organization. The synagogue won. Had it lost the contest, Judaism would not have survived the fall of the Temple. The covenant of Ezra made it clear that all are equal before God, as long as they are willing to listen, to study, and to obey God's word. The very character of Judaism is expressed here. Judaism demands understanding; it requires study, which it considers a form of worship. Obedience without understanding is truly blind. The Jew is commanded by his religion to study Torah.

What We Mean by Torah

Torah means "Instruction." The people who entered the covenant promised to walk in God's Torah and, furthermore, to obey the laws. The term "Torah" has acquired several meanings, however. They become clear as we follow the narrative of Ezra's covenant.

1) The people have gathered. Ezra brings the "Book of the Torah" to read from. He brought a parchment scroll upon which the Five Books of Moses, the Pentateuch, was written. In its narrowest sense, Torah means the same today. It stands for the scroll of the Pentateuch. Each congregation must have at least one of them for public reading.

Scroll of the Torah, open at the beginning of the Ten Commandments (Exod. 20: 1ff). The silver "hand" points to the last word of the line, which is the first word of the text of the Commandments, since all Hebrew writing is from right to left. The Torah scrolls are hand written on parchment with a special goose quill and hand made ink. Placed behind the Torah in this picture are the silver ornaments which decorate the scroll.

2) Ezra, and later the people, read the Torah. The term now stands for the *content* of the scroll and of all holy books. This is its wider meaning.

3) The Levites give sense to the reading, so the people will understand. They interpret the source readings. This also is Torah. The term now stands for all the interpretations of the Scripture. Taken in its widest sense, the term Torah thus stands for all the commentaries to the Scripture. But these commentaries and interpretations are the results of the experiences of the Jewish people, of their encounters with history, their way of life throughout the centuries. Life itself is an interpretation of our relationship to God. Torah in the fullest meaning of the term thus is synonymous with "Jewish Heritage." It is important to remember it. Torah *contains laws,* but it is *not simply law;* it is *instruction.* The meaning of the word Torah changes with the context in which it is used. It stands for "the Spirit of Judaism"; it is the essence of Judaism. Jews are the people of Torah, but they are not a legalistic people. Judaism is based on Torah, but it is not simply a religion of law. It calls for the dedication of the heart and the soul and the spirit. Misinterpretation of the term "Torah" has led to profound misunderstandings of the character of Judaism.

Written and Oral Torah

Ezra presents the Torah to the people as, literally, the word of God. Orthodox Jewry regards it as such to this day. This implies that every word and every letter has a meaning; a divinely dictated text must be regarded as precise in every detail. In this spirit the written Torah was explained and interpreted, very much as a court of law interprets the meaning of the words of the Constitution. The method of interpretation used through the ages was based on Greek principles of logic. For many

38

centuries all interpretations were transmitted by word of mouth only, and therefore called "Oral Torah." Later they were written down in a work, called the Talmud, which we shall discuss.

From the very beginning we have these two sources of authority: the "Written Torah"—Scripture—and the "Oral Torah." Oral Torah complemented, interpreted, and frequently gave the full meaning of an otherwise obscure passage of the written word. In Oral Torah we have evolution. In applying the principles of law to practical situations, rabbis added new meaning to existing legislation and established precedents. The weight of an interpretation and of a precedent depended both on its logical argument and on the authority of the interpreter. A comment or decision ascribed to Moses himself would have authority of force almost equal to the written word itself, since Moses received his interpretations directly "from Sinai," that is, from God. Just as the Constitution remains incomplete without the decisions of the court explaining and enlarging it, so does Written Torah remain incomplete without Oral Torah explaining and evolving it. The judge who becomes interpreter of Constitution and law must meet two requirements: the first is absolute loyalty to the Constitution, and the second is a thorough knowledge of law combined with the power of clear and critical thinking. The same applies to the interpreter of Torah, the rabbi. His ordination grants him the authority to render decisions. They must be based on a thorough knowledge of the sources and be the result of critical thinking; above all, they must be rooted in a spirit of full allegiance to Judaism and its tradition. While modern rabbis have functions in many other fields, the traditional rabbi of Europe was primarily a "judge," an interpreter of traditional law to meet practical situations. The judge has authority supported by the Written Torah in demanding obedience to his ruling, for the right to interpret was granted to the judges and rabbis on the basis of the word of Torah itself.

If there arise a matter too hard for thee in judgement . . . then thou shalt come unto the priests, the Levites, and unto the judge that shall be in those days; and thou shalt inquire; and they shall declare unto thee the sentence of judgement. And thou shalt do according to the tenor of the sentence . . . and thou shalt observe to do according to all they shall teach thee. According to the Torah which they shall teach thee, and according to the judgement which they shall tell thee, thou shalt do; thou shalt not turn aside from the sentence which they declare unto thee, to the right hand nor to the left (Deut. 17:8-11).

Ezra, who stands in his pulpit to read the Torah, and the Levites, who explain it, all stand squarely on this foundation of identity in evolution. Thus Judaism could and did absorb the best in other civilizations and religious philosophies. It could amalgamate ideas, it could grow, and yet it has remained the religion of Torah, as Jews have remained the people of the Torah covenant.

The Jewish encounter with Hellenism tested the strength of the people to absorb and to reject.

HELLENISM

Conflict and Rebellion: The Maccabees

For over one hundred years, the Jewish community rests sheltered in the shadow of a salutary neglect. History tells us nothing of this period, which must have been a time of inner spiritual consolidation. Then the land and the people are caught again in the current of world history. Alexander the Great becomes master of the world. Disciple of the philosopher Aristotle, he is conqueror as well as missionary of Greek thought and ideals. His kindness to the Jews earned him their eternal gratitude. They named their children Alexander; they wove beautiful legends around his appearance. As he arrived, the high priest and the elders went out to meet him. Alexander, descending from his chariot, bent the knee to Simeon, the High Priest. His men asked him, "A king, great as thou falls on his knees before this Jew"? He answered, "The vision of this priest's appearance once came to me, to lead me on to victory." [7]

Alexander's early death cut short his work. His empire was divided up between contending generals. Judah, for a while, was attached to the kingdom of Egypt ruled by the Ptolemies; then it fell into the sphere of the Seleucids, who ruled over the kingdom of Syria, the eastern portion of Alexander's erstwhile empire. King Antiochus Epiphanes of Syria was faced with the problem of unifying the various national groups of his polyglot empire. He saw only one solution: unity in Greek culture, unity through Greek religion. During the first third of the second century, the Jews thus found themselves threatened in their most precious possession, their faith, and they rebelled. The revolt had its start in a small rural community. Mattathias, an ancient priest of the House of Hasmon, gathered his sons and followers around him. Freedom of Religion was their slogan, their battle cry. Judas Maccabaeus, one of Mattathias' sons, became general of the small army of the faithful. On their banner, they wrote the initials of the scriptural quotation "*Mee Kamokha Ba-elim YHWH*"—Who is like unto Thee among the mighty, O Lord?. These initials spell the word "*M* (a) *K* (a) *B Y*," giving Judah his title: Maccabee.[8] They won their battles and rededicated the desecrated temple; the

---

[7] Talmud; Yoma 69 a.
[8] Exodus 15:11. Another derivation is from Maccabee the Hammerer, hammering down the enemy.

festival of dedication, Hanukah, has been celebrated evei since. It tells everlastingly of the victory of faith over force.

Judah falls in battle, but his brothers make peace in freedom. One of them, Simon, becomes king, the first in the dynasty of the Hasmoneans, combining the royal crown and the priestly robes, as priest-king of an independent Judaea. But too much power corrupts. The priestly office becomes a veneer for the worldly ambitions of its occupants, and family intrigues in the royal house lead to terror and civil war. Murder runs rampant in the family. Two brothers, Hyrcanus and Aristobulus, stalemated in their struggle for the crown, eventually call on Rome to settle their quarrel. In 63, the brothers appear before Pompey, and the Roman decides in favor of Hyrcanus, the weaker of the two. On his arrival in Jerusalem, Pompey enters the Temple as a sightseer would and penetrates the holy of holies, the inner sanctum where only the high priest was permitted to go in fear and trembling, and that only once a year. Pompey found it empty, the ark long disappeared, the invisible God needing no visible reflection of His presence. But Pompey is bewildered. These Jews, do they pray to nothing? Are they atheists? He cannot understand their faith, and misunderstanding, eventually, is to breed contempt. Pompey's was an act of sacrilege as far as the Jews were concerned. It clearly demonstrated, however, the new order of things. The privileges of king and priest had gone to Rome; the Hasmonean king is without power, Rome rules. Hyrcanus is given an advisor by Rome. His name is Antipater. He is not of Jewish descent, but an Idumaean, member of a people who had been conquered and forcibly converted by the Hasmoneans, without ever accepting the faith of Israel in good conscience.

Antipater is shrewd, ruthless, and skilful. Maneuvering between the contending powers in Rome, he enhances his own position by undermining the royal house of the Hasmoneans. His son, soon to become king of Judaea, completes the work of destruction. His name was Herod, and he was a monster. His enemies—real and imagined—were murdered by the hundreds, and their property confiscated for the royal treasury. To legitimize his claim to the throne, he married Mariamne, a Hasmonean princess. He had other wives, but he loved Mariamne ardently, yet in insane jealousy he murdered her. She had borne him two sons, who grew to manhood; haunted by a growing madness of suspicion, he saw even in them conspirators against his life, and led them to their death. Thus came to its end the once proud house of the Hasmoneans. Only one small grandson of royal blood survived. His name was Agrippa, and he became the friend of Rome's emperor Claudius and was able to give his people four final years of peace (41-44) before the commonwealth collapsed. Herod restored the Temple in Jerusalem; he had it rebuilt in grandiose splendor, for the sanctuary was a world famous place. It was not an act

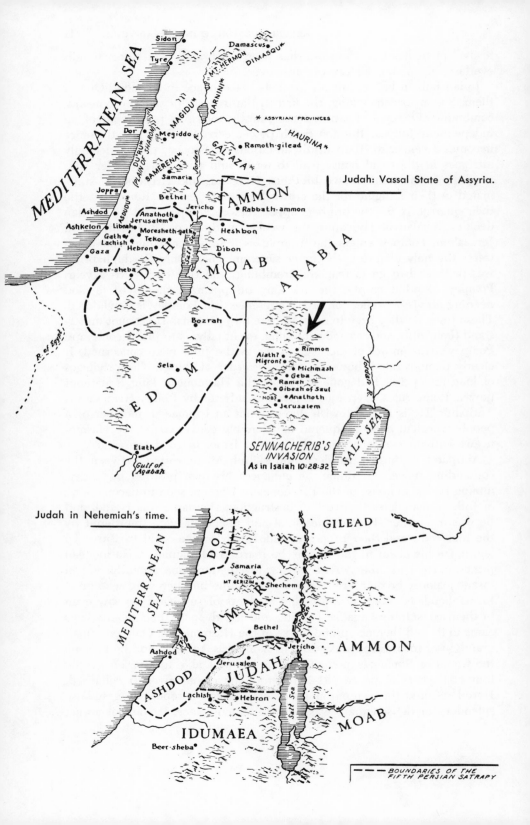

MEDITERRANEAN SEA

Sidon
Damascus
DIMASQU
MT. HERMON
Tyre
QARNINI
* ASSYRIAN PROVINCES
Megiddo
MAGIDU
HAURINA *
Dor
DU-RU
(PLAIN OF SHARON)
GAL-AZA
Ramoth-gilead
SAMERENA *
Samaria
Joppa
Judah: Vassal State of Assyria.
Bethel
AMMON
ASDUDU
Anathoth
Jericho
Rabbath-ammon
Ashdod
Jerusalem
Ashkelon
Libnah
Moresheth-gath
Heshbon
Gath
Tekoa
Lachish
Gaza
Hebron
Dibon
Beer-sheba
JUDAH
MOAB
ARABIA
R. of Egypt
Bozrah
Rimmon
Aiath?
Migron?
Michmash
Sela
Geba
Ramah
Gibeah of Saul
NOB?
Anathoth
EDOM
Jerusalem
Jordan R.
SENNACHERIB'S INVASION
As in Isaiah 10:28-32
SALT SEA
Elath
Gulf of Aqabah

Judah in Nehemiah's time.

MEDITERRANEAN SEA
DOR
GILEAD
SAMARIA
Samaria
MT GERIZIM
Shechem
Bethel
Ashdod
Jericho
AMMON
ASHDOD
Jerusalem
JUDAH
Lachish
Hebron
Salt Sea
MOAB
IDUMAEA
Beer-sheba

BOUNDARIES OF THE
FIFTH PERSIAN SATRAPY

of piety or repentance. Over the portals of the Temple Herod placed the Roman eagle, a graven image abhorrent to the Jews. Salvation, to Herod, did not come from Him whose glory dwelt in the holy halls, but rather lay with Rome. As he lived so did he die, unrepentant. He had the leaders of the people placed in jail with orders that they be killed as soon as the news of his own death became known, in order that there be no rejoicing in the hour of his parting. But this was too much even for his henchmen; his wish was not carried out. Actually, though unbeknown to him, Herod's reign spelled death to the last remnant of Judaean independence. The country was divided up among his heirs, who became rulers in name only. Rome sent procurators to Judaea, Roman governors who held the real power in their hands. Herod had ruled from 37 to 4 before the Christian era, and the memory of the "Idumaean slave," as the tortured people had called him under their breath, remained accursed. Edom was also the epithet hurled by the Jews against Herod's master, Rome.

Maccabean Palestine.

The procurators deserved the people's hatred. Frequently replaced, they used their term of office to enrich themselves quickly. They resided in Caesarea, the city and seaport built by Herod in honor of Caesar Augustus. Among them was Pontius Pilate, who held his office all too long, from 26 to 36. He found pleasure in trampling underfoot the Jews' most sacred religious beliefs. In arrogant defiance of their laws, he set up the royal eagles in Jersualem. The people appeared before him in the arena of Caesarea to petition for a change. He surrounded them with his troops, giving them a choice. They could yield, or they might accept immediate death. As the people bared their necks, ready to die for their faith, even Pilate had to yield. Soon afterwards he appropriated vast sums of the temple treasury for a building project. When the people appeared before him again, asking for redress of grievances, he had them beaten down. The country seethed with unrest; many felt that a new Judas Maccabaeus was needed to restore freedom by force of arms. Galilee was a hotbed of rebellion; Jerusalem, especially at festival times, was a cauldron of boiling emotions. Pontius Pilate had only one answer: excite the people to fever pitch, then slaughter them. Without a moment's hesitation, without the slightest trace of qualm he could, therefore, order the execution of Jesus of Nazareth, whose beliefs and ideas he distrusted. Pilate eventually carried his cruelties so far that Rome discharged him and called him back home. Joseph Caiaphas, the high priest he had appointed, was also discharged. Rome appointed a new one, for the office of high priest had become a political plum. Only Rome could appoint a man to this powerful office; the people's opposition meant nothing.

In 64 the last of the procurators, Gessius Florus, arrived. So brutal was the man, so horrible his deeds, that complaints could no longer be silenced. To meet the situation, Florus hit on a truly devilish plan. He would incite the people to rebellion, taunt them, humiliate them, until their patience broke. Then he could justify his administration and his mismanagement by pointing to the rebelliousness of the Jews. He succeeded. The people rise and the Romans are pushed back. So severe are the Roman losses that Nero decides to send his best commander to the scene. In 67, Vespasian marches his legions from Syria into Judaea. They are met by an army in Upper Galilee. The Jewish commander, Josephus Flavius, is the guardian of the approaches to the land—and Josephus surrenders. Later on, perhaps torn by remorse, he becomes a historian, the most important source for the historical events of his time. His works, "Jewish Antiquities" and "The Jewish War," have become classics. In these books, he hopes to explain to the Romans that Judaism and Jews are worthy of respect. At the moment, his betrayal leaves the road to Jerusalem open. Slowly Vespasian advances. Then Nero dies, Vespasian returns to Rome to become emperor, placing his son Titus in command

of the armies. In the year 70, Titus has finally encircled the capital city
of Jerusalem. While the enemy pushes ahead, civil war rages within the
city. The parties disagree about the conduct of the war. The radicals,
called Zealots, eventually seize the power. In the struggle storehouses are
burnt down. Hunger becomes an ally of the enemy. On the ninth day of
the Jewish month of Ab, in spite of heroic defense, Jerusalem falls; the
Temple goes up in flames. Titus, the conquering hero, returns to Rome
in triumph. An arch is erected in his honor. On it can be seen to this day
the holy candelabrum carried in triumph to Rome, followed by Jewish
prisoners in chains. Rome strikes a coin, bearing the inscription "Judaea

Details from the Arch
of Titus, Rome.

Capta." It shows the "widow" of Judah dejectedly weeping her fate, under a tree whose fruits she will no more enjoy. A conquering Roman soldier watches proudly. But Judah cannot be captured. In 1958, the Israeli government struck another medal in celebration of the new state's tenth anniversary. On one side it shows the replica of the Roman coin. On the reverse, under the caption "Israel Liberata," it presents a mother proudly holding her child to the rays of the sun of freedom. She is standing under the fruit tree, which has grown tall and sturdy. At her side is her husband, kneeling, planting a new seedling to grow to health and strength with the child and the land.

Vespasian was never to know that he himself had helped lay the foundations of Jewish survival. During the last days of the struggle for Jerusalem, a great rabbi, Johanan ben Zaccai, secretly met the general. The rabbi knew that Jerusalem was doomed. He asked Vespasian's permission to open a small school of Jewish studies in the little town of Jabneh, and the Roman could see nothing wrong with that. Immediately, Johanan sets up an academy, and obtains for it the authority in matters of Jewish religion which had resided in the Sanhedrin, the Supreme Court of Jerusalem. Its head, the "patriarch," is recognized by Jewry all over the world as their supreme spiritual leader. The donations, once sent to the Temple, are now given to the school. Before the sun had set over Jerusalem, it had risen over Jabneh. The city had been destroyed, but the spirit had remained unharmed.

This spirit found expression in political action as well. Twice the Jews rebelled. In 116, they rose up against Trajan; and in 132 they rebelled against Hadrian. The emperor now realized that he could not destroy the Jews unless he broke their faith. He therefore prohibited the practice

Coin struck off to celebrate the tenth anniversary of Israel.

Entrance to the catacombs at Bet Shearim, burial place of Rabbi Judah the Prince, editor of the Mishnah.

of Judaism. Not long ago, archaeologists found letters dating from this final rebellion, which was led by Bar Kokhba and ended in defeat, suffering, and heroic martyrdom. But Hadrian had come too late. The reorganization of Judaism had taken hold. The emperor might forbid the Jews by punishment of death to enter the ruins of Jerusalem, but he could not eradicate their faith. He might change the name of the colony from Judaea to Palestine, but he could not wipe out Judaism. He tortured to death the leaders of the people, their rabbis, and used the most sophisticated methods of inflicting pain in torture. He only succeeded in immortalizing them. The story of their martyrdom is recalled in the liturgy of the Day of Atonement, the holiest day of the Jewish year. They have become symbols, standing for the uncounted millions of Jews who laid down their lives for their Jewish heritage, and who, in dying, lived, and, in defeat, prevailed.

Hadrian's edict was rescinded by his successor, Antoninus Pius. But the lesson it had taught remained deeply etched in the consciousness of the people. Resistance must be spiritual. The Academy was rebuilt in Upper Galilee. Under the leadership of the patriarchs, it carried out its work of interpreting Torah. The Oral Torah grew apace. But the patriarchs realized that Oral Torah was in danger unless it was put in writing. One more persecution and the bearers of tradition might be wiped out. Judah the Patriarch undertook the task of editing and setting down the basic principal rulings of Oral Torah. The work, the Mishnah, was completed in about the year 200. By this achievement, Judah earned for himself the title "Rabbi"—*The* Teacher—accorded him by a grateful posterity. So venerated was his personality that his grave became a shrine for pilgrims, and Jews all over the ancient world carried their dead over thousands of miles that they might rest near the tomb of the master. His grave was discovered by Israeli archaeologists in a group of beautiful catacombs at Bet Shearim. In our day, pilgrims are coming again to visit it.

The academy continued for another two hundred years. It closed its gates around 425, when the Christian head of Palestine assumed the title patriarch. The Crusades (11th cent.) ultimately ended Jewish creativity in Palestine. The land fell into deep slumber, to be awakened again in ages to come. The center of Jewish life and creativity moved to Babylonia once more, but Zion was never without a Jewish settlement, and remained a force in the hearts and souls and minds of the Jews. It was enshrined in their prayers and songs, for it was God's will that it should be theirs.

The years whose history we have sketched were a period of turmoil and of restlessness. But this is only one part of the story, the political one. Culturally and spiritually, these were years of highest attainment. The concepts of normative Judaism were hammered out during this period, as we shall see.

The Inspiration of Greek Thought

After Ezra's reconstruction, the future of Judaism rested on two pillars: study and interpretation of Torah, and observance of Torah. The rabbis who emerged as leaders of the people were very much like the Puritan divines in Colonial New England. They interpreted Scripture and supervised its practical application in the life of the nation and of the individual. However, they differed from the Puritans in several essential points. The Puritan clergy had the power of the state behind it to enforce rulings; the rabbis depended on the power of their example and their word. The people followed them by free choice. The Puritans observed strictly the letter of the law; conservative in outlook, though forced by conditions to accept progress, they would have liked to restore to life a theocratic society which had died several thousand years before. The rabbis, living in this society, were deeply aware of changing times and conditions, and were prepared to meet new situations in the spirit of an evolving Torah. Open to new ideas, provided they met the standards of the divine word, they had to evaluate one of the most powerful spiritual and intellectual forces ever to have appeared on the stage of western civilization—Greek culture.

There was much good in Greek thought, and this the rabbis accepted. The rabbis saw in Aristotelian logic a supreme instrument for the development of thought and discussion, and built their legal deductions on Greek logic. They accepted the Platonic ideal of universal education. Everyone, be he rich or poor, has the duty to develop his abilities as far as his intelligence permits, and the state must supply the facilities for the schooling of all children. In their own lives they exemplified the spirit of stoic fortitude and courage; man must do his duty bravely without expecting rewards, and must retain his inner balance in joy as well as in sorrow. They even debated the possibility of writing holy books in Greek, the ancient world's universal language, distinguished by clarity and universal acceptance.[9] Egyptian Jews actually used Greek to such extent that they forgot Hebrew almost completely. Above all, like Greek assemblies, they *made* laws through interpretation of Scripture, promoting legislation that went beyond Scripture and transformed the character of Judaism.

But many principal ideas of Greek philosophy had to be refused. The Greek thinker could permit himself to let his mind roam, inquire freely into every field of thought, and arrive at any conclusion, provided he had followed the rules of logic. Epicurus had thus arrived at the conclusion that there are no gods to interfere in man's life, there is no hereafter with rewards or punishments, and man should simply seek happiness in prudent living. To the rabbis this was heresy. It denied God and immortality, and it served as an object lesson to the rabbis: thought unguided by faith may lead man astray. "Epicoros" (Greek *Epikoureios*) became an epithet and warning. The source of truth to rabbinic thinking lay, not in man's reason, but in God's Torah, to which man should apply his reason. And God, not man, was the center and the measure of all things. The Greeks, worshipping man, might glorify his body in its nudity at their games, their gymnasia, and in their sculptures. To the rabbis this was immoral. They had to turn down Plato's ideal state, for it was not the blueprint of a better world under God, but a caste state and an armed camp. Even stoic thought had to be rejected, much as the stoic spirit of brotherhood was admired. The pantheistic stoic philosophers held that God is simply the sum total of the world around us, while the rabbis believed in a transcendent God, who had *made* the world and all that is therein.

The rabbis could not agree with Aristotle, who spoke of *experience* as the one great source of all knowledge. *Torah,* the revelation of Sinai, was to them the ultimate source of all wisdom, and it had been given, not simply that men might know facts, but that they might act in the spirit of truth, fulfilling God's commandments and handing down God's word from generation to generation. Education to them was not simply nourishment of the intellect, it provided the food for life under God. Interpretation, therefore, must always protect the spirit of Torah, never tear it down. This is how they put it:

Moses received the Torah at Sinai and handed it down to Joshua, and Joshua to the Elders, and the Elders to the prophets; and the prophets handed it to the Men of the Great Assembly, who proclaimed three principles: Be deliberate in judgement, raise many disciples and make a fence around the Torah (Abot 1:1).

---

9 Talmud; Megillah 8 a, b.

Yet the rabbis did not believe in simple learning by rote, or in transmission of unexplained doctrine. They agree with Aristotle that the pursuit of reason is both man's ultimate task and his ultimate source of complete happiness. Influenced by this thought they went beyond Aristotle by way of implementation.

The Greek philosopher could see no way for the poor people to partake of the happiness of study. They had to work for a living; they had no time. Only the rich and well-born have the means and leisure to pursue knowledge to the fullest degree. Even some Jews of the time, like Jesus ben Sirah, agreed with him; knowledge is the privilege of the well-born, and the masses have to remain ignorant and obey. To the rabbis this was undemocratic. If knowledge is man's greatest happiness it may be denied to no man. But if it is so great a treasure then man can well do without many of the other luxuries of life, even without some of its necessities. This was their reasoning when they stated:

This is the road to Torah: be satisfied with bread and salt for food, a little water for drink, sleep on the ground, accept a life of privations, but toil in Torah. And if you do this "Happy shalt thou be, and it shall be well with thee (Psalm 128:2)." Happy shalt thou be in this world; and it shall be well with thee in the world to come (Abot 6:3).

Let the student reduce his needs to a minimum to acquire Torah; his life will be happy—and the future of Israel will be assured.

By transforming the Greek concept of education into the universal study of Torah, the rabbis fashioned the Jews into the people of the Book. In accepting and rejecting the teachings of other cultures, the rabbis were conscious of the fact that they were not "philosophers," they were "fathers." They were not simply "lovers of wisdom." Fully conscious of their function as spiritual fathers of their time and of all times, they even collected all the masters' ethical pronouncements that they might serve as guide. The small book which contains these maxims is called "Chapters of the Fathers." This Jewish term for the masters was later taken over by the Catholic Church, which speaks of its great teachers as "Church Fathers." It is a Jewish term, giving evidence of the responsibility which attaches to knowledge. He who possesses it becomes a spiritual father to those whom he influences. He may not keep his knowledge to himself, neither may he simply dispense it. He must use it as a means of education to develop mind and soul, thought and character. Thus were the "fathers" of Judaism, of whom we shall hear more. But we find the influence of Hellenism in the late books of the Bible as well as in the Talmud.

How to acquire wisdom and how to preserve it became the subject of the late books of the Bible, written in Hellenistic times: Job, Proverbs, Ecclesiastes. These books address themselves not simply to Israel, but speak of men everywhere. Job, tragic hero of suffering and tragic cleansing, is "Everyman"—he resides in the land of Uz, and he is not a Jew.

Proverbs

Proverbs starts with a characteristic opening:

The Proverbs of Solomon, the son of David, king of Israel:
To know wisdom and instruction;
to comprehend the words of understanding;
to receive the discipline of wisdom, justice, right and equity;
to give prudence to the simple,
to the young man knowledge and discretion;
that the wise man may hear and increase his learning;
and the man of understanding may attain to wise counsels
to understand a proverb and a figure;
the words of the wise and their dark saying (Prov. 1:1-6).

For a moment we seem to hear Plato's ideas as understood by a Jew. Wisdom, justice, right, and equity are similar to the virtues of Plato's three castes: wisdom, courage, temperance. The simple is to have prudence, it is the virtue he needs in daily work. The young man requires knowledge and discretion as he sets out to tackle the world with courage. The wise must increase his learning, and must be able to draw conclusions. But now comes the change. What do we mean by wisdom? To the Jewish author wisdom means Torah:

The fear of the Lord is the beginning of knowledge
but the foolish despise wisdom and discipline (Prov. 1:7).

The Platonic ideal of study and example becomes reverence for God, Torah, wisdom, and religious discipline.

The Book of Job

The Book of Job shows Greek influence in its style. Written in the form of a Platonic dialogue, it is fiction. Some of the ancient rabbis maintained that Job never existed as a real person.[10]

Job, as the story goes, is a good and pious man. Yet he is deeply afflicted—he loses his fortune, his children, his home, and his health. Covered with boils, he sits in the dust. Why should that be? Why should the righteous suffer? Isaiah had already taken up the subject, concluding that suffering may be a test of strength and faith. The book of Job comes to the same conclusion, but first it analyses other possibilities. Job is visited by his friends. They wish to help him understand the reason

---

[10] Talmud: Baba Batra 15 a.

for his suffering. Eliphaz says: "They that sow iniquity and sow mischief, reap the same." [11] Bildad adds, "Behold, God will not cast away an innocent man, neither will He uphold the evildoers." [12] Their simple position is that sin brings retribution. If Job is punished, he must have sinned. "Nemesis" is the Greek term expressing it. Zophar outlines it: "Oh that God would speak and open His lips against thee . . . know that God exacteth of thee less, than thine iniquity deserves." [13] Actually, the slight allusion to God's mercy leads beyond Greek thinking. Job could resolve the problem in one of two ways; he could admit that there might be some hidden guilt in him, or he could simply reach the conclusion that there is no God. He accepts neither of these solutions, because they are unacceptable to the Jewish author. The history of his people gives ample evidence of the fact that the innocent does suffer. The deepest convictions of his heart affirm the existence of God. Job is certain he is not a sinner: "My foot has held fast to His steps, His ways have I kept and turned not aside; I have not gone back from the commandment of His lips, I have treasured up the words of His mouth more than my necessary food." [14] He is equally convinced of God's existence. "I know that my Redeemer liveth." [15] A fourth friend is therefore introduced to present an acceptable answer; his name is Elihu. "God speaketh in one way, yea in two, though man perceiveth it not . . . then He openeth the ears of men, and by their chastisement sealeth their decree. . . . He delivereth the afflicted by his affliction and openeth their ear by tribulation." [16] Man must accept sufferings as a test of faith, and in accepting, he will find insight and strength. Isaiah had said it before, "they that wait for the Lord will renew their strength." Here, the story might come to an end, but it does not. God Himself speaks to Job:

Where wast thou when I laid the foundations of the earth?
Declare if thou hast understanding.
Who determines the measure thereof, if thou knowest?
or who laid the cornerstone thereof,
when the morning stars sang together
and all the sons of God shouted for joy (Job 38:4-7)?
The wing of the ostrich beateth joyously . . .
for she leaveth her eggs in the earth
and warmeth them in the dust,

---

[11] Job 4:8.
[12] Job 8:20.
[13] Job 11:4-6.
[14] Job 23:11-12.
[15] Job 19:25.
[16] Job 36:15.

and forgetteth that the foot may crush them
or that the wild beast may trample them.
She is hardened against her young ones as if they were not hers;
though her labor be in vain, she is without fear;
because God hath deprived her of wisdom,
neither has He imparted to her understanding (Job 39:1,2,13-17).
. . . Declare thou unto me: Wilt thou even make void My judgement?
Wilt thou condemn Me that thou mayest be justified (Job 40:8)?

Why does God speak directly, after Elihu has made the point clear?
God must speak to dispel three possible doubts. In the first place, Elihu
is only one of four speakers. Three have seen in suffering a punishment
for sin, while Elihu sees in suffering a test of strength. But who is right?
God appears as final arbiter, to endorse Elihu's view against the opinion
of the majority. Suffering is a test. Without God's direct interference another doubt might continue to linger in Job's and the reader's mind: can
we really be certain that there is a God when we see so many good
people suffer? God, therefore, appears to Job, and his doubt regarding
God's existence is resolved. Finally, Job needs reassurance. While it is
possible that the good may suffer, does he belong to this group? Perhaps,
in his case, suffering is indeed the wages of his sins? God sets his mind at
peace; Job realizes that God certainly would not speak to him if he were
a sinner; to hear the voice of God is the reward of the pious.

While speaking to him, God adds a point which Elihu has not mentioned: Man must not simply submit to the test, he must accept it
willingly and *joyfully*. All of creation shouts in joy at the destiny God
has set for it. The ostrich's labor may be lost, yet its wing beateth joyfully.
The bird has no discernment, it does not know why its eggs should be
crushed. It only knows that God has set a task, and that His will must
prevail. Thus the ostrich fulfils it in the knowledge that the loss was
ordained by God and therefore is good. Man, in accepting his tests willingly, justifies God, and therein lies man's ultimate justification.

God and Satan

The Book of Job opens with a prologue in heaven, in the form of
a dialogue between God and Satan.

And it came upon a day that the sons of God came to present themselves before the Lord, and Satan came also among them. And the Lord said unto
Satan: Whence comest thou? Then Satan answered and said: from going to
and fro in the earth and from walking up and down in it. And the Lord said
unto Satan: Has thou considered my servant Job, that there is none like him
in the earth, a wholehearted and upright man, one that feareth God and
shunneth evil? Then Satan answered and said: Doth Job fear God for nought?

. . . Thou has blessed the work of his hands. . . . But put forth Thy hand now and touch all that he has, surely he will blaspheme Thee to Thy face. And the Lord said: Behold, all that he has is in thy power (Job 1:6-22).

Here Satan is God's antagonist. He is not very powerful but rather a kind of public prosecutor who wishes to obtain indictments. Yet there is definitely a controversy between God and Satan. How did the idea of two opposing forces originate? It too is the result of conditions during the Hellenistic age, a period when ideas were exchanged widely among various religions and nations. The principle of dualism came from Zoroastrianism, a Persian faith which held that the world is divided between the forces of Light and Truth, embodied in the god Ahura Mazhda and his retinue of "angels," and the forces of Darkness and Evil, represented by the god Ahriman. These two forces fight for supremacy on earth. It is foreordained that Light will win, but only after a cataclysmic conflict at the end of days. This idea spread through the wide open Hellenistic world; the controversy between God and Satan is its reflection in Judaism. The antagonists are not equal, however. Satan is at most the force that wishes to promote evil but is forced to promote good, for he too is a servant of God. Satan has come to symbolize man's evil inclinations. But Judaism feels that these inclinations serve a good purpose; they are a necessary condition of freedom. God desires that all men have the freedom to choose between good and evil. If we could not make such a choice, and did not have the opportunity to overcome temptation, we could not consider ourselves truly free. Man has the choice between good and evil; that is his freedom. He is expected to choose good; that is his glory. It must be admitted, however, that both Judaism and Christianity have retained elements of dualistic beliefs, even though they have striven mightily against such a world view.[17]

Angels, the Redeemer, and the world to come

Zoroastrianism proclaimed two ideas: the principle of dualism, and, related to it, the prediction of a world-wide battle at the end of days. For a long time, Judaism had rejected both of them. Isaiah (II) had proclaimed categorically:

I form the light and create darkness; I make peace and create evil;
I am the Lord that doeth all these things (Isa. 45:7).

Opposition to dualism cannot be expressed more strongly. His predecessor, the first Isaiah, had also rejected the idea of an eschatological conflict. Nevertheless, these non-Jewish concepts did take hold in Jewish theology. In Job we have Satan, God's antagonist. In the prophecies of

---

[17] Gnostic dualism also affected and challenged Jewish thought.

Daniel we hear of a final heavenly battle to settle all conflicts in the world.[18]

At that time shall Michael stand up, the great prince who standeth for the children of Thy people; and there shall be a time of trouble, such as never was ever since there was a nation even to that time. And at that time thy people shall be delivered, everyone that shall be found written in the book. And many of them that sleep in the dust of the earth shall awake, some to everlasting life, and some to reproaches and everlasting abhorrence. And they that are wise shall shine as the brightness of the firmament; and they that turn many to righteousness, as the stars for ever and ever (Dan. 12:1-3).

Daniel was written after a period of persecutions. King Antiochus had set his mind on the annihilation of Judaism. History seemed to be moving away from reason rather than toward it. Isaiah had predicted a human solution to all conflict; Daniel saw no hope. To resolve it required the intervention of heavenly powers. Michael, champion of Israel, will do battle for his people against the forces of evil. The people have a heavenly representative, a guardian angel. This is a new concept of Zoroastrian origin. Previously the term "malakh," angel, simply meant messenger of God. When Abraham is visited by three messengers who announce the birth of a son, they are simply "men." The author of Job, however, speaks of the "sons of God," a heavenly court. Now, in Daniel, we are given actual names; Michael is one of them. He is to bring salvation, although it is not made clear what is meant by this deliverance. Does the author envision a restoration of political and national freedom, or is it salvation in a world to come? Both elements are represented in Daniel's prophecy, and both of them will remain components of Jewish belief. There will be a time when a Redeemer will come, to bring peace and brotherhood to a suffering world. There will be a day when the dead will rise, a day of judgement, and of resurrection to life everlasting. But there is also that life everlasting which the souls of the departed enter upon their parting from the body. Jewish thinking has continued to wrestle with the problem. Yemot Hamashiah, the days of the Redeemer, and Olam haba, the world to come, are not the same. When the day of resurrection comes, will those who dwell in God's world return to this one to live? Jewish philosophy has argued the point. In actual life, Jews have never been too much concerned over the interpretation of the fine points. The rabbis taught: "Better is one hour of repentance and of good works in this world than all the life in the world to come. And better is one hour of spiritual calm in the world to come than all the life of this world (Abot 4:22)." It is a quiet warning against being obsessed by the thought of the future

---

[18] See also Isaiah 24 and Ezekiel 38-39, where human warfare is enlarged to cosmic proportions.

world. Repentance and good works here and now are the important things. The task of the hour, well fulfilled, carries its own reward. Yet the ultimate vision of a world to come stands in the background as uplift and comfort. Judaism has remained less concerned with the hereafter than have other religions, a fact rather surprising when we realize that it was exposed to the concept since its earliest days in Egypt. But Judaism is a faith of action; let man be God's co-worker in this world, and He will receive him later in such fashion as His divine will may have devised.

The second concept expressed in Daniel's words is that of a Redeemer. Fulfilment need not be excluded from this world. Even when all earthly means seem to have failed, there is still hope for the redemption of our own society—even though it may come only through divine intervention. In subsequent centuries, as defeats multiplied and trials grew, the ancient prophecy [19] for a redeemer of the House of David acquired ever greater super-human radiance. The Messiah, the Anointed One, would appear when Israel and the world were worthy, or when conditions were so hopeless that only a divinely ordained—but human—personage could set it right. Then God would be established and Israel restored in the world.

The failure of the House of the Hasmoneans to maintain both political independence and righteous rule, and the failure of Bar Kokhba, once hailed by Rabbi Akiba as Messiah, only strengthened the faith in a Messiah emerging out of the House of David when the time, in God's plan, was ripe. Israel could prepare for his arrival only by repentance, self-improvement, and service, combined with patient waiting in unfaltering faith. Thus hopes for national restoration were fused with those of world redemption into one glorious vision and perennial task.

The messianic concept has given eternal strength to the Jew. Orthodox Jews of today may expect a real person to arise, reformed Jews may see in the Messiah simply the symbol of a world at peace, when "the lion shall dwell with the lamb." All of them will toil and strive fervently to make mankind worthy of the time of a Messiah, when human brotherhood will have been established, and all men will live in peace with each other. Nothing else will suffice as qualification for the Messiah. This moving force in thought and action is an unceasing challenge for the Jew, for he must help to make a better world. It is the very reason for his existence. Perhaps we can understand now why there may be Jews, not religious in the usual sense, who still consider themselves faithful to their heritage.

The last verses of the prophetic books of the Bible contain a prophecy by Malachi, a contemporary of Ezra:

---

[19] See Isaiah 9;6; 11:1-5; Jeremiah 23:3-7; 30:8-9; 33:14-26; Amos 9:11-15; Zachariah 9:9 ff.

Remember ye the Torah of Moses my servant,
which I commanded unto him in Horeb for all of Israel
even statutes and ordinances.
Behold I will send you Elijah the prophet
before the coming of the great and terrible day of the Lord.
And he shall turn the heart of the fathers to the children
and the heart of the children to their fathers;
lest I come and smite the land with utter destruction (Mal. 3:22-4).

These verses may have been written at a later date. In them Elijah is
seen as messenger of peace and redemption. The writer sees the *possibility* of a terrible day, but it is not inevitable. Let the Jewish people
uphold Torah in daily living, then—with the aid and guidance of God's
messenger—the hearts of mankind will be attuned to each other, and
even the eternal conflict between the generations will come to an end.
Then the day of the coming of God will not lead to destruction. The
choice is placed in the hands of man: brotherhood or destruction. Brotherhood is the hallmark of the messianic age. Failing to achieve it, man
seals his own doom. But if he makes an honest effort, Elijah, God's messenger, will stand by his side as his helper.

Every Passover, as Jews celebrate the deliverance from Egyptian
bondage, a cup filled with wine and intended for Elijah is placed on the
festive table. It is a reminder and a challenge. Liberation is not complete
until all the world is free. In spite of all setbacks, we may not give up.
Jews, throughout the centuries of their own misery, have always prepared
the cup of Elijah. He will surely come, as long as mankind waits and
hopes and—above all—works for his arrival.

THE SECTS: SADDUCEES, ESSENES, PHARISEES

Judaism absorbed those elements of Hellenism which it found useful,
and which could be interpreted in conformity with the spirit of Jewish
tradition. Such a development must be directed. Caught amidst the currents of the time, the Jews had several choices. They could follow the
prevalent trend of Hellenism; they could resist all influences from without, and seal themselves up against them; or they might chart their
course between the currents, independent, yet guided by them. Each of
these approaches was tried by an influential segment of Jewish society.
These were the *sects*. Each of them arose in response to the spiritual
and practical problems of the period.

The Sadducees

The Sadducees saw the only way to preserve Torah in strict
obedience to the *written* word. They opposed any new interpretation of

the Pentateuch (as undertaken by the Pharisees). The wellborn, wealthy and conservative members of Jewish society belonged to this group. They were opposed to any new idea, such as resurrection. Some of the wealthy Sadducees liked the man-centered appeal of Greek philosophy. Most saw in Temple and its ritual the guarantee of Jewish survival. For the sake of the Temple they were willing to appease the ruling power, Rome. To them, it was a necessary, life-saving compromise. After all, the garments of the high priest were kept in the vaults of the Roman garrison, guarded by the legion, to be handed over only for services on Yom Kippur. And Rome would give them to those who had gained her favor by compliant servility. A Caiaphas could become high priest by Pontius Pilate's appointment, although many of his own people did reject him. The Sadducees had no faith in evolution of Torah. They rejected the whole body of interpretation, the entire Oral Law. They wished to retain the written Torah pure, followed and interpreted it in severe strictness. Josephus has described them as a group of hard personalities.

The Sadducees . . . deny fate (divine ordination) completely; they maintain that God has nothing to do with the actions of man. Good and evil are completely in the power of man's will; he may choose one side or the other entirely according to his own preference. Furthermore, they deny the immortality of the soul, they deny the world to come with its rewards and punishments. While the Pharisees are kind to each other and promote peace and concord for the sake of the community's welfare, the Sadducees are unfriendly, even to each other. They are cold to their own fellows and equally cold to strangers (Josephus, Jewish War II, 8:14).[20] (Immortality is not in the Pentateuch).

The solution of the Sadducees would have caused the fall of Judaism with the destruction of the Temple.

The Essenes

The Essenes moved to the opposite extreme. Rejecting the world, they turned down its civilization in its entirety. They saw in the turmoil of the time simply a prelude of the fast approaching end. To them, the day of judgment was at hand. Some Essenes became hermits, clothing themselves in garments like those once worn by Elijah, and wandering preachers, like John the Baptist, calling the people to repentance before it was too late. They immersed themselves daily to be purified by an act which held spiritual symbolism. Some of them did no longer found families, for the end was so near; others permitted marriage for the sake

---

[20] *Josephus*, II, Henry St. John Thackeray, trans. (Cambridge: The Loeb Classical Library, Harvard University Press, 1927), p. 385. The author has not entirely adopted this translation.

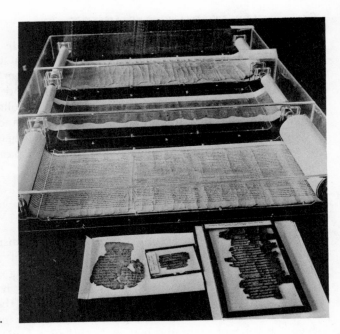

The Dead Sea Scrolls.

Parchment scroll, "The War of the Sons of Light against the Sons of Darkness," from the Dead Sea Scrolls.

of procreation. Thus, they added to the tension of the time. Some Essene groups banded together in monastic orders, so that they might become the remnant of Israel to be saved on the day of doom. They submitted to a rigid discipline of prayer, work, purification, and fellowship repasts. We know of their lives from the Dead Sea Scrolls, which contain a "Manual of Discipline" for one of their orders, and excavations have brought remnants of monasteries to light. All of them rejected the idea of a creative evolution in Judaism and submitted passively to God's will as predestined fate. As Josephus explains it:

The Essenes teach, that all is determined by fate (divine ordination), and nothing happens that is not preordained (Josephus, Jewish Antiquities XIII: 5:9).[21]

Had this solution been accepted by the Jews, Judaism might have continued to exist for a while after the destruction of the Temple. But it would have become fossilized, its creative vitality gone.

The movement of the Essenes has nevertheless had a great deal of influence upon Christianity. The rite of immersion, the sacramental meal at which wine and bread were passed around, the monastic orders, and even the concept of predestination have had a lasting impact on all or some of the Christian denominations. To Judaism, the Essenes are largely past history.

The Pharisees

The Pharisees have given Judaism its character and its strength. They rank among the greatest masters of humanity, as teachers and as representatives of highest ethical perfection. They carried forth the work of the prophets, and accepted the challenge of history to find the road of creative synthesis between assimilation and separation. Judaism has followed this road, and proudly considers itself heir to pharisaic teaching.

The origins of the pharisaic movement go back further than those of the two other groups. Since the day of Ezra, interpretation of Torah had become a major function of Jewish leadership. This called for men of great intellectual ability, combined with uncompromising faith and exemplary life. Only such a group could give the people the full meaning of the living Torah and command their allegiance. Thus a body of teachers was formed in Ezra's time, or shortly thereafter, men who had authority, the "Men of the Great Assembly." Out of it developed the organization of the "Perushim," or Pharisees. Perushim meant the "Separated Ones," the group within the group, the congregation within the

---

[21] *Josephus*, VII, Ralph Marcus, trans. (Cambridge: The Loeb Classical Library, Harvard University Press, 1943), p. 313. The author has not entirely adopted this translation. A further and detailed description of the Essenes can be found in Josephus, Jewish War II, 8:2-13 (*op. cit.*, II, pp. 369-384).

congregation. They regarded themselves as the shocktroops of Jewish survival, and were so regarded by the people, who called them "Kedoshim." The term means Saints, and should be understood in the sense in which the Puritans or later the Mormons were to use it, a band of men utterly dedicated to the preservation of their heritage. With the emergence of Pharisaism, the religious future of the people no longer lay in the hands of the priests, a caste composed of the descendants of Aaron; it lay in the hands of all those who wished to give their lives over to the task. Some of the Pharisees were priests, others were sons of converts, some were wealthy, others desperately poor. They showed their mettle in the time of the Maccabees, when they really came into their own. Liberal in ideas, they were strict in the observance of the law. They had to be, lest their broadmindedness be misunderstood as compromise. Only he who is exacting toward himself can afford to be lenient toward others. Thus they were able to absorb the best other cultures had to offer, but would accept it only if it helped to strengthen Judaism. Being firmly anchored in tradition, they could be universalistic in outlook; being utterly rooted in their heritage, they had the flexibility to adjust Judaism to changed conditions, after the Temple had been destroyed. They saw the Temple go up in flames and the state collapse, and their hearts were broken. But they knew that this was not the end. Judaism was not the Temple, Judaism was not the state, Judaism was the Torah. They would give their lives rather than permit the fence around the Torah to be broken down. Josephus said of them:

The Pharisees declare that some but not all is the work of fate, but that many things can be attained or omitted by the free will of man (Antiquities XIII; 5:9).[22]

To the Pharisees, man is master of his fate, though its complete master is God. But if God is all powerful and knows everything, does He not know and determine man's future actions? How then can man be free? Judaism accepts this as a question beyond human capacity to solve.[23] God's thought processes are not bound by the logic of humans.[24] The eternal tension between God's knowledge and power and man's freedom remains. "All is in the hands of Heaven (God), except for the fear of Heaven (which is man's)."[25] This is the Pharisaic position, and it has remained the position of Judaism. Perhaps we can understand now why Judaism has never taken any of its defeats as final, why it has never given up. Man is free to rebuild, while to yield is indeed the mortal sin.

---

22 *Op. cit.*, VII, p. 311.
23 Talmud: Berakhot 33b.
24 Efforts to give a logical answer have not been lacking. See Saadia and compare with Maimonides.
25 Talmud: Berakhot 33b.

4

The
Tannaim

With the fall of the Temple, the sects disappeared, and the Pharisees became the masters of the entire people. Individually, each of them held the title "Rabbi," teacher; collectively, the group became known as "Tannaim," the Teachers. In addition to the example of their lives, they have given us a summary of the Oral Law, as they had developed it through the centuries. It is a great work called the *Mishnah*. They were not rabbis in the sense in which we speak of a rabbi today. Although ordained, they were not professionals, and did not make a living from Torah. In a largely agricultural community, many were farmers or day laborers; others were cobblers or blacksmiths or carpenters. Even the poorest among them were agreed that "man may not make the Torah a spade to dig with (a source of income)," nor a crown for self-glorification, for "he who takes profit from the words of the Torah displaces his life (Abot 4:7)." Were they not all simply links of tradition? And unless each link is like all the others, the chain breaks. Thus, they arranged the "Chapters of the Fathers" in chronological order, and recorded the ethical sayings of the masters in sequence. We shall quote some of them, for these men were the master builders of Judaism.

THE MEN AND THEIR IDEALS

Simeon the Pious is the first mentioned by name. He was the high priest who appeared before Alexander the Great and succeeded in moving the king to mercy. His words, in a sense, are the testament for all the future: "On three things stands the world: On Torah, on Worship, on Acts of Kindness (Abot 1:2)." His disciple was Antigonus of Sokho; the rabbi's name being Greek was one of the acceptable features of Greek civilization. His ideals were Jewish, reflecting the teaching of Sadducees:

Be not like servants, who serve the master for the sake of reward; but be like servants who serve the master without any thought of receiving any reward;— and may the reverence of Heaven be upon you (Abot 1:3).

Antigonus touches a theme which has been repeated with variations throughout Jewish religion: the service of love. The reward should not be man's primary motivation in the service of God—not even the hope of a reward in the hereafter; neither should man be deterred from sin by fear of future punishment. Love of God must be man's sole guiding force. But love may lead to neglect of duty. As man loves God he knows also that he is loved by God. This may lead him "to take it easy," for he knows that loving forgiveness is always at hand. Antigonus is aware of the danger, and adds, "may the reverence of Heaven be upon you."

As we follow the generations of masters we come to Simeon ben Shetah. Simeon was *his* name, Shetah that of his father; "ben" stands for "son of." Since there were no second names, men were known by their own and that of their father. History tells us that he was the brother of the only reigning queen of the House of the Hasmoneans. Under his guidance, she gave the people a respite of peace. It is said that he enacted the compulsory education law in Judaea. From his position we understand his injunction to the courts. Law had become arbitrary, a tool in the hands of corrupt politicians. Therefore he admonished,

Examine the witnesses, with repeated care. And watch your own words (in cross examination), that they may not learn from them how to lie (Abot 1:9).

Simeon did more than talk. Using his influence, he opened the halls of the Sanhedrin, the Supreme Court, to the members of the Pharisaic group. Up to that time, only the wealthy, the nobles, the influential—in other words the Sadducees—had been privileged to hold these high positions. Against their highhandedness and partiality he established the ideal of justice as the Pharisees understood it. He knew how easy it was for a judge to put words in the mouth of a witness, and to get the evidence he wished to have. Such "justice" was abhorrent to the Pharisees.

Neither personality nor political considerations may be permitted to color judgement in a court of law. Mercy, however, may and should prevail. This basic principle has prevailed from Simeon's days—even to modern times.

Yoshua ben Perahyah carried Simeon's injunction into the sphere of daily living: "Get yourself a teacher, acquire a friend, judge everyone in his favor (Abot 1:6)." Study, fellowship, and charity in judgement make life distinguished.

When the leadership of the academy went to Shemaya and Abtalyon, a new precedent was established. The two men were not of Jewish descent, but were descendants of Sanherib, emperor of Assyria, who had destroyed the kingdom of Israel. Now his children's children were the leaders of Israel. They were truly beloved, as the Talmud tells us:

Once (at the end of the Yom Kippur service), the following event occurred. As the high priest emerged from the Temple, all the people rushed to him. But as they saw Shemaya and Abtalyon, they left him and turned to them. Shemaya and Abtalyon went over to the high priest to greet him, and he said to them, "May the sons of the foreigners find peace." They (the people) replied, "The sons of the foreigners will find peace, as they do the work of Aaron (to pursue peace), not so the son of Aaron (the high priest), who has not been doing it (for he had insulted the masters by his reflection on their background) (Yoma 71b)."

The words of these two rabbis reflect their past experiences, elevated to universal principles.

Shemaya said: Love work, hate lordly distinction, do not get intimate with the powers that rule (Abot 1:10).

The lesson of the Assyrian court had not been lost on him.

Abtalyon said: Ye wise, be careful with your words, or you may become guilty of banishment; to be banished to a place of evil waters; and the disciples who come after you may drink and die, and the Name of Heaven may be desecrated (Abot 1:11).

Abtalyon expresses a warning against self-banishment into the province of error. He knew of the pleasures of a non-Jewish culture, especially in the field of philosophy. He saw clearly how hazardous was the path followed by the Pharisees, as they walked on the razor's edge of acceptable and unacceptable doctrine. Some drank so deeply from the waters of Greek philosophy that they fell away. It happened later to Elisha ben Abuya, who became Aher—"Another One." Abtalyon recognizes the need for successful synthesis, and out of his own experiences he feels compelled to point to the dangers of the road and advise infinite caution.

To give a picture of the daily lives of these men, a story may be told of one of them. He is not mentioned in the "Chapters of the Fathers," but he typifies their way of life. His name was Abba Hilkia, his story is found in the Talmud.

Whenever the world needed rain, our masters sent to him, (that he should pray for it). Once when the world needed rain, the masters sent a pair of masters to him. They went to his house but did not find him in. They went to the field and found him digging. They offered him the greeting of peace, but he did not respond. As night fell, he gathered some wood, put the wood and his spade upon one shoulder and his coat on the other. Along the road he did not put on his shoes, except when he had to cross a stream, then he put them on. When he crossed a thorny hedge he raised his coat. As he reached the outskirts of town, he was met by his wife, and she was well adorned. As he reached the house, his wife entered first, then he followed, then our masters. He sat down to eat his bread, but did not invite the masters to join the meal. He passed out the bread; to the older of his sons he gave one piece, to the younger two. Afterwards he spoke (secretly) to his wife: "I know that the masters have come on account of the rain. Let us go to the upper room and pray for mercy. Perhaps the Holy One be He blessed will listen and rain will come. But let us not take credit for ourselves." They went to the upper room, he went into one corner, she into the other. And as the clouds floated in, the first ones came from the side of his wife. Then both went down and asked them, "Why did the masters come?" They replied, "We were sent by our masters to ask you to pray for God's mercy, namely rain." He replied, "Blessed be God, who has made it no longer necessary for you to call on Abba Hilkia." They replied, however, "We do know that the rain has come on account of you, our master. But explain to us your strange behavior. Why did you not turn to us when we gave you the greeting of peace?" He replied, "I am a day laborer and do not wish to tarry" (for even one moment of the time he had contracted to give his employer). "Why did the master put the wood on one shoulder and the coat on the other?" (When the coat would have protected his shoulder from the heavy load). He replied, "It was a borrowed coat, and I had not borrowed it for that purpose." "For what reason did the master go barefooted except when crossing the stream?" "On the road I can see (dangerous spots and avoid them, therefore can save my shoes), in the water I cannot see." "Why did the master raise his cloak when going through thorns?" "This (skin) heals easily by itself, the other (the coat) does not." "Why did your wife meet the master, all adorned?" "That I might not be tempted to cast eyes at a strange woman." "Why did your wife enter the house first, and only then you yourself, our master, and then ourselves?" "Because I did not know you." (He wanted to protect his wife from the strangers). "Why did the master eat his bread and did not say to us, 'Come and eat'?" "Because there was not sufficient bread and I did not wish to accept your thanks in vain." (He knew they would have refused and felt undeserving of their thanks since the offer was not made in sincerity). "Why did the master give two pieces to the younger and only one to the older?" "The older is at home, the younger at school (and works harder)." "Why did the clouds drift in on your wife's side first?" "Because she stays home and gives bread to the poor, and quickly stills their hunger; I can only give them money and not still their hunger right away. Perhaps there is another reason too. We have evil neighbors here, and I prayed to the Almerciful that he should make them die; but she prayed that they might repent and He should change their hearts and make them good (Taanit 23a, b)."

The poverty and piety, the patience and the honesty, the charity and the consideration for others, the love of learning and the strength of self-analysis, the deep humility and modesty, the profound love of wife and family which characterized this man are fully typical of all the Pharisees. He is not a saint, and he knows and admits it, and his love for his wife is hallowed by a deep respect. These were the qualities which made the Pharisees great. Thus they became the eternal teachers of Judaism. Perhaps the greatest of them, during the time of the temple, was *Hillel.*

When Torah was forgotten in Israel Ezra restored it; when it was forgotten again, Hillel came from Babylonia and established it again. (Sukkah 20a).

Hillel was the true antagonist of Herod, in whose time he lived. Herod was destructive, Hillel was a builder; Herod was tyrannical, Hillel typified patience; Herod saw in the people a tool for his ambitions, Hillel regarded himself as a servant to his fellowman; Herod cared nothing for the survival of Judaism, Hillel laid its firm foundations.

When Hillel opened his academy at Jerusalem, another famous rabbi, Shammai, headed another one. The two schools became friendly opponents. Hillel was poor, Shammai was rich. Hillel realized that the Torah is for man, not man for the Torah. Hillel's decisions always considered the needs of the people and their circumstances; Shammai followed strictly the letter of the law. But in the face of bitter controversies, their friendship endured. In the end—so it was related—"a voice was heard from heaven; 'Both the words of the House of Hillel and the words of the House of Shammai are the words of the living God. The decision, however, is to be according to the House of Hillel (Erubin 13b).'"

Nothing shows more clearly the freedom which Judaism grants to difference of opinion, if based on sincerity of intent, than the position of respect and approval both schools enjoyed. But Hillel's decisions, rather than Shammai's, became the norm. To Hillel, the human being came first; Torah was given to him as a precious heritage, it was the instrument which elevates him; through Torah man becomes God's co-worker, living by Torah he reaches his full stature. Without Torah he is nothing. But what is Torah without man? In Hillel's life and teaching we find a deep reverence for man; his body, his soul, the society he creates. The law of Torah must serve man, not destroy him.

One of Hillel's early experiences in life may have helped to shape this outlook. He was a descendant of the House of David, born and reared in Babylonia. As a young man, he migrated to Jerusalem to study under Shemaya and Abtalyon, the leading rabbis of their time. He completely disregarded his physical needs in order to study. Then came a dramatic experience. The Talmud tells about it. "Hillel was very poor."

Every day he would hire himself out for two small pieces of silver. Half of his earnings he gave to the doorkeeper at the academy for admission, the other half he used for the upkeep of his family and himself. One day he earned nothing, and the doorkeeper would not let him enter. So he climbed unto the roof, that through the skylight he might hear the words of the Living God revealed by the mouth of Shemaya and Abtalyon. We are told that it was on the eve of the Sabbath. It was deep winter, and snow fell on Hillel and covered him. In the morning Shemaya said to Abtalyon, "Brother Abtalyon, this house which is ordinarily light, is very dark today; is it a cloudy day?" Then they looked up, and saw the shape of a man on top of the skylight. They went up and found Hillel covered by three feet of snow. They removed the snow, pulled him down, washed him, rubbed him, sat him near a fire. They said: "This man deserves that the Sabbath be profaned in his behalf (Yoma 35b)."

This may well have been the turning point in Hillel's life. He had learned from his masters themselves that the Sabbath may be profaned for the sake of any man's life, and may have rejoiced to know that in his case they saw his life truly worthy of preservation by the promise it held. He learned anew that the Torah is for man, for this had been a well-established principle. It was based on an interpretation of a verse in Scripture: "Ye shall keep my statutes and mine ordinances, which a man shall do; *and ye shall live by them* (Lev. 18:5)." If the observance of a commandment would crush a life to death, the commandment may be broken. Eventually, Rabbi Jonathan ben Joseph was to put it pointedly: "Scripture says, 'The Sabbath is holy for *you* (Exod. 31:14).' This means it is given to *you* (man) not you to the Sabbath (Yoma 85b)." This principle has remained fundamental; but Jews have used their discretionary powers with extreme caution, as if to say, "God has given us the right to break the Torah when life is at stake, but let us bend backward before we resort to it; let us be certain that this is the only way out."

Hillel, however, was led to a new appreciation of the value of human life by this episode. He, and Judaism after him, could not see any dualism between body and soul. The body is God's holy creation. Was not man made in the image of God; was it not then man's duty to keep this image clean and well preserved? (Vayikra Rabba 34); nourishment helps to preserve the house which shelters a precious guest, the soul. The soul, however, is more precious than the body; only as the soul's vessel does the body acquire significance. Physical satisfaction should never be an ultimate goal; he who strives for it exclusively will find only disappointment:

The more flesh (luxury), the more worms (in death),

the more possessions, the more anxiety,
the more wives, the more witchery,
the more maid-servants, the more indecency,
the more men-servants, the more robbery,
the more Torah, the more life,
the more discussion, the more wisdom,
the more counsel, the more understanding,
the more charity, the more peace.
He who acquires a good name acquires (a treasure) for himself;
he who acquires words of Torah acquires life in the world to come (Abot 2:8).

This knowledge of man's worth leads to responsibility. We must love our fellowman, he is precious; and we must help him to find his way as a child of God.

Be of the disciples of Aaron, loving peace and pursuing peace;
loving all men and leading them to Torah (Abot 1:12).

It is not surprising that Hillel's patience became proverbial.[1] No one ever succeeded in making him lose his temper, and the stories of his love became legend. His philosophy of life won him friends, not only among his people, but among heathens as well; it made friends for Judaism, the faith from which he drew it.

Once a heathen came to Shammai and said to him: "You may convert me if you can teach me the Torah while I am standing on one foot." Shammai threw him out and the heathen came to Hillel, who converted him by saying to him as follows: "Do not do to thy neighbor what would be hateful to you were it done to you. This is the whole Torah, all else is commentary. Now go and study it (Shabbat 31a)."

This is the golden rule, as Hillel formulated it. It means the same in its negative form as in its positive version. If it is hateful to me to find my neighbor refusing me help, then I must help him. The only difference, perhaps, is this: the negative form contains a word of caution. There may be occasions in life when you would wish to offer help, but your neighbor may wish to meet his problems by himself. Don't force your help upon him; develop sympathy for his state of mind, and stand by. Love thy neighbor, Hillel says, but love him always. It is not enough to lead him out of a difficulty; you must be his guide by leading him to Torah. "Now go and study it," he admonishes the heathen; "love people and lead them to Torah" is his maxim. We must place our total life in the service of our fellowman, to make his life fuller and more meaningful and happy. This is the pressing task of every individual.

---

[1] Talmud: Shabbat 31a. A story of a wager made by a man who felt sure he could make Hillel lose his patience—and lost his bet.

If I am not for myself (doing the work, if need be alone), who will be for me?
If I am for myself only, what am I (my life is meaningless)?
And if not now, when (will it be done) (Abot 1:14)?

Jews have venerated Hillel, the Pharisee. His words and his example have remained a lamp unto their feet on their road through history.

Hillel had eighty disciples. So great were they, that Johanan ben Zaccai was considered the least of them.[2] Yet so great was Johanan that he became the leader in the rebuilding of Judaism after the fall of the Temple. Hillel's ideals inspired all who came after him.

Johanan had five disciples, each of them deserving to carry on the work after the master's death. He tested them to discover their qualities:

Which is the right way for man to follow?
Rabbi Eliezer said: a kindly eye. Rabbi Joshua said: a good friend.
Rabbi Yose said: a good neighbor. Rabbi Simeon said: vision of the future.
Rabbi Eleazar said: a good heart.
Then said Rabbi Johanan: "I accept the view of Rabbi Eleazar ben Arakh rather than yours, for in his words your words are included (Abot 2:13)."

The way of a good heart was Hillel's teaching. In their own way all of the five men saw part of it; but they did not see all of it. Rabbi Eliezer and his colleagues elaborated:

Let the honor of your fellow man be as dear to you as your own; don't be easily angered; return (to God in repentance) one day before your death— every day (Abot 2:15). Rabbi Joshua said: A wicked eye, evil impulses and hatred of man put a man out of the world (2:16). Rabbi Yose said: Let the property of your fellow man be as dear to you as your own; Prepare yourself for the study of Torah; it will not be yours by inheritance; Let all your actions be for the sake of Heaven. Rabbi Simeon said: When you pray, do not make your prayer a matter of routine, rather make it a plea for mercy and compassion before God, the Ever-Present, as Scripture says: He is a God full of grace and compassion, long suffering and abundant in mercy, and repenteth Him of the evil (Joel 2:13). Be not a sinner in your own eyes (Abot 2:18). (Appraise yourself adequately, do not feel inferior, love yourself decently). Rabbi Eleazar said: Be ardent in the study of Torah; know how to meet the argument of the Epicurean (the Greek humanist, the heretic) and know before Whom you are toiling, Who is your Master to reward you for your labor (Abot 2:19).

Hillel's ideas speak through all these words, and all of these principles became ground rules for Jewish living. Many rabbis followed, all speaking the same language.

We hear it in the words of Simeon ben Gamaliel:

---

[2] Talmud: Sukkah 28a.

Not study is the decisive thing but the deed (Abot 1:17).
The world is maintained by three things: truth, justice, and peace (Abot 1:18).

Eleazar ben Azariah elaborates:

He whose wisdom exceeds his deeds, to what may he be compared?
to a tree whose branches are many and whose roots are few.
The wind comes, uproots it and turns it over.
But he whose deeds surpass his wisdom, to what may he be compared?
to a tree whose branches are few, but whose roots are many.
Even if all the winds in the world come and blow against it
it cannot be moved from its place (Abot 3:22).

Gamaliel, son of Judah the Prince, was leader of his people. He had honor and prestige and wealth. Hence he warned against selfish ambition:

May all who work in behalf of the community, work *with them* for the sake of Heaven;
then the merit of their fathers will sustain them,
and their righteousness will abide forever.
And as for you (do not worry about the ultimate success and your share in it)
I bring you great reward, as if *you* had achieved it (Abot 2:2).
Do His will as if it were thy will; cancel out thy will before His (God's) (Abot 2:4).

In Rabbi Tarphon's words we find the rule applied to daily living:

It is not (necessarily) thy duty to complete the work;
neither art thou free to desist from it (Abot 2:21).

They were willing to give to Caesar that which was Caesar's, and to pray for the government, as Rabbi Hanania pointed out:

Pray ye for the welfare of the government; without the fear of it, man would swallow his neighbor alive (Abot 3:2).

They did not need power, even full political independence, as long as God was in their midst, and

As two sit together and the words of their discussion are words of Torah, the Glory of God is in their midst—even when one sits in occupation with Torah, God appoints unto him a reward. . . . When three eat at a table, speaking words of Torah it is as if they partake of God's own table (Abot 3:3-4).

Ben Zoma condenses it into simple principles of life:

Who is wise? He who learns from every man.
Who is a hero? He who conquers his evil passions.
Who is rich? He who is happy with his share of life.
Who is deserving of honor? He who honors all men (Abot 4:1).

These men were Pharisees. They and many others shaped the ethics and the faith of Judaism in the spirit of the principles we have quoted. World-wise, with deep insight, humility, and faith, they saw in Torah their guide. Love of man was their motivation, action for God and man was their battle cry. Among them there was Rabbi Akiba.

Akiba was an ignorant shepherd who fell in love with his master's daughter. She loved him, but would not marry him until he consented to study Torah. They married in secret, and then told her father. In rage, he cut off her support, so she supported her husband. He studied for 12 years and returned with a host of disciples. She came to meet him, fell on her knees and kissed his feet. Akiba presented her to his disciples, saying: "What we are today, you and I, we owe to her (Ketubot 63a)." For 40 years he taught Israel. He had survived the fall of the Temple. Fervently patriotic, he placed his hopes in Bar Kokhba and supported him with the power of his prestige in his uprising against Rome. The rebellion failed. In reprisal, Emperor Hadrian prohibited the study and practice of Torah. Unmindful of danger, Akiba went on teaching. Asked why he did not give up, he replied with a homely parable: "A fox once called out to the fishes in the brook: 'Come ashore and escape the dangers of being caught by the big fish of prey.' 'No,' they replied, 'water is the element of our life. If we leave it we perish. If we stay, some will die, but the rest will live.'" Akiba concluded: "Torah is our element of life. Some of us may perish in the trials of these days; but as long as there is Torah, the people will live." Akiba was among those who gave their lives. They tore off his flesh with red hot pincers. The disciples wept, but Akiba smiled: "Does it not say, 'Thou shalt love the Lord thy God with all thy heart and all thy soul and all thy might?' The soul, that means my life, should I not smile, now that I may serve Him with all my life?" [3]

Akiba was not the only martyr in the course of Jewish history. There was Judah ben Baba, who ordained the most brilliant of his disciples, when ordination was against Roman law. He took them to an open field, and made them run for their lives when he saw the legionnaires approaching. Placing himself in the path of the soldiers, he was pierced by their spears; but the bearers of Torah escaped.

Ten of the masters were martyred then, and millions followed them. With their dying breath they affirmed the unity of God as Akiba had done: Hear, O Israel, the Lord our God, the Lord is One. Judaism does not confer sainthood; yet those who gave their lives for God and Torah are remembered as Kedoshim, Saints. By their lives they sealed the covenant, by their death they preserved the Household of Israel.

---

[3] Berakhot 21b.

THE PAINTED ONES

Like any great movement, Pharisaism found in its ranks members that did not belong. They had joined, not in a spirit of idealism, but from motives of self-interest and the desire for self-aggrandizement. The leaders of the Pharisees were well aware of them and condemned them severely. In biting irony, the rabbis called them "Painted Ones," whose piety was but painted on, a veneer designed to hide a heart of selfishness. Thus in the mouths of the rabbis, the term "Pharisee" could be highest accolade or scathing rebuke.

Rabbi Joshua used to say: "A mad pietist, a cunning villain, a 'Pharisaic' woman and the scourge of the Pharisees lead society to destruction (Sota 20 ff.)."

In explanation, the terms are clarified:

A mad pietist: he would not save a drowning woman; it is not "decent."
A cunning villain: he sees the judge alone, in chambers, before the start of a litigation.
A Pharisaic Woman: a pray sister with an evil heart.
The scourge of the Pharisees: seven unworthy types of
Pharisees, namely:
the egotistic Pharisee: he hopes to gain by his show of piety;
the overmodest Pharisee; he walks with mincing steps;
the bleeding Pharisee: he walks with eyes closed, lest he be temped; he bleeds from hitting his head on the obstacles into which he has bumped;
the bent-over Pharisee: he demonstrates his "humility" by standing and walking in bowing position;
the dutiful Pharisee: he has "never" shirked his duty, and constantly asks for new tasks to perform;
the Pharisee of "love," who makes a show of his love of God;
the reverent Pharisee, making a show of his reverence for God.

This sarcasm, which overstates the point, clearly shows the concern the rabbis felt over the penetration of unworthy people into their ranks. Their spirit is reflected in words which Jesus speaks to hypocrite Pharisees: "You Pharisees make clean the outside of the cup and the platter; but your inward part is full of ravening and wickedness . . . ye tithe the mint and rue and all manner of herbs, and pass over judgement and the love of God: these ought you to have done, but not to leave the other undone . . . . you love the uppermost seats in the synagogues and greetings in the markets. . . . Woe unto you scribes and Pharisee hypocrites, ye are graves which appear not, and the men that walk over them are not aware of them (Luke 12:39-44)." We can almost pick the different types of "painted ones," who are mentioned here in equal sharp rebuke.

But why did the rabbis permit these people to remain members of the group? Because as humans we cannot look into the hearts of men to determine their true motivations. The Talmud points this out; after listing the various kinds of false Pharisees, it goes on: "How do we know, who is true and who is not? Rabbi Nahman said: 'The hidden is unknown to us; we see but what is in the open. But the Great Judgement will bring punishment to those who wrap themselves in cloaks (of righteousness against their true convictions).'" Then the Talmud adds a historical quotation: "King (Alexander) Jannai (of the Hasmonean dynasty) said to his wife (Salome Alexandra, to whom he left the crown): Be not afraid of the Pharisees, nor of the non-Pharisees, but fear the hypocrites, who pose as Pharisees." [4] It is one of the tragedies of history that the "Painted Ones" came to represent all of the Pharisees in the common usage of the term. This is an injustice of history to one of the great ethical movements in civilization.

There could not have been too many hypocrite Pharisees. The masses of the people have a good sense of judgement; they feel the difference between honesty and the lack of it. These masses followed the Pharisees. Never in history has there been a rule as detailed, farreaching, and completely affecting every moment of every person's life, as was the rule the Pharisees imposed upon themselves and the people. Only the Puritans in early America had a similarly extended set of ordinances: what to wear, how far to walk, what to eat. Still, it was not as detailed as that of the Pharisees, and it could be enforced, because the Puritans had behind them the awesome power of the State. The Pharisees had no power to enforce and to coerce. Why then did the people obey them? There is one basic answer: because they loved them. Some of the people may also have realized the reasons for these rules: the people of God must be held together against the influx of foreign ideas and practices. The land and the Temple had become precarious possessions; no one knew how long they might serve as unifying forces. The Torah would live forever. The deeper its impact, the greater would be its life-preserving power. If the multitudes did not understand the reasons, they still followed, simply because they felt the greatness of these men, their warmth, their love, their open hearts, and their sincerity. Thus came into existence the Republic of which Plato had dreamed, where the wise are kings by virtue of their wisdom. It was a Republic striving for the Idea of Ideas, the Living God. In it, even as Plato had seen it, the routine of life was strictly regulated in faith, thought, and action. It was truly based on "temperance," the full acceptance of their duties by all levels of the people. Unconsciously, the people had translated a Greek blueprint into a higher reality. Yet there

---

[4] Talmud Sotah 22b.

were profound differences. This "commonwealth," in which an Akiba could rise from shepherd to master, existed simply by the consent of the governed, and had no closed castes. This society had as its goal to make real the rule of God and to safeguard the eternity of the Jewish people. It was everyone's duty to rise to ever greater perfection and leadership. "Ye shall become holy, for I, the Lord your God, am holy (Lev. 19:2)." Among the nations of the world, such a spiritual community could not be understood; it stood alone. Misunderstanding led to prejudice against it. The Pharisees actually demanded of their people a decision of super-human gravity. In following Pharisaism as a way of life, they had to expose themselves to misunderstanding and attack on the part of the world. In surrendering Pharisaism, they would surrender their future and jeopardize their survival. The people accepted Pharisaism. They accepted the minute details of observance, designed to be constant reminders of their unique position according to the will of God. They had faith in the leadership of their rabbis; history has proven that they made the right choice. At the same time, they exposed themselves to "anti-Semitism," which is a modern term for a very old malady.

ANCIENT ROOTS OF ANTI-SEMITISM

Faith was the link which united the Jews of Judaea with those of the rest of the world. From every province of the vast Roman Empire and from Babylonia, they sent their Shekel to Jerusalem for the upkeep of the Temple, and later for the support of the office of the patriarch. To Palestine they sent their letters of inquiry concerning difficult questions of observance and law, to receive authoritative direction. The patriarch's decision established the dates of the festivals, at a time when a fixed calendar was not yet in operation. Law, commandment, and custom held them together, wherever they might live. Among the non-Jews, the strength of this union called forth admiration or misunderstanding or hatred.

The God concept of a loving Father in Heaven, which Judaism held up to a disillusioned world, drew many into the ranks of the Jewish faith. Aquila, translator of the Scripture into Greek, supposedly was a close relative of the Emperor Hadrian; [5] of Rabbi Meir it was even said that he was a descendant of Nero. All this is doubtful. It indicates, however, that influential Roman circles were interested—even to the point of joining. Some Romans accepted Jewish beliefs without formally adopting the faith. Jewish missionaries were active, and synagogue membership grew.

---

[5] Tanhuma Mishpatim.

What the strong admired was foolishness in the eyes of the scoffers. To them, Rome was good enough in its beliefs and practices. To accept the creed of a small, downtrodden nation was more than folly. It bordered on treason; it undermined the established way of life. Thus we may understand Juvenal's satire:

Some, sons of a father who observes the day of the Sabbath,
worship nothing but clouds and a spirit in heaven,
and differentiate not between human flesh and that of the swine
from which their father abstained. Soon they shorten their foreskin.
Trained to hold Roman law in contempt,
they study with care Jewish law to obey and revere it,
and all that Moses transmitted in secret a book.
It forbids them to show the right way to any but those who accept the same rites,
and permits them to guide to the well (of their wisdom)
the circumcised only and none of the others.
At fault is the father, however, who every seventh day
turned lazy, taking no part in the tasks and duties of life (Sat. XIV, 96-106).

Juvenal is not the only ancient writer who mentions and attacks the Jews for their arrogance, as a small defeated people, in rejecting some of the forms of a "superior" civilization. In the demagogue's mouth, this was then enlarged to spell disobedience to law in general. Scripture puts it in the mouth of Haman, persecutor of the Jews, supposedly during the Babylonian exile, but actually occurring during the period of Syrian persecution:

And Haman said unto King Ahasuerus, There is a certain people scattered abroad and dispersed among the peoples in all the provinces of thy kingdom; their laws are diverse from those of every people; neither keep they the king's laws; therefore it profiteth not the king to suffer them (Esther 3:8).

Accusation is the prelude to action and persecution. At a time when religion was the cement which held the realm together, it was easy to point to the Jews as disloyal. The divine or semi-divine emperor could unify only those of his subjects—or so he thought—who looked up to him in worshipful reverence. The Jews did obey his laws; they prayed for him; they did not pray *to* him. Thus they became disturbers of unity in the Empire.

Juvenal puts his finger on another problem. Jews could invite their neighbors to their homes and into their faith, but they could not reciprocate. They could not eat the food of the Romans because of the dietary laws, and they could not respect their gods. This violated the tenets of common Roman courtesy; it was national arrogance.

Actually, the causes went deeper. The success of Jewish missionary activity showed clearly that something was rotten in Roman society. In fact, Roman society was rotten throughout. Family life had broken down, adultery and murder had become sports. By their lives and conduct the Jews held up a mirror to the high and mighty of Rome. And what they saw, when they were sober enough to face their own image, was terrifying. Rather than change their own image by changing their ways, these Romans decided to smash the mirror. Rather than admit their shortcomings, Roman writers defamed the Jews. By what right did these poor farmers and poverty-stricken artisans criticise Rome? It started with the defamation of the God of the Jews. He was a phantom in the sky, according to His detractors. These Jews might even be atheists. Then the religious practices of the Jews were attacked. Juvenal, and, later on, Tacitus,[6] call them lazy because they observe the Sabbath. Thus might be disguised the relentless exploitation of the poor by the wealthy in Rome; there the poor were never given a moment of rest.

The Jews were accused of having no aesthetic sense because they failed to appreciate the statues of Rome, provided by extravagant spending. Their defamers declared that the true reason was because the God of the Jews was really an ass's head, worshipped in the Temple of Jerusalem. The Jews lived their own lives, finding pride in their families and strictly upholding the Torah's principles of sexual morality. Their haters had an answer for that too, which would please the libertines of the promiscuous city: the Jews were really descendants of lepers, expelled from Egypt in the times of Moses. They were outcasts and did not mix simply because they could not join the others. It is no wonder that the rabble in Alexandria and Rome took the hints and started to slaughter the Jews. The slanderous statements were contradictory, but what did it matter as long as they helped to arouse emotions? In the contrary, this contradiction made it harder for the Jews to refute them. If they laid one accusation, another one could be leveled at them. Philo,[7] the philosopher, and Josephus,[8] together with others, tried to combat slander with fact. They did not succeed. The rumors did not rest. To kill criticism the haters had to destroy the critic's reputation or the critic himself—for they did not intend to mend their own ways.

---

[6] Hist. IV.

[7] Philo headed a delegation of Jews to the emperor Caligula to demand justice after a grave pogrom at Alexandria. His opponent was Apion, one of the earliest professional anti-Semites, who had aroused the emotions of the Alexandrian rabble by his vituperative speeches. Caligula sided with Apion, who flattered the emperor.

[8] Josephus: Antiquities XIV, 10. He describes here some of the problems the Jewish community had to face, especially in connection with the religious observance of the Sabbath, when they were not permitted to work or perform military duties. This called for special enactments, releasing Jews from work on the Sabbath, and led in turn to opposition by others. Julius Caesar stands out in Josephus' story as a man of great understanding and tolerance.

The forces which triggered anti-Semitism in the ancient world are still at work, and for the same reason. Judaism has been an implied rebuke to immorality, both private and public. By its survival, Judaism has demonstrated that the moral principle cannot be suspended. Jews have become the symbol of a divinely established morality, and of the victory of this morality over the forces of license and tyranny. Jews themselves have certainly not been free from weakness, and have failed again and again to live up to God-given rules. By their survival, however, they have become symbol of divine providence. Emperors and dictators may declare themselves to be gods, they may rage and destroy, but in the end, the divine will survives; it assures eternity. This may be one reason Hitler could not tolerate the Jews. They pointed to the limitations of his omnipotence. This may be the reason why communist Russia finds them "unassimilable," and may explain why dictatorship and pogroms almost always go hand in hand, and Jews can be free only in democracies under God.

The rabbis and the people accepted Roman prejudice as a price for survival. They could look toward the future with hope in their hearts. The knowledge of God, as taught by Judaism, was spreading among the noble and wise. Eventually Judaism might be understood, and then prejudice would vanish. But it was not to be—new sources of prejudice soon developed.

5

Tenakh: The Holy Scriptures

Three gigantic works were produced by the Pharisees and their immediate spiritual descendants. These are the canon of Holy Scriptures, which they edited; the great edition of the Talmud, consisting of Mishnah and Gemara; and the basic order and portions of the Prayer Book.

The Jewish Bible consists of those books which the Christians call "Old Testament," although Jews do not use the term. True, the work is old, reaching back into the dim past of Jewish beginnings; but Jews feel strongly that no higher ethical principle was ever expressed, no deeper love ever expounded in any work which followed Jewish Holy Scriptures. Nor did God ever replace His covenant with Israel and with the world by a new one. This view is in fundamental disagreement with Christian and Islamic thought.

The Pharisees who edited the Bible were fully aware that theirs was a task of momentous import. The Word of God was being preserved for eternity. No doubt must be left that this Word could ever be changed, revised, or altered; it was the immutable rock for all generations, for all the world, for all ages. No passage of doubtful meaning could be admitted, lest there be misunderstandings. This called for careful selection among the many worthy books then in existence. Unless the rabbis were certain in their minds that a book was written under the guidance of "Holy Spirit," they omitted it from the canon of the Book. The rabbis were indeed critical analysts of the Bible; their methods differed, however, from those of modern biblical criticism. They applied moral judgements.

Since they considered Malachi the last of the prophets, no works written after him could be included. We know that some of the books of the Bible stem from a later date, but the rabbis assumed that their authors had lived further in the past. Beyond that, they passed on the merits of every one of the books. Did Ecclesiastes contain sufficient spiritual inspiration, or did its words simply contradict each other? [1] Was it too negative, too skeptical in its approach to life? Should a torrid love song like the Song of Songs be included? Sometimes personal experience affected the decision. It was Rabbi Akiba who insisted that the Song of Songs be included, by stating "If all the songs are holy, Solomon's Song of Songs is the holiest of them all." [2] Akiba knew the power of the love of a woman. Without it, he would never have risen to greatness, and his life would have been without meaning. Without it, Torah would have been lost to him, and he to Torah. The Song was thus interpreted as an allegory of God's love to Israel. The rabbis' views on the authorship of the biblical books are frequently in contrast to modern criticism. They held that books had been written by men whose names were affixed to them as authors. They ascribed the authorship of Judges, of Samuel I, II, and of Ruth, to the prophet Samuel; Jeremiah was considered editor of Kings, I, II, and of Lamentations, together with the book that bears his own name; Hezekiah headed a board who published Isaiah, Proverbs, Song of Songs, and Ecclesiastes; the Men of the Great Assembly were regarded as editors of Ezekiel, the Twelve Minor Prophets, Daniel and Esther; Ezra wrote the books bearing his name and that of Nehemiah and Chronicles. David was editor of the Psalms, which had been composed by many others as well as himself. Moses composed the Pentateuch and Job. [3] Some rabbis held that Moses could not possibly have written the last verses of the Pentateuch, which deal with his death and burial; others disagreed, claiming that God dictated the final words to him before the prophet's death.

The rejected books were to be "hidden" from the general reader, lest he be confused and consider them holy. But the works had already been translated into Greek before they were taken out of circulation, and we have them. They are still called "Hidden Books" or "Apocrypha." Among them are the Books of Sirah, Esdras, Tobit, Judith, the Story of Susannah, and the Books of the Maccabees, which are the source of the festival of Hanukah. Maccabees were excluded from the canon simply because they came too late.

---

[1] Shabbat 30b.
[2] Yadayim, 3:5.
[3] Baba Batra 14-15.

THE DIVISIONS OF THE BIBLE

The Bible is divided into three main sections: The Torah or the Five Books of Moses, also called Pentateuch; the Prophets; and Collected Writings, also called Hagiographa. These main sections were again divided into books and paragraphs. Originally, there were neither chapters nor verses. These were added by a monk during the Middle Ages and have been universally adopted. Torah, N'vee-im (Prophets), and Ketubim (Collected Writings) make up the Bible. Using the first letters of the three sections, Jews have called it TeNaKH.

Torah

Used in a narrow sense, the term stands for the Five Books of Moses: Genesis, Exodus, Leviticus, Numbers, and Deuteronomy. They tell the story of the world's beginning by the Word of God. The patriarchs step onto the scene of history, and Israel's enslavement in Egypt is related. Moses, the Master, appears to lead his people to freedom under God. The Ten Commandments are revealed, laws are proclaimed, a Tent of Meeting is built and the rituals prescribed. We hear the solemn injunction, "Thou shalt love thy neighbor as thyself (Lev. 19:18)," and the words of sacred benediction are made known:

The Lord bless thee and keep thee.
The Lord make His face to shine upon thee and be gracious unto thee.
The Lord lift up His face upon thee and give thee peace (Num. 6:24-26).

The eternal Jewish affirmation of faith is established:

Hear, O Israel, the Lord our God, the Lord is One.
And thou shalt love the Lord thy God with all thy heart and with all thy soul and with all thy might. And these words which I command thee this day, shall be in thy heart. Thou shalt teach them diligently unto thy children and shalt speak of them when thou sittest in thy house and when thou walkest by the way, and when thou liest down and when thou risest up. And thou shalt bind them for a sign upon thy hand, and they shall be for frontlets between thine eyes. And thou shalt write them upon the doorposts of thy house and upon thy gates (Deut. 6:4-9).

These are the words the Jewish child learns when he begins to speak. They are pronounced daily. To his last dying breath, every Jew is to rehearse them, that his soul may wing upward as he releases it in absolute faith, "the Lord is One." Millions of martyrs have uttered it at the very moment when they witnessed for Him in supreme sacrifice.

Holy Ark with three Torah Scrolls. Each of the Scrolls contains the Pentateuch, or five books of Moses. When not in use, they are clothed in mantels and decorated with crowns and breastplate. Note also the pointer to be used in reading the text. Over the Ark and its curtains we find the tablets of the Ten Commandments surmounted by an eternal light.

Torah Scroll in its mantle.

The Torah in life and worship

The instructions of Torah are Israel's holy heritage and guide. So important are they that they are repeated in public reading year after year. The five books are divided into sections or portions, one of them to be read each Sabbath. The first words of each portion are used as its title, so every week of the Jewish year can be clearly marked. It is the week of such and such a portion, or Sidrah (sometimes called Parshah). "On the first day of the week of Shemot" then means, "on Sunday of the week leading up to the reading of the Sidrah Shemot" (the first of the Book of Exodus). The portion of Torah thus becomes motto for the week.

The Five Books of Moses are written on a parchment scroll by men who have devoted their entire lives to copying the words of holy writ, using special ink and goosequill for their work. The congregation may have one or several scrolls, which are kept in the Holy Ark and form the congregation's holiest possession. Each scroll contains the full text. If a congregation has several scrolls, it can use a separate one for special holy day readings; if it has only one, it must be rolled to the place of special readings. As Torah is the "crown of life," a silver crown is frequently placed on it. It is wrapped in a precious mantle and may (in addition) have a breastplate, on which small, changeable silver plates tell of the place to which the scroll is rolled. There is a silver hand strung by a chain around its neck, to be used as pointer. At the appointed time, the Ark is opened while the congregation rises. A scroll is taken out and solemnly borne to the reading desk. As it is read, the congregation follows the text in its own printed books—the words are chanted following an ancient, well-defined set of modes. But the scroll itself contains neither vowels, punctuation, nor musical annotations; these must be known by the reader. The weekly portion is again divided into sections, and different members of the congregation are called to step to the reading desk to witness and follow the reading from the scroll itself. This is an honor, and those who approach pronounce a blessing to Him "Who has given the Torah."

Traditionally, every person is to prepare himself for the weekly reading by reviewing the text beforehand, for every word has meaning and significance. Every word is "alive." If the slightest error is found in a scroll it cannot be used until the error has been corrected. If it is old and has become totally worn out, it is buried, just like a person.

N'vee-im: Prophets

The second division of the Tenakh takes us through Israel's turbulent history after the conquest of the land, and presents the great personalities of the prophets. Its first section deals mainly with events, as judges, prophets, and kings walk through its pages. This section is called "Early Prophets," and contains the Books of Joshua, Judges, Samuel I and II, and Kings I and II. Here we meet Joshua, the successor to Moses, who led his people into the Promised Land and divided it among the tribes. Judges pass in review; among them are Deborah, woman-general and leader, Samson the prankster, and Samuel, who gives the people the king they have requested. Saul is presented in victory and terrible defeat, a man of moods whose picture is drawn in all its dramatic contradictions. David, darling of the people, emerges, fighting for his life against Saul and tied by tender bonds of tragic love to Jonathan, Saul's son. David rises to power, a genius as ruler, but failure as father; a man of passions, but great enough to repent them. Solomon succeeds him, inheriting a powerful kingdom. He builds the Temple, but his glory is not to survive him—the kingdom is divided after his death. The Northern Kingdom, vainly called to repentance by Elija and Elisha, by Amos and Hosea, eventually falls. The Southern Kingdom collapses later, and Jeremiah mourns its destruction, holding out hope at the same time for its restoration.

The second section, "Later Prophets," gives us the writings of the literary prophets. We meet the three "major" prophets in the Books of Isaiah, Jeremiah, and Ezekiel. Twelve "minor" prophets are represented with longer or shorter excerpts from their teachings: Hosea, Joel, Amos, Obadiah, Jonah, Micah, Nahum, Habakkuk, Zephaniah, Haggai, Zechariah, and Malachi. In their writings we find the events of Israel's and mankind's history weighed, measured, and evaluated under the aspect of eternity. Man's worth is shown, his social duties outlined, his hope rekindled by the knowledge of God's love which the prophets proclaim.

Have we not all one Father, has not one God created us? Why do we deal treacherously every man against his brother (Malachi 2:10)?

As we read these works we are uplifted, not by the message alone, but by the grandeur of the prophetic style, which is virile and tender, heroic and lyric, in turns. That men of different background could rise to such power of expression testifies to the divine inspiration which moved their hearts and their lips. In style and in content, these books belong to the greatest achievements in all of human civilization.

The prophets in worship

Not all of the writings have found a place in worship. Selected chapters were chosen by the rabbis to be recited after the reading from the Torah scroll on holy days. The selection is called "Haftarah," and is keyed to the special day on which it is read, or to the Torah portion which it follows. On the afternoon of the Day of Atonement, for instance, the Book of Jonah is read with its twofold message: we cannot run away from the tasks God has set us, and God's love extends to all His creatures, even the animals. We must bring our fellowman back to Him, for all—regardless of creed—partake of His salvation. Again, on the Sabbath when the story of Jacob's death is read from the Torah scroll, the story of David's death is recited from the prophets. The Haftarah too is chanted, though the chant is slightly different from that used in reading the Torah. It can be recited from a regular, printed book, preceded and followed by blessings "for the Torah and the prophets."

Ketubim: Collected Writings

The third division of the Tenakh rounds out the message. In it we find Psalms, Proverbs, Job, Song of Songs, Ruth, Lamentations, Ecclesiastes, Esther, Daniel, Ezra, Nehemiah, Chronicles I and II. The books vary greatly in character. *Ezra* and *Nehemiah* give an account of the work of spiritual and physical reconstruction performed by settlers returned from Babylonian exile under the leadership of the two men whose names the books bear. *Chronicles* reviews history as a march through time toward the permanent establishment of the House of David. *Daniel* envisions cataclysmic events "at the end of days," and sees the finger of God's hand literally writing words of judgment and of doom on the walls of the dwellings of the wicked.[4] But the righteous are saved in the fiery furnace of a world aflame.[5] Having steadfastly refused to bow to idols, they deserve salvation. *Proverbs* extols the values of wisdom and rises to a lavish praise of virtuous women. *Job* vindicates God's ways.

The Five Scrolls

The five remaining books are known as the "Five Scrolls." Written on individual scrolls, they were recited on special occasions of the year as part of public worship. The Song of Songs, Ruth, Lamentations, Ecclesiastes, and Esther deal with the various facets of love, both human and divine.

THE SONG OF SONGS, one of the greatest love songs ever written, sings of the ecstasies of love. The shepherd and the shepherdess are in love and share delights which even Solomon, in all his glory, can never experience. In unashamed rapture he dwells on the beauties of her body, her hair, her eyes, her lips, teeth, and breasts. He knocks at her door in

---

[4] Belshazzar in Daniel 5.
[5] Daniel 3.

the dark of the night, and she responds: "I have put off my coat; how shall I put it on? I rose up to open to my beloved . . . (5:2-5)." The power of love overwhelms them; it is elementary, it is life itself, it is eternity. It is one of the two forces which no man can escape, "for love is strong as death (8:6)," and he who loves is dead to the world. But death is the end and love the beginning. Death is defeat and love is victory. And human passion, created by God, is good. It reflects the passionate love of God for His creation.

THE BOOK OF RUTH speaks of the love for an ideal. Ruth the Moabite has married a Jewish husband and lost him after a short period of married bliss. Poor and widowed, she remains true to the ideals of Jewish life which she has embraced. Even the entreaties of her mother-in-law, who wishes her to start life anew, cannot sway her. "Where thou goest I will go . . . Thy God shall be my God (1:16)." Such is the compelling force of Torah that it calls forth a love which conquers all blandishments of life. When Ruth marries again, hers is the love of maturity. David the king is the offspring.

LAMENTATIONS reveals the agonies of non-requited love. Jerusalem has been destroyed, has become a widow. Her children, the people, have been carried into exile. Has God withdrawn His love? Through bitter tears we see a ray of hope. The people will renew their love for God, and God surely will restore His. "Turn us unto Thee, O Lord, and we shall be turned. Renew our days as of old (5:21)."

ECCLESIASTES deals with love perverted into pleasure; it has led to cynicism. There is nothing left for him whose strength of passion has deserted the body; life has become a vanity. But the rabbis would not let us yield to hopelessness. They added a last verse: "The end of the matter, all having been heard: Fear God and keep His commandments, for this is the whole man (12:13)." Resignation is the wisdom of advanced age; it can also bring happiness. Loving dedication to duty has its rewards, and spiritual love never dies, but lives on to guide others.

ESTHER glorifies sacrificial love. Married to a heathen king by royal command, Esther uses her position to rescue her people from the imminent threat of extermination. She has to risk her own life to effect their deliverance, but her love for her people and her sense of duty are greater than her desire for self-preservation. Sacrificial love leads to heroism.

The five scrolls in worship

Both nature and history demonstrate the workings of love, and so the five scrolls are read at appropriate times. At the spring festival of Passover, the Song of Songs is recited. It is the time of the year when nature bursts out in bloom, when passion predicts new life, when divine and human love renew themselves. Shabuot, the summer festival, celebrates the giving of the Ten Commandments. It is a moment of loving rededication to the ideals of Judaism, at a time when the harvest is on the way, promising fulfilment. How we use it depends on our strength of character. The Book of Ruth shows us the way. On the Fast Day of Ab, commemorating the fall of the Temple, we read the Book of Lamentations. The agonies of the past will not lead us to despair, but rekindle in us that love which will call forth God's redeeming love in return. On Sukkot, fall festival, the harvest is in, the leaves begin to fall, winter is at the gate. Another year is gone, another round completed in eternal monotony; but we get older. Not cynicism but loving dedication to the future must be the answer to melancholy and sadness. Ecclesiastes shows the way. Purim brings us the Book of Esther, the only one still read from a handwritten scroll. We give thanks for the rescue of our people, but we remember that it resulted from a heroic faith in God and from a dedicated love.

These are the sections of "Ketubim." There is one more, the Psalms.

The Psalms

The Psalms are unique among the books of the Bible. In all the others God speaks to man; now the human soul responds. And this response runs the gamut of emotions. There is jubilation, "Bless the Lord, O my soul, O Lord my God, Thou art very great (Ps. 104)." For He is the Lord of creation. There is confident hope, "Our soul has waited for the Lord; He is our help and our shield (Ps. 33:20)." "He restoreth my soul (Ps. 23:3)." There is longing, "As the hart panteth after the water brooks, so panteth my soul after Thee, O God. My soul thirsteth for the living God (Ps. 42:2-3)." There is outcry in pain, "Save me, O God; for the waters are come in even unto the soul (Ps. 69:2)." There is the plea of the repentant sinner, "Return, O Lord, deliver my soul; save me for Thy mercy's sake (Ps. 6:5)." And there is the climactic unison of a united mankind, "All that has the soul's breath, praise the Lord (Ps. 150:6)."

In the Psalms we find all the teachings of the Torah and the Prophets once more repeated by man, who has made them his own. The grandeur of God's creation is affirmed, "The heavens declare the glory of God." But creation acquires meaning only as it makes manifest the greatness of God's law, "The Torah of the Lord is perfect, restoring the soul (Ps. 19:2 and 8)." Confronted with his task as co-worker of God, man realizes his limitations and his strength (Ps. 8), and out of this contrast there arise problems. The wicked use their power for evil, yet they flourish. The Psalmist asks why, the question discussed in the Book of Job. There, it was instruction by God; here it is affirmation of God, given by the sufferer who has acquired faith; affliction is a road to God. Again and again, man is exposed to suffering; and over and over again the Psalmist cries out, in agony, in despair, but eventually in victory born of unconditional faith. In this faith the sinner turns to God, who will surely forgive. The certainty of God's guiding presence gives him confidence even in the face of death (Ps. 23). Though he speaks in the first person, the Psalmist thinks not only of himself; it may be the "I" of the household of Israel he has in mind, or the "I" of mankind as a whole. For the Psalmist's outlook is a universal one. In Isaiah and Micah we find the blueprint of a world where the Torah shall go forth from Zion, and all mankind unitedly receive God's blessing. In the Psalms this is accepted.

> The Lord has been mindful of us; He will bless us;
> He will bless the House of Israel,
> He will bless the House of Aaron,
> He will bless them that fear the Lord,
> both small and great.
> The Lord increase you more and more,
> you and your children.
> Blessed be ye of the Lord
> Who made heaven and earth (Ps. 115:12-15).

Israel is a household, and the family of Aaron is the priestly household within Israel, as Israel is within the world. But the blessing extends to all that fear God. "O Praise the Lord, all ye nations; laud Him all ye peoples (Ps. 117:1)." That God is good to all His creatures is the Psalmist's basic conviction. In Psalm 145—which is recited three times daily in orthodox Jewish worship—the Jewish philosophy of life is well expressed. The Psalm follows the Hebrew alphabet, each line beginning with one of its letters—this is a fairly common device; the Psalm also uses "parallelism," a poetic form in which the second line paraphrases the first. It opens with the name of the author, in this case David. The Book of Psalms mentions a number of others as well, among them Moses (Ps. 90), Asaph (81; 82; 83), and the Sons of Korah (84, 85). Then the poem begins.

I will extol Thee, my God, O King—and I will bless Thy name for ever and ever.
Every day will I bless Thee—and I will bless Thy name for ever and ever.
Great is the Lord and highly to be praised—and His greatness is unsearchable.
One generation shall laud Thy works to another—and shall declare Thy mighty acts.
The glorious splendor of Thy majesty—and Thy wondrous works will I rehearse.
And men shall speak of the might of Thy tremendous acts; and I will tell of Thy greatness.
They shall utter the fame of Thy great goodness—and shall sing of Thy righteousness.
The Lord is gracious and full of compassion—slow to anger and of great mercy.
The Lord is good to all—and His tender mercies are over all His works.

All Thy works shall praise Thee, O Lord—and Thy saints shall bless Thee.
They shall speak of the glory of Thy kingdom—and talk of Thy might;
to make known to the sons of men His mighty acts—and the glory of the majesty of His kingdom.
Thy kingdom is a kingdom for all ages—and Thy dominion endureth throughout all generations.
The Lord upholdeth all that fall—and raiseth up all those that are bowed down.
The eyes of all wait for Thee—and thou givest them their food in due season.
Thou openest Thy hand—and satisfiest every living thing with favor.
The Lord is righteous in all His ways—and gracious in all His works.
The Lord is nigh unto all them that call upon Him—To all that call upon Him in truth.
He will fulfill the desire of them that fear Him—He also will hear their cry and will save them.
The Lord preserveth all them that love Him—but all the wicked will He destroy.
My mouth shall speak the praise of the Lord—and let all flesh bless His holy name for ever and ever (Ps. 145).

God is Creator; Nature speaks of Him, mankind is invited to praise Him. He is gracious, compassionate, merciful, slow to anger, easy to forgive; He is our support; he sustains mankind and every living thing with favor. God is righteous even as He is loving. He does answer prayers, and He will establish justice. How significant it is that the word "Israel" is never mentioned; God is the God of "all flesh." Even at the solemn moment when the Temple, Israel's national sanctuary, was dedicated, the universality of God was proclaimed. We find it in the 24th Psalm, most probably composed for the procession to the Temple. The Psalm is written in antiphonal style, two choirs responding to each other. One asks,

Who may ascend into the mountain of the Lord, and who shall stand in His holy place?

The other responds:

He that hath clean hands and a pure heart . . . (Ps. 24:3, 4).

Not the Jew, not Israel alone, but everyone with a pure heart has access to God. Isaiah, it seems, takes this very basic principle, which the people had accepted, as source for his severe rebuke. "When you make many prayers, I will not hear; Your hands are full of blood . . . Wash you, make you clean, put away the evil . . . learn to do well; seek justice, relieve the oppressed . . . (Isa. 1:15-17)."

Those who are clean are admitted regardless of background, those who are not are rejected—even though they be Israel. Thus the Psalm always affirms what the prophet teaches. While Malachi complains, "Have we not all one father, why do we deal treacherously every man against his brother (Mal. 2:10)?" the Psalmist takes the affirmative stand on the value of brotherhood, "Behold, how good and how pleasant it is for brethren to dwell together in unity (Ps. 133:1)." There is no Psalm which does not end on a note of victory, for such is the faith of its poet. There is no emotion which is not mirrored, no situation in life that is not described. Nature, man, individual, nation, Israel, mankind, past, present, and future, all are drawn into the circle of contemplation. So deep is the faith of the Psalms that even the Day of Judgment becomes a day of joy:

Let the heavens be glad, and let the earth rejoice; . . . let the field exult and all that is therein; then shall all the trees of the wood sing for joy; before the Lord, for He is come; for He is come to judge the earth; He will judge the world with righteousness and the peoples in His faithfulness (Ps. 96: 11-13)."

Jewish strength and realistic optimism found their source in the Psalms. How can powers and forces and men ever frighten a people who are so certain of God's love for all mankind that even the Day of Judgment becomes a day of joy? They know that God's love is so great that His mercy will prevail even in judgment. The Psalms have thus become a second Pentateuch, a second "Torah" to the Jew, in their instruction, in their testimony to God's love and abiding goodness. The rabbis, therefore, divided the Psalter into five "books" similar to the five books of Torah. Torah is instruction, and the 150 Psalms are the living affirmation of Torah.

The Psalms in worship

Many of the Psalms were composed for use in ancient Temple worship, and for special occasions. There was a special Psalm for every day of the week; Psalm 92, for example, is designated as the Psalm for the Sabbath. Sometimes the instruments to be used for the performance of a Psalm are indicated, and the annotation "Selah" was a directive for the choir master to shift his voices into a higher key.

The significance of the Psalms in the life of the Jew throughout his history can hardly be overestimated. He found in the Psalms an outlet for his feelings, an answer to his questions, a comforter in his distress. To this day, there are many to whom the Psalter is a daily companion, and certainly a friend in times of trouble. In sickness, people will recite Psalms; in prayer for others, they may select verses whose first letters spell the name of the dear one for whom they pray. In drought or flood, in times of war and in moments of great joy, whatever it be, there will be a Psalm to answer questions and express the deepest emotions.

Public worship begins and ends with Psalms. The Sabbath is hallowed by recitation of special Psalms; holy days are distinguished by the recital of "The Praise," the Hallel, consisting of Psalms 113-118. Psalms are quoted in the poetry of prayers. The very structure of the morning and evening prayer follows Psalm 19, as praise to God, the Creator of Nature, leads to thanksgiving for His Torah.

At special occasions, such as the eve of the Day of Atonement, the pious would stay awake to recite the entire Psalter in responsive reading, following an ancient traditional chant. There was no better way of reflecting on God's greatness and love, on His creation, on man's frailty and need for repentance, and—finally—on the purpose of the world, the kingdom of God, where His love would embrace all for ever and ever.

HOW THE TENAKH WAS TRANSMITTED: THE MASORAH

Recent discoveries have proven that the versions of the Tenakh which we have are remarkably accurate. For this we owe another debt of thanks to the rabbis of old. They knew the importance of accuracy, especially when it came to the preservation of the word of God. Thus, they recorded the exact number of letters, words, and paragraphs in the books of the Tenakh. They indicated where the middle of a book might be found, by word count, by letter count, or by verse count. Occasionally a letter is written larger or smaller than might ordinarily be the case. These deviations are based on tradition; the rabbis made a list of them. They counted how many times a word might occur in the Torah. Guided by these notes, thousands of scribes have copied hundreds of thousands of scrolls; and all the scrolls are alike. For this great achievement we pay tribute to the humble men of Masorah of Tradition.

HOW THE TENAKH ORIGINATED: MODERN CRITICISM

Before the rabbis started their work of editing and correcting, a great many versions had already come into existence. With them there had appeared spelling errors, some of which had been reproduced in the text commonly used. If the rabbis discovered those errors, they would make a note to leave the text untouched, but to read it differently. They preferred this approach to a correction, which might create more confusion than it remedied. Many errors, however, were not discovered until scholars poured over the texts to provide critical editions. The work of these scholars in correcting errors in spelling is called "lower biblical criticism."

More important than lower criticism is the so-called "higher criticism" which goes to the subject matter itself. This form of critical Bible study reached its height in the middle of the nineteenth century. Its chief representatives were the German scholars Wellhausen and Graf. It all started with the discovery that, in the Book of Genesis, God is referred to in different terms. The story of creation uses the term "Elohim," and later we find two terms, "Yahweh" and "Elohim." Eventually, we shall have only one or the other. The critics concluded that these different terms were used by different authors. The first was an author who lived in Judah during the ninth century. He was an inspired man, who collected the written documents which he found, and perhaps some oral traditions, and molded them into a great work upon which he impressed the stamp of his theology. God, Creator of the world, is the Savior of His people. He led them out of Egypt, gave them Moses, and brought them back to the land of the fathers, where they were to emerge eventually as a strong nation under David. When he spoke of God, this author always used the term YHWH. Thus he became known as the Yahwist, and the documents as "J" documents (J after the German spelling of YHWH). A century later another author, who lived in the Kingdom of Israel, produced a literary work; and since he applied the term "Elohim" in speaking of God, he became known as Elohist, and his document as "E" document. He, too, went over the history of Israel, but with a somewhat different emphasis. God is somewhat more removed from the people; the miracle power of Moses and his uniqueness are stressed more emphatically. These two sources were woven together. Actually, we do not have the two source documents; it was the task of the higher critics to separate them as strands of the one biblical text we actually have. One hundred years after J and E, a third great work was produced, Deuteronomy. It stressed the covenant of Sinai as the central event in the history of Israel. The critics called it document "D." Eventually, a fourth work was written. It was an account of the religious development of Israel, emphasizing cult and ritual. Composed by a group of Priests in the sixth century, it became known as code "P." Thus we have the basic "J" document, upon which all the others are superimposed, the whole Scripture forming a lacework of interwoven parts.[6] This was the discovery of the critics, who then went to work to disentangle the net. In their enthusiasm as discoverers, they went quite far in dissecting the Bible on the basis of style and vocabulary and cast doubt on many biblical events, even when there was no need for such a doubt. They pointed out that the events had been recorded many years after they had taken place, which made the reports untrustworthy. Recent archaeological discoveries have shown, however, that the reporting of the Bible is much more accurate historically than the early Bible critics assumed, and we are cautioned against hasty conclusions on the basis of mere hypotheses. We may assume the Scripture to be generally correct in its historical report beginning from the time of the patriarchs.[7]

---

6 Anderson, *op. cit.*, pp. 35 ff., 160 ff., 225 ff.

7 Albright, *op. cit.*, pp. 255 ff.

BIBLE IN TRANSLATION

The power of the Biblical style can be felt even in translation. It has influenced the speech of every country and civilization. Frequently it created civilization, even in translation. Luther did not merely establish his Reformation on the basis of his great translation of the Bible; he actually created a unifying German language, without which Germany would have fallen apart into numerous different language groups. The British King James version gave strength to the English language which served as uplift when Winston Churchill used it to rally his people to the defense of the country and restore their courage in the midst of the Battle of Britain in World War II. The Bible in translation deeply influenced the style of the Puritans, even as its laws shaped the character of the New England society. Thus, it has remained an everlasting root and source of American language, custom, and law.

Historically speaking, the earliest translation was into Greek. According to legend it was undertaken by 72 scholars, called to Egypt by Ptolemy in the third century before the Christian era.[8] Actually, it may have been commissioned because the Jews in Egypt were about to forget their Hebrew. The translation was called Septuagint, which means 70, after the number of translators who collaborated in producing it. It was completed before the rabbis canonized the books of Scripture, and this was fortunate. It still contains the "hidden books," or Apocrypha.[9] The translation of the Septuagint is not always strictly in conformity with the text. Sometimes the translators would paraphrase rather than translate with exactitude. This shortcoming was remedied in a new translation by Aquila, who was a convert to Judaism,[10] and lived during the life of Akiba. At the time of the Tannaim the Bible was translated into Aramaic, the language spoken by the common people, rather than classical Hebrew. Saadia later translated it into Arabic. In the fourth century, St. Jerome translated the Septuagint translation into Latin. It was called Vulgate, and all Catholic translations are based on it.

A new Bible translation is a difficult undertaking. Throughout history great translations have injected new vigor into the societies from whose soil they emerged.

The second great work produced by the rabbis was the Mishnah.

---

[8] Talmud: Megillah 7a.
[9] See p. 79.
[10] See p. 74.

6

The
Mishnah

At the time of Akiba's death Rabbi (Judah the Prince) was born (Talmud: Kiddushin 72b)." Before the sun of Akiba had set, the sun of Judah had risen. Judah, who became the Prince or Patriarch of Palestine in the year 170, saw to it that the chain of tradition remained firm and strong. He had real spiritual and temporal power, and he ruled by wisdom and wealth, by strength of personality, and depth of knowledge. His people loved and revered him; the Roman emperors, among them Marcus Aurelius, the Stoic, treasured his friendship. Yet the future was uncertain. Akiba's martyr's death still overshadowed the life of the generation, and history might repeat itself. Could Oral Torah survive another purge of its masters? Rules and ordinances had become so numerous that it was difficult to find scholars who retained them all in their memories, though they did nothing but study. Judah concluded that the ever-growing body of tradition could no longer be transmitted orally, even in times of peace and during periods of undisturbed study. Should unrest develop, then tradition would surely be lost. Wisely, Judah decided to edit in written form the oral tradition of the past. But the problem existed that such a code might prevent the organic growth of Jewish religion, dam up the living stream of a growing, changing, ever-evolving Torah. Judah may have been aware of this, for he set down only the guide lines, the basic ideas. He prepared a brief, concise text, which could become source for further discussion. He carefully included the views of opposing schools and scholars, both of the past and of his own time. Minority opinion some day might become majority decision. The work was made easier since "lecture notes" of older masters could be used. Akiba had already removed the prohibition against written records; he had admonished his disciples, especially Rabbi Meir, to collect and write down decisions, views, and opinions. Now the work was arranged systematically, enlarged, and clarified.

In six sections, or Orders, Oral Torah was codified. This is the Mishnah, the "Review." Its decisions were based on the Written Torah, and had been developed on the basis of discussion. Logical principles worked out by Hillel had been applied to the interpretation of Scripture. Freedom of criticism and of dissent had always been permitted in Judaism, it has remained hospitable to divergent opinions. They, too, were "words of the living God."

Included in the Mishnah were "takkanot" ordinances, which formed the "fence around the Torah." Some of them might be for a specific period only, while other ordinances were permanent. The day-by-day guidelines of law, ordinance, and practical rule, mapping out the Jewish way of life, are called *Halakhah*, the "Walk" in life. "Ye shall kindle no fire throughout your habitations on the Sabbath day" is a halakhah, directly based on written Torah (Exod. 35:3). With it there went another body of instruction which gave direction and showed the underlying principles of practical observance, explaining the spirit of the law. These ideas and ideals were taught by maxim and parable, by preachment and wise counsel, and were also based on interpretation of Torah. They were called *Haggadah*, "Preaching." We find them in the body of the Mishnah, but also in a separate work, arranged as a commentary of the Scripture, following its text. This commentary is called *Midrash*, the "Search" (for Meaning). Halakhah and Haggadah are closely related; one directs actions, and the other shows their purpose—to bring man to God. The following Haggadah may serve as an example:

Rabbi Simlai lectured: 613 commandments were handed down to Moses;
365 of them are prohibitions, corresponding to the days of the year;
248 of them are laws of action, corresponding to the bones and limbs
of man.

Rabbi Hamnuna said: When David came, he reduced the commandments to eleven, for we read in Scripture:
A Psalm of David; Lord, who shall sojourn in Thy tabernacle;
who shall dwell upon Thy holy mountain?

He that *walketh uprightly* and *worketh righteousness;*	2
and *speaketh the truth* in his heart,	3
that hath *no slander* upon his tongue,	4
nor *doeth evil* to his fellow,	5
nor *taketh up a reproach* against his neighbor;	6

in whose eyes a *vile person* is *despised*, 7
but he *honoreth them* that *fear the Lord;* 8
he that *sweareth to his own hurt* and *changeth not;* 9
he that *putteth not out* his *money on interest;* 10
nor *taketh* a *bribe* against the innocent; 11
He that doeth these things shall never be moved (Ps. 15).

When Isaiah came, he reduced the commandments to six; for it is said:
He that *walketh righteously* and *speaketh uprightly,* 2
he that *despiseth* the *gain of oppression,* 3
that *shaketh* his *hands from* holding of *bribes,* 4
that *stoppeth* his *ears from hearing* of *blood,* 5
and *shutteth* his *eye from* looking upon *evil,* 6
he shall dwell on high (Isa. 33:15-16).

When Micah came, he reduced the commandments to three; as it is said:
It hath been told thee, o man what is good and what the Lord doth require
of thee:
only to *do justly,* 1
and to *love mercy,* 2
and to *walk humbly with* thy *God* (Micah 6:8). 3

Then Isaiah came again, reducing them to two, as is said:
Thus saith the Lord:
Keep ye *justice* and do *righteousness* 2
for my salvation is near to come (Isa. 56:1).

Then came Amos and reduced them to one:
Thus says the Lord to the House of Israel:
Seek ye Me and live (Amos 5:4). (Talmud Makkot 23-24) 1

Although the interpretation seems playful, arbitrary, without regard for
the historical sequence among the prophets, the message is beyond misunderstanding. Rabbi Simlai points out: Keep away from evil every day
of the year, but serve God with every fiber and limb in your body; Rabbi
Hamnuna makes it clear that there must be a purpose behind the commandments, and it must be understood. Practice must not obscure meaning—justice, mercy, humility, in a life devoted to the search of God. Thus
halakhah and haggadah do not contradict each other. Halakhah, however,
constitutes the main body of the Mishnah.

ORGANIZATION OF THE MISHNAH: THE ORDERS
AND THEIR CONTENT

As we list the six Orders of the great work, we find life in its totality
passing in review through its books (Tractates), their chapters, and their
paragraphs.

ZERAIM (Seeds), the first Order, deals with the laws of agriculture. Its first book is *Berakhot,* Blessings. Since nature and its rewards depend on God, man's relationship to God forms the first subject. The order of the service is explained, the rules for daily benedictions are laid down, and instructions are given on how to say grace, and how to give thanks for God's special favors. Here we find the blueprint for Jewish worship.

The other books deal with tithing and charity, which become duties as soon as we gather the harvest prepared for us by divine love.

MOED (Appointed Days) is the second Order. In it the rules for the festivals are explained. Its first book is *Shabbat,* its second *Erubin.* Both deal with the laws of the Sabbath, the first giving the details of work prohibition, the second providing the rules against moving goods in workaday toil. The Sabbath, as observed according to these laws, becomes a day of otherworldliness. Worries disappear, a new soul of peace transposes life and regenerates it. Without the Sabbath, Jews would never have survived; they would not have found the strength. *Pessahim* is the third book. It deals with the celebration of the Feast of Passover, including the sacrifice once offered in Temple courts. In this book we also find the outline of hymns, songs, and story for the celebration of the first night of the festival, the Seder. The family of today still gathers, passes the wine, breaks the unleavened bread, and rehearses the story of deliverance from Egypt. Ritual and words are those laid down in the Mishnah.

Shekalim speaks of the offering of the Half-Shekel. Ordained in Scripture (Exod. 30:11-16), the Shekel later became a free-will offering of World Jewry for the upkeep of the Temple and of the schools.

Yoma (the Day), discusses the great and awesome Day of Atonement. On this day the Children of Israel throughout the ages approach God in penitence, to confess their shortcomings and their sins, and to ask Him for forgiveness and for guidance throughout the year to come. The service, as once performed in the Temple, is outlined here, and the road to spiritual renewal is sketched out.

Sukkah (Tabernacle) speaks of the festival of Tabernacles. A festive booth is to be built, and people are invited to leave their homes to show symbolically that protection rests with God alone. He is our fortress. In happy procession of thanksgiving, palm branches, myrtles, willows, and citron are carried in festive bouquet around the altar. The book relates the joyful exuberance of the last day of the feast, when rabbis danced in measured abandon before God, Giver of all good things.

Yom Tob (Holiday) gives the rules applying to all holy days.

Rosh Hashanah (New Year) lays down the regulations for the New Years Day, when the ram's horn is sounded, calling the people together to shout for joy before the Lord, but also to review in earnest search their lives during the year gone by. The book tells us about the calculations of the calendar; how the rabbis determined it from month to month, from season to season, from year to year, as witnesses testified that they had just seen the emerging sickle of the new moon.

Taanit (Fast Day) deals with days of fasting.

Megillah (Scroll) details the regulations pertaining to the reading of the Scroll of Esther on Purim and matters relating to holy objects.

Moed Katan (Minor Holy Day) discusses the observance of minor holy days, the period between the first and the last days of Passover and Tabernacles. Only the first and last days are major holidays; the others are minor ones with limited observance of special rules.

Hagigah (The Festival Sacrifice) lays down the rules for the holiday pilgrimages to Jerusalem which were once obligatory, and deals with individual sacrifices and other regulations of ancient festival observance.

NASHIM (Women) is the third order, containing marriage and divorce laws. Among its books are *Kiddushin* (Sanctification of Marriages), *Ketubot,* dealing with civil laws of marriage, *Gitin* (Divorce), and others. The ritual of the Jewish marriage ceremony is based on these books, as are the laws of religious divorce proceedings observed to this day. Judaism disapproves of divorce, for the family is the unit of life, but Judaism is realistic enough to recognize that divorce may become necessary. However, the bond made in the presence of God must be resolved in religious rite. Actually, these laws had civil power; at the time when they were established, they alone were the law of the land.

NEZIKIN (Damages) forms the Code of Civil and of Criminal Law, which was public law when Israel was independent. In its civil law section (including *Baba Kamma, Baba Metzia, Baba Batra*) it deals with ownership, damages, trade, commerce, and liabilities. It also details the laws against idolatry. In its section on criminal law (including *Sanhedrin, Makkot*) it sets down the ground rules regarding courts from the Sanhedrin down; it lays down the laws of evidence, trial procedures, and penalties. At the end of this Order we find *Abot*, the Sayings of the Fathers. It is the only book dealing *exclusively* with ethics, as if to say: ethics is superior to formalized law; it prevents where the law punishes; it is spiritual, not simply physical; it is the foundation of all law. Procedure and the letter of the law are important, but the spirit alone will give them true meaning.

KADASHIM (Holy Things) deals with the laws of Temple sacrifices. It also lays down the dietary rules which have been so important in Jewish life (Tractate *Hulin*).

TAHAROT (Purifications) states the laws of ritual purity and impurities, of immersion required for Temple service, and how they are to be performed.

This is the Mishnah: its six Sedarim (Orders), its Masekhtot (Tractates), which make up the Sedarim, its Perakim and Mishnot (Chapters and Paragraphs) into which each tractate is divided. Through all of its laws breathes the spirit of a deep reverence for God and for the dignity of Man, and the very deepest concern with justice and mercy. A sample of the Mishnah may make this evident. It is taken from the Order Nezikin (Damages) and the Tractate Sanhedrin (Court), and deals with the rules of evidence, trial procedure, sentencing, and the execution of sentence.

EXCERPTS FROM THE MISHNAH: SANHEDRIN

Chapter 3. (1)   Litigations are tried before three judges, each party choosing one, and the two parties agreeing on the third; this is Rabbi Meir's view. The Rabbis ruled however, that the two judges appoint the third one. Each litigant can reject the judge chosen by his opponent; this is Rabbi Meir's view. The Rabbis state however, that a party can reject a judge only if he can show that (the judge) is related to the opposition or unfit. If both are fit and experienced neither can be rejected. Each party can declare the witnesses of the opposition to be unacceptable; this is Rabbi Meir's view. The Rabbis say, this is only possible upon proof that the witnesses are related to the opposition or (morally) unfit. . . . (3) The following are considered (morally) unfit: a gambler, a usurer, a person who races pigeons (as professional gambler). . . . (4) The following are considered relatives: father, brother, uncles on both sides, brother-in-law. . . . (6) How the witnesses are to be examined. First all of them are brought into court and instructed in regard to giving evidence. Then they are sent out of the room; only the most important witness is told to remain. The judges interrogate him: How do you know this man owes (the debt in question)? If the witness replies, 'He told me he owed the money' or 'somebody told me,' his evidence is without merit. He must clearly state, 'In our presence did this man state that he owed money to the other.' Then the other witness is brought in and examined (the same way). If their testimonies are in agreement, the case is debated by the court. If two of the judges are of one opinion and the other of opposite opinion, the decision is in favor (of the majority). If one judge states that he does not know who is entitled to the judgment, additional judges are added.

Chapter 4. (1)   Both civil cases and capital offenses require examination of the time element (when the act was committed), and careful scrutiny in regard to the act itself; for it says in Scripture: the same law shall apply to both (Lev. 24:22). How do the two kinds of cases differ? Civil cases are tried before three judges, capital cases before twenty-three. In civil cases argument may start either with (a debate on) guilt or on innocence. In capital cases the trial may be opened only with an argument in favor of the accused. In civil cases a majority of one is sufficient for a verdict; in capital cases a majority of one is sufficient for acquittal but a majority of at least two is required for conviction. In civil cases judgement may be reversed in favor or against either litigant. In capital cases judgement may be reversed in favor of the accused but not against him. In civil cases everyone (of the disciples present in court) may present an opinion either in favor or against either of the litigants. In capital cases anyone may present an opinion favorable to the accused but not against him. In civil cases a judge may reverse his opinion (in the course of the trial). In capital cases an opinion unfavorable to the accused may be reversed, but anyone who spoke in favor cannot reverse himself. Trials in civil matters are conducted in day time, but may be carried into the night to be completed. Capital cases may be tried during day time (only), and must be concluded in day time. Civil cases may be concluded in one day . . . but in capital cases the verdict must be on the day following the trial. Hence there cannot be any trials on the eve of the Sabbath and on the eve of any holiday. . . . (3) The court sat in a semicircle, in order that they could see one another. Two court recorders sat in front of them . . . to take down the words of the judges for conviction and those of the judges for acquittal. . . . (5) How did they instruct the witnesses in capital cases? They were brought into court and instructed as follows: Perhaps the testimony you are about to give will be based on guesswork or on hear-say; perhaps you know the facts from the mouth of another witness or some reliable person; or perhaps you are unaware that we shall cross-examine you later. Remember that a capital case is different from a litigation. In litigations you can compensate (for an error) and be forgiven. In capital cases the blood of the person convicted and sentenced and the blood of his descendants (he might have had otherwise) lies on your conscience. Thus did it happen to Cain of whom is said, 'the blood of thy brothers cries out to me (Gen. 7:27)!' Not simply the blood of thy brother, but of all his descendants as well. . . . God created *one* man only, Adam (from whom the whole world sprang), to teach you that he who destroys one single soul is deemed by Scripture as having destroyed a world, and he who keeps alive one single soul is deemed by Scripture as having sustained a whole world. Furthermore, God created only one person to promote peace in the world; that no one may say to his fellow man: 'my ancestors were more distinguished than thine.' . . . Yet, should you now feel, why bother with the whole thing? Remember Scripture says: 'If any person sin, and one is a witness or saw it or knows it, if he does not speak up, he will bear sin (Lev. 5:1).' Should you say: 'Why should we become guilty in the blood of this man?' remember it is written: 'When the wicked perish there is joy (Prov. 11:10).'

Chapter 5. (1) The witnesses are examined on seven different items: When did the crime take place: in which seven year cycle, in which year, in which month, on which day of the month on which day of the week, at what hour, at which place; do you know the (accused) man, have you warned him against committing his crime? (If not, he cannot be convicted). . . . (2) The more thorough the examination the better it is, and the examiner deserves praise. Ben Zaccai once questioned them about the stems of the leaves on a fig tree (under which the crime had been committed). What is the difference between the examination on the time element and on the matter of the crime itself? In the first, if he does not know, his testimony is invalid; in the second, even if both say they don't know, their evidence is (otherwise) good. In either case, if they contradict each other their evidence is invalid. . . . (4) The second (witness) is brought in and examined. If their evidence is in agreement, the discussion (of the judges) starts with an argument in the accused's favor. Should any of the witnesses declare that he has a point in the accused's favor, or if any of the disciples states that he has a point against the accused, they are told to keep silent. (The witnesses cannot argue, nor can the disciples argue, except in favor of the accused). If any of the disciples has anything to say in favor of the accused, he is permitted to step up (to the judges' seats) and may remain there for the rest of the day. If there is substance to his words, they listen to him. Even if the accused states that he has something to say in his own favor, they listen to him. But there must be substance to his words. (On the other hand he can never testify against himself). (5) If they find for acquittal, he is acquitted forthwith; if not, judgement is postponed for the next day. During the day, the judges remain together in pairs, eat little, do not drink wine. Early the next morning they return to court. Those who had previously been for acquittal declare: 'I have been for acquittal and hold this view now.' Those who had been for conviction can change their opinion toward acquittal; but those who had been for acquittal cannot change their views. If they are in error (in their statement) the court recorders remind them. If they find (the accused) innocent, they discharge him; if not, they take a vote. Twelve for acquittal and eleven for conviction sets the accused free; twelve for conviction and eleven for acquittal sets him also free. If one of the judges says, 'I don't know,' they add judges. Even if twenty-two are for conviction and one says, 'I don't know,' they add judges; up to a total of seventy-one. If thirty-six convict and thirty-five acquit, the judges go on debating until one of the convicting judges changes his mind to acquittal.

Chapter 6. (1) If he is convicted (to stoning) they lead him to the place of stoning. . . . A man stands at the door of the court house with a flag in his hand; another is placed a little further away, where he can see the first one; he is on a horse. If one of the judges says, 'I have something to say in favor of the accused,' the man waves his flag, the rider chases after the procession with the convicted and halts it. Even if the accused says he has something to say in his own favor, he is permitted to return, even four and five times. There must be substance to his words, however. If they find for acquittal, they discharge him, if not, they lead him out to stoning. (4) The stoning place (was a wall which) had the height of two men. One of the witnesses pushes (the convicted man) down sidewise. If he falls on his heart, they turn him over. If he is dead, the duty is fulfilled, if not, the other (witness) throw a stone at his heart. If he is dead (then) the duty is fulfilled; if not, all of Israel stone him. As it is said: 'The hand of the witnesses shall be at him first, and the hand of all the people thereafter . . . (Deut. 17:7).

It is not surprising that executions were extremely rare. If one happened once in seventy years, the court which handed it down had to bear the stigma of being a court of murderers. Thus did the spirit of Torah prevail, as reverence for God built mercy into law; for man is created in His image.

Palestine after the Mishnah

The work continued, and new questions arose. The Mishnah called for new interpretations. Out of discussions grew another work, the Talmud of Jerusalem. Its significance, however, remained minor, because the center of Jewish life and learning moved to Babylonia.

7

The
Babylonian
Talmud

Man's most valuable quality is foresight (Abot 2:13)."
Two of Rabbi Judah's great disciples felt that the
time had come to find a new center for the study
of Torah. Conditions in Palestine were unsettled.
Thus Abba Areka, Abba the Tall, a giant of a man both physically and
intellectually, moved to Babylonia. He was joined by Samuel, a brilliant
colleague.

BACKGROUND OF THE BABYLONIAN TALMUD

The Babylonian Jewish community was large, wealthy, and happy.
Several million Jews enjoyed freedom and prosperity in the lands of the
Tigris and Euphrates. They formed an autonomous state within the kingdom of Persia and, later, under the Califs, almost comparable to one of
the States which make up the United States. At the head of the Jewish
community stood the "Exilarch" (Resh Galuta). Descendant of the
House of David, he was "governor" in the full political sense of the word.
The central government expected him to collect the taxes which his
people had to pay; in return, he had a free hand. Taxation was heavy, but
life was abundant. The yield of the farmlands was rich, and the crafts-
man's product was highly valued. In many households the men could
enjoy the luxuries of leisure in pleasant surroundings, and the women

those of lipstick, rouge, and eye shadows. They were a proud community, proud of their Jewish heritage, and concerned that it should survive in purity.

The Exilarch might be a man of learning, but this was the exception. He depended, therefore, upon the heads of the two great academies, at Sura and Nehardea, for guidance and assistance. They were the chief justices and the spiritual heads of the community, and the importance of their offices was reflected in their title, *Gaon,* which means Excellency. Abba Areka and Samuel became the heads of these two academies. (Later the School of Nehardea was transferred to Pumpedita).

Mishnah and Gemara: The Talmud

So great was Abba's prestige and influence that he eventually became known simply as *Rab,* the Master. Rab henceforth was used as title for all the Babylonian masters, while the title *Rabbi* remained for the teachers of the Mishnah, the Tannaim. If we hear of *Rabbi* Judah, we know immediately that he was a teacher of Mishnah, a Tanna; when the term Rab is used, as in *Rab* Ashee, we know he was a master of Babylonia, an Interpreter or *Amora.* Under the leadership of Rab and Samuel and their successors, the rabbis went over the entire text of the Mishnah, almost word by word and sentence by sentence, discussing, debating, and finally voting. Their whole discussion was taken down in writing. This is the *Gemara,* the "Completion" of Mishnah. Mishnah and Gemara combined are called the Talmud, the "Compendium of Learning."

The masters of the Gemara did not spend all their time at the academy, for they were not professional scholars. They assembled only twice a year, in Spring and in Fall, for one month each time. These meetings were called *Kallah,* "Assembly." At each assembly they were given "homework" for individual study and general review at the next meeting.

The debates were recorded. Based on thorough preparation, they were both cordial and heated; at times very much to the point, they were frequently rambling. Thus the Talmud is not a dead compendium of conclusions. Through it breathes the living spirit of discussion, of question and answer, of bon mot and jest. But such exchange of thoughts makes difficult reading, especially when there are no quotation marks. The Talmud is a difficult book which must be studied, rather than merely read. We would not fully understand it today had it not been for a great medieval commentator, Rashi. He wrote a running commentary to every sentence and word which we find printed at the margin of every Talmud edition. One of the difficulties lies in the rabbis' frequent use of the method of "free association." It has been said that only a man acquainted with the method of Talmud, as was Sigmund Freud, could have invented, or re-discovered, the method of free association, which has been so important in the exploration of the mind in psychology and psycho-analysis.

When the mass of the Talmud became too great for any one man's memory, it was written down. Twice revised, it was edited under the direction of Rab Ashee and his disciple Rabina, around the year 500 of the Christian era. We call it the *Babylonian* Talmud. Everything is in it, Halakhah and Haggadah; the discussions encompass every field of human knowledge, from law to medicine, from biology to geology to astronomy. Life in its entirety passes in review.

The Talmud has been translated into English.[1] Some parts make fairly easy reading, while others call for guidance by an experienced tutor. Thus, even as written down, it has remained—in a sense—Oral Torah. It still can be mastered only through discussion and personal instruction.

Method and Organization

In its method, the Talmud follows the orders of the Mishnah and its subdivisions. Each Mishnah is quoted verbatim, then followed by Gemara, the debate and explanation. It would be difficult to find one's place in the Talmud, which consists of many heavy folio tomes, were it not for a truly ingenious arrangement. In all editions of the Talmud, the paging is the same. If we find an annotation behind a quotation from the Talmud, for instance Baba Kamma 83b, we know that the quotation is found in Tractate Baba Kamma, which is in the "Order of Damages" dealing with civil law. Opening the Talmud at the right, since all Hebrew writing is from right to left, we shall find the quotation on the back of leaf 83. What we read gives us an idea of the talmudic method:

Mishnah: A man who inflicts a bodily injury on his neighbor has to make five payments, namely: damages, payment for the pain inflicted, doctor's bills and other medical expenses, payments for loss of time and for the inflicted humiliation.

(By) Damages (we mean): If he has cut off his hand or broken his leg . . . then . . . (the injured man's present earning power is to be compared with his previous earning power and the damages to be assessed accordingly).

Gemara: Is this procedure correct? Does not the Almerciful (God) say otherwise?, (namely): An eye for an eye (Exod. 21:24)?

(Answer) This (literal interpretation) does not make sense, for we have learned (differently; namely:) If someone has blinded his fellowman, you might think he should be blinded too; or if he has severed his fellowman's hand, (you might think) his hand should be cut off; or if he has broken another's foot,

---

[1] *Babylonian Talmud,* ed. I. Epstein (London: The Soncino Press, 1953). The translations in this text are the author's own.

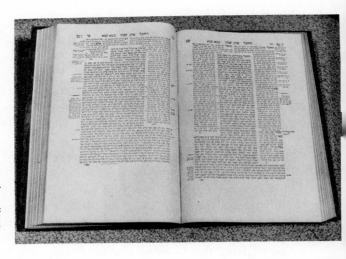

The Talmud, open to the quotation which is translated in the text. Text is in center of page, commentaries on the margins.

(you might think) his foot should be broken. (But this is not the case, for we read in Scripture) "He who strikes a man (shall be punished)," and we read also "He who strikes an animal (shall make compensation)." (In both instances the biblical terminology is the same, hence the disposition of the cases must be the same). Just as in the case of an animal, monetary compensation is ordered, so in the case of a man: monetary compensation is meant. If you argue that Scripture says "Ye shall take no ransom for the life of a murderer who deserves death; he shall surely be put to death (Num. 35:31), (which seems to show that in the case of crimes against human beings monetary compensation is not acceptable; then I tell you) for the *life* of a murderer you may not take any ransom, but you may allow compensation for the limbs of a person which will not grow back again. . . ."

The elaborate argument should not deceive us. In legal cases the exact terminology of basic law is scrutinized by lawyers today as in years gone by. According to the rabbis, the Bible was basic law, and every nuance of it had to be examined. But there is more to this interpretation of the scriptural verse "an eye for an eye." Judaism had long outgrown the concept. Now the Gemara points out that this could never have been Jewish justice. We must remember that the Gemara does not hold with a theory of historical development. To the rabbis, the word of Torah is perfect and unchangeable. If this word does not agree with the ideas of justice as the rabbis held it, then the fault lies not with the Torah but with human error in interpretation. The only solution then is to re-interpret the Torah in order to establish the true intent of the law in line with its spirit of justice and of love. Interpretation may sound tortuous; it is simply the effort to adjust law without abolishing the word of Torah. In our particular case it may be pointed out that a one-eyed man who has gouged out one eye of a two-eyed person would lose his sight completely were the principle of "eye for an eye" to be applied. He would then receive a punishment completely out of line with his crime. The victim of

105

the crime can still see, while the other one would be blind. This is not justice.

In this spirit Jewish law evolved. While Torah and Talmud have remained the core of Jewish religion, the process of evolution has continued. The ideals of love and justice for God and man have never changed, nor has the search for knowledge and for wisdom among the Jewish people.

BABYLONIAN JEWRY AFTER COMPLETION OF THE TALMUD

The completion of the Talmud did not spell the end of Jewish creativity; yet the work had been completed none too soon. Storms shook the world. Persecutions took place in Persia. Islam, the religion of Mohammed, began its victorious march. The prophet himself had learned much from the Jews in Arabia. Disappointed in his expectations, that they would join his new faith, he became antagonistic toward them. But never in Islamic history do we find extended persecution as cruel as that which characterized the nations of the West. The year of Mohammed's death, 632, saw the transition of Babylonia from Persian rule to Islamic rule. The relationship which developed between the two religions was excellent. Cultures were fused as Islam conquered country after country. Persian ideas were grafted on Jewish thought and combined with Greek philosophy. Arts and sciences flourished, but contacts with the world and with philosophy created doubts in many Jews. A Jewish sect arose which recognized only the written Torah, rejecting the tradition of the Talmud. This group, the Karaites, had to be fought. Aristotle's arguments had to be met by reason. This led to the development of Jewish philosophy. If Aristotle was right, how could the Torah be right too? If he was wrong, it had to be proven. Jews in general had never before viewed their faith from without. They lived *in* Judaism; it never occurred to them to step out—as the philosopher must—to view it from the outside and to talk *about* it. The Jewish Hellenist Philo, a significant philosopher, had done it, but he had remained practically unknown in Jewish circles. Conditions were different now; the issues had to be met.

The man who addressed himself to all these issues was the Gaon Saadia (882-942). He was a philosopher whose thoughts deserve detailed discussion. He wrote in Arabic, the language his people knew best, and translated the Bible into Arabic, a translation still used by the Jews in the Middle East. At the same time, he compiled a Hebrew grammar and re-edited the prayer book. From his pen flew tract after tract against the Karaites. He was a man of battle and his life was stormy; he stands at the end of the great masters of Babylonia. New centers of learning were soon to develop.

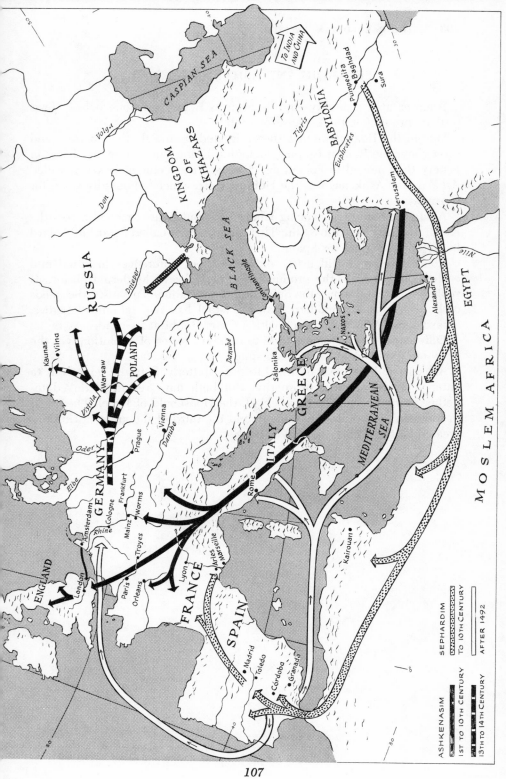

Jewish dispersion.

ASHKENASIM
SEPHARDIM

1ST TO 10TH CENTURY
TO 10TH CENTURY

13TH TO 14TH CENTURY
AFTER 1492

SEFARDIC AND ASHKENASIC JEWRY

Islam created a mighty empire, even as Rome had done before. Jews settled throughout the expanse of both.

Within the Roman Empire they migrated from Palestine to Italy and throughout the Roman Empire, including France and Germany. Later in history they moved to Poland and Russia. This sector of Jewry is called *Ashkenasim*. Ashkenas was the Hebrew word which supposedly stood for Germany.

Along the road of advancing Islam, Babylonian Jews moved across the North African coast into Spain. This community is called *Sefardim*, Sefard in Hebrew standing for Spain.

These groupings still exist, and with them differences in ritual and custom, and even in the pronunciation of Hebrew. Modern Hebrew, as spoken in Israel, follows the Sefardic pronunciation. To satisfy the needs of both groups, the modern State of Israel has two rabbinical bodies, Sefardic and Ashkenasic, each with a Chief Rabbi at its head.

Differences in environment led to different forms of evolution, yet the body of Israel is one. There is no split.

Ashkenasic Jewry was destined to suffer bitterly. Sefardic Jewry was to enter a period of great prosperity. But both have remained linked together as members of one household, the Household of Israel. They held in common the Torah, the Talmud, and the third of the great institutions created by the rabbis, the Prayer Book.

8

Prayer
and the
Prayer Book

Call, supplication, thanksgiving, intercession, all this is prayer. It is man speaking with God. Reflection on the meaning and purpose of life is prayer as long as it takes place in the presence of God. It may be my life, or the life of the community, or the purpose of creation; as long as I reflect on it, it becomes prayer. Thus the study of Torah and Talmud are—in a wider but very real sense—prayer. They are communication with God and His world; they are communion with God.

WHAT WE MEAN BY PRAYER

Jewish prayer is as old as Judaism. It is based on an intimacy with God which dares to ask and to challenge. Abraham, pleading with God for the preservation of the wicked city of Sodom if there be only a few good people in it, can say: "It should be far from Thee to slay the righteous with the wicked; shall not the judge of all the earth do justly (Gen. 18:25)?" This is not familiarity; there are in these words the utmost of respect, trust, and affirmation. But out of this very affirmation grows the question. In the same spirit, Moses can plead with God. The people have sinned grievously, they have made a golden calf. They are to be punished: "Whosoever has sinned, him will I blot out." And Moses appeals to divine mercy, until God agrees to spare the people and to lead them to their land. Then Moses goes a step further: "Show me, I pray

Thee, Thy glory." This is denied him, not because the plea is regarded as unjustified, but because it reaches beyond man's capacity. Man may ask, but must know that God determines how much may be granted to short-lived mortals. But Moses is told the qualities of God, that knowledge of them may serve to guide man's life and direct his thoughts and actions: "The Lord, the Lord, God, merciful and gracious, long suffering and abundant in goodness and truth; keeping mercy unto the thousandth generation, forgiving iniquity, transgression and sin—clearing the guilty however, that He will not (Exod. 33, 34:6-7)." These qualities are revealed that man may have guidance in emulating God and in finding Him through imitation. They are made known in order that man may appeal to them, calling on divine mercy when guilt has engulfed him. The rabbis were so certain of this mercy that they changed the final part of the verse for use in prayer. They ruled to omit its last part, and the verse as now quoted reads: ". . . forgiving iniquity, transgression and sin—clearing the guilty." This is Jewish prayer, a dialogue with God Who is infinitely merciful, and submission to His will, Who is infinite in love.

Jewish prayer is reflection. The farmer who brings his first fruits to the Temple is given a formal prayer (Deut. 26:5-10). It is almost philosophical, meditating on the help God has given His people in all the trials of history. He rescued them from Egypt and brought them to their land, whose fruits are presented to Him in gratitude.

Jewish prayer may be spontaneous, coming from the heart. Hannah, mother of Samuel, is praying for the child so far denied her. She "spoke in her heart, only her lips moved, and her voice could not be heard (I Sam. 1:13)." Her petition is answered.

So important is prayer that Solomon's Temple is dedicated not to ritual and sacrifice, but to prayer, the simple, heartfelt outpouring of those who come to worship. "What prayer and supplication soever be made by any man of all Thy people Israel—who shall know, every man the plague of his own heart—then hear Thou in heaven (I Kings 8:39)." Not the Jew's prayer alone, but all prayer directed to God deserves to be answered. "The stranger, that is not of Thy people Israel, when he . . . shall pray toward this house, hear Thou in heaven, Thy dwelling place, and do according to all that the stranger calleth Thee for (I Kings 8:41-43)."

Prayer runs through the pages of Torah like a silken thread, holding together its history and people, and linking man to God. Prayer, even supplication, is always affirmation. He who petitions affirms God, whom he addresses. Thus the Book of Psalms is called *Tehillim*, Book of Praises. It might have been called Book of Prayers, but this would have narrowed down the meaning of prayer, for all prayer is praise. Judaism needed no theology in a narrow sense, no "Science of God," no philosophy; Prayer took their place. He who prayed knew to whom he prayed, His glory, His power, His majesty, and His love. God simply was. He was there, He was near. Formal prayer was the system of Jewish philosophy, simplified, made accessible to everyone.

THE BERAKHAH

To translate this philosophy into life, the rabbis surrounded the life of the Jew with prayer. The individual Jew can always follow the promptings of his heart in finding the words by which he reaches out to God. At the same time, a formula of prayer was devised: the Berakhah, the Blessing. This Berakhah is the unit of prayer, with a definite form: "Blessed are Thou, God, our Lord, King of the world." The Psalmist had used it: "Blessed art Thou, O Lord, teach me Thy statutes (Ps. 119:12)." Now every occasion was hallowed by blessing.

Over fruit growing on trees one says: 'Blessed art Thou, God, our Lord, King of the Universe, who createst the fruit of the tree' . . . Over wine one says: 'Blessed . . . who createst the fruit of the vine' . . . Over fruits of the ground one speaks: 'Blessed . . . who createst the fruit of the ground.' Over bread one pronounces: 'Blessed . . . who bringest forth bread from the earth.' Over anything which does not grow from the earth one says: 'Blessed . . . by whose word all was created.' . . . After a meal everyone shall say grace (Mishnah Berakhot 6:1, 3, 6).

Over comets, earthquakes, thunder, storm and lightnings, over mountains, hills, oceans, rivers and deserts (a blessing is pronounced by the beholder) . . . Over rain and on getting happy news one says: 'Blessed . . . who art good and art doing good.' On receiving evil tidings one recites: 'Blessed . . . the true judge.' . . . It is man's duty to bless God for the ills that befall him holding hidden good, even as he gives blessing for the good that comes to him, though it holds hidden ills, . . . Has he built a new house or bought new clothes, he shall pronounce praise: 'Blessed . . . who hast kept us alive, hast sustained us and hast brought us to this (happy) time (Mishnah Berakhot 9:2, 3, 5).'

This is not formalism, it is existential theology. Man's thoughts constantly revolve around God as center of the world. As he gathers enjoyment from this world, he realizes that everything really belongs to God. He may have grown his food or bought it. Legally it is his, but ideally it is God's. The Berakhah is man's request for God's permission to use it. As man contemplates nature and history, he recognizes God as their master and himself as God's steward. In sorrow, he praises Him, Whose judgement is truth. Thus mourners offer blessing at the moment of their bitter grief, the moment of parting from a dear one.

Prayer reflects an unconditional faith. It combines respect with love, reverence with intimacy; it is the relationship of the child to his father. In every condition of life, the Jew is aware that God is his Father. "For Thou art our Father . . . our Redeemer (Isa. 63:16)." As the Jew sets out on his rounds of work, he is admonished: "Be strong as a leopard, swift as an eagle, speedy as a gazelle, courageous as a lion to do the will of thy Father Who is in heaven (Abot 5:20)." As he approaches God in contrition, admitting his errors in life, he cries out: "Forgive us, o our Father, for we have sinned . . . bring us back, o our Father, to Thy Torah." [1] And then he knows that forgiveness is assured to the penitent. "Blessed are you Israel, for He before Whom you try to cleanse yourselves and Who indeed purifies you, He is your Father, Who is in Heaven (Akiba's words in Yoma.8:9).

It is no contradiction that the rabbis set aside special periods during the day for prayer. Man may forget his father, if he is invisible, unless he takes time to remember him. A man may lose his philosophy of life unless he reviews it at specified times. Were we asked to pray only when the urge occurs to us, we might not pray at all. Overindulgence in prayer might equally lead to diminished respect. If a subject were to greet his king every hour of the day, he would weary his lord and his greeting would become cheap (Tanhuma). Intimacy may never become familiarity. "When thou prayest always remember before whom thou standest," is the admonition of the Talmud (Berakhot 28b). Naturally, prayer must be more than words, repeated without thought. Such a prayer would be an insult to the Father. It must be an outpouring of the heart. "A person who regards praying simply as a duty to be performed, his prayer ceases to be supplication (Berakhot 4:4)." "One may not go to prayer, except in the spirit of solemn earnestness. The pious masters of the past used to meditate for a full hour to collect their thoughts before they started formal worship; in order to direct their hearts to their Father in heaven (Berakhot 5:1)." Thus, body and soul must be completely attuned to God. "Even if the king should greet him, the worshipper may not interrupt his prayer to return the greeting (Berakhot 5:1)."

This then is the character of formal worship in Judaism. Into the set form is poured the spontaneity of the human heart.

STRUCTURED WORSHIP: PERIODS OF PRAYER

"Thou shalt love the Lord thy God with all thy heart and all thy soul and all thy might. And these words . . . thou shalt speak of them . . . when thou *liest down* and when thou *risest up* (Deut. 6:5 ff.)." Twice a day the words must be rehearsed, in the morning, as guidepost for the day, and in the evening, as yardstick in the review of the day's accomplishments. The morning and evening prayers have their foundation in these words of Scripture. An afternoon offering was presented in the Temple of old. It resulted in an afternoon prayer which serves as a pause

---

[1] From the Amidah see p. 116.

of reflection in the midst of our work: how well have we done so far? What must we yet do to give the day true meaning? Thus we have three daily prayers: Shaharit, the morning prayer; Minhah, the afternoon prayer; and Maarib, the evening prayer.

On Sabbath and holy days, a special ritual was performed in the Temple of old; it resulted in a special prayer, the *Mussaf*. It follows the Torah reading of Shaharit. On days of fasting a concluding prayer of special fervor formed the climax of the day. It has been retained on the Day of Atonement, and is called N'eelah, closing prayer; it brings this holy day to its conclusion.

All these prayers are very similar in structure. They follow the simple logic of spontaneous thought.

THE STRUCTURE OF THE MAIN PRAYERS

If we were to meet a great personality, perhaps the Head of State, to offer homage or to present petitions, how would we act?

From the moment of arising, our *preparations* will be keyed to the event.

Then, in *reflection,* we prepare ourselves for the meeting.

If we are part of a delegation we *call* them together.

Arriving and standing before the Head of State we pay our respect, *affirming* his greatness and goodness.

Then we present our *petition* or *render homage.*

Following our petition we may speak of our own shortcomings which may actually make us unworthy of special favors. *Confessing* we express trust.

Now we *listen* to the words spoken by the Head of State, in reply and admonition.

With a word of reverence and a *pledge of allegiance* we take our leave.

This is the structure of Jewish worship.

In the morning we start with special *preparation,* followed by *reflection.* All other prayers open with *reflection,* leading to the *call to worship* when public service is offered. This is followed by *affirmation,* and *petition* or *homage.* Petition leads to *confession of sins.* At appointed days we then receive the Word of God as found in *Scripture.* With a *pledge of Allegiance* we take our leave.

The Morning Prayer

PREPARATION.   On opening his eyes, man gives thanks to God who has restored his life to him. Attending to the needs of his body, he contemplates in gratitude on the wonderful organism which God has given him, and its miraculous functions. He realizes that this body is the precious vessel of the more precious, pure soul, which is in our trust that we preserve it to surrender it to Him intact when the time He has appointed comes, and to receive it again in life eternal. Then we reflect in gratitude that God is the source of our strength, of food and clothing and of freedom, and we pray for guidance, that we may not fall into sin and temptation, but remain God's co-workers throughout the work of the day. The Torah will be our guide, and we bless Him who has given it to us.

Our preparation is completed. These prayers, now recited in the synagogue, once were offered at home as man got ready for his encounter with God throughout the day.

REFLECTION. Through Psalms, recited by the congregation in unison or responsively, we put ourselves in the mood for the solemn meeting. "Serve the Lord with joy (Ps. 100)"; "I will extol Thee, my God and King (Ps. 145)"; "Hallelujah, Praise ye the Lord (Ps. 150)."

THE CALL TO WORSHIP is issued. The leader intones: "Bless ye the Lord to Whom all blessing belongeth." The congregation responds: "Blessed be the Lord, to whom all blessing belongeth, unto all eternity."

AFFIRMATION. The congregation is conscious of standing in the presence of God, and affirms His power and His love.

Our attention is drawn to the wonders of nature. Day follows day, and night follows night. He has made it and keeps it thus by His eternal law of nature. In a Berakhah we affirm it in gratitude.

To give direction and meaning to our day, He has given us the Torah as guide, and bestowed on us the power to fulfil His will by free choice, while nature *must* follow its divinely ordained law. This act of divine love must call forth within us a response of love. Affirming God's goodness in giving us the Torah, we plead for strength to respond to it in loving obedience. A Berakhah expresses gratitude and pledge.

In token of our love, we now pronounce the Affirmation of Faith: Hear O Israel the Lord our God, the Lord is One . . . And thou shalt love the Lord thy God.

The Proclamation of Faith has awakened in us the consciousness that, throughout the generations, the people of Israel have thus affirmed Him, not only in times of happiness but equally so in times of great hardship and persecution. They knew and we know that He, who is the Master of history, will never abandon us, but shapes events to His purposes. In a Berakhah we affirm God, the God of History, as the Redeemer of Israel.

PETITION OR HOMAGE. On the days of the week we now offer our petitions. On festive days, when cares recede, we render homage. The prayer is called *Amidah*, which means a prayer recited while the congregation stands. First silently, then in public repetition we spread our needs before God. These are prayers of the individual, but they are framed in plural form. All human wants are basically alike; we should remember it and include our fellow man in our supplications. The Amidah will be discussed in detail.

CONFESSION OF SIN follows here on weekdays in acknowledgement of the fact that our petitions are not based on any claim to righteousness. On festival days, Psalms 113-118, the Hallel-Praise, are recited instead.

THE WORD OF GOD is now received as it is read from the Torah on days appointed for Torah reading, followed on holy days by a prayer for America, our country.

THE PLEDGE OF ALLEGIANCE. With Kaddish and Adoration we take our leave. They will be discussed in greater detail.

The Nineteenth Psalm and the Pattern of Jewish Worship

As we review the order of Jewish worship, we find that it closely follows the structure of the nineteenth Psalm.

God is Lord of Nature: The heavens recount the glory of God (1 ff.).

God is the Source of Torah: The Torah of the Lord is perfect, restoring the soul (8-11).

Man Petitions God: Errors, who can discern them; from hidden ones cleanse Thou me (13-14).

Plea: May the words of my mouth and the meditations of my heart find grace before Thee (15).

Adoration: Thou, O Lord, art my Rock and my Redeemer (15).

Amidah: The Concerns of Petition

The Amidah consists of a series of short petitions, each a Berakhah. They are arranged in logical order.

THE FIRST CONCERN: CONTEMPLATION OF GOD

1) *God of history.* We come to God because He alone rules the world and makes history. He has the power to help us, and He has helped us. From Abraham's days He has been our shield, and He will bring redemption to our children's children.

2) *God our daily helper.* We turn to God because He never forgets the needs of even the smallest of His children; sustaining the living, healing the sick, freeing the captives, granting life eternal to those sleeping in the dust, He will surely consider our wants, insignificant as they may appear.

3) *God's holiness.* We throw our cares upon Him, for He is unique and beyond compare. He is holy. In the repetition of the Amidah the whole congregation proclaims: Holy, holy, holy is the Lord of hosts, the whole earth is full of His glory (Isa. 6:3).

THE SECOND CONCERN: HOMAGE OR MAN'S SPIRITUAL NEEDS.[2] On festive days, only one Berakhah of homage and thanksgiving is now

---

[2] See Samson R. Hirsch, *Versuche über Jisroel's Pflichten* (Altona: 1837), pp. 647 f. His effort to show that petitions for spiritual and material gifts alternate is not convincing.

offered. The Amidah continues with the third concern. On weekdays, our needs are revealed before God.

1) The need for understanding. Without knowledge and understanding, our lives are wasted. We ask for "knowledge, insight, and understanding."

2) The need for Torah. But knowledge may be applied to unholy purposes. We plead for guidance through Torah: "Lead us back, O our Father, to Thy Torah."

3) Forgiveness of sin. Sin has been the obstacle, it has estranged us from God's Torah. We plead: "Forgive us, O our Father, for we have sinned."

THE SECOND CONCERN CONTINUED: MAN'S PHYSICAL AFFLICTIONS

4) Conciliation of conflicts. Turning to our physical needs, we find both the world at large and ourselves torn by strife and inner conflict. May God redeem us from them: "See our affliction, conciliate our conflict, and redeem us soon."

5) Sickness and health. Conflict is the disease of the soul, sickness the affliction of the body. Health is our most precious physical possession. "Heal us, O Lord, and we shall be healed."

6) Want and sustenance. Our daily bread is man's basic need. We pray for freedom from want. "Bless unto us, O Lord, this year and all its produce for good, and give blessing unto the entire earth."

THE SECOND CONCERN CONTINUED: ISRAEL'S NEEDS

7) Plea for rescue. Israel, persecuted in many lands, has special problems, and stands in need of rescue from oppression. We pray: "Sound the great shofar for our redemption, lift up the banner to gather our exiles."

8) Prayer for justice. True redemption comes only through justice, established under God. Without justice there is no liberty. The prayer pleads: "Bring back our judges as of once ago . . . thereby removing from us sorrow and suffering. Reign Thou over us, Thou alone . . . and confirm us in judgement."

9) Abolition of evil. This prayer was added in times of bitter persecution, frequently based on malicious slander. May God free society from evil and malice: "Be there no hope for slanderers, may evil disappear in an instant."

10) Vindication of the just and pious. May the steadfast hope of the pious for freedom and justice be vindicated soon and "may we never be put to shame as in Thee we trust."

THE SECOND CONCERN CONTINUED: THE WORLD'S NEEDS

11) Redemption and the rebuilding of Jerusalem. May Jerusalem be built as reality and symbol, that it again be God's dwelling place. Then will mankind unite in brotherhood as the Word of God goes forth from Jerusalem and all Jews will have peace: ("David's throne be-

ing established") "Return to Thy City of Jerusalem in mercy . . . rebuild it soon . . . as a building for eternity."

12) The Messiah. May he come soon, may his age dawn speedily, that war will vanish and peace may reign. "Make the shoot of David
. . . soon to spring forth . . . we are waiting always for Thy help."

13) Divine response: may God hear our prayer. This last of the
middle petitions encompasses all of them: "Hear our voice, O Lord our
God, have mercy and compassion upon us, and receive our prayer in
mercy and grace."

THE THIRD CONCERN: MAN'S MOST PRECIOUS GOODS. On festive
days, as well as on weekdays, the Amidah continues here.

1) The opportunity of worship. Through worship we recognize
true worth. False worship leads to false values. May God so guide our
hearts that our worship be pleasing to Him. Restored to "the Halls of
His House," it is right worship.

2) The quality of gratitude. Gratitude is the hallmark of true
worship. But the prayer does not ask for the strength to be grateful, it
expresses gratitude for God's presence, for our lives, for His goodness,
for nature, and for His abiding help. "Thy kindness never ceases."

3) The gift of peace. It is the most sublime of all gifts. With
this prayer the Amidah reaches its climax: "Grant us peace." In the
repetition of the Amidah, the priestly benediction is pronounced: "The
Lord bless thee and keep thee. The Lord make His face to shine upon
thee and be gracious unto thee. The Lord lift up His face upon thee and
give thee peace (Num. 6:24-26)."

More of the *Pledge of Allegiance*

Two additional prayers deserve attention. One is the *Kaddish*. The
other, a poem composed by Rab for the New Year's Day, was found so inspiring that it was transferred to every one of the daily services. It is
the *Alenu*, the Adoration.

The Kaddish *(sanctification)*

The opening words of the Kaddish are based on a prophecy by
Ezekiel: "I will magnify Myself and sanctify Myself; I will make Myself
known in the eyes of many nations; and they shall know that I am the
Lord (Ezek. 38:23)." Ezekiel tells of the conflicts of time to come, when
the whole world will be drawn into battle. Out of it, God will emerge in
all His glory, and His majesty will be vindicated. The Jew, not waiting
for the end of days, glorifies Him now. This is the theme of the Kaddish.

It is a very old prayer, written long before the fall of the Temple, in
Aramaic, the vernacular of the people. Formerly recited at the end of
rabbinical lectures in the great academies, it is offered today as opening

and concluding proclamation marking the sections of public worship. It is recited by mourners as evidence of their faith in God, for God's greatness must remain beyond doubt and question, even in moments of supreme agony. Its central affirmation is the unison testimony of the congregation: "May His great Name be blessed for ever and ever." The words of the Kaddish show clearly the development of Christian worship out of the sources of Judaism.

Reader: Magnified and sanctified be His Great Name throughout the world Which He has created according to His will. May He establish His kingdom during your life, your days and during the life of all the House of Israel. To this say ye: Amen

People: Amen; May His great Name be blessed for ever and ever.

Reader: Blessed and lauded, glorified and lifted up and exalted and enhanced and elevated and praised be the Name of the Holy One, Blessed be He, although He is high above all blessings, hymns and lauds and uplifts that can be voiced in the world. To this say ye Amen

People: Amen

Reader: May there be abundant peace from Heaven, and life for us all and for all Israel. To this say ye Amen

People: Amen

Reader: May He who establishes peace in the heavens above, make peace for us also and for Israel. To this say ye Amen.

People: Amen

Kaddish at the beginning of worship, such as Mussaf or the afternoon prayer, becomes both call to worship and affirmation of God's holiness. At the end of worship it is a plea for universal recognition of God, and all Jews must work for it. At the end of a period of study it points to the fact that study of Torah is not an end in itself, but must lead to action in the building of God's kingdom on earth. Given different musical settings for various holy days, it becomes the theme for the individual festivals.

Adoration: The prayer that was added

With the Kaddish, public worship originally came to an end. Yet there was a prayer in the Mussaf of the New Year's Day, so beautiful in the vision of the future it presents, so poetic in its expression, so universal in its outlook, that it was taken into the three daily services, as their fitting conclusion and as a challenge for the day's work. It is the Adoration. It reflects the *task*, the *dedication*, and the *hope* of every Jew. Beginning with a call to Israel to bend the knee to God, if need be alone in a heathenish world, it ends with the certain assurance that the day will surely come when all mankind will worship Him.

The Task: Unto us the task is given to praise the Lord of All, to present the greatness of the Creator of the world. It is given to us, for He has not made us like pagans of the lands (who know Him not) . . .

The Dedication: Therefore we bend the knee and bow down to give thanks unto the King of the kings of kings, the Holy One blessed be He. He stretched forth the heavens and established the foundations of the earth. The seat of His glory is in the heavens above, the majesty of His power in the loftiest heights. He is our God, there is none else.

The Hope: We therefore hope in Thee, O Lord our God, that we may soon behold the glory of Thy might, when Thou wilt remove evil from the earth and all idolatry will wholly be wiped out, and the world be set aright under the Kingdom of the Almighty, and all humanity will call upon Thy name. When Thou wilt help the wicked of the earth to turn to Thee. May all the inhabitants of the earth become aware and understand, that unto Thee alone every knee must bend and every tongue pledge allegiance. Before Thee may they bend the knee, giving glory to Thy Name. May they all accept the yoke of Thy Kingdom, and mayest Thou rule over them for ever. For the Kingdom is Thine, and to all eternity Thou wilt reign in glory, as is written in Thy Torah: "The Lord shall reign for ever and ever." And it is said: "The Lord shall be King over all the earth. On that day the Lord shall be One and His Name shall be One."

With this outlook all Jewish worship ends.

The Afternoon Prayer

The afternoon prayer, called Minhah, after the special offering in the Temple, is simple: Psalm—Amidah—Repetition of Amidah—Confession of sins—Kaddish—Adoration—Kaddish. Its significance lies in the fact that the Jew can find a moment in the midst of a busy day to put his worldly pursuits aside, commune with God, and renew within himself the knowledge that all success depends on divine mercy.

The Evening Prayer

The evening prayer parallels the morning worship. A short *Psalm* puts the worshipper in the mood:

Bless ye the Lord, ye servants of the Lord, that stand in the house of the Lord in the night seasons (Ps. 134). And He being full of compassion forgiveth iniquity . . . (Ps. 78, 38). Save, O Lord, answer us, O King, on the day we call (Ps. 20:10).

The call to worship, as in the morning, invites the worshipper to affirm *God, Lord of nature and Giver of Torah:*

By His word He bringeth on the evening twilight . . . He createth day and night. He rolleth away light from before darkness and darkness from before light . . . Ever-living God rule Thou over us forever. [From nature the thought turns to *Torah*] With eternal love hast Thou loved us, the House of Israel . . .

Torah and commandments hast Thou taught us. Therefore, O God our Lord, when we lie down and when we rise up, we will meditate on Thy commandments. . . . May Thy love never depart from us.

The *Affirmation of Faith*, Hear O Israel, is recited.

God is affirmed as *Master of history:* "He redeemed us from the hands of kings, our King who redeems us from the hands of all our oppressors."

So far, the character of evening worship is the same as in the morning. The sounds are somewhat more quiet, in tune with evening peace. Now the worshipper feels that he wants to include a prayer for protection during the night, and a special petition is added:

Grant us, O Lord our God, to lie down in peace, and raise us up again, O our King unto life. Spread over us the tent of Thy peace. Direct us aright through Thine own good counsel; help us for Thy Name's sake. Be a shield about us. Keep away from us every enemy, pestilence, sword, famine, and sorrow. Protect us from evil desires that may confront us or follow us, but shelter us in the shadow of Thy wings. For Thou, O God, art our Protector and Deliverer. Guard our going out and our coming in unto life and peace, from now on and for evermore. Blessed art Thou, O God, who guardest Thy people Israel for ever.

In silent Amidah, the worshipper pours out his needs before God. With Kaddish and Adoration he takes his leave.

On Retiring

The day is done. As he retires the Jew once more gives thanks to God, recites the Affirmation of Faith, "Hear O Israel, the Lord our God, the Lord is One." Then he ends the day with the hymn that started it, and serves as theme for all he does.

Lord of the World who hast been ruling for eons ere creation came,
And all was made by Thine ordaining; as King Thy Name then found acclaim.
And afterwards when all's completed alone wilt rule in majesty;
Thou always wast and Thou art now, and through eternity shalt be.
And Thou art One, no second person compares to Thee nor Thine associate be;
'Without beginning, without end, the power Thine and souvereignty.
Thou art my God, living Redeemer; in pain Thou art the strength I need;
My banner Thou and my protection; salvation's cup Thou givest when I plead.
Into Thy hand I put my soul when I'm asleep to wake with cheer;
And with my soul my body too; Thou God art with me and I shall not fear.[3]

THE STRUCTURE OF WORSHIP

The following table may clarify our picture of the structure of worship.

---

[3] In the Hebrew version God is addressed in the third person: "The Lord who has." The author feels that in the second person the poem comes closer to our mode of thought and speech. This translation and all translations in this chapter are by the author.

Morning	Afternoon	Evening	Mussaf
BENEDICTIONS ON ARISING—			
REFLECTIONS			
Psalms of Reflection	Psalm of Reflection	Psalms of Reflection	Psalm
CALL TO WORSHIP	Kaddish as Call to Worship and Affirmation of God	Call to Worship	Kaddish
AFFIRMATIONS			
God, Lord of Nature		God, Lord of Nature	
God, loving Giver of Torah		God, loving Giver of Torah	
The Affirmation of Faith:			
Hear, O Israel!		Hear, O Israel!	
God, Lord of History		God, Lord of History	
PETITIONS:			
		Evening Prayer and paraphrase of Amidah (on weekdays)	
Amidah	Amidah	Amidah	Amidah
Repetition of Amidah	Repetition of Amidah		Repetition of Amidah
Individual penitence (on weekdays only)	Individual penitence (on weekdays only)		
Festive Psalms: 113-18 (only on festivals)			
TORAH READING	(Sabbath and Fast Days)		
(Mon., Thu., Sabbath, Festivals, and Fast Days)			
CONCLUDING PRAYER			
Kaddish	Kaddish	Kaddish	Kaddish
Adoration	Adoration	Adoration	Adoration
Kaddish	Kaddish	Kaddish	Kaddish

PUBLIC AND PRIVATE WORSHIP:
WHAT IS A CONGREGATION?

Wherever ten men are gathered together, they can form a congregation for the purposes of public worship. They may appoint one of their midst to be their leader. He need not be a rabbi; as long as he has the ability to lead a service and is of upstanding character, he is qualified. Public worship differs from private prayer in many respects. The call to worship is pronounced only in public worship; kaddish can be recited only in the "congregation"; formal reading of Torah from the holy scroll requires the presence of a *minyan,* a quorum of ten. In the morning and afternoon services, the Amidah is repeated and the sanctification from Isaiah included: "Holy, holy, holy is the Lord of Hosts, the whole earth is full of His glory (Isa. 6:3)." This may be done only in public worship.

Valuable as is the prayer of the individual, public worship is considered more meaningful. The congregation represents the "Household of Israel." As people worship together, they influence each other, link their souls, and bind their hearts together. In a small way, they reflect Israel as they stand before God, one in spirit and fellowship. Prayer offered in communion with others is less likely to be selfish prayer. As selfishness departs, responsibility grows, so the congregation represents the entire Household of Mankind, the brotherhood of man, for whom they pray.

But why ten? As the rabbis point out, the term "Congregation" is used in the Bible in connection with a group of ten. Of the twelve scouts Moses had sent to Canaan to explore the enemy's strength, ten came back with a discouraging report: "We cannot conquer our enemy!" They have forgotten God to whom all is possible, and God, referring to the ten, calls out: "How long shall I bear with this evil *congregation* (Num. 14:26)?" This is a typical example of rabbinical interpretation of Scripture (Mishnah Sanhedrin 1:6). The congregation of the scouts in the Bible defeated God's plan; the true congregation of worshippers is to promote it, and to speed up the coming of His kingdom by deepening the love of man for God, and of man for man.

CHANTS, SINGERS, AND POETS

Prayer is not simply recited, it is chanted. Torah and prophets are read to the congregation in a chant based on *modes,* short musical figures which are used in various combinations. The free chant of the Torah has no bars or meter, but follows the flow of the words; the Gregorian chant of the Catholic Church has been profoundly influenced by it. There are

CANTILLATION OF TORAH

zar – ko   se - gol   mu - nah

mu — nah   re - vee —— a   ma - pah   pash - to   zo - kef ko - ton

zo - kef go - dol   mer ho tip   ho mu - nah   es - nah - to   po - zer

te - lee - sho ke - ta - no   te - lee - sho ge - do - lo   kad - mo ve az - lo

az - lu   ge - resh ger - sha - yeem   ⊗►dar - go   te - vir   te sif

pe - sek   sof po - suk

The Hebrew notations are on top of each line at the beginning
of the mode.

⊗   at end of portion

Cantillation of Torah (Western European).

123

annotations for the music found in the printed Hebrew Bible, but not in the scroll from which the reader must recite. So he must know the chant by heart. The recitation of Torah is an art which can be learned only through many years of study.

Similar modes are used for the prayer recitatives. Like the Torah recitatives, some of these are very old too. They were given names, just as the German Mastersingers of the late Middle Ages would give names to their "modes," their basic building stones of hymn and song. A very old theme, for instance, has the title *Me-Sinai*—"From Sinai"—as if to say that this melody was given at Mount Sinai. Another tune carries the name *With eternal love,* because the second benediction of the evening prayer, "With eternal love . . . ," was recited in this special tune. Beyond these basic themes, Jewish music shows the influences of many ages, many lands, and varied conditions. We find in it the trills and embellishments of the mediaeval troubadour, the majestic hymns of German choral music, the optimistic major key of Western music, and the introspective minor key of slavonic song. We recall in it the Palestinian shepherd's plaintive voice, and the Yemenite camel driver's endless desert litany. Thus a superstructure was built on top of the basic modes. Varying from country to country, it bears the marks of Jewish dispersion. Since most Jews in America, Europe, South Africa, and Israel trace their origins to Eastern Europe, the mood of slavonic melancholy can be found in much of Jewish music today. Modern Jewish music came into its own during the period of Romanticism, so the style of a Mendelssohn, Schumann, or Tchaikovsky is quite prevalent in music of general use in synagogues. It is only in our day that composers of first rank have taken up writing music for Jewish worship. They have combined traditional tunes with their own creative imagination, and have given us enduring works. Two composers may be mentioned as examples. Ernest Bloch, writing in a Palestinian spirit, using traditional chant, and giving it a Wagnerian-inspired modern orchestration, has created in his Sacred Service a work of great general appeal. Darius Milhaud has written a sacred service based on the age-old musical traditions of the Jews in the Provence. Other composers have followed this example, and men like Leonard Bernstein, in his "Jeremiah Symphony," have used the chant of the synagogue in symphonic music. These are hopeful signs of a revival of Jewish music in a fusion of tradition and modern idiom.

Jewish interest in music has given us the cantor. Traditionally, any adult may lead the service, but congregations have always liked to hear singers with good voices, especially on holy days. They trained their soloists for many years; youngsters might start as choristers, standing next to the cantor while accompanying and observing him, hoping that someday they might be as great. By imitation, the young people became cantors themselves, professional leaders of the service, and then they trained a new generation. Eventually, cantors also got conservatory training and learned to write down the music which they created. The great cantors would draw audiences from far and near; by voice and depth of feeling they could truly move multitudes. Modern cantors receive regular religious and musical training for their work. Some have gone on the stage; men like Jan Peerce and Richard Tucker have transplanted some of the character of cantorial song to grand opera.

Throughout the Middle Ages, cantors were often their own lyricists, writing poems for special occasions and adding them to the various sections of public worship. We also find rabbis who wrote for special services. Hymns, litanies, responsive readings, and meditations were created. Some were of great literary value; others merely followed the style which was in vogue in the writer's country, and were transitory products. These poems, called piyutim, are still in existence and use. We have, from the hands of these writers, a complete set of prayers for the days of penitence, the *selihot,* and a collection of elegies for days of communal mourning, the *kinot.*

Thus did the *paitanim,* the poets, help to give expression to the individuality of each occasion and holy day, and cantors created special theme songs for every festive occasion. By tradition, each holy day has a tune which is its "leitmotiv," and by which it can be musically described.

THE SIGNS: AUDIO-VISUAL REMINDERS

Words will yield a fuller impact of their meaning when they are reinforced by reminders. The holiday theme is an audible reminder; it awakens associations throughout life of happy celebrations, of childhood events, of parents, of family, and of pious observance. Visual reminders are even more powerful, and there are three which are constantly employed: Tallit, Tefillin, and Mezuzah. They are adjuncts to worship.

Tallit

"Speak unto the children of Israel and bid them make fringes on the corners of their garments . . . that ye may look upon it and remember all the commandments of the Lord and do them; and that ye go not about after your own heart and your own eyes, after which you may be inclined to go astray (Num. 15:37-41)." The four cornered robe was the garb of daily wear in ancient times; it still is among the Bedouins. The fringe, which by command had to be attached to it, became a constant reminder to the wearer of the garment to stay within the bounds of decency, morality, and ethics. It never permitted him to forget God's law. Four cornered robes are no longer in daily use, but a special one is worn in the service; it is called the Tallit. It can be long and wide, permitting the wor-

Tallit and Tefillin, visual reminders and adjuncts to worship.

shipper to wrap himself in it, or draw it over his head if he wishes to exclude the world entirely as he communes with God. It may be just a "prayer shawl," short and narrow. It became the stole in Christian worship. It is worn in daytime only, the time when one can "look upon it" and see it by the natural light of God's sun. The leader of worship, however, wears it even at night. As the Jew puts it on, he is always careful to have the ribbon on top facing outward, for the Tallit is a robe which must not be worn upside down. It is the robe clothing the worshipper in the visual garment of responsibility.

Tefillin

Hear, O Israel, the Lord our God, the Lord is One. And thou shalt love the Lord thy God with all thy heart and all thy soul and all thy might. And these words . . . thou shalt bind them for a sign upon thy hand, and they shall be for frontlets between thine eyes. Thou shalt write them upon the doorposts of thy house and upon thy gates (Deut. 6:4-9).

Bind them upon thy hand, have them between thine eyes; this is meant figuratively: let God guide the work of thy hand, let Him give you vision. The commandment was, however, seen in a narrower sense as well, as an order to have visual reminders of these spiritual rules. The words about the love of God, written on small parchment scrolls, are encased in a small black parchment cube. A leather strap permits the little box to be "bound upon the hand." Actually, it is placed on the upper left arm and the straps wound down the arm to the hand. Thus—visually —the hand is placed under God's command to act in the spirit of love; the arm with its strength submits to His rule; placed on the left arm, the commandment faces the heart—symbolic seat of human urges—directing its desires creatively. A similar small receptacle with the same words in it is attached to a strap which can be placed on the head. Man's mind is thus encircled by the commandment of love, which sets man's limitations and lifts him up. This is worn during morning worship on weekdays. On the Sabbath the "Tefillin" are not used, for they are a *sign*, and so is the Sabbath. ("It is a sign between Me and the Children of Israel forever—Exod. 31:17.") The Sabbath surrounds the Jew with an atmosphere of holiness; no other reminder is needed. This rabbinical ruling—based on identity of terms used in the Torah—is a good example of rabbinical exegesis, but also of rabbinical psychological insight. Visual demonstrations are very helpful in getting ideas across; educators know that. But pile too many of them together, and the purpose will be defeated, the idea forgotten. Learning by doing has been the motto of Judaism throughout the centuries, but it has had the wisdom to balance demonstration against instruction.

Mezuzah

"Write them on the doorposts . . ." the words of love. This command also led to the creation of a visual reminder, the Mezuzah—literally, Doorpost. A small scroll containing the words is encased in a container and affixed at the door posts of the house. It invites those who enter to bring with them the spirit of love, in order that the home may remain a sanctuary of the Lord; it admonishes those who go out into the world to carry the spirit of love into their affairs, that humanity may become a kingdom of priests. There are other reminders, among them the wine, the palm branch, the candle, and the shofar. All of them are means of education; none of them have sacramental character, or bring to man any dispensation of divine grace. They are designed to bring man nearer to God by making visible to him God's presence, God's love, and God's command.

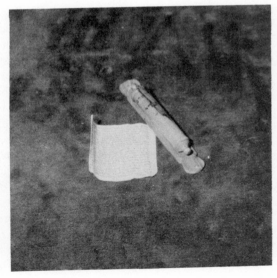

Mezuzah—parchment scroll and container. Written on parchment in the style of the Torah, the scroll contains the portions from Deut. 6:4-9, and 11:13-21. The scroll, rolled up and placed in its container, is affixed to the door.

WORSHIP AND THE JEWISH PERSONALITY

Worship was spontaneous before it was cast in permanent form. It was the expression of the Jewish character, and reflects to this day the character of the Jew. How does he look to us, this worshipper, seen through the mirror of his prayers? He is optimistic and he loves life regardless of the many scars it has inflicted upon him. He begins every day with a song. He is decently aware of his body, neither considering it deserving of neglect, nor regarding it as a source of sinfulness. He believes in immortality; he holds very dear his soul, which has been the gift of God, and which came pure to him; there is no original sin. Man is free to work out his destiny, and with the help of God can become His co-worker. Our worshipper is aware of his smallness, but also of the abundance of God's mercy. He rejoices in his task in the world, and finds happiness in the intimacy which binds him directly to the Absolutely One God, to Whom he can talk directly without intermediary, and Who will reedeem him. He looks at nature as God's magnificent creation. But while the Deist says that God is no longer regulating the world, to the Jew, God is there, in nature, in Torah, and in history. With God revered as master of history, vision becomes world-wide; the Jew's prayer becomes one for all humanity, his hope one for a world for the Messiah, at peace, and his expectation a return to Zion. In action or, if need be, in suffering, the Jew hopes to bring closer this future under God. Thus he is positive in his outlook; he does not hate. There is no hatred in Judaism; and Jews have been able to make peace with their persecutors by forgetting evil; there is to be no vindictiveness, simply the hope that evil may vanish. This is unique in human history.

Jewish prayer represents strength. The weak person leans on God as Helper, the strong person praises Him as Challenger; it has frequently been remarked by observers that Jewish prayer is mainly praise. Even evil can be good. It can be a divine test and challenge. Jewish prayer is expression of gratitude, of readiness for service, and a hope for peace, and so is Jewish life. Let it not be said that all Jews approach this ideal; but without it as an ultimate, the Jew would never have survived the trials of the ages. He knew that God was with him individually; in his congregation he built a society of equals, a true democracy without priest or intermediary, without class distinctions, and he felt certain that under God this society would someday, if only he persevered, become universal.

Thus did the Pharisees and Rabbis of old fortify their people with the weapons of faith. They gave them the completed edition of Torah, the Written Word; they gave them the Talmud, the Oral Torah; they gave them prayer and the prayer book. The people needed it. They had to meet a daughter religion which had come to power, and which was not always kind to the mother. The religion was Christianity.

9

Dissent, Disruption, Dialogue

fter centuries of misunderstandings and disruptions, Judaism and Christianity have begun to move toward a genuine dialogue. It is in this spirit that the inquiry of this chapter is conducted.

PROLOGUE: PHILO OF ALEXANDRIA

Philo, who lived from the year 20 of the pre-Christian era to the year 40 of the Christian era, was a great, good, and pious Jew. He was a member of the Jewish aristocracy in Alexandria, but his life was utterly simple. He was a philosopher and wished to devote his days to thought and study. In their moment of need, however, he was ready to close his books and step in the breach for his people. Courageously he faced the mad emperor Caligula to plead with him against an edict which would have placed the emperor's statue in the Temple of Jerusalem. Courageous as a representative of his people, he spoke up against anti-Semitic attacks against them. Philo revered the Torah, though he could read it only in Greek translation, and bore down on the members of his community who relaxed their observance of the commandments. Deeply convinced of the value of Judaism for all mankind, he actively promoted missionary activity by Jews and undertook to write works of explanation for the gentile world, in order to attract them to the faith of Israel. The messengers of the Christian church were later to follow the pattern established by Jewish missionaries.

Philo lived in two worlds, the world of Jewish thought and practice, and that of Greek philosophy, and he hoped to show that both of them were actually one. He felt that their message was identical. Plato was the great master he followed, and the School of the Stoics influenced him deeply. Plato tells us that the world in which we live is transitory, without abiding reality. Men come and go, things are created and disappear. This cannot be the real world, for the real world must be eternal, unchanging, and of different stuff. It does not exist here on earth, but in a realm of the spirit, the realm of Ideas. How can we penetrate this realm? The road is a difficult ascent from the dark cave of our imagination to the sunlight of true knowledge; philosophy, the use of reason, can lead us onward, because in philosophical dialogue the dross of faulty thinking is melted away. Eventually we shall reach the high plateau, when the vision of reason reveals truth and reality, the Ideas. Then reason stops; but there is a still higher level, the source from which all reality springs, the Idea which is creator of everything in the world. Plato calls it the "Good"; he might have called it God. How do we find God? When our reason has guided us as far as possible, then—in mystical experience— God may reveal himself, as in a flash, in intuitive enlightenment. The stoic thinkers added to this. If we wish to find God, we must follow reason only and cast aside all passions and emotions. Guided by reason, man will know and do his duty. We should know, the Stoics say, that God pervades the universe—God *is* the universe. The world is governed by reason, and in God's plan all is well.

Philo follows these teachings. He is a Stoic, turning down luxuries and pleasures, living in utter simplicity. Duty is the watchword of his life. Philo is also a mystic; God is far removed and can be seen only with the inner eye of men immersed in contemplation. God is all spirit, and through the spirit he is found. The body, like all earthly things, has no reality. Body and soul stand in contrast to each other; the body temporary, holding us down; the soul eternal, lifting us up. The mystical approach to God will be found later in St. Paul; the dualism of body and soul entered the teachings of the Christian Church.

If God is found only in the vision of the soul, if He is revealed only in the flash of mystical enlightenment, why should we search for Him in the events of physical history, why should we try to find Him through obedience to commandments? Philo tries to answer this question. The early history of the Jewish people and all the commandments are to him the visible means by which God wished to reveal the great truths of reason to simple people; they are allegories. In this spirit does he, for instance, explain the verse in Genesis: "And Terah took Abram his son . . . and they went from Ur of the Chaldees to go into the land of Canaan; and they came to Haran and dwelt there (Gen. 11:31)." Philo claims that the root of the word *Terah* means *to explore*. Terah then is not a name but means explorer; Haran is not a place name either, it means *excavation, self-perception*. The story of Terah's migration thus has a deeper meaning.

The information that Terah left the land of Chaldea and migrated to Haran . . . is given us, not with the object that we may learn as from a writer of history, that certain people . . . became emigrants, . . . but that a lesson . . . of great service to human life may not be neglected. What is the lesson? The Chaldeans are astronomers . . . Holy writ addresses to the *explorer* (Terah) of the facts of nature certain questions: "Why do you carry on investigations about the sun? . . . Mark my friend not what is above and beyond your reach, but . . . yourself should be the object of scrutiny. Go in spirit to Haran, 'excavated land' . . . learn to *know thyself* . . . This character (who seeks to know himself) Hebrews call Terah, Greeks Socrates. For they say that 'Know thyself' was likewise the theme of life-long pondering to Socrates. [1]

Philo then goes on to say that Abraham, Terah's son, strove further. He wanted to know God, wanted to advance beyond the knowledge given by the senses. And so Abraham left Haran and migrated again, toward the vision of God. Terah and Abraham are not so much historical persons; they are personalities who show us how we can reach God. Philo tells us of Moses at the burning bush. This too is an allegory. Moses wanted to know how God causes all things to happen; the bush, burning without being consumed, told him that men can never understand the reasoning of the Divinity. [2] The history of the Bible is an allegory; it describes in story form how man should find his way to the great, mystical God, Whose works are beyond *full* human understanding; it is a road which leads through reason to vision. Philo actually uses the same method employed by the Stoics to explain the mythology of the Greeks; the hero-gods are not real, they simply embody a lesson.

In similar manner, Philo explains the commandments as a visual means to teaching ethical lessons. The Sabbath teaches the power of God, who created all; circumcision portrays the "excision of pleasure and all passions." [3] Unless we grasp the inner meaning of the commandments, their observance is meaningless, for the practice is like the body and the meaning like the soul. But Philo warns his people never to think that they might abandon the commandments, as long as their meaning is kept in mind; the commandments must be observed. We can easily see, however, how small a step it was for St. Paul to declare later that observance of commandments was not necessary—they actually dragged down men's faith, as the body debases the soul.

---

[1] Philo, "On Dreams," from *Three Jewish Philosophers*, Part I (Philadelphia: Meridian Books and Jewish Publication Society of America, by arrangement with East and West Library, London, 1960), pp. 52-62.

[2] Philo, "On Flight and Finding," *op. cit.*, pp. 65-66.

[3] Philo, "Soul and Body of the Divine Laws," *op. cit.*, pp. 40-41.

Thus did the Great God wish to lead us toward the good life, pleasing to Him. He has given us the world and the power of reason and of self-improvement as an act of *grace,* and without divine grace our souls will never rise to Him. Through grace we are given the joy of His vision; without grace we are but weak mortals.[4]

Our response to grace is *faith.* Of Abraham it is said "he trusted in God (had faith) (Gen. 15:6)." Philo quotes the verse and then states: "To trust in God alone . . . this is a task for a great and celestial understanding which has ceased to be ensnared by aught of the things that surround us." And "after faith comes the reward. . . . That reward is joy." [5] Grace on the part of God—though unmerited by man—and faith as man's noblest response, will become central ideas in Christian theology.

Of even greater influence, however, has been Philo's concept of *Logos,* the "Word." If God is so supreme, so far removed, so perfect and abstract, can we conceive of Him as coming down from His remoteness to make a physical universe? Philo does not think so. According to Torah, God created the world by His word; the Greek term for Word is Logos. Logos, to Philo, is the sum of God's thought, wisdom, and power. Out of these the world was created. But Philo sees another meaning in the term Logos. The Book of Proverbs speaks of wisdom as God's first creation: Wisdom speaks: The Lord made me as the beginning of His way, the first of His works of old (Prov. 8:22). Philo interprets this verse in a very strange way. He says that God released an angel or creative agent to build the world according to God's plan. The angel is called "Wisdom"; this is what is meant by "Logos." The Logos is God's wisdom, a part of God; it is also apart from God—His messenger, His son. By His Logos, His Son, Israel is protected.

This hallowed flock (Israel) He leads in accordance with right and law, setting over it His true Word and Firstborn Son, Who shall take upon Him its government like some viceroy of a great king; for it is said in a certain place (Exod. 23:20): Behold I am; I send My Angel before thy face to guard thee in the way.[6]

Philo's concept of the Logos is confused; sometimes it is God Himself, or the principle of reason, and sometimes it is not God but an angel. By his very vagueness he surrounded his ideas with a mystery which deepened their influence upon later thinkers, above all on the Christian theologians. Thus it is reflected in the Gospel of St. John: In the beginning was the Word (Logos), and the Word was with God, and God was the Word (John 1:1).

---

[4] Philo, "On Grace," *op. cit.,* p. 76; see also p. 32.
[5] Philo, "On Faith," *op. cit.,* p. 89.
[6] Philo, "The Lord Shepherds Me," *op. cit.,* p. 30.

Philo's influence upon Jewish thinking was insignificant, although he did affect Jewish mysticism to a degree. In general, Jews have seen in God, not a philosophical Deity, but the living personal God who is Master of nature and Master of history. Christian theology, on the other hand, is deeply influenced by Philo, even though all of his thoughts did not originate with him. He was not a creative thinker, but a man of universal knowledge who became a channel through which Greek and Jewish ideas flowed and partially merged, but never mixed completely. Philo wished to show that Hellenism and Judaism could be merged; he hoped that he might inspire seekers of wisdom to join the Jewish faith. In this he failed, but he did aid Christianity. Mysticism, the vision of the mystic's God, the dualism of body and soul, the downgrading of the commandments, the idea of grace, the overreaching importance of faith against actions, and above all the idea of the Word of God assuming bodily form, as Son of God, all became basic Christian concepts. Philo never understood these terms in the sense in which Christianity was later to interpret them, but he brought them together out of his own thought and many other sources. This Jewish philosopher, who went far afield, became a powerful influence in Christianity.

JUDAISM IN DISSENT

The great problem in a dialogue of religions is that ideas which are self-evident to one religion may be strange to another. Many religious ideas are caught rather than taught; they are linked to childhood recollections, holy traditions, books sanctified by the faith of believers, creeds and customs hallowed by the blood of martyrs. These ideas are then "simply true" to the faithful, who cannot understand why others do not share them. People may actually be shocked to learn that there can be doubt in anyone's mind regarding these religious truths. We must keep this in mind when we engage in a religious dialogue, and respect the religious convictions of others even though they are directly opposite to our own.

Judaism disagrees in its theology with some of the most fundamental doctrines of Christianity.

1) To Judaism God is absolutely One. The Trinity of Father, Son, and Holy Ghost still forms One God to the Christian. To the Jew these would be three persons; he cannot understand that God could be so divided and still be One, and so the Trinity is not acceptable to Judaism.

2) To the Jew God has no form, nor has He ever nor will He ever assume any form. The Jew cannot understand the Christian doctrine that

God took the form of man in Christ. It is contrary to his most fundamental beliefs.

3) To the Jew no human being has been or ever can be divine.

4) To Judaism no human being has been or ever can be perfect; no personality in Jewish Holy Scriptures has ever been described as perfect.

5) The Jew does not believe in an intermediary between man and God. Everyone comes to the divine Father directly, and has immediate access to Him and to salvation.

6) Christianity holds the doctrine of Original Sin. When Adam and Eve sinned in the Garden of Eden all their descendants were contaminated by this sin, man becoming sinful by nature. Judaism, as we saw in our discussion of Jeremiah and Ezekiel, maintains that the sins of the fathers are *not* inherited by their children. Man's soul is pure as it comes to him and not tainted in any way.

7) Christianity teaches that *faith* in Christ leads to salvation. Judaism demands obedience to divine commandments; man must be God's co-worker in the world.

8) Christianity believes in sacraments. They are means of divine grace, physical means by which God reaches out to mankind. Judaism has no sacraments.[7]

9) Christianity links salvation to faith in Christ; only faith brings salvation. Judaism maintains that "all the righteous of the peoples of the world have a share in the world to come."[8] Adherence to basic laws of justice and humanity is all that is needed. Judaism recognizes Christianity as a good and holy road to God—for Christians; Judaism has the same view in regard to Islam, Buddhism, or any other ethical religion to the degree that they ennoble man and bring him to God. Judaism sees no reason for anyone to change his faith, and would like the other religions to feel the same way.[9]

---

[7] The author is aware of the differences of view between Catholics and Protestants regarding sacraments, but has felt that a detailed analysis goes beyond the scope of this book. The same also applies to the idea of the necessity of faith in Christ, which has been presented here in greatly simplified form.

[8] Joshua ben Hanania in Tosefta Sanhedrin 13:2, a widely used quotation. Also: "Among the righteous of the peoples of the world some are priests of God, as for instance (Emperor) Antoninus (Tanna debe Elijahu Zuta 20)"; "I call to witnesses heaven and earth that on everyone, be he Jew or non-Jew, man or woman, manservant or maidservant, the holy spirit can rest on him; it all depends on his conduct (Tanna debe Elijahu Rabba 10)."

[9] An expression of this principle is found in Micah's "Utopia": "For let all the peoples walk each one in the name of its god—but we will walk in the name of the Lord our God for ever and ever (Micah 4:5)." A plurality of religions is approved, provided they are ethical. For the idolatrous, and often immoral cults of Antiquity, the Bible has only contempt (see Deut. 7:25-26). For later Jewish views on the relationship between Judaism and Christianity, see our discussion of Maimonides, Mendelssohn, Hirsch, Cohen, Rosenzweig, and Buber.

10) Christianity has looked at Judaism as a "forerunner," with an inferior concept of ethics and a less developed ideal of divine and human love. Judaism does not consider Christian ethics or the Christian concept of love to be an advancement; it is rather a restatement. Judaism finds nothing in New Testament ethics which cannot be found in Jewish ethics. It regards New Testament ideals, as expressed, for example, in the Sermon on the Mount, as simply an expression of traditionally held Jewish beliefs.

11) Judaism, therefore, does not regard the New Testament as divine revelation. Jewish scholars find in it a substantial core of Jewish ideas. They hold that the New Testament was written many years after the events, a view shared by Christian scholars, who speak of "sources" (called Q from the German word *Quelle*, which means source).[10] The New Testament, according to Biblical (Christian) criticism, was written possibly as late as 100 years or more after Jesus had died.[11] Many events were told in retrospect, and thereby given new meaning. During the years between the death of Jesus and the composition of the New Testament, an oral tradition developed. The life and acts of Jesus were transmitted from father to son; Jewish scholars believe that, in that process, stories of miracles commonly told of many saintly people came to be ascribed to Jesus.[12] The New Testament was written in part by non-Jews who had no emotional ties with Judaism, at a time when the Jewish people had lost status in the Roman world. To Jews it contains indications that the writers wished to dissociate themselves and the new faith from both Judaism and the Jewish people. This accounts for the anti-Jewish statements found in it, of which the Gospel of St. John offers the best example. In the process of oral transmission and of eventual composition, the personality of the historical Jesus became obscured. This, fundamentally, is the Jewish view.

May the Christian reader pause here for a moment and reflect. To him the name of Jesus evokes deep stirrings of love; the Jew lacks this emotional attachment. He has deep reverence for the faith of Christians, sharing with them the love of God and a complete set of ethics. In viewing Christian history, however, the Jew's approach is simply scientific, analysing it with the same objectivity which might be applied by both Jew and Christian to the study of Islam. To the Jew, Jesus is a human personality, teacher, and reformer, whose influence has been a mighty force in bringing the knowledge of God to the peoples of the world.

---

[10] This parallels the conclusions of biblical criticism in regard to the Old Testament; the true historical personalities of many of the personalities of the Old and New Testaments have become obscured.

[11] See Albright, *op. cit.*, pp. 358 ff.

[12] Leo Baeck, *Das Evangelium als Urkunde der Juedischen Glaubensgeschichte* (New York: Schocken Books, Inc., 1938), p. 15 f.

EARLY CHRISTIANITY: THE JEWISH VIEWPOINT

The history of early Christianity may be divided into three periods.

THE LIFE OF JESUS.   At this stage there is absolutely no conflict between Judaism and Jesus. Jesus is a devout Jew who considers himself to be the Messiah and gathers a group of followers around him. The rest of his contemporaries disagree with this view, but will defend his right to hold it. Jesus is not the only one to consider himself a Messiah, either then or later in Jewish history.

THE MINISTRY OF PAUL.   Paul sees Jesus as God, and carries this message abroad to a world yearning for spiritual guidance. He patterns his missionary activity on similar work done by Jews in behalf of Judaism. Paul demands faith in Christ; only faith brings salvation. The Jews must have this faith and may dispense with or observe the commandments of the Torah; the Gentiles are saved by faith alone and are specifically forbidden to follow the commandments. Failing in faith, the Jews are rejected. But Paul wants the Jews to accept Christ and then be restored by God to their former place of distinction. Paul himself has a lasting concern with the fate of the Jews; he is proud to be a Jew. Actually he believes to have found the true *Judaism*, but his concepts of Christ as God and of the abolition of the laws of Torah lead out of Judaism and are not acceptable to it.

THE PERIOD OF DISSOCIATION.   It begins with the Roman destruction of the Temple in Jerusalem in the year 70. The new Church wishes to build a wall between itself and Judaism in order that it might be recognized as a different body. Gentiles assume leading positions, and anti-Jewish statements find a place in Christian writings, including the New Testament. Christianity becomes a state religion in Rome. The Council of Nicaea, convened under the Emperor Constantine in 325, establishes Christian dogma and makes a complete break with Judaism, which is now regarded as an inferior religion and its people as a nation despised by God.

To make their full impact clear, these events must be examined in greater detail.

The Life of Jesus

From the Hills of Galilee comes the master. He is a pious Jew, brought up in the spirit of Pharisaic tradition, who loves his people and feels profound agony at their oppression by Roman rulers. In deep faith in God, who is Israel's Father in Heaven, he goes out to his brethren to teach and guide them. He teaches nothing new, nothing not already found in Torah and rabbinic instruction, but he has the wonderful gift to simplify and to bring near to all the commandments of ethical life as found in Jewish teaching. His is a virile strength; anger may take hold of him, and love reaches out to all he meets. His is the power to attract and hold followers. A small band of devoted disciples attach themselves to him; he leads them, and tells them that he will help Israel. The thought comes to them all that he may be the Messiah. He will restore the people. Living as a Jew and interpreting Torah, he makes it abundantly clear to them that Torah must be strictly obeyed. "Think not that I am come to destroy the Torah or the prophets. I am not come to destroy but to fulfil. For verily I say to you, till heaven and earth pass, one jot or one tittle shall in no way pass from the Torah till all be fulfilled (Matt. 5:17-18)." This is the idea Isaiah's vision had pointed out: in the end the Torah will be fulfilled by all mankind. Meanwhile, Israel is the light of mankind, the salt of the earth (Matt. 5). As he comes to Jerusalem, a leader from the always rebellious Galilee, his messianic preachings are brought to the attention of the Roman procurator, Pontius Pilate. Taking no chance of having a potential troublemaker on his hands, Pontius Pilate has Jesus arrested and executed in Roman fashion by crucifixion. Like many Jewish martyrs before him, Jesus accepts his fate in quiet dignity and in submission to the will of God. In life and in death his fate resembles that of other Jews with messianic ideas, including John the Baptist, who may have headed a similar Jewish messianic movement, may have inspired Jesus, and certainly met a very similar end.[13] What was Jesus' relationship to his community, especially those who disagreed with his messianism? If they knew of him, they had no argument with him. He had a right to his opinion and belief; this had always been a basic Jewish principle. The schools of Hillel and Shammai were at the height of their influence and controversies. Those who heard of Jesus' death surely grieved for him as another Jew who had been murdered by the Romans.[14] It had become a matter of tragic monotony. Jesus was simply a man who expounded the Torah, teaching very much like the

---

[13] Enslin holds that John the Baptist was an independent preacher with a message similar to that of Jesus, whose personality was being transformed into a forerunner and thus built into the New Testament narrative. See Morton Scott Enslin, *Christian Beginnings* (New York: Harper & Brothers, 1938), p. 149 ff.; also Maurice Goguel, *Jesus and the Origins of Christianity* (New York: Harper & Bros., 1933), pp. 264 ff. Later messianic movements will be discussed in their places in history.

[14] The trial of Jesus by a Jewish court (Sanhedrin) is difficult to explain in view of the provisions of Jewish law (see above). There are contradictions on details in the gospels. Samuel Sandmel (*A Jewish Understanding of the New Testament*: Cincinnati: Hebrew Union College, 1957) points out that some Jewish scholars have refuted the procedures of the trial in detailed analysis; then he continues: "The entire trial business is legendary and tendentious (p. 128)." We may assume it to be the result of later Christian antagonism against Judaism.

other rabbis while giving his own point of view. He differed by thinking of himself as the Messiah who would free Israel from bondage, and died for it at the hands of the Romans.

The Ministry of Paul

After Jesus' death a new personality enters the scene of history, to give new leadership to the grieving disciples. He is Paul of Tarsus; and he will give Christianity everlastingly the imprint of his genius and his ideas. Paul brings with him the mysteries of oriental religions, of bread and wine, of sacraments, of death and resurrection, which are not altogether unknown to Jews in the Hellenistic world either. Like many Jews before him, he is fired by the missionary spirit. The world must be given new ideas leading to salvation. Paul is a visionary. He sees Jesus, not the man and his work, but Jesus as God. From here a new theology develops. The law is but an instrument in preparation for Christ's coming; faith in God and in Christ is the sustaining power. Abraham, the father of the Jews, had no commandments yet to fulfil; he "believed in God (had faith), and it was counted him for righteousness (Rom. 4:3)." Faith alone sufficed for him; it will suffice for all the nations of the earth. As far as Israel is concerned, they too will find salvation only through faith, and only if they are not simply the children of the flesh but rather the children of the promise, of faith (Rom. 9). Israel's law was needed as the "schoolmaster" to bring men to Christ and faith. Jews may abide by their observances but, without faith, observance is ineffective for salvation, meaningless, and harmful. This is similar to Philo's saying that the people of the world need only faith.

But to Philo the Torah must always be observed by Jews. In fact, this is derived from basic Jewish teaching, which maintains that all the righteous of the world have a share in the hereafter. Paul, however, demands from all a firm faith in Christ, and in this faith all men become alike. He does not wish the Gentiles to adopt Jewish law, and rebukes them for it. (Gal. 3). In establishing Christ as God, and in abolishing the law of Torah, Paul has stepped beyond the bounds of Judaism; but Paul has no animosity against his people. He speaks of "We who are Israelites and to whom pertaineth the adoption and the glory and the covenants and the giving of the law, and the service of God, and the promises (Rom. 9:4)." And he proudly affirms: "I say then, has God cast away His people? God forbid. For I also am an Israelite, of the seed of Abraham, of the tribe of Benjamin (Rom. 11:1)." Thus, for Paul, Judaism is permitted to observe the commandments if it deepens the observance by faith in Christ, while the Gentile world is enjoined to come to God through faith in Christ. Both Jews and Gentiles are alike before God, and both religions would have lived side by side, Christianity with the hope that Judaism would accept Christ and be restored to glory. "Rejection" did not have the awesome implications it was to have later. Paul's principle of Christ as God is not Jewish, but Paul's practical solution might have maintained peace and harmony. But Paul saw the end of days in the near future. This did not come about, and so the change came.

The Period of Dissociation

Up to the fall of the Temple, and even to the failure of the Bar Kokhba rebellion, there was prestige in the attachment of the new faith to Judaism. The Gentile world knew of Judaism and its missionary activities; the Christian messengers could build on these foundations. Now a change took place. Rome was incensed against the Jews. When the Temple fell, many Christians saw in it a sign of divine displeasure against the Jews and began to move away; after Bar Kokhba, Jewish religion was prohibited for a while, and Christian spokesmen emphasized the fact that the new faith had nothing to do with the proscribed old religion. Gentiles had assumed leading positions in the Church, and no bonds of affection and family spirit bound them to its Jewish past. This new trend is mirrored in the Gospels. The term "Pharisees" is used in a derogatory sense; by this time Pharisaism had become *the* doctrine of Judaism; thus, all of Jewry was implicated. An ever-growing distance is established between Jesus and the Jews. He who had said that "no jot shall pass from the Torah" now is reported as saying: "It is written in *your* law (John 8:17; 10:34)." He will have no part in it. "The Jews" are mentioned again and again as the adversaries, and Pontius Pilate, the Roman, is exonerated. The Jews demand the death of Jesus and assume the responsibility for all generations: "His blood be on us and on our children (Matt. 27:25)." This would establish a new kind of inherited sin, something which Judaism denies. Hence no Jew could have said it. In Matthew, Pontius Pilate then turns Jesus over to the soldiers to be crucified (27:27). In John, however, he delivers Jesus to the *Jews* to be crucified (19:15-16). The only name of the Jewish disciples which is not translated into Greek is Judas, the traitor. Of the others, Johanan becomes John, Mattityahu becomes Matthew, Simon becomes Peter, and Saul becomes Paul.

From this source great suffering has come to the Jewish people. They were branded throughout their generations as killers of God. They have never been able to understand why they were accused of murdering a fellow human being, nor why any crime of the fathers should be held against the children. They have been unable to explain why they should be guilty, even according to Christian dogma, when it was ordained in the divine plan that Christ should die for the sins of the world. He did not die on account of the Jews but in conformity with an eternal will, if we follow the report of the Gospels themselves.

The Split is Completed

As Christianity increased her power, it bore down ever harder on Judaism and Jews. Restrictions were imposed on the building of synagogues and freedom of worship; the rights of citizenship were gradually whittled down. The Council of Nicaea (325) changed the date of the Christian Easter, which had previously been observed at the same time as Passover.

. . . it appeared an unworthy thing that in the celebration of this most holy feast we should follow the practice of the Jews, who have impiously defiled their hands with enormous sin, and are, therefore, deservedly afflicted with blindness of soul. . . . Let us then have nothing in common with the detestable Jewish crowd.[15]

The observance of the Sabbath was forbidden to Christians, only Sunday was to be observed (Council of Laodicea; 343-348).[16] St. John Chrysostom (end of fourth century) hurled his curse against them: God hates you! [17]

The pall of the Middle Ages fell upon Jewry in Christian lands, not to be lifted until the eighteenth century. Of their conditions, their trials, and their inner life, we shall speak. The dialogue was not resumed until the 20th c.

The Dialogue is Resumed

World War II claimed six million Jewish martyrs. Christian conscience was aroused: Theological anti-Semitism must never become a source of Jewish persecution again. Already in 1958, Reinhold Niebuhr had counselled Protestants against missionary work among Jews, and upheld the dignity of the Jewish faith.[18] Martin Buber called for dialogue on the Jewish side. But it was the saintly Pope John XXIII who changed the Catholic-Jewish relationship radically, and with it Christian-Jewish relations in general.

When Pope John called an Ecumenical Council for the purpose of "updating" the church, he specifically ordered a statement on the Jews. It was promulgated by Pope Paul VI in 1965.

Although being the result of compromises, the decree of Vatican II (as the Council has been called) has created basic new doctrines: "The Church acknowledges the spiritual ties binding it to the Jews . . ." Although "the Jews did not accept the Gospel in large numbers, many

---

[15] Jacob R. Marcus, *The Jew in the Medieval World* (Philadelphia: Meridian Books and Jewish Publication Society of America, by arrangement with East and West Library, London, 1960), p. 105. © 1938, Union of American Hebrew Congregations, Cincinnati, Ohio.

[16] *Op. cit.*, p. 106.

[17] Malcolm Hay, *The Foot of Pride* (Boston: The Beacon Press, 1950), p. 32.

even opposing its spreading . . ., God holds the Jews most dear for the sake of their fathers, for God does not repent His gifts . . ." "The Council recommends and wishes to foster understanding and respect resulting from biblical and theological studies and from a fraternal dialogue." ". . . what happened in Christ's passion cannot be charged against all Jews then alive without distinction, nor against the Jews of today." ". . . the Jews should not be presented as rejected and accursed by God, as if this followed from the Holy Scriptures . . ." ". . . the Church decries hatred, persecution, and displays of anti-Semitism directed against Jews at any time and by anyone."

The American hierarchy had been particularly insistent on a statement. Although the decree is frequently ambiguous, its implementation proved it to be of greatest value. In 1969, the Archbishop of New York and the bishops of the area issued orders of implementaion, opening wide the doors of cooperation, while strictly forbidding any missionary activity. These have become universal in the United States. *A Secretariat for Catholic-Jewish Relations* has been established at the Vatican, in the United States and in many countries. Textbooks are being examined and statements derogatory of Jews are eliminated. The Protestant Churches have followed the example of Catholicism. In 1970, a Jewish Consultative Committee met for the first time with the World Council of Churches at Geneva. This holds the promise that the dialogue with all of Christianity will continue to grow, and be a dialogue of equals. Ultimately, a dialogue with Islam is to be earnestly sought. While these endeavors, above all the declaration of Vatican II, explicitly hold that they are not motivated by political considerations, the end result can be of great political impact. It can help bring peace to the Middle East, and this would be a great spiritual achievement. Good will and mutual understanding of emotions on all sides will be able to bring this about. It may bring all faiths, even those not yet included, into a brotherhood of man under God, all over the world.

---

[18] *Pious and Secular America* (New York: Charles Scribner's Sons, 1958), pp. 107 f. and 111 f. he writes, If we measure the two faiths by their moral fruits the Jewish faith does not fall short. . . . Rosenzweig . . . define(s) the relationship of Christianity and Judaism as two religions with one center, worshipping the same God but with Christianity serving the purpose of carrying the prophetic message to the Gentile world. . . . It is certainly a better definition than those which prompt Christian missionary activity among Jews. . . . These activities are wrong, not only because they are futile and have little fruit to boast for their exertions. They are wrong because . . . the two faiths, despite differences, are sufficiently alike for the Jew to find God more easily in terms of his own religious heritage than by subjecting himself to the hazards of guilt feelings involved in a conversion to a faith, which, whatever its excellencies, must appear to him as a symbol of an oppressive majority culture . . . .
. . . there is the strange miracle of the Jewish people outliving the hazards of the diaspora for two millennia, and finally offering their unique and valuable contributions to the common Western Civilization. . . . We should not ask that this peculiar historical miracle fit into any kind of logic or conform to some historical analogy. It must be appreciated for what it is.

10
Challenge
and
Response

The character of a community is determined by the specific challenge it has to meet, and by the response it finds. Early Spanish Jewry had to adjust to a succession of invading peoples. The Romans transplanted Jewish settlers to the Iberian peninsula; Rome was displaced by Germanic tribes, the Vandals and the Visigoths; then came the Arabs, who established a glittering civilization.

SPAIN

In the Islamic sphere of influence, Jewry was generally free to participate in the political, intellectual, cultural, and economic growth of society as a whole, and they made the most of it. Called to political office, Jewish leaders saw in their honors a challenge to promote the spiritual growth of Judaism. They became sponsors of Jewish poetry and philosophy; they drew to Spain the leading masters of the Talmud. The Babylonian academies faltered and eventually faded away, but Torah found a new home in Spain.

Hasdai and Samuel the Prince

Hasdai ibn Shaprut, royal political advisor, physician, and inspector of customs during the tenth century, stands in contact with Jewish communities everywhere. A wondrous tale reaches his ears. Far away, on the steppes of Southern Russia, a whole nation had been converted to Judaism several hundred years ago. Could it be true? Hasdai sends a letter to the king of this foreign people, the Chazars, and receives an answer: the story is true. After careful examination of the Christian, Mohammedan, and Jewish faiths, King Bulan of the Chazars had decided that, "trusting in the mercies of God and the power of the Almighty, I choose the religion of Israel. . . ." [1] This had happened c. 740, and for 200 years the Chazars had followed the Torah. They were to exist to the thirteenth century, when they were defeated, their remnants joining the Jewish or Christian communities. Hasdai had forged a link; in due time the story of the Chazars was to serve as background for a great philosophical work by one of Spanish Jewry's great writers, Judah Halevi. Hasdai surrounded himself with Hebrew poets and writers who brought about a revival of literary studies and poetry; the study of the Talmud flourished.

Under the sponsorship of Samuel, called the Prince by his people, the development continued during the eleventh century. Samuel was by trade a grocer, a dealer in spices; he was also a scholar who knew Arabic literature to perfection, and spoke and wrote seven languages. Thus he came to the attention of the king of Granada, who appointed him his vizir. A great talmudist, Samuel found time to direct a Jewish academy of learning and to write commentaries himself. Thus intellectual life flourished; commentaries to the Bible were composed, and works were published in the fields of grammar, philosophy, and Talmud, a good many of them written in Arabic. Jewish translators rendered many of these works into Hebrew, while monks translated Greek philosophy and Islamic thought into Latin. This was the road by which Greek thinking eventually entered the western world. Jewish and Islamic thinkers became the first scholastics —without them, western scholasticism might never have developed.

Gabirol

The works of one of these Jews had a strange fate. His name was Solomon ibn Gabirol (1021-1069). He was sickly, poor, and yet alive. With his pen Hebrew poetry, from prayer to drinking song, acquired new beauty. His philosophical work, *Well of Life*, was translated into Latin under the title *Fons Vitae*. For many centuries it was taken for the work of a Christian philosopher of the Neo-Platonic school, until it was discovered that the Jew Gabirol and the "Christian" philosopher Avicebron were one and the same man.

There were, among the Spanish Jews, world travelers like Benjamin of

---

[1] Marcus, *op. cit.*, p. 230.

Tudela, who kept a diary which tells us of the life of Jews in many lands. Another, Bahya, a communal judge, wrote a book called *Duties of the Heart,* which has kept its popularity throughout the ages. Let your heart direct your actions, he advises, for without your heart's love your actions and your faith are meaningless. And then there was Judah Halevi.

Judah Halevi

Judah Halevi (1080-1140), one of the most tender souls, was a poet extraordinary, philosopher, and lover of Zion. Born in Toledo, he became a physician. The art of healing had called many Jews and was to call many more in the service of mankind. Judah, suffering in his own heart with every affliction he witnessed in his fellowmen, found medicine a natural call. He traveled and studied for many years, then settled down, first in his hometown, then in Cordova. Friends surrounded him, for he was a poet of great charm. Spring, the beauties of love, the grandeur of nature, and the fury of the elements—he knows them all, and he sings of them:

> But yesterday the earth drank like a child
>   with eager thirst the autumn rain.
> Or like a wistful bride who waits the hour
>   of love's mysterious bliss and pain.
> And now the Spring is here with yearning eyes
>   midst shimmering golden flower beds,
> On meadows carpeted with varying hues,
>   in richest rayment clad she treads.
> She weaves a tapestry of bloom o'er all,
>   and myriad eyed young plants upspring,
> white, green or red like lips that to the mouth
>   of the beloved one sweetly cling. . . .
> Come, go we to the garden with our wine,
>   which scatters sparks of hot desire,
> Within our hand 't is cold, but in our veins
>   it flashes clear, it glows like fire.[2]

But there is another call, more powerful than healing; there is another love, more persuasive than that of women or of Spring. It is the call of Zion, the love of Jerusalem. There he wishes to go, a humble pilgrim, yearning for his God. Leaving his home, he reaches Egypt after a stormy voyage, then moves on toward the promised land of his hopes and dreams. Whether he ever reached the holy city we don't know. A legend has him killed under the galloping hoofs of a horse as he lies on the ground kissing the soil of the beloved spot, his face turned in ecstasy toward Jeru-

---

[2] Translation by Emma Lazarus in *A Golden Treasury of Jewish Literature,* Leo Schwarz, ed. (New York: Holt, Rinehart & Winston, Inc., 1937), p. 577.

Moses Maimonides.

salem.[3] The legend speaks for the love in which he was held by his people, who saw his life as a symbol of the Jewish people themselves, of their hopes and prayers and aspirations. His was the spirit of their march through history toward Zion, beholding it from afar, illumined by its radiance, but unable to reach it as war and disaster galloped over their bodies, prostrate in worship and longing. Judah's philosophical work *Chuzari*, uplifted by the same spirit of love, builds the story of the Chazars and the conversation of the king with the wise men of three faiths into a dialogue. The basic principles of Judaism are explained philosophically and contrasted with those of other faiths. We shall discuss it in a later chapter.

Moses Maimonides

The greatest of the Spanish masters was Moses ben Maimon, Maimonides. He belongs to the leading philosophers of the ages. When he was born in 1135, Spanish Jewry was in a difficult position. A fanatic islamic sect had come to power and forced the Jews either to migrate or accept Islam. Many Jews yielded, at least outwardly, while observing their faith in secret. Maimonides' family chose to leave Cordova. For ten years they moved from city to city and from country to country, and young Moses had the opportunity to learn from all the experts he met. Talmud, philos-

---

[3] See his *Elegy to Zion*, which will be discussed in Chapter 11.

145

ophy, medicine, mathematics, and astronomy were among the subjects of his studies. He became one of the few "universal men" of history, who knew everything that could be known in his day. After a sojourn in the Land of Israel Maimonides finally settled in Egypt, where he became court physician and head of the Jewish community of Fostat (Cairo). He died in 1204, after a life in which he made every moment count; his supposed grave is found in Israel.

Of his works

Moses' first concern was preservation of the Torah; to it he dedicated all his works, including the three extensive ones:

a) A commentary to the Mishnah, written in Arabic during the period of travel. Maimonides strove to create a synthesis of Jewish thinking and philosophy, and of Jewish ethics and the ideas of Aristotle.

b) A code of Jewish Law, embracing the entirety of all talmudic legislation. Maimonides gave it the title *Mishneh Torah*—Repetition of Torah, or *Yad ha-Hazakah*—Strong Hand.

c) A great philosophical work to explain Judaism in the light of philosophy, especially to those who had become bewildered by the conflicting claims of Torah and Aristotle. Maimonides called it: Guide of the Perplexed.

Some observations on his works

a) Maimonides was a young man of 33 when he completed his Mishnah commentary; he had encompassed all of Aristotle, and was able to embody Aristotle's ethics in it. His "Eight Chapters" of introduction to the Sayings of the Fathers, dealing with Aristotle's ethical thoughts, and fused with Jewish tradition, are still popular.

Since he was a systematic thinker, Maimonides also tried to condense the basic beliefs of a Jew in the form of a creed. It was as if he wished to say to his generation: you may build other philosophies into the structure of your thought, but never forget the basic tenets of Judaism. Subsequent periods have framed Maimonides' Articles of Faith in poetic form. One version, the Yigdal, is a hymn sung in the synagogue. His ideas, to this day, express basic beliefs of traditional Judaism.

1) I believe with a perfect faith that the Creator, blessed be He, created and leads all creation; and that He alone did fashion, does fashion and will fashion everything.

2) I believe . . . that He is One, and that there is no Oneness like His; He alone is our God, who was, is and shall be.

3) I believe . . . that He has no body, nor any bodily shape. . . .

4) I believe . . . that He is the first and the last.

5) I believe . . . that only to Him is it meet to pray, and to no other.
6) I believe . . . that all the words of the prophets are true.
7) I believe . . . that the prophecy of Moses our master is true, and that he is the father of all prophets, those before and those after him.
8) I believe . . . that the Torah now found in our hands was given to Moses. . . .
9) I believe . . . that this Torah is not subject to change, and that there will never be another Torah from the Creator. . . .
10) I believe . . . that the Creator knows all the thoughts and deeds of man. . . .
11) I believe . . . that the Creator rewards those who obey His commandments and punishes those who transgress against them.
12) I believe . . . in the coming of the Messiah; though he tarry, I expect him daily.
13) I believe . . . in the resurrection of the dead. . . .

These principles have been attacked, for they would have established a dogma resulting in reading out of Judaism those who did not abide by all of them, and Judaism has never insisted on a body of belief. Many of Maimonides' articles of faith are no longer held by Jews who, nevertheless, have a full claim to be considered devoted adherents of Judaism. Yet the principles constitute a foundation. Reinterpreted or maintained in their original meaning, they are guidelines for all religious Jews of all denominations. The impact these principles have had can be seen in the martyrs' hymn in the Warsaw Ghetto. They fought the Nazis with a song on their lips: Ani Ma-amin, I believe!

b) Maimonides wrote his *Mishneh Torah* because he felt that the law of the Talmud needed clarification and codification. Having witnessed persecution and experienced homelessness, he realized the danger threatening Jewish law in times of turmoil.

"All the laws, given to Moses at Sinai, were given with their meaning," he begins his introduction; then, setting forth the history of tradition, he concludes:

At this time, the tribulations have become heavy, . . . and the wisdom of our wise has vanished, . . . hence all the commentaries . . . of the Gaonim . . . have become difficult to understand, . . . not to speak of the Talmud proper . . . calling for wide knowledge, wisdom, and much time for research. . . . Hence I Moses ben Maimon, . . . trusting in God, have studied all these books and determined to . . . prepare a clear digest of all the works . . . so that the entire Oral Torah shall be arranged clearly for everyone . . . without the arguments of debate . . . In summary it is my purpose that no one henceforth will have to consult any other work on any of Israel's laws . . . but this work be a compendium of the entire Oral Torah . . . I have called this work "Mishneh Torah" (Repetition of Torah), since henceforth anyone who first reads the

Written Torah and then this book will know the entire Oral Torah and will need to read no additional work.[4]

This was to be a compendium where a rabbi might find an answer to any question quickly and authoritatively; it was more, however. It was a complete digest of the Oral Torah, written by a man who had explored every possible aspect and detail of it. Culled from the vast expanse of innumerable opinions in the Talmud, the final decisions are systematically arranged by subject matter. Mishneh Torah has never lost its influence. It may have been superseded by later commentaries, but it has permanently shaped the thinking and feeling of Jews in their feasting and fasting, in their celebration of Sabbaths and festivals, and in their approach to God through thought and action.

Through the centuries, the rules of repentance have been one of the sources of deep spiritual inspiration.

What is complete repentance? If a person has both opportunity and strength to repeat a previous sin, but resists it, as a result of repentance and not on account of fear or weakness (that is perfect and complete return to God). . . . But even if he has sinned throughout his entire life, yet repents on the day of his death and so departs, all his sins are forgiven him. . . .

What do we mean by repentance? The sinner must cast off his sin, banish it from his thoughts, determine in his heart never to commit it again. . . . He must confess with his lips, putting in words the thoughts, the determinations of his heart . . . without change of heart . . . confession does not help. . . .

Has he committed a sin against his neighbor, hurt him or cursed him or robbed him, he can never obtain (God's) forgiveness until he has restored unto his neighbor whatever he owed him and has received his pardon . . . Even if he has hurt his neighbor by words only, he must plead with him till he forgives. . . .

Let no man be cruel, and unforgiving, but let every man be easy to appease and slow to anger; when his foe asks him for forgiveness, he must forgive with all his heart and soul. Even if his enemy has wronged him grievously, he must not bear any grudge (Teshubah II).

Let man consider himself . . . and the world equally balanced between merit and guilt. One individual sin tilts his own scale and that of the world toward guilt and brings destruction, one individual good deed tilts his own scale and that of the world in the direction of merit bringing help and salvation.

He who separates himself from the community, even though he has not committed any sins, but stands apart from the congregation of Israel, not partak-

---

[4] *Mishneh Torah,* Hebrew (Lemberg: Salomon Rapaport, 1811), p. 1a-b. Translation by the author. All other translations from Maimonides' Mishneh Torah are from the same edition. The publisher states on the title page that it was "duly censored by the government," a reflection on the problems Jews had to face even in publishing their own literature.

ing in their actions, nor sharing in their tribulations . . . as if he did not belong to them, he has no share in the World to Come (Teshubah III).

Of the things that prevent repentance: He who sees his son get into bad company and does not prevent him while the son is still under his responsibility. . . . (Teshubah IV).

Do not think that repentance is required only for sins of commission, such as adultery, robbery and theft; man must also repent the sins of rage, hatred, jealousy, cynicism, greed for wealth and honor, ambition, gluttony and similar ones . . . Actually these are harder to repent. . . .

Think not that even after repentance man is far from the status of the pious on account of the sins he has committed. On the contrary, he is beloved and dear to the Creator as if he had never sinned; his reward is even greater, for he has tasted sin and has renounced it, and overcome his desires . . .

Israel cannot be redeemed except through repentance. . . . Great is repentance, it brings man close to God's presence; . . . it brings home those who were far away. Yesterday only, he was far from God, . . . today he is beloved, and precious, close and dear to Him . . . yesterday separated, . . . he is enveloped today in divine glory. . . .

It is a grave sin to tell a repentant sinner "remember thy former deeds" or to mention his former conduct in order to put him to shame (Teshubah VII).

Let no one determine to fulfil the commandments of Torah . . . in order to receive blessings . . . or to be worthy of life to come; nor stay away from sins . . . to escape punishment . . . or from fear of losing life eternal. It is wrong to serve God in this way, for in that case man would serve God from fear, and this is neither the level of the prophets nor of the sages. This form of service is only for the ignorant, the women and children whom one must bring up to serve God from fear until their minds mature and they can serve Him from love . . . (Teshubah X).

In other sections, Maimonides offers more wise counsel.

The wise man is distinguished by wisdom and character . . . and should be recognized by his actions, in eating and drinking, in marital relations, . . . in walk and talk, in dress, . . . in business . . . He is not a glutton but eats only what is needed to sustain Him . . . he eats only in his own home, at his own table, not in public, . . . drinks wine only to digest his food better. He who gets drunk commits a sin, becomes contemptible and loses his wisdom. If he gets drunk in the presence of the common crowd he desecrates the Name of God. . . . (His marital relations) . . . he conducts in holiness. . . .

A wise man never hollers or screams like the beasts, never raises his voice much . . . He talks softly to all men . . . He should never exaggerate, that his speech does not sound arrogant. He should always greet others first, in order to be well liked; he should always judge everyone in his favor, he always relates the good of his neighbor, never speaking adversely about him . . . He loves peace and pursues peace, if he finds that his words are useful and listened to he speaks, otherwise he keeps still. . . . The wise does not walk erect and proud . . . he lowers his eyes as if in prayer and walks along as one who minds his own business. . . . The clothes of the wise are pleasant and clean; he may have no dirt or spots on his garments. He may not dress in garments of either great luxury . . . or great poverty, . . . but wears average, simple, and useful clothes. . . .

The wise man . . . supports his family within his means and does not burden himself with debt. He shall—personally—live below his means in order that he can maintain his family above his means.

This is the way of a prudent man: first he finds work to sustain him, then he buys a home, then he takes a wife. . . .

It is forbidden to give away all one's property, even for holy causes, for man would then be a burden to others . . .

The business of the wise must be transacted in truth and faith; his yea must be yea, his nay must be nay. In accounting he must be strict with himself; he shall be liberal when buying from others. He shall pay cash right away, shall not underwrite other people's debts, shall not give power of attorney to others. . . . In litigations, if the court decides in his favor, he shall be forgiving to his opponents, and help them out by loans and assistance. He must never push his neighbor out of business, and never—in all his life—must he harm any human being.

This is the rule: it is better to belong to those who are persecuted than to those who persecute others; better it is to be among those who are humiliated than among those who humiliate others. He who guides his life by these rules may apply to himself the word of Scripture: "He said to me: Thou art My servant, Israel, in whom I will be glorified (Isa. 49:3)." (Deot V).

Life in its totality is a divine commandment. This is the lesson Maimonides has for his brethren in happy times and in hard ones. To prepare for such a life children must be well educated.

Every province, district and city must have teachers. Citizens of a town that has no school deserve to be excommunicated until they appoint teachers . . . Children should be sent to school when they are six or seven years old, depending on the health and strength of the child . . . The teacher may chastise them to make them respect him, but he may not beat them harshly or in anger. . . . A maximum of 25 children may be instructed by one teacher. If there are between 25 and 40 children an auxiliary teacher has to be employed. A class of over forty children requires two teachers (Talmud Torah II).

Maimonides is advanced in his thinking; all facets of life are discussed and have been influenced by him.

c) *The Guide of the Perplexed* established Maimonides as a leading philosopher. It shall be discussed in detail later on. It is a response to his disciples' asking of disturbing questions. Reason is Maimonides' ultimate yardstick. Accepted and denounced by Jewish orthodoxy and the

Christian Church alike, this work towers in history, influencing thinkers throughout the ages.

The End of Spanish Jewry

Spanish Jewry needed these guidelines. For several centuries Jewish life was peaceful, but the kings of Castile moved slowly southward. "Reconquista," the crusade for the reconquest of Spain, was policy and battle cry of mediaeval Christendom. In their war against the Moors, the kings actually used Jews as counselors, collectors of taxes, and financiers. Some Jews, among them Samuel of Toledo, became rich. His house was later taken over by the famous painter El Greco, and the synagogue he built can still be visited; it is now a church. The kings made the policy and spent the money; the Jews, however, became the object of hatred, for they were the tax gatherers. Tension grew; in 1391 it broke. Mobs stormed the Jewish sections, and congregation after congregation was wiped out. Thousands of Jews were murdered, while others took refuge in the shelter of Christianity. But it was a precarious shelter; they could not escape the hatred of the people. Accused of still observing Jewish law, many practiced their faith in secret worship. The people called them "Marranos," dirty fellows; to the Church they were heretics. Having once accepted Christianity, they had committed the impardonable sin of heresy. The Inquisition was set up against them, and many died. Some families retained their faith secretly throughout the ages, to profess it openly again only in the twentieth century.

Those who had remained Jews found their position more and more difficult. Restrictions were piled upon restrictions; disputations between rabbis and clerics were ordered, in which the rabbis could win their point but never their case, for it was foredoomed; yellow badges were introduced, to be worn as marks of "shame." In the meantime, the Moors were pushed back further and further. Finally, in 1492, Granada, the last Moorish stronghold, fell. Now the Jews were the only non-Christian element left; they, too, must go. Ferdinand and Isabella issued the edict: the Jews must get out, leaving their property behind. By tragic coincidence, the date set was the anniversary of the fall of Jerusalem. Turkey, Holland and other countries gave them shelter; Venice, Bordeaux, Naples, Genoa, and Amsterdam were to profit from their ability.

Watching those whom the unbending will of Torquemada, the Inquisitor, had sent into exile is Christopher Columbus, about to set sail for a new world. In his diaries he speaks movingly about the Jews and their plight. Was Columbus himself a Marrano? There are indications that this may have been possible.[5] We don't know. But strange are the ways of history or of Providence. On the days the Jews were expelled from Spain, ships set sail which were to open up a new world, and in this world Jews were to have a freedom they had never known before. The edict prohibiting Jews from living in Spain eventually was permitted to lapse and formally revoked in 1969.

CENTRAL EUROPE

The Life of Ashkenasic Jewry

As soldiers and suppliers with Caesar's legions, the Jews may have reached the Rhine. Following the routes of the Roman Empire they traveled as far as England. When Hitler, in 1933, branded them as aliens, they had lived in Germany for almost two thousand years, the group with the longest record of permanent settlement within Germanic territory.

With the arrival of Christianity their lot turned to suffering. The power of the State now stood behind the teachings of the Church, and the Fathers of the Church developed the principles upon which Church and State based their relationship. For St. Augustine, the Church is the divine instrument of government in the world, the State is its servant, and the Emperor—no longer divine—is its arm. This new order has no room for Jews. Historically, they were considered extinct as a nation; their Temple was gone and their country destroyed, all by their own doing. By rejecting Christ they had turned down their chance for salvation. But why should God have willed their survival? Would it not be better to wipe them out? No, says St. Augustine, their survival is also part of the divine will. By their humiliation they are the living witnesses of the truth proclaimed by the Church. Their law is an instrument of their education, and education eventually will open their eyes. At the end of days they will find their way to Christ.[6] The Jews must be preserved, for their survival is part of God's eternal plan, but they must be exposed in every way to the truth of Christianity, and they must live in shame and humiliation. This doctrine has shaped Jewish destiny through many centuries. It is responsible for suffering, but also for the preservation of the Jews in the Christian world of the Middle Ages. It explains the cruelty of rulers and rabble, but also the frequent kindness of the popes. How could the Jews find their way to the Church unless the Church exhibited a Christian spirit of love? Jewish religious law was never restricted, for it served as a means of education; yet, at the same time,

---

[5] See the essay on Columbus in Cecil Roth, *Personalities and Events in Jewish History* (Philadelphia: Jewish Publication Society).

[6] See N. N. Glatzer, *Geschichte der Talmudischen Zeit* (New York: Schocken Books, Inc., 1937), pp. 73 ff.

attendance at Christian services was frequently forced upon them. They were both set apart from the world and drawn into it, and their fate remained closely interwoven with that of the West. Their status, dependent on the will and strength of rulers and popes, fell slowly but inexorably; their suffering grew, and suspicion against them developed into prejudice.

The chaos which followed the collapse of the Roman Empire brought them agonies; each ruler treated them as he pleased and exploited them as he wished. When Charlemagne consolidated the realm, he showed kindness to them; it was a Jew who carried out the emperor's embassy to Harun Al Rashid. When Otto II (973-983) saw the need for expanding trade, he invited the Calonymus family of Lucca in Italy to settle in Mainz. (The date is debated; 917 has also been given recently as a likely date.) They served as merchants, forming the link between peasants who produced goods and lords who did not know how to dispose of them for profit. Permitted to buy real estate, the House of Calonymus proudly exhibited the imperial eagle granted the family as a symbol of royal favor and protection.

Pillar of the Calonymus House at Mainz. Part of the main window, approximately three feet high, it dates from about 1000. The imperial eagle on top testifies to special imperial favor and protection. The bearded figure in the medallion represents the emperor, before whom the owner of the house appears naked and humble to plead for continued protection. It was destroyed in the air raids of W.W. II.

Window of the Calonymus house, showing its wealth and the adoption of contemporary styles by Jews throughout the ages.

But favors and protection had to be bought, and bought dearly. At first only a few families enjoyed them, then they were extended to whole congregations. Always revokable, these patents of protection had to be renewed again and again. The emperor had called them and shielded them; thus the Jews became the emperor's personal property, exploitable any way he wished. He might squeeze them, as you squeeze a sponge, to get the money he needed. Or he might present the lives and belongings of the Jews of a city to one of his friends or vassals; this meant persecution, exploitation, expropriation, and—frequently—exile. Homelessness and death were always nearby. As imperial power grew weaker, so did imperial protection, and dukes and barons often acted on their own. But Germany was deeply split, and this saved the Jews many times. One duke would expel them, but his neighbor would readmit them. It was a sad merry-go-round, but it explains why Jews never left the soil of Germany. The situation was different in England and France, where royal power had broken the might of the barons and had unified the kingdom. A royal edict expelled the Jews from England in 1290, and they were not to return until the seventeenth century; in 1394, France followed suit.

In this life of sufferings, there were moments when agony turned into nightmare. The first crusade was one of these periods. In 1095, Pope Urban appealed to the Western world to gird itself for battle against the infidels who had conquered the holy places in Palestine. This was the beginning of the crusades, which had no religious end results at all. The masses who followed the appeal were a mixed lot. High-minded knights were joined by adventurous rabble looking for loot. Why go to Palestine to avenge the blood of Christ, they reasoned, when infidels who could be plundered and exterminated without risk lived right within their midst? And so they poured over the Jewish communities along the Rhine. In vain the bishops tried to stem the inflamed fury of the mob. The Jews fought with heroism, but they were overwhelmed. The centers of Jewish life in Western Europe—Mainz, Worms, Speyer, Trier, Cologne —all were wiped out. In the wall of the ancient cemetery of Worms we find a simple plaque. Next to the Kaddish and prayer for all dead, it contains one word: [4]856, the year of the Hebrew calendar corresponding to 1096. It recalls the sacrificial death of thousands who had the choice between conversion or death, and chose to die.

Degradation continued. Squeezed out of trade, rejected by the craftsmen's guilds, prohibited from owning and cultivating land, the Jews were permitted only one occupation—the lending of money. How far they had fallen; a people tied to the land for millennia, farmers and creative artisans throughout the ages, they were denied the very crafts they understood and loved. They were merely a ready source of funds for

Memorial Tablet honoring the martyrs of 1096. The Hebrew date is in the lower right hand corner; the rest is the prayer for the dead and the Kaddish.

Memorial tablets in the cemetery wall for "Twelve Overseers" of the Congregation of Worms, massacred in 1096. The two tablets are for the same men; the right one, containing only the words "Twelve Overseers, (4)856," is older. The stonecutter seems to have been either unskilled or hurried; the last letter of the word "Overseers" is missing. (Destroyed in W.W. II.)

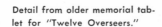

Detail from older memorial tablet for "Twelve Overseers."

155

their rulers, who would exploit them whenever they wanted. But worse was to come. The Lateran Council of 1215, presided over by Pope Innocent III, mightiest of popes, made a new ruling. Jews had to wear a yellow badge and a grotesque hat in order to be recognized immediately and given scorn and abuse. Then came the Black Death which scourged Europe in 1348, the bubonic plague brought in from the Far East. One-third of Europe's population perished. Who was considered guilty? The Jews; they were accused of having poisoned the wells. Hysteria was master; for two years Jewish congregations and their people were systematically exterminated. Hundreds of congregations were wiped out. Fortunately, Poland had already opened her gates to German Jews, permitting them to come as a needed and useful element. Thousands migrated to form great new centers of Jewish life, where piety and learning were to reach new heights.

When it was all over, the German princes realized that they had lost a source of income, and resettled their Jews. But the Jews had to live in small narrow streets in special sections of town, which could be reached only through guarded gates. Locked up at night and on special Christian holidays, insulted when they stepped out in their marked garments, they had lost access even to God's fresh air and the beauties of nature which they treasured. As their number grew, story had to be piled upon story of narrow houses in dingy streets, for the *ghetto* was never enlarged.

They were haunted by libels which aroused the mobs. They were accused of secretly entering churches to pierce the holy host, which made no sense; why should they, when they did not believe in transubstantiation? But the mob had no ear for theological subtleties, or—for that matter—for simple reason. The Jews were charged with killing Christian children to use their blood for Passover worship. This libel had been lodged against the early Christians by their pagan enemies, who deliberately misunderstood the meaning of the Christian miracle of the Mass, and now Christians used it against Jews. The popes raised their solemn voice against this horrible libel. It was untrue, declared Innocent IV in a papal bull (1247), adding that Jews must be treated with compassion. Yet it was brought up again and again, against the voices of popes and religious leaders.

They were even denied the consolations of their holy books. Listening to slanderous accusations that the Talmud contained blasphemies against God and Christ, the Inquisition burned hundreds of copies in public.

It is not surprising that the Jews withdrew into a shell. But they did maintain contact with the surrounding world as far as conditions permitted. And it is miraculous that they kept their zest for life.

The world into which they withdrew was the realm of the Talmud. The small child, upon learning to speak, was taught an affirmation: "The Torah which Moses has commanded us, it is the heritage of the congregation of Jacob (Deut. 33:4)." As he recited these words, the child was told, "Close your eyes, little child, to all that is around, the trials and the humiliation, but also all your earthly goods. All this, truly, is not yours. Your heritage is within, the Torah; it is your only assured heritage, no one can take it from you."

Yet Jews remained in touch with the world, partially because of the number of friendly Christians who maintained pleasant contacts. We gather this from ordinances forbidding Christians to be guests in Jewish homes; we even know of Christian converts to Judaism, who were promptly burned at the stake as heretics. The yellow badge was introduced with the official explanation that common dress of Jews and Christians had led to very close associations, even to marriages.

The Jews in their daily lives used the language of their countries. Rashi, the commentator of the Bible, gives the French word for terms hard to explain in Hebrew—his people understood French. In Germany they spoke German, and dressed as much like the rest of the population as permitted. When they were driven out of Germany and went to Poland, they took their German with them, and it became Jewish or Yiddish. They retained it through the centuries, a moving tribute to the culture which had helped form them, and which they had helped to develop while its representatives tortured them to the blood. Yiddish is a German dialect into which have filtered terms from Hebrew, Polish, Russian, and other languages. Its development after the thirteenth century did not follow the linguistic development of the German language, so it has retained an archaic character. Of German origin is the *caftan*, the long black garb of the Polish Jew. It was the dress of the mediaeval German; discarded by the rest of the world, it became the "Jewish" garb.

They may have been separated, but they were not secluded. German music entered their lives, as Christian musicians played at their weddings and festivities; church music entered the synagogue; from the Catholic Church they adopted the custom of lighting a candle on the anniversary of the death of a dear one, now an integral part of religious observance by all Jews. They listened to the songs of the Troubadours and even produced a Troubadour, a Minnesinger of their own, Süsskind of Trimberg, who visited the castles of the knights and struck his harp to sweet lyrical songs.

In return they gave philosophy and medicine to their Christian neighbors. Always famous as physicians, serving the highborn and the lowly, they were the only ones who could read and write at a time when writing one's name was a mark of great literacy among the rest of the world. It has been said that they, rather than the Phoenicians, had invented the alphabet back in antiquity.[7] In any event, they certainly made the

---

[7] David Diringer, *The Story of the Alphabet* (New York: Thomas Yoseloff, Inc., 1960).

art of writing universal to all their members, and in this way they could help their neighbors. Their travel made them a link between cultures, transmitters of ideas and philosophies, although often they had to travel against their will.

Retaining their zest for life, they liked to dress well when they could, and furnished their homes and synagogues as aesthetically as possible. Games and music of all kinds played a part in their lives. They loved to dance, and almost every community had its dance-house. They even copied the carnival plays and frolics of their neighbors on the Jewish "carnival" feast of Purim. This may have been partly escape, but was probably more than that. It stemmed from their knowledge beyond doubt that life was worth living as a Jew, for God was with the Jews in trial now and in eventual vindication when His time came.

The Jewish community of the Middle Ages met the challenge of their destiny by devotion to Torah and Talmud, by a deepening of their inner life and of family love. They developed a society regulated in every detail by the letter of Torah and Talmud, and yet not one that was gloomy. They knew they suffered for God, and in this knowledge they could laugh and make merry. This message was confirmed in the teachings and the worship of the synagogue, which called them three times a day at the knock of the beadle's staff as he walked down the streets, rapping at windows to arouse the people.

Synagogue Buildings

In the ancient Rhenish city of Worms there stood until 1938 the old and hallowed synagogue of the ghetto. It was about 900 years old, a monument to German civilization. The Nazis blew it up, and the German government has rebuilt it in replica form—unfortunately, as a museum, for there are hardly any Jews left in Worms. It is a small synagogue, for Jews were not permitted to erect large ones; its plan is the same, however, as that which has been followed by builders throughout the ages, in small synagogues and in stately ones, in simple structures and in monumental edifices. There have been modifications, but they have remained minor.

The synagogue of Worms was built in Romanesque and early Gothic, the styles of the time; it may even have been planned by the same architect who erected the famous cathedral in whose shadow it nestled. The worshipper entered the rounded gate; at the right hand post he could see a deep depression in the stone where pious worshippers had touched it lovingly to carry their fingers reverently to their lips. A step led down to the sanctuary in conformity with the word: Out of the depth I call unto Thee, O Lord. The building measured perhaps 50 by 50 feet. In front was the holy Ark, containing age-old scrolls of the Torah;

Exterior of ancient Synagogue at Worms; entrance to women's part is at left rear. The caved-in side wall (left front) is connected by legend to a miracle. The mother of Judah the Pious, while bearing the child, pressed against the wall to escape a speeding knight's carriage. The wall caved in to give her room, thus preserving her and the child.

Interior of Synagogue at Worms. The Ark in front is covered by a curtain and surmounted by three crowns —priesthood, royalty, and, most precious of all, Torah. In front of the Ark, level with the auditorium, is the reader's desk, facing the ark; it is surmounted by a small pulpit, facing the people, for the rabbi's sermon. To the right is the Hanukah candlestick. The reading desk for the Torah is in the center of the auditorium; the women's section, originally walled in, is in the North Transept.

steps led up to it, an eternal light shed its glimmer over it. The light, like the eternal lamp found in the Temple of old, is symbolic of God's eternal presence. At the foot of the steps, facing the Ark, was the reading desk of the cantor, who brought the prayer of the congregation to God. His position was not elevated, for he spoke out of the midst of the people. In the center of the building stood the "Bimah," an elevated reading platform from which Scripture was read as the people gathered around, as their fathers had done at Mount Sinai. When the worshipper faced the Ark, he also faced east, toward Jerusalem. At the left, toward the front, there was a transept; this was the women's section, where they sat separated from the men, as is still the practice in orthodox synagogues, where women are seated in the gallery. But this synagogue had no gallery. The women entered by a different gate, and there was originally a wall between the two sections in order that neither the men nor the women be disturbed by each other's presence during wor-

Ritual bath attached to the Synagogue of Worms. Orthodox women still follow the law of immersion, and modern bath houses exist for that reason.

Rashi Chapel, Worms.

ship. There was a window in the wall; at it there once stood a woman cantor who followed the service and led the women in prayer and song. Stepping out of the synagogue into the courtyard, the visitor found the entrance to the ritual bath, used by pious women to purify themselves every month before returning to their husbands' love and embrace. Cut deep in the rock, it reached to the level of the nearby Rhine, so that living waters from the river might form the basin of its font. A small niche in the wall offered a place to undress. These were heroic women, who braved cold and darkness and damp murkiness to fulfil the law of marital purity.

Next to the bath was the entrance to the Bet Hamidrash, the room of study. It was called Rashi chapel, for Rashi, the great commentator, was once thought to have taught there. It was a small room too, Romanesque or early Gothic, perhaps 20 by 15 feet; one wall was straight, the other slightly circular and broken by windows. Stone benches surrounded the walls, surmounted by a great elevated stone chair with arm rests cut out of the wall, a lamp, a table of later date, and books. That was all, yet here was one of the great sanctuaries of Jewry, a place hallowed by masters, graced by students, and filled with an atmosphere of devotion and with memories of sanctity.

Modern synagogues may have made changes. The Bimah has frequently been moved to the front to allow more space for the worshippers. The cantor then faces the people from an elevated chancel in order to be heard better. Few synagogues have steps leading down into the sanctuary. Conservative and Reform synagogues permit mixed seating, to keep the families together; if they have galleries, they just serve the overflow.

Orthodox synagogue at Mainz, where the author worshipped as a child; it was destroyed by Nazis in 1938. Bimah (platform) for Torah reading is in the center. Cantor's desk, level with congregation, is in front facing the Ark; above it is the pulpit for the sermon. Note eternal light, Hanukah menorah, and women's gallery (top right).

Front of the synagogue of Capernaum (second century of the Christian era). The center served as a resting place for the Ark of the Torah, which could be removed.

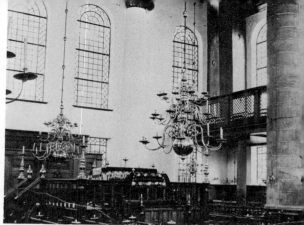

Spanish and Portuguese Synagogue
in Amsterdam.

Most, but not all, synagogues face east. The holy Ark may be veiled by
a curtain, as in Worms, or not, depending on various traditions. Additional symbols have frequently been added; the Star, the Lion of Judah
(from Gen. 49:9); the seven branched candlestick, early symbol of Judaism, and found in the Temple of old facing the holy of holies; and the
two tablets, as reminder that once the Ark contained these holy tables.
Sefardic synagogues seat the worshippers facing each other across a
center aisle, rather than directing them toward the Ark. All this is minor.
The Torah in its Ark is still the center of worship and instruction, and
will so remain for ever; the eternal light will glow. Where a pulpit is
added for the preacher, it is secondary to the pulpit for the Torah. Above
all, every synagogue has its school, and, in modern congregations, the
school plant is larger than the sanctuary, for the study of Torah is the
center of life and beginning of wisdom. Through Torah, Jewry has been
kept alive; Torah was its response to the challenge of mediaeval persecution. *Shul,* school, is what they called their House of God.

Baltimore Hebrew Congregation, Baltimore, Maryland.

FRENCH-GERMAN JEWRY RISES TO EMINENCE

On the ancient Jewish cemetery of Mainz, cleaned up several years ago at the suggestion of this writer, there can be found a simple stone. It says "Erected in memory of Gershom ben Judah." Behind this name the history of great achievement unfolds.

Gershom ben Judah

Gershom was born in France c. 960 and decided to move to Mainz, making it a center of Jewish learning. There he died in 1040. Posterity

Supposed tombstone of Rabbenu Gershom in the old cemetery of Mainz.

titled him *Light of the Diaspora,* for he was a teacher of teachers. Western Jewry called him "Rabbenu Gershom," *our* Rabbi Gershom. Thus Mainz, Speyer, and Worms, cities on the Rhine, became a world center of Jewish learning. Their academies attracted hundreds of disciples from all parts of the world; inquiries in problems of religion were sent to the masters, and their ordinances had binding power throughout Ashkenasic Jewry. From these schools there emerged liturgical poets, philologists, and experts in Jewish law. Gershom collected talmudic commentaries from various sources and began combining, editing, and organizing. Thus, once again, he summed up the work of generations. Sefardic Jewry was doing the same thing, but Spanish Jews were busy with the affairs of the world; only rarely would an average man find time to pore over heavy tomes in extended study. Sefardic commentaries had to be digests, simplifications. Maimonides knew that. German Jewry, secluded as it was, found in the Talmud a relief from life, a challenge and escape, and so German commentaries went into depth. Interpretation was piled on interpretation. An inner world of freedom was being explored. Literally woven around the Talmud itself, these commentaries became part of it, and without them the Talmud is almost beyond understanding. Social conditions did indeed affect the character of Jewish learning.

But Gershom was also a man of action, and became famous for his decrees. He ruled for all times that no letter may be opened by anyone except its recipient; that divorce requires mutual consent of both parties; and that polygamy, not yet forbidden by Scripture although long out of usage among Ashkenasim, was prohibited for all generations.

Rashi

The schools of Mainz and of Worms drew into their ranks a man who was to become the greatest of all commentators, indispensable for the study of Bible and Talmud. His name was *Rabbi Shelomoh* ben *Yitshak*, affectionately called *Rashi* by contraction of the first letters of his name.

He was born in 1040 in the city of Troyes, France. As a young man, drawn to the academies of the Rhine cities, he studied under the disciples of Rabbi Gershom, returning home to France at the age of 25. He probably never occupied the chair in the chapel of Worms which bears his name, though he may well have sat on one of the benches. In Troyes he opened a school. Soon hundreds flocked to him, for he was a man of infinite kindness and humility. He did not wish to make his teaching a profession and to take money for it, so he eked out a living for himself and his family by cultivating a vineyard and selling the wine. In his love for his people and for tradition, he realized that they needed a guide through the Talmud, and he set to work to compose it.

Word by word, sentence by sentence, he went over the entire text, explaining simply, elucidating deeply. When he was done, he revised it, and then did the same for the entire Bible. No talmudic scholar today can do without Rashi's commentary, and no reader of the Bible can get a full understanding of it without the simple, lucid, and yet penetrating commentary which Rashi appended to every word and sentence. Rashi did indeed open the gates of the Talmud; through him, Bible and Talmud became the common heritage of all, contributing to the emotional stability of Jews in times of trouble. Before he died, he had reason to be grateful that he had returned home, as he witnessed in grief the destruction of the centers on the Rhine during the first Crusade. When he passed on in 1105, he had set himself an everlasting monument and given Jewry a priceless gift. His immediate successors wrote additions, or "Tosafot," to his Talmud commentary, and when we open the Talmud we find the text in the center, Rashi's commentary on the inside margin, and the "additions" on the outside margin of each page.[8]

Of Rashi's style

Behind the simplicity of Rashi's style stands a scholar of tremendous knowledge, a universal genius, exegete, philosopher, theologian, and grammarian. The world of the Talmud is at his fingertips. There stands also a man of true humility, who, at times, will say simply: "This

---

[8] See illustration, p. 105.

verse I do not understand." A few examples may be given of his method:

Genesis 1:1—Text: In the beginning God created the heaven and the earth

Rashi: In the Beginning. . . . Why did the Torah start with Genesis? Because "He has declared to His people the power of His works, giving them the heritage of the nations (Ps. 111, 6)." Should the people of the world ever say to Israel, you have robbed the inhabitants of Canaan of their land when you took it, then you may answer: the whole earth is the Lord's, He created it, and He gives it to whom He wishes; giving it to them by His will and taking it from them, to give it to us.

Rashi, in a few words, has dealt with the origin of property and with the ethical provisions that attach to it—obedience to God.

In the Beginning He Created: . . . explaining the verse simply, this is its meaning: In the beginning of creation the earth was unformed and void and full of darkness; then God said: Let there be light. The verse does not intend to teach us the order of creation—this came first, then that—for then the text should have read differently. Instead of "Bereshit"—"in the beginning of . . ." it should have read "Borishonah"—"in the beginning" (the first form indicates that the word is connected with the next one; it is in status constructus); hence we must read "in the beginning of God's creation." Should you insist that the verse tells us God created the heaven first, then you have the problem, that water was there already; for it says: "God's spirit hovered over the face of the waters." The verse has not told us anything about a previous creation of water; but it is certain that water was there before the earth.

Rashi applies logical and critical analysis of the text, concluding: *a*) that the text does not give us the order of creation, and merely states that in the beginning of God's work of creation the earth was void; *b*) the water was created before the earth; *c*) the text must be understood as logic commands. This is bold biblical criticism.

God created: (The term for God is Elohim, which is also the term for "judge"; later the term "YHWH Elohim" is used in combination; finally only the term YHWH is used, which stands for the God of history, according to tradition the God of mercy): At first God (Elohim) planned to establish the world on justice, but He saw that it could not exist; so He added the quality of mercy (Elohim YHWH). That is the reason for the change in terms. (Eventually the world was established on mercy alone.)

The modern critic may smile at the "primitiveness" of the statement. May we not forget, however, that Rashi wrote one thousand years ago, with keen perception and bold analysis of textual problems.

Another verse may be added, the first of the Ten Commandments.

Text: I am the Lord thy God who brought thee out of the land of Egypt, out of the house of bondage.

Rashi: Who brought thee out of the land of Egypt: The purpose of your deliverance was that you be My servants. Or another explanation: At the Red Sea He appeared unto them as Lord of Battle, now—at Sinai—he appeared to them like a patriarch full of mercy. He wanted to make it clear to them: If I appear unto you in various ways do not say, these are different powers; I am He who brought you out of Egypt, I am the same.

Rashi asks himself why Egypt is mentioned in the Ten Commandments; it does not seem to belong. In giving his explanation he presents the total of the Jewish view of life: Israel is God's servant, He alone is their Master; should it appear that He acts strangely toward them, may they remember that He is infinite and infinite are the facets of His Being. Knowing that He is the One God, their God, they will remain steadfast and true. This is the meaning of the first commandment (which ends here, according to Jewish tradition).

The childlike simplicity of Rashi's writing must not deceive us. His thought is penetrating. To the simple or the hurried reader, he gives a satisfying answer; to the scholar, however, he opens new avenues of research and study. He is the commentator for all.

THE STRUGGLE FOR SURVIVAL: THE CODES

In theory it was a fine idea to let *all* Jews escape from the tyranny of life around them to the peace and serenity of the world of Talmud. In practice it did not work; the plan was too ambitious, and conditions most unfavorable. The study of Talmud calls for concentrated effort over many years under the guidance of great teachers. There was not enough time; overnight, congregations might be expelled, books burned, rabbis imprisoned. All that stood between peace and homelessness was the whim of the ruler, the stroke of a pen in the hand of a king, an inflammatory sermon arousing the mob to frenzy, a libel, or greed. The leaders of the congregations saw it daily; fugitives crowded the Shul; friends who might have been wealthy yesterday were destitute today. And the Jews took care of their own, through individual charity and community chest organization, demonstrating the spirit of family. The members regularly tithed themselves in accordance with biblical law. Very frequently this was not enough, so they gave more.

Ever since talmudic times, collectors of charity had gone from house to house, week after week, to take up the collection. The Commissioners of Charity made the distribution, and if the funds were insufficient, they had to borrow on their own security. Only it was not called "Charity," it was called "Tzedakah," *righteousness.* To help a brother in need was simply an act of righteous, decent living, nothing more. Orphan and widow, destitute and hungry had always been cared for; funds had always been found to ransom prisoners and to send money to the Holy Land. Now the demands grew into a flood of appeals, as wave after wave of homeless poured in, and cries for help were heard from every side. And the hosts of today might be the beggars of tomorrow. Beginning with the period of the Crusades, conditions became less and less favorable to universal study; they deteriorated after the Lateran Council of 1215, and practically disappeared after the Black Death of 1349. New solutions had to be found; among them was emigration, or return to Palestine. In 1286 a great Rabbi named Meir of Rothenburg tried it— and failed. Recognized during his voyage, he was returned on order of the Emperor Rudolf of Habsburg. Emigration could not be permitted, the emperor felt; it drained the imperial treasury, and an example had to be made. Meir was imprisoned for the rest of his life (to 1293). He could have been ransomed, but he refused for fear that it might then

Tombstone of Rabbi Meir of Rothenburg in the old cemetery of Worms (left). Next to him is the stone of Suesskind Wimpfen, who paid the ransom for the release of the rabbi's body with the provision that he be buried next to him. The stones on top of the monuments are "visiting cards" of those who have prayed at the graveside, a custom originating when stoneheaps formed the markers of the graves.

Detail from the tombstone of Rabbi Meir.

become a habit of rulers to capture rabbis for the purpose of extorting ransom. Yet the ransom had to be paid, after the rabbi's death, for the privilege of burying his body. For the time being, migration on a large-scale basis was impossible.

A new approach was sought. If all the laws, rules, and customs were once again collected and presented systematically, then Jewry would be surrounded by a wall of observances and practices which would shield it against spiritual decay. The simple, hurried man might not be able to study, yet he could practice the Torah. The more minute the details, the higher would be the fence of protection; Torah became a psychological defense mechanism. Individual communities frequently had their own customs and practices added to general observance. A great disciple of Rabbi Meir, Rabbi Mordecai ben Hillel, began the work of compilation of all the decisions made by the rabbis, including those of the German-French academies. Then the work was cut short; Mordecai and his family died martyrs' deaths at Nuremberg in 1298, when Jews in Southern Germany were wiped out on the libelous claim that they had desecrated a sacred host. In this case, as in the Black Death accusation against the Jews and in so many other cases, the popes vainly vindicated the Jews in official pronouncements.

Again a rabbi chose emigration as a solution; he was a colleague of the martyred Mordecai named Asher ben Jehiel. He succeeded in getting to Spain, where Jews still enjoyed freedom, and was soon appointed Rabbi of Toledo, opening a school to which students flocked from all parts of the world. In him, German Jewry lost its leading intellect, but his migration had great consequences. Asher knew that Jewry needed a code, a guide to action; he realized it more now than he had before his sad experiences; and he undertook to write it. By the strength of his background he brought about a synthesis of the German masters and the Spanish ones. What he began, his son, Jacob completed in 1340. The work was in four volumes and called *Turim*, the Rows, after the four rows of precious stones which decorated the breastplate of the high priest of old.

In 1492 Spanish Jewry collapsed and Turkey opened her gates to many of the homeless. The Sultan could see the benefit he was deriving from this influx of intelligent people with great skills and wide connections. Some Jews were soon to rise to great power; one named Joseph was made a Duke. The Sultan was also ruler of Palestine, and Joseph succeeded in getting a charter to rebuild Tiberias as an industrial center; the project failed, but migration to Palestine gained new impetus. Safed, high in the hills, became a center of both Jewish learning and mysticism. Here a new plan was conceived to assure Jewish survival. Safed would be the world center of Jewry, where rabbis were to be ordained by a central Jewish body; a first group of men were actually granted ordination. Opposition arose immediately. The idea was not acceptable to the other rabbis of Palestine, and had to be abandoned. It appeared that a code would again be the only solution. One of the band of Safed-ordained rabbis decided to write it. His name was Joseph Karo (1488-1575). Not a man of soaring inspiration, but a rather pedestrian scholar with a very systematic mind and a profound memory, he based his work on the "Four Rows" of Jacob ben Asher. Written very simply and in a rather dry style, so that everyone could read it, he called it *Shulhan Arukh—The Well-Prepared Table*. It became a classic and has remained to this day *the* guidepost for traditional Jewry and *the* authoritative code for orthodox Jewish practices. It has completely fulfilled its author's expectations, and become a means of unifying Jewry and guarding its survival.

Before the Shulhan Arukh was universally accepted, however, it had to pass one hurdle. Karo was a Sefardi and had followed the decisions of the Sefardi masters. In many instances Ashkenasi Jewry followed different customs, and its masters had rendered different decisions in the law. German Jewry would not accept the Shulhan Arukh as it came from the pen of Karo. A Polish rabbi of the city of Cracow set to work to remedy the situation. He added footnotes expressing the views of the Ashkenasic authorities. Sometimes they were more lenient, sometimes more strict. The decision of which school to follow depended on custom and environment; yet in problem cases the individual rabbi had and has the right to individual decision and choice. In this power of ultimate decision lies the authority of the rabbi, conferred to him by his ordination.

The name of the Great Annotator, who spread a "Cover" on the "Prepared Table" was *R*abbi *M*osheh Isserles (1530-1572); he and his commentary are known by his initials, R'MO.

The Shulhan Arukh

The work as we have it gives us all the laws, ordinances, rules, and regulations governing the life of the Jew. Karo gives the Sefardic decisions, R'MO adds the Ashkenasic ones. The work is divided into four "Rows," following the division made by Jacob ben Asher.

1) Orah Hayim: *The Way of Life* contains all the laws of religious observance, from awakening in the morning to retiring at night; prayers, benedictions, Sabbath, festivals, and their rules.

2) Yore Deah: *The Teacher of Knowledge* deals with dietary laws and similar regulations.

3) Eben ha-Ezer: *The Stone of Help* contains the rules of family relationships: marriage, divorce, and others.

4) Hoshen Mishpat: *The Breastplate of Judgement* deals with civil law and similar items.

We shall include quotations from the work in our discussion of Jewish observances, which are based on rulings laid down in the codes. The development leading up to the Shulhan Arukh gives us an insight in the functions and authority of the traditional, or orthodox, rabbi.

Authority and Functions of the Orthodox Rabbi

The orthodox rabbi has two major functions. He sees to it that the rules laid down in the codes are strictly observed. In addition, he renders decisions in problematic religious cases. In doing so, he will lean primarily on the Shulhan Arukh, yet he may use all the source material at his disposal: Scripture, Talmud, Rashi, Maimonides, Jacob ben Asher's Four Rows, Shulhan Arukh, R'MO, and many others. Weighing the merits of a case, he hands down a ruling, often with a detailed opinion. This ruling, in turn, sets a precedent for the future. Thus the *responsa* of leading rabbis, from the earliest days to the present, have aided the evolving development of law and practice. Whether this slow progress meets modern needs, and the Shulhan Arukh is still to be regarded as absolute foundation, is a main argument between the different Jewish "denominations." Shall it be kept, changed, or abolished?

11

The
Jewish
Year

Almost all Jewish festivals have a twofold foundation. They are connected with the cycle of nature, its awakening, flowering, and maturing, and they are also tied to religious events in Jewish history—the birth of the nation, its development, and its maturing under God. Deprived of their intimate contact with nature and regulated by the strict rules of the Shulhan Arukh, the people of the ghetto came to lay greater emphasis on the religious background of the festivals, though never quite losing sight of their character as holidays of nature. Only in modern Israel, however, has the twofold character of the Jewish holidays recovered its full expression.

Of all the holy occasions, only the Sabbath has remained unaffected by the changes of times and seasons and calendar. It marks the eternal steps of God through history. Eternity is measured, as it beats in unchanging rhythm the movement of time, while events and forces and men are playing the symphonic poem of history. The Sabbath is the heartbeat of history. The holidays are the natural pauses of reflection within the year; their dates follow the calendar, and the calendar follows the seasons.

· THE JEWISH CALENDAR

On the fifteenth day of the *seventh month* when ye have *gathered in* the fruits of the land ye shall keep the feast of the Lord (Lev. 23:39).

Choosing this biblical verse as our point of departure, we discover two facts. The Jews counted the months, from the first one in Spring, which was the date of their deliverance from Egyptian bondage, right through the year. To count the months they had to follow the phases of the moon, but their holidays had to coincide with the seasons of sowing and harvesting as well, so they had to be adjusted to the cycle of the sun. The Jewish calendar is a lunar calendar adjusted to the sun year.

In ancient days this adjustment was a simple matter, because every new month was officially pronounced by the high court in Jerusalem. People who had seen the first emerging sickle of the new moon appeared before the court as witnesses; they were examined, and upon their evidence the court declared the first day of the new month. Messengers were then sent throughout the land to give the people the news. Depending on the moon, or on the arrival of the witnesses, a month might have 29 or 30 days; the people had to know exactly, for the date of the holidays depended on it. But the messengers could only cover the territory of Palestine in the period between the first of the month and the holidays. The Jews in the diaspora were never quite certain about the length of the preceding month. To be sure that they were observing the holiday on the appointed date, they celebrated for two days. Thus it came that holy days are observed for one day in Israel and for two days among traditional Jews throughout the world.

If Spring was slow in coming and the grain not yet ripe, the high court would declare a leap year, which meant adding one complete month. Thus the moon year was adjusted to the cycle of the seasons by actual observation of nature itself. An additional check through astronomical calculations afforded balance.

The problem of the calendar arose with the end of the patriarchate in Palestine. A permanent calendar had to be worked out for all times. This was the work of Hillel II (c. 350), who did an excellent job, for his calendar still works to perfection. His task was not easy; he had to adjust the moon year to the sun year. The moon year has 354 days, the sun year has 365 days, which means an annual difference of eleven days. Then he had to see to it that certain holy days would not fall on certain weekdays; the Day of Atonement, for example, was not to fall on Friday or on Sunday. It is a day of fasting and complete work prohibition, and would have interfered with the preparations for the Sabbath, or the Sabbath would interfere with the preparations for the fast. To achieve the proper balance, the Jewish calendar includes seven leap years in 19 years. Each leap year has one additional month, so sun year and moon year are equalized over a period of 19 years:

19 *sun* years of 365 days		6935 days
19 *moon* years of 354 days	6726 days	
add 7 leap months of 30 days	210 days	
Total	6936 days	6935 days

Name and length of month	Begins between	Holy Days Hbr. Date	Name	Character	Biblical source
TISHRI 30 days	Sept. 6-Oct. 4	1	Rosh Hashanah–New Year	major	Lev. 23:23-25
		2	Rosh Hashanah †	major	
		3	Fast of Gedaliah ‡		II Kings 25:22-25 Zach. 7:5; 8:19
		4-9	Days of Penitence (includes entire period from Tishri 1 through 10)		
		10	Yom Kippur–Day of Atonement	major	Lev. 23:33-36
		15	Sukkot, Tabernacles	major	Lev. 23:33-36 Deut. 16:13-17
		16	Sukkot *	major	
		17	Sukkot	intermediate	
		18	Sukkot	intermediate	
		19	Sukkot	intermediate	
		20	Sukkot	intermediate	
		21	Sukkot	intermediate	
		22	Sh'mini Atzeret– Concluding holy day	major	
		23	Simhat Torah– * Festival concluding Torah cycle of the year	major	
MARHESHVAN 29 or 30 days	Oct. 5-Nov. 4			minor	
KISLEV 29 or 30 days	Nov. 5-Dec. 3	25	Hanukah		none (Apocrypha: Maccabees)
		26	Hanukah		
		27	Hanukah		
		28	Hanukah		
		29	Hanukah		
		(30)	Hanukah		
TEBET 29 days	Dec. 5-Jan. 2	1	Hanukah		
		2	Hanukah		
		(3	Hanukah) §		

		18 Fast Day ‡		none (Talmud)
SHEBAT 30 days	Jan. 3-Feb. 2	15 Arbor Day–Planting season	minor	
ADAR I (Leap Y. only) 30 days	Feb. 1-Feb. 11			
ADAR (Adar II; L.Y.) ‖ 29 days	Feb. 1-Mar. 13	13 Fast of Esther ‡	minor	Book of Esther
		14 Purim	minor	Book of Esther
NISSAN 30 days	Mar. 13-Apr. 11	15 Passover (Pessach) –Exodus from Egypt *	major	Exod. 12; Lev. 23:4-8
		16 Passover *	major	Deut. 16:1-8
		17 Passover	intermediate	
		18 Passover	intermediate	
		19 Passover	intermediate	
		20 Passover	intermediate	
		21 Passover	major	
		22 Passover *	major	
IYAR 29 days	Apr. 12-May 11			
SIVAN 30 days	May 11-June 9	6 Shabuot–Giving of Ten Commandments	major	Exod. 19-20; Lev. 23:15-21; Deut. 16:9-12
		7 Shabuot *		
TAMMUZ 29 days	June 10-July 9	17 Fast Day–‡ Conquest of Jerusalem	major	Zach. 7:5; 8:19
AB 30 days	July 9-Aug. 7	9 Fast Day–Destruction of Temple ‡	major	Jer. 52
ELUL 29 days	Aug. 8-Sept. 6			

* These days are not observed in Israel and are not obligatory for Reform Jews. Their observance is optional for Conservative Jews.

† This day is observed in Israel but not obligatory for Reform Jews.

‡ Fast Days are not obligatory for Reform Jews.

§ The sixth, seventh and eighth days of Hanukah can fall on the 30th of Kislev and the first and second of Tebet; or on the first, second, and third of Tebet, depending on the length of the Month of Kislev. Scripture counts the months from Nissan, month of the Exodus which established the nation; the usual count is from Tishri, as will be explained.

‖ This includes the beginning of Adar in regular years.

Within the 19 sun years there are a number of leap years too. These, and other slight differences, were taken care of by varying the length of the years. Some regular Jewish years have 354 days, some have 353 days, and some have 355 days. Leap years have 30 days more than these. In that way all the differences between sun years and moon years are equalized, and the holy days fall on the right days of the week as well.

The date of a Jewish holy day might move back and forth within a span of 30 days of the sun year, but no more. For example, the first day of Passover moves as follows: April 12; April 1; now comes a leap year, placing it on April 19; April 9; March 28; now comes a leap year: April 17, and so forth.

The dates of holy days nowadays are exactly fixed, but Jews in the diaspora still observe two days where Israelis observe only one. There is actually no reason for the observance of a second day, since we know the exact date, and so Reform Judaism has eliminated the observance of the second days, while others have retained it in deference to tradition and custom. Since 1969 its observance is left to congregational option in Conservatism.

The years are counted from the "creation of the world." Using the genealogy in Genesis, simple addition provides the total of years since Adam. In writing, the thousands may sometimes be omitted. The plaque commemorating the death of the martyrs in Worms read 856, and means 4856, or 1096. The list on pp. 174-75 may help us to understand the Jewish calendar. It shows the Hebrew months and their length, the holy days observed in them, and the date of the month when they begin. It gives the character of the holy day, which shall be explained in detail, and its biblical source. It also shows the relationship of the Jewish months to the general calendar.

THE SABBATH

Remember the Sabbath Day to hallow it (Exod. 20:8).
Observe the Sabbath Day to hallow it (Deut. 5:12).

The Sabbath is a Semitic invention which grew naturally from observation of nature as the farmer divided the cycle of the moon into its four phases. Close concern with the phenomena of the sky was an early Semitic trait. The Jews have given the Sabbath its twofold spiritual meaning. It is a day of universal rest, making real the principle of universal equality of master and slave, employer and employee, lord and servant. It is furthermore a time of spiritual recreation and restoration.[1] *Remember* the Sabbath, Torah says, remember its message for daily living: God is the Creator of the universe, all creation is the work of

---

[1] See page 23 regarding the two meanings in the Ten Commandments.

His hands and dear to Him; all humanity are His children. Your task is to act as steward of God's creation and as brother to every child of God. *Observe* the Sabbath, the Torah adds, lay down thy work at the behest of thy divine Employer, the Owner of all; rest thy body and revive thy spirit. "Remember and Observe were spoken in one divine breath," [2] the rabbis once stated; the first was a special appeal to Israel as a *spiritual function* by which Israel would teach the world, the second a call to the entire world demanding *social action* (Pesikta R. 23). The two cannot be separated.

The Sabbath makes humanity human; Judaism considers it the holiest of days. Whether we observe it on its original day, Saturday, as does Judaism, or on Sunday, as do Christians, or on Friday in the fashion of Islam, the Sabbath is so fully part of our lives that we take it for granted and fail to consider the horror that would descend on us were it ever abolished. As I write this book I remember it well, for I had to spend time in one of Hitler's concentration camps, where there was no Sabbath, no day of rest, no day to look forward to for relief and a quiet breath. The toil was endless, the future hopeless; deep depression descended on the imprisoned sufferers. Relief could be found only in retreat to dullness of mind; soon we all ceased to think in human terms, and became merely vegetating beasts of burden, no longer living. Only in this way could the unendurable be endured, without the mind cracking. We had ceased to be human, and so the world had ceased to be divine creation. Once this condition had been universal. From this stupor Judaism rescued the world by giving it the Sabbath. To have given the Sabbath to mankind is one of Israel's greatest distinctions; all other social legislation is based on it. All men had to be recognized as human beings before efforts could be made to improve their lot. This is the reason why the Sabbath is the only holy day enjoined in the Ten Commandments; its significance has been world-shaking, its establishment one of the most revolutionary steps toward human progress.

To the Jews, the Sabbath has been the supreme comforter in trouble. No wonder they counted the days of the week in their relation to it: first of the Sabbath, second of the Sabbath, and so on. It became symbolic of the covenant between God and Israel (Exod. 31:12-17); its desecration was equal to a denial of God Himself (Num. 15:32-36).[3] Prophets emphasized that without social justice during the week, Sabbath was without meaning (Isa. 1:13-14); yet observed in its twofold challenge, it guarantees Israel's eternity and binds the people together in indestructible unity (Isa. 56:1-7, Jer. 17:21-27). Restoration of the Sabbath in purity

---

[2] Talmud Shebuot 20b; Rosh Hashanah 27a.
[3] The punishment for the violator of the Sabbath was the same as that of the blasphemer; see Leviticus 24:10-24.

was the prime step in Nehemiah's work of religious and physical restoration (Neh. 13:15-22); the Rabbis of old remarked sagely: "As Israel has kept the Sabbath so did the Sabbath keep Israel alive." The Sabbath provided even the most downcast with a "taste of the world to come"; it gave him strength and courage.

Work Prohibition

Rest excludes work, and the term had to be defined; if left to individual interpretation, the master might decide that the tasks of his servant were not work. This must not be, for all must be treated alike. Written Torah states that "God rested from all His work (Gen. 2:2)," but man cannot rest from every last bit of work and survive. Oral Torah reasoned that the world is God's sanctuary and took its clue from that (see Isa. 66:1). All work once connected with the sanctuary Israel built for God, the Tabernacle in the desert, shall cease. Israel's rest will then correspond to God's rest; both rested from all tasks linked to the making of the sanctuary; God in His world, Israel in the Tabernacle. The work on the Tabernacle was performed by divine ordinance; rest from it, in all its forms, is then to be regarded as divinely ordained. According to the Mishnah (Shabbat), this led to the prohibition of 39 basic kinds of work:

1) The growing and preparation of food: plowing, sowing, harvesting, and so forth; baking, cooking, broiling; a total of eleven prohibitions.
2) Clothing: shearing, washing, bleaching, spinning, weaving, sowing, and similar work; a total of thirteen prohibitions.
3) Leather work and writing: catching of animals, slaughter, skinning, tanning, preparation of furs, preparation of parchment, writing, erasing, and so on; a total of nine prohibitions.
4) Shelter: building, demolition for the purpose of rebuilding; two prohibitions.
5) Fire: kindling and extinguishing; two prohibitions.
6) Work completion: the final hammer stroke and touch; one prohibition.
7) Transportation: Moving objects from one private domain to another, or into public domain, or within public domain, or from public to private domain; one prohibition.

To these basic prohibitions, secondary ones were added by the rabbis to prevent preparation for future work, for this would cancel out the idea of Sabbath rest. The handling of tools, of the implements of work, and of raw materials was prohibited. The intent is basic. Physical effort as such does not constitute labor, regardless of how strenuous it may be; creative effort *is* work, regardless how small the physical effort involved. A city surrounded by a wall may constitute a single dwelling in this sense. All people are moving within the same confines, but walking 2000 cubits (about 3/4th of a mile) beyond a city is travel, and is prohibited. The use of vehicles violates the rest of animals, the use of the automobile or the turning on of electricity calls for the creative act of producing fire, and these actions are prohibited according to the traditional interpretation of the law.

Under those conditions rest was complete, and the spirit took over. But the Sabbath was not a day of gloom and of joyless worship; it had no Puritan harshness. Of festivals the Talmud states: "Half is for God, half is for you (Betza 15 b)." Food, drink, song, the afternoon nap, and the leisurely walk in the fields or on river banks are all part of the traditional Sabbath. Many a boy would find his girl during the strolls young people took in the afternoon of the day; consummation of married union was part of the holy day's joys.

Modern life and conditions have changed Sabbath observance; liberal interpretation has modified its laws for liberal Jews; the restlessness of our age and lack of direction of the people have brought about an erosion in its observance. He who has not fully tasted it will never know how much he has lost; and those who have brushed it aside in hasty living have denied themselves one of the greatest of joys in human life.

Traditional Sabbath Observance

The Jewish Day starts with the night preceding it. "It was evening and it was morning" says Scripture (Gen. 1), putting the night before the day. This is a logical arrangement for the farmer and the artisan. Their day ends when night falls; as they rest, their thoughts turn to the morrow and its duties. The Sabbath and all holy days begin on the preceding evening; Friday night is one of the highlights of the week; it is Sabbath.

Friday

Piety added the last daylight hours of the day to the Sabbath; hours of preparation preceded it. Bathing, preparing of hair, body, and clothes were ordained. The house shines, and the white tablecloth, carefully guarded during the week, covers the table. The candlesticks gleam, and the goblet and decanter of wine stand next to father's plate. Two twisted loaves of bread are set next to the wine. This double portion is a reminder of the twofold measure of Manna given to Israel in the desert to last through the Sabbath; the loaf is called "Hallah," and the two are covered by an embroidered cloth, as dew once covered the Manna.

While the sun was still high the food was prepared. Fish have been a traditional dish. Cut in slices, the meat was removed without cutting the skin, then it was chopped up, mixed with bread and spices, and replaced in the fish; the fish was "filled." *Gefillte Fish* has remained a favorite and famous Jewish dish, although prepared more simply today in form of fish balls. With fish went meat. A Jew might starve throughout the week, but the Sabbath meals had splendour. He was to have three during the day, and they were the meals of a king.

As the shadows lengthened, the women took their main dish for the day to the baker, where it would cook overnight in his great oven, or they might place it in their own oven. The ingredients were raw: meat, beans or barley, and water. Tomorrow it would be perfect, heavy, tasty, and hot. It was called *Shalet* or *Cholent*, from the French word "chaud," which means hot. Heinrich Heine, the German poet who forsook his Jewish faith but never lost his romantic love for Judaism, has called the Shalet by the term used by another German poet, Schiller, as epitome of divine joy. Heine called it "Daughter of Elysium." He was not far wrong.

Dusk is falling; all is ready; it is the moment to relax. I have seen people in the poorest sections of Jerusalem at this hour, their houses gleaming, their faces radiant, their children around them, and the greeting on their lips: Shabbat Shalom, the peace of the Sabbath be with you. Father then gives the final reminder: Now kindle the Sabbath lights. Then he goes to worship.

Mother, mistress of the home, lights the candles. There are at least two, a double portion of light compared to the one small portion of the week. Spreading her hands, she speaks the blessing: "Blessed art Thou, O Lord our God, King of the world, Who hast sanctified us by Thy commandments and commanded us to kindle the Sabbath light." She remains standing in front of the lights; in silent meditation she asks God's blessing upon her home, her husband, her children and her dear ones. The Sabbath has arrived.

The men go to worship. Psalms open the devotions as the Sabbath is welcomed: "Come let us sing unto the Lord . . . (Ps. 95)." Among the mystics of Palestine there was a custom of going out into the fields in solemn procession to welcome the Sabbath Bride as she entered the town. Solomon Alkabez, friend of Joseph Karo and member of the Safed circle of mystics, put it in poetic form, and it became one of the most popular hymns of the synagogue.

Come my friend the Bride to meet;
the Sabbath in person we will greet.

As the hymn reached its last verse, it was the custom, in the synagogue where I worshipped as a child, for the whole congregation to turn around and face the door, as if the Sabbath were physically coming.

Come then in peace, crown of thy spouse,
come also in joy to jubilant praise,
amidst thy faithful, God's very own folk
come ye, O Bride, come ye, O Bride.

With a courtly bow the congregation received her. The Sabbath had
come.

Now the Sabbath Psalm is sung; it is Psalm 92. It starts with a hymn
of thanksgiving: Give thanks unto the Lord with all the instruments of
the orchestra, with all the emotions welling up in the hearts of all men,
for God's works and thoughts are great and deep. Then the Psalm turns
to reflection. Man cannot understand God fully. Wickedness and injustice succeed and flourish; how can that be? The Sabbath gives the
answer. The victory of evil is but for a moment; the work of evildoers
has no future, but the righteous, firmly planted in the house of the Lord,
will flourish forever, to declare "that the Lord is upright, my Rock, there
is no flaw in Him." In the shelter of the Sabbath the Jew reviews life
in general and his own life in particular; in God he has found his life
to be good.

The evening prayer follows; then the Kiddush, the blessing over the
wine, is pronounced. This is the blessing to be spoken at home, but
once there were many wayfarers who had no home and were fed in
the side room of the synagogue; for them the blessing was given at this
time, and it has remained.

The father returns from the
synagogue and blesses the
children of the family.

The men return home, and according to legend two angels go with them, a good one and a destructive one. If the home is filled with Sabbath spirit the good angel blesses: May it be thus next week also. But if there is no Sabbath spirit, the destructive angel has his say: May it be likewise next week. And always the other angel, against his will, has to respond Amen, so be it.[4] Thus did the rabbis recognize the psychological significance of habit which breeds habit for better or for worse. The family welcomes the angels: Peace be with you; may your coming, your blessing, and your going be unto peace. Then the parents lay their hands upon their children in blessing. To the boys they say as Jacob had taught: God make thee like Ephraim and Manasseh (Gen. 49:20). The girls are blessed with the words: God make thee like Sarah, Rebecca, Rachel and Leah. Then they continue blessing all of the children: The Lord bless thee and keep thee. The Lord make His face to shine upon thee and be gracious unto thee. The Lord lift up His face upon thee and give thee peace (Num. 6:24-26). As the father looks around, he recognizes the source of all his blessings, of his home, his children, his Sabbath table; it is his wife. Without her there would be only emptiness, but through her he is rich. In her honor, he sings the verses of Proverbs (31:10-31): A woman of valor. "The heart of her husband trusteth in her . . . she does him good . . . all the days of her life . . . many daughters have done valiantly, but thou doest excel them all . . . a woman that feareth the Lord she shall be praised."

The family washes the hands and gathers around the wine and bread on the table. These two are the most perfect gifts of food and drink, a blend of God's bounty and man's ingenuity. They are the most perfect symbols for giving thanks.[5] The father raises the cup. (Cup, *kos*, derives from the word *kosas*, that which is measured out by God—man's destiny.) He prays that it may be a cup of salvation. He speaks the Kiddush, pronouncing the Sanctification of the Sabbath. He relates the Scriptural story of the First Sabbath, when "the heaven and the earth were finished . . . and when God rested from all His work . . . and blessed (Gen. 1:31; 2:3)." He blesses God for the wine: "Blessed art Thou O Lord . . . who createst the fruit of the vine." He gives thanks to God, "Who hast sanctified us by Thy commandments and hast been pleased with us; for in love and favor Thou hast given us Thy holy Sabbath as a heritage in remembrance of the work of creation. . . ." Father drinks from the cup and passes it to the members of his family. Then he offers thanks for

---

[4] Talmud Shabbat 119b.

[5] This explanation is given by Franz Rosenzweig in his "Star of Redemption." Franz Rosenzweig: *Der Stern der Erlösung*, © 1930 by J. Kaufmann Verlag, Frankfurt am Main, Part III, p. 65.

the bread, breaks it, and passes a portion to each member of his house-hold. The meal begins.

Even the poorest is bidden to have Sabbath lights and Sabbath bread. He may have to beg for it, to borrow for it, to starve for it during the week, but the Sabbath must be honored. There is only one exception. If, in providing for the Sabbath, he would lose his human dignity, the rabbis say: Treat thy Sabbath as a weekday rather than depending on others in thy need (Shabbat 118).

The meal is completed, Sabbath hymns are sung, the Torah portion of the week may be discussed, grace is offered, and then the family retires.

In our days, a late Friday night service has been introduced in many congregations. It wishes to serve those who cannot come in the morning on the next day, nor are able to attend earlier services on Friday. It is a good institution and is followed by a congregational fellowship hour with blessings, food, and song. But it is at best a pale replica of the tradi-tional Friday evening in Synagogue and home, offered to a Jewish com-munity where many have lost the capacity to provide a true home celebration.

Sabbath day

Worship fills the morning; the Torah is read, a different portion every week. The whole family attends worship. As the family returns home, blessing is again recited over the cup of wine, and with it the fourth commandment, the ordination of the Sabbath, is repeated. After a brief repast, the family members step out to visit friends or the sick, the mourners, and the newly wed. Early afternoon brings the main meal with the Shalet, table hymns, and grace. An afternoon nap becomes a "delight," as the rabbis once stated it. This is typical of the earthiness of Judaism, its realism, its ability to give enjoyment a spiritual char-acter. Judaism has never been ascetic; it hallowed decent earthly pleas-ures, and thereby survived.

The sun begins to set. Afternoon prayers are recited in the synagogue, then the family takes its walk. Returning home just before dusk, it gathers once more for the third meal. Jewish mysticism developed this hour into a time of mystical union. As night shadows slowly rose, disciples used to listen to their rabbi as he pierced into the darkness of the coming night and into visions of eternity.

Three stars in the sky proclaim the end of the day. Once again the people assemble for worship, and in Psalms 144 and 67 they express their faith and their hope.

> Blessed be the Lord my Rock, who traineth my hand for the struggle and my fingers for the battle (of life).

Thou art my lovingkindness and my fortress . . .
O God be gracious unto us and bless us,
cause Thy face to shine upon us,
that Thy way be known upon the earth
Thy saving power among all nations.

After the evening prayer has been completed a last farewell is offered to the Sabbath. Light and the cup which have welcomed the day gently usher it out. This is Habdalah, prayer of Separation. The cup is filled, and a twisted candle, like a torch, is lighted. This is the beginning of the first day of the week when light was created; God, giver of light, therefore, is blessed. A box of spices, often with the shape of a tower, for God is the Tower of Salvation, is also used. It offers a last sniff of the sweet smell of the Sabbath. May it accompany all into the week.

The prayer of Habdalah begins with words of confidence:

Behold God is my salvation; I will trust and have no fear;
For God is my strength and song and He is become my salvation . . . (Isa. 12:2-3).

I lift the cup of salvation and call upon the Name of the Lord (Ps. 116:13).
Blessed art Thou, O Lord . . . who createst the fruit of the vine.
Blessed art Thou, O Lord . . . who createst all kinds of spices.

As the reader waits, the spice box is passed among the members, giving them their last sweet breath of the Sabbath.
From the hand of the child who has held the candle the reader takes it and speaks:

Blessed art Thou, O Lord . . . who createst the illumination of fire.

Slowly the reader passes his hands beneath the flame, watching the play of lights and shadows, for a blessing must always lead to practical use. Then he takes up the cup again and completes the blessing:

Blessed art Thou, O Lord our God . . . who didst make distinction between holy and not-sacred; . . . between the seventh day and the six days of work. Blessed art Thou, O Lord, who makest distinction between holy and not-sacred.

The candle is extinguished in a drop of wine poured from the cup. The wine is consumed, and the Sabbath has ended. The people who have greeted each other on Friday evening with "good Shabbos" now wish each other "good Woch," a good week. It is an ancient Yiddish greeting.

Once a special Sabbath Lamp used to grace every home. It hung from the ceiling and could be raised and lowered. In its star-shaped bowl oil was poured on Friday evening to give light during the Sabbath meal. At the end of the Sabbath the lamp was raised up again to the ceiling

Sabbath lamp and Habdalah objects: cup, spice box in form of a tower, candle, and plate into which wine is poured to extinguish candle.

for another week, and the medieval Jew used to say: "As the lamp comes down, sorrow goes up to vanish; as the lamp goes up again, sorrow comes down once more." But as the lamp went up the Jew began to count: "This is the first day toward the next Sabbath." It was this hope which upheld him, this forward look which kept him alive and proud.

THE DAYS OF AWE: HIGH HOLY DAYS

Of Days and Seasons and Years

The Jewish day ends with the beginning of the night. At that moment, a new day of the calendar starts, following the way of life of farmers and workers. Their day is done when their work is done. Then they review their accomplishments, relax, and make plans for the next morning. The same is true of the Jewish year. When the farmer has gathered in his harvest his year comes to its end; that is in the fall, and then a new year starts for him. That is the reason why Judaism observes New Year in autumn. It links the date with the creation of the world, which is said to have taken place at this time. Actually, we may say that the farmer, who has completed the chores of the summer, turns his creative thought toward the year to come. In this sense this is a moment of creation.

After his crop is in, he takes stock of his achievements and failures; he devises new plans to remedy errors he may have made. Judaism has said: you must also have a spiritual stocktaking; how much goodness have you sown, or have you failed? And if you have failed, how are you going to improve yourself and your work? The Jewish New Year's Season became a period of spiritual accounting; it calls for an evaluation of our life and work before God. It is a time of repentance. The first ten days of the New Year, including Rosh Hashanah and Yom Kippur, New Year's Day and Day of Atonement, are Days of Awe. After these days are over, there comes Sukkot, Feast of Tabernacles, a time of thanksgiving for the good harvest. First, however, we must repent, "do teshubah." Teshubah is the Hebrew term for repentance; literally it means "return," return to God and the right way of life.

The Ways of Teshubah

Maimonides explains some of its ways in Mishneh Torah:

This is the way of Teshubah. The sinner parts from his sins, banning them from his thoughts and pledging in his heart never to commit them again. . . . Everyone must make spoken confession, he must speak out, revealing his innermost feelings in tearful prayer to God; he must be sincere about it. He must improve in charity, showing kindness to others to the very limit of his ability and means. . . . Let him confess openly . . . but only his transgressions against his fellow man, his sins against God he need not reveal to others (Teshubah II).

Let him, above all, examine himself regarding those sins which we easily rationalize away. Maimonides mentions five of them:

1) He who accepts an invitation to dinner from a host who has not enough to feed his own family commits a sin; but he rationalizes that, after all, he was invited.

2) He who uses an object given him as bond for a poor man's loan commits a sin; but he likes to believe that use never harms a tool.

3) He who looks with desire at another's wife, excusing himself that he has, after all, not touched her; he is committing a sin.

4) He who tries to rise to honor by defaming his neighbor commits a sin; but he consoles his conscience by claiming that the other was not around to hear it, and that he was but using him as frame of comparison to demonstrate his own achievements. It is a sin.

5) He who holds the innocent in suspicion, becalming his inner voice of truth by claiming that "mere" suspicion is no injury. He has sinned.

Maimonides then adds five more items, habits which become traits of character and then are hard to throw off—we must beware of them: defamation of others, gossip, irascibility, evil thoughts, and bad company. He continues,

Do not think that teshubah is required only for grievous acts of commission, such as adultery, robbery or theft. We must equally examine ourselves and cast away evil traits of character: wrath, hatred, envy, cynicism, greed for wealth, craving for honors, and similar ones. If we find them in us we must repent them; and this may be very hard indeed.[6]

Teshubah is renewal of heart expressed in action. Man may sin against God, but this is sin easily erased. In communion with the Allmerciful the penitent pours out his soul in utter privacy to Him and to Him alone; God, who knows the emotions of the heart, forgives. Sins against fellow-man are not so readily obliterated. God will forgive them only if man has first sought and obtained reconciliation with his neighbor. The sinner must spare no effort of appeasement, but the fellow to whom he appeals must be considerate too, and may not cruelly turn down the earnest plea for forgiveness. Conduct, from then on, is the final proof of teshubah; it alone brings ultimate pardon.

Days of Repentance: Preparation

Man should repent every day, for God is always near—and so is the day of death. The daily Amidah contains the plea: "Forgive us, O our Father, for we have sinned." The Days of Awe, however, emphasize the task of teshubah to the exclusion of everything else.

It begins with the month of Elul. Every day, at the end of public worship, the ram's horn, the "shofar," is sounded, to call man, to awaken him, to admonish him, and lead him to teshubah. The week before the New Year's Day intensifies the preparation. Rising before dawn, the congregation joins in special prayers while the stars still dot the sky, and continues them until sunrise, the hour of morning worship. It approaches God in deep humility. Not by our merits do we appear before Him, for all men are sinners; we come to Him because of His great mercy, for "He, the Lord is merciful and gracious, long suffering, abundant in goodness and truth; keeping mercy unto the thousandth generation, forgiving iniquity, transgression and sin, acquitting the sinners (Exod. 34: 6-7)." This appeal stands in the center of all pleas, and around it poets have woven prayers of great beauty and deep feeling. Thus prepared, the Jew celebrates the first of the great Days of Awe, Rosh Hashanah, the New Year's Day.

---

[6] See also pp. 148 ff.

Rosh Hashanah

In the seventh month, in the first day of the month, shall be a solemn rest unto you, a memorial proclaimed with the blast of horns, a holy convocation. Ye shall do no manner of servile work. (Lev. 23:24, 25).

Before we may enter the act of repentance, we must be reminded that it is God before Whom we repent, Whose standards we have failed to apply as yardsticks in life. Rosh Hashanah is the reminder. Sin is hardly mentioned, confession not yet heard; only the greatness of God is rehearsed, His love and mercy held out to us. Affirmation of God is the theme of Rosh Hashanah.

The eve

The service is of utter simplicity, a regular evening service followed by the kiddush. At home, the table is set, the children are blessed, kiddush recited, bread is broken. The loaf of bread is often shaped in the form of a wheel, a reminder, that "a wheel goes through the world"; those who are on top now may find themselves at the bottom a year hence. May they always be faithful stewards of the earthly goods they enjoy at the hand of God. Those who eat their bread in tears this year may enjoy it in ease a year from now. May they never lose faith in Him, the source of man's destiny. The hope that the year be sweet is expressed symbolically as bread and sweet apple are dipped in honey and then passed to the members around the table, with the prayer: "May it be Thy will, O God, to renew the year unto us as a good year, full of sweetness." The meal ends early as grace is recited; and the family retires with the wish extended to all friends in synagogue and home: "May you be inscribed by God unto a good year."

The day

The synagogue is draped in white, color of purity. The mantles of the Torah scrolls, the curtain of the ark, the cover of the pulpit, all are white. In some congregations all men wear the white robes in which they will some day be buried. These are reminders of death, but also of life beyond death and life on earth as well, when equality will rule and all men be dressed alike in the garments of purity and of love. They are symbols of God's future kingdom on earth. This longing for the Kingdom is one of the basic themes of the high holy days. Every Amidah speaks of it:

Thus, Lord our God, implant the awe of Thee in all Thy works, reverence for Thee in all of Thine creation. That all Thy works may fear Thee and all creatures bow to Thee. May they all form one communion to do Thy will with a perfect heart; even as we know, O Lord our God, that dominion is Thine,

strength is in Thy hand, might in Thy right hand, and that Thy Name inspires awe in all that Thou hast created . . .

Therefore, O Lord our God, grant honor unto Thy people, good reputation to
them that revere Thee, hope to them that seek Thee, confidence to them that
wait for Thee; joy to Thy land, gladness to Thy city, speedily in our days.
Then may the just see and be happy, the upright exult, the pious rejoice in
song; may iniquity close her mouth and all wickedness be consumed like smoke
when Thou makest the rule of arrogance to pass from the earth. Mayest Thou,
then, O Lord, rule over all Thy works as it is written in Thy holy words: The
Lord shall reign for ever, thy God O Zion from generation to generation,
Hallelujah.

The morning prayer of Rosh Hashanah follows the regular pattern,
but it is embellished with special poetry. As the Amidah is concluded,
a special petition is offered to "Our Father our King." In the form of a
litany, it affirms that we have no king but Him, and pleads for a good
year, a year free from war, from sickness, from evil, a year of forgiveness
and peaceful living. Then the Torah is read to the people. It is the story
of Abraham who was ready to sacrifice his own son in obedience to a
divine command. But God does not want sacrifices which diminish human
life and extinguish it, He rather calls us to those sacrifices which will
enrich life by adding to it new dimensions of service.

Now the Shofar is sounded. It is a ram's horn, with a weird, primitive
sound. This is the natural voice of the horn, produced without concern
for key and harmony, the very voice of nature and creation. The shofar
was the original instrument in the desert; its signals called the people

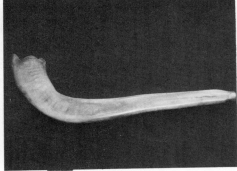

Yemenite Jew with earlocks, wearing a
Tallit, sounding the Shofar at Mount
Zion, Jerusalem.

Shofar, the ram's horn, which is sounded on the New Year and at the very
end of the Day of Atonement.

together when they were to hear the word of God. It was blown at Sinai, as the Bible reports, to accompany God's voice as He revealed the Ten Commandments.

Three different types of blast pour forth from it when it speaks during the Rosh Hashanah service: *Tekiah*—long and straight; *Shebarim*—three times broken; *Teruah*—whimpering sound of nine broken notes; then follows Tekiah again.

In desert days of wandering, Tekiah called the people to attention; Shebarim and Teruah were the signals to break camp and to prepare for departure; Tekiah again was the signal to march in a new direction.[7] Similarly, Tekiah is the signal awakening the slumberer from the complacency of daily routine living; Shebarim commands to break with the past in a spirit of broken-hearted sorrow; Teruah symbolizes the response of a penitent people, weeping at their sins; and the final Tekiah is the triumphant affirmation of victory over sin and temptation, the resolve to move in a new direction along the right road.

And now, aroused by these sounds, the congregation is ready to proclaim God in the fullness of His power. The Mussaf Amidah has three special benedictions only used on Rosh Hashanah: God is affirmed as *King* of the universe; He is praised as supreme *Judge*, Who remembers all His children for good; and He is glorified as the world's *Redeemer*, sounding the *shofar* of redemption. After each benediction the shofar is sounded in His honor.

The concept of Rosh Hashanah is universalistic. It is conceived as judgement day for all the world. A poem of the liturgy expresses this concept in majestic beauty and simple grandeur. It was composed by Calonymus ben Meshullam of Mainz, scion of the family called by the German emperor to the Rhenish city.[8]

Let us speak of the great holiness of the day, for indeed it is a day of awe and dread. On it Thy Kingdom is exalted, Thy throne established in mercy, and Thou sittest upon it in truth. In truth Thou art judge, accuser, and all-knowing witness. Thou writest and sealest, recordest and numberest. Thou rememberest all that we forgot. Thou openest the Book of Remembrances, and each deed speaks out by itself, for it is sealed by each man's own hand. A great shofar is sounded; a still, small voice is heard. The angels stand in fear; panic and trembling seize hold of them and they cry out: "See the Day of Judgement," as the host of heaven themselves are arraigned in judgement; for in Thy sight not even they are pure. And all that live Thou makest pass before Thee as a flock of sheep. As the shepherd counts his flock, making each

---

[7] An explanation given by Samson Raphael Hirsch in his "Chorev," *Versuche über Jisroel's Pflichten,* (Altona: 1837), pp. 182 ff.

[8] The story can be found on p. 153.

pass beneath his staff, so doest Thou record and number, taking account of every living soul, appointing a limit to every creature's scope, setting down his destiny.

On Rosh Hashanah the sentence is inscribed, on Yom Kippur it is sealed: how many shall pass away and how many shall be born; who shall live and who shall die; who shall complete the span of man's life and who shall not complete it; who shall perish by fire and who by water; who by the sword and who by wild beasts; who by hunger and who by thirst; who by quake and who by plague; who shall have rest and who shall go wandering; who shall be serene and who shall be distraught; who shall have ease and who shall be afflicted, who shall be rich and who shall be poor; who shall be brought low and who shall be raised up.

But Repentance, and Prayer, and Works of Goodness annul every severe decree. For thus is Thy Name and thus is Thy glory, that Thou art slow to anger, easy to appease. Thou desirest not the death of the guilty, rather that he turn from his way and live. To the very day of his death Thou waitest for him. If he returns Thou wilt right away receive him. In truth Thou art their Creator, Thou knowest their urges, that they are but flesh and blood. After all, man's origin is dust and his end is dust. He earns his bread at the hazard of his life. He is like clay, easily broken, like the grass that withereth, like the shadow swiftly passing, like the cloud floating by, like the wind rushing along, like the dust blown away and like a dream that vanishes. But Thou art King, the Living, Everlasting God.

This hymn has had an interesting history. It was taken over by the Church and adapted to form one of the great pieces of liturgical poetry: Dies Irae.[9]

This day of wrath . . . as dread grips us, for the Judge is come and come again . . . to judge the living and the dead . . . and the trumpet is sounded . . . Death and nature are in consternation as all creatures appear before the throne. The written book will be presented in which everything is contained, that all the world be judged. The Judge will be seated, every hidden fact will appear, nothing will remain veiled. . .

Yet in the Rosh Hashanah liturgy the "day of wrath" becomes "a day of mercy," for He who made man knows his weaknesses and understands and pardons.

The afternoon

People are called out to the banks of rivers and streams. Watching the waves hurrying down to the sea, they recite the last verses from the Book of Micah: "And Thou wilt cast their sins into the depths of the

---

[9] The relationship was suggested in an article by Professor Eric Werner, of the Hebrew Union College, in *The Jews: Their History, Culture, and Religion*, 3rd ed., Louis Finkelstein, ed. (New York: Harper & Brothers, 1960).

sea (7:19)." It is probably a mediaeval German custom which found its place in Jewish observance. Jacob Grimm, the German historian, tells about it as he found it in Petrarch, who once saw crowds of people walk to the bank of the Rhine in the City of Cologne on St. John's Day. In silent prayer they strew herbs and flowers upon the waves, and later told the poet their reason. They hoped that, with these herbs, they were casting out all the misfortunes in store for them for the coming year; the waves would carry all their troubles to the sea.[10]

Thus have cultures and faiths influenced each other, giving and taking and accepting as their very own what others once had started.

Between Rosh Hashanah and Yom Kippur

One week elapses, making the entire penitential season one of ten days: two days of Rosh Hashanah, seven days between, one day of Yom Kippur. We call it the Ten Days of Penitence. This is the week of implementation. Not with good resolutions alone but with one full week of his new life behind him does the penitent approach God on Yom Kippur. During the week he rises early for penitential prayers. One day of fasting is included, officially to commemorate the assassination of Gedalia, a tragic event related in Jeremiah and the Book of Kings (Jer. 40; II Kings 25:22-25). Gedalia, royal governor of Babylonia in Judah and a faithful Jew, was murdered by his own confused countrymen, and with his death complete disaster broke. It may not have happened at this particular time of the year; the importance of a fast lies in its call to reflection, self-examination, and penitence. This fast quickens all of these attitudes and deepens the spirit of teshubah. As Yom Kippur arrives, the Jew is attuned to it.

Yom Kippur: Day of Atonement

Howbeit on the tenth day of this seventh month is the day of atonement; there shall be a holy convocation unto you, and ye shall afflict your souls. . . . And ye shall do no manner of work in that same day; for it is a day of atonement, to make atonement for you before the Lord your God. . . . It shall be unto you a sabbath of solemn rest, and ye shall afflict your souls; in the ninth day of the month at even, from even to even, shall ye keep your sabbath (Lev. 23:27-32).

Sabbath of Sabbaths, this day is called. Neither food nor drink touch the lips of the Jew for its 24 hours. There is no other task for him but

---

[10] Jacob Grimm, *Deutsche Mythologie* (Göttingen: 1835), pp. 330 f. The date of Petrarch's visit to Cologne, according to Grimm, was before 1340.

teshubah. The day is spent away from the world, in the house of God, in the realm of prayer.

The eve

The preceding day is given over to preparation. As the afternoon advances a festive meal is eaten; it is considered as much a duty as the fast to follow. Jewish law wished to prevent anyone from being more pious in his own way than the command demanded; no one is permitted to fast for an additional day. The candles are lit, and, with them, a light to burn through the 24 hours of the fast. Parents bless their children with a special blessing. Friends greet each other: "Gemar hatima tova, may the seal affixed by God be on a good verdict for the year to come." In conformity with the call for castigation, people may wear soft non-leather shoes, which increase discomfort by their lack of support. The men may be dressed in the white robes of eternity. Memorial lights for the departed burn throughout the night and day.

The service starts with the Kol Nidre prayer, well known for the

Entry to the synagogue on Yom Kippur Eve.

haunting tune which expresses more than the words to which it is set. The words themselves are simply a declaration of dispensation from ascetic vows taken as special acts of piety and then neglected; the tune expresses all the longing of the soul for God, reflects on sorrow and hardship, and soars in its final passage to heights of triumph and of faith. Then follows the motto of the day: "The Lord spoke: I have forgiven according to thy word (Num. 14:20)." This forgiveness rests on man's full confession, which is offered after the regular evening prayer.

Our God and God of our Fathers, may our prayer come before Thee; hide not Thyself from our supplication, for we are not arrogant and stiffnecked to say before Thee, O Lord our God and God of our fathers, that we are righteous and have not sinned, for indeed, we *have* sinned.

This is the key to all repentance, to the long enumeration of sins which follows: we have sinned. Speaking in the plural, the members of the congregation are aware of their responsibility for one another, having failed to set the right example, to give the right guidance and support.

We have become guilty, we have committed treachery, we have robbed, we have spoken slanderously . . . we have gone astray, we have led astray . . . May it therefore by Thy will, O Lord our God and God of our fathers to pardon us all our sins, to forgive us all our iniquities and to grant atonement unto us for all our transgressions: for the sin, wherein we have sinned before Thee under compulsion and by free will; and for the sin, wherein we have sinned before Thee by hardness of heart . . .

And the recitation of trespasses stretches on; it will be repeated again on the morrow, first in silent meditation giving everyone the opportunity to add his own personal concerns, then in public utterance as expression of mutual responsibility.

The service ends, but some of the pious worshippers will remain to recite responsively the entire Book of Psalms.

The day

Solomon ibn Gabirol,[11] philosopher and poet, has given the motto to morning worship:

Judge of all the earth maintaining it through justice
life and mercy grant this poor folk
accept our morning prayer as our offering,
the morning offering once offered daily.

Who clothes Himself in love as a robe, Thou alone art exalted;
We have no works to plead for us, so remember the fathers sleeping at Hebron;

---

[11] We have discussed his life on p. 143.

May they arise in lasting memory before the Almighty,
instead of the morning offering once offered daily.

Who turnest to mercy to lead man to life
Turn to Thy folk in mercy, show them grace that they may live;
The seal of life impress upon their face; that it be there forever,
like the offering of the morning once offered daily.

Scripture reading is God's word to man. After Torah the prophet
speaks: God demands social action. This is the message of the fast:

to loose the fetters of wickedness, to undo the bands of the yoke,
and to let the oppressed go free, and that you break every yoke . . .
to deal thy bread to the hungry, and that thou bring the poor that are
cast out to thy house;
when thou seest the naked that thou cover him;
and that thou hide not thyself from thine own flesh (Isa. 58:5-7).

The Mussaf relates the story of the solemn service in the Temple, when
the high priest made confession for all, invoking the awesome Name of
God. And when the congregation heard the Name they fell on their
knees and prostrated themselves. At this moment in the service, the
congregation still fall on their knees. At any other time, this might be a
sign of humility or a symbol of the burden which presses the Jew. The
Jew must stand, stand up for God amidst the storms of the world and
the denial of His sovereignty. Only on Yom Kippur, removed from the
world and all its problems, experiencing in his heart a foretaste of a
future yet to be built, when all mankind will invoke His Name, only
then may he kneel down. At this moment it cannot possibly be mis-
construed: he kneels in adoration and proclaims: "Praised be His Name,
His glorious kingdom is for ever and ever." Thus past and present and
future are linked. The departed are remembered on Yom Kippur, that
their lives may be an inspiration to the living and their example guide
them to work for the future, when all mankind may acknowledge God
and Him alone.

Afternoon and conclusion

The story of Jonah is recited. He was the prophet who tried to
run away from his divinely given duty and could never escape. He was
also the prophet who had to learn the lesson that all men are God's
children.

Should I not have pity on Niniveh—says God—that great city in which there
are more than hundred twenty thousand people who cannot discern between
their right hand and their left hand, and much cattle too (Jonah 4:11)?

Contrastingly, the martyrs' lives and sacrifices are brought to mind, that we may learn the meaning of devotion.

As shadows lengthen, the concluding prayer, offered only on the Day of Atonement, begins. It is a last plea for mercy, a renewed expression of repentance.

Open unto us the gate, at the time that the gate is being closed,
as day has almost waned.
The day is waning, the sun is waning fast, let us enter Thy gates!

Once more prayer ascends:

Our Father our King we have sinned before Thee.
Our Father our King we have no King but Thee . . .
Our Father our King seal us in the Book of Life . . .
Our Father our King be gracious unto us and answer us; indeed we are lacking in merit; deal Thou with us in mercy and lovingkindness and save us.

The stars have risen in the sky, flames flicker in burnt out candles, as the Ark is opened. The congregation stands in awed silence. This is the moment of affirmation, of the vision of God's Kingdom. Slowly, word by word, the people recite in unison:

Shema Yisrael . . . Hear, O Israel, the Lord our God the Lord is One.
Barukh Shem . . . Blessed be His Name, the glory of His Kingdom is for ever.
Adonay . . . The Lord He is God!
The Shofar is sounded, Tekiah: onward into life!
The Ark is closed; the day is done.
Habdalah leads into the week.

THE THREE PILGRIMAGE FESTIVALS

Three times a year all thy males shall appear before the Lord thy God in the place which He shall choose: on the Feast of Matzot (Passover), on the Feast of Weeks (Shabuot), and on the Feast of Tabernacles (Sukkot) (Deut. 16:16).

Next to the high holy days, these festivals constitute the major holy days of the year. Passover, festival of freedom, celebrates the deliverance from Egypt; Shabuot, festival of revelation, commemorates the giving of the Ten Commandments; Sukkot is the festival of thanksgiving and of divine protection. In times of old the people made pilgrimages to the Temple in Jerusalem at these times. We shall talk of Sukkot first, for it arrives immediately after Rosh Hashanah and Yom Kippur, and then follow the course of the year.

Sukkot: Feast of Tabernacles (Booths)

On the fifteenth day of this seventh month is the feast of tabernacles for seven days unto the Lord. On the first day shall be a holy convocation. Ye shall do no manner of servile work. . . . On the fifteenth day when ye have gathered in the fruits of the land ye shall keep the feast of the Lord seven days. . . . And ye shall take you on the first day the fruit of goodly trees, branches of palm trees, and boughs of thick trees, and willows of the brook, and ye shall rejoice before the Lord your God seven days. . . . Ye shall dwell in booths seven days . . . that all your generations may know that I made the children of Israel to dwell in booths, when I brought them out of the land of Egypt: I am the Lord your God (Lev. 23:34-43).

The good harvest is in. We give thanks for it and for all material blessings provided by God. His sheltering hand has protected us during the year; His Providence watches over us always. When the Pilgrim Fathers of America wished to give thanks for whatever food they had, and for divine guidance across stormy seas to a new land, they chose the festival of Tabernacles as their pattern. They knew their Bible well. Some historians believe that this is the origin of our American Thanksgiving Feast.

Symbolic expression of gratitude for God's *protection* is the Sukkah, the festive booth. Symbolic expression for His *blessings* is the festive plant offering. *Sukkah* is a small hut covered by branches instead of a firm roof. It is decorated with fruits, flowers, and wall coverings to make it attractive. Traditionally, members of the family would take their meals in it, except in rainy weather.

In many European villages the small Jewish houses had special added gables whose shingles could be replaced by a roof of branches; this made the sukkah complete, for it is the roof that matters. Man steps out of the protection of his home, places himself beneath the starry sky, and feels perfectly protected, for God is his guardian. In ancient Israel, the harvest celebration in the fields took place in such huts; in orthodox congregations of today, every member has a Sukkah, and the children have the joy of visiting them all during the holiday. In every congregation there is at least one Sukkah, at the synagogue; and the congregation assembles in it to break bread and give thanks.

With thanksgiving for divine protection goes gratitude for divine blessings. It is expressed in the cluster of special plants brought to the Temple: a citron, a branch of the date palm, myrtles, and willows of the brook. These plants represent all the types of vegetation brought forth by the earth. The citron has beauty, smell, and taste; dates have no smell, but

The family takes its meal within the Sukkah.

A hasidic Jew with Lulav branch. The branch itself is not visible; the myrtles, willows, and citron can be seen.

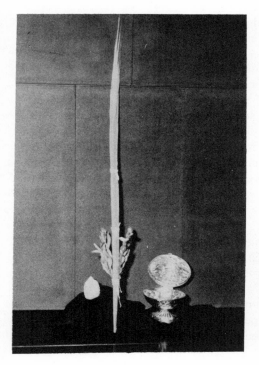

The festive branches used on Sukkot, tied together in a bouquet. Lulav, a palm branch, is in the center, with three myrtle branches to its right and two branches of willow to its left. The citron, Etrog, is to the left. This is the way the worshipper holds them. The silver receptacle, in the form of an Etrog, holds the citron when it is not in use.

198

they have a sweet taste; myrtles have no taste but a pleasant smell; willows of the brook have nothing exceptional about them, and yet, like many similar plants, they are essential on earth. The rabbis saw a parallel to human society in these four plants: there are people full of wisdom and helpfulness; others may have knowledge but lack human understanding; others may be kind, yet lack great intellectual gifts; finally, there are those who have no traits of distinction, but are just simple human beings. All of them form one great human family in which all are essential, no one expendable.

The festive bouquet is waved during the recital of the Hallel, the Psalms of thanksgiving (Pss. 113-118). "Praise the Lord for He is good, His mercy endureth for ever." As each word is recited the branches are pointed in a different direction of the compass—North, East, South, West, Upward, Downward. From the four corners of the earth, from heaven above, and from the earth beneath have come God's blessings. He is everywhere and to be thanked in every direction.

As the Mussaf reaches its end, thanksgiving is once again expressed, this time by solemn procession with all the branches around the synagogue and the altar, in the same manner as in the days of the Temple. The Torah is taken from the Ark to head the procession; behind it walk the members of the congregation, palms in hand. It is truly humanity walking before God. I remember it from my childhood—every member had his palm, forming a waving forest of branches during the Psalm, and a grand procession behind the Torah. As the procession advances the Reader begins the chant and the congregation responds:

The Plea: Hoshanah, Save us, God, we beseech Thee; The Answer: Hoshanah
For Thy sake, O our God   Hoshanah
For Thy sake, O our Creator   Hoshanah
For Thy sake, O our Redeemer   Hoshanah
For Thy sake, Thou who seekest us   Hoshanah

During the first and last days, which are full holidays, all work, except preparation of food and all that goes with it, is prohibited. The intermediate days are observed in worship and by eating in the Sukkah, but there is no work prohibition. In former times, the last day of the festival was a time of merrymaking, when dignified rabbis danced and sang and played; all of Jerusalem was wrapped in joyful abandon—within the bounds of decency. They came to watch Rabbi Simeon ben Gamaliel juggle eight burning torches.[12] Thus was pleasure woven into the fabric of Judaism. By hallowing it, they eliminated the excesses which might otherwise result from too much denial or too little regulation, and so formed the character of the Jew.

12 Talmud Sukkah 53a.

From gaiety they turned to serious business, and gave thanks for the blessing of water. The last day of Sukkot officially concludes the summer. After the Jew leaves the Sukkah, he prays for rain.

Some of this abandon has been retained in modern observance. The final day of the festival is called Simhat Torah, Joy of Torah. On that day the cycle of scriptural readings is completed and begun over again. Before the Torah reading, all scrolls are taken from the Ark and carried around the synagogue in joyful procession. Children with little flags in their hands form the escort. They will receive sweets and fruit. One of the elders of the congregation is honored by being made Hatan Torah, the Bridegroom of the Torah. To him is read the final paragraph of the Torah. (The Torah itself is the Bride.) A young married member is honored as Hatan Bereshit, Bridegroom of the Beginning; to him are read the first verses of the new cycle: In the beginning God created the heaven and the earth. In this case, creation is the Bride.

In rejoicing with Torah, the long season which started in penitence ends. With Torah in hand, thanksgiving in his heart, certain of God's protection and willing to be His witness, the Jew steps into the dark wintery months of the year. He knows that he will emerge from winter's night unto a new spring, for God is with him.

Lights in Winter's Night: Hanukah

What is Hanukah, and why is it celebrated? The historian has a simple answer: the name of the festival means "Dedication," and it is observed to commemorate the victory of the Maccabees over the Syrians, and the rededication of the Temple which had been desecrated by the enemy.[13] The Talmud tells a different story.

What is Hanukah? The Rabbis teach: On the twenty-fifth day of Kislev the days of the Feast of Hanukah begin. There are eight of them, days on which there may be no public mourning nor fasting. When the Greeks (Hellenist-Syrians) entered the Temple they desecrated all the oil in the Temple. After the leaders of the House of the Hasmoneans had overcome and defeated them, they searched all over and finally found just one little cruse of oil still bearing the seal of the high priest; just enough oil to last for one day, (in the holy candelabrum of the Temple). But a miracle happened, it burnt for eight days, (until a new one could be prepared). The following year it was ordained that these days be observed with songs of praise and thanksgiving (Shabbat 21b).

The explanation is important, not only for what it says but for what it omits. It makes very clear that Hanukah is not a victory celebration in the usual sense; Hanukah proclaims a divine miracle, not a human vic-

---

[13] The story has been told on pp. 46 ff.

tory. Courage, determination, military toughness have always been prime characteristics of the Jew. When Abraham learned that his nephew Lot had been made a prisoner, he armed the men of his clan and defeated a vastly superior army (Gen. 14). Joshua and Gideon, Saul at his prime, and David were supreme strategists and daring and fearless soldiers. The Scripture is so confident of the courage among Israel that it makes the ruling to issue a call before battle: let those who are afraid stay home, we do not want them lest they discourage others (Deut. 20:8). The Maccabees outfought a powerful enemy with their strategy, fearless courage, and supreme mastery of the art of war. Even in defeat the Jews proved no mean enemy. The war against the Jews was the most difficult campaign Rome had fought since she defeated Hannibal, the invader of Italy. Titus, their general, did not get his triumphal arch for nothing. The Bar Kokhba rebellion nailed down the elite of the Roman legions for years. During the crusades, the Jews of Mainz took up arms against the hordes that attacked them until they were pushed into a corner and literally clubbed down by an overwhelming mass of attackers. We are reminded of the Battle of the Warsaw Ghetto, when a small band of starving Jews took on the entire Nazi might with arms smuggled in from outside. None of the conquered peoples had dared to engage the conqueror in open warfare the way these inadequately armed people did. And they held out against tanks and flamethrowers until the Nazis shut off the watermains and saturated the area with incendiary bombs. Even then, they had to take on the fighters, man by man, in the midst of the flaming inferno. The victories of the Israelis over large armies are but recent history; and he who wishes to lay eyes on a soldier whose toughness is written right on his face and body need only go to Israel today.

The rabbis of old knew all of this, but they wished to stress the *source* from which this strength has come to the Jew. When Jews have fought for a cause, the cause has given them courage. The rabbis have pointed out that the courage of the Maccabees came from the light of God which burned in their hearts, and which they rekindled in the Temple. It was the flame of faith which wrought the miracle. The flame which burned for eight days symbolizes the miracle of Jewish survival. This is Hanukah. Its motto is expressed in the prophetic portion read during the festival: "Not by might nor by power but by My spirit (will ye prevail) says the Lord of Hosts (Zach. 4:6)."

The holiday itself is of minor character; there is no work prohibition. At night the lights are kindled on a nine-branched candelabrum, a menorah. One light is the serving candle whose flame touches the others, calling them into life. Beginning with one candle the first night, an additional flame is added every evening until the number reaches eight, for the miracle increased with every day. The light should be made visible to the outside, that the miracle be proclaimed far and wide. If placed in the door, it should be on the left, so that the Mezuzah will be to the right, and the person in the middle surrounded by his faith. Every male member of the household must light the candle. If a man has to borrow to buy the candles, he must borrow; even if he be on public welfare, he must kindle it, for it is truly the lamp of Jewish survival. It may not be used for practical purposes, for reading or for work; it is holy.

As it is lit the blessings are recited:

Blessed be Thou, O Lord . . . who hast sanctified us by Thy commandments and commanded us to kindle the Hanukah light. Blessed be Thou, O Lord . . . who hast wrought miracles to our fathers in ancient days at this season.

Then a hymn, whose author is unknown, is sung, speaking of God's help in ages past. Its tune is a strange mixture of a soldiers' song from the Thirty Years' War in Germany (1618-1648) and a Lutheran chorale; yet the hymn is an integral part of Jewish observance.

Since work is not forbidden, a strange custom developed. While the candles burn the family engages in work which is not work; it plays a friendly game. Card-playing was prohibited in a number of communities; the ancient congregation of Mainz pronounced a solemn ban against it, with one exception: during the celebration of Hanukah. Again, there is in the framework of Jewish religion itself a time and a place for everything, and nothing is carried to excess. While grownups play cards, children play "dreidel" (from the German *drehen*, to turn). A spinning top has four sides, each side inscribed with a Hebrew letter: *N-G-H-S*. The letters are the initials of a Hebrew sentence: *Nes Gadol Haya Shom*, a great miracle happened there. To the child *N* stood for *n*othing, and he got nothing out of the kitty; *G* meant *g*etting it all; *H* gave him *h*alf; *S* meant *s*et or put one in. Religion was never forgotten. In order to play, the children got some nuts as chips, and a few pennies; and that was the extent of Hanukah presents. In our days the festival has been overemphasized in its significance, and become a kind of counterpart to Christmas. This it is not, neither in character nor in observance. It is only a minor festival, and Jewish parents should not try to compensate their children for Christmas, either by lavish gifts or Christmas trees. Christmas trees belong in Christian homes, for they are linked with the deep spiritual significance of the birth of Christ to every Christian heart. We must not take Christ out of Christmas, and intelligent Christians should join with intelligent Jews in preserving the tree as a Christian symbol. Christian parents may invite Jewish children to share the happiness which comes to Christian homes out of the wellsprings of faith. Jewish parents should give Jewish meaning to the lives of their children by observing Jewish festivals whenever they occur, and may in turn

Seven-branched candelabrum, symbol of Judaism, on the
capital of a column in the synagogue at Capernaum; note
also the Shofar.

invite their Christian friends to share with them the happiness which
Jewish faith can give to human souls.

The Menorah, the seven branched candelabrum of the Temple, rightly
became the coat of arms of the Jews; it is the symbol of Judaism. It is
found on the ancient synagogue in Capernaum, on Jewish graves in the
Jewish catacombs of Rome and Bet Shearim, and on the Great Seal of
the State of Israel. It tells of an eternal light of divine origin, but tended
by man. Not by might but by My spirit will ye prevail.

THE FAST OF TEBET follows directly after Hanukah. It commemorates the siege of the walls of Jerusalem, and actually seems to say: you
have been celebrating quite a bit; perhaps you have overdone it. Stop
for a moment and reflect.

THE FIFTEENTH DAY OF SHEBAT is the beginning of planting season.
Spring sends out its first, timid feelers, and hope begins to sprout. For
a brief moment the daily routine is interrupted for a very minor hour
of celebration. Children are given fruit. They enjoy the fruits of the
past; they, in turn, are seed of the future. May they learn not only to
enjoy but to plant too; may they develop the potential which God has
planted in them. In modern Israel children plant trees. They will watch
the trees grow, hoping that their own development will keep step with
that of the tree and that ultimately each child may reach his full height
of body, mind, and spirit, and produce fruit which will nourish others.

THE FAST OF ESTHER immediately precedes the merry feast of

Purim. Purim resembles carnival time, and has adopted many of its features. The fast calls us to order. Tomorrow you will be gay, but today reflect on life and its duty. If you rush into escape without a sense of purpose, you may lose yourself and find it difficult to get back in the proper channels.

The Merry Feast of Purim

Purim is the feast when getting drunk becomes a duty. The feast is based on the legendary story of the Book of Esther. King Ahasuerus of Persia has discharged his queen for disobedience. Looking for a new queen, he holds a beauty contest, and Esther, a Jewish beauty, wins the crown. She has not revealed that she is a Jew and ward of the wise man, Mordecai. Mordecai remains her advisor, and sits in the outer court of the palace to be near her. There he overhears a plot to assassinate the king; he reports it, the culprits are hanged, and the event duly recorded in the royal chronicle. The king then appoints a new vizir, Haman, who immediately commands everyone to prostrate himself before him. Mordecai refuses, since he will bow down only to God. Haman broods revenge, not only on Mordecai, who is too small for him, but on all the Jews. He tells the king that a subversive group needs wiping out for the good of the country, and Ahasuerus, without asking questions, grants him the right. The thirteenth day of Adar is chosen by lot to be extermination day. The term for "lot" is "Pur," hence the name Purim. Mordecai requests Esther to see the king immediately. To enter the king's chambers without being summoned means death, but Esther is willing to sacrifice herself. She enters, the king receives her graciously, and accepts her invitation to dine with her and to bring Haman with him; he even agrees to dine with her a second night and to bring Haman again. After the first dinner he cannot sleep, so he has the chronicle read to him; he learns of Mordecai, who has saved his life and has received no reward and appoints Haman to lead Mordecai in procession through the City of Sousa. This is upsetting to Haman, who has just built a gallows to hang Mordecai, but worse is to come. Esther reveals to the king Haman's plot, and tells the king that she is Jewish too. Haman is hanged, Mordecai made vizir, the Jews are saved.

Then Mordecai and Esther enjoined the Jews regarding the days of rescue:

that they should make them days of feasting and gladness and of sending presents to one another and gifts to the poor (Esther 9:22).

As night falls on the preceding day, evening worship is conducted in the synagogue; then the Book of Esther is recited from a handwritten scroll. It will be repeated again the following morning.

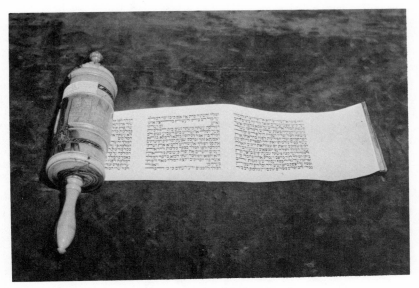

The scroll of Esther, containing the Book of Esther, hand written in the style of the Torah. It is used for the reading of the book on Purim.

The forenoon finds friends sending gifts to each other as Esther commanded, and also sending presents to the poor. This shows the spirit of Jewish charity. No one knows that he receives a present because he is poor, and no one will feel embarrassed. The giver may always say: I am not sending you this gift because you are poor but because you are my friend.

At noon the merrymaking takes over. Masquerades were introduced in the spirit of carnival which is celebrated around the same time. The festive meal is taken in the afternoon, and drinking is a duty, "until one does not know the difference between 'blessed Mordecai' and 'cursed Haman.' Until one does not know . . . in Hebrew, Ad delo yoda. This became the name of the Purim feast in modern Israel, observed with carnival parade and in great exuberance: Adeloyoda.

The Talmud relates this story.

Raba and Rab Zera celebrated the Purim feast together; and when they were all drunk, Raba got up and killed Rab Zera. The next day he pleaded with God for mercy, and God revived Rab Zera. The following year Raba said to Rab Zera: Would the master please come that we may celebrate the Purim feast together. But Rab Zera declined and said: Miracles do not happen every time (Talmud, Megillah 7b).

The Rabbi had indeed gone too far; he was human, so he was forgiven and his deed wiped out. There is a time even for getting drunk. Thus Judaism curbs excess by permitting it for a moment, in the name of God. Never ascetic, Jews have kept their balance. Among Jews, who could make even drinking an act of religion, alcoholism has never been a major affliction, nor drunkenness a major problem. The Shulhan Arukh, code of religious practice, lays down a rule ordaining drinking until sensibility is lost, but already R'MO, in the sober mood of Ashkenasic Jewry, adds:

Some say that he need not drink that much; just a little more than usual. Then he will fall asleep and no longer know the difference between "cursed" and "blessed." He who does much and he who does little are equally right, provided that every one's intention be for the sake of Heaven (God).

Take your choice, but do it for the sake of God.

European Jewry under Hitler found some distant comfort in the words "Cursed is Haman"; in Hebrew they read *Arur Haman*, predicting the fate of the Haman of our time, Adolf *Hitler*.

As Purim ends, Pessah knocks at the door.

Pessah (Passover): Rebirth in Freedom

In the first month on the fourteenth day of the month during the twilight hour is the Lord's Passover; and on the fifteenth day of the month is the Feast of Matzot (unleavened bread, plural form of matzah) unto the Lord; seven days shall you eat unleavened bread. On the first day you shall have a holy convocation; you shall do no work of labor . . . on the seventh day is holy convocation . . . (Lev. 23:4-8). Observe the month of "The Green Corn" and prepare a Passover unto the Lord thy God, for in "the Month of the Green Corn" did the Lord thy God lead you out of Egypt by night. Offer a Passover sacrifice of the flock and the herd in the place which the Lord will choose for His Name to reside there. Thou shalt not eat leavened food with it; for seven days shalt thou eat matzot, unleavened bread, bread of affliction; for in great hurry didst thou go forth from the Land of Egypt. Thus shalt thou remember the day of thy departure from Egypt all the days of thy life. And there shall not be seen any leaven in all thy domain for seven days . . . (Deut. 16:1-3).

Pessah is the Independence Day of the Jewish people, when God gave the people their freedom in order that they might have the inalienable rights of life, liberty, and the pursuit of duty, with which the Creator has endowed all men. Pessah is the festival of freedom, the festival of Spring which marks the onset of harvest time in the Holy Land. The first barley was cut on Pessah and offered in the Temple. It is the festival of creation; nature and man are reborn.

The German poet Goethe has seen the relationship between nature and man clearly, and in his drama *Faust* gives it poetic expression. It is Easter Sunday; Faust and his disciple join the citizens of their town in their holiday walk beyond the gates of the medieval city. Faust, the philosopher, speaks:

From icy bondage streams and brooks are freed
by Spring's life-giving lovely light;
in valleys hope and happiness swell seed,
while weak old winter, creeping out of sight
back to the rugged mountains must proceed. . . .
Turn around and from this height look down
backward on the litttle town.
See how the motley crowd with one accord
surges from the hollow gloomy gate!
Each suns himself with joy to celebrate
the Resurrection of the Lord.
'Tis *they* are resurrected from their past
from dingy rooms in shabby houses cast.
from bondage to their trade, by toil harassed,
from crowded street and narrow alleyway,
from oppressive roofs and gables gray,
from the church's sacred night
all are guided to the light (Faust, I, Act II).[14]

In Judaism it is the resurrection not of One Person but of the People, for in Judaism it is the *community* which gives meaning to individual lives. By doing our duty to mankind, we become holy and free. This is the story of Pessah. The Jews were redeemed from Egypt, freed from the house of bondage that they might proclaim liberty to all and work with all their might to bring it about. They had to be slaves first to feel the bitterness of oppression. Israel has never hidden the fact that they had been enslaved by Egypt. To be a slave is no reason for shame; it is only shame to enslave others.

The unleavened bread, the *matzah*, serves as a symbol of both slavery and freedom. In Egypt there was little time amidst toil to bake real bread, so matzah had to do; it was the bread of affliction. When the moment of their redemption came, there was again too little time to bake bread for the journey, "because they were thrust out of Egypt and could not tarry (Exod. 12:39)"; matzah became the symbol of freedom. It is to be eaten for seven days, because it was on the seventh day after departure that Israel crossed the Red Sea, leaving their foe behind for good. This accounts for the length of the festival, which lasts for seven —or eight—days. The first days, moments of departure, are full holidays; the middle days, period of marching, are intermediate holidays; the last days, hour of complete liberation, are again full holidays.

---

[14] Johann Wolfgang von Goethe, *Faust, A Tragedy*, Part One, trans. by Alice Raphael (New York: Holt, Rinehart and Winston, Inc., 1930, 1955), pp. 35-36.

Not only must matzah be eaten, leavened food may neither be consumed nor stored. This calls for a great spring housecleaning preceding Pessah. Everything made with starch or through fermentation of grain has to be removed from the house; even the last crumb of bread has to go. "Hametz," leaven, includes a great variety of items: bread and pastry, alcohol made of grain, tablets made with starchy binders, and medicines containing grain spirit; the list is endless. The only solution to the problem, for traditional Jews, is to replace all dishes and cooking utensils used during the year and have only special Passover dishes during the feast. Commercially produced Passover food has to be supervised in preparation to make certain it contains no hametz. On the night before the holiday, a search is made throughout the house for the last remnants of leaven. "One must search for the hametz by the flame of a light (Pessahim 1:1)." This march through cellars, rooms, and attic became a joyful event for the children, who gathered small pieces, (left on purpose) and burned them the next morning in a huge bonfire. We may reflect for a moment on the value of such complete housecleaning, especially at a time when people in medieval towns simply permitted accumulated dirt to breed disease. Pessah became truly liberation "from dingy rooms in shabby houses cast."

Man was truly reborn, the leaven of time and habit cast out, the house cleaned, and the spirit renewed. We understand why Philo sees in matzah a symbol of purity, contrasting it with the "leaven of impurity." For matzah itself consists of only flour—guarded throughout the year against premature fermentation—and water. Quick kneading and baking prevents rising. No ingredients may be added. It is flat and thin, for heat has to penetrate it quickly to bake it to a crisp.

Of course, the Passover sacrifice ceased with the end of the Temple in Jerusalem. None of the ancient sacrificial service is still performed, nor has it been performed for almost 2000 years. Prayer has long since taken its place, but the story of freedom is still told on the eve of the festival in a family rite of great beauty, warmth, and inspiration. It is called the Seder.

The Seder

The term means "order," for the service follows a definite order, based on the guide of the *Haggadah*, the Story. It traverses Jewish history from its beginning to its eventual culmination in universal, messianic peace. The meal is part of the service; it becomes truly a Lord's Supper. The words spoken go back to Temple days; in the tenth chapter of the Mishnah dealing with Pessah, we find the outline of the Haggadah.

THE SEDER TABLE. Every precious decoration the family possesses is brought out. At each place stands a cup, and next to it a copy

A family group at the Seder table.

of the Haggadah. Each cup will be filled with wine four times, and four times it will be emptied. This corresponds to four promises God made to Israel, all of which have been fulfilled:

I will bring you out from under the burdens of the Egyptians;
I will deliver you from their bondage;
I will redeem you with an outstretched arm;
I will take you to Me for a people (Exod. 6:6-7).

But there is a fifth promise: I will bring you into the land. This promise speaks of ultimate redemption for all mankind, and this promised land is still far off for humanity. But if man works for it and never gives up hope, it will surely be reached with the help of God. Its messenger, according to Malachi, is Elijah, the prophet.[15] For him a fifth cup is placed in the center of the table. No one drinks from it, but everyone is aware of the truth that the salvation of mankind is not a tale but can become a reality, today or tomorrow, if we hold out the cup of Elijah.

Also in the center of the table, near the seat of the head of the house, is the Seder Plate. It contains three matzot, the bread for which God is to be blessed, which will be broken, and shared. The matzot stand for

[15] As mentioned on pp. 56 f.

Table set for the Seder. Note the Seder Plate near the head.

the three family groups in ancient Israel, the Priests, the Levites, and the Israelites; all of them were redeemed and led to freedom. On top of the plate several symbolic foods are arranged: a roasted shankbone, reminder of the Passover lamb (therefore roasted); it is not eaten; an egg, ancient symbol of spring, symbol also of Temple offerings; it is not eaten. The egg, closed all around, is yet the birthplace of new life. It tells of the miracle of resurrection in nature, as timid plants pierce through a heavy shell of hardened soil to grow and bring beauty and food to the world. The other foods on the plate are used in the service: sprigs of parsley, used as in times of old, as appetizers; salt water in which the parsley is dipped, reminder of the bitter, salty tears shed by the slaves in Egypt, and reminder of the salty Red Sea, which opened up to form a highway to freedom; bitter herbs—lettuce or horseradish— reminder of the bitter life in Egypt; haroset, a mixture of apples, nuts, cinnamon, and wine, brownish in looks, like the mortar the Israelites had to prepare; the bitter herbs are dipped in it.

THE SERVICE.   Like the symbols on the table, the service alternates between memories of hardship and joy in freedom. The family reclines in cushioned chairs, as free men. Mother lights the festive candles and speaks the blessing. The entire family raises the cup, reciting the kiddush, and everyone partakes of the wine. Father pours water over his hands from a pitcher to clean them, for he is about to distribute the parsley among his family members. He takes the sprigs, dips them in salt water, and passes them around that all may partake. All these are symbols of freedom and well-being; they mark the beginning of a wealthy man's meal. But here we stop.

There is poverty in the world today as there was in the past; may we remember it and do something about it. Father breaks the middle matzah into two unequal parts, like a poor man who has only one piece of bread, and breaks it to keep something for the future. The big piece is wrapped in à cloth for later use, and put away. The small piece is shown to all: "This is the bread of affliction which our fathers had to eat in the land of Egypt." But what about those who may be poor and homeless right now? We must call them in: "May all who are in need come and celebrate with us." The memories of slavery and want have stirred us to immediate action. Now the story can go on. It turns to the past.

THE PAST.   The key person of the Seder is the child, who must carry on the Jewish ideals which the celebration calls to life, and understand the meaning of freedom and its obligations. To him are given the basic questions which will spark the answers. The child asks:

Why is this night different from all other nights?
Tonight we eat no bread, only matzah, symbol of enslavement;
Tonight we eat bitter herbs, symbol of enslavement;
Yet tonight also, we dip our herbs in condiments, symbol of freedom;
and tonight we sit in cushioned chairs, symbol of freedom.

The father answers: We were slaves and God made us free. He points out that there are two kinds of slavery, physical enslavement, and spiritual enslavement of those who do not know God. Israel has suffered from both, and has been freed by divine grace. We must constantly review the message of Pessah; the ancient rabbis, learned as they were, never ceased to study it, and father tells a story about it. He speaks of the four types of children, bright, bad, average, and simple; they must all be taught in their own way to understand the meaning of freedom. Then he goes on to make it clear that persecution and godlessness are not events of the past; they happen every day, and every day God helps those who trust in Him. In gratitude to Him, who has been Israel's Redeemer in all ages, the whole family lifts the cup and partakes of the wine. This is the second cup.

THE PRESENT has arrived. All wash their hands. The matzot are broken and, with a blessing to Him who "has commanded us to eat matzah," everyone eats his portion. The bitter herbs are dipped in the haroset and after blessing God, "Who has commanded us to eat bitter herbs," the family consumes them. From horseradish and matzah father makes a sandwich in memory of Hillel, who used to eat in this manner. Hillel was the man who truly carried into life God's commandment to love our neighbor. Then the meal is served, to be concluded by the piece of matzah previously put aside, in remembrance of the ancient Passover offering. But where is it? The little children, too small to understand even the simple words of the Seder, have been encouraged to "steal" it. It is a way of entertaining them, of giving them something to remember for next year when they may be able to understand more. Perhaps it will teach them not to wait for the old generation to relinquish religious leadership to them, but to "steal" it early. Father ransoms the piece with a little gift to the child, then all may eat and the Seder proceed. Grace is now recited by the family, and the third cup is emptied in gratitude for the gifts of the present.

THE FUTURE enters. A child opens the door, a welcome for Elijah. By this time, tired and a little drowsy, the child may actually feel him, coming in and taking a drop of the wine from his cup; did you not notice the ripples? Once, however, the opening of the door had a terrifying meaning; Jews looked outside to see if there were any evil spies, hoping to accuse them later with that most horrible of slanders, the use of Christian blood on Pessah.[16] The door is closed again, and Psalms are recited: Praise the Lord for He is good, His goodness endureth for ever. The hymn whose tune became the theme song for Pessah is sung: God of Might build up Thy Temple soon.

The hour is late and the children sleepy. Charades adapted from German folk songs of the fifteenth and sixteenth centuries keep them awake a little longer: Who is One? God is One; What is two? Two is for the two tablets of the Ten Commandments; What is three? Three stands for the three patriarchs, and so on. And then the final song, telling in childlike words of God's ultimate triumph in a world of injustice:

My father had a little kid—but the cat ate the kid—the dog killed the cat—the stick beat the dog—the fire burnt the stick—the water quenched the fire—the ox drank the water—the butcher killed the ox—death claimed the butcher—but God wiped out death.

The death of the little kid led to the defeat of death itself. When you must suffer, little child, don't lose your faith in God. In His plan all has meaning, and in His great design life will triumph over death. With this

---

[16] As discussed on p. 156.

note the Seder ends, as the family raises the cup for the fourth time, a toast of faith to the future.

Bedtime prayers are omitted in the Seder night, for it is a night of protection. (Russian Jewry, unfree at present, is remembered with special Matzoh.)

The days of Pessah

Public worship follows the regular order of the service for festivals. The Torah reading tells the story of the Exodus.

On the first day of the festival the congregation include a prayer for dew. At the end of the Sukkot festival they had prayed for rain during the winter; now they ask for life-preserving dew in the words of the eighth century poet Eleazar Kalir:

> Our God and God of our fathers:
> Dew, precious dew unto Thy land forlorn;
> pour out our blessing in Thy exultation,
> to strengthen us with ample wine and corn
> and give Thy chosen city safe foundation—in dew . . .
> For a blessing and not for a curse—Amen
> For life and not for death—Amen
> For plenty and not for famine—Amen.[17]

Beginning with the third day of the festival, half of the Hallel Psalms of praise are omitted. Jubilation has to be curbed, for some of God's children, the Egyptians, perished as a consequence of Israel's liberation. The ancient rabbis put the admonition in the mouth of God: "The works of My hands are drowned in the sea, and you want to sing (Sanhedrin 39b)?" God rebukes the angels who rejoice at Israel's salvation. There is no human being, no creature, no enemy who is not deserving of deep compassion. Only compassion makes one truly free, and this too is a lesson of Pessah.

The counting

From the second night of Pessah, the days and weeks are counted leading to the festival of Shabuot, which falls seven weeks later, and thus has the name "Festival of Weeks." The counting constitutes the link between the festival of physical liberation, Passover, and the day of spiritual liberation, when, according to Scripture, the Ten Commandments were given. Freedom *from* restraint, we are admonished, may easily lead to license, unless it leads to freedom *for* the tasks which God has set for us.

---

17 Rabbinical Assembly of America and United Synagogue of America, *Sabbath and Festival Prayer Book*, Rabbi Morris Silverman, ed. (Hartford: Prayer Book Press, Inc., 1946), p. 180.

Shabuot

In the third month after the children of Israel were gone forth out of the land of Egypt, the same day came they into the wilderness of Sinai. . . . And the Lord came down upon Mount Sinai . . . and God spoke all these words saying: "I am the Lord thy God . . . (Exod. 19:1-20, ff)."

And ye shall count unto you from the morrow of the day of rest . . . even unto the morrow after the seventh week shall ye number fifty days. . . . Ye shall bring out of your dwellings two . . . loaves of fine flour . . . baked with leaven for first-fruits unto the Lord. . . . And ye shall make proclamation on the selfsame day; there shall be a holy convocation unto you; ye shall do no manner of servile work (Lev. 23:15-22).

This is a feast of revelation in the wonders of nature and those of the spirit: The Ten Commandments, according to Jewish tradition. The harvest is in progress, and all of God's spiritual and physical blessings have become visible. In Temple days they brought an offering of first fruit and of bread. Their animals were decked out with wreaths and garlands, and the required pilgrimage made to lay at the altar the best of their fruit in thanksgiving.

Today synagogues are adorned with flowers; the Torah scrolls bear wreaths. The Ten Commandments are read, and this is the only time during the year when the reading of God's word is interrupted by a man-made poem of deepest appreciation for the gift of Torah:

> Before the words of God Supreme
> today are read
> for this my theme
> approbation will I seek
> these my sentences to speak.
> Were the sky of parchment made
> a quill each reed, each twig and blade,
> could we with ink the oceans fill,
> were every man a scribe of skill,
> the marvelous story
> of God's great glory
> would still remain untold.[18]

Many congregations in America have introduced a service of confirmation on Shabuot. Young people who have completed their basic religious school education, usually through junior high school years, pledge their allegiance to God and Torah on this Day of Revelation. The form of the service varies from congregation to congregation, depending on the size of the confirmation class and the character of the congregation. They have one thing in common—the act of rededication

---

[18] *Ibid.*, p. 185.

of parents and children to Torah, which "is a tree of life to those who hold on to it, and those who uphold it will find themselves enriched."

Days of Mourning

Summer is punctuated by two days of mourning and of fasting. The 17th of Tammuz commemorates the day when the walls of Jerusalem were breached and regular Temple worship came to an end. Jewish mourning is not only for the fall of the Temple but for our sins which caused it, and which cause destruction always. A three week period leads up to the saddest day of the Jewish year, Tishah b'Ab, the ninth of Ab, the day when both the first and the second Temple were destroyed.

TISHAH B'AB. For 24 hours the congregation fasts; no leather shoes are worn. The congregation sits on low stools, the curtain of the ark has been removed, and the lights are dim. In the evening the Book of Lamentations is recited. In the morning dirges are sung, composed by various poets and reflecting on Israel's tragic fate through the ages.

Judah Halevi, the great poet, expresses the theme of the day to perfection:

> Zion, wilt thou not ask if peace's wing
> shadows the captives that ensue thy peace
> left lonely from thine ancient shepherding?
>
> Lo, west and east and north and south—world-wide
> all those from far and near, without surcease
> salute thee: Peace and peace from every side.
>
> To weep thy woe my cry is waxen strong;—
> but dreaming of thine own restored anew
> I am a harp to sound for thee thy song.
>
> Thy God desired thee for a dwelling place;
> and happy is the man whom He shall choose,
> and draw him nigh to rest within thy space.[19]

Sadness merges into hope. No service of worship ever releases the people in sorrow, for hope is the lifeblood of the Jew. An ancient saying said, on the ninth day of Ab the Messiah will be born. The meaning is simple: out of agony redemption will come. The sufferings of the ages are but the birthpangs of a new world—if only we understand it.

Three weeks after Tisha b'Ab, the month of Elul comes again, and the shofar is once more sounded announcing another year with new hopes, new opportunities, new trials, and new rewards.

---

[19] Judah Halevi in *A Book of Jewish Thoughts*, Nina Salaman, trans. (New York: Bloch Publishing Co., 1943), pp. 99 ff.

12

The Road
of Life

A man without children is as if he were dead (Talmud Nedarim 64b)." Every person's life has a purpose. Simply to live out one's span is not enough—we must do something for the future. Children guarantee the physical survival of the group, and so they should be brought up in such fashion that they will safeguard spiritual survival as well. A man with no children, who has not influenced posterity, has not truly lived. That is the meaning of the talmudic saying quoted above. To have children is a command of the Torah: *Be fruitful and multiply* (Gen. 1:28). Children are the promise of Israel's eternity as the people of Torah.

Rabbi Meir once said: When Israel approached God to receive the Torah, God said to them: "Bring me guarantors that you will observe it." The people replied: "Our forefathers whose piety is the model of our lives, they are the assurance that we will keep the Torah." But God replied: "Your guarantors need guarantors themselves, for I have found fault with them." "Then let our prophets stand up and vouch for us," the people said; but God replied: "Even with them have I found fault." Then the people of Israel said: "Our children will guarantee observance of the Torah through eternity." God accepted the guarantee and thereupon gave them the Torah (Shir Hashirim Rabba 1:4).

BIRTH

The birth of a child is a moment of great rejoicing. If the child is a girl, the father will be called to the Torah at its next reading, to offer a special blessing for his wife and child; in the blessing the name of the newborn baby is mentioned before God, completing the child's naming. If the baby is a boy, he has to be initiated in "the covenant of Abraham" by the act of circumcision.

Circumcision

On the eighth day the flesh of his foreskin shall be circumcised (Lev. 12:3). According to Scripture, Abraham was the first to receive the commandment; circumcision was the seal of the covenant between God and Abraham (Gen. 17,10ff). It transformed him into a Jew. From that time on, all male children had to undergo the rite. Anthropologists have many theories about its origin. To the pious Jew it has always been a commandment of God to be observed in obedience to the divine will. In our own time, the hygienic value of the operation has been recognized so fully that it is now performed routinely on all male children.

The rite is considered so important that it has to be performed exactly on the eighth day, as Scripture states, even if the eighth day falls on a Sabbath or on Yom Kippur, when work is otherwise strictly prohibited. The first week of the child's life becomes a period of preparation. First of all, it must be decided if he is strong enough; if the slightest doubt exists, circumcision has to be postponed. Then, is his father ready to assume his responsibilities as a guide to Jewish living? To make the father's readiness visible, a special celebration used to be held on the Friday evening after the child's birth. Friends gathered in the home of the father to study some Torah and partake of refreshments. The atmosphere of Torah was strengthened in the home of the child, and the parent was well-prepared.

The rite itself is to be performed by a *Mohel*, a pious man specially trained in the techniques of the operation. The skill of these men was and frequently is quite remarkable. To be a mohel is an honor and a great distinction; to be called as officiating mohel was a privilege eagerly sought. Nowadays, being a mohel is a profession for which professional fees are charged; the pious mohel of the past, however, would never think of taking a fee for his services. It was *he* who received a reward, to bring a child into the fold of Judaism. I have known some of these men. I knew one, highly skilled in his holy work, but by profession a businessman. He frequently neglected his business to travel to distant towns for the performance of his sacred task. He was never paid for his service or expenses, but often he would pay to help a poor family observe the happy occasion in dignity.

During the middle ages and in Eastern Europe, the act was often performed in the synagogue; today it is performed in the hospital or the home. Traditional custom calls for a quorum of ten to be present.

Two chairs are arranged in front of the mohel. One is for a relative, a grandfather or an uncle, who has the honor of holding the child during the operation; he becomes the child's godfather. The other chair remains empty; it is—symbolically—the chair of Elijah the prophet, guardian of Israel's eternal covenant with God.

Grandmother or aunt brings in the child, an act which makes her his godmother. The little boy is dressed in special finery, swaddled in precious swaddling cloths. As the child arrives all rise to greet him: "Blessed be he that cometh in the Name of the Lord." The mohel offers a prayer for divine assistance in the operation, then recites the blessing: "Blessed art Thou, O Lord . . . who hast sanctified us by Thy commandments and commanded us to perform circumcision." The father of the child then adds his blessing: "Blessed art Thou, O Lord . . . who hast sanctified us by Thy commandments and commanded us to enter him in the covenant of our father Abraham." By the time the father completes his blessings, the mohel has usually completed the operation in one swift stroke. He joins with the assembly in the response to the father's prayer: "As he has entered the covenant, so may he come to enter the realm of Torah, of marriage and of good deeds. Amen."

The blood has been wiped off the operated surface, the skin pushed back and secured that it will not grow back again, and the wound has been dressed. Now the mohel raises the cup of wine and with his blessing gives the child his name. "Our God and God of our fathers: preserve this child unto his father and mother; and may his name be called in Israel:———." A drop of wine is passed to the lips of the child, father finishes the cup, and the baby is returned to his mother. The cup used at circumcision is frequently the gift of the godfather to the child. It will be used again in the boy's life on festive occasions, including his wedding. It will become a treasured heirloom, a link in the chain of generations. Right now, after the child has been placed once again in his mother's arms, the cup is lifted in benediction at the beginning of a happy meal in which the friends join.

Modern circumcision ceremonies have become most informal affairs, held in hospitals, with only the closest relative present. As long as rules are observed this is acceptable; but frequently the religious part is completely forgotten. The attending physician performs the operation in routine fashion, on the third day, or whenever he considers best. This is an unhappy development; circumcision, to be religiously meaningful, should be observed on the eighth day as specified by Torah and in the manner hallowed by law and tradition.

Jewish Names

Family names came late into Jewish use, and then frequently upon the insistence of the government. Traditionally and for synagogue use, a person bears his given name together with that of his father: Isaac son of Abraham, or, in Hebrew, Yitshak ben Abraham. The same applies to women: Miriam daughter of Amram, Miriam bat Amram. The given name is carefully chosen for the child. Among the Ashkenasim, it is the name of a departed grandparent or great grandparent, whose life sets an example to his namesake and whose memory is perpetuated in his children's children. The Sefardim choose living relatives, in order that the child may have their guiding influence in his life. These are the names bestowed on children at circumcision or in the synagogue; today the giving of the name is frequently surrounded by a bit of ceremony and forms part of Sabbath worship. Sometimes a certificate is issued, to make sure the child will not forget the Hebrew name received; in all cases it is recorded. For it is by this name that a boy will be called to the Torah; these names will appear on the Hebrew marriage certificate; someday they will be inscribed on tombstones and memorial plaques, and the children will remember their dear ones by these names in memorial prayers for the dead.

Eventually it became customary to give the child a civic name also. This too was combined with a ceremony, which was observed when the mother left the house for the first time after her confinement. Her first visit was to be to the synagogue. Upon her return, all the children in the neighborhood were invited to assemble around the baby's crib. They recited in Hebrew the first verse of each of the Five Books of Moses, which the child was eventually to learn; they added the blessing of Jacob, and concluded with the last sentence of the Books of Moses. Then the crib was lifted high, all the children trying to help. "How shall we name the baby?" And all the children responded with the baby's civic name. Then they received sweets and cookies. A bond had thus been fashioned between the children from early youth, and the older ones had been given to understand that they had to help the little one in his learning of Torah and in his efforts to make a name for himself and to rise to achievement in life. It was a beautiful custom; unhappily, it has vanished.[1]

The civic names are chosen in conjunction with Hebrew names in a number of methods. The simplest way is to use Hebrew names in both the synagogue and outside. These names are hallowed, and they are beautiful: Abraham, Sarah, Rebecca, Jacob, Rachel, Miriam, Judith, Joseph, David, Michael, Samuel, Deborah, Esther, Ruth, Naomi, Judah, Israel, and many others.

English versions of Hebrew names may also be used: Johanan and

---

[1] The verses to be recited by the children, not usually found in prayer books, are included in S. Behr, *Seder Avodat Yisrael*, (Berlin: Schocken Books, Inc., 1937).

John are the same name, so are Miriam and Mary, and Hannah and Anne.

Names may be translated from the Hebrew: Simhah becomes Joy. The meaning of a Hebrew name may be sought and then an English name looked for which has the same meaning. For example, in the Book of Genesis, Judah is compared to a "lion's whelp" (Gen. 49:9); if Judah stands for Lion, then "Leo" might be used as a corresponding English name for the Hebrew Judah. Leo means lion in Latin.

The most commonly used method, and the least acceptable, is to choose an English name beginning with the same letter as the Hebrew name: Maurice to correspond with Moses, Richard with Ruben, or—as in German-Jewish families of the past—Sigmund with Solomon.

Family names developed later and from many sources. A family might claim to be descended from the priests of old. The Hebrew word for priest is "Cohen." From there we derive the names Cohn, Cohen, and Cahn; or from the abbreviation of the words *Kahen Tzedek*, righteous priest, we have the name Katz. Other families may claim to belong to the tribe of Levi and therefore bear the name; or their name may be an abbreviation of the term "*Segan Levaya,*" Overseer of Levites, and may be spelled Segal, Siegel, or similarly.

Another, rather simple, method was to use first names as family names, either in the original Hebrew or in translation. Benjamin, Judah, and Isaac, are historical examples. The Hebrew Dov would be translated into Bear, or Beer, or Berlin (little Bear); the Hebrew Tzevi would be translated into Hirsch, Herz, Hertz, or (in French translation) Cerf. These names could then be first names or family names. The list is long.

Places of origin frequently gave Jews their names: Oppenheimer, Milhaud, Prager (from Prague), Warshavsky (from Warsaw), and so on.

Their trade accounted for some names: a ritual slaughterer of cattle was called Schechter, and the name has remained in different spellings: Schector, Schectman.

Following general medieval custom, many Jewish houses had emblems which gave their occupants names and designation. A family which had a red shield in front of the house might be called Red Shield or Roth Schild or Rothschild. Other distinguishing features of dwelling places also led to names. In the German city of Fulda, an ancient Jewish family lived in a house which had a broad flight of stairs leading to its door. In 1672 the abbot of Fulda contemplated moving the Jews out of the city, except for the oldest Jewish families in town. So he exempted the Jew "Hirtz on the stair" from the edict. The order was revoked but the name stuck. "On the stair," in old German, means "uff der Trepp." The name "Trepp" has been held by the family ever since.

Eventually the government required all Jews to adopt family names.

This led to abuses by small government officials. If a Jew wanted a pleasant sounding name he might have to bribe the official. But then he would get a name like Valley of Roses—Rosenthal; Mountain of Flowers—Blumenberg or Blumberg; and so on. He might choose his profession: merchant—Kaufmann or Kramer. Eventually, the names might be changed again, as Jews migrated to new countries.

All these were official names. Among themselves, Jews simply used their Hebrew names for identification until the nineteenth century. As my father told me, there were at one time three related families Trepp in the city of Fulda. All of them had sons whose names were Judah, so they called them by their father's name. One was Simon's Judah, another was Isaac's Judah, and the third was Solomon's Judah. When the Jewish philosopher Moses, Son of Mendel, migrated from Dessau in Germany to Berlin during the eighteenth century, some people called him by his birthplace—Moses Dessau. Others called him by his father's name—Moses Mendelssohn.

An Archaic Custom: Pidyon Haben

According to a very ancient tradition, the first child of the family, if he was a boy, was to be destined for the priesthood, which was later taken over exclusively by the tribe of Levi and the family of Aaron. To release the boy for secular pursuits, a member of the family of Aaron takes it upon himself to serve in his stead. The little ceremony is largely without meaning and purpose, yet pious families have retained it as an occasion of thanksgiving. Only rarely can it be observed, which may be a reason for its retention. It can take place only if the first child of both father and mother is a boy and neither parent belongs to the family of Aaron or the tribe of Levi themselves. Naturally we have no proof regarding the family trees of the people, since it is all based on tradition, but this matters little. There are no longer any priestly functions to be performed.

Education and Bar Mitzvah

When the children begin to speak, they are taught to pray. In former times, when a boy was one year old he was taken to the synagogue by his father for a brief moment. He was brought into the sanctuary after the Torah had been read, to offer a small gift. The swaddling cloth used at his circumcision had been made into a wrapper for the Torah scroll, to be wound around the parchment. It had been embroidered with the child's name, birth date, and the wish that he grow up to Torah, marriage, and good deeds. From then on the boy's name was symbolically woven around the Torah. Congregations had hundreds of these "Wim-

The child is dedicated to the Law of Moses after the first year of his life.

pels;" they were extremely useful for historical research. Polish Jewry did not have the custom, and the treasure houses of German synagogues have unfortunately been destroyed.

In Talmudic and medieval times, boys had to go to school from the age of five; girls learned their reading and writing at home. Life in school was hard and the hours long, lasting well into the night. The Talmud made the law that every father had to teach his son an honest trade. But there was little to teach children in the ghetto of the middle ages; trades and skilled crafts were not open to Jews. Talmud became a full-time occupation.

Beginning with the age of thirteen—the onset of puberty—the boy is considered responsible for his religious acts; up to that time the responsibility rests with the father. Girls, maturing earlier, became responsible at the age of twelve. Now the boy can be counted among the ten making up the quorum for public worship, for he is "Bar Mitzvah"—son of the commandment. For the first time in his life he is therefore called to offer blessing for the Torah in public. His father gives thanks for having brought his boy that far. If the youngster was a good talmudic student, he might give a lecture on a talmudic subject he had carefully prepared with a teacher, showing his potential as a scholar. In this simple manner children were introduced to their duties; Bar Mitzvah is a state of responsibility into which a Jew enters automatically on his thirteenth birthday. No ceremony is required. The emphasis on ceremonial admission and celebration is of late origin, and frequently overdone.

In modern practice, the Bar Mitzvah speaks the blessings of the Torah, and reads the portion from the prophets for the Sabbath of his celebration, using the traditional chant of the synagogue. He may present a short address, an adaptation of the talmudic discourse once delivered, or he may offer prayer. He may listen to a charge by the rabbi and receive the rabbi's blessing. If he is able, the boy may even be permitted to lead portions of the service. All these practices vary with different congregations. The one important thing for the Bar Mitzvah to know and for his parents to remember is this: Bar Mitzvah is not the end but rather the beginning of Jewish responsibilities and studies.

Girls grew into their responsibilities without ceremony. In our day, with an ever-growing recognition of equality among the sexes, congregations have evolved a so-called Bat Mitzvah ceremony for girls. Practices still vary, but the idea is becoming more and more popular.

Toward Marriage

Jews used to marry young; the Talmud suggests the age of eighteen.[2] Frequently the young man was unable to support a wife at that age. Rather than postpone marriage, the girl's father might support the new family, especially when the young man was a promising talmudic scholar. He would go right back to his Talmud, and his father-in-law would take care of him and his wife for a while. But many times it happened that the husband was so completely immersed in Talmud that he could never make a living, a task which then fell to his wife for the rest of her days.

MARRIAGE

A wife may be acquired in three ways; and gains her freedom in two ways: She is acquired by silver, through contract and through marital cohabitation. She gains her freedom through a Bill of Divorcement and by the death of her husband (Mishnah Kiddushin 1:1).

As husband and wife are worthy God's Glory dwells in their midst (Sota 17a).

Two aspects of marriage are here revealed to us. Marriage is a legal contract, as two people assume certain obligations, but it is more than that. It is a union which partakes of the divine, and in which God Him-

---

[2] Chapters of the Fathers 5:24.

self reveals His glory. Jewish wedding rites reflect both of these aspects.

In ancient Israel, betrothal and marriage were kept about one year apart. A girl betrothed to a man was bound to him, as he to her. They could not live with each other, neither could they get a separation without a full divorce. Secure in the knowledge of having found a husband, the future bride prepared her trousseau and made all preparations for married life. The day of her wedding bound her once more to her betrothed, but now in full marriage bonds, both legal and divine. As time went on it was found that the separation of two binding acts did no longer work. To be bound to each other without being married was hardship for both groom and bride, and so the two acts were united in one ceremony. The Jewish wedding rite now comprises both the ancient act of betrothal and the vows of marriage.

Preparation

As a man takes a wife, he assumes grave duties and solemn obligations; as a woman entrusts her life unto a man she makes the most momentous decision regarding her future. Both should seek the advice of the rabbi, that he might counsel them, help them bring God into their future home, and give it happiness. After the rabbi has made certain that there are no religious or legal obstacles to the marriage, the date of the wedding may be set.

The Betrothal: First Part of the Marriage Ceremony

Since it is a legal act, marriage requires two witnesses not related to the couple or to each other. The rabbi, as the bride and groom stand before him, makes certain that they truly wish to join their lives together, and that they are doing so by their own free will and consent. He asks the question; they affirm their intent. Raising the cup of wine, the rabbi blesses God, by Whose word betrothal and marriage have come into being, and the couple share the cup. The betrothal ceremony is ended, and leads directly into the marriage rites.

Marriage Rites: Second Part of the Marriage Ceremony

Anyone of three legal acts ties the knot, as the Mishnah points out. The marriage ceremony includes all three of them and leaves no doubts.

Legal acts

a) Two people may become man and wife by living together and building a home. Thus there is built over the heads of the couple a canopy, a home, called the Huppah. The groom takes his bride under the Huppah, into his home to live with her. It is not a very realistic act, and so it is not very essential. In the old congregation of Mainz a Tallit was spread over the heads of the couple; in medieval days, the hood of the groom's headgear was simply placed on the head of his bride. But Huppah has become synonymous with wedding in Jewish usage; the newborn child is blessed: God make him grow up to Torah and to Huppah and to good deeds. Parents hope to see their children under the Huppah; in traditional practice they lead them there, the two fathers leading the groom, the two mothers leading the bride. It is the parents' great joy.

b) A man may acquire a wife by "silver"—by handing to her something of value with the expressed declaration that he wishes to marry her by this gift. As she accepts it, she becomes his wife. Early in history this valuable gift was presented in the form of a ring; thus it has remained and has been followed by other faiths.

Standing under the Huppah the groom places the ring on the finger of his bride and solemnly speaks the words: "Be thou consecrated unto me—as my wife—by this ring according to the law of Moses and Israel." The bride accepts the ring, and the two are married. She may wish to give him a ring, an act which carries emotional meaning but has no legal significance.

c) Contract legalizes marriage. In the shelter of the Huppah the groom has placed the ring upon the finger of his bride, and now the rabbi reads the contract previously witnessed, the Ketubah. It states that the husband promises to honor and cherish his wife, to support her in decency, to love her in truth, to take care of all her needs "down to the shirt off my back," to provide for her in case of his death or in the event of a divorce. The wife, in turn, promises to fulfil her duties in sincerity and truth. The three legal acts uniting a man and a woman have been performed, and now God's blessing is invoked.

The Divine blessing

The cup is raised as the rabbi recites the blessing:

Blessed be Thou, O Lord . . . who createst the fruit of the vine.

Blessed be Thou, O Lord . . . who createst all to Thy glory.

Blessed be Thou, O Lord . . . Creator of man.

Blessed be Thou, O Lord . . . who hast created man in Thine image and likeness and given him the capacity for eternal self perpetuation. Blessed be Thou, O Lord, Creator of man.

May Zion, childless now, rejoice, when her children are gathered in her midst in joy. Blessed be Thou, O Lord, who givest joy to Zion through her children.

Make these beloved mates to rejoice in great joy, as once Thou didst give joy to Thy creatures in the garden of Eden. Blessed be Thou, O Lord . . . who makest groom and bride to rejoice.

Blessed be Thou, O Lord . . . who has created joy and gladness, groom and bride, jubilation and exultation, delight and satisfaction, love and brotherhood, peace and friendship . . . Blessed be Thou, O Lord who makest rejoice the groom with his bride.

The cup is handed to them; they share it. Thus will they share the cup of life throughout the years to come. May God reside in their home, and may their "cup," their measured fate, always be a blessed one. The rabbi pronounces them husband and wife in accordance with State law and with Jewish law.

Customs

The ceremony is ended, yet custom has added a few more rites. The rabbi may address the couple during the ceremony; he will most surely bless them with the ancient blessing of the Torah: the Lord bless thee. . . . A glass may be broken in symbolic recognition of the sorrows of Israel since the time of its dispersion. It is a beautiful custom, for it reminds us that even in moments of supreme happiness we may not think of ourselves alone; our heart must always turn to those who may be burdened. It was the custom to lead the couple to the privacy of a room together, that they might officially break their fast; for on their wedding day, just as on Yom Kippur, groom and bride must fast and confess their sins before taking their solemn vows. Actually, groom and bride were now really alone—perhaps for the first time in their lives. The third of the three knots had been tied, not only symbolically but in reality.

Practices surrounding weddings

When betrothal in its ancient meaning was abandoned, engagement in the modern sense took its place. Celebrated in the family and among friends, it was a moment when bride and groom would exchange gifts. He gave her a preciously bound prayer book, in which some day the names of the children would be recorded; she gave him the Tallit he would wear at worship.

In the medieval congregation, weddings were public events. Rabbi and dignitaries, preceded by candle bearers, met the groom at his home and accompanied him to the courtyard of the synagogue; then they returned to meet the bride and escort her. The ceremony took place in the synagogue or in its courtyard, under the open sky, "that their seed might multiply like the stars in heaven." Under a shower of wheat, mixed with coins, the young people stepped out from under the Huppah. The wheat was symbol of their blessing, the coins a reminder to be charitable;

The wedding ceremony is performed under the Huppah.

they were not for the newlyweds, but for the poor. The groom was led home first, that he might meet his bride at the doorstep and lead her into the house. He welcomed her, taking her hand and putting it at the post of the house, for now it was her house and she was its mistress. Then the couple retired and the festivities began. The musicians struck up, young people began to dance, and the dance house was filled to overflowing as festivities lasted for seven days. On the Sabbath of his wedding week, the groom was again escorted by the leaders of the congregation as he went to the synagogue, where he was given a seat of honor. And the day was filled with music and dancing; Christian musicians were engaged, since law forbade the playing of instruments on the Sabbath. A new home had been founded in Israel, so the people rejoiced.

MARRIED LIFE

Children are the glory of the family, and every family was to have at least one son and one daughter, if God was gracious.[3] The welfare of

---

[3] Mishnah Yebamot 6:6.

the offspring was the first concern. The rabbis advised young men to marry wisely, not for money, but for beauty, and above all to look for the daughter of a wise man who might take hold of the family in emergencies and bring up the family well should the husband die.[4] They suggested that people look for contrasting qualities in their mates; the tall man ought to find himself a small wife; the pale girl a darker fellow, in order that the children be normal in their physical features.[5] But procreation was not the sole justification for sex, every wife had a right to ask it of her husband as a pleasure to be enjoyed.[6] Judaism has always considered the gifts of the body to be good. If there was danger to health in case of conception, contraceptives were permitted by the Talmud. Three situations are mentioned in particular: three women may use a sponge (as contraceptive) during intercourse—a minor, a pregnant woman, and a woman breast-nursing her child. The minor is granted this permission because she might die from a pregnancy, the pregnant woman since additional semen might harm her embryo, and the nursing mother since she might be forced to wean her child too early (due to new pregnancy, her milk might dry out), which might endanger the child's life (Talmud Yebamot 12b). Later generations ruled against contraceptives with greater severity.

Yet for almost two weeks out of every month, husband and wife were forbidden even to touch each other. During the monthly period and seven days thereafter they were to be apart. Only after the wife had immersed herself in a specially arranged ritual pool were they to come to each other again. Orthodox people still abide strictly by this law, which may be a reason for the low divorce rate in Jewish life. Most marriages of the past were arranged by matchmakers, yet they endured. Husbands did not get tired of wives they could not approach half of the time. Families based on piety, duty, and parental responsibility had good foundations.

Women's Status in Religious Law

Woman's position in the home was one of dignity and power. She was endowed with the privilege of kindling the lights of the Sabbath, for to her belonged the authority in the home. The education of the children lay in her hands. Her husband, who greeted her every Friday night with the Hymn of Praise from Proverbs, knew how much she meant to him. Many a Talmudic scholar found in his wife the support of his family while he gave his life to study. The Talmud speaks of all Jewish women

---

4 Talmud Pessahim 49a-b.
5 Talmud Berahot 45b.
6 Shulhan Arukh, Eben ha-Ezer 76.

when it points out that "for the sake of the pious women were our fathers redeemed from Egypt (Shemot Rabba 1)." They found food for their families and gave courage to their husbands. Generation after generation, women were the stay and stability of the home. Abraham is advised by God to dismiss his son Ishmael, as long as Sarah so desires (Gen. 21:8-12); Rebecca, and later Rachel and Leah, advise their husbands on the important decisions in life (Gen. 27:46; 31:1-16). This is far different from the inferior position of women in other civilizations of the time. Miriam, sister of Moses, becomes a national heroine; she saves the life of her brother. (Exod. 2:4). The tale may well have served as pattern for the New Testament story of the birth of Jesus. Moses is exposed to the waves, since Pharaoh wishes all male children to die; Jesus is born at the time when Herod orders the murder of babies. Moses is the rescuer of Israel, and so is Jesus. Moses is exposed to the elements in a basket made of grass and reeds; Jesus is born in an exposed stable and covered by hay; Moses is lifted up by the wise daughter of Pharaoh, Jesus is visited by the wise men. Above all, Moses is rescued by his sister Miriam, who becomes his virgin mother by saving his life; Jesus is given life by Miriam too—Mary—his virgin mother. It speaks for the tremendous respect in which women were held that Miriam, a woman, could influence history so deeply as a national heroine at a period when all heroes were men of brawn, cunning, and military prowess. In Jewish history we even find at least one woman who was outstanding as a soldier and general; she was Deborah, judge and leader of Israel (Judges 4:4-5,32).

Legally, however, the position of women was inferior from the beginning and deteriorated as Jewish isolation led to ever more stringent legislation.

From the day she entered her husband's home, her hair was veiled, sometimes even cut; her beauty was not for the world to see. Her voice was not to be heard in public. She could be neither judge nor witness. She could refuse to accept a bill of divorcement, but could not initiate divorce proceedings of her own. If her husband disappeared without a trace she could not remarry, for his death had to be certified by witnesses before she was free. These are problems which have remained unsolved to this day for orthodox Jewry.

In the days of the Temple, at festive occasions, she originally took her place with the men. When it was found that this lacked decorum, she was banished to the gallery. When men still turned to the women sitting in the gallery, a curtain was drawn, a partition which still remains in orthodox synagogues.

Women could not be counted among the ten who form the quorum for public worship. Originally she could be called to the Torah like the men; gradually this privilege too was taken from her. Joseph Karo still states in the Shulhan Arukh:

All may go up to the Torah on the Sabbath, up to a total number of seven to be called; even a woman and a child who knows to Whom we pray, may go. The Rabbis have said however: a woman should not be called out of respect for the congregation (Orah Hayim 282, 283).

Women are not called to the Torah. Some congregations have tried to reverse the trend, but women themselves were initially opposed. Now, however, more and more women are demanding this right.

Women were always freed from the observance of religious duties which had to be performed at specific times. It was felt that their duties in the home, or their condition, might prevent them from attending to these obligations. In a society in which fulfilment of Torah was sign of distinction, this dispensation alone branded them as inferior in the minds of many. There was joy when a girl was born, but somehow the boy was the fulfilment of his parents' hopes. The story is told of Rashi, who was grieved, for he had no son, until God appeared unto him in a dream to promise him that his daughters' husbands and children would bring glory to him.

Why did women accept all this? Because they had the love and respect of their husbands, and because they knew that theirs was the greatest task of all: the raising of their children in the fear of God, in respect for their elders, and in love of Torah. These women accepted inequality, holding on to that position of superiority which was theirs uncontested: to be the builders of the generations of the Jewish people. Lately, women have *organized* to advance their full equality.

It would indeed be unfair to perpetuate their position of inferiority in our own time. Talmudic law was framed at a time when women simply were not equal; the Jewish woman, then, had many more rights than her contemporary in other cultures. Conditions have changed, and changed laws must give full rights to women. This is being implemented in *Reform* and *Reconstructionism,* adjustments being considered in *Conservatism.*

Divorce

Divorce was rare, and usually discouraged, but it could be granted. "When a home is broken by divorce, the altar even sheds tears (Gitin 90b)." When there was no hope, when living together became impossible, divorce could be obtained. No "guilt" had to be proven. A man could get a divorce if his wife bore him no children for ten years. A wife could ask the court to force her husband to divorce her when his conduct or type of work made it impossible for her to live with him. But when Jewish jurisdiction ceased, women lost this recourse. According to orthodox law, a degree obtained in general court is not sufficient to dissolve a marriage; there has to be a Jewish religious divorce, performed before a religious court of three rabbis with two witnesses present. A Bill of Divorcement is made out on request of the husband; the document must be written in conformity with exact and detailed regulations. As tne wife accepts the document from her husband, she is divorced. Ninety days later she may remarry. She may marry her husband again, but only if she has not married anyone else after her divorce. Since it is a binding principle in Judaism that "the law of the land is *the* law," no Jewish divorce may be granted without a preceding civil divorce.

SICKNESS AND DEATH IN TRADITIONAL OBSERVANCE

Health and Sickness

"One may not live in a town without a physician (Jerushalmi, Kiddushin 4:12)." To get competent medical help is a duty, for life is man's most precious gift. In this spirit, Jews have always seen in the art of healing a divine calling. Maimonides was a physician; there were many others before and after him. So famous were they that kings and bishops called them in their need. Queen Elizabeth I of England had a Jewish physician at a time when no Jew was permitted to set foot in her realm. The unhappy man, accused of treason by his enemies, paid with his life for the privilege of serving her.

Everyone must do his utmost to keep his body in good condition, and use competent medical help restore it to health and strength. He must also assist his neighbor in times of sickness. He who visits the sick takes a portion of his ills away from him, for he brings courage to his fellowman. But human resources are limited; healing comes from God, who is "physician of all flesh." To Him we pray, and prayer may spell the difference between life and death, and between a quick recovery and lingering illness. In silent Amidah we may add personal petitions for friends and dear ones to the plea for the general health of mankind. When a person falls seriously ill, and his life is in danger, friends may offer a special benediction after the reading of the Torah, or they may assemble to recite Psalms in supplication for his speedy return to well-being.

As Death Approaches

As a Jew nears the end of his earthly road, his friends will be around him. He may not recognize them any more, but throughout life he has had the comfort of knowing that he would not have to face eternity alone, that his companions in life would go with him praying, at least to the portals of life everlasting.

Among all communal organizations, none has traditionally enjoyed greater prestige than the "Holy Fellowship," men and women of proven worth and piety who hold the privilege of attending to the dying and the dead. Theirs are acts of love, performed without compensation; for there is no greater love than the love extended to those who cannot even say "thank you" any more.

The Jew's last words are to be his affirmation of faith: "Hear, O Israel, the Lord our God the Lord is One." As a person reaches his end, the men or women of the "fellowship" traditionally take turns staying with him. They spend the time in prayer; they confess his sins with the dying person, or for him. They recite with or for him the affirmation of faith, repeating it during his last moments, in order that with his last breath he might proclaim "Ehad"—He is One!

Preparing the Dead

During the last moments, the patient is not to be needlessly touched or moved, for any manipulation may hasten his death, and it is not for man to shorten another's span of life even by a hair's breadth; God alone determines the length of our days and years. When a person has died, a feather is placed on his lips to be sure he has breathed his last. This procedure originated at a time when physicians had no more definite way of making certain that death had come. They close his eyes and take him off the bed unto the dust whence he has come. His friends of the "fellowship" then make his coffin of simple rough wood.

When the coffin is completed, they wash the body and cleanse it, reciting the words Ezekiel spoke to the people in ancient days: "And I will sprinkle clean water upon you and ye shall be clean; from all your defilements and all your blemishes I will cleanse you (Ezek. 36:25)." Tenderly they dry the body and clothe it in the simplest of garments put on with loving care: white linen trousers and shoes, a linen shirt, the linen robe he had worn on Yom Kippur, a belt, and a cap. Women are given similar white garments. His Tallit is placed around his shoulders, and the body wrapped in a white shroud. Thus robed in purity, he is laid in the coffin. This custom of equal robes and equal coffins developed in ancient Israel as a result of a rabbinical ordinance. Before then, the poor frequently denuded themselves in an effort to give lavish funerals to their dear ones; now all are equal, and the dead no longer impose unduly on life. Embalming is forbidden, for all that came from the dust is to return to it.

It is considered an honor for the dead to be returned to the earth, his final resting place, as quickly as possible; thus funerals were often held on the very day of death. They may not be conducted on the Sabbath, but are permitted on the second day of holidays. Modern life has changed many of the customs, and this is regrettable; there is grandeur and there is deep love in the ancient customs.

Burial

As the body is taken to its resting place, friends and the members of the congregation join the procession. A eulogy may be offered, except on holy days. At the moment of their most bitter grief, the mourners put a tear in their garment; on the left—over the heart—for father and mother; on the right for other relatives. At the same time they bless God, "the righteous Judge." The body is lowered into the grave, also prepared by loving hands, and the children put the first shovels of earth upon the coffin. It is the last token of respect and of love; children are returning the mortal remains of their parents to the earth whence God has formed man. Then they stand to recite the kaddish: "Magnified and sanctified by the Name of God." By glorifying God in the hour of their bereavement, they give testimony to the piety of their dear ones and witness to their teachings. They demonstrate to the world that their parents have given them such faith in God's absolute goodness that the children can praise Him in public even now. Passing through two rows of friends, the mourners return home. "May God comfort you among those who mourn for Zion and for Jerusalem" is the parting greeting of the assembly. Once home, the mourners take off their shoes and sit on low stools for seven days.

The Period of Mourning

The first meal is brought by friends, lest the mourners forget to nourish themselves in their grief. Morning and evening worship is conducted in the home; the families of the community come to visit. Only on the Sabbath may the mourners leave their home. As the Sabbath is ushered in they enter the synagogue, are met by the rabbi at the door, and escorted to their seats with the words: "May God comfort you."

Shivah, the seven days of mourning, is ordained for father and mother, son and daughter, brother and sister, husband and wife. During this period the thoughts of the bereaved dwell upon their dear ones. Their reading is from the Book of Job. Friends speak to them of death as trial and act of grace.

Two vessels are sailing the seas; one setting out from sheltered harbor to unknown destination; the other returning from strenuous voyage. As the ship comes home the people rejoice. Even so is life. Yet we rejoice when birth sends out the child on the uncertain voyage of life, should we not find comfort when the ship finally reaches the sheltered harbor of God's peace (Shemot Rabba 48:1)?

For three days we may surrender to full expression of grief; from the fourth day, restraint is in order. After 30 days life must return to normal;

mourning comes to an end, except for father and mother. They are remembered for a full year. Every day, morning and night, the sons say Kaddish in the synagogue, up to the end of the eleventh month. Then life restores itself.

In his work *Peace of Mind,* the late Joshua Loth Liebman, rabbi and psychologist, has shown us how deep a psychological insight is reflected in Jewish mourning customs. He points out that repressed grief can be a source of neuroses and of physical diseases. Then he goes on to say: Traditional Judaism had the vision to provide all the procedures for healthy-minded grief which the contemporary psychologist counsels . . . Where traditional Judaism was psychologically sound in its approach to death much liberal religion has been unsound. We moderns have assimilated from our environment a sense of shame about emotionalism and a disinclination to face the tragic realities of life, both leading to unwise repression and emotional evasion. Liberal rabbis and liberal ministers alike are continually committing psychological fallacies.[7]

Yahrzeit

The years pass, but parents are never forgotten. The anniversary of their death, called Yahrzeit (from the German: Jahr-year and Zeit-time, meaning anniversary), is observed in all homes. A light burns from evening to evening. This custom, probably taken from the Catholic church, was first assailed by the rabbis, but is now firmly established. Kaddish is recited by the children on the day itself and on the preceding Sabbath. Study of Torah, giving of charity, perhaps fasting as call to repentance, set the day apart. If possible, children visit the graves of their dear ones, placing a little stone on the tombstone in parting. This custom originated in ancient days when stone heaps marked the graves; each visitor thus added to the upkeep of the grave by placing a stone on it. Today, the stone has become the "calling card." On Yom Kippur and on the last day of the Pilgrimage festivals the names of the departed are remembered in memorial services. Some congregations have memorial plaques on which children may have the names of their parents inscribed. A light will be kindled on the plaque, near the name, to burn on Yahrzeit and during memorial services on the Sabbath preceding it.

As grandchildren bear the names of their grandparents, the chain endures.

DIETARY LAWS

Of all religious laws and observances, the dietary laws have had the major share in fashioning and maintaining the distinctive character of the Jewish community.

---

[7] Joshua Liebman, *Peace of Mind,* © 1946 by Joshua Loth Liebman, by permission of Simon and Schuster; p. 123 f.

Purpose and Background

A great deal has been said about the background and purpose of these laws. They have been traced back to taboos existing even before the emergence of the Jewish people, and they have been regarded as health laws. There is truth in both of these explanations. In many cases the sanitary character of certain laws is almost self-evident. Jews have always insisted on cleanliness in food preparation, on forms of meat inspection, on purity of foods; these ordinances were based on religious laws, but helped to preserve health. The prohibition of certain kinds of sea food, such as shellfish, was a sound measure, especially in Palestine, where heat could lead to immediate spoilage. To the Jew, however, these laws have had a different meaning. He saw three basic motivations for them:

1. They are God's laws. He knows their purpose, even though mortal man may not be able to grasp it. They are to be observed in obedience to His will, in affirmation of His sovereignty. He has willed it, and we shall obey.

2. They are considered a means of preserving the uniqueness of the Jewish community. Unable to share their neighbor's table, Jews were tied to one another in closer communion, retaining their identity, and perpetuating their heritage.

3. They might be regarded as symbolic acts, expressing belonging to a group. Fraternal orders have their symbols, such as the handshake, by which the fellows recognize and are drawn to each other. Dietary laws equally have the power to bind the members of the community in close fellowship to one another, to their history, and their tradition. They build the spirit of family. Of these three, the first is the most important; the others emerged from it.

The Laws

Jewish dietary laws center around a number of basic regulations and prohibitions which form the fabric of observance and of practice.

PROHIBITED FOODS. There is no prohibition of any vegetable food. Regarding foods of animal origin, the Scripture sets definite rules in Leviticus 11 and Deuteronomy 14.

a) Cattle. "Whatsoever parteth the hoof and is completely cloven footed, and cheweth the cud . . . that may you eat (Lev. 11:3)." As examples are listed the ox, the sheep, the hart, the gazelle, the wild gazelle, the antelope, and others (Deut. 14:4-5). Both characteristics, parted hoofs *and* chewing the cud, must be present to make the meat permissible. This excludes those animals which have only one of these characteristics: the camel and the hare, which have no parted hoofs; the pig which does not chew the cud. They are "unclean" (Lev. 11:4-7).

b) Fish. "Whatsoever has fins *and* scales in the waters, in the seas and in the rivers, those you may eat (Lev. 11:9 and Deut. 14:9)." Again both conditions must be met: fins and scales. This eliminates all shellfish, but also eel and sturgeon, which have no scales.

c) Birds. The Bible gives a list of "unclean" birds, mostly birds of prey; all others may be eaten. Since the exact meaning of the Hebrew terms for these birds has become obscured, only those birds are permitted which have always been regarded as "clean." This includes chicken, geese, ducks, pigeons, and turkeys.

d) Swarming things with wings are prohibited, with the exception of locusts and grashoppers (Lev. 11:20-23). Yet they are not commonly eaten, and thus are regarded as prohibited.

e) Swarming things on the earth, from mice to crocodiles, are prohibited (Lev. 11:29-30).

In general, we find that all animals which live by the destruction of other lives, be they wild beasts or birds, are prohibited. Did the law possibly wish to convey a message of peace and a call to peaceful living?

RESTRICTIONS REGARDING PERMITTED FOODS. Even the permitted animals may be consumed only under certain conditions. The following are prohibited:

a) animals that have died on their own (Lev. 11:39; Deut 14:21);

b) animals that have been torn by others (Exod. 22:30);

c) all blood (Lev. 7:26);

d) certain animal fats, even of permitted animals: "It shall be a perpetual statute throughout your generations in all your dwellings, that ye shall eat neither fat nor blood (Lev. 3:17)."

e) certain sinews: "therefore the children of Israel shall not eat the sinew of the thigh vein . . . , because (the angel who wrestled with Jacob) touched the hollow of Jacob's thigh; namely the sinew of the thigh vein (Gen. 32:33)."

None of these and the following prohibitions apply to fish, however.

PREPARATION OF MEAT. *a) Slaughter.* Animals must be killed; if they die of natural causes they may not be used. There has to be a definite method of slaughter. Scripture merely states: ". . . and thou shalt kill of thy herd and of thy flock . . . as I have commanded thee (Deut 12:21)." The verse is significant. According to rabbinical interpretation, it holds a direct reference to the Oral Torah, whose binding power is thereby clearly established. Written Torah gives no further instruction regarding the method of slaughter.

By tradition, it is established that animals and birds must be killed by cutting through the arteries and veins and the windpipe at the neck. The knife must be sharp, without the smallest nick in it. The severing must be performed in one continuous stroke, without interruption, without downward pressure, and without meeting any obstacles in the animal's throat. If any of these conditions is not met, the animal may not be eaten. The slaughtering of an animal thus becomes a highly skilled task; the "shohet" who performs it must have both technical knowledge and learning in the law. He will examine his knife before and after the cut. If he finds the slightest nick in it, as he goes over its edge with his finger, he will proclaim the animal forbidden for use. He will do the same if he notices any other irregularity in his performance. In order to perform his office, the "shohet" obtains special certification from the rabbi.

Animal physiology has shown that the Jewish method of slaughter may be considered the most humane possible. A cut with a very sharp knife produces no pain sensation for a moment; we have all noticed that when cutting ourselves with a very sharp, clean-edged instrument. The same applies to the animal. At the time when pain ordinarily might be felt, the blood has already been drained from the brain through the artery of the neck, the brain has stopped functioning, and no pain sensation can develop. To spare the animal unnecessary suffering may have been the actual intention of the law. At the same time, the rapid drainage of blood makes the meat better fit for longer preservation.

b) Animals that have been torn may not be eaten. This means animals who have lost their power of survival (for at least another year) through either disease or injury. The shohet, therefore, has to examine the animal for signs of disease. If he finds damage in the lungs, an ulcerated stomach, or a discolored brain, the meat cannot be used.

c) Fats and sinews then have to be removed. The Jewish butcher learns to do that, so he too must be a responsible person. The sinews in the hind quarter of the animal are very difficult to remove. This part, therefore, is frequently not used at all, unless the butcher has the knowledge and skill to cut out the forbidden portions and has been certified to that effect by the rabbi.

d) Blood has to be eliminated. This is generally the task of the housewife. She soaks the meat in water for about one half hour; then she covers it with salt on all sides and leaves it for about one hour. After the salt has been washed off, the meat can be prepared for consumption. Another method which may be used consists in broiling the meat and permitting the blood to flow out freely; this is the only method permitted in the preparation of liver.

The meat must be fresh. If it has been stored for three days before all blood has been taken out—or at least been softened through washing—it can no longer be eaten.

When the entire process is completed, the meat is fully "kosher," which means "all right."

Kitchen utensils which have been used in connection with forbidden foods cannot be used in a "kosher" household. This includes knives, pots, pans, bowls, and plates. Kosher dishes cannot be washed with soap which contains animal fats, but they can be washed in detergents. Modern detergents and pure vegetable foods, such as beans in cans, may carry the seal of the Union of Orthodox Congregations, which testifies that their manufacture is supervised and their ingredients usable. The seal is a "U" in a circle—ⓤ—and is found on a great many products on the shelves of general food stores.

MEAT AND MILK. At three different places Scripture states: "Thou shalt not seethe the kid in the milk of its mother (Exod. 23:19; 34:25; Deut. 14:21)." This threefold prohibition was interpreted as conveying three different messages: you may not eat meat and milk products together; you may not cook those products together; you may not use any mixture of them. Originally, fowl was not included in the prohibition, for it has no "mother"; eventually, it was added too.

Meat and milk products may not be served together; there is to be no butter at a meat dinner, no ice cream to follow it. A waiting period has to be allowed between the consumption of meat and milk dishes.

The two may not be cooked together. But the law goes further. As meat is cooked, its juices penetrate the pores of the pots; as it is cut, they enter the knife; as it is served, they seep into the chinaware. The same applies to milk. The kosher household, therefore, has two complete sets of dishes, from cooking pots to spoons. They may never be used together or washed together. If they get mixed up by mistake, they may sometimes be cleansed by boiling out or by burning out the food, as the utensil is brought to red heat. Very often, however, the dishes have become useless. Only glass, which has no pores, can be used either way.

A kosher home must have two sets of dishes; it may have three, the additional one to be used for foods in neither category, such as fruit. In addition, it has to have complete duplicate sets for Passover, when the year-round dishes cannot be used, since they have been permeated by grain products.

These dietary laws imposed such a regimen of observance and self-discipline upon members of the community that they could never forget their identity. Friends may eat only among those friends whose conscientiousness is beyond question. Questions in "Kashrut" situations can be decided by the rabbi. This was and is one of the primary functions of the orthodox rabbi. He did not have to be a preacher, for dietary law observance was in itself an eternal message. It has held up to the people the power of Torah, its authority, and its eternally binding force.

Some modern Jews do no longer feel bound by the laws of kashrut; their reasons will be explained later. Others wish to maintain it in their homes as a symbol of Jewish belongingness; among them are those who will obey some of the rules without accepting all of them. These people will eat some or all regular foods when they are away from home. Others will simply deny themselves *some* foods, such as pork, as a matter of religious discipline. But there are a great many Jews who obey the dietary laws without compromise and who find happiness in doing so. To them, the technical problems of having a kosher home have become routines of life and present no major obstacles. Their enforced separation from the stream of society is real, but it is accepted cheerfully as the price to be paid for obedience to a command in which they see the word of God and a safeguard for survival.

THE WEARING OF THE HAT

No Jewish custom is more difficult to explain than the wearing of the hat in the synagogue. The Torah has no ruling about it. The Talmud observes simply:

Men sometimes have their heads covered, and sometimes go bareheaded; Women always cover their heads; children always go bareheaded (Nedarim 30b).

This points to complete freedom of choice as far as men were concerned. At another occasion a revealing story is related.

Chaldaean (astrologers) told the mother of Rabbi Nahman ben Isaac: "Your son will be a thief." (To prevent him from falling into thievery), she never permitted him to go bareheaded but told him: "Cover thy head that thou mayest have the fear of God, and ask Him for mercy." Once he sat under a palm tree studying Torah; suddenly the cloth fell off his head. He raised up his eyes, noticed the palm tree and was gripped by temptation. He climbed up the tree and tore off a bunch of dates with his teeth (Sabbath 156b).

The head covering seems to have been a veil to shield a susceptible boy from the world and its temptations by screening his view of it. When he lost his veil, he succumbed. The wearing of a head covering obviously was not a general custom; otherwise there would be no point to the story.

In the Shulhan Arukh we find three rulings, each more restrictive than the one preceding, indicating a process of evolution. The first ruling states: "One may not read from the Torah with uncovered head (Orah Hayim 282:3)." The prohibition applies only to the public recital of the Torah. There is nothing said about any rules at home or even at prayer. Actually, there is an implied possibility that people may have been worshipping bareheaded as late as the sixteenth century, and were told to cover their heads when Torah was recited by them to the congregation.

The next ruling deals with decorum in the synagogue. The Shulhan Arukh states: "One may enter the synagogue with one's staff, knapsack and purse; but some prohibit entering with a long knife or uncovered head (Orah Hayim 151:6)." The rules have been tightened; no murderous weapon may be brought into the House of God, and some consider bareheadedness to be repugnant in contact with God.

Finally, the Shulhan Arukh states categorically: "One may not walk four cubits with uncovered head (Orah Hayim 2:6)." This applies to all places and conditions, at home, at work, and in prayer.

In viewing these laws, we conclude first of all that the law and custom had remained fluid until very late in Jewish history, hardening at a period when strictness and literal interpretation reached their height. It is possible, therefore, that the story of the Talmud was given a universal significance; covering of the head prevents sin and should be universal. But another explanation may be suggested as well. In the Middle Ages the king kept his head covered while his courtiers bared theirs as sign of humility. In the same manner, the Torah reader, as spokesman for God, was to have his head covered, symbolically expressing the majesty of God whose word he proclaimed. What about the rest of the congregation? To the medieval Jew, the Jew-hat was a mark of humiliation imposed by the Christian community. He may have responded by making it a badge of honor. Forced upon him as means of identification, it became for him an emblem of self-identification. In the synagogue where he was free to develop his own pattern of conduct, he insisted on the hat to demonstrate his defiant individuality. It was as if he wished to say: You force us to wear a hat in the street in distinction from you, we equally choose to wear it in the House of the Lord, where you remove it. We wear it, for we deem ourselves royal princes rather than outcasts, and may keep our heads covered in the presence of the King of Kings.

Thus the hat of humiliation may have been transformed into a crown of distinction. It was a token of self-identification, and an act of defiance against unjust law and against oppression. It showed a lack of pride not to wear it in the synagogue, hence it was forbidden. The Jew, linking himself more intimately to God the deeper he sank in his status in the world, eventually would wear his hat always; he lived always in the immediate presence of God. It was the symbol of Jewish pride and self-respect.

This emotional attachment may explain why Jews have held on to the wearing of hats with such tenacity. No change in Jewish practice has met with greater resistance than the rule of American Reform Judaism permitting worship with uncovered heads. Many Reform congregations who accepted the rule for their members have retained head coverings for their rabbis and cantors. As a custom, anchored in the emotions of the people, the covering of the head has exerted a greater power than many a well-established law which was modified or abolished.[8] It may be considered a symbol of the principle of identity in difference, which the Jews have championed with great determination. We have a right to be different, it says, and so has everyone; since our non-conformism does not harm society, we have an equal right to be respected and treated as equal citizens. So has everyone else under equal conditions.

---

[8] Head covering as a sign of humility was indeed practiced by an ancient rabbi, "for the glory of God is above my head" (Talmud Kiddushin 31a).

13

Forces and Counterforces

U ntil the time of the Renaissance in the western world, religion had been the unifying force in a life founded in the one Catholic Church. From that time on, however, religion and secular pursuits were to be separated; the one religion developed into several religions as a result of the Reformation. Following the banner of religious ideals, nations made wars against each other which soon ceased to be religiously motivated and became contests for national power and instruments of political conquest. Some of these wars wrought terrible destruction. During the Thirty Years War, which lasted from 1618 to 1648, Germany was utterly devastated. It was as if the forces of the apocalypse had been turned loose in battle before the end of days. No wonder that expectations were aroused of a speedy arrival of Christ, who would usher in the millennium; no wonder that Jews, too, saw signs of the coming of the Messiah.

The Jews were caught in the maelstrom of conflicts as men's souls broke asunder and societies disintegrated. The split personality of the western world was reflected in its attitude toward the Jew; it was mirrored in the attitude of the Jew himself.

Humanism called for a return to the original sources of ancient literature. Latin, Greek and Hebrew works were studied in their originals; the results were sometimes startling. The Humanists who studied the Hebrew Bible developed doubts in the accuracy of the Catholic version; some were drawn to Jewish commentators such as Rashi. In the end their discoveries aided the forces of dissent within the Catholic Church, and contributed to the Reformation.

An Example: Venice

Humanism itself exerted a mighty force upon the Jews, especially in Italy, home of the Renaissance. The Jews wanted to become an integral part of the Western World, but governments, full of anxieties at the new forces which were closing in, did not wish to admit any more nonconformists than necessary. Thus we find the strange example of the Jewish community in Venice. Jews taught Christian Hebraists and held philosophical debates with Christian scholars; they translated Italian works into Hebrew; they engaged widely in the newly invented art of printing, while Christian printers were the first ones to issue complete Hebrew texts of Bible and Talmud in print. Jewish composers moved into the stream of baroque music. The association of Christians and Jews was close, until the government clamped down. It was during the Renaissance that the Jews of Venice were forced to move into the ghetto, their rights restricted. Even there they continued their contacts, calling the leading architect of the time, Longhena, builder of the famous church Santa Maria della Salute, to erect a synagogue for them —in the ghetto, on the second floor of a house, so that it would be undetectable as a synagogue from without. Thus was government law followed.

Luther

Strange indeed were the results of the Reformation in Germany and in England. Luther favored the Jews in his early career. He hoped to convert them to his creed; had it not been purified of "popish abominations"? The Jews refused to follow him, and his friendship turned into implacable hatred. Persecution remained their lot.

England

In England, great upheavals followed the rule of Queen Elizabeth I. A king, Charles I, was executed; a militant sect of protestant purists assumed power. They were the Puritans, led by Oliver Cromwell. Fervently hoping for the advent of Christ, he held the view that the Jews had a share in the scheme of salvation. They had to be fully dispersed among the nations of the world before Christ would return; hence they had to be in England, too. He established contact with the leader of Dutch Jewry, a scholar named Manasseh ben Israel (1604-57), and entered into negotiations with him. Manasseh was invited to England to present his case; no formal legislation was passed, but Jews were informally permitted to return to the land from which they had so long been excluded. Reformation and messianic hopes had become a blessing to the homeless.

Eastern Europe

Eastern European Jewry presents a different picture; it reflects the fate of the general population. The progress started by the Renaissance stopped at the Iron Curtain. This curtain, which today separates Free Europe from Communist Europe, is not a creation of the twentieth century. For centuries the Elbe river, which flows from the Bohemian mountains through the center of Germany to the North Sea, has been a boundary. To its east there has always been enslavement, growing in severity; to the west, freedom slowly emerged. In Eastern Europe the commercial and—later—the industrial revolution were slow in taking hold. While in the west an evolving civilization brought more and more power to the middle classes, and eventually to labor as well, eastern Europe saw the reversal of the process. The landowner, the lord of the manor, became more powerful as the peasant sank deeper into the despondency of serfdom. The distinction between the classes grew. This condition has remained to the twentieth century. Russia admitted no Jews. They were forced on her in the 18th century by acquisition of a slice of Poland, where large masses of Jews lived. As all people suffered, Jews suffered doubly.

Even under Polish rule Jews had been oppressed. The Church opposed any humane intentions of the rulers. The Jews remained a distinct community, and were eventually given internal self-government, supervised by the king. They developed a complete internal autonomy, from the *Kahal,* the communal organization, to the *Council of the Four Lands,* their central administration. Thus they lived a life separated from the outside world, from which they could not learn and with which they had neither language nor culture in common. In its loneliness, homelessness, and hopelessness, Eastern European Jewry immersed itself ever more deeply in the realm of the Talmud, analysing, dissecting in hairsplitting dialectic every word, every phrase of the book. Torah—written and oral—was *the truth;* all legitimate interpretation was contained in it. The masters of the Talmud therefore could never be wrong. When there was disagreement among them, it meant that each had expressed one aspect of the total truth. The student of the Talmud had to conciliate all these views by means of reasoning, debate and a new twist to reconcile contradictions. Debate and more debate led to ever narrower alleys of discussion and thought, far removed from the highway of Talmud. Clear evidence of that withdrawal could be found in every aspect of life. There was no progress. The German garment was forever retained as the *caftan,* and so was the German hat. Commandments were taken in their most literal meaning. "Ye shall not round the corners of your head; neither shalt thou mar the corners of thy beard (Lev. 19:27)." These rules, designed to prevent effeminacy or practices connected with heathen worship, now became absolute commandments. The corners of the head, the sidelocks at the temples could not be touched; the beard could not be cut at the side. Thus a strange looking Jew emerged in self-styled uniqueness. He was forcefully secluded, and, by his actions, removed himself even further.

The seventeenth century brought frightful sufferings to the East European Jews. Whenever the masses rose against their oppressors, their fury was deflected upon the Jews. The Jews were slaughtered, and the misery of the poor remained the same. In 1648, the Cossacks under Chmielnicky rose against the Polish gentry; the uprising was broken, but hundreds of thousands of innocent Jews lost their lives. Death or baptism was their choice; again they chose death.

It is not surprising, then, that Jews withdrew further and further into the realm of the Talmud and more deeply into the mysticism of the Cabalah, that mystical tradition which supposedly had come down the centuries from the days of the Mishnah.

Messianism

Then the dam burst all over Europe. Expectation of the end was in the air. There arose in the City of Smyrna, in Turkey, a young, handsome, fascinating man. His name was Sabbatai Zevi (1626-76), and he proclaimed himself the messiah. The power of his appeal was overwhelming. Never in history had Jewry accepted a messiah who had proclaimed himself as such, for they knew that only world events would testify to the fact that the messiah had come. A world at peace, a world of brotherhood, a world of humanity under God would be his credential. This time, however, they followed the voice, for the cup of their suffering had been filled to overflowing. They did not listen to the voice of their rabbis. They sold their homes, their belongings, they bought carts to carry a few things, and they were on the way. From Greece and Turkey, from Italy and Germany, from Holland, Poland, and Russia, an endless stream moved to Palestine. And then came the blow. Sabbatai, captured by the Turks, was given a choice. He might testify to his calling by dying a martyr's death, or he might disown his mission and be converted to Islam. He chose conversion, but his followers could not accept this deception. The excitement continued, as other messianic movements followed; mysticism grew and became popular. The disappointment was tragic beyond measure.

But Jewry could not be left to despair. Leaders arose who gave it new hope by means of a creative adjustment to the conditions of the time.

Elijah, the Gaon of Vilna.

Eastern Europe had the "Gaon of Vilna," Elijah ben Solomon (1720-1797); it also had Israel "Baal Shem Tov," Master of the Divine Name (1700-1760). German Jewry, living under the somewhat brighter reflection of the light of the Age of Reason, found a leader in Moses Mendelssohn (1729-1786).

The "Gaon" of Vilna

Elijah ben Solomon acquired his name "Gaon" by his wisdom and unparalleled mastery of Jewish sources, combined with his wide knowledge of secular subjects. Gaon, once the official title held by the heads of the Babylonian academies, was now bestowed on him by his people in recognition of his greatness. He realized that Judaism must be pulled back unto the highway of reason; talmudic study must once more be in line with sound principles of thought; the underbrush of dialectic must be cut. Secular knowledge is essential, and his own commentaries follow this approach; they are lucid, simple, and clear. Worship in his own synagogue was simplified, too; he did away with a great many of the piyutim, those pieces of poetry which had accumulated over the years and had obscured the clear pattern and meaning of worship; he sought to improve fervor by greater use of unison prayer. Above all, he called for a return to reason, to study in meaningful ways. He saw clearly that Judaism is the religion of reason, the faith of intelligence, based on the tradition of Torah, the Book. He realized that

Judaism must remain in touch with its intellectual and cultural surroundings in order to evolve naturally. As far as his community was concerned, he failed. Thousands worshipped him personally and called him a Saint, but they retained the method of dialectic and maintained their hostility to non-Jewish cultural influences. This has been most unfortunate. Had the Gaon prevailed, Eastern European Jewry might have found a gradual adjustment to modern ways without giving up their deep Jewish fervor. Their descendants, thrown unto the modern scene of American and western civilization, might have been less confused, and their children been less tempted to discard completely the heritage of their fathers.

The Baal Shem: The Hasidim

Many worshipped the Gaon, but followers of the Baal Shem did not. Under his influence, there emerged a movement which was to have profound influence upon Jewish life and philosophy: Hasidism. Inwardness, joyful awareness of God in nature, exultation, acceptance of the menial tasks of life as divine challenges; these were some of its features. Study was secondary. So great has been the impact of Hasidism that it deserves special discussion (see Chapter 14). It was something not known before in this form. In vain did the Gaon raise his voice; the movement grew. Some of its effects can be seen in the new State of Israel, in the philosophy of Martin Buber, and in the influence Buber has had on modern thought in general.

Moses Mendelssohn

Moses Mendelssohn in turn gave direction to the entire development of western Jewry and deserves special treatment in a later chapter. Out of his work grew the synthesis of Judaism and culture which the Gaon could not effect among his people.

Baruch Spinoza

There was one land which gave Jews freedom of movement and of thought; it was Holland. It produced a Jew who was lost to Judaism because he lacked spiritual discipline. His name was Baruch Spinoza (1632-1677). Spinoza, son of a marrano family returned to Judaism, and widely read in philosophy, was confused. The lines between Judaism and Christianity were blurred for some of these men and women who had been Christians at the surface and Jews in secret. It is not surprising that Spinoza, schooled in rationalistic thought by study of Maimonides and modern thinkers, compared the ideas of the emerging enlightenment with both religions, and developed an opinion of his own.

Spinoza's way of thinking stood under the influence of the great

French philosopher Descartes (1596-1650). Descartes had stated that we must have a basic principle of knowledge which is absolutely certain, completely beyond question, and immediately evident. Is there anything in the world of which I can be certain; is it not possible that all is but a dream? He answers, indeed I have no right to take anything for granted; I must doubt everything. But then I know that I have doubt; and to doubt means to think; and to think means to exist. How could I think if I did not exist? From this point Descartes moves to a proof of the existence of God, and from there to that of the reality of the world. Descartes' universe is a dualistic one: body and soul, matter and mind, world and God. He offers us a key to unlock the secrets of the things around us; it is mathematics.

Spinoza follows Descartes. To him mathematics is more than a key to the world; it is absolute law. The universe is based on logical and mathematical necessity. Only thus can God be understood, for only through reason can he be found. In his search for such certainty, Spinoza must abandon the God of Israel who speaks to man, who loves and wishes to be loved, who is father to all his children, and full of mercy. There is no certainty of such God, in a mathematical sense. The mathematical God can neither be worshipped nor can he have been the author of Torah and commandments. The Torah then, according to Spinoza, was not given by God but written by a number of men, and not necessarily those who are considered authors of its various books. The commandments are merely a practical invention which once had the purpose of preserving the ancient Jewish state.[1] Wilfully, Spinoza breaks the law.

Yet—perhaps as a result of his Jewish background—Spinoza feels compelled to reject the dualism of Descartes. Unity is his principle, and the one God is seen in absolute oneness. Out of this synthesis emerges Spinoza's thought. He combines the mathematical God, based on Descartes ideas, with the Oneness of the God of Israel, and arrives at *Deus sive Natura*, the God who is identical with Nature. He is neither more nor less than all of nature; he can be found through reason and worshipped through logic. Everything becomes a "mode of God," everything we do is part of him. But logically, as we can see, this leads to the conclusion that good and evil are no longer opposites in human life; evil as well as good is one of God's modes. In that case, where is the ultimate

---

[1] Benedict Spinoza, *The Political Works* (incl. The Tractatus Theologico-Politicus), ed. and Trans., with Introduction and Notes, by A. G. Wernham (New York: Oxford University Press, 1958). In chapter V (pp. 95 ff.), Spinoza writes: "Sacred rites make no contribution to blessedness, and those prescribed in the Old Testament, and indeed in the whole law of Moses were concerned only with the Jewish state, and thus with temporal benefits alone. As for Christian rites, like Baptism, Lord's Supper, festivals . . . they were instituted only as symbols of a universal church and not as things which make any contribution to blessedness, or have any intrinsic sanctity."

imperative for ethical action? Spinoza does not seem to see the dilemma in which he finds himself. He does not see that, in his system, good and evil cease to be necessary choices of man. He fails to recognize that his system allows for no movement forward, onward, or upward. All is God; in this pantheism the universe, in final analysis, stands still.

Spinoza lived a calm life, free from emotions and ambitions. He lived the life of reason. Study to him is worship; this too was a Jewish heritage. His philosophy has appealed to the emotions of later generations.

The rabbis in Amsterdam, however, had no choice. They excommunicated him. He had courted excommunication by his defiance of Jewish tradition, he had refused to yield in either his actions or his opinions, and he had rejected their plea. Had he remained a member in good standing of the synagogue, his philosophy might have taken all hope from the people. If Nature is God, if all is a mode of God, what then is the meaning of all our suffering through history? The persecuted is no better than his persecutor. If God does not speak, to whom shall we turn in our distress? Who will give us hope? Who will sustain us? How can we survive? To the rabbis, either Spinoza had to be eliminated or Judaism would collapse; their choice was obvious.

The significance of Spinoza is that he makes clear the infinite difficulty facing the Jew. Judaism allows freedom of thought, but it demands a self-imposed restraint. The lines are not drawn through ordinances by church bodies, but from within, from the inner God awareness of the Jew, from his inner relationship with his people, his tradition, his spiritual heritage, and the living future of his faith. Freedom of thought may lead to many different answers, all of them within Judaism. Hillel and Shammai were among the first to argue, and the words of both were "the words of the living God." They were concerned with the strengthening of the Torah and of the faith; their intent made their opinions holy. This explains why there can be so many different views among Jews in the fields of theology, philosophy, and practice; in spite of the differences, there is *one* Judaism. In all the varieties of expression the underlying ideals of God and Torah are retained; the different schools all work "for the sake of Heaven." Spinoza threw these Jewish ideals overboard; he did not care for the preservation of Judaism and its ideas, so he tore it down. The intent was more destructive than the act might have been. For that reason he could no longer be a member of the "shul"—the school-synagogue. Excommunication in Judaism is extremely rare, and Spinoza's has remained a unique case. He had to be excluded, for every Jew in good standing is a teacher to his fellow-Jews. He may make mistakes, and that is understood, but Spinoza emphasized that he had made no mistake; that was his philosophy. This made him unfit to be a teacher of Jews, a member of the shul. His teaching, if it had succeeded, would have destroyed the living God, and hope, and Judaism itself, for this was the effect he intended.

14

Hasidism

asid is the "pious one," but pious in a special sense, for he is a mystic. Hasidism is almost as old as Judaism itself. Its rebirth in Poland after the collapse of messianic expectations can be understood. The masses lived in misery; was there any hope? Hasidism held out to them the promise of salvation, not only through the agency of one man, a Messiah, but through the work of all. It would involve not merely a physical return to Israel when the time was ripe, but the spiritual restoration of the Kingdom of God, to be promoted now. Throughout history, Hasidism has held greatest appeal and reached highest development in times of disappointment, when hopes have been quashed; it became the antidote to despair.

Ezekiel

Israel was in exile; the first Temple had been destroyed. The people were disheartened, doubtful of their future. This was the moment of Ezekiel's vision:

Now it happened . . . that the heavens were opened and I saw visions of God . . . (Ezek. 1:1).

Thus begins the narration of one of the great mystical experiences. The prophet tells of his vision of the heavenly throne surrounded by the

chariots of heaven. It is *Maaseh Merkabah*, the "Event of the Chariot."
The chapter gives us some basic ideas regarding the character of Jewish
mysticism. The initiates could expect direct mystical experience as a
result of preparation, through fasting, meditation, and separation from
the world. A God concept and vision are vouchsafed which are veiled
to the average man, yet the content of the vision may be made public.
The revelation is not the property of the individual who has the experience; it is not *his* revelation, but *universal* revelation which comes only
to the pure and the perfect. Ezekiel does not keep his revelation to
himself, he reveals it.

THE RABBIS OF THE TALMUD did not look kindly upon the study
of mysticism; it might lead astray, out of Judaism. The Mishnah makes
this clear:

The mysteries of creation may be taught not even to two students at a time.
"Maaseh Merkabah" not even to one student, except he be a sage and grasp it
out of his own understanding. He who ponders over four things had better not
been born. (The four are:) That which is above, that which is below, that
which is before us and that which is behind us. He who does not protect the
honor of his Creator, it were better for him had he not been born (Hagigah
2:1).

The dangers of speculation can clearly be recognized from this Mishnah;
the Jewish God concept itself is at stake, and with it the very essence
of the Jewish faith. The Gemara goes into further details:

"Maaseh Merkabah may not be taught even to one student," (says Mishnah).
(Gemara:) Rabbi Hiya taught, you may tell him the main ideas. Rabbi Zera
said: (Even) the main ideas you may tell only to the head of the court of
justice, and to one who is full of fear and awe in his heart. Rabbi Johanan once
said to Rabbi Eleazar: Come I will teach you Maaseh Merkabah; but he replied, I am not old enough for it. When he was old enough Rabbi Johanan had
died. So Rabbi Assi spoke to him and said: Come, I will now teach you Maaseh
Merkabah. But he replied: Had I been worthy I should have had the privilege
of learning it from your master, Rabbi Johanan. . . .

The rabbis taught: Four entered the paradise (of mystical speculations):
Ben Azai, Ben Zoma, Aher and Rabbi Akiba. Ben Azzai saw and died;
Ben Zoma saw and lost his mind; Aher saw and lost his faith; only Akiba
entered and emerged in peace (Hagigah 13-15, selections).

Only the initiated were now given mystical instruction, and, in turn,
transmitted it only to a small group of the select. It became "special
transference," in Hebrew, *Cabalah*. It could not be transmitted to the
ignorant in whose mind it might create havoc, and whose soul it might
subvert from the teachings of Judaism.

German Hasidism: Judah Hahasid and His Followers

The crusades had left the communities of the Rhineland desolate, and had spread their terror throughout the holy congregations of Germany. In their wake we find a new flowering of mysticism in Germany. Centered in Worms and Regensburg during the twelfth and thirteenth centuries, it has as its masters Judah and his son Eleazar of the Calonymus family. *The Book of the Pious* is one of their great works; "Hasid" means "Pious." The piety demanded by the group called for more than average religious observance; it called for unconditional love, absolute selflessness, and complete self denial. Man must develop a spirit of absolute serenity while renouncing the gifts of the world; he must live an ascetic life and submit to a discipline much stricter than that of Torah and Talmud. In trembling love the Hasid must link his soul to God in a spiritual passion which excludes all earthly physical passion. Ascetic denial of the world thus goes hand in hand with absolute unselfishness. The Christian Church has given the world a saint in whom we find the same spirit and outlook. He is St. Francis of Assisi (1182-1226), a contemporary of Judah. As the mystic pores over the words of the Torah, he finds new meanings in them. Tradition has taught that every word of Torah had been spoken by God Himself. Like the Talmudists, the mystics held that every word and every letter had its definite purpose, for God does not waste words. But the mystics saw meaning behind meaning. They explained Scripture not only literally, but also allegorically, symbolically, and mystically. Combinations of letters, meaningless to literal explanation, may reveal new mystical insights. Hebrew letters also serve as numbers, hence the letters of a word can be added to reveal new meanings. And the hidden meanings of the word conveyed more than knowledge—they gave creative power. They revealed God anew; and he who understands the very deepest meaning of the word resembles God in his power to shape and affect events. He acquires this potency, if, like God, he is entirely unselfish, never asking anything for himself. He who understood the secret meaning of the "Divine Name" was "Master of the Name," Baal Shem, and could change the world. *All* the words of Torah were realignments of the Name.

As there are hidden meanings in the word, so there are hidden forces —our surroundings abound with good agents or evil spirits and demons which affect people. They sometimes reveal themselves in dreams, and can be driven out through the use of the Divine Name. A person can protect himself against them by wearing a charm, perhaps a small scroll containing holy words of secret meaning. A woman in childbirth can be shielded from danger to herself and her child by an amulet worn around her neck, or by protective inscriptions hung around the room.

Later, at the beginning of the seventeenth century, we hear of a Master who is able to fashion a homunculus, the *Golem*. Rabbi Loew of Prague makes a clay figure which comes to life when a strip of parchment inscribed with the name of God is placed in his mouth.

These beliefs in demons and evil spirits were held by Christians too. We have seen that Judah and St. Francis shared similarities in outlook. Throughout the centuries mysticism forged a close link between Jews and Christians; the fraternity of mystics transcended the boundaries of faith.

Zohar: The Book of Radiance

Toward the end of the thirteenth century, a book was written in Spain which was to become the textbook of the mystics. Its author, Moses de Leon, called it Zohar, Book of Radiance. Some have held that he was only a compiler of ideas which had come to him through oral transmission. This is not likely,[1] but he did ascribe the origin of Cabbalah to Rabbi Simeon be Johai, who lived during the second century of the Christian era. According to legend, he had fled from the Romans, and spent 13 years in a cave of the Judaean mountains. Miraculously supplied with food, he devoted his time to mystical speculations. From this life in seclusion, the Zohar supposedly emerged. It contains several sections, among them a commentary to Scripture, revealing its hidden meanings, and also deals with the mysterious powers contained in the letters that make up the name of God. It pictures the seven "palaces of light" that unfold before the inner eye of the mystic in prayer and are vouchsafed unto the pious in life after death. It takes us through Paradise, and tells us of the lives and deaths of great masters of mysticism, and of their teachings.

Some of the ideas of Zohar

To the Zohar, God is *En Sof*, the Infinite. We know nothing of Him, and cannot penetrate the hidden recesses of His Being. He has divided the universe into an upper world, and a lower world in which we live, fashioned by an outpouring of Divine Radiance. The Zohar

---

[1] This view is held by Gershom G. Scholem, who considers the work to have been authored by Moses de Leon. See Gershom G. Scholem, *Zohar, The Book of Splendor* (New York: Schocken Books, Inc., 1949), pp. 12 ff., and *Major Trends in Jewish Mysticism* (New York: Schocken Books, Inc., 1946), pp. 156 ff. These two works have been a major source of the author in the preparation of this chapter.

compares the universe to a nut which has a core surrounded by a number of shells, each protecting the other. The inner shells, closer to the core, are softer and more precious. As we move outward the shells get cruder. God the Infinite is the center of the universe. Each of the shells surrounding Him is further removed from Him. As God created the world He emerged from the recess of His Being and made Himself known to man by assuming a number of attributes; He moved through ten spheres to come to the point where He fashioned our universe. These are called *Sephirot*. God moves further and further down toward man. The mystic, in turn, tries to move up through the Sephirot to the En Sof, the Infinite.

Man is endowed with body and soul, the soul being a higher shell. In life man must try to help God by creating higher spiritual values, shells closer to the core. By his contemplation, his prayers, but also his actions in the world, man must aspire toward *Devekut*, the cleaving to God, the immersion in God. He who has earnestly striven to fulfil this task finds his soul pure and undefiled at the end of the road through life. Then it may return to God. But he who fails may find himself in hell or purgatory, where his soul must dwell ten times the length of its sinfulness on earth; his body, too, is cruelly punished. Only on the Sabbath will it find rest.

How deep the impact of these teachings has been can be shown from an experience of my own life. On Sabbath afternoon, during the hour of dusk, we were supposed to refrain from drinking water, "for this water is for the souls to refresh themselves before returning to the punishment of the week." And at the end of the Sabbath the cantor would stretch the recital of the openings verses of worship, in order "to give an additional moment of rest to the souls."

The Zohar also speaks of transmigration; souls go from body to body by way of purification. Man actually has a threefold soul. Upon death one part travels on earth to comfort the troubled and intercede for them; the other rejoices in an earthly paradise and rises to the heavenly one on the Sabbath; the third soul returns to God and eternal bliss. If the highest soul is refused entrance to the eternal paradise because of its sins, then the other two walk dejectedly on earth. If the lowest soul finds great sorrow in the world, it bestirs the higher ones to appear before God in pleading. Thus man performs his work through eternity. In the eternal conflict between good and evil, he can promote the good both here and throughout eternity, and he can help God, who has willed the conflict and wishes it resolved.

There is one moment on earth when the bliss of absolute union is felt. It occurs in the sex act, which makes God rejoice. In this act all separateness vanishes, and creation is its blessed fruit. If performed on the

Sabbath, then the holy day will be further enhanced by it. The act should be performed in joyful surrender, and in the presence of God.

Thus God descends and man ascends; God released the world, and man returns it to Him, catching glimpses of the bliss of perfect union.

Rabbi Isaac Luria (1534–1572)

Spanish Jewry had fallen. Its wealthy members had become wandering beggars, its radiant culture extinguished. There appeared a new mystical movement at Safed in Palestine. Isaac Luria, an Ashkenasic Jew born at Jerusalem, started the movement. His disciples called him by the initials of his name: Ashkenasi Rabbi Isaac, or ARI. The word (pronounced Aree) means lion in Hebrew. Safed was a good place for such a movement, because it was close to the tomb of Simeon ben Johai, and the Ari made frequent pilgrimages to this resting place of the mystic's "patron saint." He came to think of himself as the forerunner of the Messiah. On Sabbath he clothed himself in white, the garment of purity. He developed further the ideas of the Zohar.

Some ideas of the Ari

The world is an emanation of God. But how can that be? Does not God fill the whole universe? Has He not filled it from the beginning? He is the universe; how then could it be created? Luria has a significant doctrine called *Tzimtzum*. In order to create the world, God withdrew into Himself, thus leaving part of the universe void. We may perhaps compare it—though inadequately—with a container completely filled with water. If the water is compressed, by freezing, for instance, part of the vessel would be empty. Thus did God withdraw, leaving room for creation. Then He created the world out of the void, exiling Himself from the world in order to create it.

Then God's radiance was poured out into the shells, filling them. But the lower vessels, the outer shells, could not take the power, and broke. The "Breaking of the Vessels" constitutes the tragedy of life—evil. It creates the upheavals and convulsions of human history. The divine sparks have become scattered, God's "Shehinah," His Radiance, has been exiled. Through history the break may be mended, the sparks gathered, and unity re-established. Man, making history, thus helps God. Had Adam not sinned, the act of restoration would have been fulfilled through him. But since he did sin, the task evolved upon mankind, and, above all, the Jew. The Jewish community, as the Zohar had already pointed out, is the image of the divine Shehinah; God dwells in their midst, and their actions immediately bring divine reaction. The task of restoration is called *Tikkun*. The Jew, through obedience to Torah and through prayer, has in his hand the capacity to accelerate or postpone the eventual restoration. When the task is fulfilled, the Messiah will come. The Jew must strive for *Devekut*. Every prayer must be filled with *Kavanah*, the mystical intention to bring about the unification of God's Name. Every act, even menial labor, serves this goal, and can lead to the eternal Sabbath. There is nothing outside God; there is nothing without God; there is nothing which does not vitally affect both God and man. Life is an eternal confrontation of man with God in the work of salvation. Joy and ecstasy at this distinction must fill every moment of our days, especially the outpouring of our prayers.

Hasidism in Russia and Poland

Sabbatai Zevi had turned out to be an impostor, his messianic movement a cruel joke of history. Hasidism arose in response to a terrible hopelessness. Its master was Israel Baal Shem (Master of the Divine Name) of Miedzyboz. He was not a learned rabbi, but a man of great love who mingled with the people and taught them by simple parable. His movement brought hope to thousands; his teachings reflected those of the mystics who had preceded him. God has sent the world out of Himself, yet dwells in it. He cries out for salvation, but salvation can come only through man's cooperation. The unity of the world broke with Adam's sin; it broke again when Israel had to go into exile, thus a twofold exile has to be removed. Only through man's actions can this be accomplished, and everyone contributes to the fate of the world and of God Himself. Every act is holy. In everything man does he stands before God; he must hear His voice, His command. This word of command is not necessarily contained in formalized law, but is received out of the permanent confrontation of man with God, the permanent relationship of "I and Thou." This does not call for self-denying acts of ascetic character. On the contrary, it demands that we live our lives fully and sanctify every moment of them. Every moment becomes worship.

Henoch was a shoemaker. As he joined the upper leather with the sole, he united God with His Shehinah (His Radiance).[2]

Everyday work is thus hallowed; it must be performed with the right Kavanah; it must be rendered in joy.

This does not mean that the performance of the commandments has been suspended, but it does mean that it is meaningless without the

---

[2] Martin Buber, *Deutung des Chassidismus* (Berlin: Schocken Verlag, 1935). Scholem (*Major Trends in Jewish Mysticism*, p. 365, fn. 101) discusses the origin of the Enoch legend, which may go back to German medieval Hasidism.

right intent. A secular act could acquire greater value before God than a commandment, provided the act is performed correctly. It may mean that eating and drinking in joy before God becomes communion with Him.

Once the Hasidim sat together drinking; the rabbi entered; his looks were not friendly. They asked: "Are you displeased Rabbi, to find us drinking? After all is it not said that Hasidim who sit together drinking are counted as if they studied the Torah?" The rabbi replied: "Many a word in the Torah can convey holy meaning in one place and a different one in another. In one place we read: 'Do *thee* not *make* hewn work'; in another Moses is commanded: '*Hew* unto *thee* two tables of stone.' The latter work is holy, the former is not. In the latter sentence the term 'thee' follows the act; in the former it does not. Thus it is in every action. If 'thee'—thy self-interest—precedes an action and motivates it, then the act is unholy; if it follows it—and God's will comes first—it is holy." [3]

Subjecting oneself to the call of God makes for holiness. This is no-where more evident than in prayer. Prayer is acceptance of God's rule, of the yoke of His kingdom; prayer calls for complete abandonment in God. Prayer is ecstasis in the fullest sense of the word—to be beyond oneself. The Hasidim would pray with their entire bodies, swaying and jerking, excitedly reaching out for God as a drowning man would. They could dance before Him with the same abandonment. Prayer must burst forth from man's innermost depth in order to be vital, to reach God.

Hasidism depended greatly on the personalities of the masters. Many groups emerged, each gathered around a *Zaddik*, a righteous master. They would come to him as often as they could, especially for the high holy days, to spend a few precious days in his presence, bringing their needs, written on scraps of paper, that he might heal them by his mirac-ulous powers. In him they saw a human being so perfect, so fully able to concentrate upon his task to help God and man, that God's grace could not possibly be denied him. To them he was a personality so powerful that he might well influence the powers on high. As a man free from vanity and selfishness, he was to them the true co-worker with God in the work of salvation. In his presence they felt exalted and hallowed. The cryptic words of his instruction held deepest meaning for them. The Zaddik was surrounded by his courtiers, disciples who attended to his every need. With them he would spend the twilight hours of the departing Sabbath. The third Sabbath meal—a piece of fish, a drink of whiskey—and the rabbi's words, or even his silence in medita-tion, became hours of communion and of unity. Thus did they taste the moment of redemption in the midst of their toil, and the spirit of salva-tion in the midst of persecution.

---

[3] Martin Buber, *Der Grosse Maggid* (Berlin: Schocken Verlag, 1937), pp. 287 f.

Further developments

Hasidism eventually decayed. The forms remained, but the spirit fled. Zaddikim formed dynasties, the sons succeeding to their fathers' office; they established veritable courts. The swaying remained but the ecstasis fled. The garment was retained, but the living spirit died of the very disease which Hasidism had so valiantly tried to combat: formalization and ritualization. There are still Hasidic groups in existence, but there is little in them of the vital spirit of the past.

The Impact of Hasidism

Yet Hasidism has had a profound impact upon Jewish life and religion. Modern Israel reflects some of its ideals. Here Jews went to work to build. No task was too difficult, no job too lowly, no duty too insignificant. In all of them they saw a challenge; though secularized, it was work of redemption, so they gave their utmost. Hasidism has thus helped to create the spirit of equality in Israel; everyone's work is of highest significance, and so is every person. In the spirit of Hasidism, pioneers

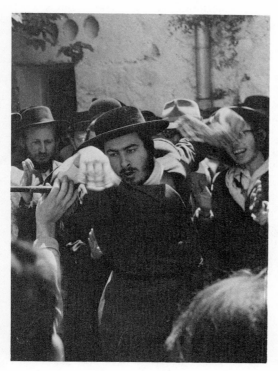

Hasidim dancing at religious festivities.

developed unparalleled endurance and unflinching dedication to their goals, but also joy, exuberance, dance, and celebration.

Hasidism has inspired the work of modern Jewish thinkers, especially Martin Buber, who was formed by it, and whose influence is reaching out into the world at large. Standing up to God, hearing His command out of the task of the moment, finding Him in the eternal dialogue of "I and Thou," these are the foundations of Buber's thinking. They are Hasidic ideas. The shortest road from man to God goes through humanity, and the goal of all human striving must be the unity of all men in unity with God. Both Buber and Hasidism see it thus. This is the way to redemption; this leads to the coming of the Messiah.

The Hasidim found God existentially, by living before Him. Their message and their goal—as interpreted by Buber and exemplified in Israel—are reaching into the field of universal ideas discussed and evaluated in general philosophy and theology. From the point of view of general impact, Hasidism is one of the significant contributions of modern Jewry to religion as a whole.

15

Darkness
and Light

Rabbi Israel of Rizin used to say: "The Messiah will come first to the Land of Russia." Similarly, this story was often told: A Hasid, disciple of Rabbi Motel, uncle of the Rabbi of Rizin, once visited his Zaddik. As he prayed in the inn—his face turned toward the wall as was his custom—suddenly there stood a man behind him and said: "I have measured the entire face of the earth with the steps of my foot, yet nowhere have I found an exile equal in harshness to that in Russia." The Hasid turned around and saw the man disappearing in the doorway of Rabbi Motel's house. When he followed him, he was no longer there. In vain did the Hasid inquire about him.[1]

THE AGONY OF RUSSIAN JEWRY

No exile was harsher than that of Jewry living in territories that fell to Russia during the 18th century. The great majority of Jews had lived there since the Middle Ages. Deeply pious, living only for their Judaism, they formed the reservoir of Jewish survival. Now they fell into ever deeper poverty. Even the internal self-government they had once enjoyed was taken away from them; all the councils were permitted to do was collect taxes for the Czar. Sinking deeply into despondency, they had only Torah

---

[1] Martin Buber, *op. cit.*, pp. 295 f.

to sustain them spiritually and intellectually, but, as they were cut off from life, they lost themselves in overly refined talmudic disputations, and embittered their days in acrimonious battles between Hasidim and Mitnagdim, the followers of the Gaon. The rabbis formed the elite. Children, from the tenderest age, were pressed into the routine of eternal study. They knew none of the joys of normal childhood. Hayim Nahman Byalik, himself a product of this environment of Torah, Russian persecution, and poverty, and later poet laureate of Israel (1873-1934), has put it in words:

And when thou goest forth alone, at nightfall,
wandering in one of these, the sacred cities . . .
thine ear will catch the murmur of a voice,
thine eye will catch the twinkle of a light
set in a window, and a human form—
a shadow like the shadow of death—beyond,
a shadow trembling, swaying back and forth,
a voice, an agony, that lifts and falls,
and comes toward thee upon the waves of silence. . . .
A prisoner, self-guarded, self-condemned,
self-sacrificed to study the Law. . . .
Within these walls, within this prison house
six years have passed above his swaying form:
within these walls the child became the youth,
the youth became the man, fore-ripened, swift,
and swift as these went, swifter yet were gone
the cheeks' bloom and the luster of his eyes. . . .
Six years of hunger, years of sleeplessness,
six years of wasting flesh and falling cheeks—
And all to him as if it had not been.
He knows that Jews have studied thus of old,
He knows the fame and glory they have won.[2]

Fame and glory? Certainly not in the world; possibly with God. It was not a matter of glory; it was a simple matter of necessity, if they wished to retain their sanity and emotional balance.

Russia was in turmoil; the tyranny of the Czars became intolerable. Jews were made the scapegoats to deflect the wrath of the people. Czar Nicholas I (1825-1855) embarked on a policy of enforced conversion. Persecution followed persecution, pogrom succeeded pogrom. Jews were restricted in their movements, forced to live in the overcrowded provinces of Poland. They had no outlets for any commercial activity. As paupers, they traded among themselves. To force their children into conversion, the Czar issued an edict forcing Jews into military service for 25 years,

---

2 Haim Nahman Byalik, "The Matmid," Maurice Samuel, trans., A *Book of Jewish Thoughts* (New York: Bloch Publishing Co., Inc., 1943), pp. 53 ff.

beginning at the age of 18. To make sure that the necessary number of conscripts was available, children were torn from the laps of their mothers to be "prepared" for their service. They were placed in special army units, and their lives became a hell on earth; there was no chance of promotion, except by conversion; there was no chance of relief, outside of conversion, except death. Many succumbed or yielded; many remained faithful to the teachings of Judaism they had received as children. Sustained by their faith, they endured years of harassment.

The Russian government had a firm policy of extermination: let one third of Jewry be converted, another third die, the final third emigrate, and the problem is solved. It tried everything, from schools for Jewish children, designed to estrange them from their faith, to terror, restrictions, and force. There was daily insecurity, and there was poverty. From time to time there were major pogroms. Those of Kishinev and Homel in 1904 shocked the civilized world. Nicholas I was dead by that time, but the policy of persecution remained very much alive. Even after World War I it continued. The White Army, defeated in its effort to dislodge the Bolshevic regime, took out its frustration on the Jews of the Ukraine by slaughtering them. Rumania similarly persecuted its Jews. Poverty and persecution led to gigantic migrations during the nineteenth and early twentieth centuries to Germany, England, and above all, the United States.

Jews in present-day Russia are subject to discrimination and grave insecurity. Many wish to emigrate to Israel. They have pressed for this right under great personal risk. To some extent the government has had to yield, but, in 1972, demanded a ransom of up to $37,000—for each would-be emigrant, depending on his education. Many of the three million Jews will remain. So far, all have been denied access to Jewish sources of strength. No prayer books have been printed since the revolution. Most synagogues have been closed. Opportunities in life are restricted. Their identification papers are stamped "Jew". As in the days of the Czar and Stalin they may yet be scapegoats again. By persecuting Jews, the USSR also hopes to gain favor with the Arabs whom they wish to dominate. In the free world, governments, churches and upright Christians have joined Jews in protest and pressure against this spiritual genocide. 77 U.S. Senators voted for U.S. sanctions against the ransom laws. Many Congressmen joined. Basically, Judaism is the living indictment of communism and of all totalitarianism. It proclaims that only God is supreme, the state, the dictator is not. The survival of the Jews over man-made ideologies of power is testimony to the truth they profess. Thus Judaism must be oppressed if totalitarian regimes, including communism, are to be vindicated.

And shouldst thou wish to know the Source
from which thy tortured brethren drew

in evil days their strength of soul
to meet their doom, stretch out their necks
to each uplifted knife and axe,
in flames, on stakes to die with joy,
and with a whisper "God is One"
to close their lips?

And shouldst thou wish to find the Spring
from which thy banished brethren drew,
'midst fear of death and fear of life,
their comfort, courage, patience, trust,
an iron will to bear the yoke,
to live bespattered and despised,
and suffer without end?

If thou, my brother, knowest not
this mother, spring and lap and fort,
then enter thou the House of God,
the House of Study old and gray
throughout the sultry summer days,
throughout the gloomy winter nights,
at morning, midday or at eve;
perchance there is a remnant yet,
perchance the eye may still behold
in some dark corner hid from view
a cast-off shadow of the past,
the profile of some pallid face,
upon an ancient folio bent,
who seeks to drown unspoken woes
in the Talmudic boundless waves;
and then thy heart shall guess the truth
that thou hast touched the sacred ground
of thy great nation's House of Life,
and that thy eyes do gaze upon
the treasure of thy nation's soul.

And know that this is but a spark
that by a miracle escaped
of that bright light, that sacred flame
thy forbears kindled long ago
on altars high and pure.[3]

THE DAWN OF THE AGE OF ENLIGHTENMENT

In the West the process of liberation, started in the Renaissance, progressed. Spiritually and intellectually, it reached its high mark in the eighteenth century, the "Enlightenment." The most glorious attainment of

---

[3] Haim Nahman Byalik, "The Fountain," P. M. Raskin, trans., *op. cit.*, pp. 57 ff.

this age, and everlasting witness to its greatness, is the United States of America. Its founding fathers testify to the nobility of this great century. America's Basic Scriptures, the Declaration of Independence and the Constitution, are the firm foundations of our freedom.

European developments did not lead to complete success. Had developments there equalled those in America, the War of Independence and the French Revolution might have been avoided. Liberty and the rights of man would have been found through reason alone. Still, the movement was on the march; Reason became the guide. In the light of Reason, there was no cause for discrimination against the Jews. Reason was to break down the gates of the ghetto; intellectually at first, later physically, but not without struggle.

Suddenly emerging into the world—from the middle ages, as it were—Jews had to justify their faith and their existence in the light of reason. Philosophical foundations had to be laid to qualify Judaism as a separate ideology. Its value had to be shown; its contribution to the life of its own members and to the world had to be demonstrated. The task was a twofold one. To its own adherents, Judaism had to justify its ideals, principles, teachings, and laws, for the members were becoming philosophically schooled. To the world at large, Judaism had to explain itself. How does the Jewish God concept, the stories of creation and revelation, stand up under the scrutiny of philosophy? How do Jewish ethical systems compare with those developed by philosophers? What is the meaning of the commandments? When Judaism and philosophy disagree, how can this disagreement be explained? Can both sides be right? What is the ultimate goal of Judaism?

To the Jew of the past, this question was of minor significance. He lived his Judaism, and found its value existentially as he obeyed the commandments. The community was totally Jewish; mutual influence and example exerted a strong pull. The situation during antiquity and throughout the middle ages was substantially the same.

There were exceptions, however. In times of relative freedom Jews would ask questions. This happened in Hellenistic Alexandria; it occurred again in the times of the Gaonim in Babylonia; it led Spanish Jewry into great perplexities. It has been our concern ever since the Age of Enlightenment.

At the hour of emancipation, the masses of people had to be adjusted to totally new conditions; they had to be led out of slavery and equipped for a life in the world. The thinkers among the Jews had to be given a philosophy of life out of the sources of Judaism. The task was difficult, but Jewish philosophical thinkers had guideposts. They had the works of earlier philosophers written at times when similar conditions had called for similar answers. To some of these earlier philosophers we shall now turn.

16

On Jewish Philosophy

Baghdad of the tenth century was a dazzling city of beauty, splendor, and luxury. It was also the center of learning. Plato and Aristotle had just become known in Arabic translations and had disturbed the tranquil waters of thought and religion. Schools sprang up and constantly debated. In Islam, the rationalistic group of the Kalaam argued with the mystics and with orthodox theologians; the Mutazilites, within the Kalaam, used allegorical interpretation of the Koran, as Philo had once done for Torah. Christianity, Zoroastrianism, Manichaeism, all made themselves felt and had their representatives. There was so much confusion of ideas that many divorced themselves entirely from religious doctrines and became freethinkers.

What were Jews to believe? Islam taught that the Torah had been replaced by the Koran. Christianity advocated the principle of the Trinity—God is in Three Persons. Zoroastrianism and Manichaeism held that the world is torn between two equally powerful forces: Good and Evil, Light and Darkness, God and the Devil, who are fighting for supremacy. All of these ideas were contrary to Jewish beliefs. In addition, there was the Jewish sect of the Karaites who denied the validity of Oral Torah and considered only written Torah as binding.

SAADIA: THE BOOK OF DOCTRINES AND BELIEFS [1]

It was a world in ferment in which Saadia arrived. Born in Egypt in 892 and educated there, he came to Babylonia in 915 and was appointed Gaon, or President, of the Academy of Sura at the age of 36. He was a man of iron will who ran into trouble as if he had sought it. Before long, he was embroiled in bitter conflict with the exilarch who had appointed him. This cost Saadia his position and condemned him to enforced leisure. It turned out to be a blessing for posterity, for Saadia wrote. Just before his death, he was reinstated in office and the argument settled. He died in 942.

Of His Ideas

Saadia's fundamental position is very simple and at the same time startling: Judaism teaches nothing which is contrary to reason, and which is closed to reason. The truth, transmitted through revelation, can also be found through reason. Does that make revelation superfluous? No, replies Saadia. Revelation gives us the truth in advance, that we may be guided by it right now. Otherwise it might take us centuries of hard work to find it, or we might lack the perseverance ever to arrive at it. In the meanwhile we would be without guidance in life. We may compare the process to a teacher who finds his students trying to divide some money among themselves. They have difficulties in solving their problem, so the teacher gives them the answer which permits them to settle their affairs. Then the teacher says: "I want you to find out how to arrive at the solution yourselves." Revelation does the same thing. It helps us perform the rules of religion and to lead the right kind of life. Ultimately, however, "approval of all things He has commanded us, and disapproval of all things He has prohibited us He has implanted in our reason." [2] St. Thomas Aquinas will say that there are mysteries, such as the character of the Trinity, which for all eternity surpass the power of understanding; they must be accepted. Saadia proclaims Judaism as the religion of reason. Later thinkers will use his theory in a way not intended by him, making their own reasoning the final arbiter of what is to be retained and what is to be changed in Judaism. To be the religion of reason has remained one of Judaism's claims to distinction.

---

[1] This translation of the title of Saadia's work follows Alexander Altmann's; see his explanation in "Saadia Gaon: Book of Doctrines and Beliefs," *Three Jewish Philosophers* (Meridian Books and Jewish Publication Society of America, by arrangement with East and West Library, London, 1960), Part II, pp. 19 ff.

[2] *Ibid.*, p. 97.

Saadia next asks, how can we accept tradition as true? How do we know that the Torah is really God's word? His answer is that we must put faith in reliable tradition. After all, our entire life rests on faith in the truth of other peoples' words. Without such faith we could not transact business, we would not trust the other's word, we could not transact the affairs of state, we could not even establish families without faith that the future will resemble the past of which we have learned. Our knowledge comes from four roots: sense-perception, reason, knowledge by inference as we draw conclusions from preceding premises, and, especially for "Believers in the Unity of God," reliable tradition. The revelation at Mount Sinai took place in front of an entire people; it was public, excluding any possibility of deception. We must accept the report as true.

Now Saadia endeavors to prove philosophically the truths which revelation has handed to us. Has the world been created as the Bible says, or has it existed from eternity as Aristotle claims? How do we know that God is One?

A number of proofs are offered. Among them, Saadia states the following: Our world is finite. It is finite in size; it must be equally finite in strength and force and power. No finite thing has infinite strength, hence it cannot have existed forever, for this would require infinite strength. It must have been created in time, since it cannot have been in existence forever. It must have been created by an infinite power—God.

All things on earth come and go; they are composed of numerous parts, and eventually break down. There must have been a time when the parts were first put together, as there is the moment of their separation and decay. This shows that the world is not eternal. Even time is not eternal; at any given moment, time comes to an end.

God alone, who is beyond time, is eternal. God alone is infinite. But this means God is totally different from the world, He is *beyond compare*, and none of the characteristics of the world can apply to Him. *He* is the Creator, *it* is creation. We must understand that nothing that applies to the world applies to God. All the bodies in the world can be counted and numbered. Since God is absolutely different from the world, number must not apply to Him. He can only be *One*, completely outside the category of number. As creator He possesses *life, power,* and *wisdom.* Without these He could not create. But we must not think of them as three different attributes. They are all part of His oneness; only our language is incapable of expressing them in one single word, hence we use three terms in expressing what is really one.[3]

---

3 The five attributes of God are in italics.

The world is the creation of a free-creating, transcendent, One God. He put it into being at a given moment in time. He rules it, and rewards and punishes its creatures. He has given us a body and a soul. Without a body, the soul could not exist in the material realm of nature; without a soul the body would be deprived of its power to reason, to exhibit courage, and to have human drives and urges. As we can see, Saadia uses Platonic and Aristotelian ideas, but arrives at his own conclusions. He combines Greek philosophy and Jewish doctrine.

Reward and punishment are for our own good; they are the results of obedience or disobedience. But in order to obey God we must have freedom of will. How can man have a free will if God knows beforehand what man will do? If God knows it, I am bound by it; if He does not know it, He is not an all-knowing God. Saadia brushes off this argument as a case of careless thinking. God's knowledge is not the cause of things. Man is free to act, and God simply knows what man is going to decide.

Should one object "If God knows that a certain person will speak, is it possible for that person to be silent?" We answer quite simply, that if a person was to keep silent instead of speaking we should have said in our original statement that God knew this man would be silent.[4]

Man's final goal is to be worthy of redemption. He may suffer in this world to make amends for his sins; then he will arrive in the world to come in complete purity, and rejoice in eternal bliss forever. Suffering thus comes to us as an act of God's goodness as well as of His justice.

If man has followed the commandments, his soul will depart in purity. Through obedience to commandments which he understands, such as honesty, he improves himself and society; these commandments were only restated and amplified in revelation, since reason leads us to them. Through his obedience to the religious commandments, he has helped himself in ways not yet known to him, but he has also stored up rewards in heaven. Thus law is intended for man's ethical growth. The soul, separated on death from the body, will be reunited with it on the day of resurrection. Then body and soul will be judged. After the resurrection there will come the day of the Messiah, and all generations will witness the restoration of Israel.

Saadia's conclusions are those of Bible and Talmud. To him, the tradition of Judaism is holy and true, but reason is the supreme yardstick. If man will but think the problems through, he will arrive at the same truths. Meanwhile, may he follow the law of God and gain happiness. Saadia is satisfied that he has vindicated Judaism philosophically.

---

[4] *Ibid.*, p. 123.

JUDAH HALEVI: THE KUSARI [5]

Judah Halevi is a poet, the singer of Zion for which his soul yearns. His philosophy is poetic, expressing more positively than any other philosopher the idea of Israel's chosenness. Israel is a miracle of creation; Israel's purpose is to serve as the religious heart of mankind. Israel's election passes human understanding; Judah Halevi is infinitely proud of it. His philosophical work is set in the frame of a story, a dialogue, reflecting somewhat the style of Plato. It rests on the search of Bulan, king of the Chazars, to find the right faith.[6]

The king, having been told by an angel that his "intentions are acceptable to the Creator, but not the actions," first calls a philosopher, whose arguments leave him cold; rationalism holds no answer. A Christian explains his faith, but the king remains dissatisfied. Christian dogma runs counter to reason; it can be accepted by those who have had a great spiritual experience and then undergirded it by logic. It is good for Christians; for him, the rational seeker, it holds no appeal. The Islamic scholar has an easier position; his concept of One God is logically sound and reasonably acceptable. Like the Christian thinker, however, he constantly refers back to Judaism as mother religion. Since both are agreed that Judaism is the foundation of their faiths, the king calls the rabbi in an effort to go to the root of things.

The Jewish master speaks of God, who chose Abraham, Isaac, and Jacob, led Israel from Egypt through the desert to the land of their heritage, gave them the Torah, sent to them prophets, and spoke to them of rewards and punishments. God is presented as the God of history, not as a deity of the philosopher's speculations. He spoke to the people in public, at Sinai; he spoke to all of them, not only to one man, as in the case of Mohammed. Two things are thus made clear. Philosophy can err when it comes to metaphysics; that is the reason there are so many schools of thought. Private communication is not trustworthy as a source of history.[7] Philosophy has its function, but it is limited. The static God of the philosopher, end result of human speculation, does not commit us to any action.[8] But Israel's God is the living Lord of history, who has sent out the call to action, desirous to lift up mankind to Himself. In *public* revelation Israel received His word.[9] There is no doubt that the Jew, and only he, has an absolute foundation for true tradition,

---

[5] Judah Halevi's life; see p. 144.
[6] See p. 143.
[7] *Das Buch Kusari* (Leipzig: 1869), I, 1; IV, 13.
[8] *Ibid.*, I, 81 ff.
[9] *Ibid.*, I, 87.

and has the true religion. Responding to the divine appeal, we must seek God in fulfilment of His commandments, yearn for him with all our heart and soul. Thus—and not through mere intellectual activity— shall we truly find Him.

From that point on, Judah has easy going. Has the world existed from eternity, as Aristotle said, or has it been created in time? The philosopher had no tradition of true worth to give him an answer; he had to speculate. He saw the generations roll by and concluded that the world was eternal. Had he lived among a people with a true tradition, he need not have speculated, he would have been assured of the right answer: the world was created. Is the message of tradition true? It must be, for God would not give us anything contrary to reason. Torah and reason cannot disagree, yet there are questions which cannot be answered by philosophical reasoning. Creation is one example. Judah thus disputes Saadia's argument that all is ultimately open to reason. Saadia used reason to prove God; Halevi finds God necessary to validate reason. In the God of Israel and the Torah of Israel lies the one and only source of absolute truth, and all other religions are man-made. But why did Israel alone receive the truth? Why not the others? Judah's answer, which is the core of his thought, is a confession; it is no longer philosophy. It is the answer of the heart, which needs no philosophical proofs. The answer sets Israel aside as a special work of creation, and makes the faith of Israel different in quality from any other. It is the proud answer of a man of conviction, his and his alone. We may reject it, yet it has had the power to sustain many through ages of darkness.

Give me a little time to explain to you the greatness of the people. Good evidence lies in the fact that God chose this people unto Himself from among the peoples of the world; that the divine spirit rested upon the whole multitude of the people, raising them to such level that He could speak with them in Person. This divine spirit extended to their women also, for there were women prophets.

How did this come to pass?

Previously the divine spirit had rested only on individuals, descendants of Adam who was absolutely perfect . . . , having been created by God. . . . He was created with the power . . . to receive the soul in its perfection; he also received an intellect in the fullest measure attainable to man; beyond this intellect he was given the divine power enabling him to cleave to God, grasp the spiritual and acquire truth without great effort, simply by meditation. This is why we call him "son of God," and those among his seed, who are like him, are called "sons of God."

He had many sons, but none of them was worthy to take Adam's place except Abel, who was like him. And when Cain, Abel's brother, murdered him in envy of this distinction, Set was given Adam in his place as son of distinction. . . . Set's son of distinction was Enoch, and thus it continued until Noah. The continuity always resided in individuals, all of them resembling Adam, all of them called "sons of God." They were perfect physically, mentally, in length of days, in wisdom, and in strength. By their live's spans we keep count (of the world): from Adam to Noah, from Noah to Abraham. Sometimes the divine spirit did not rest on one of them, such as Terah, but his son Abraham was a disciple of his grandfather Eber, even of Noah himself. Thus did the divine spirit come down from ancestors to children's children. Abraham was the son of distinction of Eber, whence he was called (H)Ebrew. Eber was the son of distinction of Shem and Shem of Noah; therefore Shem inherited the lands of moderate climate, of which the most central and precious is the land of Canaan, the land of prophecy. . . . Abraham's son of distinction was Isaac; (and Abraham) removed all his other sons from the land, in order that it remain for Isaac. Isaac's son of distinction was Jacob; Esow was expelled since Jacob had claim to the land. Jacob's sons were all deserving of the divine spirit; thus this place, so uniquely fitted for God's spirit, became theirs in common. This was the first time that the spirit of God had come to rest on an entire community. Previously it had rested only on individuals.[10]

Israel is the chosen people, God's own chosen son of distinction. The glory which once rested on a few divinely selected individuals only, from Adam to Jacob, resides in all of the people Israel, the men and women and children. No other people, no other personality outside of Israel, is granted it. Ideally, Israel should be united with the land of Israel, a piece of earth especially chosen for the descendants of Jacob. But even in far away lands the Jewish people have a function. God sustains them wherever they may be, for Israel is the heart of humanity.

Israel, among the peoples of the world, compares to the heart within the body, the most afflicted and yet the healthiest of all the organs. The heart is constantly threatened by diseases, by sorrow and distress, by fear, hostilities, hatred, love, and anxieties; it is subject to the dangers of imbalance; it is affected by harmful food and drink, strain, work, sleep, and lack of rest. The other organs remain unaffected by these influences . . . But its very sensitivity, which is the source of all its sufferings, gives it the capacity to throw off these afflictions before they become rooted in the body. Thus does Israel bear the afflictions of the world. We are in distress even while the world is still enjoying rest. The sufferings meted out to us help us to deepen Torah within ourselves, to cleanse ourselves from all sludge that may stick to us. Through our virtue and our correction the divine spirit is made to persist in the world.[11]

Mighty powers have fallen, but Israel lives; it is the teacher of mankind and its suffering servant. This is Judah's explanation of why Israel alone was given the Torah, and why Israel is eternal. But as servant of God the Jew need not renounce the world to live a life of asceticism.

---

[10] *Ibid.*, I, 95 ff.
[11] *Ibid.*, I, 36 ff.

He need but fulfil God's commandments, and do so joyfully, and direct his faculties to serve Him. "He who can command his intellectual and physical faculties to follow his will, him we call 'pious'." [12] Plato and Aristotle are combined with the traditional Jewish outlook on life. The "pious" resembles the wise in Plato's Republic; Abraham's God, found in yearning search, is contrasted with the "Eternal" of Aristotle, merely an object of philosophical thought.[13]

Judah Halevi's discussion of causality, and his proofs of God, follow, with variations, the methods of scholasticism. His ideas on the Jewish rationale of existence, his emphasis that God's existence is made manifest in the religious life, his view of the importance of the Land of Israel, are important contributions he has made.

Judah, theoretically, speaks to a heathen king who wishes to be converted. What about converts? Judah answers that they too partake of Jewish distinction. The mass of the Jewish people, including converts, will not yet reach the highest state of perfection, that of the pious and the prophets. Only a few will be given this grace. When the time of the Messiah comes, then all Jews, including all the converts, will reach this highest level, and will bring mankind to a full understanding of the glory of God.

With pride in his heritage, Judah combines a truly Jewish concern for all mankind. For the sake of mankind Judaism is in the world; for the sake of mankind Jews suffer. Endowed with the special genius of religion, they bring to mankind the knowledge of God and the happiness of the messianic age.

Judah Halevi restates Biblical and Talmudic doctrine. Jews throughout the ages have been uplifted by his poetic words, to persevere, to remember the land of Israel, and to serve humanity.

MOSES MAIMONIDES (1135-1204)

In the panorama of western civilization, a few personalities stand towering above the rest. These are the men who encompassed the totality of knowledge available to their period, evaluated it critically, and carried it beyond the frontiers of their time. Among this select group we may count Aristotle, St. Thomas Aquinas, Leonardo da Vinci, Goethe—and Moses Maimonides. He is philosopher, physician, biologist, codifier, and commentator. Disciple of Aristotle, he remains a deeply religious man; Torah is the lodestar of his life's journey. Reason is man's greatest endowment, and the Torah, divine and infallible, *is* reason; although Aristotle's

---

[12] *Ibid.*, III, 5; for detailed characterization of the pious see III, 2 ff.
[13] *Ibid.*, IV, 16.

Supposed tomb of Maimonides shown at Tiberias.

philosophy is also based on reason, he is but human. When Aristotle disagrees with Torah we must show where his human error lay; and when the words of Torah seem to conflict with reason, philosophy can shed new light upon their deeper meaning, and resolve the conflict.

These convictions motivate Maimonides to write his "Guide of the Perplexed." Aristotle's thought had left doubts, bewilderment, and anxiety in the minds of many faithful and thoughtful Jews of the time. Had Aristotle proven the Torah wrong? Judah ibn Aknin, Maimonides' favorite disciple, gave expression to the bewilderment of his generation when he addressed the beloved master and asked him to resolve the dilemma. In response, Maimonides explains that he has written his book, not for the instruction of the masses, nor as a beginners' text in philosophy, but for the religious thinker, well schooled in Torah and philosophy, who is confused and is inclined to feel that . . .

if he is guided by reason, he may have to *reject* some terms (of Torah) as he understands them, and may think that he has rejected the *foundations* of Torah. Yet . . . in *refusing to follow* reason and by turning his back to it, he discovers that he has acted *against his intellectual* integrity.[14]

The task will also entail a new approach to statements in Scripture which lead to confusion if taken literally, but yield themselves to symbolic interpretation.

---

[14] Moses Maimonides, *Guide of the Perplexed,* trans. and annotated by M. Friedlander (London: Tuebner & Co., 1885), Introduction.

But Maimonides did not write his work simply to check a process of erosion in faith. True, those persons who live and move within the faith without doubts and uncertainties will not need his book. But the master considers the study of philosophy a higher level of intellectual life. He salutes those who are engaged in the pursuit of reason and are drinking deeply from the wellsprings of universal knowledge. In explanation he invents a parable of his own. A great King, God, dwells in a palace at the very center of town. Among his subjects some do not even dwell in town; they reside in the countryside. They are the ones who are removed from the City of God, without faith and thought. Their features may be human, but actually they are no better than the apes. From this pseudo-human level one may move into the city in the hope of eventually seeing the king. But the city also offers two roads. Some of the city dwellers have not even seen the palace; their backs are turned to it. These are people who *do* think, but their views are all wrong; they move in the wrong direction, they are caught in error. Others have set out to reach the palace. These are the people who cleave to Torah and fulfil its commandments, but have remained ignorant. A smaller group have reached the palace and now walk around it to find the entrance. Even earnest students of Talmud may belong to that group; they strive, without getting through to the fundamentals of faith. Mathematicians and logicians also are counted among this element; they too remain on the outside of true knowledge. A few have entered the palace courts and have made progress within its halls. They are the seekers for the roots of faith, students of great works and of nature, critical minds. Those who have gained insights to the limit of human capacity have reached the inner court. Reason has guided them in matters divine; theology is their occupation. The great sages of Israel belong to this group. He who has covered all these steps and is capable of devoting himself entirely to an intellectual contemplation of God, he who studies nature to find Him in its order, he is the man who has reached the king's chamber. This is the level of the prophet.[15]

Like Aristotle, Maimonides maintains that only reason makes us human; it is man's great distinction over all the other creatures. The pursuit of reason gives us greatest happiness. Unlike Aristotle, he is convinced that reason gives fulfilment to human life only if it leads to the knowledge of God. Like the Talmud, he demands obedience to God's commandments as a first essential step on the road to God. It must lead to a study of tradition, to studies in Judaism. Beyond that, Maimonides envisions a higher level: philosophy leading to theology and culminating in a direct intellectual conversation with Him, as far as human limitations will permit it. This is prophecy.

---

[15] *Guide* III, Ch. 51; II, pp. 279 ff.

Prophet and Philosopher

No one becomes a prophet overnight. First he must be a philosopher; he must travel as far as humanly possible toward a true knowledge of God. Then, in a flash of illumination, God reveals to him the highest truth. But not every philosopher becomes a prophet, even if he is fully prepared for it. God may withhold the gift of prophecy from him; God acts in His own, miraculous ways. Jews produced prophets while other nations did not, because the visions of others are simply not true. This applies especially to those prophets who make the claim that God spoke with them directly. Scripture testifies that only Moses was given this privilege. To him God spoke "mouth to mouth; as a man talks to his fellow (Exod. 33:11)." The other Jewish prophets were addressed by an angel only. Should a prophet make the claim that God has talked with him directly, he is a false prophet. Even if such a prophet produces miracles to substantiate his claim, he is still false. Moses did not need any miracles to prove his immediate contact with God; the whole people *saw* him speak to the Lord; they were eyewitnesses. Miracles prove nothing. The word of Torah stands: Moses, who *publicly* spoke with God directly, is the only prophet so chosen and ever to be chosen. This explains the superiority of Judaism over all other faiths; it is based on a unique, personal revelation of God, never to be repeated. It is therefore the one true and abiding faith.[16]

The philosopher rates beneath the prophet but ranks highest on the scale of human achievement. He has the task to apply reason to the knowledge of God.

God

God is the cornerstone of Judaism; He is One. What can we know about Him? To Judaism He is the Creator of the universe and Father to His children. Aristotle also recognizes One God, but he is different, the Unmoved Mover. Aristotle holds that everything in the world has an inner drive to fulfil its potential. An acorn, for instance, has an inner drive to become an oak tree. The goal *for* which all things strive Aristotle calls *form*. The oak tree is the *form* of the acorn. In turn, the acorn is *matter* of the future oak tree. In another example, the child is the *matter* of the *man;* to be a man is his goal, his *form;* he is a *potential* man. When he is a man his potential has been realized. Matter is potentiality, form is reality. When the acorn has grown into a tree, when the child has grown into a man, new goals develop. The oak tree has a purpose; the man has a purpose. A new *form* is there. In the beginning the oak

---

[16] *Guide* II, 32, 35-37, 42; also Mishneh Torah, Hilhot Yesode Hatorah VII-VIII.

tree was the *form* of the acorn; now, fully grown, it is *matter* for a new form. Thus matter becomes form, and then form becomes matter. This goes on until we come to a final form. Everything strives toward this form, and the final form serves nothing else; it never becomes matter. This final form is God. God cannot do anything, God cannot move, God cannot serve any cause. He is absolute *form*. God becomes the Unmoved Mover. Everything moves toward Him; He does not move at all. In human terms, we may explain it by the example of a man who is in love with a woman. She does not know him, she does not do anything for him, she is unmoved. Yet she moves him to many activities; he looks for her, comes near her, works hard to gain her attention and be worthy of her.

God, then, cannot be the creator of the world. Aristotle accepts that and concludes that the world has existed forever. But Maimonides cannot accept it. The Torah describes God as Creator who fashioned the world at a certain period in time. Maimonides follows Aristotle as long as he can, then sets out to disprove him. If there are forces in everything to lead it from potentiality to actuality, from matter to form, who gave all creatures this force? The answer must be God. If there is a goal toward which everything moves, there must also be a starting point. The existence and progress of the world leads us to the conclusion that it must have been started. There must be a first cause for it. God is the first cause, the Creator. Oak trees might or might not exist; nothing exists by necessity. But the first cause must exist by necessity, because if there were no first cause nothing else would exist. There must be a Creator-God. He alone could create the world out of nothing. This means that He is totally different from His creatures who cannot create out of nothing, and do not exist by necessity. But what is He like? Maimonides answers: we shall never know. All we know is *that* He is, we cannot know *what* He is. Our thoughts cannot comprehend Him, nor have we words to express Him.

Whatever we say about God is inaccurate. Let us give a few examples.

a) If we say: "The man exists," we actually say two things: (1) there is such a thing as a man; (2) he is here. But of God we cannot state *two* things, He is one. His essence and existence are the same.

b) If we say: "One man," we also state several things, namely: (1) men exist; (2) they do not exist by necessity—we can think of a world without man; (3) it so happens that one man is here; there might be more men here, too. Can we say that of God? Can we think of a world without God? Can we think of more than one God? Certainly not. This shows that we simply have neither the faculty nor the words to express what God is.

c) If we say: "the man is tall and handsome and intelligent," we have said a number of things: there is (1) a man into whom are woven (2) tallness, (3) handsomeness, (4) intelligence. We have put *four* units together; but God is absolutely *one* unit.

We really can get no idea of God; His Oneness is unlike any oneness we can understand, His existence unlike any existence we can grasp. Our statements about God can only be negative statements. We can only say that He is *not* like anything we understand. We call this negative theology. This does not mean we deny His existence, we simply state that we have no comprehension of Him; nothing compares to Him. We cannot give him any positive attributes.[17]

God's attributes and the Bible

But this is not the way it is put by the Bible. It speaks of God being merciful and gracious; it even mentions the voice of God, the hand of God, the eyes and ears of God, the mouth of God. Maimonides explains that the Bible uses these expressions to explain God's presence to simple people. They cannot understand philosophical explanations, so they must be helped to visualize. When it is said, God is merciful, it means *we* feel an *effect* of mercy. When we learn of the voice of God, this means the effect of God on *us* is like a voice speaking. The acts of the One unknown God have *numerous* effects on us. This is all the Scripture means to say when it uses anthropomorphisms; neither voice nor hand nor eye can be ascribed to God. Maimonides gives fire as an example of nature. It blackens, whitens, melts, hardens, burns, and cooks, depending on circumstances. An ignorant person might think fire has many powers, but heat is the one source of all these effects. And so it is with God; we see the effects, but there is just one source—God, whose character we do not know.[18]

God's providence and man's free will

One of the most serious problems of theology has been the question of man's freedom of will. If God knows beforehand what man will do, how can man be free to do as he wishes?[19] Maimonides can give us a very simple answer. The whole problem arises only if we believe that God thinks the way humans do. Actually, we do not know how God's thought-processes operate. He may know all, and yet we may be free. What is a paradox for us need not be one for Him, whose "thoughts are

---

[17] *Guide* I, 50 ff.
[18] *Guide* I, 26, 35, 50 ff.
[19] See p. 268 for Saadia's contrasting opinion.

not like your thoughts (Isa. 55:8).'' We do not know.[20] We can be sure, however, that we are free. God watches over all His creation. He does not interfere in nature, because he has built into it the laws which guide it forever in the right direction. To man, however, He has given freedom, and with it admonitions to help him find the right way. God's Providence operates in the inwardness of man.

Miracles

But do miracles interfere with the course of nature? Some miracles, related to us in Scripture, must be taken allegorically, such as the talk between God and Adam in the Garden of Eden, or the voice of Balaam's ass. These did not really happen. Other miracles were not created in the moment of need, but were included in the work of creation. When God made the world, He foresaw that at certain times and under certain conditions a deviation from the regular order of its course would be necessary. He provided for certain emergencies in history by setting up His creation in such fashion that variations of events would take place at the right time and location.

Creation of the world: why Aristotle disagreed

Aristotle held, the world could not have been created in time, because creation out of nothing is impossible. For Maimonides creation is an incontestable fact. It can be proven philosophically, as Maimonides has done. Time does not apply to God, for before God created it there was no time. All else must also be the result of creation. For Jews, the testimony of the Bible is proof. Why did Aristotle fail to see the philosophical necessity for a created world? He based his conclusions on the present state of things, like an orphan boy stranded in early infancy with some male companions on a deserted island. The boy has never seen a female creature. As he grows up he asks about the origin of man, and is told about the growth of the embryo in its mother's womb, where for nine months it neither breathes nor feeds itself nor walks around. The boy now must choose between accepting the explanation, or relying on his own experiences. His own experience, as a grown man, tells him that no one can survive for even a few moments without breathing. Trusting in it, he may reject the explanation given him about the beginning of human beings. This was Aristotle's situation. He could only judge by his own experiences; he had no tradition, and therefore excluded any thought which might have led him in a direction contrary to his own experiences. That was his mistake. He erred in assuming that the creation of the world *as a whole* follows the same principles as the creation of the

---

[20] Mishneh Torah, Hilhot Teshubah V.

things *in* it. *In* the world, creation out of nothing is impossible. But this is a law of nature that had to be created also. It cannot be applied to creation as a whole. Philosophy cannot explain creation out of nothing. Hence we must abide by the reliable report of Torah: God created. Why God created it in time is unanswerable, as we cannot comprehend God. To Maimonides, Aristotle's argument has become so weak that we must follow the teachings of religion. Since Torah has given us an explanation of the world's beginning we can philosophize freely, and need not worry that immediate experience seems to contradict our philosophical conclusions.[21]

Why creation—what about immortality?

Why did God create the world? Certainly not for the sake of man, who is of no use to the universe. Again, we don't know, for the will of God is inscrutable, but the purpose of the world surely is to perform God's will.[22] Scripture tells us that He created the world because it was good to do so. Upon us rests the obligation to give meaning and purpose to our lives, and to gain understanding so we will be worthy of communion with God in the life of immortality. What is this life of immortality? Certainly not an earthly paradise transposed into eternity. God, whom we cannot describe, has prepared for us a life which is equally beyond our description. But life in the world to come must not be mistaken for the messianic age here on earth, when Israel will be restored and, through it, all of mankind. The pious of Israel will be awakened at that moment, to witness and rejoice in Israel's restoration.[23]

Just Average Good People

Not everybody can reach the inner chamber of the king and be a prophet; nor can he enter his courts and be a philosopher. Most people remain on a lower level. Among this mass there are also different stages of perfection. Maimonides follows Aristotle in listing the aims for which we strive. The lowest goal is wealth and possessions. Health and physical perfection is a higher aim, but both of them are self-centered. Morality is a worthier object of our ambitions. It makes us just and gives us love for our fellowman. Most commandments tend to lead us to such ethical conduct; we are to be servants and helpers for our fellowmen. But moral virtues have meaning only in society. A person who is totally isolated would not need them. How could he improve himself? By reaching the fourth level, which is search for God, from whom the principles of our lives derive.[24] Since we live in society, we have the

---

21 *Guide* II, 17.
22 *Guide* III, 13 and 25.
23 Mishneh Torah, Hilhot Teshubah 8-9.
24 *Guide* III, 54.

duty and opportunity to combine search for God with obedience to commandments which lead us to morality.

The Meaning of the Commandments

The commandments of Torah have social significance. The principles of faith raise the Jewish people to spiritual perfection. Maimonides finds himself confronted with the task of explaining the social function of the Jewish commandments. In many cases this is easy; the Sabbath law, for instance, can easily be explained in a rational way. It provides rest for everyone. There are other laws, however, which do not yield so easily. Here Maimonides uses a thoroughly modern approach; he explains them scientifically. The most striking example occurs in connection with the laws of animal sacrifices, which are explained psychologically. At the time when Israel was delivered from Egyptian bondage, all the nations of the world offered animal sacrifices to their gods. God realized that it would be asking too much of the people to make them change completely their form of worship. Changes had to come gradually. God permitted them, therefore, to offer animal sacrifices, and even taught them how to offer them, in order that they would not follow the crude customs of the heathens, and that their hearts be directed to Him. Yet He always had in mind to lead them to true worship, namely through prayer. He ordered them to build one single temple, as the *only* place where animals might be sacrificed. But prayer and supplication, *which are true worship,* may be offered at any place and at any time.[25]

The implications of this theory are far-reaching. While Maimonides himself abides faithfully by all the commandments, the theoretical foundation for a new approach is laid. It will demand that every commandment justify itself in the judgement of reason; it will evaluate ancient law on the basis of historical analysis. Maimonides, in his capacity as philosopher, sees Judaism as an evolving faith, which it is. This concept, however, was alien to the thought of his time.

After Maimonides

It is understandable that Maimonides' views drew the violent opposition of his own and of subsequent generations of rabbis. His philosophy opened avenues for the complete re-evaluation of tradition which was to be undertaken by the nineteenth century.

At the same time, his influence upon Christian scholasticism has been profound. He may be considered the father of Christian scholasticism, for it was he who gave St. Thomas Aquinas the idea and the scope of

[25] *Guide* III, 32.

his endeavors, to combine and to harmonize Aristotle with the principles of faith.[26] Aquinas' method and conclusions frequently directly follow the reasoning of Maimonides, and many other philosophers throughout the ages have been influenced by him.

MOSES MENDELSSOHN (1729-1786)

Background

The princes of the tiny German State of Anhalt were enlightened men. They opened the gates of their principality and of its capital city, Dessau, to Jews who wished to settle there. Jews came and founded a congregation in 1672. Their most influential member was Moses Benjamin Wulff, Court-Jew to the duke. Being a Court-Jew was a unique calling; one could become rich and influential, or one could lose one's head. Many princes appointed Jews to serve them as financial advisors,

Moses Mendelssohn.

[26] Concerning the influence of Maimonides on Christian scholastics, including St. Thomas Aquinas, see Isaac Husic: *A History of Jewish Mediaeval Philosophy* (New York: Meridian Books, Inc., 1960), pp. 306 ff.

budget directors, tax collectors, and scapegoats, all combined. The Jew had to devise new sources of income for the prince, new means of taxation; he had to collect the taxes, and serve as buffer between the prince and the people. If all went well, the Court-Jew gained wealth and prestige; but if the people rebelled against the heavy burden of taxation, then the Jew would be thrown to the wolves. Tried, found guilty of mismanagement, and hanged, he cleared his master, who then looked for his successor. In their position, many Court-Jews became benefactors to their brethren, obtaining for them the privilege of establishing residence, of trading, and of establishing congregations. In Dessau, Moses Benjamin Wulff gave prestige to the little congregation. He was a true leader and an enterprising man, even founding a printing press where Maimonides' great work, *The Guide of the Perplexed,* was reprinted for the first time in centuries.

Next to the Court-Jew in influence came the rabbi. David Fränckel was a learned man, soon to be called to Berlin to serve as chief rabbi. Close to the bottom of the official hierarchy was Menahem Mendel, Hebrew teacher and Torah scribe of the congregation; he performed the routine chores. But Mendel had a son who was to give new direction to Jewish thought. He was called simply Moses, Mendel's son, or Moses Mendelssohn.

Life

Mendelssohn's intellectual brilliance is recognized early; his own curiosity drives him to study. But he is a sickly child, undernourished and overworked. He falls ill; his growth is stunted, his back hunched. Fortunately, the brilliance of his mind is not affected; the peace of his soul remains undisturbed, for he is a deeply religious person. Rabbi Fränckel is impressed by the boy's ability, and accepts him for private instruction. Maimonides' work comes off the press at Dessau just at this time, and young Moses gets the chance to study the work of the great Moses. It was to have lasting impact upon his thought.

The rabbi leaves for his new position in Berlin. Mendelssohn, 14 years old, decides to follow the rabbi as his disciple. As he arrives at the gate of the city he pays the toll charged for cattle, dogs, and Jews. He is permitted to take up temporary domicile in the capital of Frederick the Great, enlightened despot—except when it comes to Jews. Mendelssohn is desperately poor. He cuts notches in his loaf of bread, to make sure he will not eat too much today and then go entirely hungry on the morrow. Yet he loves Berlin; it is a city alive with ideas, a metropolis of the spirit. From Talmud he moves to general studies: Locke, Leibnitz, Spinoza. He makes friends, and wants to stay in Berlin, but he has no residence permit. Finally he finds "domestic employment" in the home of a Jewish silk manufacturer who has such a permit; as domestic servant he can stay. Eventually he will become a partner in the business; his days of poverty will be over. Against his true inclination, he will always remain a business man.

He is introduced to Lessing, poet, critic, playwright. A deep and lasting friendship develops. Later in life Lessing will use Mendelssohn as model for the hero of his play *Nathan the Wise;* through him, he will appeal to the conscience of mankind in behalf of religious equality. At present Lessing helps Mendelssohn polish his German style to glittering perfection. He persuades him to publish his first book, *Philosophical Discourses.* The work creates a sensation; the entire intellectual world, and even the king, take note. Greater distinction is to come. In 1763 Mendelssohn is awarded first prize for an essay submitted in competition to the Prussian Academy. Among the competitors is Immanuel Kant, who is given honorable mention. Kant's work is actually deeper, but Mendelssohn's style is clearer. His fame grows, he marries, his home becomes a center for the literary world, but he has no permanent residence permit. His Christian friends plead with him to petition the king for the privilege. For a long time Mendelssohn refuses to "beg for that permission to exist which is the natural right of every human being who lives as a peaceful citizen." [27] But Frederick has no intention to grant this *natural right* to *a* Jew, though he may be persuaded to bestow the *privilege* of residence to *this* Jew. Frederick does not like Jews; he likes them even less when they are successful in the fields of literature and philosophy. The king himself is ambitious without getting very far. He does not even write in German—his literary works are composed in French. A story—possibly not true—throws a clear light on the relationship between Frederick and Mendelssohn. The philosopher has criticized the king's published poetry. Called to task, he replies: "He who writes is like a person engaged in the game of bowling; he must permit the boy to tell him how many pins he has thrown. Whether king or peasant makes no difference." But it makes a difference when a Jew wants a residence permit. Frederick grants it grudgingly when Mendelssohn, on repeated urgings of his friends, finally applies; he really cannot refuse, he is too famous. But when the members of the Academy petition the king to grant his approval for Mendelssohn's admission, he turns them down flat.

Actually, Mendelssohn is a totally new type of Jew, devoutly pious and faithfully observant of every one of the commandments, and also a liberal thinker, a philosopher of the Enlightenment, who takes his

---

[27] Mendelssohn to Marquis d' Argent, quoted in Joseph S. Baron, *A Treasury of Jewish Quotations* (New York: Crown Publishers, Inc., 1956), p. 420.

place proudly among the guiding minds of his time. This kind of Jew had not existed for centuries. Mendelssohn is a puzzle to many of his contemporaries, among them Johann Kaspar Lavater, a young Swiss Pastor. In a visit to Mendelssohn he tries to nail him down on the merits of Christianity. Mendelssohn seeks to evade the issue and eventually expresses his recognition of Jesus as a teacher of ethics. This gives Lavater a tool to challenge him publicly. A work has just been published proving by arguments of reason the truth of Christianity. According to Lavater, Mendelssohn, as a philosopher of reason, must either disprove the argument or—if unable to do so—must in honesty accept the consequences and become a Christian himself. Mendelssohn is in a difficult position; he will not give up his faith, yet he can foresee great harm for the barely tolerated Jews if he argues against Christian dogmas. As a man of peace he dislikes controversy in principle. "It has been my hope to disprove the contemptuous views commonly held about a Jew, by virtue rather than by controversial writings," [28] he tells Lavater. But answer he must; and his reply is a ringing affirmation of Judaism:

> May I point out that I did not start yesterday examining my religion . . . Years of examination have resulted in a decision wholly in favor of my religion; else I would have felt compelled to act publicly upon any negative conclusions. What indeed could tie me to a religion which is so extremely strict and, at the same time, so generally held in contempt, except the conviction of my heart that it is true. My examination . . . has strengthened me in the faith of my fathers . . . I hereby witness before the God of truth . . . that I shall abide by these my convictions as long as my soul will not change its nature.[29]

The Torah, he explains, is binding only for the Jew. "Moses gave *us* a law (Deut. 33:4)." The rest of mankind may be guided by natural religion or their own traditions. If they lead a good life in accordance with reason and morality, they are dear to God. Judaism therefore does not try to make converts; it can admire the ethical teachers of all nations, be they Confucius or Solon; it rejoices in the knowledge that these, like all good men, will find eternal salvation without change of faith.[30] Lavater had demanded an "either—or" decision; Mendelssohn replied in the true spirit of tolerant understanding. To him, child of the Enlightenment, all ethical masters of mankind deserve admiration; he is happy that Judaism bears him out. He recognizes and demands recognition for

---

[28] Moses Mendelssohn, *Gesammelte Schriften, nach Originaldrucken und Handschriften herausgegeben von Prof. G. B. Mendelssohn in sieben Baenden;* Dritter Band (Lavater, Jerusalem, Manasseh ben Israel, etc.) (Leipzig: F. A. Brockhaus, 1843), Letter to Lavater, p. 42. All translations by the author.

[29] *Ibid.*, p. 41.

[30] *Ibid.*, p. 43.

every religion; they all serve their faithful well. He feels entitled to equal recognition of his faith by all mankind. May the Jew be faithful to his own holy heritage, the Christian to his, and together they will usher in a better future for humanity under God.

Lavater apologized for his hasty challenge, but Mendelssohn is deeply shaken. The incident marks a turning point in his life, for now his major efforts will be devoted to a vindication of Judaism before a prejudiced world, and to the improvement of his own brethren. Overcoming apprehensions, he makes the treatise of Manasseh ben Israel accessible to the German reader. Manasseh had presented an outline of Judaism to Cromwell, clarifying commonly held misapprehensions and succeeding in opening the doors of Britain to the Jews. The German reader might be moved to better understanding too. Mendelssohn expresses hope that prejudice may not have closed the ears of the people to the voice of truth.[31] Then he lashes out at bigoted statesmen, who fail to see the value of the various population groups to the state. " 'People expendable to the State; useless to the State,' these are statements unworthy of a statesman . . . No country can dispense with even the humblest and seemingly most useless of its inhabitants without seriously harming itself. To a wise government not even a pauper is one too many; not even a cripple altogether useless." [32]

As far as religion is concerned, the State has no right to inquire into it or to be interested in it. It is outside its sphere.[33] Let the citizens, regardless of faith, give full allegiance and devotion to the State and they have served it as duty demands. As far as Jews are concerned, this imposes upon them a double obligation: "Devote yourselves to the ways and the constitution of the land in which you have settled, but remain equally firm in the religion of your fathers. Bear the burdens of both to the best of your ability." To Christians he appeals: "Brethren, . . . consider the *actions* of your fellowmen, calling them before the judgement seat of wise legislation; but do not interfere with (freedom of) thought and speech; which the Father of All has granted us by right as everlasting inheritance . . . Giving unto Caesar that which is Caesar's you will be giving unto God that which is God's. Love ye truth and love ye peace." [34]

But the Jews of the time had not been fully prepared to assume their obligations. Through years of ghetto life they had lost touch with Ger-

---

31 *Ibid.*, Manasseh ben Israel, "Rettung der Juden"; Vorrede p. 186.

32 *Ibid.*, p. 188.

33 *Op. cit.*, Jerusalem I, p. 261; Reference to Locke: The State's only concern is the welfare of the citizens in *this* world.

34 *Op. cit.*, Jerusalem II, pp. 355-362.

man culture and language. Mendelssohn realizes that communication creates the firmest link between people; German Jewry must build a bridge through language. The best way of fusing tradition and modern culture in his view lies in a Bible translation. Mendelssohn gives his people a Pentateuch translation in modern German, together with a Hebrew commentary. Through Mendelssohn, German Jewry stepped into German civilization holding in their hand the Bible, their proudest possession. Thus they were protected from losing their own heritage while adding a new one to it. In tragic irony, we find Jewry engaged in another Bible translation, perhaps the greatest in the German language, at the time when they were again to be separated from German tradition. It is the magnificent work of Buber and Rosenzweig, a bequest of German Jewry in symbolic recognition of a once so fruitful collaboration.

In Mendelssohn we find the beginning of this synthesis. He was a Jew in the fullest sense of the word. By his Christian contemporaries he was also acclaimed as "a philosopher of the German nation and language." [35] In his own family the synthesis did not last—his children left the faith. Under the guidance of his thought, however, German Jewry set up an ideal and a pattern which were to give all of modern Jewry its character: devotion as citizens, steadfastness in tradition. Mendelssohn's life and his religious philosophy showed them the way.

Religious Philosophy

As a philosopher of the Enlightenment, Mendelssohn belongs to a group of most distinguished and illustrious men. He shares a good many of their ideas.

Nature's God, His Ways, and His Works

We can find God through reason, says the Enlightenment. The greatest living philosophical document of the Age of Enlightenment, the American Declaration of Independence, speaks of "the laws of nature and of nature's God." Nature reveals Him; its laws testify to His presence and His goodness. Mendelssohn accepts these ideas readily. He finds support in his concept of the God of Reason in the book he has studied since childhood, Maimonides' *Guide of the Perplexed*. Subsequent examination of other Jewish philosophers has revealed to him their virtual unanimity on this point; Judaism is the religion of reason.

God is good, says the Enlightenment. Mendelssohn echoes it. God is the great educator, using rewards and punishments to lead man on the right road. God never punishes in retribution. As a teacher chastises

---

[35] J. G. Herder on Mendelssohn's death, in Bruno Strauss; *Moses Mendelssohn in Moses Mendelssohn* (Berlin: Verlag Eschkol, 1929), p. 38.

a child to guide him, so does God inflict hardships on us only to make us change our ways. When we are deserving, He rewards us as a means of encouragement, that we may persevere. There is no eternal damnation or punishment; it would serve no educational purpose, but merely be the act of a revengeful God on man no longer able to change his way.

Our reason tells us what is good; it teaches us morality, justice, love, and brotherhood. If the children of man will but follow their reason, all will be well. There is no need for any revelation to show us how to live honorably in the sight of God and man. Our intellect alone reveals to us the workings of God's Providence; it is manifest in nature. As we consider the purpose of the world and the meaning of man's life, we become convinced that we have an immortal soul; without it there would be no direction to our striving. In these views we notice the influence of Mendelssohn's great personal friend, Immanuel Kant, who develops the same thought. Our moral reasoning requires us to postulate the existence of God, soul, and immortality. Our souls are filled with awe as we contemplate "the starry sky above me and the moral law within me."

Biblical Revelations and Miracles

Reason is the absolute guide. Does that agree with the Bible, which tells us of revelations and of miracles? The revelation at Sinai requires no speculation, Mendelssohn explains. It is a publicly certified fact. This is straight out of Maimonides. What about miracles? Can we put our faith in their message? Only if the content of the message is in full agreement with reason. If the miracle is to convey an idea which is contrary to reason, then we must discard the miracle, even if it were to reveal a concept which reason cannot attain on its own. In his letter to Lavater, Mendelssohn makes it clear that he has examined Judaism in this light, and that it has met his requirements. On the other hand, so he states, the fundamental dogmas of Christianity are outside the realm of proof by reason, and unacceptable to him. This applies in particular to Trinity, Original Sin, and the Atoning Death of Christ. Mendelssohn realizes that if we trust any miracle, we must trust all of them. As David Hume, among others, pointed out, this is impossible, since the miraculous claims of the various religions are contradictory; a miracle to one religion is none to others, which may deny that such an event ever happened. We find reflections of Leibnitz, Locke, but above all, Saadia, champion of reason.

Why Judaism?

The great ideals of religion can be found only through reason. No revelation is needed. But why was the revelation at Sinai necessary?

Mendelssohn comes up with a startling answer: At Sinai the Jews received no religious ideas, no dogmas; they received a *law*. Judaism, as founded at Sinai, is *revealed law*. Mendelssohn offers two reasons for this conclusion. First, we need no revelation to arrive at the ideals of religion; our mind leads us to them. The second goes back to Saadia, who said that God gave us the *results* of reason before we could reach them ourselves. God acted like a teacher who gives his pupils the answer to a problem, in order that they can use it in practical affairs.[36] Mendelssohn says it would not be fair of God to give to Israel *alone* the end results of reason, for this would give Israel an undue advantage. While other nations are still striving for the answers, Israel could already apply them. But God has given all mankind the *same* power of mind to discover the great ideas in nature. Israel received, not facts of truth, but a law only.

The Israelites have a divine law, commandments, and ordinances . . . but no dogmas, no saving truths, no general self-evident propositions. Those the Lord reveals to us as to the rest of mankind by nature and by events, but never in words or written documents.[37]

We must understand the purpose of the law. When God saw that the other nations served idols, He called Israel to His service. The heathen world had taken the *symbols* of a faith of reason, worshipped them, and forgot the ideas for which they stood. Israel became the "priestly people"; its laws, which set it apart from the idol worshippers, are practical demonstrations of morality. In obeying them, the Jews live moral lives, and show the world how ideals can be translated into practice. By living in accordance with the law, the Jews fulfil the function "to teach these (universal ideals of religion) unceasingly among the nations, they proclaim them, preach them, uphold them by their very existence." [38] The Jew by his life reminds the world of God. The Jew may never depart from the law, even for the sake of gaining equal rights as a citizen. By doing so he would lose his purpose in God's plan. "If civil union (political equality) cannot be obtained on any other term than that of departing from the Law . . . which we consider binding . . . then, with sorrow in our hearts, we find it necessary to declare that we will rather reject civil union." [39]

---

[36] See p. 266.
[37] Mendelssohn, *op. cit.*, Jerusalem II, p. 311.
[38] *Ibid.*, p. 311.
[39] *Ibid.*, pp. 357-358.

Living in two worlds

Mendelssohn's theory has several profound consequences. It invites the Jew to live in two worlds.

1) He is absolutely bound by the law when it comes to practice. He is given complete freedom of thought. "There is not one single command in Mosaic Law telling us "Thou shalt *believe*" or "not believe" . . . Faith is not commanded. In questions of eternal truth nothing is said of believing, the terms are 'understanding' and 'knowing.'" [40] This resolves Mendelssohn's dilemma. He can be a free-thinking philosopher, and yet—in his own mind—a faithful Jew.

2) The Jew is part of the world whose principles of religion are found through reason. All of humanity must combine in the effort of discovering them. The Jew must join with people of other faith in the promotion of the ideals of the Religion of Reason. He is free in matters of dogma and belief, and may find the truth by his own speculations or accept it from others.

3) The Jew stands apart in the performance of the law. He sets an example. Obedience to Jewish law is a matter of free choice to the Jew. He need no longer fear any punishment for disobedience; there is no power in the world which could enforce the law. He is morally bound, however, to remain faithful to it. By symbolizing in his life the spirit of obedience to God, he becomes teacher of humanity. Actually, the Jew is close to the world. A teacher may be apart from his pupils; this is necessary if he wishes to serve them and teach them. The Jew is apart from the world to teach it; he works for the world, preparing the day when all humanity will serve God.

4) All peoples are equally beloved of God. The other peoples need no commandment; they have the faith of reason. Should they go astray and worship symbols, the example of Israel will pull them back. The various families of humanity find numerous ways of approaching God. God has fashioned man in different shapes and given him different methods to reach the divine. Religious plurality is built by God into the very scheme of things. Each group can learn something from the other. The divine plan for the world will be fulfilled only if we grant full freedom of conscience to everyone and permit all religions to unfold their ideals freely. They must learn to stand up proudly for their heritage, that others may profit from it.

Why should we, in the most important concerns of our life, render ourselves

---

[40] *Ibid.*, p. 321.

unknown to one another by disguise? Not for nothing has God stamped individual features on every face.[41]

Mendelssohn's Influence

Mendelssohn's influence upon Jewish religion has been profound. His ideas have been modified, his radical separation of faith from action admitted only with qualifications. It was also pointed out that he had —admittedly—no sense of history and of its processes of evolution, to which faith and law are subject. But his theories have become the starting point for the development of modern Judaism. Taking their cue from him, western orthodoxy has given a great deal of freedom of thought to its followers, while adhering strictly to the law.

Others, contrary to Mendelssohn, declared that *faith* is true revelation. Laws and practices can be historically explained; this means they can be changed or eliminated. They are only *symbols* of eternal truths. This led to reforms, which, surely, was not Mendelssohn's intent. Reform maintained that the important thing is that we represent the great ideals of ethics and exemplify them among a struggling humanity. Forms do not matter.

As law came to be regarded as expendable and thought was free, there emerged Jews whose only bond to Judaism was their emotional attachment, their family spirit.

The freethinker, in turn, had only to equate the nineteenth century with the period of universal reason; he could then cast off religion altogether. Or he might see in Christianity this realization, and accept it.

Generally speaking, Mendelssohn's philosophy permitted every Jew to become a scientist, a philosopher, or a writer. As he followed the law, he remained a faithful son of his people. As he served humanity and reason, he lived up to the highest ideals of Judaism as proclaimed by Mendelssohn.

---

[41] *Ibid.*, pp. 360-361.

17

French Revolution and Aftermath

The Enlightenment lowered many intellectual barriers, commerce and industry brought Jews and Christians together in business, but still the barriers did not fall. In 1782 Joseph II, emperor of Austria and a truly enlightened monarch, issued an edict opening the public schools and universities to the Jews, and removing a number of other disabilities. The Jews were ordered henceforth to use the German language. The idea was to remove some walls of separation without giving them full equality. It took the French Revolution to bring about a radical change. Inspired by the American Revolution, it could but follow its ideals; in America the Jews were free and equal citizens. The French Revolution brought a complete assault on the organizational unity of Jewry. Mendelssohn had seen the Jews as a group, a "nation," but also full-fledged citizens of the countries in which they lived, and dedicated to special duties by which humanity would profit. The French Revolution could see only *individual* citizens. It was either abandonment of group jurisdiction and group law, or nothing. "To the individual Jew everything," said Clermont-Tonnère in the National Assembly, "to the Jews as a nation nothing." The Jews had to make a serious decision. Unless they abandoned the inner structure of their community life, they would have to remain foreigners. They decided to follow the call of the new age which was opening up to them, the world of freedom. On September 27, 1791, Jews were declared French citizens with equal rights. There were now two countries in the world, the United States of America and France, where the Jews had acquired full citizenship.

NAPOLEON ORGANIZES A SANHEDRIN

As the colors of France and of the French Revolution were carried abroad, freedom for the Jews went with them, to Belgium, Holland, and Germany. Out of the holocaust Napoleon emerged as ruler of France. He was a dictator, but he was also a child of the French Revolution. He liberated the Jews in the countries he had conquered, at the same time setting up the central and district consistories, through which he hoped to supervise their conduct. He really had nothing to fear from a people who savored the taste of liberty for the first time in centuries, but Napoleon was suspicious. Would their religious teachings always serve *his* aims? Motivated by the same suspicion, he had asserted his power over the pope, eventually bringing him to Paris. The Jews had no pope, but once, he knew, they had had a Sanhedrin, the supreme religious authority. Nothing would be easier than to convoke a new Sanhedrin—at Paris. After due preparation, the Sanhedrin was installed with great pomp and circumstance; in its rank sat some of the most learned men in Napoleon's empire. These rabbis had an extremely difficult task in trying to meet Napoleon's demands without abandoning Jewish law. They realized that they must please Napoleon or their people would lose their hard won freedom, yet they could never be untrue to Torah. Some questions could be answered easily. Did they consider France their homeland? Did they regard Frenchmen to be their brethren? Of course they did. What about a Jewish nation? They answered: "There is no Jewish nation, only Germans, Frenchmen, and Englishmen who profess the Jewish religion." This statement was true. Jews have always been faithful citizens of the countries in which they lived, but there has been a feeling of kinship. Unfortunately, both the terms citizenship and kinship had been expressed by the term nation. Mendelssohn meant kinship when he spoke of nation. Napoleon was interested in the political aspect of citizenship when *he* spoke of nation. In the course of the years, some Jews themselves misunderstood the situation and came to feel that all ties of kinship were to be broken. They thought they could earn the right of citizenship only at the cost of denial of all bonds. We find the same tendency among immigrants from many lands who came to America and felt they had to erase completely the culture to which they were heirs.

Under the impact of Napoleon's ideas and decrees, the Jewish community became more and more atomized. Jewish authorities lacked even the power of rebuke. The State dispensed the law, including cases of family relationships, such as marriages. How difficult the position of the Sanhedrin was can be seen from their decision regarding interfaith marriages. Napoleon, man of reason, felt that religion should be no obstacle; as emperor, he maintained that a marriage approved by the State should receive the approval of religion as well. Carefully the Sanhedrin stated the principle that, according to the Talmud, State law is binding. It was made clear, however, that the Talmud also insists that Jewish religion must govern family relationships, such as marriage—unless there is a conflict with the law of the State.

Marriages between Israelites and Christians, which have been entered according to the law of the Civil Code, are binding and valid according to civil law, and—although incapable of being clothed with religious forms—do not lead to an anathema.[1]

The problems of the newly opened world thus hit Jewry with their fullest impact before there was time for any adjustment.

France granted limited liberty. The nations conquered by Napoleon were reluctant. Prussia, badly beaten by the emperor, accepted the willing and enthusiastic support given it by its Jews. In reward, it declared them equal citizens in 1812. The following year, Jewish youth laid down their lives for Prussia in the war of liberation. When the war was over, the official attitude changed back to old patterns.

JEWS AND THE CONGRESS OF VIENNA

Napoleon was defeated, and abdicated. The victorious powers met at the Congress of Vienna (1814-1815) to restore order. The people, including the Jews, came to plead for greater democracy. Finally, a commission was established to study the status of the Jews and to prepare the way to give them equal rights. This would take time. "Until then the rights already granted to them *in* the Confederate States shall remain in force." This meant the rights granted by Napoleon in the states he had ruled, but one of the copyists, on suggestion of a delegate, changed one word which cost the Jews their liberties. Signed by all the powers, the statement now read: "Until then the rights already granted to them *by* the Confederate States shall remain in force." The rights of citizenship had been granted to the Jews, but *not by* the States; they had been given by Napoleon *in* the states of his empire. Thus the Jews lost their rights. Prussia, which had granted the rights, now hedged them in by many edicts; Bavaria found means to retard and reverse the growth of

---

[1] Quoted from *Rabbi's Manual*, © 1928 Central Conference of American Rabbis, p. 172 (Historical Appendix).

the Jewish population; Joseph's tolerance edict in Austria had already died with the emperor. But the Jews were not the only ones to suffer from these reactions following Napoleon's defeat. Liberal Christians also saw their hopes dashed. Jews and Christians now joined, taking as their cause the battle for universal liberty. Jews produced fighters, such as Gabriel Riesser, who could not teach at a university because of his religion. Human rights for all was his device; with it, citizenship for Jews would go hand in hand. It took two revolutions, in 1830 and 1848, to give Jews the feeling that they were finally on the way. Unfortunately, this was not quite true. Full recognition did not come to the Jews in Germany until 1918, after World War I. And then it was only an interlude before the Nazi storm broke.

In the meantime, Jews had to adjust themselves to their "Renaissance." They had to move rapidly. Emerging from their Middle Ages, they had to cover Renaissance, the Industrial Revolution, and the Scientific Revolution all at the same time.

THE STATE ORGANIZES THE JEWISH COMMUNITY

As they gained their freedom, the Jews lost the self-government which had been part of their ghetto life. Congregations were established and supervised by the State, and served as purely religious institutions. Their organization, structure, administration, and the position of their rabbis and lay leaders followed exactly the pattern established for the Christian churches. Every Jew had to belong to the synagogue in his district. The State approved the congregational constitutions and by-laws, and published them in the official law gazette; they were public law. Congregations had the right to impose taxes upon their members, and the government revenue office saw to their collection. The rabbis had to be approved and were installed by the State, with life tenure, giving them great freedom to reform and rebuild. The lay officers had the power of the State behind their ordinances.

AN EXAMPLE: OLDENBURG

I served as the last Chief Rabbi (Landesrabbiner) of the State of Oldenburg under the system then still in operation. It was my function to supervise all the Jewish congregations, and their ministers, in the State. I should like to quote a few of the laws governing the Jewish congregations, which are significant as an example and have had great general impact. In a way, Oldenburg was a laboratory for Jewish ideas and communal organization. The founding Chief Rabbi and organizer of the Jewish community was Dr. Nathan Adler, one of the first rabbis to hold a Ph.D. From Oldenburg he was called to be rabbi of Hanover, then still under British rule; eventually he rose to the position of Chief Rabbi of the British Empire. He found the Jewish community there disorganized and in confusion, and rebuilt it on the pattern of the Oldenburg example. The Chief Rabbi of Britain is the spiritual head; the congregations are generally subject to his jurisdiction; he ordains the rabbis and ministers and supervises them. Each district has its synagogue; combined, the synagogues are represented by a governing board to which they send delegates. This was the Oldenburg pattern, still followed by the United Synagogue of the British Commonwealth, the representative body of British Jewry.[2] Most significantly, it derives its strength and prestige from an act of Parliament of 1856.

In Oldenburg, Adler was followed by Samson Raphael Hirsch, who was to become the founder of Neo-Orthodoxy. Under the Oldenburg constitution, he had the opportunity to hammer out his program. His basic work, the Chorev, was written in Oldenburg. So profound was its impact that a young man, trying to find his way, came to Hirsch to spend with him the most formative years of life. The young man's name was Heinrich Graetz, the most influential Jewish historian of modern Jewry.

Oldenburg was a workshop, reflecting the significance of German Jewry as a whole. In Germany the new ideology was forged which has influenced all of world Jewry. It was possible only as a result of the system of organization of which Oldenburg offers a sample.[3]

Here are some of the edicts.

August 24, 1827. In order to control the religious affairs and the school system of the Jews and give it supervision, a Chief Rabbi shall be appointed. Upon presentation of sufficient credentials in regard to his knowledge, general education, and good character, and after passing an examination, he shall be approved by the Grand Duke. He shall be sworn to obedience of the law . . . The Chief Rabbi shall have his seat in (the City of) Oldenburg and shall be priest (sic) of its synagogue. . . . The Chief Rabbi is responsible to the government, and shall report to it when conditions warrant. Under his supervision are the conditions in the churches (sic) and schools of the Jews in the entire State. He is responsible for appropriate order but has no judicial authority whatsoever . . . To the duties of the Chief Rabbi belong the performance of all spiritual functions, the supervision of religious services, the direc-

---

2 There are other synagogue bodies in Great Britain, since affiliation is voluntary. In addition, a lay organization, the Board of Deputies of British Jews, acts as recognized spokesman for Jewish interests. Without being endowed with any formal mandate, it has acquired great prestige in the 200 years of its existence.

3 Leo Trepp, Die Landesgemeinde der Juden in Oldenburg, 1965 Oldenburg.

tion and supervision of religious services, especially in the Synagogue of (the City of) Oldenburg; supervision over education and Shehitah.[4]

ON THE ORGANIZATION OF CONGREGATIONS:

Rasted, the third of July 1858.—We, Nicolaus Friedrich Peter, by the Grace of God Grand Duke of Oldenburg, Heir to Norway, Duke of Schleswig, Holstein, Stormarn, Dithmarschen, and Oldenburg, Prince of Lübek and Birkenfeld, Lord of Jever and Kniphausen, etc. etc. . . . proclaim . . . as follows:

I. About the Jews' Congregations

ARTICLE 1.

§ 1. The Jewish religious community in the Dukedom of Oldenburg consists of the Congregations of: Oldenburg for the County of Oldenburg; Varel for the County of Neuenburg. . . .

§ 2. Residence within the district of a synagogue constitutes membership in the congregation for every Jew in the Dukedom of Oldenburg.

§ 3. Formation of a new congregation . . . can be ordered after hearings . . . provided that the Ministry of State and the State Council approve.

ARTICLE 2. All these congregations form the "Jewish State Congregation."

ARTICLE 3.

§ 1. Each congregation has a synagogue council, which represents the congregation and is in charge of its business. It consists of a president and two assistants which are . . . to be elected for terms of four years.

ARTICLE 4. Deals with the functions of the synagogue council.

ARTICLE 5.

§ 1. The "Jewish State Congregation" is represented through the "Jewish State Council." It administers the business of the "State Congregation" and is supreme authority, directing and supervising the Synagogue Councils.

§ 2. The "Jewish State Council" consists of a) the Chief Rabbi as presiding officer; b) the presidents of all the congregations.

§ 3. The functions of the "Jewish State Council" consist of:

a) election and presentation of a Chief Rabbi, who is to be appointed by the Grand Duke. Should the Grand Duke have any objections to the appointment of the nominee, then the Council has to elect and present another person.

b) general congregational business, including the regular annual budget for salaries of Chief Rabbi. The budget for the Chief Rabbi's salary must be approved by the government.

The general ordinances obtain the force of law upon publication in the Oldenburg Gazette. . . .

ARTICLE 6.

The Chief Rabbi is appointed by the Grand Duke upon presentation by the Jewish State Council. He is sworn in by the government, which is his superior and overseer. . . .

ARTICLE 7.

For the protection of the rights of the State, the Government has the supreme

---

[4] The kosher slaughter of animals.

supervision over the entire organization of the Jewish cult. . . . From "The Landtag's Reasons for the Law" to Article 7: The Government shall no longer have the actual *direction* of Jewish affairs, as up to now, for the Jews shall themselves administer their own affairs, but only a *general supervision* to protect the rights of the State. . . .

§ 3. About the Raising of Funds. This is done by taxation.

The position of the Chief Rabbi as spiritual and administrative head was unique. Once elected, he was independent of his congregations. His people had no means of disciplining him; they could not lower his salary, for it had to be approved by the Ministry of Churches. On the other hand, he depended on the good will of his superiors in the State government. The ruler had a profound influence on the character of the Jewish community. If he was interested in the modernization of the service and of general practices, he would appoint modern rabbis, men with university education and liberal outlook. Should he decide to keep the Jewish community outside the main stream of general culture, he could at least retard the acculturation of Jews by prohibiting the introduction of new forms in the service. This happened in Prussia, where the German sermon was forbidden in the synagogue. Generally speaking, however, the trend was liberal, in the direction of reform. Pressures from without, ambition from within, opportunity for experimentation, all worked together to bring about a reformation of Judaism, which proceeded rapidly. But in spite of its speed, it can be regarded as a great success and achievement.

The new rabbis who took on the leadership of the Jewish community all agreed that changes had to take place. Judaism had to be brought up to date if the generations of the future were to be kept within the faith. They were deeply divided, however, on the extent of this reorganization.

REORGANIZATION AND THE DIVISION OF MINDS

Some rabbis had a basic inner resistance to change; if it had to come, let there be as little of it as possible.

Others, however, felt that the culture of the world can enrich Judaism, and should be incorporated in the system of Jewish life and worship. These should be made aesthetically appealing and emotionally satisfying to modern people. At the same time, the law of Torah and Talmud may not be touched; it must be performed in all its details. Out of this approach came Neo-Orthodoxy, led by Samson Raphael Hirsch.

The Reform group went further, and split. Some were so intoxicated by the spirit of freedom that they were ready to throw off all tradition and maintain only the ethical law. Samuel Holdheim belonged to this element. Others, moving more carefully, nevertheless claimed that they had the right to adjust the law, to abolish laws, to examine its fundamentals, and change them, even as the Talmud had done. Abraham Geiger was their leader.

Between these two camps we find a middle-of-the-road school represented by Zachariah Frankel. Let us stay in touch with the people, and tradition they said. Let us examine their actual feelings, study their needs, and on that basis let us proceed to remake Judaism, not by revolution, but evolution. They spoke of a "positive historical Judaism." This was Conservatism.

What these men thought and how they built will be the subject of detailed description. The tool they all used was the Science of Judaism.

THE SCIENCE OF JUDAISM

We must not forget that, at this time, no Jewish history had been written. The evolution of worship, practices, and customs was largely unknown. Mendelssohn himself neither knew nor cared for history. If Judaism was to be modernized, it had to be scientifically explored. The father of this "Science of Judaism" was Leopold Zunz (1794-1886); trained in Jewish and secular subjects, he dedicated himself to the exploration of Judaism. He was aware that knowledge of Judaism would give pride to those ready to abandon it, and as a student had founded a "Society for the Culture and the Science of the Jews." Heinrich Heine, one of its members, left his faith to get, through baptism, his "admission ticket to society." He never ceased to regret it. Zunz, however, led ever more deeply into Judaism, went on searching for Jewish literary sources. The publication of his work "The Sermon in Jewish Worship," [5] was an event. He proved that the Prussian government was wrong when it forbade the sermon in the synagogue, claiming it was a Christian practice; Jews had actually founded the institution. Beyond that, he demonstrated that Jewish literature and history are subjects of serious study which deserve attention by universities and scholars of all religions.

Other works followed. His Bible translation became a standard work; no Jewish home in Germany could be without it. Zunz saw clearly that innovations in Judaism were appropriate and could be carried out in the spirit of tradition. He was profoundly shocked however at the recklessness with which some of the reform elements tore down the hallowed institutions and denuded Judaism of all content. His significance as trailblazer and master of Jewish Science has been great and enduring. It is reflected even in this very book, which is based on the foundations laid by Zunz.

And so the modernization of Judaism began.

---

[5] Die Gottesdienstlichen Vorträge der Juden (1832).

18

Conflicts
and
Conferences

T he problem of reform in Judaism is as old as Judaism itself. Tradition has never stood still, except, perhaps, during the period just before the emancipation. There has always existed a creative tension between faith and life. Great personalities, such as Hillel, Rabbi Johanan, and Rabbenu Gershom testify to it. Saadia, Maimonides, and Mendelssohn are witnesses also. New, however, was the critical approach to the Scripture itself, to its divine origin and the authorship of its parts. The past had always explained Torah in terms of "being"; it was the eternal unchanging rock. Now Torah was explained in terms of "becoming," and Judaism seen as an evolutionary process. The results of the new approach varied with the men who undertook the interpretation; they might be conservative or radical in their approach and their conclusions. Out of these interpretations grew the various "denominations" in Judaism of today.

As rabbis, they chose their congregations as laboratories. In addition, they revived the practice of rabbinical conferences, hoping that these would bring unanimous decisions, as had the gatherings of rabbis in days of the Talmud. Two of these conferences are outstanding—Braunschweig in 1844 and Frankfurt in 1845.

The men who appeared at these conferences had in common a desire to reform Judaism in line with the needs of the new age. Those who did not approve of reforms stayed away. Eventually some of the par-

299

ticipants found the resolutions of the conferences to be so radical that they could not endorse them, and withdrew. There was another group of men who believed in modernization but considered conferences as a wrong and illegitimate approach toward reconstruction.

THREE GIANTS

Among the participants, three men stand out as leaders. Destined to link their names to the movements which they called into being, they were Holdheim, Geiger, and Frankel.

Samuel Holdheim (1806–1860)

He was the radical of the group. Only as a grown man, and under the influence of his wife, had he come in contact with secular knowledge. Born in the eastern part of Prussia, he had spent his childhood and youth in the study of Talmud, pursuing it according to the mediaeval methods of the "pilpul." The sudden transition from one world to another may have been a cause of his imbalance. The new world simply burst upon him, and he embraced it with all his heart. Only the law of the State is binding, he proclaimed. Eventually, as rabbi of the newly organized Reform Congregation of Berlin, he abolished the Sabbath in favor of Sunday observance, and solemnized marriages of Christians to Jews. His following remained extremely small.

Abraham Geiger (1810–1874)

Much more significant to the development of reform, Geiger also advocated the most drastic changes in Judaism, but in order to rejuvenate Judaism and give it meaning under changed conditions. Holdheim was a wrecker, Geiger a builder. Bold in his pronouncements, he moved much more slowly when translating his ideas into the practice of Jewish observance.

Geiger was born at Frankfurt. At an early age he began his studies of Talmud, while also being given some secular education. Then doubt came, and he thought university study might give him better insights. He went to Heidelberg, then to Bonn, where Samson Raphael Hirsch became one of his close friends. Eventually these two men were to be bitter antagonists. Geiger took his Ph.D., received rabbinical ordination, and accepted the call as rabbi of Wiesbaden. Soon he made a name for himself by founding a Jewish-scientific periodical in which he boldly called for a thorough reform of Jewish religion, and as organizer of a small conference of liberals. In 1838 he was called to Breslau. It was a position for which he was ill suited, for, in addition to being a preacher,

Abraham Geiger.

he was to make religious decisions in practical matters of Talmudic law. He himself denied the validity of the very law he was to expound and administer. The orthodox element strenuously opposed him, but, with the temper of the time in his favor, he became the leader of reform at Breslau, and used the battle that raged about him for its full publicity value. Soon he was the recognized spokesman of reform throughout Germany, and gained fame as a writer. "The Original and the Translations of the Bible" [1] was a work clearly dedicated to the spirit of evolving Jewish religion. Each generation, he pointed out, reads into the Bible its own highest ideals and aspirations. Scientific research thus guided his practical decisions. After Breslau, he served for some years at Frankfurt, then was called to serve as liberal rabbi at Berlin. Here one of his great hopes became a slowly maturing reality. A modern seminary for rabbis had been organized, called "The School for the Science of Judaism." It offered him the opportunity to train future rabbis in the spirit of reform. At the same time, Berlin gave him the outlet of a pulpit and of an active ministry. In this twofold role as teacher and practicing rabbi, he found the ultimate fulfilment of his aspirations. The school became one of the most distinguished centers of Jewish learning until the Nazis destroyed it. Among its graduates we find some of the most illustrious names in the rabbinate.

---

[1] *Urschrift und Übersetzungen der Bibel.*

Zachariah Frankel (1801–1875)

In agreement with Geiger on the need for reform, Frankel's approach was so different that he ended as an opponent of the reform movement.

He was born at Prague and received a thorough talmudic training; his mind was so brilliant that he could acquire his high school education by private study at home. He took a qualifying examination, and was admitted to the University of Budapest without ever having been to school before. He obtained his Ph.D. and ordination, and received a call to the small town of Teplitz in Austria, right near the German border. Soon he became known for his great learning, and the Ministry of Churches of the neighboring Kingdom of Saxony called him to be the rabbi of Dresden, capital of Saxony. There he became a defender of Jewish rights, and was revered, respected, and beloved.

He succeeded in having the special degrading oath for Jews abolished. His writings were modern; his approach, scientific and critical. In 1853 he was called to the position which was to give him even greater scope. A conservative seminary for rabbis had been founded at Breslau, and Frankel was to be its president. As head of the "Jewish Theological Seminary," he spent the rest of his life in education, calling to his faculty some of the outstanding scholars of his time, including the great historian Heinrich Graetz. Thus Frankel became one of the fathers of Jewish spiritual life in Germany as the seminary extended its influence throughout the entire Jewish world. It was destroyed by the Nazis, but its fame endures.

CONTROVERSY: REFORM AND CONSERVATIVE JUDAISM

The conferences which brought together these rabbis of different leanings were concerned with practical problems, not with ideology. But ideological differences immediately appeared.

Behind every problem certain basic considerations could be found. There was, first of all, the problem of "nationhood." Jews had lived in Germany for perhaps 1800 years, possibly longer. They had been set apart as a "nation," and now they were moving toward the goal of equality. From the outside world they were under pressure to amalgamate with the rest of the population. The Jews were eager to respond; they wanted to be citizens, but they also wanted to remain Jews. The problem faced by the conference was to find which of the Jewish laws were "national" laws, leftovers from the ancient Jewish state, and which laws were purely religious. The national laws would have to go; the religious laws and ideals would have to be emphasized. In that manner Jews could be both citizens and religious Jews.

Another problem dealt with religious worship. How could it be made aesthetically appealing to a generation raised under the influence of modern tastes in beauty? How could it be made meaningful and uplifting?

Cutting deeply into all considerations was the spirit of scientific approaches to religion. How could the new insights and materials presented by Zunz and his disciples be applied to Jewish law? There was also the fact that the reformers did not operate in a vacuum. They were dealing with people, a community molded by its past. True, some of its members were trying to escape, but many more were deeply attached to it, its traditions, its practices, and its holy Scriptures.

Over their thinking seemed to hover the spirit of Mendelssohn. He had taught that the law had been revealed to the Jews to set them apart. Ethical laws, based on reason, had been given to all mankind.

Geiger and Holdheim

The leaders of reform—Geiger and Holdheim—disagreed with Mendelssohn in regard to revelation. Science does not bear out *any* revelation. They agreed that Judaism has the mission to lead mankind, and also that, originally, the law had been given the Jews for the purpose of setting them apart, a nation in their own state. Since it was *not* revealed law, what purpose did it have in a modern society with Judaism only a religion? Under modern conditions the law is outmoded, even harmful; therefore the law must go, it must be abolished. This would apply to all Jewish laws, according to Holdheim. He says: the Sabbath idea is good, Sabbath rest is ennobling, but observance of the Sabbath on the Saturday leads to exclusiveness. His Sabbath worship, therefore, is conducted on Sunday. Even circumcision, the basic commandment of Judaism, leads to particularism as far as he is concerned; it must go. Other "separatistic" laws to be omitted would include dietary laws, all Sabbath prohibitions, and all dogmas which have no foundation in scientific fact, such as a personal Messiah, resurrection of the dead, or return to Zion. Such an outlook could only lead to a complete split in Judaism. Holdheim does not care whether the masses of the people will follow him or not; his influence remains restricted to a very small congregation in Germany. It is in America that his ideas will make greater inroads.

Geiger does care. In theory he agrees with Holdheim. Judaism must be purified, the "underbrush" cut out; science must be the guide for a systematic reform, with humanity as the goal. But, as a responsible leader, he knows that the unity of the Jewish people must be preserved. This involves him in contradictions, as he speaks of the people of Israel, which to him seems to have had "a native endowment . . . the genius

of religion . . ." "Judaism originated among the people of revelation." [2]
He admits that the Jews, a people of revelation, have a special gift.
This is more than a practical concession to reality; these are his emotions, his pride in his heritage speaking. Geiger will not admit that he
has broken with the past; he considers his reforms simply a historical
development. Reform "preserves carefully the bond which connects the
present with the past." [3] Holdheim does away with Hebrew, while
Geiger, in his prayer book, retains it. "The significance of the prayers
consists not only in their content, but also in their traditional forms . . .
in the Hebrew language." [4]

Thus Geiger is torn between logical conclusions and emotional attachment to Judaism—between scientific deductions and practical realities. One pulls in the direction of radical solutions, the other toward
answers dictated by his love for Judaism as a sacred heritage and by
the pragmatic fact that he is dealing with people who must not be
forced. Still, after Geiger gets through with his reforms, the foundations have been removed from beneath tradition; there is no central
authority to which the people can turn. Torah is no longer divine Word,
the binding power of the Talmud is denied, the law is rejected as belonging to another period. God is seen in deistic and scientific terms.

*Geiger's ideas led to the formation of Reform Judaism, the first of
the new "denominations." Science is master, individual conscience alone
serves as guidepost. No laws are binding, and education, sermon, worship, and the missionary ideal are the foundations of Judaism. Through
Judaism, mankind is to be led toward the fulfilment of the ideal of
brotherhood.* It should be pointed out, however, that in the intervening
years Reform has moved a good deal closer to traditionalism and conservatism.

Frankel

It was obvious that a clash would develop at the rabbinical conference between the extreme reformers and the conservative Frankel. As
long as the changes were in the spirit of the Talmud, there was no
disagreement. The second day of the holidays, which serves no purpose,

---

[2] Das Judentum und seine Geschichte (Breslau: Schlettersche Buchhandlung, 1865),
Part I, p. 61 f., also Part II, pp. 10 ff., "Judaism arose within a people; the people
were the bearers of this faith. . . ."

[3] Unser Gottesdienst, 1868, quoted by Joseph L. Baron, A Treasury of Jewish Quotations, © 1956 by Joseph Baron (New York: Crown Publishers, Inc., 1956), p. 403;
Jüdische Zeitschrift für Wissenschaft und Leben, quoted by D. Phillipson; Centennary
Papers, Cincinnati, 1919, p. 102.

[4] Israelitisches Gebetbuch, 1854, quoted by Joseph L. Baron, op. cit., p. 370.

might be eliminated. Organ music may be introduced; there is no valid talmudic prohibition against it. These reforms were in the spirit of Judaism. But the others were not in the spirit of Judaism, at least in the opinion of Zachariah Frankel.

Frankel felt that he was witnessing a form of "negative Judaism" in the proceedings of the conferences. Laws and tradition were cast out, and nothing was put in their place. Authority and tradition were denied without any new guideposts being established. The spirit of the time was no yardstick; times change, and with them their spirit. Would Judaism become a rudderless ship drifting with the currents of changing fashions and philosophies? Frankel could not let that happen, but he was also a man of science, aware that Judaism and its ideas had evolved, and its institutions had grown and changed in the course of history. They had evolved out of the spirit of the people, slowly, imperceptibly perhaps, but progressively. The people, by unspoken, unanimous consent, had discarded old concepts, introduced new ones, reinterpreted others. All we would have to do, therefore, would be approach the past of the Jewish people through scholarly research, while remaining in touch with the feelings of the living people. Out of it would emerge the change, the adjustment, the reform. "Positive historical Judaism" is Frankel's principle. According to Frankel, there exists a permanent inner tension between law and life which is constantly resolved by the people themselves. This is the lesson we learn from the study of evolving tradition, so study and research are of primary importance. Reverence and love for tradition are indispensable attitudes. The unity of the Jewish people with its past, future, and in all its branches at the present, is the paramount consideration.

If we reform, we may do so only within the limited area of talmudic law, if the people accept the reforms. The organ, for example, when generally accepted, becomes permissible; there is no objection to it within the law. For centuries, however, the organ had been banned, because the people had been opposed to it emotionally. As long as such emotional blocks exist they must be respected; when they vanish, the road is open for the change. Hebrew is another point in question. According to the Talmud, prayer may be offered in any language; emotionally, however, the Jew is linked to Hebrew, so it must remain in the service. It forges the link to the past; it constitutes a bond between Jewries in many lands; it binds the Jew to his future, the restoration of Zion. Hebrew is the essence of Judaism. And the Jews are a nation.

Frankel is able to see the difference between "nation" politically speaking and "nation" viewed as a spiritual union, as kinship, and as household. He is as patriotic as Geiger, but he realizes that Judaism creates a unity which lies outside the political. This, the very spirit of

Judaism, must be preserved. "Nation" thus becomes only a religious factor. "The spirit of the nation" is the ultimate authority regarding the lawful and the unlawful; it differentiates between living precepts and those which no longer have any meaning.

The hope of redemption, the restoration of Zion, give meaning to Jewish existence. In this hope are enshrined all prayers for human improvement and perfection, for brotherhood and peace. This is a much deeper "missionary ideal" than that of reform. Frankel has thus succeeded in combining the various elements under discussion. The law is retained as long as the people need it, want it, and are emotionally tied to it. At the same time the spirit of evolution is recognized. "Particularity" is removed from any political connotation, and becomes a purely religious element. Emancipation is not in danger.

Frankel left the Frankfurt conference in deep disagreement and sorrow, but he went on to train the generations of rabbis who were to give German Jewry its predominant character. Conservatism has become a powerful force in America as well.

Frankel's ideas have led to the second denomination in modern Judaism: Conservatism. Judaism evolves through the spirit of the people themselves. By being attuned to this spirit, by study and historical research, the leaders and members develop a traditional, yet changing, Judaism, bound by the laws which are living among the people, linked through Hebrew to the entire Jewish community of the world. It looks forward to the redemption of Zion, but its people feel deeply rooted in the countries whose citizens they are, giving them their full and proud devotion. Judaism never loses the link between its branches, its past, and its future. American Conservatism has accepted these principles while adapting and changing them to align with American thought and conditions.

NEO-ORTHODOXY

In spite of their controversies, conservatism and reform had one thing in common; they both exalted science and the conclusions of science over the doctrines handed down by tradition. Orthodox tradition had taught that the Torah had been completely dictated by God. This basic belief had served as the foundation of Judaism throughout the centuries, but to men under the influence of modern science it was no longer acceptable. When they spoke of revelation, they had to give the word a less literal meaning; it stood for the divine inspiration which God gives to great minds, not for dictation. The foundations of Judaism had been shifted. Reform based Judaism on science and individual conscience; conservatism rested it on science and the will of the people. Conservatism might be as strict in obedience to a commandment as orthodoxy, but there was a difference. Orthodoxy would say: we obey because God wants us to perform this particular law; we know that for all eternity Jews will by bound by all the rules set down in the divinely dictated Torah. Conservatism would say: we obey this law because it has always been dear to the Jewish people; it conveys a meaningful message to them. We will abide by it as long as the people—by unanimous and unspoken consent—wish to retain it. We do not exclude the possibility that, sooner or later, this law or other laws will be quietly discarded by the Jewish people and thereby become obsolete. This was a concept unacceptable to the orthodox; to them, Torah must be accepted unconditionally, because it is divine in every aspect. Yet this group realized the need for a happy relationship with worldly culture, for beauty in worship, for patriotism, and dedicated citizenship. How could it be achieved? The man who succeeded in synthesizing all these elements was Samson Raphael Hirsch.

Samson Raphael Hirsch (1808–1888)

Born at Hamburg and given a thorough Jewish and secular education, as a young man Hirsch witnessed the struggle between orthodoxy and reform in his own home town. Reform had opened its first temple and introduced a new prayer book with many innovations, resulting in widespread controversy. Orthodoxy countered by entrusting the leadership of

Samson Raphael Hirsch.

its forces to a man of modern education, its Chief Rabbi Isaac Bernays, a philosopher of romantic leanings, and a fine preacher. Hirsch thus realized by immediate experience that no old-time rabbi could meet the liberal movement on equal terms. Only rabbis with modern training and university education could hope to meet the challenge of the new age. He determined to be such a rabbi, well-versed in Talmud, and fully educated in secular disciplines. He matriculated at the University of Bonn, where he met Abraham Geiger. They studied Talmud and languages together, became friends, argued. Graduating at 22, Hirsch became Chief Rabbi of the State of Oldenburg, where he published his basic work expounding his philosophy of Judaism. Composed in the form of 19 letters addressed to a fictitious friend, who, confused and bewildered, is assumed to have asked Hirsch for guidance. How can Judaism, as divinely revealed religion, be equated with the results of science; how must a Jew live to be both citizen and true to his faith? Hirsch replies to all of these; the title of the work is known simply as *Nineteen Letters*.

It was a stirring and powerful book with instantaneous appeal. Among its readers was a young man as bewildered as the hero of the work, named *Heinrich Graetz* (1817-1891), whose gigantic work "History of the Jews" was to become a universal classic. Graetz writes Hirsch, and is invited to live with him at Oldenburg. For three years the two men work and study together. Both are children of their time, seekers, reformers, lovers of beauty. They will retain these traits for the rest of their lives, but there are profound differences between the two which eventually lead to their parting. Hirsch is absolutely orthodox. Whenever he finds his judgement in conflict with the truth revealed in Torah, he cancels his own opinion. Graetz places his own personal experience above the revelation of Torah, seeing in himself the final arbiter of truth. Hirsch will retain this outlook throughout life; Graetz, however, changes under Hirsch's influence. In the future he will no longer accept Hirsch's position. He will subject the Torah to criticism, but he will submit his judgment to the collective experience of the Jewish people. Through Hirsch, Graetz was led into the camp of Frankel, who was to call him to his seminary at Breslau. Without Hirsch he might have landed in Holdheim's camp, and we would have lost Graetz, the learned historian with his warm heart, his deep love for Judaism and the Jewish people, and his inspiring presentation of "positive historical Judaism." We see the barriers separating orthodoxy and conservatism, but also their proximity.

In 1836 Hirsch publishes his *Chorev*; he tries to explain the meaning of the divine commandments. This is in the spirit of Maimonides, but also in response to the need of the age.

From Oldenburg Hirsch is called to Emden, and then to a leading old-time eastern orthodox congregation, Nicolsburg in Austria. Immediately the unbridgeable gulf between the new orthodoxy and traditional orthodoxy begins to show. The people simply cannot understand Hirsch or his ideas. "The ancient rabbis used to read the Bible and study the Talmud," they would say, "but Hirsch studies the Bible and reads the Talmud." It is all wrong. In 1851 Hirsch is called to form an orthodox congregation at Frankfurt. Now he is in his element.

According to State law, each community in Germany was to have *one* congregation. In the larger cities, however, there existed at least two groups, the liberal and the orthodox. Large congregations, trying to meet all needs, would then establish two synagogues under one congregational administration. One synagogue would be orthodox, the other liberal. The orthodox synagogue would retain the unabridged Hebrew prayer book, there would be no organ, but it would have robed rabbis and cantors, choir, an aesthetically satisfying service, and a German sermon. The liberal synagogue would have an organ, an abridged Hebrew service, and German prayers; otherwise it would be the same as the orthodox one. Both synagogues were maintained by the taxes levied by the congregation on the entire membership. Hirsch immediately attacked this system, declaring that it was against Jewish law, since the orthodox members were contributing to the upkeep of a liberal service. He succeeded in getting his way. The Prussian government eventually granted his congregation the right to secede from the city congregation and to operate a completely separate set of institutions.

Now Hirsch made his congregation into a model community. Among the members were men of great wealth, including a branch of the Rothschild family. A magnificent synagogue was built, a gem of beauty but fully in accord with Jewish law. The service was the ultimate in perfection, with liveried ushers, gowned rabbis and cantors, and a top-hatted, morning-coated congregation. Hirsch himself was a master of the German language and a powerful preacher. His sermons attracted the people through their literary quality, beauty, and content. The members were proud to belong and enthusiastic in their support. Orthodoxy in Hirsch's surroundings became most fashionable.

In addition, Hirsch kept on writing. Among other works, he wrote a translation and commentary to the entire Pentateuch—in German. He founded a school system which would carry the children of his congregation through most of high school. Its ideal was absolute faithfulness to Torah combined with highest scholastic and educational standards. The students were expected not merely to pass their examinations but to pass them with distinction, and to carry with them a deep and abiding love and appreciation for German culture, music, art, poetry, and philosophy.

The Rabbinerseminar

The spirit of this enthusiasm, which fired his congregation, influenced all of German Jewry. In Berlin, Rabbi Ezriel Hildesheimer founded an orthodox seminary, the "Rabbinerseminar." Now all denominations had their training schools for rabbis; private study was no longer the road to ordination. Hildesheimer was attacked from two sides. The old-time orthodox groups of Eastern Europe criticized him severely for his modern approaches. The Seminary and its professors were dedicated to a scientific curriculum, differing from Breslau only in their fundamental philosophy—the divinity of Torah and not the will of the people is the guiding principle. Standards and requirements were virtually the same. Hildesheimer was also attacked from Hirsch's camp, for he did not accept Hirsch's principle of separatism. Rabbis ordained by the Rabbinerseminar served in the orthodox synagogues of unified congregations, while their colleagues ordained at the other schools might serve the liberal synagogues of the same congregation. The Rabbinerseminar produced men of great stature and influenced some American seminaries. It was destroyed by the Nazis.

The Character of German Orthodoxy

German orthodoxy accepted all of Hirsch's ideas except separatism, which made little progress. For all practical purposes the differences separating orthodox and conservative rabbis and congregations were small. The liberal synagogue in Germany was really conservative, with exception of a few synagogues. The orthodox synagogue, with its modern forms, was also conservative. The use of German prayers, the length of the service, the use of the organ, these were items differentiating them. The differences looked big at the time, but are very small when viewed from the distance of time and space. German Jewry had developed a golden mean. It is important to remember that even Hirsch's orthodoxy was a far cry from the orthodoxy of Eastern Europe, which had not changed at all. To the Eastern European Jew, ideological differences meant little. What he saw in the German synagogues of all denominations appeared about the same. Raised in the environment of hasidic exuberance or self-denying seclusion in Talmud, what did he find? A stately form of service, where the Torah was carried from the Ark in slow measured step following the beat of the choir leader's baton. He found robed rabbis, who looked to him like the clergy of the Russian church he had come to fear. He listened to a sermon quoting the rabbis of old in conjunction with Goethe and Schiller, and it made no sense to him. He watched a mute congregation in silent devotion of prayer, which to him was a pouring out of soul in ecstatic movement and voice. Thus to Eastern European Jewry, German Jewry in its entirety was "unjewish." This error has been perpetuated to our day. Actually, German Jewry had the most workable synthesis for its time and situation. It was the teacher of world Jewry. Where its example was followed and adapted to conditions, the Jewish heritage was transmitted well. We shall see its influence on English-speaking Jewry.

Hirsch's Philosophy

Hirsch is, beyond question, the father of neo-orthodoxy. He is a disciple of Mendelssohn, who hails the emancipation as a divine gift. "I bless the emancipation, when I see . . . respect for right, for human rights (prevailing): to be man among men . . . the earth is the Lord's and whosoever bears the image of being His child shall be respected joyfully as brother." [5] But the gift serves a purpose. The emancipation removed some of the burdens from the Jew in order that he may serve God better. Living among mankind, it is the Jew's task to elevate it, which is exactly what Mendelssohn had said. The task is performed, as Mendelssohn had pointed out, by obedience to the laws of Torah, by an action program. Judaism is not to be made into a set of ethical values, nor into an emotional "religion"; it is practical performance of Torah. Hirsch explains that God has given recognition to man by elevating him from an animal to the status and dignity of a human being. But man can always sink back, and will, if money, pleasures, or desires become the ultimate goals of his life. To give to all mankind an example of ideal humanity, God created the Jew. He is the teacher. The commandments are given him that he may overcome his desires and rise toward the true goal of serving God. In action, in self-denial, in the conquest of his selfish—although human—cravings, the Jew becomes the ideal man. He becomes, in Hirsch's term, "Israel-Man." What is permitted to others may be prohibited to the Jew, who, for the sake of mankind, lives in his own province, alone, separated, involved in mankind as a teacher. Israel's "particularity," which Geiger wanted to overcome by eliminating the law, is seen by Hirsch as a high contribution to humanity; it is service for mankind. "Normal" existence is not for the Jew. When the Jews wished to live "normally" in the land of Israel, the land was taken away from them. Hirsch maintains that Israel was made into a people and the land of Israel was given them only to make them more spiritual; to give them a stage on which to present the world with an ideal society dedicated to God. When they failed, they lost their land. They have to find their way back to God amidst persecution

---

[5] Samson Raphael Hirsch, *Neunzehn Briefe Über Das Judentum* (Altona: Hammerich'sche Verlagsbuchhandlung, 1836), p. 81. Author's translation used throughout.

and trials, and demonstrate to the world that it is possible to serve the Lord joyously, even in affliction. The folk character was given the Jews only to make them holy.

. . . it is a duty to fulfil as far as possible the tasks of citizenship in the state which has accepted us; to promote the goals of the state, and to see one's own welfare inseparable from that of the state. This is well possible even in the spirit of Judaism. For even the earlier independent national life was not truly the essence and the purpose of Israel's peoplehood; it was only a means for the performance of his spiritual calling. Never were land and soil the uniting bond, only the common task of Torah (was this bond). There is unity, there-fore, even though they are citizens in the lands of the diaspora; until God shall unite them as a nation on one soil and the Law of Torah shall once again be established as principle of a state, as pattern and as revelation of God, and of man's true calling. This future . . . is prophesied but may not be actively pre-pared—only hoped for. For it (this future) we are being educated that we may then, in our happiness, better exemplify "Israel" than we did the first time. This future will go hand in hand with the elevation of all mankind to all-embracing brotherhood under God, the Only One. On account of this purely spiritual nature of Israel's folk character, Israel is able to link itself most sincerely to the states (of the world). Only in one way perhaps will Israel differ. While others may regard the goods, which the state protects—such as property and the pur-suit of happiness—to be their highest goal, Israel will see in them only the means toward the fulfilment of its human vocation.[6]

Hirsch means to say that every Jew has to set an example to the world. This is his religious duty and his duty as a citizen. God has set the Jew apart to guide the world by living a model life. If he does so, he helps others and society as a whole by his example. The more faithful he is to Torah, the greater is the example he presents. By his devotion to Torah, he demonstrates how we can curb our animal appetites and release ever greater love. This is the purpose of the commandments. His non-Jewish fellow citizens watch him, and are inspired by him to pursue high ideals; he has helped them, his society, and his country. He is a good citizen. The emancipation for the first time in centuries offers the Jew an opportunity to serve God in joy and to spread His ideals among others. Up to then Jews had been persecuted in punish-ment for their failure to serve God in times of happiness, but a new era has come. The ideal Jew is he who combines to perfection worldly ed-ucation and true Judaism, using both to serve mankind. He proudly proclaims his Jewishness to the world and inspires others, by his con-duct, to follow him and pave the way for a better world. Hirsch all but denies the nationhood of Israel, calling it only a spiritual concept. In

---

[6] *Op. cit.*, pp. 79 f. The term "Israel" generally stands for Jewry. Only in modern times has it come to connote the independent state in Palestine. The terms must not be confused.

the remote future the Messiah will come for all mankind, and Israel will again be called to organize an ideal state for all other nations to imitate. Meanwhile nothing may be done to promote this event, for Torah itself forbids it. This was both traditional and universalistic, Jewish and patriotic. It gave pride to the Jew, explained to him why he should be faithful to the commandments, forged a link between Judaism and humanity, made secular education a religious function, and religious life a civic duty.

(You say about) Contact with non-Jews: "One is so set apart, immediately recognized as a Jew" (by the various dietary laws, etc.). Son of my time, who tells you to deny that you are a Jew? Be a Jew, be it in all sincerity, strive to attain the ideal of a true Jew by fulfilment of Torah by justice and love—in order that you be respected on account of being a Jew, not in spite of being a Jew; understand yourself as a Jew, spread its idea by your word, or—even better—by your life among your non-Jewish brethren. But the full degree of intimacy you may not be able to acquire if you don't eat and drink with them at their meals? Again, practice justice and love as thy Torah teaches thee: be just in deed, true in word, bear love in thy heart toward thy non-Jewish brother as thy Torah teaches thee—feed his hungry, clothe his naked, refresh his afflicted, comfort his mourners, advise his seekers for advice, aid with counsel and aid in distress and danger, unfold the whole fullness of thy "Israel-dom";—and he, will he not honor thee and love thee? Being more, however, namely a member of his family? Don't you see that you may not do that? that you may never be able to go that far? not from antagonism, but for reasons of thy calling as Israel," (to be outside as example).[7]

There is elan in Hirsch's words, a winged enthusiasm. We are reminded of Schiller's poetry, and indeed Hirsch sees in Schiller an inspired envoy of the same universal ideals handed down in Torah. Hirsch is actually more "reformed" than Frankel when it comes to ideology; in observance, however, the situation is different. Here even the smallest act is surrounded by the halo of its divinity and attains almost cosmic meaning. We can understand why he could not permit any contact with the other groups in Judaism. If his ideas were correct, then all the others were in utter error, which is perhaps a reason why his enthusiasm kindled so many hearts in his own circle. Actually, his doctrine could work only among an upper middle class, well-established, intellectually interested, and thoroughly emancipated, to whom secular culture meant a great deal. This type of orthodox Jew has now emerged in the United States. Hirsch's works have been translated into English. His influence is growing. To college educated, orthodox Jews, led by university trained orthodox rabbis, he offers a theology that permits participation in western culture

---

[7] *Op. cit.,* pp. 76 ff.

for "Torah-true" Jews. In contrast to Hirsch, modern Orthodoxy regards the restoration of State of Israel as permitted by Torah.

Hirsch's orthodoxy is the third denomination in Judaism. It is different from the old orthodoxy; we may call it Neo-Orthodoxy. Based on a synthesis of Torah and culture, it sees in "Israel" a spiritual ideal. The "Israel-Man" has an action program, the Torah, given by God. He must fulfil it, that through his example mankind be brought to God. "Nationhood" is taken in purely spiritual terms. The attachment to State seems greater in Hirsch's orthodoxy than in Frankel's conservatism. The restoration of Zion is to be left in the hand of God; the task for the people is here and now, among our non-Jewish brethren. Modern Orthodoxy disagrees with him only in its affirmation of the State of Israel.

OF DENOMINATIONS AND IDEOLOGIES: A SURVEY

This is the situation as it existed at the beginning of the twentieth century, before the emergence of Zionism.

1. OLD ORTHODOXY. The Torah is divine and must be obeyed. Questions need not be asked. Judaism lives by itself without contact with the outside world, which is basically regarded as hostile. This orthodoxy, which rejected all change, was practiced in Eastern Europe. Performance of the commandments in all their minute details was a psychological defense mechanism against the intolerable hardships of persecution. It gave the people great strength, while the expectation of a personal Messiah gave them hope.

2. NEO-ORTHODOXY. The Torah is divine, and obedience to it is service to mankind. Israel is the teacher of humanity. Secular culture is to be acquired; adjustment to modern conditions is essential, but may not encroach on the observance of Torah. Good citizenship is a divinely ordained obligation. Aesthetic values are to be fostered in worship and in life.

3. CONSERVATISM. The divinity of Torah is anchored in the consent of the people. Intuitively the people will adjust its commandments to their needs. Positive values are to be affirmed; historical study opens the gates to evaluation of Judaism. Adjustment is necessary and desirable within the framework of the people's acceptance. Israel constitutes a people. Spiritual and "national" bonds form a link; hope for restoration of Zion is a strong force. Aesthetic values are significant.

4. REFORM. The divinity of Torah compares to the divine inspiration given to poets and artists. The individual is the judge, his conscience the supreme yardstick. Laws which create a barrier between the Jew and his surroundings must be re-evaluated or abandoned. The

validity of the Talmud is reduced. The Torah is to be studied on a scientific basis. Ethical and aesthetic values are of supreme importance, and must be taught to mankind.

5. SECULARISM. Orthodoxy in Eastern Europe categorically denied the right to secular studies. A new generation, especially those who had emigrated, began to taste the beauty of worldly culture. They found no link to religion, but wished to remain Jews, so they took up the science of Judaism, its language and lore, without accepting religious obligations. They accepted the ethical teachings, especially in the field of social justice. This has led to purely secular movements dedicated to Jewish culture. Their adherents are convinced that they are good Jews. Some social action programs have been based on it.

6. ROMANTIC JUDAISM. Rationalism yielded to Romanticism. The God of Reason became the God of Emotion. This happened in the nineteenth century. Since Mendelssohn's time, law and ethics had become separated. Now many Jews, yielding to emotion, regarded themselves as children of their people without practicing anything. They became "Jews in heart," and can be found to this day.

This was carried to the point where Judaism remained an emotion of the heart even among those who had abandoned it. Heine was one of them; Disraeli, Queen Victoria's great prime minister, was another. He had been baptised as a child, yet, great romanticist that he was, he held a profound love for Judaism in his heart, identifying himself with its greatness and achievements.

All of these ideologies can be found in present-day Jewry. Subsequent developments during the twentieth century, however, have wrought a number of changes and modifications.

19
The New
Anti-Semitism

"Prejudice is thinking ill of others without sufficient warrant."[1] The Age of Reason had given freedom to the
Jews of Germany. The age-old, faulty generalizations in
regard to Jews had been dispelled by unbiased critical
thinking, but reason was soon displaced by Romanticism. Emotions once
more ruled the minds of men, for Romanticism appeals to emotions and
finds in them the guide for judgement. In addition, Romanticism looks
toward the past, glorifying times gone by, dreaming of distant places
and ancient people. As the Germans looked backward in history, they
discovered that the Jews, who now expected to be treated as equals,
had for centuries been regarded as a foreign body in the organism of
society. Blamed for the evils that had befallen mankind, they had always
been an alien element, the non-Christians in the Christian state. As the
Germans looked ahead, they found themselves confronted with grave
problems. All the other European nations had attained unification long
ago; the Germans longed for it throughout almost the entire nineteenth
century. If they could only restore the Christian State of old, they might
regain their strength, status, and glory. This was their hope. Hegel,
Germany's leading philosopher, laid the theoretical foundations. To him
history was the unfolding of the Absolute, the march of God. History
moves in triads: thesis—antithesis—synthesis. In marriage, the husband,

[1] Gordon W. Allport, *The Nature of Prejudice* (Cambridge: Addison-Wesley Publishing Company, 1954), p. 6.

with his endowments, links his strength in union to his wife in order to give life to the child. Husband is thesis, wife with her different genes is antithesis, the child, combining the two, is synthesis. Hegel maintains that history works the same way, leading to ever greater perfection. One of its glorious fulfilments was the *State* governed by a *monarch;* another was *Christianity.* In Christianity, God is becoming man. It is the synthesis of two previous stages: God facing man was the thesis, man facing God the antithesis, God and Man being One the synthesis. The *Christian State* ruled by a *monarch,* this was true fulfilment. This branded the Jews as a block on mankind's road to perfection. Hegel had proven it philosophically, according to his followers. But there was another approach, through science. This was significant; for many, the dogmas of the Church had lost their hold, while science had taken their place in the minds of intellectuals and of intellectual romanticists. As science progressed, the Jew, no longer rejected for religious reasons, was rejected for "scientific" reasons—race. Men like Gobineau in France and Houston Stewart Chamberlain in Germany advanced their racial theories. The Jews, no longer the anti-thesis to the Church, became the anti-thesis to the master race, the Aryans. The Jew could now be attacked from two sides. To the dogmatic Christian romanticists he was the non-Christian stumbling block; to the "scientific" romanticists he belonged to an inferior race.

PRESSURES AND RESULTS

The German Christian state began to apply a low, but very real, pressure. No Jew could become a full university professor, or a civil servant, or an officer in the peacetime army, unless he converted to Christianity. My father used to tell me of his own experience. By his educational background, he was entitled to take officers' training in fulfilment of his military duty. When the time came for the officers' examination, he was called to his captain, who told him: "I have done you a favor. I have scheduled the examination to take place on your Jewish holiday. Write me a letter to be excused from taking it." Why? "I know you will pass; but then you will be rejected by the officers' corps. Let me spare you the humiliation." I remember seeing my father's military passport. It said: "Promoted to the rank of sergeant—has not taken officers' examination."

The effect on the Jews was unfortunate. Denied access to many vocations and professions, they flocked to those open to them: medicine and law. If corporations refused to employ them, they could always start their own business, hoping to win acceptance if they did well. Main street stores became dotted with Jewish names, but the people of the street saw only the names on the store fronts, which spelled economic power. Envy bred more prejudice. The harder the Jews tried, the more problems they created for themselves. People neither knew nor cared that discrimination had forced the Jews into specific occupations and professions. At the same time the sociological imbalance which had existed during ghetto times continued. As Jewish names became conspicuous, the Jewish minority became ever more vulnerable. Politically weak, exposed, it offered itself as perfect scapegoat for all that went wrong. A chain reaction had begun.

The Jew was still seen by many as member of a foreign nation, international in character. If he no longer lived in a ghetto, it could only mean that he tried to camouflage his nationhood, and had entered a secret conspiracy of power. But against whom could this power be directed? An international conspiracy could be directed only against the national state. It was as simple as that.

These were the bitter fruits of German Romanticism, carried over into the period of "Realism," the time when Germany followed the policy of brutal aggression. Germany claimed that the nordic blood entitled her to mastery over others. The Jew was the opponent. The works of Richard Wagner may serve as an example of extreme German nationalism. They combined art and philosophy. He had two subjects: Christianity, as in *Parsifal* and *Tannhäuser*, and the nordic gods and men who symbolized primaeval strength, courage, heroism, fearlessness and manliness, as in the *Ring of the Nibelung*. Surrounded by a torrent of glorious music, the listener could lose himself in emotion. No wonder Hitler could not get enough of Wagner, this Romanticist of the highest order. In life, however, Wagner was a ruthless realist, ready to crush any opposition and competition. His great competitor was Meyerbeer, the Jewish composer who wrote equally spectacular, if not as enduring, operas. Wagner, as a struggling young composer, gratefully accepted Meyerbeer's generous assistance, but then, as the "philosopher," he set out to prove that Judaism and music were alien to each other in character. Jews were parasites who had cheapened and commercialized music, with no feeling or understanding for it. Yet when he needed Jewish help, both artistic and financial, he sought and accepted it. This was "Romantic Realism" in its purest form. Emperor William II surrounded his aggressive plans with Wagnerian symbols. He saw himself, and had himself portrayed, as *Lohengrin*, the knight in shining armor, blond and Christian, rescuing the princess in distress.

With the imperial household setting the pattern, even the scholars fell in line. Sociologists, like Sombart, insulted the Jews for their imbalance in professional occupations; conveniently, they took the sympton for the cause. As Solomon Schechter, head of the American Jewish Theological Seminary, once pointed out, higher Biblical criticism was at least in part motivated by the desire to deny to the Jews authorship of the Scriptures. It claimed that the Jews had stolen the material from Babylonian and Egyptian sources, and had contaminated it by their own cheap business ideology. One did not have to recognize a debt of gratitude to them for the Bible. Higher criticism, in Schechter's words, became higher anti-Semitism. The true "racial scientists" even "proved" that Jesus was not a Jew, but an Aryan.

The scientists "proved," the realists exploited the ideas. The imperial court preacher, Stoecker, was able to organize an anti-Semitic party in the German parliament, the Reischstag. It was not successful, but it kept prejudice alive. High-minded Christians organized associations to combat the evil of anti-Semitism, while Jews did the same. But they had only reason as a weapon, and reason did not work in the emotionally supercharged atmosphere of the German empire.

This was "the good old anti-Semitism," as the Jews would call it later, in the days of Nazi persecution. It ranged from a feeling of general unease in connection with the Jew, to religious antagonism, which could be eliminated by conversion. It ran the gamut from envy, which expressed the wish "to get them," to racism, which saw in extermination the only solution to the Jewish question. It could be combatted on a day by day basis, but its roots were too deep for easy elimination.

Among the Jews there were some who succumbed and accepted Christianity for the sake of promotion. They too were later captured by the Nazis. The majority retained their faith and their hope. They had lived in Germany so long that they could no longer envision expulsion or extermination. The nineteenth century was a period of great optimism throughout the world, and Jews, as perennial optimists, firmly believed in gradual improvement of conditions. And every Jew had some true Christian friends who were close to *him*, regardless of their feeling about Jews in general.

There were among those who had left the Jewish faith men who accepted the slanders and made them their own. The prime example is Karl Marx. Baptised early in life, hostile to the world as a whole, a "scientist," he took Hegel's method of thought and turned it upside down: economics is the moving force, class struggle the power in history. From Judaism he borrowed the idea of a messianic age of human equality, and perverted it beyond recognition. In doing so he expressed such hatred, venom, and spiteful scorn against Jews and Judaism that he has become a teacher of the most rabid anti-Semitism in the world. Materialist that he was, he could not help hating the God-centered ideals of Judaism.

CONTRASTS

German anti-Semitism deserves our special attention because it became an article of export. In Eastern Europe there had always been hatred, but in the West it was different. When Jews were permitted to resettle in England and France, they had been away for so long that the memory of their past status was forgotten, and they could start anew. English Romanticism viewed the Jews as the mysterious descendants of a glorious people, divinely appointed and eternal in its purpose. Sir Walter Scott and Disraeli depicted them in that light. The Jews were able, therefore, to overcome their disabilities in steady progress, even though they lived in a country where the Church was part of the State, and where any oath of office included a pledge of allegiance to Christianity. The people themselves helped. When one of the Rothschilds was elected to Parliament, he was refused his seat because his religion forbade him to take the prescribed oath. But the people of the City of London elected him again and again until the oath was changed and he could be seated.

Anti-Semitism in the West was made in Germany and exported from Germany. Even in present-day America, wherever we find it, it uses the same arguments and methods invented in Germany. There is one difference, however. The Germans accepted it because they had never had true freedom, and had never fought for their rights as citizens. They neither knew the value of liberty nor recognized that freedom is indivisible. The American people are wiser.

Since Hitler, the old anti-Semitism has become discredited. Spurred by Russia and Arab rulers, it now hides itself under the name *Anti-Zionism*. As such, it has become a slogan of the Radical Left. Seeking to divide Jewry into Zionists and non-Zionists, it is, in fact, attacking all Jews, and needs to be watched and combatted.

20
Zionism

U nder the impact of nineteenth century nationalism, a new approach emerged in response to the intolerable conditions of Eastern European Jewry. It was Zionism, which was to be triggered into a world-wide movement by an event and by a man. The event was the Dreyfus Case in France; the man was Theodor Herzl.

Heinrich Graetz once characterized Judaism as a blend of the idea of "state" and the idea of religion." [1] The ideal of Judaism is indeed a synthesis of the idea of "kinship," which unites its members, and the idea of "faith," which binds them to God. In the course of history the two ingredients were blended in different proportions. Western European Jewry emphasized the element of "religion," while Eastern European Jewry stressed the concept of "nation." In the West, Jewish life had permanence, and was creative of universal contributions. In the East, Jews had to confine creativity to their own sphere, for they truly lived in "exile." Russia too had felt the breath of the "scientific" race theory when Czar Alexander III decided to unify and pacify his restless empire on the principle of "one race—the Slaves; one religion—the Russian Orthodox Church." The Jews became the victims of this policy; their life became a hell on earth. The "Pale" the province allocated them as resi-

---

[1] Heinrich Graetz, *Die Konstruktion der Juedischen Geschichte* (Berlin: Buecherei des Schocken Verlages, 1936).

321

dence was cut down in size. Those who had leased some land and tilled the soil, were now brutally removed from any contact with the earth. All Jews had to remain in the village in whose registers their names had been recorded, and woe to the Jew whose name had not been registered or whose register had disappeared from the village administrator's file. He became a Cain, homeless, hopeless, driven from pillar to post. The Jews lost their livelihood, the last remnants of freedom, and their homes. They became sitting ducks for the raiders who swooped down to plunder and kill. It was official policy to overlook these brutalities against the Jews. Even under these conditions, it never occurred to the Jew to give up his faith. He faced disabilities, hunger, persecution, and slaughter, but he would not yield in his convictions. The idea of nationhood, however, gained an ever stronger hold on his imagination. Russia pushed the emigration of Jews. Why not go to Palestine? In the religious Jew, the age-old hope of a return to Zion came to life again. But a group of non-religious Jews was also emerging in Russia, young people, small in number but strong in spirit. To them the idea of Jewish nationhood, plain and simple, of freedom, of a land where one could enjoy life and self-respect, became a vision of compelling strength.

Organizations were founded, among them the *Hovave Zion*, the Lovers of Zion. Emissaries of terror-stricken Jewry knocked at the doors of Western Jewish philanthropists. Thousands were helped to come to the United States, but this was no solution for those demanding political nationhood. Migration to Palestine was difficult, since the Turkish government was unwilling to admit large numbers to the country. Those who arrived found the land poor and malaria-infested, and the work backbreaking. The settlers were aided by Baron Rothschild of France, who founded several colonies, running them, however, in a paternalistic fashion.

The Jews in Russia were themselves bewildered. Migration was hard, and perhaps Russia would grant eventual emancipation after all. "No," said Dr. Leo Pinsker of Odessa. Jews will never be free unless they emancipate themselves. "Auto-emancipation" became his slogan. He considered anti-Semitism "a psychosis. As psychosis it is hereditary; as a disease carried down the ages for 2000 years it cannot be cured." [2] "As long as we do not have our own homeland as the other nations, we may as well give up hope once and for all of becoming equal human beings." [3] Pinsker does not care where this homeland shall be established, as long as it guarantees sovereign rule to the Jewish settlers.

Not the "holy" land shall be the goal of our movement now but our "own"

---

[2] Leon Pinsker, *Auto-Emanzipation,* 1882; Reprint Jüdischer Verlag, Berlin, 1934, p. 8. Translation by the author.

[3] *Ibid.,* p. 18.

land. All we need is a large piece of land for our poor brethren, which is to remain our property, from which no foreign lord can remove us. Thence we will bring the holiest goods we saved from the shipwreck of our ancient motherland: The Idea of God and the Bible.[4]

The pendulum had swung in the other direction completely. To German Jewry the "land" was at best an idea. It had to be "the holy land." To Pinsker, nationhood and independence were the primary goals. God and Bible could easily be transplanted anywhere.

CULTURAL ZIONISM: AHAD HA-AM

Pinsker simply wanted a place for Jews to live in decency and freedom. Ahad Ha-Am asks a deeper question: Is a homeland going to solve all Jewish questions? A homeland will make the Jewish people like all other people; it will normalize them. But what will become of the spirit of Judaism? What will the future contribution of the Jews be to the spiritual and cultural growth of mankind? Pinsker had given no thought to the question. Like a drowning man, he was only concerned with a means of survival. Ahad Ha-Am, however, had a philosophy.

Ahad Ha-Am's Life

Ahad Ha-Am means "One of the People." He used it as his pen name, indicating modestly that he claimed no distinction, but merely intended to give form to the people's ideas. His real name was Asher Ginzberg. Born into an ultra-pious home of Hasidim in 1856, he was denied education in secular subjects, even the alphabet. It might create doubts in his mind. Brilliant as a talmudic scholar, he soon found himself attracted to general philosophy and general culture, which he was forced to study in secret. "Haskalah," the philosophy of "Enlightenment" and the movement young Russian Jews had organized to promote it, drew him. Then he traveled to see the world, Vienna, Berlin, Breslau. He came back and joined the ranks of the Hovave Zion, before long finding himself in the very center of the battle of ideas. How could Jews become free? By a nationalistic movement which would lead to an "Ingathering of Exiles" in a national state? "Lo zu haderekh," this is *not* the way, Ahad Ha-Am cried out. Physical survival, important as it is, does not spell the ultimate goal of the Jewish people. The spirit Jewish culture, must survive. This is his theme, voiced again and again, in publication after publication. Thus Ahad Ha-Am became the father of "Cultural Zionism." Never fully accepted by the official Zionist movement, it has nevertheless had great influence upon it. When Ahad Ha-Am died in Palestine (1927), he knew that he had not fought in vain.

---

[4] *Ibid.*, p. 21.

His Ideas

Every nation possesses a national spirit, Ginzberg believed. The national spirit of the Jews has found expression in the prophetic ideals of justice and righteousness proclaimed by Israel. This spirit developed when people and soil were united. To preserve it in foreign lands of exile, a wall of religious laws had been erected around the people, to shelter them from alien influences. The emancipation tore down the wall; it left the Jewish spirit unprotected, with only one remedy: a national home in Palestine. This home shall serve as spiritual core of Hebrew culture, and shall be the center from which the Torah shall go out. It is not necessary that all Jews move to Palestine, but it is essential that they all be revived and sustained by the spirit of Judaism which will emanate from Zion. Palestine, in Ahad Ha-Am's view, has two functions. The lesser purpose of the homeland is to serve as haven for the persecuted; the greater purpose is to be the wellspring of Judaism. A two-way communication will be established. Diaspora Jewry will bring inspiration to Palestine, and will in turn refresh its spirit at the fountainhead of Jewish life. The entire world will gain from the contribution which Judaism can thus make, for all nations must give of their own to the betterment of humanity.

. . . Contact with modern culture overturns the inner defences of Judaism . . . The spirit of our people . . . wants to absorb the basic elements of general culture . . . to digest them and to make them part of itself as it has done before, at various periods of its history. But the conditions of its life in exile are not suitable for such a task. In our time culture expresses itself everywhere through the form of the national spirit, and the stranger who would become part of culture must sink his individuality and become absorbed in the dominant environment. In exile, Judaism cannot, therefore, develop its individuality in its own way . . . So it seeks to return to its historic center, where it will be able . . . to bring its powers into play in every department of human culture, to broaden and perfect those national possessions which it has acquired up to now, and thus to contribute to the common stock of humanity, in the future as it has in the past, a great national culture, the fruit of the unhampered activity of a people living by the light of its own spirit. For this purpose Judaism can, for the present, content itself with little. It does not need an independent State, but only the creation in its native land of conditions favorable to its development: a good-sized settlement of Jews working without hindrance in every branch of civilization, from agriculture and handicrafts to science and literature. This Jewish settlement . . . will become in course of time the center of the nation, wherein its spirit will find pure expression and develop in all its aspects to the highest degree of perfection of which it is capable. Then, from this center, the spirit of Judaism will radiate to the great circumference, to all the communities of the Diaspora, to inspire them with new life and to preserve the over-all unity of our people . . . It will produce men in the

Land of Israel itself who will be able, at a favorable moment, to establish a State there—one which will be not merely a State of Jews but a really Jewish State.[5]

Ahad Ha-Am's thinking did contribute to the development of Israel as a world center of culture. Above all, he laid the foundations for the characteristic attitude of American Jewry toward Israel. American Jews feel as Americans, think as Americans, and call no country their own but America. They see in the Land of Israel a home for those Jews who feel its call to them and a cultural center from which inspiration to world Jewry and to all mankind may pour forth. To this end, American Jews will contribute to Israel of their substance, of their knowledge, and of their hearts.

POLITICAL ZIONISM: THEODOR HERZL

In the combat of ideas of "Political Zionism," the ideal of Pinsker was to prevail over Ahad Ha-Am's Cultural Zionism, mainly because it found a leader and spokesman of unparalleled power, ability, appeal, and dedication—Theodor Herzl.

Herzl and the Dreyfus Affair

Herzl was born in Budapest in 1860. He was wealthy, handsome, and gifted. After completing law school he became a journalist, and would have liked to be a judge, but that was out of the question for a Jew. In school and college he had been exposed to anti-Semitism, but these experiences had strengthened his conviction never to abandon his faith. Actually, he had not given the problem too much thought, accepting what could not be changed while hoping for a better tomorrow. Serving as a reporter for Vienna's leading newspaper, *Die Neue Freie Presse*, he also tried his hand as a writer, essayist, and even as a playwright. He was successful and popular. Then his paper sent him to Paris to cover the Dreyfus trial. It became the turning point of his life.

Dreyfus was a captain in the French army, a career officer, the only Jew attached to the headquarters of the French general staff. In 1894 a secret document was stolen and transmitted to the Germans. Without further inquiry the cry went up: Le Juif, voila l'ennemy, the Jew, indeed he must be the enemy, he is the traitor. Dreyfus was arrested; it was a moment of high exaltation for the militant opponents of the Republic.

---

[5] Ahad Ha-Am, *The Jewish State and the Jewish Problem* (1897), quoted from Arthur Hertzberg, ed., *The Zionist Idea*, copyright © 1959 by Arthur Hertzberg. Reprinted by permission of Doubleday & Company, Inc., pp. 266 f.

By claiming that the Jews were enemies of France, they hoped to strike a blow at the Republic and to return to power. After all, *republican* France had given full citizenship to Jews. What followed was a complete travesty of justice. Documents were forged, defense witnesses intimidated, prosecution witnesses readily perjured themselves in return for promised rewards. The German emperor, who knew the thief, refused to aid justice. Dreyfus was convicted and degraded in public ceremony. In vain did he proclaim his innocence in frantic outcry. A special law was passed permitting Dreyfus' deportation and imprisonment at Devil's Island. The trial sparked mob riots against Jews. The government yielded to mob pressure. Appeals were rejected and the champions of justice persecuted, among them Emile Zola, the famous French writer. "J'Accuse," I accuse, was his cry. It earned him a trial for libel and a prison sentence which he avoided by fleeing to England. It also earned him eternal fame as a fighter for truth and justice. But his voice had not been raised in vain. Dedicated men pursued the search for truth,

Theodor Herzl.

until eventually it came to light. The National Assembly began to realize that there was a plot to overthrow the Republic. George Clemenceau, who had fought for Dreyfus from the beginning, redoubled his efforts, giving the cause the whole measure of his ability and brilliant mind, and the full weight of his influence. Colonel Picquard, who had given up his army career to fight for justice, pushed on. None of these men were Jews, nor were many of the others who joined them. Dreyfus had become a symbol of human rights, of democracy itself. It was a case of chauvinism versus democracy, and the future of humanity itself was at stake. The Jew had been used as scapegoat, victim, and sacrifice to further the schemes of unscrupulous men. In the end, the traitors were brought to justice and convicted; Colonel Henry confessed and committed suicide; Count Esterhazy fled to England. Dreyfus was reinstated and promoted, but the specter of anti-Semitism once again had risen—and in France, of all countries, France, the land of liberty, equality, and brotherhood.

Herzl Learns a Lesson

To Herzl this came as a shock. If France, mother of freedom, could degenerate to such depravity, then there was no hope; if anti-Semitism could re-emerge so quickly and with such terrifying impact, then there was no cure for it. For the Jew there was only one answer: a Jewish State. In 1896 his brochure, *Der Judenstaat,* The Jewish State, appeared.

The Jewish State

Herzl calls the idea a very ancient one, yet his small work became the "Bible" of political Zionism. He begins with an analysis of anti-Semitism, as he sees it. It exists wherever Jews live in perceptible numbers; it is brought to new countries as Jews immigrate.

Anti-Semitism is a highly complex movement, which I think I understand. I approach this movement as a Jew, yet without fear or hatred. I believe I can see in it the elements of cruel sport, of common commercial rivalry, of inherited prejudice, of religious intolerance—but also of a supposed need for self-defense. I consider the Jewish question neither a social nor a religious one, even though it sometimes takes these and other forms. It is a national question, and to solve it we must first of all establish it as an international political problem to be discussed and settled by the civilized nations of the world in council. We are a people—*one* people.[6]

He describes the distress of the Jews. Even in progressive countries the army may be closed to them as a career, and public institutions and private business will not hire them. With the cry "Don't buy from Jews," they are pushed out of their own businesses. They are attacked in parliaments, at public meetings, in the press, from the pulpit, in the street; they find certain hotels and amusement places closed to them. "Society" in Paris keeps them out; Germany beats them up occasionally; Austria resorts to terror to keep them in their place. In backward countries, from Russia to Rumania to Algeria, murder and pillage of Jews have become commonplace. No attempt at solution has ever succeeded. There is only one answer:

Let sovereignty be granted us over a portion of the globe adequate to meet our rightful national requirements; we will attend to the rest.[7]

Herzl would set up a "Society of Jews," to be in charge of planning and negotiations. Another organization, "The Company of Jews," will direct the liquidation of assets and migration itself. Herzl is as yet not committed to Palestine as the homeland; first let the Jews simply find freedom as a nation. Even years later Herzl was willing to accept Uganda,

---

[6] Theodor Herzl, "Der Judenstaat" (1896), quoted from Herzberg, *op. cit.,* p. 209.
[7] *Ibid.,* p. 220.

offered by the British, as a Jewish homeland, but the Jews would have none of it. Palestine was the land promised by the Torah, enshrined in the hearts of the Jew. Herzl yielded.

He began to organize. He traveled, meeting kings, emperors, the pope, the sultan, making friends among heads of governments. In 1897 he called the first Zionist Congress to Basel, Switzerland. After lengthy debates, the congress established a permanent Zionist Organization and formulated its program:

Zionism seeks to secure for the Jewish people the creation of a homeland in Palestine, which shall be recognized and secured publicly and legally.

A trust fund was set up, a Jewish National Fund organized. Land acquired was to belong to the people as a whole, not to individual purchasers. This was political Zionism. The Jewish state was not to become a theocracy, Herzl declared. It will simply be a political entity.

Herzl's road was not an easy one. He faced difficulties with governments and opposition from within the Jewish community. In 1904 he died, prematurely worn out. His disciples took up the leadership of the movement. Among them was Chaim Weizmann, who was to become the first president of the State of Israel.

Reaction and Opposition

Herzl declared those Jews who would not follow him to be lost. He saw no future or value in diaspora Jewry, sentiments which have occasionally been echoed in our time by some of the political leaders of modern Israel. They were opposed then and have been emphatically opposed in our time. In his own days there were many dissenting voices. Eastern European Jewry, considered a nation among nations already, generally welcomed his plan; it offered hope for the oppressed and persecuted. Ahad Ha-Am, however, had his reservations. He could not accept a purely political Zionism, nor did he see the need for all Jews to emigrate. German and American Jewry were even more outspoken. German Jewry had developed a Judaism which emphasized religion. As religion it could prosper and develop wherever there was freedom. The German rabbis could not accept the "either-or" position of Herzl's program: "either you come with me, or—by refusing—sever all ties with Judaism." History did not bear out this fact. In addition, civic duties and love of country were seen by German Jews to be part of their religious obligations. German Jews were willing to support the venture to help their brethren in distress; they were not willing to identify themselves with its fundamental ideas. They had also been taught that the coming of the Messiah and the return to Zion were in the hand of God. The only way to promote it was through prayer and obedience to His commandments. The restoration of a Jewish state in Palestine was against God's law. Many orthodox people in Eastern Europe held the same views. My own parents, deeply pious and devout, but schooled in the religious philosophy of Samson Raphael Hirsch, held this view. They saw in Zionism an effort to force God's hand by secular means, and in Zionists people who themselves failed to live up to the principles of strict Jewish law and observance. They were certain that this was not the way of God, nor could it be a way of man permitted by Him. They hoped and prayed and yearned for the rescue of their Jewish brethren from oppression, and they invited the wayfarers to their table and promoted opportunities for migration to other lands, including Palestine. But they could not accept a Jewish State built without the miraculous, visible interference of God—at the end of days.

All these were honest arguments. Facts proved them wrong, yet it will not do to question the sincerity of those people who held them in deep conviction. In time, orthodoxy changed and organized an orthodox Zionist party, the Mizrachi, which operates within the framework of general Zionism. American Jewry has generously supported and endorsed the State of Israel before and since its birth, but it denies categorically Herzl's assertion. American Jewry views itself as a religious body of Americans with a sense of kinship, it is true, to Jews in Israel and all over the world. Yet it sees its future in America, land of the free, where freedom of religion and equality of all men are the cornerstones of both government and society itself.

Zionism, however, deserves undying credit for its courage in forging ahead. Through it, millions of Jews found life at a time when the gates of the world were closed to the masses of the persecuted of Europe. Others are still finding a haven from tribulation. Israel is a proud achievement and has instilled pride in all that seek her welfare.

THE PANGS OF BIRTH

World War I witnessed the defeat of Turkey. In the aftermath of the war the large Ottoman Empire was carved up by the victorious powers, but while the conflict was still in progress promises were made. The Arabs were to be free and were to establish several independent states. The Jews were to receive Palestine as a homeland, to dwell as friend among their liberated Arab neighbors. Chaim Weizmann, renowned as a chemist, aided the British war effort by his inventions, and used his influence to keep the government's interest in the Palestine situation. In 1917, the British Foreign Office issued the Declaration, which had been approved by other nations, including the United States:

His Majesty's Government view with favor the establishment in Palestine of a national home for the Jewish people, and will use their best endeavors to facilitate the achievement of this object, it being clearly understood that nothing shall be done to prejudice the civil and religious rights of existing non-Jewish communities in Palestine, or the rights and political status enjoyed by Jews in any other country.

Signed by Arthur James Balfour, it became known as the Balfour Declaration.

Immigration began. Land was bought from the Arabs, every acre paid for. It was either poor, barren, dried-out land, or it might be swamp land, malaria-infested. The Jews had to irrigate and drain the swamps, to sow and to plant. They buried their dead where they had fallen in battle against a pitiless nature. As the land improved, the Arabs regretted their bargain, forgetting that they had been paid well for their holdings. The British tried to appease the Arabs by restricting immigration, which they could do since they were the supervising power by mandate of the League of Nations. Yet migration continued. A university was founded early.

Then came 1933. Hitler assumed his murderous rule. Migration to Palestine became a mighty stream, while Britain still held to her restrictions on immigration, even though it might mean the difference between life and death for millions. Thousands came anyway, arriving after harrowing days at sea. They were smuggled in. Sometimes they were caught and expelled to die at sea, or be interned, or fall in the hands of the enemy. But more and more of them arrived. In 1936 pressure had reached such force that a royal commission suggested the land be divided into an Arab and a Jewish section, where Jewish immigrants might be settled. The plan could not be implemented until World War II had passed. In this war Palestinian Jews fought with heroism. Hitler's general Rommel had taken all of North Africa and was about to cut Britain's lifeline

Chaim Weizmann.

to the East, the Suez Canal. It was a Jewish division which stemmed his progress at El Alamein, saving the Canal.

With the end of the war problems increased, and Arab pressure intensified as they claimed the vastly improved and widely developed land as their own. In 1948, the British, tired of it all, carried out their revised partition plan. Let the Jews have their sector of Palestine as an independent state, if they could run it. The British garrison pulled out, and on that day the State of Israel was proclaimed, its flag the Star of David on white ground and two broad blue stripes. These were the Jewish colors, blue and white, the colors of the Tallit-fringes ordained in the Bible. Chaim Weizmann became the first president, the United States the first country to recognize Israel.

GROWING PAINS

From the moment of its birth Israel had to fight. Arab armies stood at its borders to swoop down before the new government had time to organize, but the armies never reached the center of Israel. They were repulsed. On the hills overlooking Jerusalem we can visit the graves of Jewish soldiers who gave their lives in the "War of Liberation"; rows upon rows of stones tell of boys and girls, sixteen, seventeen, nineteen, privates or colonels, who gave their full measure of devotion. Those Arabs who had left their homes to clear the advance of the invader now found themselves homeless. Their friends have refused to resettle them, preferring to use them as a political football. Israel claims that they would become a subversive force if permitted to return, but Israel will pay indemnity, and will resettle some Arabs. Left to rot in transit camps, young Arabs formed the fanatic "Palestine Liberation Front." Its purpose has been to destroy Israel through terrorism. Many Arab governments forced Jews in their countries to leave and confiscated Jewish property; Israel took the destitute *Jewish* refugees. The moneys left in Arab hands could be employed to rehabilitate *Arab* refugees among *their* brethren. The Arabs who remained in Israel became citizens of the new state.

The war ended with a truce. There still is no peace. King Abdullah of Jordan, who wanted to make peace in order to improve both countries through mutual cooperation, was murdered by his own people. "War against Israel" has remained the rallying cry of the demagogues, who find in it a means of rallying their people, for Arabs are united only "against Israel." Every offer on the part of Israel, even to sit down and negotiate, has been rejected.

In 1956 Israel had to fight another war to stop the continual raids on her borders and to gain access to the Suez Canal and international waterways, closed to Israel by Arab force. Russia had begun to supply the Arab states with arms. To forestall international war, President Eisenhower called for withdrawal, and promised his aid toward the opening of the waterways; Israel withdrew. Eisenhower was not successful. A UN force was placed along the borders to assure calm. It remained until 1967.

The Arab countries rearmed and preached war of extermination against Israel, emotions rose high. In 1967, Egypt and her allies were ready. On Egypt's demand, the UN force was removed by U Thant, Secretary General of the UN. Then Egypt closed the Strait of Tiran, Israel's only eastern access to the sea. Egypt's airforce and all the Arab armies were poised for attack. Israel could not wait. Fearing for its life, it took the offensive: the Egyptian airforce was destroyed on the ground. The enemy armies were defeated in six days (June 5-10). Then Israel declared its readiness to enter direct peace negotiations with the Arabs. But, led by the USSR, the UN took the narrowly legalistic position of condemning Israel as aggressor, and demanded that Israel withdraw immediately behind her pre-war borders before any peace negotiations with Egypt could even begin. Israel declared that these borders offered no security. The mediation attempt by the UN therefore remained unsuccessful as neither side could be moved from its position; Egypt, supported by the UN, demanded a complete Israeli withdrawal *preceding* any cease-fire and peace arrangements, Israel calling for a ceasefire *first*, with a settlement of the borders to be agreed on in direct peace negotiations. Israel was led by one of the most brilliant statesmen of our time, a woman, Golda Meir. President Nixon, who admired her greatly, had several personal talks with her in which a formula for a cease-fire was worked out. Israel promised to withdraw to new borders, but these had to be secure and had first to be agreed on in *direct peace* negotiations of the parties involved. The United States promised to provide Israel with weapons enabling it to defend itself, and has done so cautiously. On this basis, the President of the United States was able to obtain a cease-fire from Egypt. It was to be of limited duration. Although its terms were frequently violated, the cease-fire was still in force in 1972. It had been quietly extended beyond the originally stipulated period.

The USSR followed an opposite course. Joined by most of her satellites, it broke diplomatic relations with Israel and rearmed Egypt, providing it both with massive armaments and a garrison to teach the Egyptians the use of this modern weaponry. It appeared however that Russia was not willing to risk the possibility of a conflict that might escalate into a new world war. It merely desired the perpetuation of a tension in the area which would enable it to extend its power in the Mediterranean and in North Africa. Egypt did not get all the arms it desired, nor did it get the latest and most sophisticated weapons which the Egyptian army could not operate in any war situation without the active participation of Russian military personnel. Angered by the Russian position, the Egyptian government expelled the Russian garrison in 1972, but found itself compelled to ask for the return of Russian military advisors toward the end of the year. The uneasy situation continued.

At the same time, Arab terrorists escalated their activities. Their aim was to wipe out the State of Israel entirely, not merely to confine it within certain borders. They hoped to attain their goal not only through raids on Israeli border settlements, but engaged in a stepped up activity throughout the world. Planes were highjacked, letters and packages containing deadly bombs were sent to selected people throughout the world, a large group of tourists was mowed down by machineguns on arrival at the Tel Aviv airport. In the summer of 1972, during the Olympic Games at Munich, this activity reached a gruesome climax. An Arab terrorist group invaded the residence of the Israeli athletes, captured eleven men and eventually murdered them. Expressing condemnation, the UN took no action against international terrorism, in spite of the urging of the United States. Some Arab countries, such as Jordan, condemned the act, others praised the attackers as heroes and martyrs. Jordan had suppressed the terrorists quartered on its own territory. Israel maintained that these activities rested on the support of several Arab states, especially Lebanon and Syria, and engaged in raids on areas in these countries where Israel claimed the centers and staging areas of guerilla activities and international terrorism were to be found. The situation remained highly volatile.

Israel was prepared to return much of the occupied Arab territory when peace was made, except for Jerusalem, holy to Jews and economically indivisible. Free access to their holy places was to be granted to the faithful of all religions. Israel also wished to retain those areas regarded as indispensable for defense. The former borders were extremely difficult to defend. Convincing the Great Powers of these needs proved difficult. In the meanwhile, Israel cared well for the welfare of the Arabs living in the territories now in Israeli hands. They were permitted to move freely, even to cross the border into Jordan for business or visits of family. Their standard of living rose appreciably.

World Jewry recognized its bond with Israel when it was in danger. Out of the depths of its soul the spirit of oneness welled forth.

In the meantime, Israel has moved ahead in art, sciences, and industry. In its cooperative farms, the kibbutzim, it has successfully carried out a new experiment of social living. The members share according to their need, they contribute according to their strength. It is a socialist experiment, but there is no compulsion to belong or to remain in the kibbutz. The movement is slowing down, now that the country is offering increased opportunities for free enterprise. Agriculture has been pushed as far as water resources permitted. Then industries were begun, manufacturing products ranging from automobile tires to clothing, and from machinery to candy. Resources are exploited, ships and airplanes under Israeli flag carry the products to all parts of the globe. Music and theater flourish. The university, the Weizmann Research Institute at Rehobot, the Technical Institute at Haifa take their place with the best in the world. Hadassah Medical Center, endowed by American women, is one of the most modern hospitals anywhere, combining medical school, dental school, nursing school, and school of pharmacy. Health supervision permits the tourist to drink the water and milk, and to eat the food. The holy places of all faiths are tenderly cared for and supported by governments funds, while archaeologists dig deeply into the ground, bringing to light precious objects and documents witnessing to Israel's ancient glory.

In 1967 the Israeli author, Samuel Joseph Agnon, was awarded the Nobel Prize for Literature jointly with Nelly Sachs, the Jewish poetess of the Holocaust.

Israel also has internal problems. Conflicts between Western Jews and Oriental Jews have arisen. They are the result of different life styles, racial differences and, above all, the educational backwardness of Oriental Jews. Efforts are being made to overcome these conflicts and progress has been achieved. Another problem is the power of the orthodox Chief Rabbinate. Conservative and Reform Jews find themselves in an uphill struggle for recognition. It has also resulted in conflicts with modern law and majority desires. The solution awaits the coming of peace.

But the spirit of Bible is felt throughout the Land. Scripture is reader, guide and "national literature" apart from its religious significance. Its call to social justice is always heard, although the implementation of the prophetic message has to yield at times to the issues of the still existing emergency.

To the newly liberated nations of Africa and Asia, Israel has sent teachers and technicians, to guide them in their development. This was done unselfishly, in the spirit of Torah.

To the democracies of the free world Israel is a trustworthy and faithful ally, a bulwark of democracy in a troubled area. This has gained her the enmity of Russia.

To the Jews of the world, the emergence of Israel has been a thrilling realization. It has brought a revival of Judaism and a new pride in the great, vital, and virile tradition which Jewry is privileged to possess.

21

An Age of
Maturity

A had Ha-Am had imagined a two-way street, from Israel to Diaspora and from Diaspora to Israel. His was a nationalistic point of view; it was cultural nationalism. The religious thinker might have arrived at a similar conclusion—by God's plan Israel was the suffering servant, the teacher of mankind; his position was different from others, his reason for being was to be a witness. Return to the normal conditions of a life in a national state would fundamentally change this situation. People living in their homeland as free men do not ask the question, "what is the purpose of our national life?" America, to our credit, has sometimes asked it, but that is the exception. Most nations are satisfied simply to live, and prosper, and be happy, and perhaps expand. They do not measure their right to exist by any supernational or divine yardstick. This would happen to the Jews going to Israel; as a matter of fact, it has happened. "We are a nation like all other nations," many will say, "what more do you want?" Diaspora Jewry, however, must evaluate itself and Judaism in the light of eternity, in the light of its function. In a sense, Lavater had made this clear in his letter to Mendelssohn, asking him: "Show me that there is a purpose to Judaism or else give it up."

German Jewry had to meet the question directly, like American Jewry today. They lived on two planes: the culture of Germany and the tradition of Judaism. Free enough to think, to feel contented, and even to prosper, they still had many disabilities. The questions automatically came to mind: Is it worthwhile to remain a Jew? Has Judaism something to offer I cannot get elsewhere? What is the ultimate hope Judaism holds out? Does it compensate for a second class citizenship when I can have a first class citizenship simply by casting it off?

German Jewry was well equipped to approach these problems with the tools of scholarly analysis. With the rest of the educated Germans it shared a certain liking for philosophical questions. It had rabbinical leadership in all its communities, and its rabbis were well trained. Since the German public school system was organized on denominational lines, the larger communities, at least, frequently had Jewish elementary schools. The state would provide them whenever the number of Jewish children warranted it, just as it did for Catholics and Protestants. This called for a staff of well-trained Jewish elementary school teachers, holding public school teaching credentials and tenure as civil servants. The teachers, in turn, were trained in denominational teachers' colleges, where Jewish teachers were given a thorough education in Jewish subjects in addition to the courses prescribed for their certificate. This enabled them to function as ministers in small congregations, naturally under the supervision of the district rabbi. It was an ideal solution, for it provided a corps of highly trained men with good cultural as well as Jewish foundations, and the skill to teach. In addition, religion was a compulsory subject to be taken through high school. Some basic knowledge of Judaism was therefore acquired by all children, and some of it was invariably retained. Here was a reservoir for leaders, and here also were the listeners.

German Jewry had had the time to adjust and to develop a philosophy. In 1929, just before the advent of Hitler, it celebrated the 200th birthday of Moses Mendelssohn. The result of such education could be ideal. My father, who introduced me to the study of the Talmud, also analysed Schiller's plays for me, tutored me in Latin, gave me an appreciation of Rembrandt's paintings, and initiated me in the beauties of operas by explaining libretto and score before sending me to the opera house, twice a week. He told me of his grandmother, 85 years old when he was born in 1873, who took him on her lap and sang tunes she heard as a young girl and woman, works which were new in her day—Beethoven's *Ninth Symphony* and *Fidelio*, Weber's *Invitation to the Dance* and *Freischütz*, Schubert's Songs, and Chopin, Liszt, Meyerbeer, Donizetti, Verdi, Wagner, and Mendelssohn. And my father was just a businessman, as his father had been before him, who wrote poetry. All of them were profoundly religious and uncompromisingly orthodox. Indeed, German Jews were able to find a synthesis.

This is the reason they assumed the key role in the development of faith and tradition, influencing much of European Jewry. Most French

Jews, living in Alsace, the southern part of the Rhineland, were German in their culture and bilingual in their speech. English Jewry chose German-trained men for its first two Chief Rabbis. American Jewry, still in its infancy, called German and British educated rabbis to lead it, and to organize and direct its seminaries.

Out of this environment German Jews produced masters whose towering personalities may yet exert a lasting influence on Jewry in years to come. Three of them shall be mentioned: Hermann Cohen, philosopher; Franz Rosenzweig, leader of a religious and intellectual renaissance; Martin Buber, builder of bridges between East and West, between German thought and Israel, between Judaism and the world. They deal with problems which are our problems here and now.

HERMANN COHEN (1842-1918)

Cohen was the founder of the Neo-Kantian school at the University of Marburg, teacher of a generation of philosophers. He took a new look at Kant, whose thoughts had become distorted, thus he occupies his own place among the leading German thinkers of his time. But he was first and foremost a Jew. His life was shaped by his Jewishness.

Hermann Cohen.

Life

When he was barely 17, this brilliant son of a cantor at Coswig in Central Germany was already admitted to the Breslau Seminary to study for the rabbinate under Frankel and Graetz. Then he changed his mind; he wanted to be a philosopher. After studies at Berlin, he was appointed instructor at the University of Marburg. In 1876 he, a Jew, was made a full professor. This was unheard of; even Christians had to go through the ranks. But his department head, sick and ready to retire, had seen in him the only worthy successor. On his deathbed the old professor had himself carried to the meeting of the Senate of the University, where Cohen's appointment was voted on. He had his final wish. Cohen was elected, and remained at Marburg until 1913.

The Jews at Marburg were unhappy. When the high holy days came, Cohen would go away. Was he too good to join them in worship? Only later did it become clear that Cohen was going home. His father was old and could no longer carry the entire service of the holy days; the son became his assistant. The professor, standing before the Holy Ark in this little rural congregation, was leading the small folk in prayer. It was a labor of love, symbolic of the man. Judaism was dear to him, the heritage of the fathers precious. Let it be in need, smarting under attacks, calling for a spokesman, Cohen was there. He unmasked the pseudo-science of his anti-semitic opponents, powerful as they were in the academic society.

Then the break came. The government refused to grant him the funds he needed for the expansion of the department. He resigned; it was a heartbreak, but it was also a challenge. He would go to Berlin and give all of his time and knowledge to the education of his people. Again he was disappointed. He began to teach at the reform seminary, where his circle remained small, but he inspired those who surrounded him. Franz Rosenzweig was one of them.

Writing and teaching did not give him complete fulfilment. Just before the outbreak of World War I he went to Poland, planning to develop a school system for the Jewish population which would strengthen their Judaism by opening to them the culture of the world. His plan failed; it too was a casualty of war. Had it succeeded, Jewish history might well have been different. Thousands of people who later came to America would have come under his influence. They would have known enough of worldly culture not to be dazzled by it, perhaps even enough to combine it with Judaism, and to make both meaningful to their American-bred children.

But the visit to Poland was a triumph in other ways. Cohen was received as a prince in Israel, as indeed he was. Polish Jewry may not have understood his philosophy, but they could grasp his profound talmudic learning, and they could feel his deep and burning love. When he died in Berlin it was they, the immigrants, the poor, who came out by the thousands to render him final honors.

Cohen, the Kantian, based his philosophy on Reason. Maimonides, philosopher of Reason, was next to Kant, the second great master he acknowledged. But Cohen's Reason was illuminated by love; this was the burden of his life and thought. Judaism, more than any other religion, was *the* religion of Reason, perhaps the only religion of Reason. Of his works, the last sums it up, even in its title: *Religion of Reason from the Sources of Judaism.*

We cannot discuss his general philosophy here; we shall merely outline some of his thoughts on Judaism.

Cohen's Answer to Basic Questions: Judaism and Christianity

In 1880 Hermann Cohen wrote an essay, "An Affirmation concerning the Jewish Question." He later considered it the turning point of his own life. He had been living in enjoyment of his position and his success, but the essay marks the beginning of his newly deepened sense of responsibility toward his faith and people. The challenge to his conscience came from the leading German historian, Treitschke, who was an anti-Semite and desired to give scholarly respectability to his prejudice that "the Jews are our misfortune." Treitschke characterized Judaism as "the national religion of a basically alien tribe." [1] This was a two-pronged assault: the tribe was alien, the religion national, and therefore alien and meaningless to Germans. Cohen's answer proved the contrary on both counts. He gives us the meaning of Judaism in the modern world and he shows its relationship to Christianity. Judaism has given the world the ideal of absolute monotheism, of a God who is Spirit; Christianity accepted this spiritual God and is the child of Judaism on that score. Judaism proclaimed the messianic ideal to mankind; this is another of its distinctions. Messianism means that God is Father to *all* mankind; He guides His children now and will gather them in love at the end of days. Christianity has accepted that ideal too.

Christianity has in turn taught that God became Man. It has stressed the divine powers of the human being. Christianity actually said to man: You are part God; you have the gift of divine reason, which makes you *capable* of finding the law of ethical conduct within yourself. God *need not* teach you the fundamental principle of ethics. Christianity then added, you are like God in another way as well. You are *free* to de-

---

[1] Hermann Cohen's *Jüdische Schriften* (Berlin: C. A. Schwetschke & Sohn, 1924). Translations by the author. II, 74; see II, 73, for Cohen's answer to Treitschke.

velop the principles of moral law. By *capacity* and *freedom* you are like God. Without this fundamentally Christian principle, it would never have been possible for Kant to see in *man* the yardstick of all moral conduct. This Kant had done in his "categorical imperative": "Act in such fashion that the maxim of thy action can become foundation for general legislation." Man has the god-like autonomy to establish the principle, and the freedom to implement it. Judaism, according to Cohen, had never been explicit on that point. Cohen concludes, therefore, that the Christian who accepts the spirituality of God and the messianic idea is a Jew in these beliefs; every Jew who accepts the autonomy of the moral law is a Christian in this point. In life, Judaism and Christianity are far from being alien to one another; actually they are so closely knit into a fabric of beliefs that they are inseparable. Jews must continue, therefore, to exist, and to represent their contribution to mankind while recognizing the importance of Christianity. They must cooperate with mankind, while Christians must recognize that a living Judaism is essential in their midst. Cohen points out, however, that man has greater freedom according to Judaism than according to Christianity.[2] Atonement, according to Christianity, is possible only through *Christ*. In Judaism, atonement is the result of *man's* repentance. God has given to everyone the freedom to repent and to come to Him directly. And God in turn has given His pledge that He will accept everyone's act of repentance. This freedom makes us like God Himself. We are free to grasp ideas and ideals; we are free to strive for them; we are free to come to the Father. We have freedom of will, and need no intermediary. This distinguishes Judaism from Christianity.

God, World, and Jew

How did Cohen arrive at his conclusion regarding the function of Judaism? How did he come to know God?

Cohen is a disciple of Kant, who said that we shall never know what the world is really like. Our mind is a "receiving set" and all we know is the picture of the world as it appears to us. We cannot know what the true world, the "thing-in-itself" really is; it will remain hidden from us. This has significant consequences. God is a "thing-in-itself," and so are soul, immortality, and eternity. According to Kant, we do not have the mental equipment to get through to their reality. We cannot prove God. We speak of Him because we *feel* him in our hearts; we believe in immortality because it would be immoral to assume that a good person should not be rewarded for his goodness. Since we often

---

[2] *Ibid.*, III, p. 36; see also Introduction by Franz Rosenzweig I, LII.

see a good person suffering, we must assume—as moral people—that he will be rewarded in eternity, that he has an immortal soul which will receive the reward, and that there is a God who will give him his recompense. God is a "postulate of morality"; we must *act as if* He existed.

Cohen does not accept this idea. The "thing-in-itself" is not something we can never see because it is beyond our powers of perception. To Cohen, it is the ultimate in knowledge. From the moment we gain some knowledge, new horizons are opened to us. The more we learn, the greater are the new vistas revealed. Each step forward shows us more clearly how endless are the realms of knowledge. We shall never reach the "thing-in-itself," because it is so far removed, but it leads us on to deeper and deeper search. It is eternal challenge, eternal task.

God is a challenge. Knowledge moves us forward in search; moral growth leads us on toward God, the ultimate in moral perfection and the *Idea* of ethical perfection. He is the *Head* of morally acting beings. How do we act morally? By influencing nature around us. God created nature as the stage on which we can act morally, creating the world that it be a challenge and opportunity for us. He gave it to us, that we may exercise our moral powers in making it better. Thus we can grow in character and come closer to Him.

Nature and ethics have the same source and creator: God. Since they are keyed to each other in such perfect harmony, they must have been fashioned by One God, the God whom Israel affirms: Hear O Israel, the Lord our God, the Lord is One. It is the God of Maimonides, so completely One that we cannot describe Him. Cohen has broken with Kant. Not emotion, but reason, is the yardstick of morality, and God is the capstone of the universe.

Nature and morality are not one and the same; but they demand a single origin. And the oneness of God finds its scientific proof in the fact that it explains the unity of this source of nature and of morality, and with it the unity in our view of the world.[3]

In Quest of Perfection

The task of ethical perfection is eternal. We grow toward it through our work in the world of nature, so the world must be eternal to give us a limitless opportunity for growth. There must be a God to guarantee us two things: we must be certain that *we* can grow eternally to ever greater ethical perfection; and we must have assurance that there will always be a *world* which will give us the raw materials to be developed.

---

[3] *Ibid.*, I, p. 5.

Without God, to guarantee both, there can be neither world nor ethics.

This thought is symbolically expressed in the Jewish idea of the Messiah, the idea of eternal ethical growth toward God. The work will never be completed. When the messianic age comes, it will remove the obstacles to continued ethical development, such as war, hatred, and poverty, but growth will go on. "Messianism," thus, is the central pillar of Judaism." [4] Here Judaism parts from Christianity, which believes that the Messiah has already come.

The future, which the prophets have painted in the symbol of the Messiah, is the future of world history. It is the goal, it is the meaning of history. . . .

It is humanity itself which has to bring about this age of the Messiah. Men and cultures must learn to think and hope for the ideal human life, the ideal life of individuals and nations, the future of the Messiah as something in the *future* of the human race. The realization of morality on earth, its tasks and its eternal goal, this and nothing else is the meaning of the Messiah for us. . . .

The kingdom of the Messiah is the kingdom of God. Not a personal ruler is this Messiah, not a hero, but the spirit of God rests upon him and he brings justice to the peoples. . . .[5]

In explaining the Jewish concept of the Messiah, Cohen has eliminated the belief in a personal Messiah, but he has not changed the age-old Jewish idea of the messianic age and what it is to be like. Since Jews have to work for it, they must continue to exist in the world.

These concepts were hammered out by the prophets, who were the first to include all of humanity in the scheme of salvation. Even Plato excluded the barbarian from his ideal Republic. The ethical ideal of the prophets included all of mankind.[6] Thus the prophets became the founders of social religion. Not in mystical contemplation or philosophical perception do we find God and express our love for Him, but in service.

The prophets did not stop with God but put Him in relation and contact with man to act upon him and to react to Him. Thus did the problem of love arise, not in God but in relationship to man. They (the prophets) wanted to present a perfect concept of man, not through a "science of man," . . . (but through love in action).[7]

Cohen has actually gone beyond philosophical analysis. God is found out of the living relationship we establish with Him, and this contact comes into being as we serve our fellow man.

---

[4] *Ibid.,* II, p. 264.

[5] *Ibid.,* III, p. 173 f.

[6] *Ibid.,* I, pp. 306 ff.

[7] *Ibid.,* I, pp. 306 ff., "Das Soziale Ideal bei Platon und den Propheten." Cohen contrasts Plato's ideal state, *The Republic,* with Isaiah's view of the future, which we have discussed above.

The whole development of prophecy can be developed from this guiding principle. God is not the father of heroes, and these are not called beloved of God; He is the God who "loveth the stranger." The stranger in polytheistic religion is . . . "barbarian." As soon as God loves the "barbarian," regards enemy people as His own, equal to Israel who is also His possession, then the horizon of humanity is newly illuminated. Messianism demands and promotes this development which leads to cosmopolitanism. . . .

As much as the prophets demand justice and righteousness, and proclaim their God as God of righteousness, this abstraction is not sufficient for them. They address the heart of man, which to them is the only treasure house of his spirit. Thus they call forth that form of awareness which alone can meet suffering—compassion. Compassion is a basic word in the Hebrew language. Its root is "the mother's womb" (rahamim = compassion; rehem = womb). With this emotion God has compassion on the poor; with this emotion man is to discover the poor as his fellow man. Compassion, therefore, is not a passion, not a physiological effect which man may share with animals, compassion is a spiritual factor . . . The whole force of a basic philosophy of life comes to the fore in it . . . in compassion the suffering of another person becomes my own, and he becomes my fellow man.[8]

The road to human redemption is clearly shown. Ethics establishes the relationship between nations and societies; religion deepens it by adding to it *personal* compassion. Both are impossible without God. But if ethics alone were the moving force, then religions, including Judaism, could cease to exist. Compassion, however, limitless in its call, is based on religion; religion will therefore be indispensable forever. Judaism teaches it and must forever exemplify it.

Even ethics, though lower than compassion, establishes so high a goal that it will not ever be fully reached. Thus the Jew must be true to his religion to the end of days, to exemplify ethics and compassion. By living *for* his neighbor, he stays in immediate contact with God. Religion recognizes the *individual* in his unique dignity. He therefore has *direct* access to God without intermediary. In this free and direct approach to God, taught by Judaism, Cohen sees one of the major contributions of Jewish religion to the progress of religion in general. God's revelation is not a one-time experience, but is repeated with every new task man performs in love, with every effort to find God through intellect and reason. Like the world "renewed daily" in the words of the prayer book, revelation is brand new every moment.

The Soul

In order to be capable of such perfect love, man must have a pure soul, unspoiled, unsoiled by original sin. This is basic Jewish doctrine. He must be endowed with a spirit of holiness, a "holy spirit."

---

[8] *Ibid.*, I, pp. 310 ff.

The holy spirit is just as much the spirit of man as it is the spirit of God. The holy God has put His spirit in man. The human spirit thus is truly a holy spirit.[9] It relates God and man.

If man has soiled his soul, he can purify it before God.

The reconciliation of man with God, the redemption of man from sin, rests upon this concept of the purity of soul and the holiness of the spirit. Even though the soul may have become soiled it can never lose its purity. Man simply has to start this work of his redemption in all earnestness. He shall assume his justification in faith—both terms belong to the Old Testament—in all seriousness, with all the strength and power of repentance and return, in full contrition, and also in complete hope; and sin and its burden will be taken from his soul.

After the gravest sin of his life, the Psalmist lets David say: "Do not reject me from Thy presence and do not take Thy holy spirit from me (Ps. 51:14)." Apart from another place in Isaiah, which is of minor importance, this is the only place where we find "holy spirit" in the Old Testament. It is mentioned to relieve man of anxiety and the fear that sin might deprive him of the purity of his soul. Thus does Judaism guarantee God's redemption, namely by the concept of the human soul. And thus is man's salvation founded in man's own moral efforts.[10]

Sin and Repentance

Why do men sin? There are a few who act in defiant disobedience, but generally, as Cohen points out, men act sinfully because of human frailty, in "shegaga"—in error.

This is the sin, committed from ignorance, secretly . . . On a second level, this may be the sin committed by man without intent to sin. He feels that he has desecrated himself, yet cannot accuse himself . . . (But) seen from a higher point of view, are not all sins of man more or less results of error? Is not awareness darkened more or less in all of them, or perhaps not fully developed? But this may . . . open the gates to rationalizations, a danger which could be avoided only by adding to it another religious concept . . . "repentance." . . . The Hebrew word for repentance is "Teshubah," return, turning away from evil, turning toward the good, turning inward. . . .

Here we have the basic concept of pure morality: the reconciliation of man with himself . . . True repentance does not concern itself with detailed actions; it recognizes individual actions in the context of human will and desires, in the totality of the human being. No wrong exists isolated in the human personality. Repentance is the guidepost which leads individual actions to a

---

[9] *Ibid.*, II, p. 245; see also III, pp. 177 ff.
[10] *Ibid.*, II, pp. 244 ff.

harmonious way of life. Renewal of the total personality, the new heart and the new spirit, this is the idea of repentance. . . .

Among the festivals, the Day of Atonement takes first rank . . . The prophetic reading of the morning castigates a fast which fails to lead you "to break thy bread to the hungry, denying thyself to thine own flesh." . . . The prophetic portion of the afternoon proclaims in charming innocence how the chosen people think about heathens. Jonah prophesies that his God has compassion with sinful Niniveh. Niniveh repents. This is the mood of the twilight hour. The perspective, however, is provided in the morning prayer: "Give reverence of Thee to all Thou hast created, that all creation may worship Thee and that all may unite in one bond of fellowship." This is the bond of fellowship which will come in the messianic age, when all mankind will yearn for it. This covenant to be made by mankind is the transformation and the goal of the covenant God once made with Israel. The Day of Repentance is the day of this covenant. Thus our holy days of repentance are truly messianic festivals. They express the hope that the synagogue of the ghetto some day will be open as a temple of mankind. . . .[11]

Sin is the human condition. Awareness of error leads the individual to the awareness of self. *He* has sinned, he is an "I" not one in the mass. This leads man to "Teshubah." He appeals to God for compassion; God responds immediately, demanding only that man shows *compassion* for his neighbor. Reconciliation then initiates the process toward the messianic age: reconciliation of man with himself, his fellow man, with God.

On the day of justice we appeal for compassion. Both are identical. Therefore there is no damnation, no punishments in hell. The thought of it is rejected. Even punishment is mercy, consisting of sufferings of love. God judges man knowing he is but flesh and blood. God's mercy corresponds to human frailty. The flow of divine grace needs no sacraments. God's grace is built into His relationship to man. There cannot be any intermediary in this relationship. The immediacy of God is the foundation of redemption and reconciliation. God is love—no visible proof of it is required of Him.[12]

The Neighbor

Jews are indispensable for the world. As a minority they are "strangers" in every land. The stranger's function is to ennoble his majority neighbor by providing him with the opportunity to practice compassion. Jews as mankind's teacher are equally indispensable, for Judaism is the religion of reason and of love. In one of his essays,[13] Cohen gives some basic principles, which must guide our relationship with our enemies. Taken from Jewish Scriptures, they constitute minimum requirements.

---

[11] *Ibid.*, I, pp. 131 ff.
[12] *Ibid.*, I, pp. 136 ff.
[13] *Ibid.*, III, pp. 66 ff.; in "Liebe und Gerechtigkeit in den Begriffen Gott und Mensch," pp. 43 ff.

1. I may not yield to resentment against mine enemy.
2. I may not develop feelings of revenge.
3. I must be ready to help him in a positive way.
4. I must protect his human dignity.
5. I must admonish and guide him.

Quoting from the Talmud, he adds: "Hatred is equal to idolatry, incest, and murder (Yoma 9b)."

In his defense of Judaism against attack, Cohen starts with correction of errors made by Christians and ends in affirmation of Judaism. Nowhere in the Old Testament or in Jewish Writings do we find the sentence mentioned in the New Testament: "It has been told you to love your friends and hate your enemies." [14] On the contrary, love of enemy has always been a principle and teaching of Judaism; unfortunately, it has not been heeded by the world.

Quoting the statement "No one comes to the Father except through the Son (John 14:6)," Cohen makes clear that this is contrary to Jewish belief. According to Judaism, *all* come to the Father.

He is our Father, even when we do not seek Him, less find Him. [15]

Finally, he points out that love of neighbor in the New Testament is ordained simply as a command of the Old Testament, where it originated. The Jewish scribe asks Jesus to tell him the basic commandments. Jesus replies by quoting "Hear O Israel, the Lord our God, the Lord is One. And thou shalt love the Lord thy God. . . ." This is the first commandment, quoted from Deuteronomy (6:4 ff). The second commandment is quoted by Jesus from Leviticus (19:18): "Thou shalt love thy neighbor as thyself." The scribe fully endorses these answers, and Jesus then tells him: "Thou art not far from the kingdom of God (Mark 12:28 ff.; see also Matthew 23:35 ff.)." But the New Testament does not go as far, according to Cohen, as Judaism would have gone. Even had he been a heathen, "according to (Jewish) teaching regarding . . . the pious of the peoples of the world, this scribe was not only not far from the kingdom of God, he was in it." He was deserving of the messianic age and equally deserving of life in the world to come, according to prophetic teaching. Christianity attaches conditions to salvation, while Judaism simply guarantees it to "all the pious of the world." "Here lies the difference between Judaism and Christianity," Cohen concludes. [16]

---

[14] *Ibid.*, III, p. 72.
[15] *Ibid.*, III, p. 65.
[16] *Ibid.*, III, pp. 60 f.

Judaism still marches in the forefront of mankind, leading the way toward the messianic age. Cohen has answered the questions of his time. There is a purpose in Jewish survival and, if need be, suffering. Eventually all mankind will be united. Until then, the Jewish community must live for the ideal as best it can, and the congregation is a symbol of God's congregation which some day will embrace all mankind within its folds, for

God's congregation is not a special covenant of the faithful. It is, in the prophetic sense, the unification of all mankind, beyond castes and nations, in a unity of conscience, a unity of ethical humanity.[17]

Hermann Cohen's writings require concentrated reading. His works have been translated into English. His impact may be growing.

FRANZ ROSENZWEIG (1886-1929)

Another generation found another spokesman to explain the purpose and meaning of Jewish survival. Franz Rosenzweig was a disciple of Hermann Cohen, and his works make extremely difficult reading. His contacts were mainly with intellectuals, but his life itself became a symbol. It mirrored the conflicts of young intelligent Jews regarding the values of Judaism itself; it presented in dramatic unfolding the return of a noble man from the periphery to the very center of Jewish life; it bore heroic witness to the triumph of the spirit over the forces of destruction. As a symbol, it gave fortitude to thousands who were made to suffer for the spirit of Judaism a few years after his death.

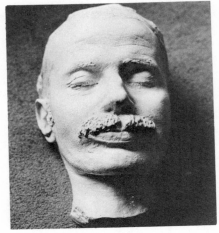

Death mask of Franz Rosenzweig.

---

17 *Ibid.*, I, p. 30.

Of His Life

His family was wealthy, cultured, and liberal, owner of a big business at Cassel. They had what may be called a Jewish home, for the family went to services on the high holy days and affirmed its liberal Jewish tradition. But religion had little influence on outlook, pattern of life, or daily practices. After a few years in the study of medicine, Franz decided to become a philosopher. Thus, instead of an M.D., he took a Ph.D., submitting as dissertation a study of Hegel's philosophical influence. The question arose, what was he going to do, and with it the more fundamental question, what was he going to believe. A brilliant cousin of his gave up his faith just then to become a Protestant. There was no difference in the general outlook of the family from that of liberal Protestantism, and by conversion one could expect full acceptance in society. But Rosenzweig's family was shocked; one need not believe too deeply, but one did not desert, even though it seemed logical. Soon enough Rosenzweig himself would have to face the decision. He served his year of compulsory military service, then went back to school. This time it was law; actually, he was searching for the meaning of his life, groping for an ideal which would give him strength. He certainly could not find it in the christianized Judaism of his environment, and he knew of no other. He had almost decided to follow the example of his cousin, but intellectual honesty compelled him to give at least some study to Judaism. He could not leave a faith he did not know. Yom Kippur came, in 1913, and he wanted to worship one last time as a Jew. His mother considered him lost and asked him not to burden her heart by his presence at worship, so he went to Berlin and found a little synagogue which seemed to suit him. And here it happened—a mystical experience, a spiritual experience. Overwhelmed by the power of the day and its worship, he found his way home. A Yom Kippur may indeed be a truly "tremendous" experience. Aime Pallière in France, Catholic seminarian-to-be, had had the same experience. Wandering into a synagogue on the afternoon of Yom Kippur, he was so deeply stirred by the sight of a congregation standing before God in silence, waiting for His revelation of grace, that he turned to Judaism, to study it, and to love it. Rudolph Otto, a Protestant, for the first time understood the meaning of "holy" when he stood in a synagogue on Yom Kippur. His work, *The Idea of the Holy,* conceived at that moment, has become a classic. Of these men we know; there may be many others we do not know. To Franz Rosenzweig it was a turning point, leading him on the road deep into Judaism. To his cousin, now a protestant theologian, who had guided him in his search, he wrote about his final decision. He will not become a Christian: "It does no longer seem to be necessary, hence in my case no longer possible. I shall remain a Jew." [18]

Rosenzweig meets Hermann Cohen in Berlin, and becomes his disciple. Then comes the war. Serving as anti-aircraft gunner in the Balkans, he catches a severe pneumonia which will leave its after effects. For the moment, he recovers and is filled with a unique, creative clarity of mind. In the trenches, on post cards, he writes his major work, *The Star of Redemption*. His mother keeps these post cards for him.

But philosophy of Judaism is only a gate which must open onto life. In order to know what it means to be a Jew, one must live as a Jew, since Judaism reveals itself existentially. From the front, Rosenzweig sends to Hermann Cohen a program of universal Jewish education for Western Jewry. Study, in Jewish tradition, is more than gathering of knowledge; it is communion with God; it forges a chain which molds men and spells survival. Cohen is enthusiastic, but when Rosenzweig is finally discharged, Cohen is dead.

He moves to Frankfurt, a center of Jewish life, and returns to observance of traditional practice and commandments. Not orthodox, he does not accept blindly whatever the law commands, but wishes to live by the commandments to find the truth they reveal, to gather their meaning for life, and this is possible only by actual performance. In Rabbi Nehemiah Nobel, who is a divinely gifted preacher, a scholar and Goethe specialist, and profoundly orthodox, he finds the man who has attained full synthesis of cultures. He begins to translate his educational program into reality by opening an adult academy at Frankfurt, dedicated to Jewish studies of the highest intellectual standard. Called "Freies Juedisches Lehrhaus," it was to serve as model for a whole system of similar institutions which sprang up all over Germany. These schools were to give guidance and new enthusiasm to people who had not opened a Jewish book for years, but who were soon to need all the spiritual strength they could muster. Schools need books, so new life came to the entire literary scene. Books on Judaism were published, scholarly tomes and pocket books, Hebrew texts were reissued. These years, just before the collapse, witnessed an unparalleled renaissance of Judaism in Germany.

In 1922 Rosenzweig feels a slight paralysis. Medical examiners come up with a ponderous phrase: "amyotrophic lateral sclerosis with progressive paralysis of the bulba." To Rosenzweig, former student of medicine, it is clear that he has a general progressive paralysis with a maximum of two years of agony. He prepares for the ordeal. In August 1922, writing becomes difficult, and in December it ceases altogether; in the Spring of 1923 he loses the ability to speak; in the fall the disease, after-

---

[18] Franz Rosenzweig, *Briefe* (Berlin: Schockenverlag, 1935), p. 71.

effect of his wartime pneumonia, stops all movement. But he can still move his thumb. Propped up on pillows, his head held by a brace, he keeps writing on a special typewriter. Eventually he can only point to the letters while his wife, with miraculous insight, completes the thoughts he indicates. A translation of Judah Ha-Levi's poetry is completed. Miraculously, he keeps on living beyond any expectation. In 1925 he starts a major work in cooperation with his friend of many years, philosopher Martin Buber. It is a translation of the entire Bible, showing the deepest understanding of both the Hebrew and German languages, revealing new meanings of the text which previous renditions had left completely untouched. The years pass, and the man who should be dead still pushes on in the fullness of intellectual and spiritual strength. Those who visited him, or participated in the religious services regularly held in his home, tell of these meetings as great spiritual experiences. There was a man unable to speak, unable to move, his head braced but frequently falling forward, but a man alert, gay, fully acquainted with everything the world around him did, suffered, and created; speaking through his eyes, answering through his wife. In the face of eternal and hopeless suffering he remained keen, cheerful, fully composed through pains and agony. In November 1929 he completed the translation of Isaiah, and on December 9th he died.

To find Judaism, one must live it. To live it, one must know it. Knowing and living will be experiences which lead beyond the realm of pain and suffering. Whatever happens, we are with God. This was Rosenzweig's answer to the basic question, what is the meaning of Judaism? Live it and you will find out, and know that living as a Jew is service to God and mankind. It may hasten humanity's salvation.

How soon German Jewry was to recognize this truth. Like Rosenzweig, it found that the ills which had their start in the war grew to overpowering proportions. Like him, it found itself in ever greater agony, but it also found meaning in its suffering by "being with the Father." They were not tired and weak when they were wiped out; they were cut down in the strength of creative manhood, still building, learning, and obeying the Torah.

To a great degree this was the result of Rosenzweig's influence, the impact of his example, of his "Lehrhaus," where study and practice were given new life, the influence of his symbolic suffering and of his courage. The gates had opened into life, and German Jewry was alive when it was felled. Its achievements are guiding us still.

Of His Thought

The place of Israel in God's plan

What was the burden of Rosenzweig's experience on the fateful

Yom Kippur which determined his entire future life? In a letter he describes the new insight he has gained. Judaism is essential in the divine scheme of the world. The Jews as a people have reached shelter in God; they have completed their spiritual journey through the world. They are *with* the Father. The rest of mankind is still on the road to Him, finding encouragement and the inspiration to persevere in the example and achievement of Israel.

Christianity recognizes the God of Judaism, not as God but as Father of Jesus Christ. It abides by the Lord (Jesus Christ) knowing that He alone is the way to the Father. He will remain Lord of His Church to the end of days. Then He ceases to be Lord and will be subject to the Father, who then will be All in All. What Christ and His Church mean to the world we are all agreed on: Nobody comes to the Father except through Him.

Nobody *comes* to the Father. But it is different for him who no longer has to come to Him, because he is already there. This indeed is the case of the people Israel (though not of the individual Jew). The people Israel, chosen by his Father, looks stolidly across the world; (it looks) beyond history toward this last point when He his Father, the very Same, the One and Only will be All in All. At the point when Christ ceases to be Lord, Israel ceases to be chosen; on that day God loses the name by which Israel alone calls Him; He will no longer be "his" God. Up to this day, however, it is the purpose of Israel's life to anticipate this eternal day in word of affirmation and in action. (It is the purpose of Israel) to exist as a living prophecy of this day, (to be) a nation of priests, enjoined to sanctify the Name of God by its own sanctity. The fate of this people of God in the world at large is known to us all. (We know of) the sufferings inflicted from without (persecution); (we also know) its internal sufferings (stagnation). It accepts them for the sake of its solitary position. Yet these sufferings of world-negation are accepted by the synagogue in the same hope of the ultimate "end" as the Church accepts the sufferings of world-affirmation . . . Church and Synagogue depend on each other.[19]

This is the lesson which came to Rosenzweig on Yom Kippur, as the congregation stood in complete absorption of God, and at peace with itself. Israel has reached God, is with Him. The Synagogue has reached the highest goal of human striving, shelter in the All-One, and there is no more struggle. Israel is the only one who has come to God, while all other nations, peoples, and religions are still on the road to Him. They must be active in history; they must march on, and lift themselves up together with the world. Eventually they will all reach Him. When that day comes, there will be no difference between Israel and the rest of the world. Meanwhile, however, Israel stands alone, misunderstood and persecuted. In order to come to God the Father, the world needs Christ, His guidance and intercession, His ideals, His comforting Godliness. When all mankind has reached the goal, the Father alone will

---

[19] *Ibid.*, pp. 73 ff.

rule. Since Israel has already reached the goal it does not need the Son. It has the Father, and the Father embraces Israel.

We recognize the influence of Hegel, to whom history is the unfolding of the Absolute, of God. Rosenzweig accepts that for all mankind, but the Jews have already completed their journey. Christianity is right and essential for Christians, just as Judaism is essential for the world. It shows the world that it is possible to come to God, and offers the image of a society that dwells in Him. It spurs the rest of mankind on their road.

The Star of Redemption

The star as symbol in Judaism

Through the ages *Magen David*, David's Shield, has been a symbol of Judaism. Rosenzweig gives a modern explanation of its meaning. Let us first try to find an explanation of how the six pointed star may have become a Jewish emblem; then we shall turn to Rosenzweig's ideas.

Was David's shield really fashioned in the form of a star? We do not know. The star is a very ancient decorative motive, found in many parts of the world. We find it in the synagogue at Capernaum, built in the second Christian century. But there it is simply one decoration among many; the menorah, the seven-branched candelabrum, is featured much more prominently. The menorah has always represented Judaism.

Magen David, the Star, from a relief in the synagogue at Capernaum. Note the inferior position of the star compared to the candelabrum (Menorah), shown on page 203. The star is just one of several pieces of ornamentation.

An eight-pointed star served as decorative pattern in a Palestinian fresco about 5500 years ago.[20] In five-cornered and six-cornered shape, the star has long been regarded as a mystical and magical sign. Mephistopheles, the Devil, is caught by it. In Goethe's play "Faust," he has lost the freedom of movement, and "the pentagram gives him pain."[21] This might perhaps lead us toward an answer. In the six-cornered star, the sphere of God (three points from above) is interlinked with the sphere of man (three points from below); in the pentagram one point is held in common. Linked to God, man's sphere is protected by Him, and evil kept away. (In the pentagram where the points are interwoven, the lines must meet exactly to make the point of linkage, or else—as in *Faust* —there is no protection. If God's sphere does not touch man's, the devil— Mephistopheles—has access.)

The school of mystics at Safed speaks of four worlds between "En-Sof," the Endless God, and our human world. There is the world of the Creator God; He has stepped out of His endlessness to fashion the universe. Then there is the world of the highest angels, surrounding the Divine Throne. It is followed by the world of lower angels. Finally there is the spiritual world model God fashioned before He created the material universe. God—four higher worlds—man's world. The six points of the star may perhaps represent them. These worlds, according to the mystics, are separated from each other by curtains through which the divine power flows. The bars of the star would be the symbol.[22]

Rosenzweig's "star"

Rosenzweig speaks of three fundamental *units* of the universe: God-World-Man, represented by the three points of the upper triangle. He also sees three basic *actions* which bind God and World and Man together: Creation-Revelation-Redemption, represented by the lower triangle. The points of the two triangles are interwoven and form the six-pointed star. In the same manner the six elements are interwoven. In their relationship to each other the points of the star explain the relationship of God to Man and World, and the means of bringing about Redemption to God's Creation by obedience to His Revelation. *God* makes the *World* through *Creation*. *God* chooses *Man* through *Revelation*. *God*, with the help of *Man's* creative work in the *World*, brings about the act of *Redemption*. God is Originator; Man is His co-worker in the work of creation; God has fashioned the world but chosen man for

---

[20] See W. F. Albright, *From the Stone Age to Christianity* (New York: Doubleday Anchor Book, 1957), p. 143.

[21] Faust, I, Act II, Scene 3.

[22] See Gershom G. Scholem, *Major Trends in Jewish Mysticism* (New York: Schocken Books, Inc., 1946), pp. 272 ff.

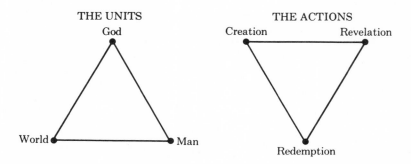

THE UNITS

God

World — Man

THE ACTIONS

Creation — Revelation

Redemption

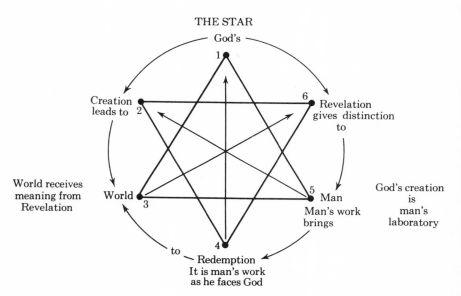

THE STAR

God's

1

Creation leads to 2

6 Revelation gives distinction to

World receives meaning from Revelation

World 3

5 Man
Man's work brings

God's creation is man's laboratory

to 4
Redemption
It is man's work as he faces God

The six corners:

1-2-3: God's (1) Creation (2) leads to World (3).

1-6-5: God's (1) Revelation (6) gives distinction to Man (5).

5-4-3: Man's (5) Work brings Redemption (4) to World (3).

The opposites:

1-4: God and Redemption face each other; God assures ultimate Redemption to World and Man.

2-5: Man and Creation face each other; God's Creation is man's workshop; he leads it to Redemption by bringing to life the message of Revelation.

3-6: The World receives meaning from Revelation, being led from Creation to Redemption.

a special task. Man must strive eternally, and the world is his laboratory; in life man finds God. Philosophy is but the gate. Judaism, being with God, holds the completed star in his hands. It is Israel's symbol. Through inward growth Israel can lead mankind to fashion the star for all of humanity under God. In the end God himself is redeemed.

We find Hermann Cohen's ideas developed into a new system. God is necessary as Creator and to give meaning and ethical impulse to the world. We also find Hegel's thoughts expressed: history is evolution. But, as Rosenzweig sees it, Judaism has completed the road through history. It responds to God through Mitzvot: constant interaction of every new revelation and response.

MARTIN BUBER (1878-1965): LIFE OF THE DIALOGUE

The Jews have always regarded themselves teachers of mankind, "a light unto the nations," speaking to them of God and His order. Mankind accepted the message but did not credit the messenger; frequently it even garbled the instruction and rejected the instructor. Martin Buber has become a teacher of mankind whose teachings spring from the sources of Judaism. Significantly, he has been recognized generally as such a teacher, and the Jewish source of his thoughts has been acknowledged. This is a tribute to the power of his ideas, the impact of his words, but it is also a tribute to the new spirit of receptiveness among Christian thinkers. It testifies to a new approach to Judaism on the part of an enlightened Christian world. To accept Buber's teachings, Christian theologians have to admit that Judaism did not cease to be creative

Martin Buber.

with the end of the Old Testament. They have to acknowledge that Judaism has continued to provide deep religious insights which are of universal value, and they have to respect Judaism as a faith alive, growing, and vital for the human race. Leading Christian thinkers have done just that, and have reversed common notions held for almost 2000 years in regard to Judaism. Buber has thus become a builder of bridges, for a bridge can be constructed only if the foundations on *both* sides are considered firm and strong. He has initiated a dialogue, for dialogue can only be carried out when both sides are convinced of each other's integrity and each other's capability to contribute something of importance. Buber's impact on modern thought has thus provided a new answer to the question asked by Jews. Judaism *does* serve a function; its survival is imperative for the good of humanity.

But Buber has also served as a bridge between Eastern Hasidism and German scholarship, between European Judaism and Israel, between religion and Zionism, between the occidental world and the orient. His hope to forge a link between Jews and Arabs may eventually be fulfilled as well.

Life

Born at Vienna in 1878, he found in his grandfather the understanding mentor of his youth. Solomon Buber was a modern Jew and a scholar who devoted his life to the exploration of the Midrash. He was openminded and permitted his grandson to explore on his own, even along paths alien to grandfather's own convictions. Thus Buber was led to the little synagogues of the Hasidim. He followed their dances, learned of their mystical fervor, and was inspired to accept their ideas. To the Hasidim, every action in life is performed in the presence of God. God speaks to man, telling him what to do in every situation, but man must listen. Every act must be carried out in response to a divine instruction, even *in behalf* of God, for God has set man on this earth to help Him restore the world to unity. Therefore, we must first listen to Him, find out what He wants, then carry it out in service of our fellow man. A slight, even menial, task may be of the greatest importance in God's scheme. We shall know it when the moment comes. Thus we must live in love of God and man, and in the joy before Him, who has hallowed us to be His co-workers and hallowed the world to be His workshop of salvation. This is the way Buber understood Hasidism; it became the root of his thoughts.

Then he entered the realm of modern scholarship, studying philosophy and history of art at the universities of Vienna, Leipzig, Berlin, and Zurich. The building of bridges had begun. He heard Herzl's call, but could not follow Herzl's idea of *political* Zionism. Ahad Ha-am, he felt, was closer to the truth, but Zionism became a formative influence in his life. He saw in it a way for the Jew to fulfill his destiny. After another period of study, at Florence, he settled down in Berlin, establishing contact with leading Jewish thinkers. Then he moved to a small, idyllic town in Southwestern Germany, Heppenheim, near Frankfurt, where he wrote, lectured, and edited a journal, *The Jew*. His works on Hasidim and Hasidism became famous. He joined Rosenzweig's "Lehrhaus." In 1923, he was called to the University of Frankfort as professor of religion, the first to occupy, in a German university, a chair established specifically for the teaching of Judaism. Rosenzweig was to have had it, but had been forced by his encroaching sickness to decline; he had prevailed on Buber to accept the call. Then came the monumental translation of the Bible in cooperation with Rosenzweig. With the advent of Hitler, Buber lost his position at the university and assumed the leadership of the great network of adult education which Rosenzweig had established throughout Germany's Jewish congregations. By deepening knowledge and love for their heritage among German Jewry, he gave them strength to face their trials. In 1938, he settled in Palestine, following the call of the Hebrew University at Jerusalem. As professor of the philosophy of society he taught, lectured, and wrote. When he died in 1965 his influence had spread in ever widening circles throughout the world.

Of His Thought

The Life of the Dialogue

Buber's ideas, found in many of the basic philosophy texts, grew out of Hasidism. "How can I know God?" That is the first question. God appears in spirit and in nature; He is everywhere, He speaks to me. He calls me every moment, and demands an answer from me. I never know in advance what He may want me to do, because it changes with the situation and the task. I do know, however, that it may always be different, and that it is addressed to *me* individually. What God demands of me is different from his demand on my neighbor; what He asks me today is different from what He asked me to do yesterday. I can find out by carrying on a dialogue, by letting Him speak to me while I speak to Him. This means I must establish an "I and Thou" relationship. Simply explained, we can state it in this manner. Two types of human relationships are possible, "I and Thou," and "I and It." If I analyze another person or use him, he is an "It" for me, an object. If I let him influence me by his total self, as in dialogue, he becomes a "Thou," a subject. My own self changes, depending on the relationship of "I and Thou" or "I and It." "I and Thou" is an existential encounter, living persons interact and get to know each other and themselves better. This must be the relationship between man and man, but also between man and God. Man must find him existentially, not in philosophy. When I permit God to speak with me, when I ask at every decision of my life, "What does He want me to do?" when I feel His unspoken word, then I have an "I and Thou" relationship with Him. Deep within my heart I experience His nearness. I "exist" before Him. Thus it was done among the Hasidim; this was "Kavanah," the directing of my total personality to Him.

I cannot blindly follow the routine of my life or even the rules and rituals of religion, for they may not meet the situation. There may be occasions when the voice of God tells me to act in new and different ways, contrary to religious commandments and tradition. If that happens, I must follow the voice of God. Buber makes a distinction between "Religiosity," the waiting in wonder at God's appeal, and "Religion," a set of rules. I must retain my "Religiosity."

Religion may acquiesce to be a compartment of life, side by side with other compartments, with its own claims and laws—in doing that it has already perverted the relationship of faith . . . He who does not give fulfilment to this relationship of faith, as fully as he can . . . this person sets a limit to the dominion of God over the world, over its unfolding and its fulfilment . . . The relationship of faith is not a book of rules which one might consult to know what to do at a certain hour. What God demands of me for this hour, that I shall experience . . . no sooner than at the hour. Even then I shall experience it only if I feel responsible for this hour as *my* hour before God, and if I carry out this responsibility toward Him to the best of my ability.[23]

Man thus "argues" with God, wrestling with God as did Jacob in the Bible; he "redeems" God, who blesses man as did the angel in the biblical story, who called Jacob "Israel"—fighter with God. With my whole soul I must strive for God. Even my evil inclinations can serve Him, as I overcome them. Only when I miss the direction to God, only when I lose my relationship to Him, only then have I done evil; then I shall feel guilty. A person who reaches a state of depravity, where he no longer feels guilty at missing God, is truly a sinner, and should he actually come to oppose God's will, then he is utterly evil and will do untold harm.

Thinking of God, and studying the works of religion, is not enough. Thought must be combined with action. This is the way the Hasidim saw it, and Buber follows them. The arena where this action takes place is society and the world. Buber takes issue with the master of existentialism, the Danish theologian Kierkegaard, who felt that we must deny the world in order to concentrate on God, and went to the point of breaking his engagement with the girl he loved, because he could not tolerate

---

[23] Martin Buber, *Die Frage an den Einzelnen* (Berlin: Schocken Verlag, 1936), p. 67.

any human being coming between himself and God in the dialogue by which he was to experience Him. Buber points out that God has given us the world of creation, that we may complete it. The road to God leads through the world, therefore I must establish a true "I and Thou" relationship with all my fellow men. I must create a close bond of unspoken understanding with all, and react with my entire person to the world, not only with my critical faculties of thought. In the "I and Thou" relationship between man and man, God is present; in the relationship to God, humanity must be present.

The individual answers God when he embraces in human embrace the piece of the world handed to him; just as God embraces His world in divine embrace.[24]

This is the Life of the Dialogue.

Unfortunately, "in our age the I-It relation, gigantically swollen, has usurped, practically uncontested, the mastery and the rule."[25] There is no dialogue any more, either between man and God or between man and man. This is the tragedy of our world, the cause of the breakdown of society and of the human personality. God has gone into eclipse, but Buber hopes fervently that mankind will find its way back.

The great dialogue between I and Thou is silent; nothing else exists than his (man's) self. That is . . . being untrue. Being true to the being in which and before which I am placed is the one thing that is needful.[26]

Buber is actually close to Hermann Cohen, for Cohen also sees in God the ultimate ideal for which we strive in service. He is also close to Franz Rosenzweig's *New Thinking*, which expresses the idea of "man bringing redemption to the world as he faces God."[27] Both of these men see a specific function for Judaism in the scheme of things. Buber addresses himself to humanity as a whole, assuring himself of universal recognition. He also sees a special function for Judaism.

Judaism

As each person hears the individual message of God, so does each community. Judaism has a special call.

The divine can awaken in the individual; but it reaches fulfilment only when individuals, awakened to the awareness of divine Allness, open up to each other, communicate with each other, help each other . . . the true place of realization is society, and true society is one in which the divine is made real

---

[24] *Ibid.*, p. 42.

[25] Martin Buber, *Eclipse of God* (New York: Harper & Brothers, 1952), p. 166.

[26] Martin Buber, *Pointing the Way*, © 1957 by Martin Buber (New York: Harper and Brothers, 1957), p. X.

[27] Franz Rosenzweig, "Das Neue Denken," in *Kleinere Schriften* (Berlin: Schocken Verlag, 1937), pp. 373 ff.

in human relationships. These are the principles of the teachings upon which the call of Judaism is based. . . . Truth made manifest in action is its goal; to strive for it its purpose and its strength. The will is implanted in it to establish the true society on earth. Its (Israel's) yearning for God is the yearning to prepare a dwelling place for Him in the midst of a true society. God's awareness of Israel is the awareness that from Israel shall come the true society; Israel's waiting for the Messiah is the waiting for the true society . . . Hence it may never consider itself as one of the nations, for it knows that it is the first fruit of fulfilment. Yet it may not consider itself better than the nations, since it has remained so far from the ideal, so far in fact, that at times it can hardly see it clearly. Hence Israel will never recognize any man as Messiah to have already come; not so long as the kingdom of God has not yet been achieved. But Israel will never cease to demand of man the effort leading to redemption, since it is man's function to establish God's glory in the world on earth.[28]

This is the specific dialogue between God and Israel, and between Israel and mankind with God present. Israel is God's people. Israel and God stand in a unique "I and Thou" relationship, *the* "I and Thou" relationship.

Zionism

This also is the source of Buber's Zionism, but he goes beyond Ahad Ha-Am. A cultural center in Palestine is not enough. As he said, the individual cannot unfold alone, so the Jew can unfold to his task only in a society of Jews. In Israel he can build a miniature society, an ideal society which will guide mankind by its example toward the kingdom of God. The Jewish state must never become simply a national state like all the others. This would pervert the ideal. Zion, the ideal always pursued, never reached, is the goal and task.[29]

Speaking more concretely, Buber sees a very practical function for the Jew and for a Jewish state in Palestine. To him, the Jew is fundamentally oriental, and the characteristic of the oriental is action, the urge to create, build, and construct. Western man is more inclined to contemplation. Since the Jew is also imbued with the culture of the west, he is the logical intermediary between Orient and Occident. Whether this analysis is correct may be questioned, yet the conclusions sound almost prophetic.

Europe must go to work and must initiate a new era to preserve the Orient and to create an understanding between it and the Occident, in order that both may work together, improving each other and joining in the common effort for humanity . . . For this world historical mission Europe is offered an intermediary, a people which has acquired all the wisdom and the art of

---

[28] Martin Buber, *Reden Über Das Judentum* (Berlin: Schocken Verlag, 1932), pp. 147 ff. Translation by the author.
[29] *Zion als Ziel und als Aufgabe* (Berlin: Schockenverlag, 1936).

the Occident, yet has not lost its oriental character, a people destined to link Orient and Occident in fruitful interaction; perhaps even called to amalgamate the spirit of the Orient and the spirit of the Occident and fuse it into a new message.[30]

In this spirit Buber can well justify the existence of Israel among the Arab states. It is a God-given task; even the geographical location of the land of Israel is God-ordained, a bridge between cultures. This is the message of Israel for today and tomorrow.

The renewal of Judaism

Every generation must accept the divine challenge. There have been generations who tried to escape it, or, even worse, generations who arrived at "pseudo-acceptance." Religion for them is primarily a matter of emotion, "inspiration," empty talk, and preachments. This empty emotionalism has perverted Judaism as well, so Judaism must renew and revitalize itself. The renewal is threefold.

JUDAISM MUST DEVELOP THE SPIRIT OF UNITY. It can be recaptured in three ways: through *study of the past*, in the holy works of Scripture and History. They relate how Israel walked with God through the ages. This must lead to *unity among the* people *living* today. In every person there is a divine presence; in the people as a whole it is a fire, sometimes burning low, but capable of being fanned to life. It safeguards eternity. Finally there is the *soul's recollection*, as the depth of our spiritual experiences are plumbed. (Rosenzweig holds similar ideas.)

This is the reason for Buber's translation of Scripture, jointly with Rosenzweig, for his call to renewed acquaintance with Hebrew, for his revival of Hasidic lore. The road to a united society must be traveled by every individual alone, but in fellowship with others.[31]

THE SPIRIT OF UNITY MUST LEAD TO ACTION. Judaism is basically an action program. Again seeing the Jew as an oriental, Buber claims that action is the oriental's way to God, while contemplative faith constitutes the road for the occidental. But action is not the same as ceremonial law, with all its detailed prescriptions; this law atomized the program of action. It was Jesus' great contribution that he replaced the observance of details with a great overall program to save mankind. Jesus acted fully in the spirit of the prophets and of Jewish tradition. He cast out ceremonialism in order that the law might be made clear, and he made it clear that "not one tittle of the law was to be abolished until it is all fulfilled (Matt. 5)." This was listening to God, working with

---

[30] *Ibid.*, p. 98.
[31] Martin Buber, *Reden an die Jugend* (Berlin: Schocken Verlag, 1938).

Him, establishing His kingdom on earth, fulfilling His law. Of the prophets and of Jesus, Buber says:

It was Jewish land upon which this revolution of the spirit emerged. It awoke in the lap of ancient Jewish communal fellowship. They were Jewish men, those who carried it abroad. Those to whom they spoke—as is always pointed out—were the Jewish people and no other. And what they proclaimed was nothing else but the renewal of religiosity of action in Judaism.[32]

"In the center of original Christianity stands the deed." Only when the Occident added its contribution did Christianity become a matter of faith. Basic Christianity is Judaism. It is a call to action before God, just as Judaism is, as Hasidism had demonstrated so clearly to Buber. In this spirit Buber builds a bridge between Christianity and Judaism by calling both to creative action in the building of God's kingdom. In great pride as a Jew, he can point out that, in answer to those who have called for a closer relationship between Christianity and Judaism, we may say:

Whatever has been creative in Christianity is not Christianity but Judaism. With that we need not come into closer touch; all we need do is to recognize it within ourselves and take possession of it. We carry it within us, can never lose it. Whatever is not Judaism in Christianity that is uncreative, a mixture of thousands of rites and dogmas; and with that—we affirm as Jews and as men —we do not wish to come in touch. This answer, however, we may give only if we overcome superstitious fright which we may hold in connection with the Nazarene Movement, and put it where it belongs: in the spiritual history of Judaism.[33]

We must not misunderstand Buber. These are words of highest praise. Judaism and Christianity in their true essence and goal are truly one in their call for action. Ceremonies and dogmas are dross in both religions. At the same time, he gives to his own people a new pride in their heritage. Judaism is the founder of Christianity, and its highest ideals are Jewish ideals. Judaism has always had a purpose: it must survive, and it must cooperate.

THE GOAL IS THE VISION OF THE FUTURE. This vision must be renewed. It is founded in Judaism because, according to Buber, the Jew has a greater sense of time and a less developed sense of space. Music is the Jew's favorite expression in art, because it relates to time.[34] (This

---

[32] Buber, *Reden Über Das Judentum*, p. 52.

[33] *Ibid.*, p. 54.

[34] Hermann Cohen equally points out that Plato's "Republic" is circumscribed in *space*, comprising only Greeks, while the vision of the prophets is limitless in space and, above all, in time, reaching to "the end of days." (*Jüd. Schriften* I, p. 325.)

may be argued.) To achieve the goal, the Jew must have a society of his own, where he can live and create freely, but this society must not live unto itself. It lives for the day when a united humanity of brothers and sisters will flourish in the presence of God. The Jew in this society does not need "religion," in the usual sense of the word. As a builder of the future he is working for God in whatever he does, an idea reflected in modern Israel. Those who till the soil are serving. Israel, the first nation to bring technical aid to the newly created nations of Africa, expresses the spirit of responsibility for mankind. The spirit of Hasidism is alive in Israel, not only in the dance and the song of the workers, but in their joyful dedication to the building of a miniature ideal society. This does not mean that Buber is the official philosopher of the State of Israel. Generally speaking, the people in Israel consider themselves simply citizens of an independent state, but one with a mission. They have guided and helped others, they have sacrificed heavily for it, and they know how to share. When peace is made in the region, the ideal will come to full fruition for Jew, Arab, and the world. Unity, action, vision of the future, these are the ideals of Judaism. They are reflected in the Jewish God concept. Unity has led to the majestic idea of the *One God; action* envisions Him as *world-creating* and *world-ruling;* the *vision* of the *future* recognizes Him as *world-loving* and has resulted in the *messianic ideal* which Judaism has given to the world.

This view of the future has been the source of messianism. In it the other two tendencies of Judaism, the idea of unity and the idea of action, find the basis for their final and complete fulfilment.[35]

We recognize an emphasis on Creation-Revelation-Redemption, understood very much as Rosenzweig had seen it. In other works Buber expresses the ideas even more concretely.[36] We also notice similarities to Cohen.

Buber's philosophy, his action program are too vague. The "deed before God" is too vast a concept, hence too empty for average people in everyday living. Buber rejects Mitzvot, the religious duties toward God established by Torah and tradition. But Mitzvah is the unifying bond of the generations. Without it there remains only a "folk-feeling" a felt relationship to God and Israel. But is this enough for authentic Jewish living? Can an average person constantly listen to the voice of God and of his people and offer constant response? Modern Jewish theologians of the existentialist school have therefore stressed Mitzvot as a response to the Metzaveh, the Commanding God. Commandment presupposes a *person* that issues it, God, and a *person* that responds, the Jew. In this manner, the "I and Thou"

---

[35] *Ibid.,* pp. 58 f.
[36] See Will Herzberg: *The Writings of Martin Buber* (N.Y.: Meridian Books, 1956, pp. 29 f. and footnotes).

Synagogue of Wiesbaden in flames, 1938.

is established, God is experienced existentially. For the rest, Buber's thoughts with their demand on total man and Jew, have been the foundation of their theology.

THE END OF GERMAN JEWRY

At the height of these achievements, German Jewry died. The majority of European Jewry was wiped out, six million of them. Exterminated in the gas chambers of Poland, at Auschwitz, Bergen Belsen, Treblinka, and Dachau, tortured in concentration camps, they went to their death proudly, knowing that there was meaning in living and dying as a Jew. Instead of doubting their heritage, they saw in their suffering a challenge to affirm God and His love. "I believe" was the song on the lips of the Warsaw fighters, remnant of Polish Jewry who made a final and heroic stand against the overwhelming might of the Nazis. I can speak of their faith, for I learned of it through survivors of the days of deportation, who told me of the weeks and years in camp, and the ordeals endured by the members of my own family who perished. I lost my mother, two uncles and an aunt on my mother's side, and my father's brother, a severely disabled veteran of World War I, together with his family. I lost many cousins and innumerable friends and members of my congregations. None of them ever weakened in spirit.

Leo Baeck

Towering among the masses there was Rabbi Leo Baeck, symbol of Judaism itself. *Leo Baeck* (1873-1956) was scholar, leader, defender of Judaism and shepherd of his people in their darkest hour. As a young man he wrote a systematic exposition of Judaism, *The Essence of Judaism,* which has become a classic. He was deeply immersed in western culture and investigated Christianity, explaining *The Gospels as Documents of the History of Jewish Faith,* and exposing the errors held regarding *The Pharisees* among Christians. (The items in *italics* are titles of some of his works.) His greatest hour came when he accepted the call of German Jewry to be its head and spokesman during the Nazi regime. With great dignity and exemplary courage he spoke for them to the diabolical rulers. When his people were taken to the concentration camps and extermination centers he felt it his duty to join them and their fate. He rejected the invitations that came to him from America and England, he went with his flock to Theresienstadt. There he gave them courage and steadfastness, taught them at the risk of his life, for the Nazis had forbidden it, and from memory, for there were no books. Slated for execution, he was miraculously spared. After the war he settled in England but also taught at the Hebrew Union College in America. Out of his spiritual experience emerged his work *This People Israel,* an existentially seen history of the Jewish people. Israel stands under an everlasting *covenant* with God. It is eternal. It suffers, it is creative in spiritual fields of human endeavor, it is witness to the eternal covenant of *God* with nature and mankind, guaranteeing the oneness of all that *man* is to bring to fruition. The Jews, people of the covenant, survive, the Torah being the "tree of life to those who hold on to it."[36] In his work *The Essence of Judaism,* Baeck stated:

Leo Baeck.

---

[36] Proverbs 3:18.
[37] Leo Baeck, *Das Wesen des Judentums* (Frankfurt: J. Kaufmann Verlag, 1932), p. 304; *The Essence of Judaism* (New York: Schocken Books, Inc., 1948), p. 271.

This is the principle of Judaism in its deepest meaning: through action we shall preach our religion. Our lives shall speak of the greatness of our faith.[37]

Many Jewish institutions bear his name to emphasize the greatness of his life and work to future generations.

With the destruction of European Jewry, the great centers of Jewish thought vanished. Germany lost some of its most creative minds in every field of cultural endeavor, but she also lost an opportunity history had given her from the very beginning of her national life, the opportunity to mature in the spirit of truth, justice, and love, by accepting fully those of her citizens who were of different faith but had given her so much. German leaders have expressed sorrow and awareness of this loss, and are trying to make whatever restitution may be possible. Whether the man in the street is aware of any loss at all is difficult to say.

With the destruction of European Jewry, the great reservoirs of Jewish learning, piety, devotion, and sacrificial living in Eastern Europe dried out. The loss is irreplaceable. With it, the responsibility for the evolution of Jewish thought has fallen on remaining Jewry. The mantle of leadership, however, was placed on two communities, those of Israel and of the United States. The emergence of Israel as an independent state is one of the few positive results of World War II. We have also been able to witness a revival of Jewish faith in the free world. These two developments actually spell the ultimate defeat of Hitler in history. Nothing was so close to his scheming mind, nothing so systematically pursued, than the extermination of Jewry and Judaism. Yet, from the graves of the martyrs, new life is springing forth in the hearts of their kinfolk.

The Jewish community in the United States had to face an unfamiliar and vital new task. American Jewry had lived as world Jewry's child, young, unhampered, unburdened with responsibilities. Ideology was developed in Europe. If there were Jews whose faith had eroded in the vastness of the empty land of the United States, they were constantly replaced by immigrants who poured in and brought with them a strong spirit and firm traditional convictions. All this was changed now. American Jewry was called upon to lead. It had to raise the funds for rescue and assume the tasks of spiritual leadership. It rose nobly to the challenge. The generosity of American Jewry stands unmatched in the history of philanthropy. Religious institutions were expanded to develop the forces for spiritual action. Then came the most serious of problems: to make the average Jew aware that he had to assume fully the responsibilities of meaningful living as a religious Jew, to make clear to him his awesome responsibility for the future of Judaism, and to elicit response. The problem is still with us, yet awareness seems to be dawning and the future holds hope. To understand the character of American Jewry, we have to deal briefly with its development.

22

Enter
America

A t the very moment when the Jews were expelled from Spain, Columbus set sail to discover a new westward passage to the Far East, an adventure which was to make him the discoverer of a new world. He opened the gates of freedom for millions of Jews in a land where they were to be citizens by right and not by sufferance for the first time in centuries.

BEGINNINGS

The New World fell into the hands of the Spanish and Portuguese. The secret Jews, the marranos, who sought refuge there soon found out that they were to find no peace under these flags, even in the new world. The arm of the Inquisition reached beyond the ocean, and the first burning of a Jew in America took place at Mexico City in 1574. But Holland, which was tolerant and had given shelter to many of the refugee Jews from Spain, was emerging as a world power. In 1631 the Dutch took Recife, then capital of Brazil, and the Jews rejoiced. Now they could openly profess their faith. Immigrants arrived from Holland, a congregation was founded, but the joy was shortlived. In 1654 Recife fell back into the hands of the Portuguese, and the Jews had to leave. Some went to other Dutch colonies, such as Surinam or Curacao; others migrated to British possessions such as Barbados, where Jews had first settled in 1628. They settled at Jamaica and any other places that accepted them.

A small number of Dutch Jews from Brazil, 23 in all, decided to move to Holland's North American colony, New Amsterdam. There they arrived in September 1654, poor and very unwelcome. Thus was begun the settlement of the Jews in what was to be the United States of America.

In Colonial America

These 23 whose arrival galled Peter Stuyvesant, governor of the colony, were the forerunners of the first stream of immigration, which was really little more than a ripple. By the time of the American Revolution there were about 5,000 Jews in the United States; by 1840 their number had slowly risen to approximately 15,000, and to 50,000 by 1850. This comparatively small number makes their contribution so much more remarkable.

The beginning was struggle for a living and for the rights of citizenship. From the very beginning they entered the struggle for equality. This was a new world, a new beginning. Toleration was the best these people could expect in Europe, but now they breathed the air of a new environment and braced themselves to fight for their freedom. On their arrival Stuyvesant made them promise that they would always take care of their own poor, a promise kept by American Jewry to this day. But then the governor tried to deny them the right to bear arms in the defense of the colony, and to this they would not agree. Letters went back and forth between New Amsterdam and Amsterdam, until Stuyvesant was overruled. The Jews' right was affirmed; they could join their fellow colonists in protecting the settlement. This meant it was now their home in the full sense of the term. When New Amsterdam became New York, the Jews could build a synagogue. When the Revolution came, the Jews rallied to the cause of freedom, pledging and giving to it their "lives, fortunes and sacred honor."

Massachusetts was another matter. The Puritans, who built a community on the principles of the Old Testament, had no room for the children of the Old Testament. Only some converts were granted permanent residence in the colony to teach Hebrew to divinity students at Harvard College. Yet the Puritans did much to weave Jewish ethics and morality into the permanent fabric of America. Every year, as we celebrate Thanksgiving, we are reminded that it is based on the biblical festival of Sukkot, feast of thanksgiving observed in the fall.

Virginia and Maryland excluded Jews for religious reasons. Rhode Island, founded on the principle of toleration, admitted them early. The Quaker State of Pennsylvania opened its gates to them, without giving

ouro Synagogue, Newport,
now a national historic shrine.

em full equality. South Carolina gave them the right to build a syna-
ogue. John Locke, the great philosopher, pleaded their cause. Locke
ad drawn up the constitution for South Carolina. In 1699 he pointed
ut: "If we permit the Jews to have private houses and dwellings among
s, why should we not allow them to have synagogues?" [1] Georgia also
dmitted them. At the time of the Revolution there were five synagogues
 the United States: New York, Newport, Rhode Island, Charleston,
uth Carolina, Savannah, Georgia, and Philadelphia, Pennsylvania. New-
ort had the most enduring of these synagogues. Built in Georgian
yle, based on the English adaptation of classical forms, as promoted by
igo Jones, famous British architect, it is still in existence. An architec-
ral gem built in 1762 by Peter Harrison, architect of King's Chapel
 Boston, it is today a national shrine. Philadelphia's synagogue set
other precedent, for it was built with contributions from Christians

---

[1] John Locke, "Letter Concerning Toleration," in *Works* (London, 1740), vol II,
 273. Quoted from Anita L. Lebeson, *Pilgrim People*, © 1950 by Anita Libman
beson (New York: Harper & Brothers), p. 74.

as well as Jews. Benjamin Franklin was the largest contributor to i
building fund. New York's synagogue was closed during the Revolutic
when its minister, Gershom Seixas, refused to remain in the city whe
the British took it. Carrying with him the scroll of the Torah, he le
for Philadelphia, and the majority of his congregation followed.

Citizens of the United States

The Jews did indeed rally to the cause of the United States. The
served in the army, and some rose to commissioned ranks. Out of the
midst came Haym Solomon, the first Polish Jew of whom we hear. A
the broker of the new government, he had the job of selling the securiti
of the new United States. They were not a good investment; the cred
of the United States was weak. Solomon spent his own funds in th
purchase of the bonds, and left his family destitute when he died.

The Federal Government proclaimed religious liberty for all, but th
battle was not over for the Jews. Jefferson and Madison bent all the
efforts toward the establishment of a "wall of separation between Churc
and State." They succeeded on the federal level, but the states wei
slow in following the lead of the constitution. This time, however, th
Jews were not alone in their fight. In Maryland, for instance, a Scotc
Presbyterian, Thomas Kennedy, took up their cause:

There are no Jews in the country from which I come, nor have I the slighte:
acquaintance with any Jew in the world . . . There are few Jews in th
United States; in Maryland there are very few, but if there were only one, t
that one we ought to do justice.[2]

It was George Washington, however, who laid down the principles c
America, finally and categorically. In a reply to a letter sent him by th
Jewish congregation at Newport, Washington wrote:

The citizens of the United States have a right to applaud themselves for havin
given to mankind examples of an enlarged and liberal policy worthy of imita
tion. All possess alike liberty of conscience and immunities of citizenship. It :
no more that toleration is spoken of as if it were by the indulgence of one clas
of people that another enjoyed the exercise of their inherent natural right; fc
happily the government of the United States, which gives to bigotry no sanc
tion, to persecution no assistance, requires only that they who live under it
protection shall demean themselves as good citizens in giving it on all occe
sions their effectual support. May the children of the stock of Abraham, wh
dwell in this land, continue to merit and enjoy the good will of the other ir

---

[2] Lee J. Levinger, *A History of the Jews in the United States*, © 1949 by Th
Union of American Hebrew Congregations, New York, p. 137.

Mordecai Manuel Noah.

abitants, while everyone shall sit in safety under his own vine and fig tree, nd there shall be none to make him afraid.[3]

Under conditions of expanding freedom, the Jewish community grew. nglish and German Jews arrived, and congregations were founded herever Jews moved. They "demean themselves as good citizens." We ear of Judah Touro (1775-1854), who was born at Newport, Rhode sland, but moved to New Orleans. Fighting under Andrew Jackson in e battle of New Orleans, he was severely wounded. As he acquired ealth as a successful businessman he became a philanthropist, found-g the synagogue at New Orleans, donating to churches, but remem-ered as the man who sparked the building of the Bunker Hill Monu-ent at Boston by giving $10,000—or one fifth of the total cost of the ructure. It was a tremendous sum in those days, and testifies to his atriotic pride in being an American. There was no good cause, Jewish Christian, to which he did not contribute with lavish generosity.

Mordecai Manuel Noah (1785-1851) was a different personality. Play-right, social leader, sheriff of New York County, judge, United States onsul at Tunis, he lead a gregarious life. In Tunis he had occasion to itness at first hand the sad plight of his Jewish brethren in the old orld. He had an idea, let them come to America and settle as colonists, ventually building their own state within the framework of the United tates. He purchased land near Buffalo, New York, and founded the com-

---

3 Quoted from A Book of Jewish Thoughts, p. 71 (with permission of Bloch Pub-hing Company, New York).

371

munity of Ararat, named after the mountain on which Noah's ar finally found rest. The cornerstone, still preserved, reads:

ARARAT—A CITY OF REFUGE FOR THE JEWS
FOUNDED BY MORDECAI MANUEL NOAH IN THE MONTH OF TIZRI,
SEPTEMBER 1825
AND IN THE 50TH YEAR OF AMERICAN INDEPENDENCE [4]

He issued a proclamation to the Jews who are "to be gathered fror the four corners of the globe . . . to be restored and enjoy the righ of a sovereign independent people,"

Therefore I, Mordecai Manuel Noah, Citizen of the United States of Americ . . . and by the Grace of God governor and judge of Israel, have issued th my proclamation, announcing to the Jews of all the world that an asylum prepared and hereby offered to them. . . .[5]

His plan failed. Thinking that Jews would rather go to Palestine, he toc up the project. Palestine must revert to its

legitimate proprietors . . . the descendants of Abraham . . . Every attemp to colonize the Jews in other lands has failed; their eye has steadily rested c their beloved Jerusalem and they have said, "the time will come, the promis will be fulfilled." [6]

This was said at a time when the Jews in Europe had to remember tha to the Jews "as a nation" nothing was to be granted. It was said by man who even in America had suffered from prejudice, yet could proudl proclaim himself "citizen of the United States." As his language gushe forth in bombastic style, it reveals a man self-reliant and proud as a fre American. In America a Jew can be a Zionist, he can be "governor c the Jews"; all this is permitted him—as to all others—on the firm founda tions of American liberties. This was truly a new spirit at a time whei in Europe, conversion was the only "admission ticket to society," a Heine had said.

In America a Jew rose through the ranks to the highest commissio in the Navy of the time, that of Commodore. Uriah P. Levy (1792-1862 reached his goal, even though he had to fight bitterly to break dow prejudice. Prejudice was far from dead, it still exists today, but her in America it was possible to combat it, and the law opened the op portunity to a Jew for aspiration to high office. It could never have er tered any Jew's mind in any other country at the time. America offere the opportunity and, with it, the trials of freedom. Freedom create problems which the Jewish community was soon to experience.

---

[4] Museum at Buffalo, N.Y. Quoted from Lebeson, *op. cit.*, p. 206.
[5] *Op. cit.*, p. 207.
[6] *Ibid.*, p. 209.

Uriah P. Levy.

The Problems for Judaism

The community started out small in number, poor in worldly goods, and far removed from the centers of Jewish life. Originally it was Sefardic, but soon newcomers from all parts of the world joined it. The American synagogue was free from state supervision, yet it had considerable power. It was a spiritual haven, gave emotional security to the immigrants, and perpetuated the customs of the old country in an alien surrounding. It was a piece of home for the homesick. When there were no public schools it undertook the education of the young. It provided kosher meat, and supervised the religious life of the community and of individuals. No one had to join it, but no immigrant could live without it. What the synagogue lacked was ordained leadership. There were a few rabbis from Europe in the United States at about the middle of the nineteenth century. There were none before. The "hazzan," or cantor, could read the service and teach the children. The leadership of the synagogue, however, lay in the hands of the "parnass," the president and his board of trustees. They decided on the form of the service, which was usually orthodox; they maintained discipline; they would either permit or request their hazzan to preach a sermon, for he could not do so without their permission.

373

The results, generally speaking, were not happy. Laymen became the arbiters of religious observance and practice; and when rabbis eventually appeared, they found themselves subject to the direction of the laity, even in spiritual matters. The effects of this condition are still with us today. Judaism did not develop organically. A congregation might retain a practice, a form of prayer, simply because they had always done it that way. Rituals of minor importance might be considered important because they were tinged with nostalgia: thus did we see it "at home." Without trained leadership there could be no authoritative decisions. Communities might split up into different congregations over a minor point of liturgy or practice. Sefardic Jews saw it one way, German Jews another, Russian Jews a third. The people began to feel that the synagogue was there to serve *them*, rather than challenge them to serve *God*. Worship became a matter of nostalgia, of emotion, leading to varied consequences. In orthodoxy it tended to permit different standards of religious conduct: one is religious in an old fashioned way when one attends the synagogue, but outside one goes with the world. Sabbath observance fell sharply, even among the leaders of the community, Jewish practices were abandoned, but synagogue worship did not change. Eventually the gulf between life and worship grew so wide that worship became meaningless, even distasteful, to many. There were as yet no leaders like Samson Raphael Hirsch, Zachariah Frankel, or Abraham Geiger to guide American Jewry as German Jewry had been guided. In time they were to come.

At the same time powerful forces of dissolution were at work in American Judaism. The spirit of "Enlightenment" pervaded the air. Jews would have to cope with it, but laymen could not be expected to do so. The frontier beckoned, and Jews moved with the population. Many Jews no longer lived in closely-knit religious communities. As a matter of fact, they were frequently compelled to live all by themselves, without any Jewish contacts. They were peddlars, moving from place to place, roaming all over the plains, pushing westward. For weeks or months they might not see another Jew. Eventually Jewish fervor would weaken, as the lure of the environment became more powerful. They became estranged, the call of Judaism no longer reaching them across the prairies. They settled down; they got adjusted; they intermarried.

Lack of leadership, divided and feuding communities, bossism in the synagogue, an outmoded form of worship, wide dispersion, and the pull of American enlightenment, all these were destructive factors. The future looked grim for American Jewry.

There were some who saw clearly the need for reform in Judaism. One of them was Isaac Harby of Charleston, South Carolina. He was an educator, and realized that something had to be done if American

Judaism was to be saved. A synthesis had to be created of Judaism, Americanism, and Enlightenment. This he expressed in a letter to Thomas Jefferson, dated January 14, 1826.

With patience and industry we hope, in a few years, to be able to establish a mode of worship, simple and sensible; suited to the liberality of the age, improving to the Israelite and acceptable to the Deity. The example set by the University (of Virginia), which owes its noblest characteristic to your judgement and philanthropy, offers a bright pattern to any similar institution in our country. May you, honored sir, live to see your warmest wishes realized in the results.

With sentiments of gratitude and admiration,

I am your ob't serv't
Isaac Harby [7]

That Harby wrote to Jefferson shows the spirit of the time. Jefferson saw in education an instrument of moral improvement, and religion to him served the same purpose.[8] The form of religion mattered little to the Deist as long as it served the improvement of the worshippers.

Harby's hope eventually was to come true, but only after many struggles. A new stream of migration brought with it both vastly increased numbers of immigrants and the men eager and trained to undertake the task of reform.

GERMAN IMMIGRATION

By 1875, the number of Jews in America had risen to about 250,000. The majority of these immigrants had come from Germany. Jews from Bavaria had arrived early in the century; the cruel government of that German state had prohibited marriage for the majority of them, and America offered freedom. Christians as well as Jews came in large numbers after the failure of the German revolution of 1848. In its wake, the German states enacted severely repressive laws against the idealists who had dreamed of and worked for democracy in Germany. America gained some of its most valuable freedom fighters in these immigrants from Germany, whose descendants were to distinguish themselves through subsequent generations. The German Jews settled along the Eastern Seaboard or moved west to Cincinnati and St. Louis, where large scale settlements of Germans were already in existence. My father told me, as one of his earliest recollections, how his father's brother, now well-

---

[7] *Ibid.*, p. 211.
[8] See Northwest Ordinance, Article III: "Religion, morality and knowledge being necessary to good government and the happiness of mankind, schools and the means of education shall forever be encouraged."

established at St. Louis, visited the old home town in Germany, bringing gifts to all the children. Jews followed the gold rush to California, where they founded congregations even before the Golden State had become part of the United States.

With them there came rabbis. Max Lilienthal was one of the earliest arrivals. As a young rabbi in Germany he had been invited by the Czar of Russia to develop a Jewish school system in which religious and secular studies would be combined. After a few years he found that he was to prepare the masses for wholesale conversion, so he fled in terror. America offered him a new and creative future. In 1846, Isaac Meyer Wise set foot on the shores of America to become the great organizer of its Jewish community. Nine years later, David Einhorn arrived after a stormy rabbinical career in Germany. His ideas were so radical that he could find no pulpit in the land of his birth. Intoxicated by the spirit of progress, he saw in his own age the beginnings of the messianic period of universal brotherhood. Calling upon his people to embrace this world of human equality, he urged them to abolish most forms of religious observance and cast off all the laws of the Talmud, which were to him just walls of separation. He was to have great influence on American Jewry. All these men were reformers. They had been preceded by the leader of a new orthodoxy in America, Isaac Leeser, who came in 1824 and was to assume spiritual leadership for the Jews of practically the entire country, at least for a while. Yet he was not a rabbi. We shall hear more about him and the others.

A new type of lay leader also arrived from Germany, men capable of building great fortunes and willing to put their wealth at the disposal of their brethren. Among them were the Straus family, Jacob Schiff, the Lehmans, and others. They were typically German in their thoroughness and their love for organization. Thus a system of charitable institutions was developed which had no equal in Jewish history; millions eventually were rescued, rehabilitated, and transformed into proud and creative American citizens. But the position of the layman became ever more important and powerful in all fields of Jewish life, including religion.

Since they were organization minded, they founded their own fraternal order when blocked from membership in general ones. It was called B'nai B'rith, Sons of the Covenant. Started in 1843 as a benevolent organization of German Jews, it cast off its exclusiveness, grew rapidly, and has spread all over the world. Its growth continues. B'nai B'rith has served the causes of Jewish charity and philanthropy. Through its Anti-Defamation League it has combatted anti-Semitism, and through its Hillel Foundations has brought Jewish inspiration to students on many university campuses, in America and abroad.

The Civil War found the Jews on both sides of the line. Six thousand Jews served in the Union Army, 1200 in the Confederate Army. Judah P. Benjamin rose to cabinet position in the Confederacy. David Einhorn, rabbi of Baltimore, had to flee for his life, having preached in fiery wrath against the crime of slavery. For the first time a Jewish chaplain was appointed; Abraham Lincoln issued the directive. There was also anti-Semitism, then, as so often, a result of general tension. Judah Benjamin's appointment drew anti-Jewish reaction. U.S. Grant accused the Jews of crossing the lines and, faithful to the historical pattern of anti-Jewish action, issued an order expelling *all* Jews from his sector of operations. But Abraham Lincoln intervened directly and the order was revoked. The President listened carefully to the Jewish delegation presenting their case, and then—with his characteristic twinkle—said: "and so the children of Israel were driven from the happy land of Canaan." "Yes," was the reply, "and they have come to father Abraham's bosom to seek protection." [9] In America anti-Semitism has always been outside the law; in Europe it was officially sanctioned. This has given American Jewry the will to fight against it and against all forms of discrimination, which are contrary to the law and spirit of America, a perversion of American ideals, and a subversion of her constitution.

As American Jewry cast its roots more deeply in the soil of America, the need for a reconstruction of Judaism to serve Americans became imperative.

ADJUSTMENT AND REFORM

Isaac Leeser (1806–1868)

When Leeser, in 1824, came to the United States from Neunkirchen, Westphalia, he had neither rabbinical training nor any idea that he would ever be a rabbinical leader. He took a job as a clerk in a business house at Richmond, Virginia; then an article attacking Jewish customs appeared in a Richmond paper. Leeser replied; in clear and dignified words he defended the faith of his fathers. Obviously there was no one but this young clerk who had the courage and background to speak in defense of Judaism, for it was on the strength of his letter to the paper that Leeser was appointed minister, or "hazzan," of the venerable synagogue at Philadelphia. The officers of the congregation did not know it then, but they had made an outstanding choice. Leeser was deeply orthodox in the spirit of Moses Mendelssohn, which meant living in two cultures. The pattern of his Mendelssohnian thinking can be seen clearly.

---

[9] Levinger, *op. cit.*, p. 199.

Isaac Leeser.

Leeser had started his career in public defense of Judaism. Now, for his own people, he translated the Bible and the prayer book into English, and he founded a periodical, "The Occident and American Jewish Advocate." Traveling all over the country, he gave guidance and inspiration to his widely scattered co-religionists. There is a difference between Mendelssohn and Leeser, and we shall find it in all of the reformers in America as compared with those in Germany. The Americans are not given to theoretical thinking; they are not "pure" philosophers and theologians, but are developing the basic ideas taken from Germany. They are practical men, reflecting the American character as a whole. It can be found in the life and work of the man who became the great Jewish organizer of the century, Isaac Meyer Wise. Leeser first welcomed his support, but eventually was to regard him as his great antagonist.

Isaac Meyer Wise (1819–1900): Master Builder, Father of Reform

Wise was born at Steingrub, Austria, and grew to manhood during the rule of Metternich. It was a period of reaction, and it taught Wise to hate tyranny and to fight it with all his strength. He received his ordination in Europe, and served for some time. Then, as a man of 27, inspired by the liberal ideas of the Reform movement in Germany, and by the vision of civil liberties in America, he emigrated, hoping to graft modern Jewish thought on the tree of Judaism in the United States. Wise was no radical reformer, but even his moderate ideas were to get him into trouble. Called to a pulpit at Albany, New York, he immediately came into conflict with the power of orthodox lay leadership. Standing up to his ideals of a reformed service which would meet modern needs, he found himself harassed by lay leaders disagreeing with him, and eventually was bodily attacked in his own pulpit. Among his Christian friends who learned of the incident were the justices of the New York Supreme Court. They suggested that he give up the rabbinate, since it would bring him only heartaches, and were willing to admit him to the ·bar after a pro forma examination. They felt sure that he would bring distinction to the bar, and find honor, peace of mind, and happiness for himself. But Wise had strength of character, deep convictions, and great dedication.[10] He refused the flattering offer and eventually

[10] Jacob R. Marcus, *Memoirs of American Jews,* II (Philadelphia: Jewish Publication Society of America, 1955), pp. 120 ff., relates Wise's own story of the struggle.

Isaac Meyer Wise.

accepted a call to Cincinnati, ready for the slow uphill fight in behalf of American Judaism.

Following the example of Isaac Leeser, he started a journal, "The Israelite." In it he asked the question:

Why do Jews respect each other so little; why is there so much strife in their midst; why do they copy slavishly the Christian customs, be they good or bad; why that humility before any Christian whether he be deserving of respect or not? [In answer he points to the century-long oppression which has demoralized the Jew.] It has robbed him of his self-respect, has killed all pride in him. There is only one solution: the Jew must become thoroughly Americanized. He must, within himself, develop the self reliance and self assurance for which America stands. Then will he hold his head high as becomes a free-born man.[11]

Americanization and Reform were the two goals to which Wise dedicated his life. Reform was needed to give new strength to Judaism. Wise had no intention to make Jewish religion more "comfortable," he rather wished to give it more power, and to restore the faith of the people. Both aims were to be served by the new prayer book which Wise had already advocated in Albany. It was called *Minhag America*, the Custom of America. Even Leeser approved, writing in his "Occident" that the book would create unity out of the numerous divergent customs which divided congregations and their members. With every immigrant bringing his own customs from home, dissension was inevitable and Americanization was retarded. Wise's Prayer Book thus would create unity among the members, and a uniform practice among congregations, inevitably strengthening Judaism. At the same time, it would eliminate the pull of the old country, the attachment to the past, and replace it by an American spirit. This would help Americanization.[12] Leeser understood Wise's aims well. He had met Wise in 1847, and the two men had been impressed by each other. Their ideas, at the moment, were identical. Leeser was in accord with Wise's plan to organize an "association of Israelitish congregations in North America to produce one sublime and grand end, to defend and maintain our sacred faith." [13]

Now, as rabbi in Cincinnati, Wise called a conference to be held in Cleveland in 1855. It was to consider the articles of "Union of American Israel," which were to be acceptable to all. They give us a good idea of Wise's own convictions at the moment:

The Bible is of divine origin. The Talmud contains the traditional, legal and logical expositions of Biblical laws which must be expounded and practiced

---

[11] Quoted from Marcus, *op. cit.*, pp. 133 ff.

[12] Lebeson, *op. cit.*, p. 311, quotes Leeser's statement.

[13] Quoted from Ismar Elbogen, *A Century of Jewish Life* (Philadelphia: Jewish Publication Society of America, 1944), p. 124.

according to the comments of the Talmud. The resolutions of the synod in accordance with the above principles are legally valid; statutes and ordinances contrary to the laws of the land are invalid.[14]

This was clearly a conservative position, a common meeting ground for all views. But the men of extreme Reform, rabbis like Einhorn, schooled on the doctrines of Geiger and Holdheim, would not go along with Wise's moderate principles. To them the Talmud was no longer binding; the spirit of the age was to be considered first, radical reform was the watchword. Wise had to make an extremely difficult decision. He knew that the orthodox congregations would not follow him if he moved further toward reform; he was equally aware that he needed the liberal congregations to build an American Judaism. He moved toward reform. His friends, like Lilienthal, supported him, but opposition grew. Finally he decided to organize a union of congregations which might be a meeting ground for all, regardless of religious outlook. The call went out through Wise's own congregation. Rabbis and representatives of communities throughout the West and Middle West gathered at Cincinnati. As a result of this conference, the Union of American Hebrew Congregations was founded in 1873. Its aims:

to establish and maintain institutions for instruction in the higher branches of Hebrew literature and Jewish Theology; to provide means for the relief of Jews from political oppression and unjust discrimination, and for rendering them aid for their intellectual elevation; to promote religious instruction and encourage the study of the Scriptures and the tenets and history of Judaism—all this, however, without interfering in any manner whatsoever with the worship, the schools or any other of the congregational institutions.[15]

This was the pragmatic approach, and Wise hoped to bring about a real union of all congregations, which would have given great strength to American Judaism. Unfortunately, the orthodox congregations, in spite of the neutrality of the program, did not join. Still, the Union of American Hebrew Congregations has remained a meeting ground for various types of congregations. This has been its strength and its weakness, its strength lying in the freedom granted its members in matters of worship and practice. Reform Judaism has never said to its adherents, "You may not observe certain practices, or you must observe others." It has never, for instance, insisted that only the Union Prayer Book may be used, or that worship must be conducted with or without hats. It has simply stated that a Jew who, in good conscience, accepts or rejects certain regulations, principles, and customs, remains a good Jew—even if his decision is contrary to the regulations set down in the Talmud.

---

[14] *Ibid.*, p. 125.
[15] *Ibid.*, p. 126.

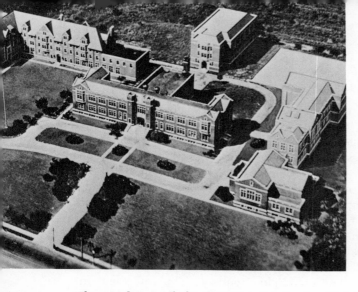

Hebrew Union College—
Jewish Institute of Reli-
gion, Cincinnati, Ohio.

The weakness of this position lies in the fact that there is no longer a central organization which rules on the law nor a basic code which is regarded as authority. Each individual congregation is ultimately free to establish its own form of religious practice and observance. Frequently the lay leaders, as men of influence, become final arbiters in the field of religion. In the past, Torah, Talmud, and Shulhan Arukh were the law; now law was whatever a congregation decided it was. This has frequently led to conflicts, changes, and battles between opposing factions striving for power. Member congregations of the Union of American Hebrew Congregations have varied greatly in ritual, practices, and forms of worship. Union has come into existence among congregations, but the unity of which Wise had dreamed did not materialize.

To redeem the situation as far as possible, and in order to safeguard the future of Judaism, Wise now engaged in the second of his great projects, the establishment of a theological school. Here rabbis would be trained to guide their flock; native rabbis for native congregations. Uniformly educated, they might be able eventually to introduce uniform practices in all congregations. Wise hoped that a unified American Judaism might still come into existence. The school, the Hebrew Union College, founded in 1875, would serve all branches of American Jewry. This expectation, too, of forming an "inter-denominational" school, was doomed to disappointment. The school remained a seminary for liberal rabbis, but as such it has grown in size and distinction with the growth of Reform Judaism. Today it is the oldest rabbinical training school in America. To its campus at Cincinnati it has added the Jewish Institute of Religion at New York, a rabbinical school founded by the late Rabbi *Stephen* Wise. The names of both schools have been combined to Hebrew Union College—Jewish Institute of Religion. A branch at Los Angeles provides training and extension services on the West Coast. A campus at Jerusalem offers education and research opportunities in Israel. All rabbinical students are required to study there for one year. The Hebrew Union College has produced great rabbis, cantors, and educators. Its graduates have ranged from radical reform to traditional conservatism, although the school's character has been reformed.

In 1889 Wise added a third organization, the Central Conference of American Rabbis. Thus he became master builder of American Jewry. Later, when conservative and orthodox groups saw the need for union and regeneration, they copied his pattern in every detail: a union of congregations, a theological school, and a rabbinical organization.

The Development of Reform Judaism

Changing times have influenced the outlook of Reform Judaism. In 1885, 19 rabbis, led by Reform's leading theologian Kaufmann Kohler, met in unofficial conclave and arrived at a set of guiding principles. This so-called Pittsburgh Platform may be regarded as the high water mark of "classical" reform. Going much further than any of the German reformers—except perhaps Holdheim—ever did, it is extremely radical and humanistic: Jews are simply a religious group, and definitely not a nation. There is no resurrection, no hereafter, and Bible and Talmud are no longer binding, except as ethical guides. It is the mission of Israel to bring the knowledge of God to the world. Fifty-two years later, at Columbus in 1937, a new balance sheet was drawn up in the form of a "platform." "The threads of historical continuity in the practice of the Jewish faith" were recognized, the significance of Torah and Talmud was stressed again, and Judaism was once again recognized as a way of life; practical observances and creative expression were enjoined. The peoplehood of Israel was affirmed:

. . . Judaism is the historical religious experience of the Jewish people. Though growing out of Jewish life, its message is universal. . . . Reform Judaism recognizes the principle of progressive development in religion and consciously applies this principle to spiritual as well as to cultural and social life. . . . Revelation is a continuous process. . . . The Torah, both written and oral, enshrines Israel's ever growing consciousness of God and of the moral law. It preserves the historical precedents, sanctions and norms of Jewish life. . . . Being products of historical processes certain of its laws have lost their binding force with the passing of conditions that called them forth. But as a depository of permanent spiritual ideals the Torah remains the dynamic source of the life of Israel. Each age has the obligation to adapt the teachings of the Torah to its basic needs in consonance with the genius of Judaism . . . Judaism is the soul of which Israel is the body. Living in all parts of the world, Israel has been held together by the ties of a common history, and above all, by the heritage of faith. Though we recognize the group-loyalty of Jews who have become estranged of our religious tradition, a bond which still unites them with us, we maintain that it is by its religion and for its religion that the Jewish people has lived. . . . In the rehabilitation of Palestine . . . we affirm the obligation of all Jewry to aid in its upbuilding as a Jewish homeland. . . . In Judaism religion and morality blend into an indissoluble unity. . . . Religious practice: the religious life . . . the home . . . the synagog . . . education . . . prayer. . . . Judaism as *a way of life* requires in addition to its moral and spiritual demands, the preservation of the Sabbath, festivals and Holy Days, the retention and development of such customs, symbols and ceremonies as possess inspirational value, the cultivation of distinctive forms of religious art and music and the use of Hebrew, together with the vernacular, in our worship and instruction.[16]

This was more in line with Wise's original ideas. It came close to the concept of "positive historical Judaism," which has been the guiding principle of conservatism since Frankel established it in Germany. In short, reform has become more conservative because its members have desired it. Hebrew has been brought back into the service; customs such as the kiddush and the Bar Mitzvah have been restored. Confirmation, however, has been retained. It had been introduced by Reform to take the place of Bar Mitzvah, but now it has become an act of consecration. Young people who have had three years of additional study and Jewish practice since Bar Mitzvah solemnly affirm their faith at an age of greater maturity, on the basis of better knowledge and several years of responsible Jewish living.' The value of confirmation has not been diminished by Bar Mitzvah; on the contrary, it has been enhanced. Bar Mitzvah itself, frequently considered the terminal point of Jewish education, has become what it always has been supposed to be—a gateway to deepened Jewish loyalty and extended studies.

The confirmation ceremony has been copied by all the other branches of Judaism; pragmatically speaking, it offered motivation for young Jews to continue their Jewish education beyond Bar Mitzvah. It now involves another significant factor: while Bar Mitzvah is only for boys, confirmation recognizes the equality of woman in religion as in American life. Confirmation, no longer a copy from Protestantism, has become a Jewish institution in the American synagogue. Individual Reform synagogues, free to construct their forms of worship, have brought back many other ceremonies: the Tallit and head covering, at least for rabbis, the Sukkah, the Lulav, the Shofar, and the Seder. The individual is urged to give greater Jewish meaning to his life by home study and observance. The cantor has been restored to his function in the synagogue, and a school for cantors has been added to the theological seminaries. Jewish archives, museums, summer camps for children and adolescents, retreats for adults, and laymen's institutes have been developed to give depth to Jewish living. One of Reform's greatest achievements

---

16 Yearbook, Central Conference of American Rabbis, Vol. XVIII, pp. 97-100, © 1937 by C.C.A.R.

has been in the field of education. From primer to advanced texts, the education series produced by the Reform movement have blazed new paths. Even a Jewish day school movement has been initiated by several congregations.

True to its ideal that Judaism be a light unto the nations, the Reform movement has developed a widespread program of teaching ethics to the community at large. Radio and television programs serve the cause. The Jewish Chautauqua Society sends rabbis to colleges and universities, that they may lecture on the character of Judaism and its message; it demands that the presentations live up to the highest demands of scholarship. Books on Judaism have been widely distributed to college libraries. Through its center at Washington, D.C. and the social action committees in individual congregations, the Jewish ethical point of view is transmitted to lawmakers and nation.

The hope for the future of Israel in the land of Israel has been revived. Some of the great zionist leaders have come from the ranks of the reform rabbinate. The prayer book once more includes prayers for Jerusalem.

This work is carried out by the Union of American Hebrew Congregations, which counts between 600 and 700 congregations in its ranks. Affiliated with it are Brotherhoods, Sisterhoods, Temple Youth Groups, and Educator and Administrator Organizations. The movement has spread throughout the free world. It is organized as "The World Union of Progressive Judaism."

A Jew need not follow the dietary laws in order to be considered a good Jew, yet, if he does, his actions are given approval as an act of Jewish affirmation. He need not wear a hat in the synagogue, but he may do so. He need not observe two days of the holidays, yet many reform rabbis regularly preach in orthodox congregations on the second days of festivals.

This trend has brought the movement severe criticism from the old-time classical reform element, which claims that Reform is swinging back to Orthodoxy. It has been countered by a re-assertion of the basic outlook of Reform. It does not consider itself called simply to abolish the past, but rather to evaluate the past and to reject and adopt that which is meaningful for the living generation. At the same time Reform permits individual interpretation. This permissiveness has in turn been criticised by the Conservative movement, which claims that "halakhah," Jewish law, must be considered binding in principle. Actually, permissiveness does present a danger. It may lead to a breakdown of religion. A number of Reform rabbis have been keenly aware of the problem, and have advocated a return to at least a guide for Jewish observances. Individual rabbis have published such guidelines, based on modern interpretation of talmudic law.

What then must Reform Jews observe? They must observe the Sabbath, the holy days, and the rituals relating to birth, marriage, and death. They must educate their children in a Jewish way, formally and by setting examples, and must pray and study and give their homes a Jewish atmosphere. They must be aware of the missionary function of the Jewish people in the world, and work for social justice, carrying forward the fight for human rights to all.

The contributions of Reform Judaism to Judaism as a whole are significant, yet in the vagueness of its program it can exist and survive only if the individual members and the community constantly re-evaluate and apply its message. The line that exists between meaningful adjustment and comfort-seeking abandonment of Jewish tradition is very thin. In order to live, it must demand of its leaders and members a fervent dedication to Judaism and the will to make it vital and strong. It can flourish if its adherents dedicate themselves to the study of Judaism, its past and present, its tradition and its meaning. It can survive if parents and children carry it from the synagogue to their homes, from holy days to the days of the week, to establish it as a way of life for themselves and their posterity. It must not be timid in its demand for personal sacrifice. Some decades ago, some of its leaders changed the day of rest from the Sabbath to the Sunday. They yielded to people's search of comfort, only to find that the vast majority of the people themselves rejected the change and the rationalizations which made it feasible. It was contrary to the spirit of Judaism. Reform must demand a maximum program; it was set up to do that. Then it will remain a powerfully creative force.

The Reform movement was founded in the days of German immigration, built on the ideology of Jews from Germany, imbued with the spirit of German idealism and American democracy. As Jews from Eastern Europe came to this country and joined its ranks, Reform found itself compelled to transform its outlook and character. It is a sign of vitality that it has been able to accomplish this transformation.

With this new immigration, new forces developed in American Jewish life, new religious movements sprang up. The next stream of immigration was to bring millions of persecuted Jews from Eastern Europe, yearning for the freedom of America and willing to take their station in the battle for human rights.

23

Migration from Eastern Europe

Between 1881 and 1920, a total of two million Jews came to the United States. In the overwhelming majority they were victims of persecution from Eastern Europe. In character this migration differed greatly from previous ones. The Jews who came from Russia, Poland, and Rumania were desperately poor, and also profoundly pious; Judaism had given them the strength to endure amidst trials and tribulations. They were tightly knit, having found strength in mutual support. The German Jews, who had preceded them, spoke German and settled among the Germans in the Middle West with whom they had much in common.

The new immigrants stood alone. Their language was Yiddish, and their strength lay in themselves. Similar to the Italian and Irish migrations, this immigration also constituted a shift from rural to urban living for the people involved. All this was to create problems. They arrived in great streams, tired, poor, yearning to be free. Indeed, Emma Lazarus, the Jewish poetess, found her inspiration for the great poem on American ideals from working among them. The poem is emblazoned on the base of the Statue of Liberty.

> "Keep ancient lands your storied pomp," cries she
> with silent lips. "Give me your tired, your poor,
> your huddled masses yearning to breathe free,
> the wretched refuse of your teeming shore.
> Send these, the homeless, tempest-tossed to me;
> I lift my lamp beside the golden door."

Emma Lazarus.

It was an exact description of the masses of arriving Jews. They did not move far beyond the golden door, but settled along the Atlantic Seaboard, the majority remaining in New York. They wanted to stay together as they had lived together in Europe. Each group organized its own little synagogue, where they practiced the customs of the past and spoke the language of the past, just as they had done in the towns and little villages whence they had come. Their rabbis, who had come with them, remained their leaders. They were learned men, well-schooled in Talmud, but strangers to worldly culture. The masses had little learning. Like the German Jews before them, they perpetuated what they had seen at home without knowing why. But these people had a strong sense of "national" unity.

Problems of Transition

The German Jews and their leaders helped them sacrificially. The job was staggering. The number of immigrants was ten times larger than the entire Jewish population of America up to that time. Transferring their own emotions to the immigrants, these German Jews decided to Americanize them as quickly as possible, and to reform them in their own image. It was not all unselfishness. German Jews themselves were not quite fully secure in the American environment, and the new and foreign element made them apprehensive. Would these newcomers jeopardize the position of the older Jewish community? Thus the German Jews both helped and kept aloof, for they did not wish to be confused with them in the public mind. A cleavage arose which only time could slowly heal. The newcomers wanted to become Americans, but on their own terms and out of their own efforts. They were willing to bring great sacrifices for their children; to give them an education, possibly through

388

college. But they wished to retain their distinctive Jewish characteristics. Thus German and Eastern Jews drifted apart emotionally.

What could the immigrants do? There was a demand for labor, but it was on the lowest level of employment. They worked in the sweatshops of the garment industry. They might get themselves a pushcart and peddle notions or vegetables. They starved. But their concern for improvement did not blot out in their hearts the Jewish ideal of social justice. Looking beyond their own needs, they became spokesmen and organizers in the labor movement. This explains the emergence of men like Samuel Gompers, cigarmaker from London and founder of the A.F.L. It was typical for Jews to want to learn, even while working. The cigarmakers appointed a reader to teach them while they were rolling cigars. They worked, they learned, they organized; Yiddish was for some time the language of the labor movement in New York. A new type of Jew emerged, idealistic, socialistic, but no longer religious. He was proud to be a Jew, but had no contact with the synagogue and desired none. It had become irrelevant to him.

Parents and Children

The religious Jew had his problems too. One of them were his children. The natural conflict between parents and children was severely aggravated by circumstances. To the father, religion was a bulwark against the world; the smallest step beyond its walls might lead to desertion. To the son in his American school, cooperation, participation, and wholehearted identification with society became an ideal, part of his education. This was more than the parents had bargained for when they sent their children to school. The fathers did not understand that, in America, cooperation would not interfere with the faith of a Jew; the sons could not understand their fathers' outlandishness. To the parents, any change in religious custom was treason: "If you don't keep it all, you may as well give it up entirely." And the children, seeing no purpose in keeping it all, gave it up. Unfortunately, the parents had neither the insight nor the equipment to explain the meaning of Judaism to their children. On the other hand, the school did explain the world along the lines of science. The contrast between unexplained tradition and the scientific world view sharpened the conflict between the generations. The children abandoned religion—but not their Jewishness. It became an emotional attachment, expressing itself in deep devotion to their parents, or in the fight for Jewish rights, or perhaps only in a love for Jewish food and a nostalgia for Yiddish tunes. As the new generation acquired means, it came to the fore in their charity, eventually finding an outlet in Zionism. The secular Jew had arrived. He was profoundly interested in Jewish culture, though not in Jewish religion.

Prejudice

Another misunderstanding arose from the rapid transition from the medieval village to the American city. Thrown into this great melting pot where all differences were to disappear, a great many of the immigrants believed that America demanded the sacrifice of their individuality. In other words, a little less Jewishness makes for a little more Americanism. Judaism was reduced to an absolute minimum.

The Jews felt at home only among themselves—the effects of many centuries of oppression cannot be wiped out in one generation or two. As their status improved, they changed their residences and moved to better sections of their town—but they remained together. As soon as one Jew started the movement to a new location, others quickly followed. Before long the new district had become a Jewish district. But this was not entirely the fault of the Jews. America has been the land of the free; it has not been a land without prejudice.

Throughout American history we find movements directed against foreigners, against Catholics, and against Jews. Racial theories found acceptance, and have been reflected in the official immigration policies of the United States; "Nordics" have been favored over immigrants from other parts of the world. Movements such as the "Know Nothing Party" had anti-Jewish trends, and so did the Ku Klux Klan. After World War I, Henry Ford became the unwitting instrument of bigotry. A political brochure, once concocted against Napoleon III, described his supposed plans for world domination. Under Czarist influence the names were changed, and the Jews were now made the secret schemers for world rule. The title of the vicious pamphlet was "The Protocols of the Elders of Zion." Ford gave it publicity in the United States. Appraised of its untruth, he apologized, yet the harm was done. The slander is still about. How many people in the world have been turned to anti-Semitism by it will never be known.

The result of this feeling of prejudice has been noticed in many ways. In times of recession, Jews found it extremely difficult to obtain employment. Again, as in Europe, they were forced to open stores on main street. And again, as their names were displayed along the thoroughfares of American cities and towns, they were accused of owning too much of America. Few realized that they followed this line out of necessity. Colleges and universities placed restrictions on the number of Jewish students they would admit, a limitation which had not existed in Germany. It forced the Jewish student, even in high school, to work twice as hard for good grades as his Christian fellow. He had to be tops to get into college. Of course it set him apart from the rest of the class. When there were opportunities, the Jew flocked to them. Civil service was one of them, and the movie industry, at a time when it was young, untried, and no one wanted to risk his time, money, and energy on it, was another. They were excluded from hotels with "restricted clientele," from certain health resorts, country clubs and Greek letter organizations. When they organized their own, they were blamed for being clannish. These conditions have improved, but have not yet been fully remedied. A curtain of separation still seems to settle between Christians and Jews at five o'clock every evening. They work together but have no social contact with each other. Homes are not open to them in normal exchange of friendly sociability. Thus Jews have remained on the outside; it has been held against them as an excuse for continued exclusion.

Constantly on guard against efforts to undermine their position, American Jews have had to form defense organizations. The American Jewish Committee, founded in 1906 in the wake of the Kishinev pogroms in Russia, was the first of these. Headed initially by Mayer Sulzberger, an outstanding judge, who was followed by Louis Marshall, a great lawyer, it was and is concerned with the rights of Jews all over the world. Rabbi Stephen Wise spearheaded the American Jewish Congress, whose intention was to give a broader *popular* base to the representation of Jewish rights than the Committee seemed to afford. Organized in 1922, it was under Wise's leadership expanded into a World Jewish Congress in 1936, as Nazi atrocities reached ever greater heights. B'nai B'rith has also entered the field of defense through its Anti-Defamation league.

The synagogue could not undertake the task. It had become atomized as each group of arrivals huddled around its own tiny congregation. The larger organizations of synagogues which gradually emerged were fighting on doctrinal lines, and unable to come to agreement. A "Synagogue Council of America" was founded to be the spokesman for all branches of religious Judaism, but only in recent years has it begun to make any impact at all. It still faces an uphill fight, both internally and in its efforts to be recognized as a spokesman for Judaism. The Jewish Welfare Board, a lay organization and organizer of YMHA's and Jewish Community Centers, has become the official agency certifying chaplains for the armed services. The ultimate approval of these men lies however with the rabbinical bodies. In interfaith projects we may frequently find Catholics and Protestants represented by their churches, while a lay organization is speaking for Judaism. Student foundations at colleges and universities, the Hillel Houses, corresponding to the Newman Clubs or Wesley Foundations, have been sponsored by B'nai B'rith. The synagogue simply has been too weak to undertake the job, but the directors of Hillel Houses are ordained rabbis.

These organizations have done an outstanding job, and lay initiative has had its good sides. In Hillel Houses and the chaplaincy, these lay organizations have had to draw equally from all branches of Judaism. The rabbis in turn, whether orthodox, conservative, or reform, have had to minister to students and soldiers of different religious convictions. This has brought greater unity among the various religious groups.

Henrietta Szold

Among the many personages who crowd the scene of these years, one great woman stands out for her lasting achievement. Henrietta Szold, born the daughter of a Baltimore Rabbi in 1860, saw the deeper needs of "defense." She became co-founder and secretary of the Jewish Publication Society, editing Jewish works which would bring inner strength to American Jews out of the sources of Judaism. Then, imbued with a deep love for Palestine, she founded Hadassah, the organization of Zionist women. In 1920 she went to Palestine to lay the foundations of the great medical work which was to bring healing to Jew and Arab alike, culminating in the great Hadassah Hospital completed in 1960. When the Nazis overran Germany, she organized "Youth Aliyah," bringing thousands of youngsters to Israel and a new life. She died in Israel in 1945, one of the truly great women of our age.

Immigration from Eastern Europe has given American Jewry both the manpower and the resources for creative and constructive efforts in every field of endeavor. It has made American Jewry the leading Jewry in the world today. In the religious field, it has powerfully influenced the development of Conservative Judaism.

The Jewish Theological Seminary of America.

Solomon Schechter.

CONSERVATIVE JUDAISM

The immigrants transformed themselves into Americans, eventually finding the European style synagogues inadequate for their needs. They admired the decorum of the reform synagogue, but missed in it the warmth and intimacy which they desired. Neither could they accept the radical departure from tradition which, at that time, was the rule. They were not at home. The very term "Reform" was repugnant to them. Out of their need Conservatism emerged. It might have come anyway; now need gave impetus to the movement.

Isaac Leeser was dead. His successor, Sabato Morais, followed in his path. He called for the founding of a traditional rabbinical seminary which got under way slowly and falteringly. It was soon to acquire status and strength, and to develop into the backbone of traditional Judaism. An inspiring leader, Solomon Schechter, was found.

Solomon Schechter (1850–1915)

Schechter was called by the leading laymen of the time to assume the presidency of the seminary. He was a remarkable man.

Born in Rumania and brought up as a talmudic scholar, he acquired his secular education at Vienna and Berlin, and was eventually called to Cambridge University in England, where he became famous. By accident a few scraps of medieval manuscripts were brought to his attention, and he followed the lead they presented. It took him to Cairo, Egypt. There, in an ancient synagogue, he discovered a "genizah," a hidden storage place of discarded books. Forbidden by religious law to destroy sacred scriptures, or even scraps of them, the Jews of Cairo had deposited them in a cellar of the synagogue. The find was a treasure house of wealth. Texts, such as the works of Ben Sirah, never known in their Hebrew version, were discovered, together with original manuscripts of Maimonides and many others. Tattered and torn as some of them were, they were nevertheless of momentous significance. Schechter carted them to Cambridge and began the work of editing. Then he was called to give up his position as one of the world's great scholars at one of the world's great universities to accept the presidency of a new, small, struggling school. That he accepted speaks for his idealism.

Schechter was deeply influenced by German Jewish scholarship and philosophy. From 1879 to 1882 he had studied at the Hochschule, the Rabbinical Seminary developed by Abraham Geiger. Ideologically, however, he became a disciple of the school of Zachariah Frankel, the school of "positive historical Judaism." He endorsed the very name of Frankel's Breslau seminary for his own rabbinical seminary, calling it The Jewish Theological Seminary of America. Like Frankel, he was interested in the organic growth of Judaism, and like him he was convinced that each generation must add its share to the unfolding destiny of the living body of the Jewish people.

The historical school has never . . . offered the world a theological programme of its own . . . Its theological position may perhaps be thus defined: It is not mere revealed Bible that is of first importance to the Jew, but the Bible as it repeats itself in history, in other words as it is interpreted by Tradition . . . Since . . . the interpretation of Scripture . . . is mainly a product of changing historical influences, it follows that the centre of authority is actually removed from the Bible, and placed in some "living body," which, by reason of its being in touch with the ideal aspirations and the religious needs of the age, is best able to determine the nature of the . . . meaning. This living body, however, is not represented by any section of the nation, or any corporate priesthood, or Rabbihood, but by the collective conscience of Catholic Israel as embodied in the Universal Synagogue . . . We may, therefore, safely trust that the Synagogue will again assert its divine right in passing judgement upon the Bible when it feels called upon to exercise that holy office . . . God's choice invariably coincides with the wishes of Israel; He "performeth all things" upon which the councils of Israel, meeting under promise of divine presence and communion, have previously agreed . . . Liberty was always given to the great teachers of every generation to make modifications and innovations in harmony with the spirit of existing institutions. Hence a return to Mosaism would be illegal, pernicious and indeed impossible. The norm as well as the sanction of Judaism is the practice actually in vogue. Its consecration is the consecration of general use—or, in other words, of Catholic Israel.[1]

Catholic to Schechter means universal, all-embracing. The Jewish people as a whole fashions its pattern of life, its interpretation of Torah.

Like Wise before him, Schechter hoped to create an all-embracing Judaism in America. Like Wise, he did not succeed. When he became president of the Jewish Theological Seminary, Kaufmann Kohler was head of the Hebrew Union College. Reform was going through a radical phase under Kohler's leadership. The two men respected each other, but Schechter saw in himself "the loyal opposition." This is important; he disagreed with all his might, but made it clear that the bond of Catholic Judaism was not then, and never could, be broken.

Organizationally, Schechter followed Wise's pattern. In the United Synagogue he laid the foundation of a congregational organization which embraces more than 600 congregations today. The Rabbinical Assembly became the national body of the world conservative rabbinate. A worldwide organization of conservative synagogues was created.

Conservative Judaism has grown to great strength, both in number and in spirit. The Theological Seminary today owns the greatest collection of Jewish manuscripts ever assembled in the world. Affiliated with it is a branch, the University of Judaism at Los Angeles, serving the western half of the United States and a Center at Jerusalem. A museum has become one of the showplaces of New York. The seminary has sponsored radio and television programs for many years. In its Institute of Religious and Social Studies it gathers scholars of all religions for research in the problems of life and the solutions religion has to offer. Schools for cantors, for teachers, and for general Jewish studies are affiliated with the seminary. Men's clubs, women's clubs, youth organizations, attached to congregations, are centrally directed. Youth camps and student organizations have been organized. The day-school idea is spreading. Numerous publications carry information and instruction to almost every conservative home, and a series of text books have been issued for religious instruction. The conservative movement has high achievements to its credit, but it has had to meet some serious problems.

The character of Conservative Judaism

In a sense, conservatism reflects the pragmatism of America. As William James has pointed out, we are reluctant to adopt new ideas. We prefer to stretch our old concepts wide enough to admit some new ones, and then try to amalgamate old and new ideas.[2] Then the stretch-

---

[1] Norman Bentwich, ed., *Selected Writings of Solomon Schechter* (Oxford: East and West Library, 1946), pp. 35 f.

[2] William James, *Pragmatism, and other Essays* (New York: Meridian Books, Inc., 1955).

ing process is renewed. At any given time this may lead to inconsistencies in thought and in action, but such is human nature. These inconsistencies are evident in Conservative Judaism, as it is constantly trying to combine the old and the new. Its growth is based on the organic evolution of the spirit of Judaism through the Jewish people, so the laity has a great deal of influence. As it accepts and incorporates new ideas and practices, they become part of the structure of Judaism; Judaism grows with the times. In this situation, the rabbi becomes advisor and persuader, rather than leader. This is a danger. The national body will sanction changes only after they have been adopted by the people. In the meantime there is experimenting, and with it conflict of views and opinions. Among the congregations there may be wide divergences of belief; some of them may be Orthodox, for all practical purposes, others may come very close to Reform. Changes in the membership of a congregation may lead to grave upheavals as new ideas—perhaps voiced by new members—wrestle with older ones. This may be one reason why a high percentage of rabbis have been known to change pulpits in some years.

But there is great vitality in conservative Judaism. After a slow start it has recently made rapid progress in numbers. Like Reform congregations, the individual synagogues can give their members what they need; they can adjust to changed needs and conditions.

Actually, the distance between the two movements has narrowed down in many instances, and they may eventually be found very close to the imaginary line that divides them. The same development took place in Germany.

Some principles

Stressing the peoplehood of the Jews, Conservatism has made efforts to maintain those characteristics which testify to the character of the Jews as a people. It is positively Zionist, and insists on the study and use of Hebrew in ever-increasing degree. In line with Schechter's thinking, it considers the experiences of the Jewish people as the basic source of revelation. True to its conservative outlook, it maintains that the laws of Judaism may not be changed lightly. Halakhah is binding, but may be interpreted and stretched. Dietary laws and strict Sabbath observance are compulsory. Through them and through Hebrew, the unity of the Jewish people is symbolically expressed and physically maintained. The Bible need not be regarded as literally revealed, but it is to be regarded as true, for it is the revelation of the Jewish people's communion with God. The truth of the Bible does not lie in its historical accuracy, but in its meaning for the life of the Jew and the life of mankind. Tradition and change confront each other in eternal, creative tension.

RECONSTRUCTIONISM

Reconstructionism is a school of thought grown into a denomination. Its roots are American. Its founder, Mordecai M. Kaplan (born 1881), was still active in 1972. One of the greatest intellects in Jewry, he has been equally distinguished by his great humanity.

The aim of Reconstructionism has been to revitalize Judaism and make it meaningful for modern, scientifically oriented Jews. Mordecai Kaplan realized that many Jews did not feel at home, intellectually and ideologically, in any of the existing "denominations" of Jewry. Yet these people quite frequently were looking desperately for a meaning of their lives as Jews and for a Jewish direction enabling them to face the future with courage. Intellectual honesty, undergirded by Mordecai Kaplan's deep love of the Jewish people and his compassionate love for every individual person, motivated him to advance his ideas, organize a congregation in New York as their testing ground, and then develop the organization into a movement that has grown into a "denomination" itself without abandoning its impact on all segments of Jewry.

Kaplan has established a *Federation of Reconstructionist Congregations* (1955); *Fellowships* (Haburot) exist throughout the country. In 1968 a *Rabbinical College* was opened in Philadelphia. Its students must also be enrolled in a Ph.D. program at Temple University in order to function as college teachers as well as rabbis upon graduation. The movement has its own press, has issued prayer books, the magazine *The Reconstructionist* serves as its mouthpiece.

In the 1970s, over 90 years old, Kaplan engaged in a teaching activity in Israel, realizing the people's search for a meaningful, modern Judaism. Reconstructionism began to cast roots there and gained affiliates.

Mordecai Kaplan

Mordecai Kaplan has been influenced by John Dewey, Achad Ha-am and Emile Durkheim. To Dewey, the value of an idea is to be measured by its effect on the *lives* of its adherents; to Kaplan, Judaism is to be measured by the help it gives the Jew to fulfil the promise of his life as a person, member of the Jewish people and of mankind. Also like Dewey, Kaplan is a naturalist; he rejects supernatural revelation and dispensation. To Achad Ha-am, Israel is the hub of Jewish life; Kaplan sees a two-way street of cultural interaction between Israel and Diaspora. Durkheim, a sociologist, has held that a people is more than the sum of its members. A people develops a spiritual ideal by which its individual members are lifted up. The common ideal unites them. It challenges every individual member to strive in his own life towards the values and ideals his people

Dr. Mordecai M. Kaplan.

has collectively developed. By identifying with his people and his people's spirit the individual person *transcends* his small, self-centered concerns and links himself to *ultimate concerns*. In return he is given an orientation in life and the security and courage that result from his sense of belonging. Interpreting Durkheim in this manner, Kaplan applied these insights to the Jewish people.

The Concept of God. Every individual and all peoples have needs, including shelter, sustenance and orientation.

In striving for the fulfilment of their needs individual persons and peoples establish *values*. For a person without shelter finding a home is a value. This value affects his life and his actions. His situation *is*: he is homeless; the situation *ought to be*: he has found shelter. The value has entered his life, it motivates his actions; he will be in search of a home, he may equally be in search of work permitting him to rent or to buy a home. The value (his shelter) is not merely his goal; it is also the *power* that makes him strive for a home and permeates his life and actions. The value leads him from that which *is* toward that which *ought to be*. Peoples also establish values. These are not simply the sum total of the values held by their members, they are more. The values of a people as a whole emerge from the collective life of the people. This had been pointed out by Durkheim. The people's values actually form the unity and the character of the people.

They see the world as it *is*, envision it as it *ought to be* to meet their needs, and try to devise *means* of obtaining fulfilment. They call their ultimate need God.

A people's *god* is this people's ultimate value; ideally this value becomes the concern of every member of the people, his ultimate concern that enters every thought and action, stands before him as his goal and gives him the power to strive for the goal. It enters his life providing him with orientation, direction and courage. If we see a people's god as *the people's ultimate value* then we must say that the people *create* their god, their ultimate value, out of their collective spirit. This is Kaplan's view.

In search of the ultimate need and ultimate value of the Jewish people Kaplan arrived at a momentous conclusion:

The Jewish people has ethical nationhood as its ultimate need and value.

Out of this collective need the *Jewish people created* its God concept: the God of ethics. This is a reversal of the common idea that *God created Israel;* Kaplan has called it his "galilean revolution."

The authors of Scripture and the masters of the Talmud and their great successors could not yet perceive this fact. A demythologization of Scripture will reveal it, and, at the same time, make Scripture and tradition meaningful for the scientifically oriented Jew who cannot accept any supernaturalistic theology. As ultimate value, God enters the life of the Jewish people and of all its members.

God is not a personal God. He is the Power which makes me follow ever higher ideals. As power, He is at the same time present *in me* to give me the strength to pursue ever higher goals.

The release and activation of this power in the individual Jew and in the Jewish people is *Jewish Religion.* Religion is therefore to be distinguished from science. Science *explains* nature and society; science states that which *is.* It does not tell me that which *ought to be.* Science does not reveal values; science does not reveal God, for God is not the same as nature. Science cannot explain the *power* that elevates man to act ethically. This power is God. God is in the consciousness of men, telling them how nature and society shall be transformed to be what they *ought* to be: in Jewish view, *ethical.* As the power that pulls man and society toward ethical perfection and tells them how to use nature for ethical purposes, God is *trans-natural.*

Jewish Religion and Practice

In order that the Jewish God remain a living force for ethical growth two conditions have to be met: God may not be merely a theological idea, He must be a real presence in every Jew's consciousness, the power that leads him. In addition, the Jewish people must exist as an organic whole and must evolve organically, in order that the *spirit* of the people may unfold within the *body* of a living people.

God must not merely be held as an idea; He must be felt as a presence, if we want not only to know about God but to know God.[3]

When I pray I feel this presence. It leads me to ethical action.

Jewish rituals and holidays have to be equally understood as serving

---

[3] Mordecai M. Kaplan, *The Meaning of God in Modern Jewish Religion* (New York: Reconstructionist Foundation, 1937), p. 244.

the twofold goal of making real the presence of God and of maintaining the Jewish people.

The Sabbath, for instance, brings to mind and heart that God is the Power which makes for salvation. But we must not think of "salvation" in a supernatural sense. The Sabbath removes from me the burden of work; it makes me feel free. It must give me the will and the strength to use my freedom in behalf of others, to build a world in which more and more people shall be free, until all are free and may rest. The High Holy Days are days of regeneration, conveying the message that God is the Power that makes for Regeneration of Human Nature. Obviously they are designed to help us cast off the evil of the past and start anew with determination to build a better world. Nothing in these days has supernatural characteristics of divine grace blotting out human sins. The other holidays hold similar messages.

These observances and rites were created by the Jewish people as *means* to follow the ideal. They are expressions of the people. They remind every member of his belongingness and show him what he *ought* to do; they serve as symbols. Every people has *sancta,* holy symbols. They may be acts, observances, or rites, but they all link the members of a people to their national ideals, history, and deepest aspirations. As Americans we have such a sanctum in our flag. When we see it we are touched by the greatness of our country, by its history, the men who fought and died for it; we are inspired to give greater allegiance to democracy, and to serve our country with full devotion. The flag has released all these feelings in us. Jewish practices are also sancta, offering inspiration and awakening the spirit of dedication. In order to have this effect, the sancta must be meaningful; the commandments and practices must have the power to arouse us. If we find that a practice and ritual no longer has any meaning for us, we should try to re-interpret it and give it new content. We should always favor a conservative approach to national sancta, but if we cannot find any meaning at all, then we may eliminate it. This is a personal matter. No stigma attaches to any Jew who has discarded practices that have become meaningless for him, even if they mean much to us. Thus do we "reconstruct" Judaism, hence the term Reconstructionism.

Kaplan's ideas have been attacked with great violence by orthodoxy, yet even this group has been influenced by them. Evaluating his philosophy, we find several problems. In denying the chosenness of Israel, Reconstructionism overlooks the fact that the will to survive did not save other groups from extinction. There seems to be a divine ordination in the survival of the Jewish people. The will of the people, tested in trial, was matched by historical developments throughout the ages over which the Jews had no control. And history, somehow, has always opened new avenues of life to a remnant of Israel. It is not unreasonable to see in these developments the guiding hand of God, but this also means that we acknowledge a God who shapes history as its Master. Reconstructionism, on the other hand, denies a personal God. It may be asked if it does not deprive us of a powerful source of strength in doing so. In scientific analysis of the God concept, we may be very logical. In moments of anxiety, of need, of guilt we may need a personal God to Whom we can talk and confess, and on Whom we can lean. This may be inconsistent, but it is also human nature.

And yet, Reconstructionism demonstrates the breadth of Judaism. Its foundation is the concept of the House of Israel, the family to which all belong. As such, it has become a source of unity; whoever is interested in Jewish survival is welcomed into its ranks. It has become a meeting ground of conservative and reform Jews and rabbis, and of secularists, because of its scientific and logical approach. Its motto is intellectual and spiritual honesty and truth. Although its doctrines may appear cold, once implemented they generate the warmth of human fellowship; no one has exemplified this better than Mordecai Kaplan himself. A logical thinker of deep convictions, he is a man of great warmth, free from narrowness of thought and free from prejudice, with an incorruptible sense of justice and an infinite measure of love.

The Character of Reconstructionism

Reconstructionism, as we have seen, holds the idea that Jews are a people, *not a chosen people*, but simply a people who wish to survive. The Jewish people is composed of those Jews who wish to live Jewishly. It does not matter whether they are orthodox, conservative, reformed, or secularists. This Jewish people has its hub in the land of Israel. This does not mean that all Jews should go there; it does mean that Israel and diaspora influence each other.

As a people, Jews are more than a religion. They are creative in many fields outside religion, for Judaism is a civilization, expressing itself in art, music, literature, and other forms. It is a civilization which never stands still—an evolving civilization. It is impossible, however, to speak of Judaism without recognizing its religious roots and basically religious character. Take away religion, and Judaism loses its strength. Judaism is "an evolving religious civilization." This civilization enhances the lives of its followers, and makes life more meaningful and more holy. It equips the Jew to serve God by serving man.

To fulfil its ideal of peoplehood the Jewish people must restore itself as an organic whole, the divisions in Jewry must be overcome. It must also strive toward fulfilment of its collective folk spirit which is *ethical nationhood*.

Kaplan links his ideas to the social message of the prophets, and gives it a modern meaning: We must all strive for the ideal society. The ideal society is reached in an ideal democracy, and a workshop of this democracy is America. Here human society has reached a higher state of perfection than anywhere else in the world, but it is far from perfect. *It stands forever in need of improvement.* To work for it is the duty of every man, of every Jew. For Kaplan the documents of American Democracy are "Scriptures" in the sense of holy scriptures. Every Jew must be fully American and fully Jew and live in *two civilizations,* the American and the Jewish. The Jewish people does not exist unto itself.

The purpose of every civilization is to make a contribution to mankind. The Jews are no exception. They serve mankind best by retaining their identity.

What distinguishes Reconstructionism, next to its naturalism, is its intellectual honesty. We must evaluate tradition, not merely retain it because it has always been thus. The reconstruction of Judaism is based on action. We must work to strengthen Jewish civilization and the bonds to Israel and between individual Jews. We must work with all men to improve our world and strengthen democracy.

Reconstructionism is intended to awaken in our people the corporate will to live and to function as a source of human good.[4]

Reconstructionism: An Example of Judaism's Flexibility

Judaism, as Mendelssohn has said, is commandment. It faces realistically the hard realities of life and calls for action. It is, as Rabbi Leo Baeck has pointed out, "classical religiousness," based on order, moral law, duty, and ethical action. It looks forward. Christianity, in contrast, is "romantic religiousness," [5] based on "the feeling of absolute dependence," [6] on faith, grace, mood, surrender, and emotion. It looks backward. Traditional Christianity demands of its faithful the acceptance of a definite cosmology and theology, requiring a measure of obedience so complete that it may include surrender of free intellectual search. There must be faith, emotional acceptance of the basic ideas of the Church. This makes a Christian.

But a great many modern persons have been schooled on the principles of science; scientific cosmology and Christian cosmology are far apart. The Christian may therefore be confronted by a dilemma: either

---

[4] Mordecai M. Kaplan, *The Future of the American Jew* (New York: The Macmillan Company, 1948), p. xvii.

[5] Leo Baeck, "Romantic Religion," in *Judaism and Christianity* (Philadelphia: Jewish Publication Society of America, 1958), pp. 189 ff. See also his essay, "The Character of Judaism," in his work, *The Pharisees* (New York: Schocken Books, Inc., 1947). Here Baeck divides the world into two "domains"—one in which the dynamic spirit of Judaism entered and man became God's active co-worker, the other where this divine spirit has not entered and the striving for the messianic future of universal justice is therefore not recognized as the task of the individual and of the society of responsible individuals. Judaism combines introspection with action.

[6] Schleiermacher's definition of religion, quoted by Baeck, *op. cit.,* p. 192.

Christianity or science. A great many seem to have chosen science, which immediately presents them with another pitfall. Science deals with matter. It has no room for introspection, which man needs so badly. In their quest for an answer, numerous earnest seekers have turned to the introspective religions of the Far East, but these religions have different ideals. To them man must wipe out his individuality, his striving, and dissolve himself in the great ocean of the universe. He is no longer co-worker with God. This then is the proposition: either Christianity or materialism or introspection; either individual striving or the denial of man's creative function in the divine scheme of things.

Reconstructionism has shown that Judaism is wide enough to permit, within its framework, the existence of a school of thought that has a scientific cosmology and theology, calls for both introspection and action, and is not materialistic. This shows that a modern solution in religion may be attempted which takes into consideration the changing outlook of changing times. There need be no dilemma for the searching modern Jew, for search is permitted, and answers may be found which satisfy the soul without antagonizing the intellect. Judaism is "classical religion," a true synthesis of ideals leading out into the ethical act.

ORTHODOXY

The immigrants from Eastern Europe were orthodox. Theirs was a pre-Mendelssohnian religion, a faith that does not doubt, that had never known of or been influenced by Samson Raphael Hirsch. American orthodoxy could not have followed him. Hirsch's orthodoxy called for a highly developed cultural awareness, general education, and a philosophical mind, none of which were found among the immigrants. In addition, Hirsch's orthodoxy was "German," its very character alien to Eastern European Jewry. They were suspicious of it; they were afraid it might lead out of Judaism.

Orthodox Jewry, on its arrival, was deeply split. Every group had its own synagogue, its own rabbi, its own individual intensity of practice and observance. These shadings were minute, yet they meant a world of difference to those who held them dear. The effects can still be felt. Although there has been a certain amount of organization in American orthodoxy, it is still far from the unity which we find in Reform and Conservative organizations. There are rivalries between rabbis trained in Europe and others trained in America, between college-educated rabbis and those who would consider this kind of training unjewish, between "left-wing," Hirsch-oriented, and pre-Mendelssohnian factions of old-time Judaism. Some of these, like the "Lubavitcher Rebbe" and his school system have appealed to many by their vitality and warmth.

Two rabbinical organizations, however, encompass the majority of orthodox rabbis. These are the Union of Orthodox Rabbis in the United States and Canada, and the Rabbinical Council of America. The outstanding rabbinical training school for orthodox rabbis is Yeshivah University in New York. Starting as a small rabbinical school, in Hebrew a *yeshivah*, it has developed rapidly into a full-fledged university of highest academic standards. Its center, the rabbinical seminary, is surrounded by other schools: a liberal arts college, a college for women, and graduate departments. Yeshivah's great pride is the Albert Einstein Medical School, an institution ranking high among the accredited institutions for the training of physicians. It is not restricted to orthodox students. In this sense, the ideal of Samson Raphael Hirsch has found fulfilment. These schools and the numerous day schools throughout the country reflect Hirsch's thoughts. For Hirsch believed that only a synthesis of Judaism and worldly education and culture could make the Jew whole. Of course, some of these schools may be in operation as a concession to the times, to give Jewish students—who, after all need general knowledge to find their way in the world—an education within a Jewish environment.

There are also a number of congregational organizations. Of these, the Union of Jewish Orthodox Congregations is the largest. Like Conservatism, Orthodoxy has thus—at a distance—followed the pattern established by Isaac Meyer Wise: Rabbinical organization, seminary, and congregational organization.

The Character of Orthodoxy

Orthodoxy regards itself as the only true Judaism. A Jew who is not orthodox is simply a sinful Jew.

Orthodoxy maintains that God personally revealed Himself at Sinai, choosing the people of Israel as a holy people. The function of the Jewish people need not necessarily concern us; it is whatever God had in mind when He fashioned them. It could be a mission to the world, but it need not be a mission. It is simply God's will that they exist. God, who is personal, directs and guides the affairs of the world and of every single person, listening to prayer and answering it in accordance with His decision. In Torah He gave His law to Israel, and Israel must obey it. The words of the Torah are literally His words, explaining why major changes in the law are impossible. Since He has ordained that there may be no fire on the Sabbath, any kind of fire is prohibited, be it the ignition in an automobile or the glow in a radio tube. For He who sees the world from eternity to eternity knew of all the modern inventions at the time He gave the law. Had He wished to except them He would have said so. The Torah did invest the rabbis with a certain limited authority to interpret the law, and this makes development possible. But it must be within the framework of the divine Torah and in line with the discussions in the Talmud. Ultimately the Shulhan Arukh and R'MO remain the basic codes to be followed. Changes, therefore, will be few and limited to individual situations. Permission was recently granted to use electric dishwashers for both milk and meat dishes; of course they may not be washed together, and certain arrangements have to be made to clean the washer between the two operations.[7]

The primary function of the Jew is to follow and obey the law. This law regulates not only religious practices, but affects practically every moment of life, from rising and washing to food and business, sex and marriage, for the individual and for society. It shapes the outlook of the orthodox Jew in philosophy, psychology, social sciences, and all the other disciplines of life. To abide by it truly and faithfully is the function of his life on earth. To him who has earnestly toiled to live up to the law, there arises hope of life eternal and of resurrection in days to come. On earth, there is the expectation of the coming of the Messiah in physical form, a man who will gather Israel from the "four corners of the earth" to its homeland, and will bring peace and brotherhood to all humanity. Orthodox Judaism is a faith which offers peace of mind to those who abide by it in all its details. It banishes anxiety, exacting great demands and holding great beauty. Man is secure.

Orthodox Jewry, in its majority, is zionistic. A small minority still feels that Israel's redemption may not be attempted by human means, but must await God's hour and supernatural interference. Those who approve of the State of Israel have hailed it as a place where the law of the Torah can be lived fully, and can actually become the constitution of the land. This has also created difficulties.

Orthodoxy and Israel

In Israel, orthodoxy is the official religion of the state; no other Jewish denomination is permitted to function. This has led to the paradox that, in Israel, all non-Jewish religions and sects may operate freely and be supported by the government, while Jews must abide by orthodox law if they wish to give any expression to religion. Many people, unable to follow orthodox religion in good conscience, have no choice but to abandon religion altogether. Movements to establish American-sponsored conservative and reform synagogues have run into strenuous opposition. The reason for this development is historical. Under Turkish rule, each religious group was placed under the jurisdiction of its clergy. When Britain assumed power over Palestine under the mandate of the League of Nations, the practice was continued, and the Jews were placed under the authority of the orthodox rabbinate, which was maintained by gov-

---

[7] Emanuel Rackman, "What is Orthodox Judaism?" in *Jewish Heritage*, Vol. 2, No. 3, p. 8.

ernment funds. Then the Jewish state was established, and it could not deny to its own rabbis the rights which the non-Jewish mandate's power had granted them. Since then, orthodoxy has organized a small political party which frequently holds the balance of power in the K'neset, the Israeli Parliament. Marriage, family, and inheritance laws are governed by religious law; so is public Sabbath observance. The school system is divided into religiously oriented and secular schools. The state itself follows Western law, which differs markedly from Torah. Orthodoxy would like to see this changed. The state claims that it is impossible to operate a modern society on principles and legislation enacted under totally different circumstances. The problem has not been solved, and is a source of continual conflict. Voices have been raised demanding complete separation of Church and State in Israel.

SOME PROBLEMS OF AMERICAN JEWRY

The American environment has made its impact felt. American Jewry and its institutions bear the imprint of the American way of life, as do its problems.

The Impact of Circumstances

Nominally, Orthodoxy claims the largest number of adherents. Its severest problem is that those who profess allegiance to it very often do not live up to its tenets and principles. Everyone, as the saying goes, "writes his own Shulhan Arukh," his own code of laws. A synagogue may be operated on strictly orthodox lines, yet outside its members follow different ways. But this is not a problem confined to Orthodoxy; it exists in all groups of American Jewry. Life with its demands has led all too many away from the synagogue and from a consistent observance of their religious duties, be they orthodox, conservative, or reform. Knowledge of Judaism is small. The Hitler period, making overwhelming demands on the financial resources of American Jews, forced a "moratorium on religion" on Jewish life in America. Fund-raising became the major task, and indeed it has saved millions of lives and made the State of Israel possible. But it pushed religion into the background; study and observance were reduced to minor importance. It was hoped that, once the emergency was over, people would revert to their religious obligations, but unfortunately the emergency is not over yet. American Jewry has had to learn to combine emergency work with constructive efforts to build its own house, both physically and spiritually, and in a physical sense it has accepted the challenge. Hundreds of new synagogues have been built within the last 20 years. Spiritually, however, the commitment leaves much to be desired. There are still many Jews who feel that, in giving of their substance, they have fulfilled their duty. There are many others who are completely lacking in the basic knowledge required for meaningful Jewish living, totally unaware of the proud heritage which is theirs.

Forces of Environment and History

The majority of American Jews today are native-born, and a high percentage are the children of native-born Americans. The antagonism of the second generation against the beliefs of the parents has lessened; it has been replaced by complacency. One lives an average, normal life. A good many people have moved to suburbia and built synagogues, because to have a religious center is part of normal American group life. They are sending their children to Sunday School; this, too, is part of the American way. Feeling uncomfortable in some gentile clubs and organizations, they have transformed their synagogues into social centers, places where one can "let one's hair down." This function of the synagogue is legitimate, it meets a need, but it has often become the central function of the synagogue, replacing worship and education; and that is not good. Attendance at worship has frequently been poor. Rabbis have sometimes been chosen by congregations on the basis of their popularity, both within the congregation and in the Christian community which they serve as ambassadors of Judaism.

Many young Jews have regarded this Jewishness of the "establishment" as unauthentic and have reacted in diametrically opposed ways. Some have devoted themselves exclusively to social action, denying its source in Jewish teachings. Some have joined the Radical Left, following communist lines and demonstrating hostility to Jewish religion and the State of Israel, siding with the Arabs. On the positive side, young Jews have reacted by demanding more allocations for Jewish education, have themselves returned to committed Jewish living. "Haburot" (fellowships) have been founded by students, engaged in experiments to make Judaism relevant. They have published magazines. Free Universities for Jewish studies have sprung up on many campuses.

There are many hopeful signs. The same Hitler terror which made rescue work the number one priority also awakened Jewish consciousness in thousands of hearts where it had long been asleep. In addition to those parents who send their children to Sunday School as a matter of social conformity, there are many who feel that their children should at least know something about Judaism, even if their homes no longer function as a true example of Jewish living. The result has been that the overwhelming number of Jewish children receive some Jewish education, in one-day schools on Sunday and, ever increasingly, in weekday Hebrew instruction and day schools. Practically every child observes Bar Mitzvah or Confirmation. After that, matters do not look so well, yet adult education is being pushed by congregations and national organizations, and the effort is meeting with widening response. Since Hebrew has become the official language of Israel, the study of it has been widely pursued.

The immigration of the Hitler years has brought to America scholars and rabbis from Europe who have put their experiences in the service of American Jewry. Among the laymen who arrived, many had been educated to combine the culture of the world with Jewish civilization, and were deeply religious. Their influx has been helpful and enriching.

We find that Jewish pride has grown. Jews who may not even know how great a treasure they possess in their tradition have won new self-assurance and self-esteem, reflected in a greater readiness of American Jewry to accept converts who come to the faith in sincerity. The State of Israel has strengthened Jewish pride. The emotional impact of the Six-Day War in 1967 has fused Jewry together. Americans of all faiths have shown increased interest in Judaism, and, subsequent to Vatican II, chairs have been established at many universities. With it, the desire to know more about their heritage has grown among Jews.

Cooperation in Faith, Key to the Future

The spiritual progress of American Jewry can be speeded up if the synagogue is given a more central place in communal life, and if the various denominations learn to work together. Today they are divided; this makes for weakness. Through cooperation they could at least begin the gigantic task of bringing in the unaffiliated. The division is ideological, but it is also organizational. National religious bodies compete for the affiliation of congregations as yet uncommitted. They compete for funds, not only against each other but against innumerable other Jewish organizations, all of which are worthy, but all of which appeal to the same constituency. The three synagogue groups depend on each other, whether they know it or not. Reform has given American Judaism the pattern of religious organization. By its nature it can experiment with new ideas and concepts, but since it grants full autonomy to the conscience of the individual, it always faces the danger of falling apart. During the period of "classical Reform," it did indeed drift far away. Conservatism has called it back and forced it to re-evaluate its position and to re-establish beloved rituals. Conservatism has strengthened the awareness of Jewish peoplehood in all of American Jewry. Conservatism, however, has insufficient guidelines. It follows the people, frequently failing to lead them. Reform Judaism is serving it by experimenting with the new, Orthodoxy is helping it by holding it to the old. In its strict adherence to norm, Orthodoxy has remained a bulwark of Jewish steadfastness and a reservoir of tradition. Both Conservatism and Reform have drawn from it. Orthodoxy faces the danger of being mere observance lacking inwardness of heart. Reform and Conservatism have aroused it to rebuild and link itself to the world. Reconstructionism, as a school of thought, has compelled all of them to clarify in their own minds the meaning and purpose of Jewish survival and the reasons for the commandments. To many a layman, this interdependence seems to be instinctively clear. Dual affiliation in two different congregations is not infrequent.

While the practice of religion may have become weaker, American Jews have a strong sense of belonging together, of communality, the sense of *Yiddishkeit*. It may reflect the universally emerging emphasis on "ethnicity." It serves as a power making for survival. Yet, only the affirmation of American Judaism as a *religious* body assures continuation, for, as Will Herberg has pointed out,[7] America recognizes religious diversity and discourages perpetuation of ethnic diversity. The significance of the synagogue is pragmatically recognized by secular and fund-raising Jewish organizations that call on it for support. Religion plus Yiddishkeit is promoted through many local community bureaus of education, serving all Jewish groups impartially.

THEOLOGICAL THOUGHT

The greatest disaster of Jewish history, characterized by Auschwitz, and the greatest fulfilment of Jewish hopes, the Restoration of Israel, have both occurred in our time. This has raised questions: Why did God cause both events? What is the place of the Jew in the divine scheme? How should he react to these events? These are theological questions to which thinkers in all Jewish camps addressed themselves. Jewish theology has therefore had a revival. Within Orthodoxy, *Rav Kook*, Chief Rabbi of Israel until his death in 1935, addressed himself early to the question.

To him, it is the characteristic of religion and the religious person to see not only the unity of God, but also the unity and harmony of the universe as a whole. The spiritual and the material belong together under God's will. Every thought and every action has its place in this unified universe. In the Diaspora, this unity was broken; Jews had no opportunity to express the spirit of holiness in the action of involvement in the physical world. With the return to Israel, this unity was again restored. Rav Kook sees in this return a messianic event. The Spiritual could be fulfilled through the physical. Seen in this light, the work of the non-religious halutz is a spiritual expression: He is a builder.

Rabbi Joseph B. Soloveitchik, considered the greatest halakhic authority in America, takes as a starting point man's loneliness, as a creature of dust. To escape it, the average man immerses himself in society; the Jew must be mindful that in every societal relationship God enters, Jews are covenanted to Him. All human relations and all Jewish conduct must therefore be based on halakhah through which God is included.[1] Halakhah is thus existential theology, whose great implications Soloveitchik has not yet worked out in detail. To orthodox thinkers, the uniqueness of the Jew is established by God. The right-wing *Conservative* Abraham Heschel wishes to evoke an emotional attachment to the life of Eastern European Jewry.

---

[7] Will Herberg, *Catholic, Protestant, Jew;* N.Y. Doubleday, 1955.

[1] Soloveitchik: *The Lonely Man of Faith* (essay).

These Jews did not question, they knew God was there and followed Him; their *total life* was Jewish, was existential theology. God is ineffable, no logic can define Him. Eastern Jewry acknowledged Him *existentially*, took a "leap to God through action"; Western Jews must do the same and relate to God through the performance of Mitzvot. They must regain the childlike wonder at God's world. In prayer they make themselves known to Him, and find Him.

To pray is to take notice of the wonder, to regain a sense of the mystery that animates all beings, the divine margin in all attainments. Prayer is our humble answer to the inconceivable surprise of living. [2]

But prayer is not the complete answer, nor is faith. The true response to God lies in the deed: Mitzvah. This includes social action.

Judaism stands and falls with the idea of the absolute relevance of human deeds. Even to God we ascribe the deed. Imitatio Dei is in deeds. The deed is the source of holiness. [3]

Judaism's special function is to sanctify time. The world sanctifies space and therefore builds cathedrals; the Jew observes the Sabbath as a cathedral of time. Heschel has written widely and masterfully.

Reconstructionist Theology has been explained; *Reform* rabbis have been widely engaged in theology and stand largely under the influence of Buber and Rosenzweig, as Eugene B. Borowitz has pointed out:[4] namely that the Jew has a unique place in history, the Jewish people are God-*given,* and they must be in dialogue with the living God, existentially found. A most distinguished representative of this group is Rabbi *Emil L. Fackenheim,*[5] who is also a philosopher. He asks, how can we understand God's way of balancing justice and mercy in the light of events? The only answer lies in faith, *emunah,* which means *trust* in Him, even if He hides from us or is in eclipse. God created the Jewish people and sustains it for ever. We must accept this truth existentially, even though it can never be proven. This means we must respond to God in Mitzvot, as Rosenzweig has taught it. *Mitzvah* means *Command.* Command presupposes a person who gives it and a person who responds. Both exist: God, the Metzaveh, Commander and the responding Jew. A direct relationship between persons

---

[2] Abraham J. Heschel, *Man's Quest for God* (New York: Charles Scribner's Sons, 1954), p. 5.

[3] *Ibid.,* p. 109.

[4] "On the Commentary Symposium: Alternatives in Creating a Jewish Apologetic," Judaism, Fall 1966, pp. 458-65; see also Introduction to "Condition of Jewish Belief" by Milton Himmelfarb, and an analysis, in conjunction with an excellent evaluation of Jewish theology, in Lou H. Silverman: *"Concerning Jewish Theology in North America: Some Notes on a Decade,"* American Jewish Yearbook, 1969, pp. 37-58.

[5] Emil L. Fackenheim: *In Quest of Past and Future.*

—God and man—is established. The Jew must respond to the living God through Mitzvah. To do less, or to deny the transcendent commanding and protecting God, would grant Hitler a posthumous victory: the destruction of the Jews. Life, existence and survival demand belief in a transcendent God. Jewish religion is not the religious experience of the people's self-transcending mind, as liberals and Reconstructionists hold. It is God's commandment. We have learned from Nazi Germany that a people's mind can self-transcend itself into evil, and that liberal humanism can deteriorate into tyranny. We cannot trust liberalism, humanism or the secular world. They have too often gone astray. We must listen to God instead. Existentially, Jews must acknowledge the transcendent God and respond to Him. Why it all happened under God's will we do not know. We do know that it happened through God, in behalf of the Jewish people, and in behalf of mankind for whom the Jews must be an eternal teacher. From Fackenheim's position it is only a short step to the *existential* acceptance of a personal Messiah, a view held by Steven A. Schwarzschild.

Richard L. Rubenstein, disciple of Mordecai Kaplan, but a deeply pessimistic thinker, takes the opposite position. In his work, *After Auschwitz,* he holds that the last two thousand years were a gigantic historical error. Jews believed that mankind would grow in ethical conduct, and that they were making a contribution toward it. Auschwitz proved them wrong. Mankind never improves. The restoration of Israel has now fulfilled Jewish eschatological expectations: the Jews are going home. As a people like all other peoples they have found rest. Now they have to reverse their whole outlook, to work not *in* history but *outside* of it. They must become pagan. This means, as Mircea Eliade has defined it, living by the cyclical recurrence of nature, away from the historical projections of history. Their life will revolve about nature. But in nature, all that is born returns to nothingness. This too we must accept.

This is the only meaningful religious option remaining to Jews after Auschwitz and the rebirth of Israel.[6] Therefore: "Accept the world in both its joy and horror without illusion. Acknowledge what in fact you already know—that in the final analysis we are of earth and to her we must be true."[7]

But the Mitzvot must be observed, especially archaic ones. They are the creation of the Jewish people, its self-expression, sancta. Rubenstein's views are exceptional as pessimism is not a Jewish trait. They reveal the impact of Auschwitz and the impact of Israel's restoration most clearly.

---

[6] *After Auschwitz,* p. 130.
[7] *Op. cit.,* p. 111.

THE THRUST OF THOUGHT AND TASK

"In action rather than theory resides the focus (of Judaism)" (Abot). This has guided the Jewish people. Franz Rosenzweig concluded his *Star of Redemption* with the words "toward life," seeing in his theological system only a prologue. Mordecai Kaplan has taken philosophy sharply to task by defining it as "the immaculate conception of the mind not sired by experience." Unlike Christianity which emphasizes belief and dogma, Judaism has been essentially action centered, but it has equally stressed study: "The unlearned cannot acquire and live by the fear of God (Abot)." Theology has been forced upon the Jew by the events of our day, for they seem to be beyond human comprehension. Mordecai Kaplan is a great theologian whose definitions have given new directions to Jewish life. We cannot know how deeply the average Jew is affected by systematic Jewish philosophy, but he does speculate. *Communality* is the result of internalized theology as well as folk-feeling: the Jews are a people and regard themselves as kinfolk.

This awareness has found expression in literature as well as theological works. Nelli Sachs, who won the Nobel Prize for literature jointly with S. Y. Agnon, concerned herself with the holocaust *(O The Chimneys)*, but her soul searing poetry is not merely a collection of dirges; it is search for the meaning of Jewish destiny under God; Agnon's mystic-laden stories do the same. Jews have written a great deal, not all of it heroic, much of it reflecting physical and psychological adjustment problems and conditions. Some have traced the experiences of the recent past in Europe and Israel (Eli Wiesel on Russian Jewry), others have gone into history, others have made the modern rabbi into the suffering anti-hero, or even the sleuth who solves murders through talmudic logic. Christian authors have frequently woven Jewish characters into their stories, where they serve as catalysts. The general public has avidly read these works, though some of them were of small literary merit. It has followed the portrayal of Jews on stage, film and television with great interest. Perhaps the individual Jew stands for *the* Jews seen as a collective person by the world. This Jew, the collective person, may have come to represent mankind in its struggle to find the meaning of life. Like Faust in Goethe's work, the Jew is Everyman, striving for salvation, going frequently astray, and yet finding it by benefitting mankind: "He who has striven to perfect himself, to him we grant salvation." (Faust, last scene)

But any collective image may degenerate into a stereotype. Throughout the centuries the Jew is all too often regarded as the embodiment of evil. This view has not been eradicated. It shows itself in the subtle caution that moves many non-Jews in dealing with any Jew. It offers food to the professional anti-Semite. It has found recent expression. Some Black radicals have embraced anti-Semitism. Believing that the Jews were generally disliked by the majority, they may have felt that anti-Semitism, for once, placed them with the majority. Some Jews may have wronged Blacks. As example: Blacks usually have settled in neighborhoods previously occupied by Jews. Many Jews retained the property and became landlords. The landlord has been stereotyped as an evil person. The Jewish landlord became stereotyped as *the* Jew, hence Jews are evil. The majority of the Black population has not been affected by this unfortunate trend. It may have been kept from making common cause with the Jews in the struggle for civil rights. Jews, in turn, have regretted that they may not help the Blacks. They may have to understand, however, that the paternalistic system of help that Jews with their strong family awareness have practiced, must be abandoned.

Anti-Semitism has been exploited by communist countries. We have seen its operation in Russia, although the government denies its existence. When Czechoslovakia was invaded by the Russians in 1968, the Jews were immediately accused of having fomented the "bourgeois" uprising, and were degraded. The freedom movement in Poland, at the same time, was equally brutally suppressed, and the pitiful remnant of the once flourishing Jewish community was so viciously attacked by the government that the world was shocked. Most of them emigrated with the aid of American Jewry. The position of Jews in all communist states, such as Cuba and Chile, is precarious. The stereotype of the evil Jew may be used at any time by leaders in their struggle for power. Jewish communality in action has shown itself not only in the assistance given these Jews for resettlement, but also by the spiritual help rendered them. Through American efforts, rabbinical seminaries have been established and are being maintained in Argentina, to provide leadership for Latin-American Jewry, hopefully in a peaceful future. (The spirit of Vatican II may aid the Jews in these largely Catholic countries.)

Guided by communism, hostile to Israel, the Radical Left has become anti-Zionist, which is just another term for anti-Semitism, as Dr. Martin Luther King, in sharp rebuke of this ideology, once pointed out. Arab leaders have used anti-Jewish stereotypes to arouse their own people emotionally for world propaganda against Israel. Jews have sustained Israel, are prepared to shoulder the burden of the resettlement of those Russian Jews who may emigrate, and to press for full civic and religious rights for those remaining. This is communality in action.

Confronted with the anti-Jewish actions of the Radical Left, Jews, traditionally liberal, have begun to reassess their position, and a trend toward political conservatism may be in the making. A serious problem to be faced by Jews is population control. Can Jews afford it after the losses Jewry has suffered? Having long been known for small families, can they continue to see their proportionate strength diminish within society? The deed, rooted in communal responsibility, will determine the future of the

Jew. It has to be based on thought, especially a greater knowledge of the Jewish heritage that will lead to practice of Judaism and the social action springing from it.

When viewed in the light of the ideal, individual Jews and communities leave much to be desired. Therefore any stereotype distorts their image. But even in the least devoted Jew there is the striving to defend the Jewish "household" and heritage. There is the deep seated need to do his part for the improvement of society. *Judaism's example of courage kindles courage. Judaism has always stressed the intent of men's hearts.* As the task is being performed with courage and conviction, in tune with the spirit of Judaism that calls for universal justice, errors may be forgiven. As George Washington stated it, "the event lies in the hands of God." And the Rabbis said, "It is not your duty to complete the task, yet you are not free to desist from it." (Abot 2:21)

THE DENOMINATIONS
SOME PRACTICAL IMPLICATIONS

In Worship

ORTHODOXY: A quorum of ten men—minyan—is required for public worship. Women, seated in the gallery, do not participate in conducting worship.

CONSERVATISM: A quorum of ten men is required for public worship. Families are usually seated together. Participation of women in conducting worship is presently being experimented with in some congregations.

REFORM: A quorum is not required but desirable. Women have equal status in the synagogue. In 1972 the first woman was ordained as a rabbi.

Sabbath

ORTHODOXY: Neither automobile nor radio may be used.

CONSERVATISM: According to a rabbinical split decision, automobiles may be used to go to worship if there is no other way of getting there; they may not be used otherwise. Radio or television may be turned on only for inspirational programs which befit the spiritual character of the Sabbath.

REFORM: No restrictions.

Wearing of Hats in the Synagogue

ORTHODOXY: Wearing of hats or skull caps is obligatory; they should always be worn.

CONSERVATISM: Wearing of hats or skull caps is obligatory at worship, even at home.

REFORM: Wearing of head covering is optional, but frequently abolished even in synagogue worship.

Divorce

ORTHODOXY: After the civil divorce, a religious divorce must be obtained by the wife from her husband. If he refuses, the woman is still regarded as being married to him according to Jewish law. She cannot remarry.

CONSERVATISM: After civil divorce, a religious divorce must be obtained by the wife from her husband. Before marriage, the groom signs a pledge to grant divorce papers if reconciliation through a rabbinical court fails. This pledge can be enforced, if necessary through the civil courts.

REFORM: Divorce in court is regarded as sufficient.

Agunah

ORTHODOXY: A woman whose husband has disappeared and is presumed dead may not remarry. Evidence of death can be based only on testimony of witnesses who have actually seen the person in death.

CONSERVATISM: The Rabbinical Assembly has been wrestling with the problem for many years.

REFORM: If a civil court declares a person to be legally dead, remarriage of the surviving spouse is permitted.

Conversion

ORTHODOXY: Preparation, circumcision, and immersion in the presence of a rabbinical court of three is required for male converts; preparation and immersion is required for female converts.

CONSERVATISM: The same ritual is required as in orthodoxy.

REFORM: A solemn pledge of acceptance of Judaism after thorough preparation is all that is required. Conservatism recognizes converts who were admitted by Reform rabbis; Orthodoxy recognizes only those converted in strict accordance with its own rules.

Dietary Laws

ORTHODOXY: Absolutely binding in all details.
CONSERVATISM: Generally binding.
REFORM: Not binding.

Prayer and the Prayer Book

The ideas of the groups are mirrored in the prayer book. Some parallels will be quoted. The basic structure of the traditional service is maintained in all of them. The orthodox prayer book is in Hebrew, although translations have been made, and readings in English are provided in some of the more recent books.[1] The English sermon has also been introduced in a great number of congregations, but the traditional service is offered in its entirety. The conservative and reconstructionist prayer books preceded the new orthodox version and served as its pattern.[2] Designed for shorter services, they offer a large selection of readings in English, to be chosen by the rabbi. The reform prayer book is more abridged and has large alterations in the traditional text.[3] Both Hebrew and English are used, but there are large sections of English prayers only. The three non-orthodox groups have regarded revision of their prayer books as an ongoing concern.

A few samples will show how the prayers reflect the ideologies of the group.

The prayer for peace

ORTHODOXY: (Traditional) Grant peace, welfare, blessing, grace, lovingkindness and mercy unto us all and unto all Thy people Israel.[4]

CONSERVATISM: (Greater emphasis on God as Father of all mankind) Grant peace, well-being and blessing unto the world, with grace, lovingkindness and mercy for all and for all Israel Thy people.[5]

RECONSTRUCTIONISM: (Follows the ideas of Conservatism, but the idea that Israel is God's people is omitted. Reconstructionism does not believe in a "chosen people") Grant peace, blessing, lovingkindness and mercy to us and to all who revere Thee.[6]

REFORM: (Israel is called to teach mankind; that is its mission) Grant us peace, Thy most precious gift, O Thou eternal Source of peace, and enable Israel to be its messenger unto the peoples of the earth.[7]

Immortality, the personal Messiah, and resurrection [8]

ORTHODOXY: (Expressing a firm belief in immortality, resurrection and a personal Messiah) Blessed art Thou, O Lord our God and God of our fathers . . . for Thine own sake Thou wilt lovingly bring a Redeemer to their children's children . . . Lord who art mighty for

---

[1] See David De Sola Pool, ed. and trans., *The Siddur,* © 1960 by The Rabbinical Council of America, Inc. (Behrman House, Inc., New York).

[2] See *Sabbath and Festival Prayer Book,* Rabbi Morris Silverman, ed., © 1946 by The Rabbinical Assembly of America and the United Synagogue of America; *Sabbath Prayer Book,* © 1945 by The Jewish Reconstructionist Foundation, Inc., New York. A two-volume high holiday book has also been published.

[3] See *The Union Prayer Book for Jewish Worship,* © 1940, edited and published by The Central Conference of American Rabbis.

[4] Author's translation.

[5] *Sabbath and Festival Prayer Book,* p. 101.

[6] *Sabbath Prayer Book,* p. 137.

[7] *The Union Prayer Book for Jewish Worship,* p. 140.

[8] All prayers are taken from the Amidah.

all eternity, Thou revivest the dead. Thou art great in saving the living, sustaining them in love. Thou upholdest the falling, Thou healest the sick, Thou freest the bound. In Thy great love Thou revivest the dead, keeping faith with those who sleep in the dust ... . Thou wilt keep faith in reviving the dead. Blessed art Thou, Lord who revivest the dead.[9]

CONSERVATISM: (The ideas are carefully phrased to permit individual interpretation. "Redeemer" is spelled with a small "r" and can mean anyone who will bring help. The terms "immortal life" and "calling the dead to life everlasting" permit both a traditionally orthodox and a modern interpretation) Praised art Thou, O Lord our God and God of our fathers . . . Thou wilt in Thy love bring a redeemer to their children's children for the sake of Thy name . . . Thou, O Lord art mighty forever. Thou callest the dead to immortal life . . . in great mercy callest the departed to everlasting life . . . Faithful Thou art to grant eternal life to the departed. Blessed art Thou, O Lord who callest the dead to life everlasting.[10]

RECONSTRUCTIONISM: (The idea of a redeemer is rejected, so is the idea of resurrection. God is a Power) Blessed art Thou, O Lord our God and God of our fathers . . . Thou wilt, in Thy love, bring redemption to their children's children. . . . O Lord mighty for all eternity, Thou aboundest in the power to save. . . . Blessed art Thou, O Lord, who in love rememberest Thy creatures unto life.[11]

REFORM: (Evades the question with a negative slant toward resurrection) Praised be Thou, O Lord, God of our fathers . . . Thou . . . bringest redemption to their descendants for the sake of Thy name . . . Eternal is Thy power, O Lord, Thou art mighty to save. In lovingkindness Thou sustainest the living . . . and keepest faith with Thy children in death as in life. Who is like unto Thee, Almighty God Author of life and death, Source of Salvation? Praised be Thou, O Lord, who hast implanted within us eternal life.[12]

Immortality, as a principle, is retained in all four versions.

The Mussaf service and animal sacrifices

In the Temple of old, animal sacrifices were offered. Maimonides, as we have seen, considered them a divine concession to the spirit of the times. The present-day rabbinate in Israel may or may not anticipate their revival; many orthodox people outside of Israel, it may be assumed, do not expect it either. But at the time the prayer book was edited, hope in the restoration of the sacrificial service ran high. The Messiah would bring it back. A special service was dedicated to the sacrifices on every

---

[9] *The Siddur*, p. 7.
[10] *Sabbath and Festival Prayer Book*, pp. 21 f.
[11] *Sabbath Prayer Book*, p. 45.
[12] *The Union Prayer Book for Jewish Worship*, pp. 33 f.

Sabbath and festival. It was called the Mussaf, and included a recital of the ancient ritual, and the hope for its restoration. The four groups have had to face the problem, and decide what to do with a prayer expressing a hope no one would even wish to see fulfilled.

ORTHODOXY retained the prayer in its ancient form. Thus we read in Sabbath worship of the orthodox synagogue:

At Sinai they (the offerings) were commanded unto us . . . May it be Thy will, O Lord our God, to lead us in joy to our land . . . where we shall prepare unto Thee the sacrifices as our duty commands . . . and the additional offering of the Sabbath we shall lovingly prepare and offer unto Thee, according to the commandment at Thy gracious will, as laid down for us in Thy Torah at the hand of Moses Thy servant, from the mouth of Thy Majesty as it is said: and on the Sabbath day two lambs. . . .[13]

CONSERVATISM, trying to avoid elimination of any prayers, has put this portion of the Mussaf in the past tense, and added a meditation. Thus it becomes a recital of an act which was once performed. The meditation explains the situation, and explains Conservatism.

Our God and God of our fathers. May there come before Thee the remembrance of our ancestors as they appeared in Thy sacred Temple in days of yore. How deep was their love of Thee as they brought Thee their offerings each Sabbath day. We pray Thee grant us of the spirit of knowledge and the fear of the Lord that lived in their hearts. May we, in their spirit of sacrificial devotion fulfil our duty to the rebuilding of Thy holy land, the fountain of our life, that we may ever be a blessing to all the peoples of the earth.

Then comes the recital of the parallel portions to the orthodox prayer book put in the past tense:

At Sinai our forefathers were commanded to keep the Sabbath; and Thou didst ordain . . . that they bring the additional Sabbath offerings . . . May it be Thy will, O Lord our God . . . to lead us joyfully back to our land . . . where our forefathers prepared the daily offerings and the additional Sabbath offerings, as it is written in Thy Torah, through Moses Thine inspired servant. The Sabbath Offering (Num. 28:9-10).[14]

Conservatism thus approves of the sacrificial cult of the past, because this is what the people once considered good. Our prayer asks for a similar spirit in our time, expressing the hope that the people's collective will may arrive at a similarly heartfelt expression of devotion. By playing on the meanings of the word *sacrificial*, it artificially ties together past and present. In Temple times, sacrificial referred to animal offerings, while today it stands for the devotion of the human heart. A not entirely successful compromise has been struck. Congregations whose members

---

[13] Author's translation.
[14] *Sabbath and Festival Prayer Books*, pp. 140 f.

still feel orthodox will be satisfied, as will congregations whose feelings have changed in regard to sacrifices, and who wish to express only those sentiments in prayer which they can actually endorse.

RECONSTRUCTIONISM, dedicated to intellectual honesty yet tied to conservative philosophy, has not been satisfied with the solution found by conservatism. In the spirit of honesty it has changed the Mussaf; in the conservative attitude of re-interpretation it has also introduced a meditation. It speaks of the "nation," and leads up to the social commitment which the memory of sancta is to arouse in us.

In ancient days, when Israel dwelt in its own land, the Temple in Jerusalem was the symbol of God's presence. The sacrifices were offered daily in behalf of the entire nation. On Sabbath, a special sacrifice marked the day's holiness. Thus did the Temple bear testimony to Israel's consecration to the God of all mankind.

The Temple has long been destroyed, yet the remembrance of it lives in the heart of our people. The form of worship practiced there belongs to a bygone age, yet it continues to awaken solemn thoughts.

Today, Israel is scattered in many lands. But when we remember the Temple, we feel that we are part of one people, dedicated to the service of God and His kingdom of righteousness. Our worship is one of prayer and praise. But when we think of the piety of our fathers, who from their meager store of cattle and grain, the yield of the shepherd's care and the farmer's toil, offered their best in the service of God, can we be content with a gift of mere words that cost us neither labor nor privation? Shall we not feel impelled to devote of our substance to the service of God? Shall we not give of our store to the relief of suffering, the healing of sickness, the dispelling of ignorance and error, and the righting of wrongs and the strengthening of faith? [15]

These are noble sentiments. The concept of peoplehood, the link of the generations, they lead us to the ideal of social action—this is the spirit of Reconstructionism. Actually, the prayer no longer has any relationship to the original. The sentiments are artificially grafted on some remnants of the ancient liturgy. Had there been no traditional Mussaf, there would have been no effort to combine modern thoughts with ancient sacrifices which, to an honest Reconstructionist, must have lost all meaning. Here, too, the effort to maintain a concept that has lost its meaning has failed; re-interpretation has not worked.

REFORM, seeing no purpose in the prayer, and true to its logical and consistent approach, has entirely abolished the Mussaf prayer. By breaking a sentimental link with the past, it has shown a radical tendency, but it has also had the most truthful approach. No worshipper can offer the Mussaf and mean it; let it be abolished, Reform says, to give way to devotions fitting for our time.

---

[15] *Sabbath Prayer Book*, pp. 188 f.

The Next Step:
A Selected Bibliography

The number of books on Judaism and its ideas is endless, and it is growing. This bibliography is designed to lead the interested reader just one step further in his search. Emphasis has been placed on books available in paperback editions. The bibliographies found in the works listed will serve as a guide to those who may wish to go even further in study and research.

GENERAL REFERENCE WORKS

Geoffrey Wigoder (ed.), Encyclopedia Judaica, 16 vols. Jerusalem, 1972, N.Y. Collier-Macmillan. *The Standard Jewish Encyclopedia, edited by Cecil Roth,* New York, Doubleday, 1959, is an excellent one-volume reference work. *Louis Finkelstein (ed.), The Jews: Their History, Culture, and Religion,* New York, Harper, 1960. *David Bridger (ed.): The New Jewish Encyclopedia,* New York, Behrman House, 1967, is a good reference work. *Leo Trepp, Judaism, Development and Life,* Encino, Dickenson, 1966 (rev. 1974).

GENERAL WORKS AND READERS

Leo Baeck, The Essence of Judaism, New York, Schocken, 1946, is a mature and scholarly exposition of Judaism; in *I. Epstein, The Faith of Judaism,* New York, Penguin, 1954, Judaism is explained by an orthodox scholar; *Cecil Roth, The Jewish Contribution to Civilization,* Cincinnati, Union of American Hebrew Congregations (henceforth to be abbreviated as UAHC), 1940, tells the story of Jewish creative participation in the cultures of the world; *Nahum N. Glatzer, In Time and Eternity,* New York, Schocken, 1946, offers a fine selection of Jewish writings through the ages.

Glatzer's three volume work, *The Rest is Commentary; Faith and Knowledge; The Dynamics of Emancipation,* Boston, Beacon Press, 1961, 1963, 1965, is an excellent anthology leading the reader from the time of the second Temple to the present. *Louis Jacobs* works include: *Faith,* New York, Basic Books, 1968; *Principles of the Jewish Faith: An Analytical Study,* New York, Basic Books, 1964; *We Have Reason to Believe,* London, Valentine, 1957. Written by the most incisive thinker of English Jewry, they offer insights into Judaism as seen by a traditional yet progressive Jew. *Buber: On Judaism,* edited by N. N. Glatzer, N.Y., Schocken, 1967.

GENERAL HISTORIES

Heinrich Graetz, Jewish History, six volumes, Philadelphia, Jewish Publication Society (henceforth to be abbreviated as JPS), 1926, is still a classical work. It has been brought up to date by *Ismar Elbogen, A Century of Jewish Life, Philadelphia,* JPS, 1946. In *Salo Baron, A Social and Religious History of the Jews,* Revised Edition, Philadelphia, JPS, 1952 ff., we have an ongoing thoroughly written scholarly work. *Meyer Waxman, A History of Jewish Literature,* four volumes, New York, Bloch, 1936 ff., is a basic work. There are numerous one-volume histories. Outstanding among them is *Max Margolis and Alexander Marx, History of the Jewish People,* Philadelphia and New York, JPS and Meridian Books, 1960. *Solomon Grayzel, A History of the Jews,* Philadelphia, JPS, 1960, *A History of Contemporary Jews from 1900 to the Present,* Philadelphia and New York, JPS and Meridian, 1960, deals with modern Jewry, emphasizing life in the United States. *Bernard J. Bamberger, The Story of Judaism,* New York, UAHC, 1957, traces the development of Judaism and its ideals down the ages; it is written from a liberal point of view. Other one-volume works: *Cecil Roth, History of the Jews,* New York, Schocken, 1970. *Leo Baeck, This People Israel: The Meaning of Jewish Existence,* Philadelphia, JPS, 1965.

COLLECTIONS OF ESSAYS AND BIOGRAPHIES

Alexander Marx, Essays in Jewish Biographies, Philadelphia, JPS, 1948, contains biographies of great personalities, including Saadia, Rabbenu Gershom, Solomon Schechter, and others; *Simon Noveck (ed.), Great Jewish Personalities in Ancient and Mediaeval Times* and *Great Jewish Personalities in Modern Times,* Washington, B'nai B'rith, 1960, includes biographies of Moses, David, Akiba, Rashi, Saadia, Maimonides, Mendelssohn, Samson Raphael Hirsch, Schechter, Herzl, Byalik, Weizmann and others, written by various contributors in popular style. *Louis Ginzberg, Students, Scholars and Saints,* Philadelphia and New York, JPS and Meridian, 1958, includes essays on Halakhah, the Pharisees, and others, and biographies of Zachariah Frankel, Solomon Schechter, and various notables.

The Bible

To list even the commentaries to individual books of the Bible would go beyond the scope of this book. We shall confine ourselves to some basic introductory works.

Soncino Books of the Bible, 14 volumes, London and New York, Soncino Press, offer the entire Hebrew Scriptures in Hebrew and English, with an excellent running commentary. *The Anchor Bible* is a monumental work, each book of the Bible having been entrusted to the most distinguished scholar in the field for translation and commentary. *The Holy Scriptures,* Philadelphia, JPS, 1917 ff., a work by a number of American scholars, may be considered the standard translation for American Jewry; a new translation is in the making. The first part of this new translation, *The Torah,* appeared in 1962 (Phila., JPS.), *Isaiah* in 1972. *Joseph Hertz, The Pentateuch and Haftorahs,* London, Soncino Press, 1938, is published in America by Bloch Publishing Company. It divides the Hebrew text according to the weekly readings for every Sabbath of the year, and provides an excellent translation and running commentary based on numerous ancient and modern commentators; there are also several essays on biblical subjects. The book can serve as introduction to Jewish exegesis; its style is popular. *Samuel Sandmel, The Hebrew Scriptures,* New York, Knopf, 1963, represents the approach of higher biblical criticism; *Th. C. Vriezen, The Religion of Ancient Israel,* Phila., Westminster Press, 1967 presents in excellent form the development of Jewish religion during the biblical period, as seen by a Christian scholar. *Martin Buber* has written on *Moses, the Revelation and the Covenant,* N.Y., Harper Row, 1958; *The Prophetic Faith,* N.Y., Harper Row, 1960; *Buber on the Bible,* edited by N. N. Glatzer appeared by Schocken (N.Y.) in 1968. From *Abraham Heschel* we have *The Prophets,* Phila., JPS, 1962. Buber's *Kingship of God,* New York and Evanston, Harper Row, 1967 deserves attention as it advances the concept of God's immediate dialogue with Israel. *Robert Gordis; Kohelet, The Man and His World,* N.Y. Schocken, 1970, his *Poets, Prophets and Sages, Essays in Biblical Interpretation,* Bloomington, Indiana U.P., 1970, and his *The Book of God and Man — A Study of Job,* Chicago, Univ. of Chicago Press, 1966, reveal insights as does *Louis Finkelstein, New Light from the Prophets,* N.Y. Basic Books, 1970. *Mortimer J. Cohen, Pathways through the Bible,* Philadelphia, JPS, 1946, is a popular reader, offering selections from all the books of the Bible with brief introductions and commentary. *Robert Pfeiffer, Books of the Old Testament,* New York, Harper, 1957, a work by an outstanding Christian Harvard professor; and *Harry Orlinsky, Ancient Israel,* Ithaca, Cornell University Press, 1954, by a Jewish scholar. *Bernard J. Bamberger, The Bible a Modern Jewish Approach,* New York, B'nai B'rith Hillel Foundations, 1956, a "Hillel Little Book," dealing with the background of the Bible, its contents, and the impact of its ideas on modern life. *Louis Ginzberg, The Legend of the Jews,* Philadelphia, JPS, 1928, is a seven volume anthology which has been republished in recent condensation under the title *Legends in the Bible,* Philadelphia, JPS, 1956. It is a valuable source of instruction and makes enjoyable reading. *William F. Albright, Archae-*

ology and the Religion of Israel, Baltimore, Johns Hopkins Press, 1942, is a work by a foremost expert in the field, and is extremely instructive, as is his *From the Stone Age to Christianity,* Garden City, N.Y., Anchor, 1957. *John Bright, History of Israel,* Phila., Westminster Press, 1959, is an outstanding work by one of Albright's disciples. *Martin Noth, History of Israel, Biblical History,* New York, Harper-Row, 1960, follows a more critical approach.

Talmud

The Soncino Talmud, London and New York, Soncino Press, 1935 ff., is a complete translation of the entire Talmud reissued now in 18 volumes. *H. Danby, The Mishnah,* New York, Oxford, 1933, offers a translation of the Mishnah. *A. Cohen, Everyman's Talmud,* New York, Dutton, 1949, gives insights into its world. *Herman Strack, Introduction to the Talmud and Midrash,* Philadelphia and New York, JPS, and Meridian, 1959, is a classical work of introduction by a great nineteenth century Christian scholar in Germany. *Morris Adler, The World of the Talmud,* New York, B'nai B'rith Hillel Foundation, 1959, is another popular introduction in the series of "Little Hillel Books." *Judah Goldin, The Living Talmud,* New York, Mentor, 1957, is a translation of the "Sayings of the Fathers" with commentary and an introduction explaining the method of the Talmud. *Joseph H. Hertz, Sayings of the Fathers,* London and New York, East and West Library, 1952, offers the Hebrew version with a fine translation and commentary. *Louis J. Newman, The Talmudic Anthology,* New York, Behrman House, 1947, uses largely midrashic material, arranged by subject headings, to convey the ethical message of the Talmud. *George F. Moore, Judaism in the First Centuries of the Christian Era,* Cambridge, Mass., Schocken, 1972, is a complete treatment of normative Judaism, as it came into existence and practice in talmudic times; the work, written by a Christian, is authoritative and comprehensive, a classic in the field. *Louis Finkelstein, The Pharisees,* two volumes, Philadelphia, JPS, 1940, is a significant work which deserves to be consulted by all who wish to understand the character and importance of the Pharisees. *Leo Baeck, The Pharisees and Other Essays,* New York, Schocken, 1947, offers some additional essays, discussion of fundamentals in the character of Judaism and contrasting it with other ideologies. *Max Kadushin, The Rabbinic Mind,* N.Y. Blaisdell, 1965, and *Jacob Petuchowski, Heirs to the Pharisees,* N.Y., Basic Books, 1970, will give an understanding of the Jewish Mind. The works on the Dead Sea Scrolls are numerous, and new discoveries will add to their number. *Millars Burrow, The Dead Sea Scrolls,* New York, Viking Press, 1955, and *Edmund Wilson, The Scrolls from the Dead Sea,* New York, 1955, are basic works. *Theodore Gaster, The Dead Sea Scriptures,* New York, Anchor, 1957, gives us a valuable explanation of the life of the Qumram community, and then presents the Manual of Discipline of the monastic group in English translation; *Yigael Yadin, Masada, Herod's Fortress and the Zealots' Last Stand,* N.Y., Random House, 1966, deals with the completed excavations of the fortress and the insights they reveal.

Prayers and the Prayer Book

Joseph H. Hertz, The Authorized Daily Prayer Book, New York, Bloch, 1960, is an orthodox prayer book, well translated, and with a running commentary by the late Chief Rabbi of the British Commonwealth. Since the orthodox prayer book is the point of departure for all other prayer books, this edition will be helpful. The various groups in America, Orthodoxy, Conservatism, Reform, and Reconstructionism, have issued their own prayer books (see footnotes) which have introductory notes explaining their scope. *A. Z. Idelson, Jewish Liturgy and its Development,* New York, Schocken, 1971, gives the evolution of the liturgy. Reconstructionism and Reform have also issued *Haggadah* versions reflecting their ideologies.

Music and Art

A. Z. Idelson, Jewish Music, New York, Schocken, 1970, offers a complete history of Jewish music throughout the ages, written in simple English with numerous musical annotations. *Cecil Roth, Jewish Art,* New York, McGraw-Hill, 1961, has many illustrations; *Rachel Wischnitzer, The Architecture of the European Synagogue,* Phila., JPS, 1964, offers a historical, well illustrated survey; *Avram Kampf, Contemporary Synagogue Art,* Phila., JPS, 1966, deals with modern, frequently daring developments.

Judaism and Christianity

Only a few introductory works can be mentioned.

Samuel Sandmel, A Jewish Understanding of the Old Testament, Cincinnati, Hebrew Union College Press, 1957, and its companion work by the same author, *The Genius of Paul,* New York, Farrar, Straus, 1958, and *We Jews and Jesus,* N.Y., Oxford U.P., 1965, are excellent studies by a modern scholar. *J. Klausner, Jesus of Nazareth,* New York, 1926, and his *From Jesus to Paul,* Boston, Beacon Press, 1961, are works of basic research in the field. *Leo Baeck, Judaism and Christianity,* Philadelphia, JPS, 1958, illuminates the differences between the two religions. *Martin Buber, Two Types of Faith,* Chicago, Wilcox & Follett, 1951, deserves study, as the meaning of faith in the two religions is examined and compared. *James Parkes, A History of the Jewish People,* Pelican, 1964, *The Conflict of the Church and the Synagogue,* London, Soncino, 1934, *Judaism and Christianity,* Chicago, University of Chicago Press, 1948, and *Anti-Semitism,* Chicago, Quadrangle, 1964, are by a Christian theologian. *(Father) Edward Flannery, The Anguish of the Jews—2000 Years of Anti-Semitism* is a very good analysis by a Catholic priest. *Charles Y. Glock and Rodney Stark, Christian Beliefs and Anti-Semitism,* N.Y., Harper-Row, 1966, offers the results of a statistical investigation of its forms today. *Arthur Gilbert, The Vatican Council and the Jews,* Cleveland, World Publishing Company, 1968, presents the background story of the Declaration on the Jews. *Jules Isaac, The Teaching of Contempt: Christian Roots of Anti-Semitism,* N.Y., Holt, Rinehart and Winston, 1964, is a significant Jewish work on the issue.

The Middle Ages

Jacob R. Marcus, The Jew in the Mediaeval World, Philadelphia and New York, JPS and Meridian Books, 1960, offers a selection of documents referring to Jews, covering the period from the fourth to the eighteenth centuries; it is a valuable collection of source materials. *Israel Abrahams, Jewish Life in the Middle Ages,* New York and Philadelphia, Meridian Books and JPS, 1960, gives us a well-rounded picture of mediaeval Jewish life. *Cecil Roth* has written a *History of the Marranos,* Philadelphia, JPS, 1959, *Personalities and Events in Jewish History,* Philadelphia, JPS, 1954, and *The Jews in the Renaissance,* Philadelphia, JPS, 1959. *Yitzhak F. Baer* a *History of the Jews in Christian Spain, I, II,* Phila., JPS, 1966. Selections from *Rashi's Commentaries on the Pentateuch* have appeared in the B'nai B'rith Jewish Heritage Classic Series, New York, Norton, 1970. Translations of the *Codes of Maimonides* are appearing in the Yale Judaica Series, Yale University Press.

The Jewish Year

S. Y. Agnon, Days of Awe, N.Y., Schocken, 1948, is an anthology on the High Holy Days by the Jewish writer who won the Nobel prize. Dealing with the Sabbath are *Abraham J. Heschel, The Sabbath, Its Meaning for Modern Man,* N.Y., Farrar, Straus and Young, 1951, and — in form of an anthology, *Abraham Millgram, Sabbath, Day of Delight,* Phila., JPS, 1944, in a series of anthologies that include *Philip Goodman, The Purim Anthology, The Passover Anthology,* and *Hanukah, The Feast of Light,* all published in Philadelphia by JPS, give the background, history and observances, the legends and customs connected with these holidays. *Hayyim Schauss, The Jewish Festivals,* New York, UAHC, 1938, presents an overview. An interpretation of the High Holy Day liturgy is offered in *Max Arzt, Justice and Mercy, Commentary on the Liturgy of the New Year and the Day of Atonement,* N.Y., Holt, Rinehart and Winston, 1961; see also *Jacob J. Petuchowski, Prayer Book Reform in Europe,* N.Y., World Union of Progressive Judaism, 1969.

The Road of Life

Milton Steinberg, Basic Judaism, New York, Harcourt Brace, 1947, offers an excellent outline of Judaism in philosophy and practice as seen by a conservative rabbi; *Hayyim Schauss, The Lifetime of a Jew,* New York, UAHC, 1950, adds to his book on the festivals.

Hasidism — Mysticism

Gershom G. Scholem, Major Trends in Jewish Mysticism, New York, Schocken, 1963, is a basic exposition of Jewish mysticism; *Zohar, the Book of Splendor,* New York, Schocken, 1949, by the same author, contains an introduction and selections from the great mystical work. Also by him, *Gershom Scholem, On the*

Kabbalah and Its Symbolism, N.Y., Schocken, 1965. *Martin Buber* has written widely on the subject. Among his works are: *Hasidism,* New York, Philosophical Library, 1948; *The Way of Modern Man according to the Teachings of Hasidism,* Chicago, Wilcox & Follett, 1951; *Tales of the Hasidim, The Early Masters,* New York, Schocken, 1947, and *The Later Masters,* New York, Schocken, 1948.

Jewish Philosophy

Julius Guttman, The Philosophies of Judaism, Phila., JPS, 1964; N.Y., Holt, Rinehart and Winston, 1964, is a basic work. *Isaac Husik, A History of Mediaeval Jewish Philosophy,* Philadelphia and New York, JPS and Meridian Books, 1958, a good overview of the period from the ninth to the fifteenth centuries. *Three Jewish Philosophers,* Philadelphia and New York, JPS, and Meridian Books, 1960, offers representative selections from the writings of Philo, Saadia, and Judah Halevi, with scholarly introductions. *Harry A. Wolfson, Philo,* Cambridge, Mass., Harvard University Press, 1947, is a classic two-volume work in the field. *Jacob S. Minkin, The World of Moses Maimonides,* New York, Yosseloff, 1957, offers a biography and cross section of his work, with explanation by the compiler. *M. Friedlander, Moses Maimonides, The Guide of the Perplexed,* originally published in 1881, is now available in paperback form. *Jacob Agus, The Evolution of Jewish Thought,* New York, Abelard Schuman, 1960, covering the period from the Bible to the nineteenth century, is not an easy book. *Alfred Jospe (ed.), Jerusalem and other Jewish Writings by Moses Mendelssohn,* N.Y., Schocken, 1969. *S. R. Hirsch, Nineteen Letters of Ben Usiel,* New York, Feldheim, 1962, is a translation of Hirsch's basic work.

Zionism

Arthur Hertzberg, The Zionist Idea, Philadelphia and New York, JPS and Meridian Books, 1960, contains the basic writings of the Zionist leaders, and gives an excellent survey of the development of Zionism; *Martin Buber, Israel and Palestine: The History of an Idea,* London, East and West Library, 1952, gives Buber's view; *Sir Leon Simon, Ahad Ha-Am,* Philadelphia, JPS, 1960, and *Alex Bein, Theodor Herzl,* Philadelphia, JPS, 1940, are good biographies.

An Age of Maturity

The works of the German Jewish thinkers are explained in a number of books. *Nathan Rothenstreich, Jewish Philosophy in Modern Times,* N.Y., Holt, 1968, offers an excellent analysis of modern Jewish thought from Mendelssohn to the present. *Samuel H. Bergman, Faith and Reason,* Washington, B'nai B'rith, Hillel Foundation, 1961, deals with the thoughts of Hermann Cohen, Franz Rosenzweig, and Martin Buber. *Will Herberg, The Writings of Martin Buber,* New York, Meridian Books, 1960, is an inexpensive paperback introducing the reader to Buber; *Maurice S. Friedman, Martin Buber, the Life of the Dialogue,*

Chicago, University of Chicago Press, 1955, is a scholarly work. Of Buber's own works, *I and Thou,* New York, Scribner's, 1937, is perhaps the most widely read. *Eclipse of God: Studies in the Relation between Religion and Philosophy,* New York, Harper, 1953, amplifies his ideas, and *Pointing the Way: Collected Essays,* New York, Harper, 1956, deals with the implications of the "I and Thou" in many fields of human endeavor, as does *Between Man and Man,* Boston, Beacon, 1955, in human relations. *Nahum N. Glatzer, Franz Rosenzweig, His Life and Thought,* Philadelphia, JPS, 1962, is a valuable biography and introduction. Franz Rosenzweig, The Star of Redemption, tr. Hallo. *Mordecai M. Kaplan, The Purpose and Meaning of Jewish Existence,* Phila., JPS, 1964, is a critique of Hermann Cohen.

American Judaism: Beginnings and Reform Judaism

Oscar Handlin, Adventure in Freedom: Three Hundred Years of Jewish Life in America, New York, McGraw-Hill, 1954, and *Rufus Learsi, The Jews in America,* New York, World, 1954, are competent works. *Jacob R. Marcus, Early American Jewry,* two volumes, Philadelphia, JPS, and his *Memoirs of American Jews,* 3 volumes, Philadelphia, JPS, 1955, give us glimpses of early Jewish life and of the growth of the Jewish community through such men as Uriah P. Levy, Manuel M. Noah, Isaac Meyer Wise, and Sampel Gompers. *Sylvan D. Schwartzman, Reform Judaism in the Making,* New York, UAHC, 1955, traces the development of Reform; *Abraham J. Feldman, Reform Judaism,* is a concise exposition of Reform together with a guide to practice. *Solomon B. Freehof, The Reform Responsa,* New York, UAHC, 1960, a technical work, gives a good indication of Reform's renewed concern with Halakhah. *Kaufmann Kohler, Jewish Theology Systematically and Historically Considered,* 1918, is a general overview favoring Reform by a man who was a leader of Reform, President of Hebrew Union College, and had been under the direct influence of Samson Raphael Hirsch and Abraham Geiger in Germany before coming to the United States, where he represents "classical" reform.

American Judaism: Later Developments: Conservatism, Orthodoxy, Present Problems

Solomon Schechter, Studies in Judaism, Philadelphia, JPS, and N.Y., Meridian, 1959, his *Seminary Addresses and other Papers,* New York, Burning Bush Press, 1959, together with *Norman Bentwich (ed.), Selected Writings of Solomon Schechter,* Oxford, East and West Library, 1946, provide good insights in the life and views of the leader and founder of conservatism in America. *Marshall Sklare, Conservative Judaism,* Glencoe, Free Press, 1955, is a study of the group, while his *The Jews, Social Patterns of an American Group,* Glencoe, The Free Press, 1958, deals with over-all aspects. Of *Mordecai M. Kaplan's* works we mention *Judaism as a Civilization,* New York, Macmillan, 1934, Yoseloff, 1957, stating his basic pronouncements on Reconstructionism, which he founded. *The Meaning of God in Modern Jewish Religion,* New York, Behrman House, 1937, develops his ideas in interpretation of practices and observances; *The Future of the American Jew*, New York, Macmillan, 1948, presents a program of regeneration in thought and action; *The Greater Judaism in the Making*, New York, Reconstructionist Press, 1960; *Religion of Ethical Nationhood*, N.Y., Macmillan, 1970. A. I. Gordon has written about *Jews in Suburbia*, Boston, Beacon Press, 1959; *Will Herberg, Protestant, Catholic, Jew*, New York, Doubleday, 1955, describes the place of religion in American life, including a discussion of the *American* forms of various religions.

The evolution of Conservative Judaism is traced by *Moshe Davis, The Emergence of Conservative Judaism: The Historical School in the Nineteenth Century*, Phila., JPS, 1963. That of Reform Judaism in two works, permitting its historical representatives to speak by *Gunther W. Plaut, The Rise of Reform Judaism* and *The Growth of Reform Judaism*, N.Y., The World Union of Progressive Judaism, 1963 and 1965. *Nathan Glazer, American Judaism*, Chicago, University of Chicago Press, 1959, is a history and evaluation of present-day Jewry, while *Will Herberg, Judaism and Modern Man*, Philadelphia, JPS, New York, Meridian, 1959, tries to re-evaluate the basic ideas of Judaism as seen by an existentialist thinker. *Abraham Heschel's God in Search of Man*, Philadelphia, JPS, 1954, *Man's Quest for God*, New York, Charles Scribner's Sons, 1954, and *Man is not Alone*, Philadelphia, JPS, 1951, offers insights in his thinking and the beauty of his style. *A. Vorspan and E. Lipman, Justice and Judaism*, New York, UAHC, 1956, deals with the application of Jewish teaching to modern life, and the functions of American Jewry to promote the ethical ideals of Judaism in the modern society.

Theological ferment is reflected in: *Jacob I. Petuchowski, Ever Since Sinai*, N.Y., Scribe, 1961. *Eugene B. Borowitz, A New Jewish Theology in the Making*, Phila., Westminster, 1968, and *How Can a Jew Speak of Faith Today?* Phila., Westminster, 1969. *Emil L. Fackenheim, Quest for Past and Future*, Bloomington, Univ. of Indiana Press, 1968. *Richard Rubenstein, After Auschwitz*, Indianapolis, Bobbs Merrill, 1966. *Arnold J. Wolf (ed.), Rediscovering Judaism*, Chicago, Quadrangle, 1965. *The Condition of Jewish Belief; a Symposium Compiled by the Editors of Commentary Magazine*, New York and London, Macmillan, 1966. *Arthur A. Cohen, Arguments and Doctrines*, Phila., JPS, 1970 (a reader with introductory essays). *Bernard Postal and Lionel Koppman, A Jewish Tourist's Guide through the United States*, Philadelphia, JPS, 1954, is a guide and history pointing to Jewish institutions, monuments, and places of interest throughout the United States.

The Holocaust and its aftermath are reflected in *Nelly Sachs* (Nobel Prize winner), *O the Chimneys*, Phila., JPS, 1968 in *Jacob Glatstein, Israel Knox, Samuel Margoshes (eds.), Anthology of Holocaust Literature*, Phila., JPS, 1969; and in the works of Elie E. Wiesel.

SOME PERIODICALS

The various denominational groups are keeping in touch with their affiliates through numerous periodical publications. Some of these frequently offer valuable essays. Among them we mention *Conservative Judaism,* the journal of the conservative Rabbinical Assembly, and *CCAR Journal,* the journal of the Central Conference of American Rabbis (Reform); The Reconstructionist Movement issues its own magazine, *The Reconstructionist.*

The Jewish Committee is sponsor of a magazine, *Commentary,* dealing with many aspects of American life and literature; *Midstream* is a similar magazine, sponsored by the Zionist Organization. *Judaism* is a very scholarly quarterly, and *Jewish Heritage,* published quarterly by B'nai B'rith, a popular and highly informative magazine on all aspects of Jewish life and faith. There are numerous weeklies. *The National Jewish Monthly* is sent to all members of B'nai B'rith. The Jewish Publication Society of America has issued an annual Year Book for many years; it is devoted to statistics of Jews in America and in the world and Jewish history during the year gone by. *The American Jewish Year Book* is also an important reference work.

Appendix

I. JEWISH POPULATION IN THE WORLD [1]

America

United States	5,900,000	Chile	35,000
Canada	280,000	Colombia	10,000
Mexico	35,000	Cuba	2,000
Argentina	500,000	Peru	4,000
Bolivia	4,000	Uruguay	50,000
Brazil	140,000	Venezuela	12,000

The number of Jews in the other countries is almost negligible.

Asia

Israel	2,500,000	Lebanon	3,000
India	15,000	Syria	4,000
Iran	80,000	Turkey	40,000
Iraq	2,500		

There are small numbers of Jews in other countries, except for Jordan and Saudi Arabia.

Europe

Austria	8,000	France	550,000
Belgium	40,000	West Germany	30,000
Bulgaria	7,000	Great Britain	410,000
Czechoslovakia	15,000	Greece	6,000
Denmark	6,000	Holland	30,000
Finland	2,000	Hungary	80,000

[1] Populations are given in round figures. They are based on information found in *American Jewish Yearbook,* © 1969 by The American Jewish Committee and the Jewish Publication Society of America.

Ireland	6,000	(7,000 in Spain)	
Italy	35,000	Sweden	15,000
Norway	1,000	Switzerland	20,000
Poland	9,000	USSR	2,600,000
Rumania	100,000	Yugoslavia	7,000
Spain and Portugal	8,000		

There are small numbers in other parts.

Africa

Algeria	1,500	Rhodesia	5,000
Egypt	1,000	Tunisia	10,000
Libya	100	Republic of South Africa	120,000
Morocco	50,000		

Small numbers in other parts.

Australia

Australia	73,000	New Zealand	5,000

II. CHRONOLOGICAL TABLE

c. 1728-1686		Hammurabi
c. 1750	Abraham migrates to Canaan	
c. 1700-1600	The Israelites migrate from Canaan to Egypt	
c. 1290-1224		Rameses II of Egypt
c. 1280	Exodus of Israel from Egypt	
c. 1250-1200	Conquest of Canaan	
c. 1200-1020	Period of the Judges	
c. 1150-1000	Philistines rise to power	
c. 1050	Samuel	
c. 1020-1000	Saul	
c. 1013-973	David	
c. 973-933	Solomon	
c. 930	Division of the Realm into the Kingdoms of Judah and Israel	

	Judah	Israel
930-915	Rehoboam	
922-901		Jeroboam I
876-869		Omri
869-850		Ahab
c. 850		Elijah
842-837	Athalia	
786-746		Jeroboam II
783-742	Azariah (Uzziah)	
750-735	Jotham	
c. 750		Amos
c. 745		Hosea
742	I Isaiah called	
742-700	I Isaiah	
c. 740-700	Micah	
722		Samaria falls; End of Israel

640-609	Josiah	
628-622		Zephaniah
621		Deuteronomy
626-587		Jeremiah

605-562		Nebuchadnezzar
605		Habakkuk
586	Fall of Jerusalem; Babylonian Exile	
c. 593-573		Ezekiel
		Patterns of the Synagogue and of Worship begun
c. 540		II Isaiah
538	Cyrus grants permission to return	
520-515	Rebuilding of Temple	Samaritans
		Haggai
		Zachariah
c. 500-450		Malachi
458 (?)		Ezra's Mission
445		Nehemiah arrives
444		The Covenant (Synagogue as permanent institution)
c. 460-330		The Men of the Great Assembly
336-323		Alexander the Great
285-150		Septuagint
		Influence of Hellenism
		Pharisaism (Development of Sects)
167	Maccabean Revolt leading to Independence	
63	Pompey captures Jerusalem; Beginning of Roman overlordship	
37-4	Herod the Great	
c. 30-10		Hillel
		Shammai
c. 10-40		Philo of Alexandria
4-39	Herod Antipas	
29	John the Baptist executed	
26-36	Pontius Pilate	
30	Jesus is crucified	
64	Florus, last Procurator, takes office	
70	Jerusalem destroyed by Titus	
		Josephus
		Johanan ben Zaccai establishes Center at Jabneh
80-110		The Scriptures are canonized
		Prayerbook is issued
116	Uprising against Trajan	
117-138		Hadrian
50-135		Akiba
132-135	Bar Kokhba Rebellion	
100-160	Simeon ben Johai	
130-160		Rabbi Meir is religious head
c. 200		Codification of the Mishnah under Rabbi Judah
217		Death of Rabbi Judah
311-337		Constantine the Great
312		Constantine becomes a Christian
325		Council of Nicaea
425	End of the Patriarchate	

Babylonia

c. 200-250	Rab and Samuel establish Center of Learning
352-427	Rab Ashee
474-499	Rabina II
500	Talmud (Gemara) completed

| 622 | | Hegira, Mohammed's flight; Spread of Islam |
| 892-942 | Saadia | |

Sefardim

before 300	Settlement in Spain
912-961	Hasdai ibn Shaprut, 912-961, establishes contact with the Jewish Kingdom of the Chazars (having accepted Judaism since *c.* 740)
1021-1069	Solomon ibn Gabirol
1086-1141	Judah Halevi
1135-1204	Maimonides
1250-1305	Moses de Leon, Master of the Name (Zohar)
1492	Expulsion from Spain; settlement in Turkey (Palestine), Holland
1488-1575	Joseph Karo (Spain and Palestine)
Palestine:	
1534-1572	Isaac Luria (The Mystics of Safed)
1567	The Shulhan Arukh

Ashkenasim

321	*Germany:* First documentary proofs of settlement, having been established earlier within the Roman Empire
768-814	*Germany:* Charlemagne; Jews serve at his court
990(?)	*Germany:* Calonymus family called from Italy to Mainz
960-1040	*Germany:* Gershom ben Judah
1040-1105	*Germany:* Rashi
1096	*Germany:* First Crusade
	Poland and Russia: Immigration begins
1179	Innocent III (Lateran Council) imposes grave restrictions (The Badge)
1220-1293	*Germany:* Rabbi Meir of Rothenburg
1290	*England:* Jews are expelled
1348-9	*Germany:* Black Death; Jews accused of poisoning wells
	Poland and Russia: Immigration to escape persecution in Germany
1394	*France:* Jews expelled, except for papal province.
1525-1572	*Poland and Russia:* Moses Isserles
1652-1655	*England:* Manasseh ben Israel discusses return of Jews to England with Cromwell. Parliament declares no legal obstacle ever existed. Resettlement starts
1648-1655	*Poland and Russia:* Chmielnicky Massacres of Jews
1626-1676	Sabbatai Zevi, the false Messiah; his movement spreads
1700-1760	*Poland and Russia:* Israel Baal Shem Tov: Hasidism
1720-1797	*Poland and Russia:* The Gaon of Vilna
1729-1786	*Germany:* Moses Mendelssohn; Father of Emancipation
1782	*Austria:* Tolerance Edict of Joseph II
1700 ff.	*France:* Jews begin to resettle
1791	*France:* Jews declared full citizens
1804	*Poland and Russia:* Restrictions of Movement of Jews (Pale)
1807	*France:* The Grand Sanhedrin, convoked by Napoleon
1812	*Germany:* Prussian Jews emancipated
1806-1860	*Germany:* Samuel Holdheim (Reform)
1818	*Germany:* The Hamburg Temple (Reform)
1794-1886	*Germany:* Leopold Zunz (Science of Judaism)
1810-1874	*Germany:* Abraham Geiger (Reform)
1801-1875	*Germany:* Zachariah Frankel (Conservatism)
1808-1888	*Germany:* Samson Raphael Hirsch (Neo-Orthodoxy)
1825-1855	*Poland and Russia:* Nicholas I, severe oppressions
1821-1891	*Poland and Russia:* Leo Pinsker; settlers go to Palestine
1881	*Poland and Russia:* Pogroms; mass migration to America begins

1856-1927	*Poland and Russia:* Ahad Ha-Am; Cultural Zionism
1860-1904	*Austria:* Theodor Herzl (Founder of Zionism)
1894-1895	*France:* Dreyfus Affair
1897	First Zionist Congress
1917	*England:* Balfour Declaration on Palestine
1919	*Poland and Russia:* Pogroms in the Ukraine
1842-1918	*Germany:* Hermann Cohen
1886-1929	*Germany:* Franz Rosenzweig
1933-1945	*Germany:* Adolph Hitler; extermination of six million European Jews
1948	Establishment of the Independent State of Israel; Jerusalem divided
1878-1965	*Germany-Israel:* Martin Buber
1967	Jerusalem reunited—after Six-Day War

America

1654	First Settlement
1655	First Synagogue, First Stream of immigration (Sefardim)
1788-1828	Isaac Harby (First Reform Movement)
1806-1868	Isaac Leeser (Modern Orthodoxy)
1819-1900	Isaac Meyer Wise (Modern Reform)
1847-1915	Solomon Schechter (Conservatism)
1848 ff.	German immigration
1881 ff.	Third and largest immigration (Eastern European Jews)
1843	Founding of Order of B'nai B'rith
1856-1941	Louis D. Brandeis, Supreme Court Justice; Zionist leader
1860-1941	Henrietta Szold
1873	Union of American Hebrew Congregations
1875	Hebrew Union College
1849-1887	Emma Lazarus, poetess
1881	Mordecai Kaplan
1886	Founding of American Federation of Labor by Samuel Gompers (1850-1924)
1902	Jewish Theological Seminary rises to eminence under Solomon Schechter
1906	American Jewish Committee
1909	Rabbi Judah Magnes tries to unite all of New York Jewry under one community organization, a Kehillah; project doomed to failure
1913	The United Synagogue of America
1915	Yeshivah College (later University) begins its rise to eminence
1917	National Jewish Welfare Board founded to meet problems of war and peace
1922	Rabbi Stephen Wise (1874-1944) organizes Jewish Institute of Religion (later merged with Hebrew Union College)
1922	American Jewish Congress
1933	United Jewish Appeal to serve the needs of dislocated Jewry
1936	World Jewish Congress
1941-1945	600,000 Jews serve in Armed Forces
1968	Reconstructionist Rabbinical College opened in Philadelphia

Index

A

Aaron, family of, 87
Ab, 86, 215
  dates of, 175
Abba Areka (Rab) 102, 103
Abdullah, King of Jordan, 332
Abir Yaakob, 8
Abraham, 5, 109, 131, 139, 189, 200
  God of, 4, 7-8
  migration from Chaldaea, 5
Abtalyon, 64, 66-67
Academies:
  in Babylonia, 103
  at Jabneh, 46, 48
    rebuilding of, 47
  at Jerusalem, 66
Adar, dates of, 175
Adeloyoda, 205
Adler, Nathan, 295
Adoration, 115, 118-119
Affirmation of faith, 2, 3, 80, 114, 120,
    121, 196, 232
Africa, 443
  Jews in, 2
Age of Enlightenment, 286-287, 384
Age of Reason, 316
  dawn of, 263-264
Agnon, S. Y., 334, 412
Agrippa, 41

Agunah, 415
Ahad Ha-Am, 323, 329, 335, 356-357,
    360, 398 (see also Ginzberg,
    Asher)
  ideas of, 324-325
  life of, 324
  picture of, 323
Aher (see Eisha ben Abuya)
Ahriman, 54
Ahura Mazhda, 54
Akiba, Rabbi, 54, 71, 74, 79, 92-93, 251
Albany, New York, 379
Albright, William F., 15n.
Alcoholism, 206
Alexander the Great, 40, 62
  empire of, map, 31
Alexander III, Czar, 321
Alexandria, Egypt, 76, 264
Algeria, 328
Alkabez, Solomon, 180
Allport, Gordon W., 316n.
Alphabet, invention of, 157
Alsace, 337
Altars, 25
Altmann, Alexander, 266n.
American Jewish Committee, 391
American Jewish Congress, 391
American Jewry, 2-3, 247, 325, 329-330,
    335, 337
  early, 368-375

American Jewry (*Cont.*):
   problems of, 373-375
  leadership of, 420
  philanthropy of, 366
  problems of, present-day, 406-409
  spiritual progress of, 408
  (*see also* United States)
Americanization, 380, 388
American Revolution, 368
Amidah, 114, 115-117, 187, 188, 231
Amora, definition of, 103
Amos, 17-19, 83, 95
Amsterdam, 249, synagogue at, illustrated, 162
Amulets, 252
Anderson, B. W., 7n., 15n.
Angels, 54-55
Anhalt, Germany, 281
Ani Ma-amin (song), 147
Animal sacrifices, 280, 417-418
Anthropomorphism, 277
Anti-Defamation League, 376, 391
Antigonus of Sokho, 63
Antiochus Epiphanes, King, 40, 55, 58
Antipater, 41
Anti-Semitism, 36, 74
  American, 320, 376-377, 390-391
  ancient roots of, 74-77
  French, 326-327
  German, 320
  new, 316-320, 413
  (*see also* Hitler; Nazis; Prejudice)
Antoninus Pius, 47
Apion, 76n.
Apocrypha, 79, 92
Aquila, 74, 92
Arabia, 106
Arabs, 330-332
  Jews and, 356
Ararat, New York, 372
Arbor Day, 175
Architecture of synagogues, 158-161
Areka, Abba, 102-103
Argentina, 413
Ari (*see* Luria, Rabbi Isaac)
Aristobulus, 41
Aristotle, 40, 49-50, 106, 146, 265, 267, 270, 272, 274, 279, 281
  and creation of world, 278-279
  God of, 275
Ark, the, 26, 82, 159, 162
  illustration of, 81, 159
Articles of faith, 147
Aryans, 317, 319
Asaph, 87
Ashee, Rab, 103-104
Asher ben Jehiel, Rabbi, 169
Ashkenasic Jewry, 108, 152-158, 164, 170, 206, 255
Ashkenism, 108, 219

Asia, 332
  Jews in, 2
Assyria, 13-14, 64
  map of, 30
Atonement, 340
Atonement, Day of (*see* Day of Atonement; Yom Kippur)
Auschwitz, 409-411
Australia, Jews in, 3
Austria, Jews in, 294, 328
Auto-emancipation, 322
Avicebron, 143

B

Baal, worship of, 17
Baal Shem, 247, 252
Babylonia, 14, 24-25, 48, 66, 101, 264, 266
  map of, 30
Babylonian Exile, 14, 25-31, 32
Babylonian Jewry, 101-106
  after completion of Talmud, 106-108
Baeck, Rabbi Leo, 365, 401
  picture of, 365
Baghdad, 265
Bahya, 144
Balaam, 16
Balfour Declaration, 331
Baltimore Hebrew Congregation, illustrated, 163
Bar Kokhba, 47, 56, 71
Bar Mitzvah, 221-223, 384, 407
Barbados, 367
Baron, Joseph L., 304n.
Bat Mitzvah, 223
Bavaria, 293-294, 375
Bedouins, 12
  (*see also* Arabs)
Behr, S., 219n.
Ben, 63
Ben Azai, Rabbi, 251
Ben Sirah, 394
Ben Zoma, 70, 251
Benediction (words of), 80
  Priestly, 117
Benjamin, 13
Benjamin, Judah P., 377
Benjamin of Tudela, 143, 144
Bentwich, Norman, 395n.
Berakhah (Blessing), 111-112
Berlin, Germany, 282, 300-301, 310, 338, 348, 357
Bernays, Chief Rabbi Isaac, 308
Bernstein, Leonard, 124
Bet Hamidrash, 160
Bet Shearim, 47
  catacombs at, illustrated, 47

Bet Yisrael (*see* Israel, House of), 2
Betrothal, 224, 226
Bible, 78, 267, 396
    as basis of Judaism, 4, 105, 411
    divisions of, 80-90
    modern criticism of, 90-91
    in translation, 92, 106, 286, 298, 350
Bildad, 52
Bimah, 159, 161
Birds, prohibition against, 236
Birth, 216-223
Black Death, 156, 168-169
Bloch, Ernest, 124
Blood, prohibition against eating of, 236-
        237
B'nai B'rith, 376, 391, 407
Bolshevics, 262
"Book of Doctrines and Beliefs," 266n.
Book of the Pious, The, 252
Book of Radiance, The, 253-255
Borowitz, Eugene, 410
Braunschweig conference, 299
Brazil, 367
Breslau, Germany, 300, 302, 308, 338
Britain (*see* England)
Brotherhood of man, 57
Buber, Martin, 140, 247, 256n.-257n., 259-
        260n., 337, 350, 355-356, 410,
        421
    life of, 356-357
    picture of, 355
    thoughts of, 357-363
        on Judaism, 359-363
        on Zionism, 360-361
Buber, Solomon, 356
Bubonic plague, 156
Buffalo, N.Y., 371
Burial, 233
Byalik, Hayim Nahman, quoted, 261-263

C

Cabalah, 245, 251, 253
Caesar, Julius, 76
Caesarea, 44
Caftan (garment), 157, 244
Caiphas (*see* Joseph Caiphas)
Cairo, Egypt, 394
Calendar, Jewish, 97, 172-175
California, 376
    (*see also* Los Angeles)
Caligula, Emperor, 76n.
Calonymus family, 153
    house of, illustrated, 153
Calonymus, ben Meshullam, 190
Canaan, 5-6, 8, 12
Canaanites, 34
Candelabrum (*see* Menorah)

Candles, use of, in worship, 157
Cantors, 26, 124-125, 159, 161, 373, 384
    schools for, 384, 395
Capernaum, 203, 352
    synagogue of, illustrated, 161
Card-playing, prohibition against, 202
Cassel, Germany, 348
Catholic Church (*see* Church, the)
Catholic Judaism, 395
Cattle, prohibition against, 235-236
Causality (in Judah Halevi), 272
Central Conference of American Rabbis,
        383
Central Europe, Jews, in, 152-162, App.
Chaldaea, 5
Chamberlain, Houston Stewart, 317
Chants, 122
"Chapters of the Fathers," 50, 62
Charades, 212
Charity, 205
    collection of, 167
    (*see also* Fund-raising; Philanthropy)
Charlemagne, 153
Charleston, South Carolina, 369, 374
Chazars, 143, 145, 269
Chief Rabbi, position of, 295, 297
Children:
    birth of, 216-223
    dedication of, illustrated, 222
    education of, 221-223, 228, 349, 385,
        403, 407
    importance of, 216, 227-228
    naming of, 219-221
Chile, 413
Chmielnicky, 245
Cholent, 180
Chorev, Hirsch, 295, 308
"Chosen people," concept of, 17-18, 269-
        271, 351
    denied, 398
Christ, 44, 134, 243, 319, 351
    atoning death of, 287
Christianity, 129 ff., 151, 265, 269, 317,
        352
    Essenes and, 60
    and the Jews, 129-130, 152
    Judaism and, 118, 126, 131-133, 284,
        339-340, 342, 346, 351, 362
    in the Middle Ages, 141, 152
    science and, 401-402
    theological differences, 134-135
    and the Trinity, 134, 256, 287
Christians:
    converted to Judaism, 157
    and Jews, relations between, 129, 140,
        141, 157, 284-287, 355-356, 407
    (*see also* Anti-Semitism: American,
        German)
Christians, 202
Chronicles, Book of, 79, 84

Church, the, 191, 234, 242-243
  influence of, 157
  and State, 152
Churchill, Winston, 92
Chuzari, 145, 269-272
Cincinnati, Ohio, 375, 380, 382
Circumcision, 36, 217-218, 303
Citizenship, 326, 371-372
  duties of, 24-25, 285, 312, 314, 398
Civil service, 390
Civil War, 377
Claudius, Emperor, 41
Clemenceau, Georges, 327
Clothing, medieval Jewish, 156-157
  (*see also* Hats)
Codes, the, 167-171
Cohen, Hermann, 21n., 337-349, 359,
  363n.
  life of, 338-339
  philosophy of, 340-347
  picture of, 337
  writings of, 339, 347
Collected Writings, 80, 84-90
Cologne, Germany, 154
Columbus, Christopher, 151, 367
Columbus "platform," 383
Command (Mitzvah), 410
Commandments, 94-95
  ethical conduct and, 279
  meaning of, 279-280
Communism, Jews and, 262
Compassion, 345
  meaning of, 343
Concentration camps, 177, 364
Conferences, rabbinical, 299-300, 302-
  304, 306
Confession, 113, 114
Confession before marriage, 226
Confirmation, 214, 384, 407
Congregation, definition of, 122
Congregations, state supervision of, 294
Conservative Judaism, 2, 230, 298, 302-
  306, 314
  in America, 306, 393-395, 408
    character of, 395-396
    principles of, 396
    and Reconstructionism, 397-402
  differentiated from Reform and Ortho-
    doxy, 414-419
  and Mussaf service, 418
  principles of, 412-413
Contraception, use of, 228
Conversion, 34-35, 348, 372, 415
  converts, 33-36, 68
  enforced, 261
  historical perspective on, 36
  to Judaism, 33-36, 157
Cosmology, 401
Cossacks, 245
Council of the Four Lands, 244

Counting, the, 213
Court-Jews, 281-282
Covenant, the, 2, 23, 36-40, 345
Covenant of Abraham, 217, 218
Creed, Jewish, 146
Cromwell, Oliver, 243
Crusades, 48, 154, 168, 252
Cuba, 413
Culture:
  Greek, 48
  Jewish, 389
  Torah and, 314
Cup:
  at special rites, 218, 225-226
  as symbol, 182
Cyrus, King, 29
Czechoslovakia, 413

D

Dancing, 158
  at weddings, 227
Daniel, 55
  Book of, 79, 84
David, 12-13, 17, 35, 79, 87, 94
  House of, 56
Day of Atonement, 84, 90, 96, 173, 345
  origin of, 47
Day of Judgment, 89
Day schools, 403
Days of Awe, 185-196
  list of, 186
Days of Penitence, 174, 192
Days of Repentance, 187, 345
Dead, the:
  burial of, 233
  mourning for, 233-234
  preparation of, 232
Dead Sea Scrolls, 60
  illustration of, 159
Death:
  anniversary of, 234
  approach of, 231-232
Deborah, 83, 229
Declaration of Independence, 286
De Leon, Moses, 253
Descartes, 248
Dessau, Germany, 281-282
Deutero-Isaiah, 19
Deuteronomy, 22-23, 91
Devekut, 254, 256
Dewey, John, 397
Diaspora, 25, 27, 32, 324-325, 329, 335,
  413
Dictatorship, pogroms and, 77
Dies Irae (hymn), 191
Dietary laws, 75, 234, 303, 385, 396, 415
  foods prohibited by, 235-236
  purpose and background of, 235

Diringer, David, 157*n.*
Discrimination, 2
  (*see also* Anti-Semitism)
Dishes for kosher cooking, 238
Dispersion:
  illustration of, 107
  purpose of, 25
Disraeli, Benjamin, 315, 320
Divorce, 97, 223, 230-231, 414-415
Dred Scot decision, 12
"Dreidel" (a game), 202
Dresden, Germany, 302
Dreyfus Case, 321, 326-327
Drunkenness, 206
Dualism, 54, 67

E

Eastern Europe:
  Jews in, 244-245, 310-311, 321, 329
    migration of, 387-391
  Messianism in, 246
Eben ha-Ezer: *The Stone of Help,* 170
Ecclesiastes, Book of, 79, 84-86
Ecumenical Council (decrees), 140, 141
Edom, 43
Education, 49, 221-223, 228, 349, 403, 407
  adult, 407
  compulsory, 63
  Reform Judaism and, 385
  Torah and, 50
Egypt, 13, 25, 57, 146, 266, 334
  migration to, 8
  under Ptolemies, 40
  religion of, 9
  (*see also* Alexandria; Cairo)
Einhorn, David, 376-377, 381
Einstein, Albert, 403
Eisenhower, President, 334
Elbogen, Ismar, 380*n.*
Eleazar, Rabbi, 251-252
Eleazar ben Arakh, 69
Eleazar ben Azariah, 70
Eliade Mircea, 411
Eliezer, Rabbi, 69
Elihu, 52-53
Elijah, 17, 57, 209, 212, 218
Elijah ben Solomon, 246-247, 261
  picture of, 246
Eliphaz, 52
Elisha, 83
Elisha ben Abuya, 64, 251
Elizabeth I, Queen, 231, 243
"Elohe Abraham" (God of Abraham), 8
Elul, 187, 215
  dates of, 175
Embalming, 232
Emden, Germany, 308

Emunah, 410
End of Days, 20-21, 55, 140
Enemies, love of, 345-346
Engagements, 226
England, 334
  Jews in, 2, 152, 154, 262, 285, 295, 320, 337
  Reformation in, 243-244
Enlightenment, the, 263, 264, 283, 284, 286-287, 374
En Sof, 253, 353
Ephraim, 34
Epicureans, 58
Epicurus, 49
Equality, human, 18, 21, 135, 195, 284, 288-289, 346
Essence of Judaism, The, Baeck, 365
Essenes, the, 58, 60
Esterhazy, Count, 327
Esther, 36, 204-205
  Book of, 79, 84-86
  Fast of, 175, 203-204
  scroll of, illustrated, 205
Ethics and ethical conduct, 8, 71
  God and, 341
  and quest for perfection, 341-343
  teaching of, 385, 413
Europe, Jews in, 2
  (*see also* Central Europe; Eastern Europe; Western European Jewry)
Excommunication of Jews, 249
Exilarch, 102, 266
Existentialism, 111, 349, 357-358, 363, 409, 410-411
Exodus, route of, illustrated, 8
Ezekiel, 2*n.*, 17, 26-28, 232, 250-251
  Book of, 79, 83
Ezra, 34-38, 60, 66
  Book of, 79, 84

F

Fackenheim, Emil L., 410-411
Faith, 34, 71, 74, 290
  affirmation of, 80
  endurance and, 29
Family of Israel, the, 5-8, 18, 421
Fast days, 97, 175, 203-204
Fasting before marriage, 226
"Father in Heaven", 112
"Fathers," 50
Faust, Goethe, 206, 353
Ferdinand and Isabella, 151
Fertile Crescent, the, illustration of, 6
Festival of Weeks (*see* Shabuot)
Fish, "gefillte", 180
Fish, prohibition against, 236
Five Scrolls, the, 84-86

Food:
  prohibited, 235-236
  Sabbath, 180
  Seder, 209-210
Ford, Henry, 390
France, 321, 334
  anti-Semitism in, 326-327
  Jews in, 108, 154, 293, 320, 336-337
  (*see also* French-German Jewry)
Fränckel, David, 282
Frankel, Zachariah, 298, 302, 304-306, 338, 374, 384, 394
Frankfurt, Germany, 309, 349, 357
Frankfurt conference, 299, 306
Franklin, Benjamin, 370
Frederick the Great, 282-283
Free association, 103
Free universities, 407
Free will, God's providence and, 277-278
Freedom:
  of thought, 66, 289
  religious, 40, 370
Freies Judisches Lehrhaus, Frankfurt, 349-350, 357
French-German Jewry, 163-167, 169
French Revolution, 264, 291, 292
Freud, Sigmund, 103
Friday, Sabbath preparations on, 179-183
Fulda, Abbot of, 220
Fund-raising, 406

G

Gabirol, Solomon ibn (*see* Solomon ibn Gabirol)
Galilee, 44, 47
Gamaliel, 70
Gaon, 103
  of Vilna, 246-247 (*see also* Elijah Ben Solomon)
Gedalia, 192
Gedaliah, Fast of, 174
Gefillte fish, 180
Geiger, Abraham, 298, 300-301, 303-304, 308, 374, 394
  picture of, 301
Gemara, 78, 103-105
  quoted, 251
Genizah, 394
Georgia, 369
German Jewry, 153-158, 170, 246, 286, 302, 306, 309, 323, 329, 335-336, 350, 357, 374, 387-388
  end of, 364-366
  (*see also* French-German Jewry)

Germany, 242
  Conservatism in, 396
  emigration of Jews from, 375
  Hasidism in, 252
  Jew in, 2, 108, 152, 154, 163-169, 262, 294-297, 302, 310-311, 316, 320
  and Nazis, 364-365
  Reformation in, 243
  Renaissance of Judaism in, 349
Gershom ben Judah, 163-164, 299
  tombstone of, illustrated, 164
Gessius Florus, 44
Ghetto, 156, 201
Gilgamesh epos, the, 5
Ginzberg, Asher, 324-325
  (*see also* Ahad Ha-Am)
Glatzer, N. N., 152n.
Gnostic dualism, 54n.
Gobineau, Arthur, 317
God:
  of Abraham, and Isaac, 4, 6, 7-8
  as cornerstone of Judaism, 275-279
  and ethics, 341-342
  five attributes of, 267n.
  of history, 10, 115
  Jewish concept of, 10, 23, 49, 61, 74, 76-77, 399
  and Job, 52-53
  of love, 7, 19, 63, 89
  and man, 254-255, 268, 344, 359
  of Moses, 8, 9-10, 12
  names of, 9, 90-91, 166
  and nature, 88, 90, 248-249, 286-287, 341
  prayers and, 109-110
  qualities of, 110
  of righteousness, 6, 19
  and Satan, 53-54
  and the universe, 353-355
  and the world, 255-256, 267-268
Gods:
  heathen, 12, 17
  Persian, 54
  Roman, 75
Goethe, von, Johann Wolfgang, 206, 272, 353, 412
Golden rule, the, 68
Golem, the, 253
Gompers, Samuel, 389
Good and evil, choice between, 54
Government, ideal, 20
Graetz, Heinrich, 295, 302, 308, 321, 338
Greek language, 49
Greek thought, inspiration of, 48-57
Gregorian Chant, 122
Grimm, Jacob, 192
Guide of the Perplexed, Maimonides, 146, 150, 273, 282, 286
Guilt, feeling of, 28

H

Habakkuk, 83
Habdalah, 184
Habiru, 7n.
Habits, 186-187
Haburot, 407
Hadassah, 392
Hadassah Hospital, 392
Hadassah Medical Center, 334
Hadrian, Emperor, 46-47, 71, 74
Haftarah, 83-84
Haggadah (rabbinic preachings), 94, 104
Haggadah (for Seder ritual), 208-209
Haggai, 33, 83
Hagigah, 97
Hagiographa, 80
Haifa, Technical Institute at, 334
Halakhah, 94, 104, 385, 396, 409, 413
Halevi, Judah, 143, 144-145, 269, 350
  philosophy of, 269-272
  quoted, 215
Hallel, the, 89, 115, 199, 213
Haman, 75, 204-206
Hametz (leaven), 208
Hammurabi, 5
  law of, 10
  stele of, illustrated, 7
Hamnuna, Rabbi, 94
Hanania, Rabbi, 70
Hanukah, 174-175, 200-203
  origin of, 41, 79
Harby, Isaac, 374-375
Haroset, 210, 212
Harrison, Peter, 369
Hasdai ibn Shaprut, 142-143
Hasid, 250
  meaning of, 252
Hasidim, 247, 261, 356-357
  festive dance of, illustrated, 258
Hasidism, 247
  decay of, 258
  Eastern, 356-357, 362
  German, 252-253
  history of, 250-259
  impact of, 258-259
  in Russia and Poland, 256-257
Haskalah, 324
Hasmoneans, 41, 56, 63
Hatan Bereshit, 200
Hatan Torah, 200
Hatred, 346
Hats, 244
  as mark of humiliation, 156, 240
  wearing of, in synagogues, 239-241,
    385, 414
Hazzan (see Cantor)
Health, 279

doctors and, 231
Hebrew, 92, 305, 384, 396
  abolishment of, 304
  Conservatism and, 413
  language, 4, 304, 305, 396
  meaning of word, 6
  modern, 4, 108, 407
  origin of term, 6-7
  Orthodoxy and, 412
  pronunciation of, 108
Hebrew Union College, Cincinnati, 381,
    395, 409
  picture of, 382
Hebrew University, Jerusalem, 357
Hegel, G. W. F., 316-317, 352
Heine, Heinrich, 180, 298, 315, 372
Helena, Queen of Adiabene, 36
Hell, 254, 345
Hellenism, 40-57
Henoch, 256
Henry, Colonel, 327
Herberg, Will, 409
Herder, J. G., 286n.
Heresy, 151
Herod, King, 41, 66
Hertzberg, Arthur, 325n.
Herzl, Theodor, 321
  and Dreyfus Case, 326-327
  picture of, 327
  and Zionism, 328-330
Heschel, Abraham Joshua, 409-411, 420
Hezekiah, 79
High holy days (see Holy days)
Hildesheimer, Rabbi Ezriel, 310
Hilkia, Abba, 65-66
Hillel, 66-69, 94, 212, 249, 299
  disciples of, 69
  teachings of, 67-70
Hillel II, 173
Hillel Foundations, 376, 407
Hillel Houses, 391
Hirsch, Samson Raphael, 190n., 295, 297,
    300, 307, 374, 402, 403
  life of, 307-309
  philosophy of, 311-314, 330, 402-403
  picture of, 307
Hitler, 77, 152, 318, 331, 357, 366, 406-
    407, 410
Hiya, Rabbi, 251
Holdheim, Samuel, 297, 300, 303-304
Holidays, 96
  meaning of, 399
  second days of, 304-305, 385
Holland, 151, 247
  (see also Amsterdam)
Holy communion, 25
Holy days:
  dates of, 174-176

Holy days (*Cont.*):
   meaning of, 399
   observance of, 386
Holy Scriptures, 87-92
   reading of, 25
   (*see also* Bible)
Holy Spirit, 78, 344
Homel, pogrom of, 262
Homer, 4-5
Homunculus, 253
Horseradish, 212
Hosea, 19, 83
Hoshen Mishpat: *The Breastplate of Judgment*, 171
House of David, 13-14
Hovave Zion, 322
Human relationships, 345-346
Humanism, 242-243
Hume, David, 287
Huppah, 224-226
   illustrated, 227
Husic, Isaac, 280*n.*
Hymns, 25, 180
   for Hanukah, 202
   for Rosh Hashanah, 190-191
Hyrcanus, 41

I

Idea of the Holy, The, Otto, 348
Identity cards, 2
Illumination, Maimonides, 146
Immersion, 36, 58, 60
Immortality of the soul, 9, 279
   views on, 416-417
Inclinations, evil (*see* Yetzer ha-ra)
Innocent III, Pope, 156
Innocent IV, Pope, 156
Inquisition, the, 151, 156, 367
Institute of Religious and Social Studies, New York, 395
Iron Curtain, origin of term, 244
Isaac:
   God of, 4
   kinsmen of, 8
Isaiah, 4, 17, 19-22, 51, 52, 54-55, 95
   Book of, 19, 79, 83, 87
   Deutero-, 19
   second, 19, 28-31, 32, 35, 54
Islam, 106, 108, 134, 135, 245, 265
Israel (Kingdom), 13, 16-18, 35
   map of, 13
Israel, origin of name, 8
Israel (people), 271-272, 288, 351, 360
   (*see also* Judaism)

Israel (State), 2, 46, 108, 312*n.*, 325, 329, 332, 385, 392, 398, 405-408, 420
   and Diaspora, 335, 413-414
   economic map of, 333
   founding of, 366
   Hasidism in, 258
   holidays in, 172, 175*n.*, 205, 247
   Orthodoxy in, 405
   problems of, 334
   tenth anniversary coin of, illustrated, 46
   (*see also* Zionism)
Israel, Children of, 2*n.*
Israel, House of, 2, 87
   symbol of, 9
Israel "Baal Shem Tov," 246-247
Israel of Rizin, Rabbi, quoted, 260
"Israel-Man," 311, 314
Israeli (*see* Israel [State])
Israelite, The (journal), 380
Isserles, Rabbi Mosheh, 170
Italy, 243
Iyar, dates of, 175

J

Jabneh, 46
Jacob, 34, 236
   House of, 21
   Mighty One of, 8
Jacob ben Asher, 169-171
Jamaica, 368
James, William, 395
Jefferson, Thomas, 370, 375
Jeremiah, 2*n.*, 17, 24-25, 79
   Book of, 83
Jerusalem, 29, 34, 44, 66, 383, 385
   academies at, 66
   fall of, 45
   love of, 144
   pilgrimages to, 97
   Temple in, 12, 14, 33, 41, 43, 45, 62, 74, 83
Jesus of Nazareth, 44, 135-137, 229, 284, 319, 361
   (*see also* Christ)
Jesus ben Sirah, 50, 394
Jew, The (journal), 357
Jewish Chautauqua Society, 385
Jewish community, state and, 294-297, 309
Jewish Community Centers, 391
Jewish day, 179, 185
Jewish Institute of Religion, New York, 382

Jewish law, 10
Jewish names, 219-221
Jewish National Fund, 329
Jewish Publication Society, 392
Jewish State, 328
  (*see also* Israel [State]; Zionism)
Jewish Theological Seminary, Breslau,
    302, 308, 338, 394
Jewish Theological Seminary of America,
    394, 397, 409
  illustration of, 392
Jewish Welfare Board, 391
Jewish year, 172-215
Jewry (*see* kind of Jewry, as Ashkenasic)
Jews:
  chosenness, 17-18 (*see also* Chosen
    People)
  as citizens, 371-372
  covenant, 2
  discrimination and prejudice against
    (*see* Anti-Semitism)
  in Europe, 2, 152-162
  as family, 2, 5 ff., 21, 87
  function of, 311-313, 420
  history of, 5, 298
  kinship among, 2
  marks of, 156
  migration of, 262, 322, 367-368
  as a nation, 2, 291-292, 302, 305-306,
    312
  as nationals, 2
  number of, in world, 1-2, App.
  occupations permitted to, 154
  orthodox (*see* Orthodoxy)
  as people, 1, 2
  persecution of, 156, 261, 322, 328,
    364-367
  pride of, 407
  as religion, 2, 302, 330, 409
  secular, 389
  status of, 153
  in United States (*see* American Jewry)
Job, 28, 50, 51-53
  Book of, 51-54, 79, 84, 86
  God and, 52-53
Johanan, Rabbi, 251, 299
Johanan ben Zaccai, 46, 69
John XXIII, Pope, 140
Jonah, 83-84, 195, 345
Jonathan, 83
Jonathan ben Joseph, Rabbi, 67
Jones, Inigo, 369
Joseph, 34
Joseph Caiphas, 44, 58
Josephus Flavius, 44, 76
  quoted, 58, 60, 61
Joshua, 12
  Book of, 83

Joshua, Rabbi, 69, 72
Judaea, 41, 47, 74
  compulsory education in, 63
Judah Hahasid, mysticism of, 252-253
Judah Halevi:
  as philosopher, 145
  as poet, 144
  quoted, 215
  (*see also* Halevi, Judah)
Judah, Kingdom of, 13-14, 18, 40
  maps of, 42
Judah, Rabbi, 47, 93, 102
Judah, tribe of, 41
Judah ibn Aknin, 273
Judah ben Baba, 71
Judah the Patriarch (*see* Judah, Rabbi)
Judah the Prince (*see* Judah, Rabbi)
Judaism:
  Buber's thoughts on, 359-363
  Christianity and, 339-340, 342, 347,
    362, 401-402
  as a civilization, 398-399
  definitions of, 2, 321, 398
  evolution of, 5
  flexibility of, 401-402
  foundations of, 18
  function of, 340
  under Hadrian, 46-47
  heritage of, 5
  ideals of, 8
  impact of, 1
  and individual responsibility, 27
  influences on, 21
  negative, 305
  philosophy and, 264, 349
  positive historical, 298, 305, 308, 384,
    394
  practice of, 399-401
  principles of, 145
  problems for, in America, 373-375
  and the prophets, 16
  reform in, problems of, 299
  as a religion, 3
    of reason, 286, 339
  and religious democracy, 26
  romantic, 315, 409-411
  science of, 298
  and the Torah, 60-61
  (*see also* Conservative Judaism; Ortho-
    doxy; Reconstructionism; Re-
    form Judaism)
Judas Maccabaeus, 40
Judenstaat, Der, Herzl, 328
Judges, Book of, 79, 83
Julius Caesar, 76*n.*
Justice, 105
  social, 20, 22-23
Juvenal, quoted, 75

K

Kadashim, 97
Kaddish, 115, 117-118, 119, 120, 121, 233, 234
Kahal, 244
Kalaam, 265
Kalir, Eleazar, quoted, 213
Kallah, 103
Kant, Immanuel, 283, 287, 337, 339-340
Kaplan, Mordecai M., 397, 400, 412
    picture of, 397
    quoted, 3, 399-400
    (see also Reconstructionism)
Karaites, the, 106, 265
Karo, Joseph, 170, 229
    quoted, 230
Kaddish, 234
Kashrut, laws of, 238-239
Kavanah, 256, 358
Kedoshim (saints), 71
    (see also Pharisees)
Kennedy, Thomas, 370
Ketubah, 225
Ketubim, 80, 84-90
Kibbutzim, 333
Kiddush, 181-182, 188, 211, 384
Kierkegaard, 358
Kings, Book of, 79, 83
Kinot, 125
Kishenev pogroms, 262, 391
Kislev, 200
    dates of, 174
Kitchen utensils, 238
"Know Nothing Party," 390
Knowledge, love of, 25
Kohler, Kaufmann, 383, 395
Kol Nidre, 193-194
Kook, Rav, 409
Korah, Sons of, 87
Koran, the, 265
Kosher, 237
Kosher foods, 237-238
Ku Klux Klan, 390
Kusari, The, Halevi, 269-272

L

Lamentations, Book of, 79, 84-86, 215
Lateran Council of 1215, 156, 168
Lavater, Johann Kaspar, 284, 287, 335
Law:
    and Covenant, 2
    ethical, 303
    Jewish, 10, 106, 288-289

    code of, 97, 146
    Mosaic, 10, 34
Lazarus, Emma, 144
    picture of, 388
    quoted, 387
League of Nations, 331, 405
Leap year, 173
Lebeson, Anita L., 369n.
Leeser, Isaac, 376, 380, 393
    life of, 377-378
    picture of, 378
Lehman, Herbert, 409
Lehman family, 376
Lessing, Gotthold Ephraim, 283
Levinger, Lee J., 370n.
Levites, 39
Leviticus, 27
Levy, Commodore Uriah P., 372
    picture of, 373
Liebman, Joshua Loth, quoted, 234
Lilienthal, Rabbi Max, 376
Lincoln, Abraham, 377
Lion of Judah, 162
Liturgy, beginning of, 25
Locke, John, 282, 287, 369
Loew, Rabbi, 253
Logos, 132
Longhena, 243
Los Angeles, 382, 395
Love:
    of animals, 23
    of neighbor, 23, 68, 80, 345-346
    of God, 23, 63, 80, 112, 346
    (see also Neighbor; Social Justice)
Lubavitcher Rebbe, 402
Lulav branch, illustrated, 198
Luria, Rabbi Isaac, 255
    ideas of, 255-256
Luther, Martin, 92, 243

M

Maarib, service, 113, 119-120, 121
Maaseh Merkabah, 251
Maccabees, 40-48
    Book of, 79
    Hanukah and, 200-201
Madison, James, 369
Magen David (star), 162, 352
    illustrated, 352, 354
Maimonides, Moses, 145-151, 231, 247, 282, 287, 299
    importance of, 272
    philosophy of, 272-281, 339, 417
    picture of, 145
    tomb of, illustrated, 273
    works of, 146-151, 273, 286, 394

Mainz, Germany, 154, 163-165, 190, 202, 225
  synagogue at, illustrated, 161
"Malakh" (see Angels)
Malachi, 56, 79, 83, 209
  quoted, 57, 88
Man:
  freedom of, 12
  God and, 254-255, 268, 277-279, 344, 359
  Plato's idea of, 21-22
  and reason, 274
Manasseh, 34
Manasseh ben Israel, 243, 285
Manichaeism, 265
Marburg, University of, 337-338
Marcus, Jacob R., 379n.
Marcus Aurelius, 93
Marheshvan, dates of, 174
Mariamne, 41
Marital purity, law of, 160
Marranos, 151, 247, 367
Marriage, 97, 223, 293
  blessing of, 225
  with Christians, 293, 300
  early, 223
  with heathen wives, 34
  preparation for, 224
Marriage customs, 226
Marriage rites, legal acts in, 224-225
Married life, 227-231
Marshall, Louis, 391, 409
Martyrs, 71, 169
  Memorial Tablet for, illustrated, 155
Marx, Karl, 319
Maryland, 368, 370
  (see also Baltimore)
Masorah, the, 90
Masquerades, Purim, 205
Massachusetts, 368
Mattathias, 40
Matzah, 206, 207, 211-212
Meat:
  kosher, 237-238
  and milk, 238-239
  preparation of, 236
  utensils used in cooking of, 238
Medicine, 157
  study of, 144, 231
Meek, T. J., 10n.
Megillah, 97
Meir, Golda, 333
Meir, Rabbi, 74, 94
  quoted, 216
Meir of Rothenburg, Rabbi, 168
  tombstone of, illustrated, 168
Men of the Great Assembly, 79
Mendel, Menahem, 282
Mendelssohn, Moses, 221, 246, 247, 298-299, 303, 335-336, 377-378

Mendelssohn, Moses (Cont.):
  background of, 281-282
  influence of, 247, 290, 303, 311
  life of, 282-284
  philosophy of, 284-290
  picture of, 281
  works of, 283
Menorah, 201, 203
  illustrated, 203
Messiah, the, 56, 260, 317
  coming of, 215, 261, 268, 272, 342, 345, 360, 413
  views on, 279, 303, 416-417
Messianism, 245, 339, 342-343, 363
Metaphysics, philosophy and (in Judah Halevi), 269
Mexico City, 367
Meyerbeer, Giacomo, 318
Mezuzah, 127, 202
  illustrated, 127
Micah, 20, 95, 134n., 191
  Book of, 83, 86
Michael, 55
Middle Ages, Jews in, 152-158
Midianites, 34
Midrash, 94
Milhaud, Darius, 124
Military service, enforced, 261-262
Milk, meat and, 238-239
Minhag America, 380
Minhah, service, 113, 119, 121
Minyan, 122
Miracles, 278, 287-290
Miriam, 229
Mishnah, the, 47, 62, 92-98, 245
  commentary to, 146
  definition of, 94
  excerpts from, 98-101, 251
  organization of, 95-98
  work prohibition and, 178
Mishneh Torah, Maimonides, 146-151
Missionaries, Jewish, 36, 74-75
Missionary activities of Christians, 129
Mitnagdim, 261
Mizrachi, the, 330
Moab, 16, 35
Modes, musical, 122-124
Moed, 96
Moed Katan, 97
Mohammed, 106, 269
Mohel, function of, 217
Monastic orders, 60
Money-lenders, Jews as, 154
Moors, the, 151
Morais, Sabato, 393
Morality, 77, 279
  reason and, 341
  sexual, 341
Mordecai, 204-206
Mordecai ben Hillel, Rabbi, 169

More, Sir Thomas, 21-22
Mormons, 61
Moses, 4, 34, 39, 79, 87, 109-110, 131, 229, 275, 284
 Five Books of, 80, 82
 God of, 9-10, 12
 vision of, 9-10
Moses ben Maimon (*see* Maimonides)
Motel, Rabbi, 260
Mourning, 233-234
 days of, 215
Movie industry, 391
Music, Jewish, 122-125, 158
 church, 157
 German, 157, 318
 at weddings, 227
Mussaf service, 113, 121, 190, 195, 199, 417-418
Mutazilites, 265
Mysticism, 245, 252-253

N

"Nabi" (speaker), 15
Nahman ben Isaac, Rabbi, 239
Nahman, Rabbi, 73
Nahum, 83
Names:
 civic, 219
 family, 218-221
 meaning of, 220-221
Naming of children, 217, 218
Naomi, 35
Napoleon, 292
Nashim, 97
Nathan, 17
Nathan the Wise, Lessing, 283
Nationalism, German, 318
Nature:
 God and, 88, 248-249, 286-287, 341
 and morality, 341
Nazis, 147, 201, 301, 310, 319, 364, 392
Nebuchadnezzar, 14, 29
Ne'elah, 113
Nehardea, 103
Nehemiah, 34
 Book of, 79, 84
Neighbors, love of, 23, 68, 346
Nemesis, 52
Neo-Orthodoxy, 295, 297, 306-314
Nero, 44, 74
New Amsterdam, 368
New Testament, 136, 346
New Thinking, Rosenzweig, 359
New Year (*see* Rosh Hashanah)

New York, 368-370, 382, 388, 395
Newport, Rhode Island, 369-370
 synagogue at, illustrated, 369
Nezikin, 97
Nicholas I, Czar, 261-262
Nicolsburg, Austria, 309
Niebuhr, Reinhold, 140, 141*n.*
Nine-branched candelabrum, 201
Nineteen Letters, Hirsch, 308, 311*n.*
Nissan, dates of, 175
Nixon, Richard M., President, 333
Noah, 6
Noah, Mordecai Manuel, 371-372
 picture of, 371
Nobel, Rabbi Nehemiah, 349
Northwest Ordinance, 375*n.*
N'vee-im (*see also* Prophets), 80, 82-84

O

Obadiah, 83
Obedience, 412
"Occident and American Jewish Advocate, The," 378
Olam haba, 55
Oldenburg, State of, 294-295, 308
 Edicts of, 295-297
On (ancient Egyptian city [Heliopolis]), 34
Optimism, 24, 89
Orah Hayim: *The Way of Life*, 170
Oral Law (*see* Mishnah)
Oral Torah:
 meaning of term, 39, 62
 written down, 47, 93
Orders of the Mishnah, 95-98
Organ music, 305
Original sin, 26-27, 128, 287
"Original and the Translations of the Bible, The," Geiger, 301
Orthodoxy, 2, 4, 314, 396
 American, 402-404
 character of, 404
 differentiated from Reform and Conservatism, 414-419
 German, 310-311
 in Israel, 334, 405
 and the Messiah, 56
 and Mussaf service, 418
 principles of, 412
 Reconstructionism and, 400
 swing back to, 385
Osnat, 34
Otto, Rudolph, 348
Otto II, 153

P

Painted Ones, the, 72-74
Paitanim (liturgical poetry), 125
"Pakhad Yitshak" (Kinsman of Isaac), 8
Pale, 321
Palestine, 29, 47, 74, 101, 328, 330, 357,
    392, 405
  and the Crusades, 154
  emigration to, 168-169, 245, 322, 331
  functions of, 324-325
  Maccabean, map of, 43
Pallière, Aime, 348
Parents, 10
Parnass (president of congregation),
    duties of, 373
Parshah, 82
Parsley, 210-211
Passover, 4, 57, 85, 96, 175, 196, 206-213
  days of, 213
  dishes used during, 238
  origin of, 57
Patriarch, 46, 93
Paul VI, pope, 140
Peace, prayer for, 416
Peace of Mind, Liebman, 234n.
Penitence, days of, 192
Pennsylvania, 368-369
  (*see also* Philadelphia)
Pentateuch, 79-80
Perfection, quest for, 341-343
Persecutions:
  in Persia, 106
  in Russia (*see* Pogroms)
Persia, 36
  map of, 31
  persecutions in, 106
"Perushim" (*see* Pharisees)
Pessah, Feast of (*see* Passover)
Pharisees, importance of, 60-62, 63, 64-
    66, 71, 365
  Painted Ones and, 72-74
  works produced by, 78
Philadelphia, 369-370, 377
Philistines, 12, 35
Philo, 76, 106, 129, 133, 208
Philosophers, 279, 286, 289
  prophets and, 275
Philosophical Discourses, Mendelssohn,
    283
Philosophy, 157
  Greek, 49, 58, 64, 106, 268
  Jewish, 106, 265-290, 394, 411
  Judaism and, 264
  reason and, 339, 411
  religious, 286
Physicians, Jewish, 157, 231
Picquard, Colonel, 327

Pidyon Haben, 221
Pilgrimage festivals, 196, 234
Pilpul (method of Talmudic study), 300
Pinsker, Leon, 322-323
Pittsburgh Platform, 383
Piut(im), 125, 246
Plato, 21-22, 49, 51, 73, 130, 265, 269,
    272, 342, 363n.
Pogroms, 76n.-77, 261-262, 391
Poland, 338, 413
  Hasidism in, 256-257
  Jews in, 2, 108, 156, 244, 245, 261, 364
  migration from, 387
Polish Jewry, 222, 338-339
Polygamy, 164
Pompey, 41
Pontius Pilate, 44, 137, 139
Pool, David De Sola, 415n.
Popes, the Jews and, 130, 152-153, 156
Population control, 413-414
Prayer (and prayers), 25, 193, 213, 256,
    257, 410, 415-416
  meaning of, 109-110
Prayer Book, 78, 108-128
  American, 380-381
    new, 398
  conservative and reconstructionist, 415
  orthodox, 415-416
  reform, 416
Predestination, 60
Prejudice, 316-319, 390-391
Priesthood, 221
Procurators, 44
Property rights, 10, 97-100
Prophecy, 54, 56-57, 274-275
  development of, 15-25
Prophets, 14-15, 79, 86, 275, 279
  Books of, 80
  early, 15, 16-25, 83
  heathen, 15
  later, 82-84
  major, 17, 83
  minor, 17, 83
  Plato and, 21n.
Protestantism, conversion to, 348
Protocols of the Elders of Zion, 390
Proverbs, Book of, 51, 79, 84
Prussia, 297
  Jews in, 293
Psalms, 25, 116, 231, 422
  Book of, 79, 84, 86-90
Ptolemies, the, 40
Pumpedita, 103
Punishment, reward and, 268
Purgatory, 254
Purim, 86, 97, 158, 175, 204-206
Puritans, 61, 73, 92, 243, 368

R

Rab (Abba Areka), 102
Rabbinerseminar, Berlin, 310
Rabbinical Assembly of America, 395
Rabbinical conferences, 299, 302
Rabbinical Council of America, 402
Rabbis:
  and the Bible, 78-79
  importance of, 37
  and Judaism, 297-298
  as judges, 39
  origin of word, 103
  orthodox, authority and functions of,
    171, 238
  qualifications for, 26, 39
  and the Torah, 48-50
Rabina, 104
Rackman, Emanuel, 404n.
Radical Left, 407, 413
Rameses II, 8
Rashi, 103, 157, 160, 165, 230, 242
  style of, 165-167
Rashi Chapel, Worms, illustrated, 160
Realism:
  German, 318
  Romantic, 318
Reason, 274
  Age of, 316
  morality and, 341
  philosophy and, 339, 411
  religion of, 266, 286, 339
Reconstructionism, 230, 397, 402, 410
  character of, 398, 400
  Conservatism and, 397-402, 414
  and flexibility of Judaism, 401-402
  foundation of, 401
  meaning of term, 400
  and Mussaf service, 419
  principles of, 401ff.
"Reconstructionist, The" (magazine),
  398
Reconstructionist Movement, 3n.
Redeemer, the, 55-56
Redemption, 268, 306
  (see also World to come; Messiah)
Redemption, star of, 352-353
Reform Judaism, 2, 230, 297-298, 300,
  301-307, 314-315, 386
  American, 240, 303, 374-375, 378-386,
    408
  classical, 402, 408
  contributions of, 386
  differentiated from Orthodoxy and
    Conservatism, 414-419
  founding of, 386
  holy days in, 175n.-176
  and Mussaf service, 419

Reform Judaism (Cont.):
  principles of, 413
Reformation, the, 92, 242, 243
Regensburg, Germany, 252
Rehoboam, 12
Rehobot, Israel, 333
Religion:
  classical, 402
  definition of, 401
  democracy in, 26
  Egyptian, 9
  ethics and, 343
  freedom of, 40, 370
  Jewish (see Judaism)
  of reason, 286, 339
  religiosity and, 358
  without social justice, 23
Religion of Reason, Cohen, 339
Religiosity, religion and, 358
Renaissance, the, 242-243
Repentance (see Teshubah)
Republic, Plato's, 22, 73-74, 342, 363n.
Responsa, 171
Responsibility:
  individual, 26
  social, 27, 195
Resurrection, day of, 55
  views on, 303, 416-417
Revelation, 266, 275, 288, 303, 306
Reward, punishment and, 268
Rhode Island, 368-369
Riesser, Gabriel, 294
Rites, meaning of, 19-20
  and righteousness, 19
Ritual bath, 160
  at Worms, illustrated, 160
R'MO, 170-172, 206, 404
Roman empire, 36, 74, 108, 152
  collapse of, 153
Romanticism, 315-316
  English, 320
  German, 318
Rome, 41, 43-44, 58, 74-76
  Arch of Titus in, illustrated, 45
Rosenzweig, Franz, 182n., 337-338, 347,
    359, 410, 412
  death mask of, illustrated, 347
  life of, 348-350
  "star" of, 353-355
  thoughts of, 351-352
Rosh Hashanah, 96-97, 174, 186
  concept of, 190
  day of, 188-191
  eve of, 188
  hymn of, 190-191
Roth, Cecil, 152
Rothschild family, 309, 320
Rubenstein, Richard L., 411
Rules of repentance, 148-150

Rumania, 393
Jews in, 262, 328
migration from, 387
Russia, 244, 260, 333
Hasidism in, 256-257
Israel and, 334
Jews in, 2, 77, 108, 321-322, 328
migration from, 387
pogroms in, 77, 261-262, 391
present-day, 2, 262
Russian Jewry, 244, 374
agony of, 260-263
Russian Orthodox Church, 244
Ruth, 35-36
Book of, 35, 79, 84-86

S

Saadia, 106, 266, 270, 299
ideas of, 266-268, 287-288
Sabbath:
abolishment of, 300, 303
laws of, 96
observance of, 1, 23, 67, 76, 172, 176-
184, 232, 233, 254, 303, 386,
396, 404-405, 414
purpose of, 23, 399
work prohibition on, 178-179
Sabbath Lamp, 184-185
illustrated, 185
Sabbath Psalm, 181
Sachs, Nelly, 334, 412
Sacraments, 20, 135, 345
Sadducees, 57-58, 63
Safed, Palestine, 169, 255, 353
St. Augustine, 152
St. Francis of Assisi, 252-253
St. Jerome, 92
St. Louis, Missouri, 375
St. Paul, 131, 138-139
St. Thomas Aquinas, 266, 272, 280
Saints, 71
Samaria, 14
Samaritans, 33
Samson, 83
Samuel, 16, 79, 102-103
Books of, 83
Samuel of Toledo, 151
Samuel the Prince, 143
Sanhedrin, the, 46, 63, 98-100
organized by Napoleon, 292
Sanherib, Emperor, 64
Satan, God and, 53-54
Saul, 12, 16, 83

Saxony, 302
Schechter, Solomon, 318-319, 409
life of, 393-395
picture of, 393
quoted, 407
Schiff, Jacob, 376
Schiller, Friedrich, 313
Schleiermacher, F. E. D., 401n.
Scholasticism, 280
Scholem, Gershom G., 253, 256n., 353n.
School for the Science of Judaism, The,
Berlin, 301
Schools:
for cantors, 384, 395
Jewish, 162, 165
day, 403
elementary, 336
Schwarzschild, Steven A., 411
Science:
Christianity and, 401-402
Judaism and, 402
of Judaism, 298
Scott, Sir Walter, 320
Sects, 57-58, 60-61
Secularism, 315
Seder, the, 96, 208
service of, 211-213
Seder Plate, 209
Seder Table, 208-210
illustrated, 209-210
Sefardic Jewry, 108, 164, 264, 373-374
end of, 151-152, 169, 255
Sefardim, 108, 219, 368-370, 374
Seixas, Gershom, 370
Seleucids, 40
Selihot, 125
Sephirot, 254
Septuagint, 92
Sermon, origin of, 25, 298
Seven-branched candlestick, 162, 203
(see also Menorah)
Sex act, 254-255
Sexual morality, 76
Shabuot, 86, 175, 196, 213-215
Shalet, 180
Shammai, 66, 249
Shebat:
dates of, 175
fifteenth day of, 203
Shegaga, concept of, 344-345
Shehitah, 296
Shekalim, 96
Shekels, 96
Shekhinah, 255-256
Shelomoh ben Yitshak, Rabbi (see Rashi)
Shem, Israel Baal, 256
Shema (see Affirmation of faith)
Shemaya, 64, 66-67
Shivah, 233
Sh'mini Atzeret, 174

Shofar, 196, 215
  description of, 189-190
  illustrated, 189
"Shohet," 237
Shul (school, synagogue), 162, 249
Shulhan Arukh, 172, 206, 239, 382, 404,
    406, 412,
*Shulhan Arukh—The Well-Prepared
    Table,* Karo, 170-171, 229
Sickness, 231
Sidelocks, 245
Sidrah, definition of, 82
Silverman, Rabbi Morris, 213n., 416n.
Simhat Torah, 174, 200
Simeon, Rabbi, 69
Simeon ben Gamaliel, Rabbi, 69, 199
Simeon ben Johai, Rabbi, 253, 255
Simeon ben Shetah, 63
Simeon the Pious, 40, 63
Simlai, Rabbi, 94-95
Simon, King, 41
Sin:
  inherited, versus individual responsi-
    bility, 26-28
  original, 135
  rationalizing away of, 186, 344
  repentance and, 344-345
  wages of, 28
Sinai, Mount, 10, 190, 267, 287-288
Sivan, dates of, 175
Six-day War, 333, 408
Slaughter of animals, 236-237
Slavery in Egypt, 8
Smyrna, Turkey, 245
Social conditions, Jewish learning and,
    164
Social Justice, 23, 177, 342, 358
Society:
  ideal of, 20-21
  in Isaiah, 19
  in Micah, 20-21
  in Plato, 21, 49, 73
  in Sir Thomas More, 21
Society for the Advancement of Judaism,
    397-398
Society for Culture and Science of the
    Jews, 298
Sodom, 7-8, 109
Solomon, 12, 83, 110
Solomon, Haym, 370
Solomon ibn Gabirol, 143-144, 194
Solomon's temple, 110
Soloveitchik, Joseph B., 409
Song of Songs, 79, 84-85
Soul, the, 113, 128, 287, 343-344
  Psalms and, 86
  transmigration of, 254
  (*see also* Immortality)
South America, Jews in, 2

South Carolina, 369
  (*see also* Charleston)
Spain, Jews in, 108, 151, 169, 253, 367
Spanish Jewry (*see* Sefardic Jewry)
Speyer, Germany, 154, 164
Spinoza, Baruch, 247-249, 282
Spinoza, Benedict, 248n.
Stalin, 262
Star (*see* Magan David)
Star of Redemption, The, Rosenzweig,
    349
State, the:
  Church and, 152, 405
  Judaism and, 294-297, 309
Stoecker, Prussian Court-preacher, 319
Stoicism, 49, 130
Straus family, 376
Stuyvesant, Peter, 368
Suez Canal, 332-333
Suffering, 29
  sin and, 28, 51-53
  undeserved, 28, 51-53
Sukkah, 96, 197
  illustrated, 198
Sukkot, 86, 96, 174, 186, 196-197, 199-
    200, 368
  festive branches used at, illustrated,
    198
Sulzberger, Mayer, 391
Sunday Schools, 406, 407
Sura, Academy at, 266
Surah, 103
Süsskind of Trimberg, 157
Swarming things, prohibition against, 236
Symbols, 162
Synagogue buildings:
  conservative and reform, 161
  German, 158-160
  modern, 161
  Sephardic, 162
  in United States, 369
Synagogue Council of America, 391
Synagogue:
  candles used in, 157
  as center of Jewish life, 2, 407
  liberal, 310
  meaning of word, 26
  music in, 157
  origin, 26
  Torah and, 37
  in United States, 391, 407-408
    at time of Revolution, 369
  women's partition, 159, 229
Syria, 40
Szold, Henrietta, 392

T

Taanit, 7
Tabernacles, Feast of (*see* Sukkot)
Tacitus, 76
Taharot, 97
"Takkanot" ordinances, 94
Tallit, 125, 224, 226, 232, 332
  illustration of, 126
Talmud, the, 25, 101
  Babylonian, 102-108
    background of, 102-106
  burning of, during Inquisition, 156
  commentaries on, 165
  illustration of, 105
  interpretations of, 164
  method and organization of, 104-106
  Orthodoxy and, 412
  and the Pharisees, 73, 78
  rabbis of, 251
  study of, 167
  translations of, 104
Tammuz:
  dates of, 175
  seventeenth of, 215
Tannaim, the, 62-77, 92, 103
Tanna, Tannaim, the, 62-77, 92, 103
Tarphon, Rabbi, 70
Tax gatherers, 151
Tebet:
  dates of, 175
  fast of, 203
Tefillin and illustration of, 126
Tehillim, 110
  (*see also* Psalms)
Temple at Jerusalem, 83, 110, 280
  burning of, 45
  first, 12
    destruction of, 14
  new, 33
    fall of, 36, 62, 86
  restoration of, 41-42
  synagogues and, 26
Ten Commandments, 4, 10, 23, 26, 80,
    86, 176-177, 214
Ten Lost Tribes, 14
Tenakh (Holy Scriptures), 78-92
  origin of, 90-91
  transmission of, 90
Teplitz, Austria, 302
Terah, 130-131
Teshubah, ways of, 148-149, 186-187,
    344
Thanksgiving Day, 368
Thant, U, 333
Theology, 249, 274, 277, 394, 409-412
Thirty Years War, 242
Tikkun, 255

Tishah b'Av, 45, 86, 215
Tishri, dates of, 174
Titus, 44-45
  Arch of, illustrated, 45
Toledo, Spain, 169
Torah, the, 37, 80, 169, 247, 284
  cantillation of, illustrated, 123
  Conservatism and, 412
  and culture, 314
  and education, 50, 162
  illustrations of, 81
  interpretation of, 60
  in life and worship, 82
  meaning of, 37-38
  oral, 39, 47, 58, 93-94, 104, 265
    digest of, 148
  Orthodoxy and, 404-405, 412
  as pillar of Judaism, 48-49, 73
  preservation of, 146
  Psalms and, 86
  Reform Judaism and, 413
  Tannaim and, 62
  written, 38-39, 58, 94, 106, 265
Torquemada, 151
Tosafot, 165
Touro, Judah, 371
Touro Synagogue, Newport, illustrated,
    369
Trajan, Emperor, 46
Transmigration of souls, 254
Treitschke, 339
Trier, Germany, 154
Trinity, the, 134, 265-266, 287
Troubadours, 157
Tunis, 371
Turim, 169
Turkey, 169, 245, 330
Twelve Minor Prophets, 79, 83
"Twelve Overseers" memorial, illus-
    trated, 155
Tzedakah (righteousness, charity), 167-
    168
Tzimtzum, 255

U

Uganda, 328
Union of American Hebrew Congrega-
    tions, 381, 385
"Union of American Israel," 380
Union of Jewish Orthodox Congregations,
    403
  seal of, 238
Union of Orthodox Rabbis, 402
Union Prayer Book, 381
United Jewish Appeal, 409

United Nations, 333
United States, 262, 264, 332
    anti-Semitism in, 320, 376-377, 390-391, 413
    Conservatism in, 306
    Jews in, 2, 370-375
United States (Cont.):
    migration to, 262, 322, 366-368, 375, 407-408
    Reform Judaism in, 240, 303, 374-375, 378-386
    (see also American Jewry)
United Synagogue of America, 395
United Synagogue of the British Commonwealth, 295
Universe, three fundamental units of, 353
University of Judaism, Los Angeles, 395
Unleavened bread, 207
Urban, Pope, 154
Utopean ideals, 21

V

Vatican II (Ecumenical Council), 140, 408, 413
Venice, Jews in, 151, 243
Vespasian, 44, 46
Vienna, 356
    congress of, 293
Vilna, Gaon of, 246-247, 261
Vinci, Leonardo da, 272
Virginia, 368
Vulgate, the, 92

W

Wagner, Richard, 318
Warsaw ghetto, 201
Washington, George, 370, 414
Weizmann, Chaim, 329-330, 332
    picture of, 331
Weizmann Research Institute, Rehobot, 333
Werner, Eric, 191n.
Western European Jewry, 321, 349
Wiesbaden, Germany, 300
    synagogue at, illustrated, 364
Wiesel, Eli, 412
William II, Emperor, 318
Wimpel, 221-222
Wise, Rabbi Isaac Meyer, 376, 378, 384, 395, 403
    life of, 378-383

    picture of, 379
Wise, Rabbi Stephen, 382, 391
Wives:
    acquisition of, 223
    purification of, 228
    status of, 228-230
    working, 223
Women, 97, 414
    position of, 10, 228-230, 384
    (see also Wives)
Work prohibition, Sabbath and, 178-179
World:
    concepts of, 267-268, 270
    creation of (Maimonides' proof), 278-279
    God and, 255
World to come, the, 55-56, 268
World Jewish Congress, 391
World Jewry, 295
World War I, 330
World War II, 331, 366
Worms, Germany, 154, 164-165, 252
    synagogue at, 158-160
        illustrations of, 155, 159
Worship:
    Bible in, 82-85, 89
    common pattern of, 25
    quorum for, 122, 414
    structure of, 112, 120-122
    (see also Prayer)
Wulff, Moses Benjamin, 281-282

Y

Yahrzeit, 234
Yellow badge, 156-157
Yemot Hamashiah, 55
Yeshiva University, New York, 402-403
    Main Building, illustrated, 403
Yeshivot, Russian, 260
Yetzer ha-Ra (evil inclination), 27, 54
YHWH (God), 9
Yiddish, 157, 387, 389
Yiddishkeit, 408
Yigdal (hymn), 146-147
YMHA, 391
Yom Kippur, 58, 74, 186, 192-193, 217, 232, 234, 348, 351
    day of, 194-196
    eve of, 193-194
        entry into synagogue on, illustrated, 193
Yom Tob, 96
Yoma, 96
Yore Deah: The Teacher of Knowledge, 170

Yose, Rabbi, 69
Yoshua ben Perahyah, 64
Youth Aliyah, 392

Z

Zachariah, 33
Zaddik, Zaddikim, 257, 258
Zealots, 45
Zechariah, 83
Zephaniah, 83
Zera, Rabbi, 251
Zeraim, 96
Zerubabel, 33
Zevi, Sabbatai, 245, 256
Zion, 29, 33, 48, 144
   restoration of, 306, 314

Zionism, 314, 321-325, 356, 360-361
   birth of, 330-332
   Conservatism and, 396, 413
   cultural, 324, 326, 398
   development of, 332-334
   political, 326-330, 356
   reaction and opposition to, 329-330
   Reconstructionism and, 413
   Reform Judaism and, 413
Zionist Congress, first, 329
Zionist Movement, 409
Zionist Organization, permanent, 329
Zohar, 253
   ideas of, 253-255
Zola, Emile, 326
Zophar, 52
Zoroastrianism, 21, 54-55, 265
Zunz, Leopold, 298, 323